Writing & Reading

Canadian Edition

Across the Disciplines

D1234249

Laurence Behrens
University of California
Santa Barbara

Leonard J. Rosen
Bentley College

Jaqueline McLeod Rogers
University of Winnipeg

Catherine Taylor
University of Winnipeg

PEARSON

Longman

Toronto

Library and Archives Canada Cataloguing in Publication

Writing and reading across the disciplines / Laurence Behrens ... [et al.]. — Canadian ed.

Includes index.
ISBN 0-321-32826-4

1. College readers. 2. Interdisciplinary approach in education—Problems, exercises, etc. 3. English language—Rhetoric—Problems, exercises, etc. 4. Academic writing—Problems, exercises, etc.
I. Behrens, Laurence

PE1417.W723 2007   808'.0427   C2005-907087-0

ISBN 0-321-32826-4

Vice President, Editorial Director: Michael J. Young
Acquisitions Editor: Patty Riediger
Signing Representative: Duncan MacKinnon
Marketing Manager: Leigh-Anne Graham
Developmental Editor: Patti Altridge
Production Editor: Kevin Leung
Copy Editor: Lenore Latta
Proofreader: Ann McInnis
Senior Production Coordinator: Peggy Brown
Composition: Janet Zanette
Permissions Research: Sandy Cooke
Art Director: Julia Hall
Cover and Interior Design: Anthony Leung
Cover Image: Johner/GettyImages

1 2 3 4 5   11 10 09 08 07

Printed and bound in the USA.

PEARSON
Longman

Contents

3 Critiquing Sources: Textual Analysis and Response   68

▪ Part II
An Anthology of Readings

Political Science

5 Homeless in the "Just Society"   151

Preface

Writing and Reading Across the Disciplines offers your favourite selections from its successful predecessor, *Writing and Reading Across the Curriculum*, in a new, concise text, fitting a one-semester course. The rhetoric section in Part I opens with a single chapter presenting key concepts of the writing process that can be understood as generic to most academic writing situations. It then devotes a chapter each to two key aspects of academic writing: representing outside sources (including summary, paraphrase, and quotation) and critiquing sources. Part I concludes with a chapter on developing research essays, a form of writing that incorporates the approaches developed in previous chapters. Several chapters on matters such as research and documentation, which were part of the previous edition, have been omitted, since many instructors already supplement this book with a handbook.

The anthology section in Part II of this brief edition offers five chapters, each offering a wide, and somewhat expanded, range of topical readings. Four chapters have been retained from the previous edition, based of their popularity with instructors, while a fifth chapter on Canadian identity—taking a cultural studies approach—has been added in response to the recent burgeoning of this interdisciplinary field.

STRUCTURE

This brief edition is organized into two main parts in place of the three in the longer text. In the first part, representing selections from Parts I and II in the longer version, the four chapters cover the writing process and three frequently used writing types. The first chapter does not take an exhaustive approach to the writing process, but provides an overview intended to help students get started in a purposeful way. The chapters that follow on the three writing types are similar to those in the longer version that dealt with summary, critique, and synthesis. We used the term "research essay" here in place of "synthesis" as one more apt and familiar, differentiating amongst three types of essay: the research argument, the explanatory research essay, and the comparison-and-contrast research essay. At the end of this chapter, we consider a fourth type of essay, the non-researched personal argument—a form written with more frequency in several disciplines over the past few years.

Part II, the Anthology of Readings, has four chapters. The Psychology chapter on "Obedience to Authority" appeals to many instructors and students, so it appears more or less intact, apart from the addition of Isaiah Berlin's powerful "Notes on Prejudice." The other chapters contain new

Canadian material. Chapter 9, "Canadian Identities," is entirely new, and contains selections by both popular and scholarly writers. Some of the writing replicates the sort produced by scholars in disciplinary publications while some is more journalistic and mainstream. By including this combination, we hope to engage the interest of students, as well as exposing them to stylistic range.

There are enough readings in each of the five anthology chapters to allow instructors to make choices on the basis of thematic appeal, so that in a 10–12 week course, an instructor might select readings from any three of the five fields. However, we encourage instructors to look for crossovers and linkages amongst readings in various chapters, so that, for example, the readings on residential schools (in Chapter 7) are germane to a reading like "The Myth of the Master Race" (in Chapter 9).

INSTRUCTOR'S SUPPLEMENTS

The Instructor's Manual can be downloaded by instructors from a password-protected location on Pearson Education Canada's online catalogue (vig. pearsoned.ca). Simply search for the text and then click on "Instructor" under "Resources" in the left-hand menu. Contact your local sales representative for further information.

ACKNOWLEDGMENTS

We would like to thank the anonymous reviewers who helped us revise this book by providing valuable feedback on the responses and needs of their students.

We are extremely grateful to Patti Altridge, who has been cheerful, efficient, and smart as an editor. We have also benefited from Lenore Latte's careful copyediting and encouragement to meet deadlines.

The University of Winnipeg generously provided us with a work-study grant to employ the assistance of Melanie Wilchowy in preparing the manuscript. Our colleagues in the Centre for Academic Writing provide a rich climate for thinking about pedagogical and curricular issues. Finally, we are grateful to our students who have helped us become more aware of and sensitive to the needs and interests of Canadian students.

1

Process, Thesis, and Paragraphs

INTRODUCTION TO THE ART OF ESSAY WRITING

First-year students are sometimes told by their more experienced peers that essays are easy, that they can be written almost according to formula and still fetch reasonable marks from most professors. And it is true that all essays have in common a basic structure: each has an introduction, followed by an orderly series of claims and support, in turn followed by a conclusion, all held together by devotion to an overarching claim or thesis. Though the details change from subject to subject and occasion to occasion, we can be fairly confident in our work if we keep in mind Aristotle's simple description of another complex form of text—Greek tragedies. Essays, like Greek tragedies, must have a beginning, a middle, and an end, or they don't work.

However, if the art of writing essays could be adequately mastered simply by following a few structural principles, essays would not be the challenging enterprise that their name (from the Old French *essaier*, to try, to test—not necessarily to succeed) suggests they are. First, the people who take a formulaic approach underestimate the central role that must be played by the essayists themselves. The essayists must use their own imagination to find an interesting angle on the topic, develop a thesis or insight that makes sense of the angle, and explore that thesis through a paper that carefully unpacks and tests the angle's logic. Writing about any topic, whether one has a personal interest in it or not, requires the probing, connecting, questioning, shaping activity of the individual mind, not only "essaying" previously unfamiliar ideas and connections between ideas, but reflecting on whether they make sense of the topic.

Of course, this demand that the essay actually make sense of things further complicates the task. Not only must the essay be a well-crafted line of argument with its own structural integrity, but it must also accurately represent that portion of the universe that is its topic. Depending on the topic, the need for accurate representation might require essay writers to observe with extreme attentiveness the behaviour of grizzly bears first-hand (though seldom in first year), or examine distant galaxies through a telescope, or recollect a 10-year-old experience in detail, or intently read and reread a poem or philosophical treatise, or conduct interviews with survivors of a natural disaster. Care is required because essays collapse if they are based on faulty observation. For example, an eloquently argued essay on Shakespeare's *Macbeth* is no good if its claims are based on misquotations and misreadings; an essay on the

1

safety of genetically modified foods, no matter how beautifully constructed as a fluid series of logically connected claims, cannot work if it has the facts wrong, or relies on faulty sources, or fails to consider important aspects of the issue. Essays, then, demand a dual focus—on both claims and support, writing and reading, the mind's eye and what it sees.

Full engagement in the process of writing a successful essay—reading, thinking, and, sometimes, observing—involves much more time than students often expect—particularly if, as is often the case, you became accustomed in high school to getting good grades for "night-before" efforts that were short on research and contemplation but perhaps graced by a spirited manner. The single most important advice we can give you for doing well on university and college writing assignments is to give them the time they demand and to spend that time productively.

THE RECURSIVE WRITING PROCESS

Keep in mind that an essay is not finished when the required number of pages is full: On the contrary, essay writing is a "recursive" process—one that goes over the same territory many times in the interests of shaping the best possible expression of the material. The intense concentration required is more akin to that for painting a canvas or carving a sculpture than that for running a 100-metre race. Although successful writers vary in the particular techniques they employ and the amount of time they devote to each one, generally the recursive process involves the following three main stages.

1. Planning or pre-writing

In this stage, writers analyze the requirements of the writing challenge before them. They might have to decide on a topic if it is not supplied, or choose one from a limited selection. They try to find an angle that interests them and work at "unpacking" the topic to explore possible approaches to writing about it. Sometimes they use techniques such as freewriting or pro–con lists to generate and collect ideas in writing.

Focused Freewriting: Writing to Explore a Topic

1. Don't STOP.
2. Don't worry about CORRECTNESS.

Let's say you are asked to write about biotechnology in a biology class, and you are uncertain about how to start. Freewriting can often help you narrow your topic and identify a "real" subject that interests you. Time yourself, allowing for about 10 minutes of non-stop writing. Use this opportunity to write about whatever comes to mind, to capture in writing things you already know about the topic as well as connections you might not have considered previously. Don't stop to evaluate your ideas, since the whole point is to find out the flow and direction of your thinking; don't stop to correct yourself as you go, since worrying about surface expression tends to block the flow of ideas. Freewriting on the topic of biotechnology might look like this:

What to say about biotech ... I never think about it very much why would I since I don't need any radical cures thank goodness and my family is OK so we don't have experience with transplants or whatever extremes they experiment with. I did hear about operations on embryos and how Canada needs to pass laws to make it illegal to do stem cell research, like they just passed laws in Britain I think. But there's GM foods, too—that's something that affects me, all the alterations they are doing to crops and animals, at least to animals through the sort of feed they get, so that they say kids are maturing earlier with all the hormones or steroids that are in the feed that cows eat and that get into the meat and the milk. That doesn't sound quite right. That could be a place to start looking ....

Point/Counterpoint/Defence Outline

Another way to get started is to outline ideas. On the informal level, there are scratch outlines, containing key words and ideas that the writer wants to explore. More formal outlines often list all the main supporting points. The following represents the start of a three-column outline. This kind of outlining helps you to generate ideas, since it invites you to list your points of support, arguments running counter to each of these, and justifications explaining why your points prevail or how they can be modified to reflect the counter position.

Working Thesis: People have the right to shop wherever they choose, but they should not let convenience and cheap prices win out over supporting the Canadian economy and maintaining a sense of individuality.

SUPPORTING POINTS	OPPOSING POINTS	DEFENCE
"Everything's starting to look the same, everybody buys all the same things" (Ortega 104).	People will buy what they like at a cheap price, regardless of how many other people have the same product.	We all have a right to have some choice in our lives, regardless of how wealthy we are.
People who are against Wal-Marts are regular people.	Supporters of Wal-Mart call protesters "elitists for opposing a purveyor of low-priced goods" (Ortega 104).	The desire to exercise personal taste and being selective about where you shop are not solely privileges of the rich.
Wal-Marts are taking too much money from other businesses.	Many businesses are not run efficiently or competitively, and are blaming Wal-Mart for their shortcomings.	Businesses cannot always find ways to be more competitive or unique when they face a giant competitor.
Local businesses are noted for giving generously to the community and charities.	Wal-Mart does give to the community.	"Except for one high school scholarship per year, Wal-Mart gives very little back to the community" (Norman 105).

As in the above examples, writers usually develop a working thesis (though they continue to fine-tune it in the next stage: drafting) and they try to find whatever research sources they need. If they cannot find the sources they need to support their preliminary thesis, or if their view of the topic changes unexpectedly as a result of information and ideas encountered in the research process, they revise the thesis. (We discuss this important process of finding a topic and developing a thesis later in this chapter.) Some writers develop a detailed formal outline that is almost a point-form version of their whole essay before they go on to the drafting stage; others use mind maps or minimal lists of the five or six main points. Whatever the particular techniques employed, the overall aim of the pre-writing stage is to put oneself in an excellent position to begin drafting.

2. Drafting and redrafting or revising

Again, successful writers approach this phase in different ways. For some, the first draft is very drafty indeed; it is written quickly and intensely, with the writer trying to plough through from beginning to end, knowing that there will be ample time for radical revision. Other writers work and rework each paragraph or block of paragraphs as they go along rather than revising their whole draft at different sittings, and then do one last reworking of the whole essay. The important thing at this stage is to ensure that the final draft ends up being the best possible execution of your thesis for your particular audience.

It is obvious that revising well involves effective rewriting of material; what is less obvious perhaps is that it involves particular troubleshooting skills such as looking for gaps or repetitions in the argument and identifying unsupported claims. Instructors are providing you with an excellent opportunity to develop these troubleshooting skills when they set up peer-feedback workshops. Such workshops also provide you with the opportunity to hear from actual readers of your work before you submit it for grading.

3. Editing and proofreading

Time should be reserved at the end to attend to such micro-level issues as style (Is the language used always appropriate for the audience? Is it as clear and dynamic as you can make it?), correct usage (Are comma splices and sentence fragments avoided? Is everything spelled correctly?), typing (Are there any keyboarding errors?), and complete documentation (Is there a citation for every single usage of every single source, and a reference list at the end?). Because it is often hard to see your own mistakes, particularly if you have been working on an essay so long that you're feeling a bit stale about it, writing instructors often set up peer-editing workshops that focus only on this final stage of the writing process.

At this stage, access to a well-thumbed writing handbook that goes over stylistic options and grammatical issues can be helpful, as can the writing tools available in word processors (spell checker, thesaurus, grammar checker), though they are neither infallible in error detection nor always wise in their counsel. All of these editing aids, including peer feedback, should be used as sources of possible improvements rather than correct answers. Writers know their work best and should always weigh their options carefully rather than obediently following advice.

In Chapter 4 on developing a research essay, we go over several examples of writing assignments as they move through some of these stages.

THESIS AND THE STRUCTURE OF ARGUMENTS

The goal of this careful recursive process is to produce an essay that communicates its thesis in a well-crafted structure of claim and support. Crudely put, an academic essay usually looks something like this:

Thesis (X) in an introduction
Claim 1 (often a claim that the opposition doesn't counter)
Claim 2 (a reason for believing X)
Claim 3 (another reason for believing X)
Conclusion where X is reasserted in a larger context

Sometimes academic writing is so blatantly structured this way that the whole line of argument—the structure of claim and support that develops the thesis—can be picked up simply by reading the first sentence of each paragraph and stringing them together. But even if the argument is not so readily apparent, a successful academic essay will invariably have a solid structure of claim and support on closer inspection. Even if an essay is, as the novelist Virginia Woolf says about painting, "on the surface, feathery and evanescent, one colour melting into another like the colours on a butterfly's wing . . . beneath it must be clamped together with bolts of iron"[1] —or else it's a failed attempt because it can't carry the weight of the thesis.

WRITING A THESIS

A thesis is a one-sentence summary of a paper's content. It is similar, actually, to a paper's conclusion but lacks the conclusion's concern for broad implications and significance. For a writer in the drafting stages, the thesis establishes a focus, a basis on which to include or exclude information. For the reader of a finished product, the thesis anticipates the author's discussion. *A thesis, therefore, is an essential tool for both writers and readers of academic material.*

The previous sentence is our thesis for this section. Based on this thesis, we, as the authors, have limited the content of the section; and you, as the reader, will be able to form certain expectations about the discussion that follows. Based on that thesis statement, you would expect us to define a thesis; to describe ways that a thesis is used; and to focus our discussion on academic

[1] Virginia Woolf, *To the Lighthouse* (Harmondsworth, U.K.: Penguin, 1968), 194.

material. As writers, we will have met our obligations to you only if in subsequent paragraphs we satisfy these expectations.

The Components of a Thesis

Like any other sentence, a thesis includes a subject and a predicate, and consists of an assertion about the subject. In the sentence "Sir John A. Macdonald and Louis Riel were equally key figures in Canadian Confederation," the subject is "Sir John A. Macdonald and Louis Riel" and the predicate is "were equally key figures in Canadian Confederation." What distinguishes a thesis from any other sentence with a subject and predicate is that *the thesis presents the controlling idea of the paper.* The subject of a thesis must present the right balance between the general and the specific to allow for a thorough discussion within the allotted length of the paper. The discussion might include definitions, details, comparisons, contrasts—whatever is needed to illuminate a subject and carry on an intelligent conversation. (If the sentence about Macdonald and Riel were a thesis, the reader would assume that the rest of the paper contained comparisons and contrasts between the two leaders.)

Bear in mind when writing thesis statements that the more general your subject and the more complex your assertion, the longer your paper will be. For instance, you could not write an effective 10-page paper based on the following:

Democracy is the best system of government.

Consider the subject of this sentence ("democracy") and the assertion of its predicate ("is the best system of government"). The subject is enormous in scope; it is a general category composed of hundreds of more specific subcategories, each of which would be appropriate for a paper 10 pages in length. The predicate of our example is also a problem, for the claim that democracy is the best system of government would be simplistic unless accompanied by a thorough, systematic, critical evaluation of *every* form of government yet devised. A 10-page paper governed by such a thesis simply could not achieve the level of detail expected of college and university students.

Limiting the Scope of the Thesis

To write an effective thesis and thus a controlled, effective paper, you need to limit your subject and your claims about it. Two strategies for achieving a thesis of manageable proportions are (1) to begin with a working thesis (this strategy assumes that you are familiar with your topic) and (2) to begin with a broad area of interest and narrow it (this strategy assumes that you are unfamiliar with your topic).

1. Begin with a Working Thesis

Professionals thoroughly familiar with a topic often begin writing with a clear thesis in mind—a happy state of affairs. These professionals usually know their material, are familiar with the ways of approaching it, are aware of the questions important to practitioners, and have devoted considerable time to the study of the topic; they are naturally in a strong position to begin writing a paper. Not only do professionals have experience in their fields, but also they have a clear purpose in writing, they know their audience, and they are comfortable with the format of their papers.

Experience counts—there's no way around it. As a student, you are not yet an expert in the field of scholarly topics and therefore don't generally have the luxury of beginning your writing tasks with a definite thesis in mind. Once you choose and devote time to a major field of study, however, you will gain experience. In the meantime, you'll usually have to do more work than the professional to prepare yourself for writing a paper.

But there are occasions in academic writing situations when you need to draw on experience (when writing the Personal Argument, for example); in a similar fashion, when you write in-class essays, you need to develop a thesis quickly, without the luxury of reflection and research, but relying instead on your experiences studying and preparing the course material. There might be other non-academic occasions when you need to write about a topic in order to make a point. Let's say, for example, that you are an expert on backpacking and are asked by your sports-store employer to write a short piece discussing the relative merits of backpack designs. Your job is to recommend which line of backpacks the sporting-goods chain should carry. Since you already know a good deal about backpacks, you may already have some well-developed ideas on the topic before you start doing additional research.

Yet even as an expert in your field, you will find that beginning the writing task is a challenge, for at this point it is unlikely that you will be able to conceive a thesis perfectly suited to the contents of your paper. After all, a thesis is a summary, and it is difficult to summarize a presentation yet to be written—especially if you plan to discover what you want to say during the process of writing. Even if you know your material well, the best you can do at the early stages is to formulate a *working thesis*—a hypothesis of sorts, a well-informed hunch about your topic and the claim to be made about it.

Once you have completed a draft, you can evaluate the degree to which your working thesis accurately summarizes the content of your paper. Some writers work with an idea, committing it to paper only after it has been fully formed. Others begin with a vague notion and begin writing a first draft, trusting that as they write they'll discover what they wish to say. Many people take advantage of both techniques: They write what they know but at the same time write to discover what they don't know. If the match is a good one, the working thesis becomes the thesis. If, however, sections of the paper drift from the focus set out in the working thesis, you'll need to revise the thesis and the paper itself to ensure that the presentation is unified. (You'll know that the match between the content and thesis is a good one when every paragraph directly refers to and develops some element of the thesis.)

2. Begin with a Subject and Narrow It

Let's assume that you have moved from writing about the realm of things learned through experience to addressing a specific scholarly question, say writing a paper for your government class. Whereas you were once the professional who knew enough about your subject to begin writing with a working thesis, you are now the student, inexperienced and in need of a great deal of information before you can begin to think of thesis statements. It may be a comfort to know that your political science professor would likely be in the same predicament if asked to recommend backpack designs. She would need to spend several weeks, at least, backpacking to become as experienced as you; and it is fair to say that you will need to spend several hours looking for sources before you are in a position to choose a topic suitable for an undergraduate paper.

Suppose you have been assigned a 10-page paper in Political Science 104, a course on social policy. Not only do you not have a thesis—you don't have a subject! Where will you begin? First, you need to select a broad area of interest and make yourself knowledgeable about its general features. What if no broad area of interest occurs to you? Don't despair—usually there's a way to make use of discussions you've read in a text or heard in a lecture. The trick is to find a topic that can become personally important, for whatever reason. (For a paper in your biology class, you might write on the digestive system because a relative has stomach troubles. For an economics seminar, you might explore the factors that threaten banks with collapse because your great-grandparents lost their life savings during the Great Depression.) Whatever the academic discipline, try to discover a topic that you'll enjoy exploring; that way, you'll be writing for yourself as much as for your instructor. Some specific strategies to try if no topics occur to you: Review material covered during the semester, class by class if need be; review the semester's readings, actually skimming each assignment. Choose any subject that has held your interest, if even for a moment, and use that as your point of departure.

Suppose you have reviewed each of your classes and recall that a lecture on AIDS aroused your curiosity. Your broad subject of interest, then, will be AIDS. At this point, the goal of your research is to limit this subject to a manageable scope. Although your initial, broad subject will often be more specific than our AIDS example, we'll assume for the purposes of discussion the most general case (the subject in greatest need of limiting).

A subject can be limited in at least two ways. First, a general article such as an encyclopedia entry may do the work for you by presenting the subject in the form of an outline, with each item in the outline representing a separate topic (which, for your purposes, may need further limiting). Second, you can limit a subject by asking several questions about it:

Who?
What aspects?
Where?
When?
How?

These questions will occur to you as you conduct your research and see the ways in which various authors have focused their discussions. Having read several sources and having decided that you'd like to use them, you might limit the subject "AIDS" by asking *who*—AIDS patients; and *which* aspect—civil rights of AIDS patients.

Certainly, "the civil rights of AIDS patients" offers a more specific focus than does "AIDS"; still, the revised focus is too broad for a 10-page paper in that a comprehensive discussion would obligate you to review numerous particular rights. So again you must try to limit your subject by posing a question. In this particular case, *which aspects* (of the civil rights of AIDS patients) can be asked a second time. Six aspects may come to mind:

- Rights in the workplace
- Rights to hospital care
- Rights to insurance benefits
- Rights to privacy
- Rights to fair housing
- Rights to education

Any *one* of these aspects could provide the focus of a 10-page paper, and you do yourself an important service by choosing one, perhaps two, of the aspects; to choose more would obligate you to too broad a discussion and you would frustrate yourself: Either the paper would have to be longer than 10 pages or, assuming you kept to the page limit, the paper would be superficial in its treatment. In both instances, the paper would fail, given the constraints of the assignment. So it is far better that you limit your subject ahead of time, before you attempt to write about it. Let's assume that you settle on the following as an appropriately defined subject for a 10-page paper:

the rights of AIDS patients in the workplace

The process of narrowing an initial subject depends heavily on the reading you do. The more you read, the deeper your understanding of a topic. The deeper your understanding, the likelier you are to be able to divide a broad and complex topic into manageable—that is, researchable—categories. In the AIDS example, your reading in the literature suggested that the civil rights of AIDS patients was an issue at the centre of recent national debate. So reading allowed you to narrow the subject "AIDS" by answering the initial questions—the *who* and *which* aspects. Once you narrowed your focus to "the civil rights of AIDS patients," you read further and quickly realized that civil rights in itself was a broad concern that also should be limited. In this way, reading provided an important stimulus as you worked to identify an appropriate subject for your paper.

3. Make an Assertion

Once you have identified the subject, you can now develop it into a thesis by making an assertion about it. If you have spent enough time reading and gathering information, you will be knowledgeable enough to have something to say about the subject, based on a combination of your own thinking and the thinking of your sources. If you have trouble making an assertion, try writing your topic at the top of a page and then listing everything you now know and feel about it. Often from such a list you will discover an assertion that you then can use to fashion a working thesis. A good way to gauge the reasonableness of your claim is to see what other authors have asserted about the same topic. In fact, keep good notes on the views of others; the notes will prove a useful support or counterpoint to your own views as you write, and you may want to use them in your paper.

Next, sketch several different versions of a thesis, looking for one that best fits your present perspective on the topic:

1. During the past few years, the rights of AIDS patients in the workplace have been debated by national columnists.
2. Several columnists have offered convincing reasons for protecting the rights of AIDS patients in the workplace.
3. The most sensible plan for protecting the rights of AIDS patients in the workplace has been offered by columnist Anthony Jones.

Keep in mind that these are *working thesis statements*. Because you haven't written a paper based on any of them, they remain *hypotheses* to be tested. After completing a first draft, you would compare the contents of the paper to the thesis and make adjustments as necessary for unity. The working thesis is an excellent tool for planning broad sections of the paper, but—again—don't let it prevent you from pursuing related discussions as they occur to you.

Notice how the three statements in our example differ from one another in the forcefulness of their assertions. Statement 3 is *strongly argumentative*. "Most sensible" implies that the writer will first explain several plans for protecting the rights of AIDS patients in the workplace. Following the explanation would come a comparison of plans and then, finally, a judgment in favour of Anthony Jones's plan. Like any working thesis, this one helps the writer plan the paper. Assuming the paper follows the three-part structure we've just inferred, the working thesis would become the final thesis, on the basis of which a reader could anticipate sections of the essay to come.

Statement 1, by contrast, is *explanatory*:

During the past few years, the rights of AIDS patients in the workplace have been debated by national columnists.

In developing a paper based on this thesis, the writer would assert only the existence of a debate, obligating himself merely to a summary of the various positions taken. Readers, then, would use this thesis as a tool for anticipating the contours of the paper to follow. Based on this particular thesis, a reader would *not* expect to find the author strongly endorsing the views of one or another columnist. The thesis does not require the author to defend a personal opinion.

Statement 2 *does* entail a personal, intellectually assertive commitment to the material, although the assertion is not as forceful as the one found in statement 3:

Several columnists have offered convincing reasons for protecting the rights of AIDS patients in the workplace.

Here we have an *explanatory, mildly argumentative* thesis that enables the writer to express an opinion. We infer from the use of the word *convincing* that the writer will judge the various reasons for protecting the rights of AIDS patients; and, we can reasonably assume, the writer herself believes in protecting these rights. Note the contrast between this second thesis and the first one, in which the writer committed himself to no involvement in the debate whatsoever. Still, the present thesis is not as ambitious as the third one, whose writer implicitly accepted the general argument for safeguarding rights (an acceptance she would need to justify) and then took the additional step of evaluating the merits of those arguments in relation to each other.

As you can see, for any subject you might care to explore in a paper, you can make any number of assertions—some relatively simple, some complex. It is on the basis of these assertions that you set yourself an agenda in writing a paper—and readers set for themselves expectations for reading. The more ambitious the thesis, the more complex will be the paper and the greater will be the readers' expectations.

Using the Thesis

Different writing tasks require different thesis statements. The *explanatory thesis* often is developed in response to short-answer exam questions that call for information, not analysis (e.g., "List and explain recent modifications to Canadian legislation on the rights of same-sex couples."). The *explanatory but mildly argumentative thesis* is appropriate for organizing reports (even lengthy ones), as well as essay questions that call for some analysis (e.g., "In what ways are the recent modifications to Canadian legislation about same-sex couples significant?"). The *strongly argumentative thesis* is used to organize papers and exam questions that call for information, analysis, *and* the writer's forcefully stated point of view (e.g., "Evaluate recent modifications to the legal status of same-sex couples.").

The strongly argumentative thesis, of course, is the riskiest of the three, since you must unequivocally state your position and make it appear reasonable—which requires that you offer evidence and defend against logical objections. But such intellectual risks pay dividends, and if you become involved enough in your work to make challenging assertions, you will provoke challenging responses that enliven classroom discussions. One of the important objectives of a university education is to extend learning by stretching, or challenging, conventional beliefs. You breathe new life into this broad objective, and you enliven your own learning as well, every time you adopt a thesis that sets a challenging agenda both for you (as writer) and for your readers. Of course, once you set the challenge, you must be equal to the task. As a writer, you will need to discuss all the elements implied by your thesis. If you can't do it, change your thesis to one you can fulfill.

To review: A thesis (a one-sentence summary of your paper) helps you organize and your reader anticipate a discussion. Thesis statements are distinguished by their carefully worded subjects and predicates, which should be just broad enough and complex enough to be developed within the length limitations of the assignment. Whereas "topic" (from *topos*, the Greek word for "place") is a neutral description of the territory you explore in an essay, thesis is opinionated. It is the main claim—or, if you will, the central organizing insight—you make about that territory:

> Topic: Modifications to the legal status of same-sex couples
> Thesis: Same-sex couples are still far from enjoying the same legal rights as heterosexual couples.

The thesis is not always stated conveniently in one sentence or in one place, but a successful argument always has an implicit thesis that can be deduced from the argument itself. Both novices and experts in a field typically begin the initial draft of a paper with a working thesis—a statement that provides writers with enough structure to get started but with enough latitude to discover what they want to say as they write. Once you have completed a first draft, you should test the "fit" of your thesis with the paper that follows. Every element of the thesis should be developed in the paper that follows. Discussions that drift from your thesis should be deleted, or the thesis changed to accommodate the new discussions.

BUILDING A STRONG THESIS STATEMENT

There is no one formula for writing a strong thesis statement, but the following approach is well suited to any essay in which you are expected to develop a thesis that takes alternative views into account. In this approach, the writer starts with his or her basic (simple) claim about the topic, then expands on it to provide the rationale for the claim, then incorporates the likeliest opposition to the claim.

Simple—just state your main claim about the topic:

- a one-clause sentence: X

"College and university students are the hardest-working demographic group in Canada today."

Expanded—better for you and the reader because it *forecasts* your argument by providing the rationale for your main claim:

- a two-clause sentence: X *because* Y

"College and university students are the hardest-working demographic group in Canada today because they typically work part-time or even full-time while going to school."

Or use another clause (Z) to acknowledge the opposition to X. This works well in an argumentative essay where the position taken is likely to be attacked:

- *Although* Z, X or *Even though* Z, X

"Even though being a student is generally regarded as easier than working for a living, college and university students are the hardest-working demographic group in Canada today."

Better yet, do both. Acknowledge the opposition right away, and then support your claim:

- *Even though* Z, X *because* Y

"Even though being a student is generally regarded as easier than working for a living, college and university students are the hardest-working demographic group in Canada today because they typically work part-time or even full-time while going to school."

This statement forecasts the movement of a whole essay. In this case, the thesis promises that the essay will compare the workloads of students to those of other demographic groups. The essay will support the main claim that students are the hardest-working group by showing that they are unique in combining the double workload of employment and study, and it will refute the common perception that being a student is easier than working.

Now, ask yourself: If I prove this thesis, will my reader be persuaded that X is true—that students are the hardest-working people in Canada? If not, revise the thesis. Finally, ask yourself, "So what?" If you ask yourself this about your thesis statement and no good answer comes to mind, it still needs work, because your reader will be asking "So what?" as well.

■ EXERCISES

1. Choose one of the chapters from Part II and try to identify the thesis in the first paragraphs of each of the readings.
2. Choose a topic and write a thesis statement for it. Now get some practice at expanding your options by writing three more thesis statements on the same topic, all of them significantly different in perspective and purpose from the first.
3. Read the following thesis statements and decide whether each one is weak or strong. Consider the criteria discussed in this chapter when making your decision:
   - Is it clear? Is it brief enough to be held in mind while writing a paper? Is it logical? Does it avoid careless or sensationalistic language?
   - Does it go beyond mere topic description to make a claim about a topic?
   - Can that claim be proved? Would it be hard to research?
   - Is the claim ambitious enough to be written about in an essay? On the other hand, is it so ambitious that its promises could not be fulfilled in the time and space typically available for an essay?
   - So what? What difference does it make whether it's true or not? Why would anyone care?

   If you have time, explain your evaluation and propose a better version.

   1. This essay will examine the health risks of eating potatoes.
   2. We have come a long way since human beings first crawled out of caves.
   3. College and university students are the hardest-working demographic group in Canada today.
   4. Although Canada's anti-Jewish immigration policy during the Nazi Holocaust has been blamed on the prejudice of a few officials, the main reason for its adoption can be found in Mackenzie King's sensitivity to the political climate of his country: anti-Semitism was a vote-getter.
   5. Margaret Laurence's writing is full of hot sex scenes.
   6. Princess Diana was murdered by the Royal Family.
   7. There is no need to be overly concerned about street gangs. After all, human beings have gathered into groups based on shared interests since the dawn of time.

8. Globalization of the economy is happening all around the world. More and more governments take their orders from big business. Some companies have more influence on the course of history than governments do. Students have been in the forefront of demonstrations against globalization. One of these demonstrations was at Quebec City, where anyone who approached the security fence was tear-gassed.
9. Same-sex couples are still far from enjoying the same legal rights in Canada as heterosexual couples.
10. Although they are typically organized around ideals of love and compassion, religions sadly also produce intolerance and hatred for others.

PARAGRAPHS: FORMING AND SHAPING IDEAS

What Paragraphs Do

Paragraphs are made up of sentences that focus on one topic or idea and develop it fully. The indentation that marks the start of a new paragraph is like a pause to tell your readers that there is some separation between the idea you have been developing and the one that you will develop in the paragraph ahead. Of course, the new paragraph is related to the previous one because both deal with some aspect of your thesis, but it is common for each paragraph to offer a fresh or altered approach.

As you have probably noticed when you are reading, paragraphs vary in length and complexity. Paragraph variety is often recommended as a way to appeal to readers. Yet the length of a paragraph is not entirely arbitrary, since it is often governed by the complexity of the concepts you are treating. Complex ideas sometimes require a long paragraph or even several paragraphs to explore their components adequately. If several paragraphs are needed to treat one idea, a shift to a new paragraph means that the writer is refocusing to take a new angle or present a new stage of thought.

The following sections provide some guidelines to help you think about shaping paragraphs and make choices about developing details. Some writers are conscious of forming paragraphs even in early drafting stages. These writers often work from an outline of main, or topic, ideas, and thus approach essay writing by building a series of paragraphs that address different elements of the thesis. Other writers are more concerned with using their draft to explore ideas and they do not worry about paragraph structure until returning to the draft to make revisions.

At some stage in the writing process, it can be useful to remember that most projects require three types of paragraphs—introductory, concluding, and middle paragraphs that build the body of the essay—and that helpful guidelines exist for shaping each of these. You also need to remember that these guidelines are not rules, and should be applied to each writing situation with flexibility, depending on your purpose and the material you are working with. Many visual artists whose work is eventually unconventional began by first learning to draw human and still-life figures. Analogously, once you have an understanding of the basic forms of paragraphs, you will probably want to explore modifications or variants to decide what is suitable in a given writing situation.

Introductions: Some General Guidelines

Frequently, the purpose of the introductory paragraph is to announce your topic and identify how you intend to approach it; to do this, you often need to include your thesis sentence. This enables readers to understand your intention from the outset—whether it is, for example, to explore, illustrate, or demonstrate your idea. Like other paragraphs, introductions usually contain some generalizations alongside more specific details. What makes an introduction different from the paragraphs of development following it is that its purpose is to announce the main argument or the "big idea."

The *purpose* of an introduction is to prepare the reader to enter the world of your essay. The introduction makes the connection between the more familiar world inhabited by the reader and the less familiar world of the writer's particular subject; it places a discussion in a context that the reader can understand. For example, addressing the complex and specialized topic of advances in genetics and biological sciences, Henry Friesen opens "Canada and the Genomic Revolution" (pp. 411–416) by referring to the ancient wisdom of Lao Tzu, using a rhetorical strategy likely chosen to reassure his audience that important truths are abiding, not overwhelming.

Writing Introductions: A Basic Approach

Although there are many ways to build opening paragraphs, you may find it helpful in the drafting process to have a basic or conventional pattern in mind. Perhaps the most basic organizational pattern is to move from general to specific. You begin on relatively general grounds, often by telling the reader what the topic area is, what book you will examine, what controversy you will enter, or what situation you will analyze. The next few sentences often narrow or restrict your topic, so that you clarify some of your decisions about taking a specific approach to your topic; this sometimes involves sorting out why certain areas of the topic concern you and others do not. Finally, the last sentence of your opening paragraph often gives your thesis—what you mean to say or contend about your specific topic.

Visually, a general-to-specific introduction can be compared to a funnel or top-heavy triangle, since it begins broadly, and narrows toward a point. To see an example of an opening paragraph that follows this pattern, look at the student-written research argument, "A Vote for Wal-Mart" (p. 126), noting the highlighted thesis at the end of the paragraph; the other student-written model in that chapter, "If a Tree Falls but Nobody's Listening," (p. 147) takes a similar approach, moving steadily toward a thesis statement by the end of the introduction. One of the biggest problems with writing an opening paragraph occurs if you try to cover too much. Remember that an introductory paragraph needs to familiarize readers with your focus and approach, and that substantive commentary presenting your evidence should come in the paragraphs to follow, which aim at developing your thesis idea. Yet length of introduction is largely a matter of personal or corporate style: There is no rule concerning the correct length of an introduction. If you feel that a short introduction is appropriate, use one. For example, look at how Jack Layton grabs the reader's attention by beginning his journalistic essay about the need for serious and purposeful responses to the problem of homelessness with a single sentence that takes a provocative swipe at superficial responses: "It couldn't have been worse timed" (p. 161).

On the other hand, you may wish to break up what seems like a long introduction into several paragraphs, as Stanley Milgram does in opening "The Perils of Obedience" (p. 221); in the first paragraph, he defines his key term ("obedience"); in the second, he establishes the historical significance of human obedience; and then in the last sentence of the third paragraph, he presents his thesis: "The extreme willingness of adults to go to almost any lengths on the command of an authority constitutes the chief finding of this study and the fact most urgently demanding explanation" (p. 214).

Writing Introductions: Some Advice about Getting Started

A classic image: The writer stares glumly at a blank sheet of paper—or a blank screen. Usually, however, this is an image of a writer who hasn't yet begun to write. Once the piece has been started, momentum often helps to carry it forward, even over the rough spots, which can always be fixed later. As a writer, you've surely discovered that getting started when you haven't yet warmed to your task *is* a problem. What's the best way to approach your subject? With high seriousness, a light touch, an anecdote? How best to engage your reader?

Many writers avoid such agonizing choices by putting them off—productively. Bypassing the introduction, they start by writing the body of the piece; only after they're finished the body do they go back to write the introduction. There's a lot to be said for this approach. Because you have presumably spent more time thinking about the topic itself than about how you're going to introduce it, you are in a better position to begin directly with your presentation. And often, it's not until you've actually seen the piece on paper and read it over once or twice that a "natural" way of introducing it becomes apparent. Even if there is no natural way to begin, you are generally in better psychological shape to write the introduction after the major task of writing is behind you and you know exactly what you're leading up to.

Perhaps, however, you can't operate this way. After all, you have to start writing *somewhere*, and if you have evaded the problem by skipping the introduction, that blank page may loom just as large whenever you do choose to begin. If this is the case, then go ahead and write an introduction, knowing full well that it's probably going to be flat and awful. Set down any kind of pump-priming or throat-clearing verbiage that comes to mind, as long as you have a working thesis. Assure yourself that whatever you put down at this point (except for the thesis) "won't count" and that, when the time is right, you'll go back and replace it with something that's fit for eyes other than yours. But in the meantime, you'll have gotten started.

Conclusions: Some General Guidelines

One way to view the conclusion of your paper is as an introduction worked in reverse, a bridge from the world of your essay back to the world of your reader. In the student-written sample argument, "A Vote for Wal-Mart" (pp. 126–129), the concluding paragraph reiterates the thesis idea that Wal-Mart is successful because it serves customers well; the last paragraph even echoes a key term, "the villain," from the introduction. A conclusion is the part of your paper in which you restate and (if necessary) expand on your thesis. If the form of an introduction at its most basic is like a funnel or top-heavy triangle, the conclusion can be pictured as an inversion of this—as inverted funnel or bottom-heavy triangle. Usually the first sentence offers a recap of the thesis idea. This can be relatively brief, since your readers should be fairly clear about your main contention and expect the conclusion to offer a general reminder of the gist.

Important in some conclusions is the summary, which is not merely a repetition of the thesis but a restatement that takes advantage of the material you've presented. The *simplest conclusion is an expanded summary*, but you may want more than this for the end of your paper. Depending on your needs, you might offer a summary and then build onto it a discussion of the paper's significance or its implications for future study, for choices that individuals might make, for policy, and so on. You might also want to urge the reader to change an attitude or to modify behaviour. Certainly, you are under no obligation to discuss the broader significance of your work (and a summary, alone, will satisfy the formal requirement that your paper have an ending); but the conclusions of better papers often reveal authors who are "thinking large" and want to connect the particular concerns of their papers with the broader concerns of society.

Here are two words of advice about writing conclusions. First, no matter how clever or beautifully executed, a conclusion cannot salvage a poorly written paper. Second, by virtue of its placement, the conclusion carries rhetorical weight. It is the last statement a reader will encounter before turning from your work. Realizing this, writers who expand on the basic summary-conclusion often wish to give their final words a dramatic flourish, a heightened level of diction. Soaring rhetoric and drama in a conclusion are fine as long as they do not unbalance the paper and call attention to themselves. Having laboured long hours over your paper, you have every right to wax eloquent. But keep a sense of proportion and timing. Make your points quickly and end crisply.

Here are some possible approaches to writing effective conclusions:

1. Statement of the Subject's Significance

It can be effective to discuss the broader significance of what you have written, moving from the specific concern of your paper to the broader concerns of the reader's world. Often you will need to choose amongst a range of significances. A paper on bullying in public schools, for example, might end with a discussion of how bullying plays out in homes, businesses, and organizations or of how bullying is related to other social problems. You want to provide readers with one more reason to regard your work as a serious effort, but you don't want to overwhelm your reader or move too far from your main focus.

2. Call for Further Research

In the scientific and social scientific communities, papers often end with a review of what has been presented and the ways in which the subject under consideration needs to be further explored.

3. Solution/Recommendation

If the purpose of your paper is to review a problem or controversy (perhaps to discuss contributing factors) it can be appropriate to recommend a solution based on the knowledge you've gained while conducting research.

4. Anecdote

An anecdote is a briefly told story or joke, the point of which in a conclusion is to shed light on your subject. The anecdote is more direct than an allusion. With an allusion you merely refer to a story ("Too many people today live in Plato's cave . . . "); with an anecdote you actually retell the story. The anecdote allows readers to discover for themselves the significance of a reference to another source—an effort most readers enjoy because they get a chance to exercise their creativity.

5. Quotation

A favourite concluding device is the quotation—the words of a famous person or an authority in the field about which you are writing. The purpose of quoting another is to link your work to theirs, thereby gaining authority and credibility for your work. Your choice of source should be suitable to your thesis, and you should consider what your choice says about you. Suppose you are writing a paper about the homeless in Canada; you set a very different tone if you choose to conclude with a line from a comedian like Mike Myers or from a governing minister. Make sure you identify the person you've quoted, and follow documentation conventions.

There is a potential problem with using quotations: If you end with the words of another, you may leave the impression that someone else can make your case more eloquently. The way to avoid this problem is to make your own presentation strong.

6. *Question*

Questions are useful for opening essays, and they are just as useful for closing them. Whereas the opening question promises to be addressed in the paper that follows, the concluding question leaves issues unresolved, calling on readers to offer their own solutions. Alternately, if you raise and answer a question in your conclusion, you challenge the reader to agree or disagree with your response and thus to assume an active role.

7. *Speculation*

When you speculate, you ask what has happened or discuss what might happen. This kind of question can stimulate the reader because it opens to question the unknown.

▨ EXERCISES

1. Look at the two full-length student-written model essays in Chapter 4. How would you describe the pattern of the conclusion in each?
2. Look at the concluding paragraphs of some of the professional essays in this book to see if you can find examples of the seven approaches described above.

Middle Paragraphs: Paragraphs of Support

While it is important to write carefully crafted introductions and conclusions because they catch readers both coming and going, paragraphs in the body or middle of the essay make up the remaining 98% of your essay and are therefore worth some consideration. Middle paragraphs are sometimes called paragraphs of support because they typically demonstrate or support some element of the thesis or main idea. Yet, common general purpose aside, middle paragraphs do many things—raise questions, provide examples, analyze arguments, develop interpretations—and take different shapes. Those that work best tend to be unified (focusing on one idea) and complete (providing enough detail about that one idea). Paragraphs also need to be presented in a coherent way, so that sentences are not choppy but smoothly linked together.

Unity

A paragraph should be about *one thing*. It should discuss one point rather than several or, if the point is complex, one aspect of the point. Paragraphs that try to cover too much ground can seem thin or underdeveloped, conveying the impression that the writer's thoughts have ranged far and wide but have not been deep.

One way to ensure that a paragraph is unified is to develop it from a topic sentence—a sentence that announces the general paragraph idea. This sentence controls the paragraph, since everything that follows it offers some level of support. For example, after announcing the paragraph topic in the topic sentence, the next sentence often restates the topic in a more refined or restricted version. From there we get the specific support—the facts, illustrations, statistics—that serve as evidence.

It helps some writers to think about the topic sentence as an umbrella sentence that "covers" the paragraph. In this way, it works like a small version of the thesis sentence, which can be seen as the umbrella sentence that covers the essay as a whole.

Many paragraphs do not state a topic sentence directly, but convey the paragraph topic tacitly, by implication. If one of your paragraphs seems unmanageable and appears to lack unity, you might try to summarize it in a sentence, which can then function as an organizing topic sentence. You can decide whether to incorporate this sentence into the paragraph directly or just use it to help you focus and redirect the paragraph.

In the following example, the first paragraph builds from a direct topic statement, while the second paragraph implies the topic idea.

Direct Topic Sentence

Narrative writing has become increasingly influential across the curriculum in the last 10 years. Before that time, most disciplines favoured an objective tone and the recital of facts, but using the personal voice to treat the realm of material experience became more popular with the spread of postmodern skepticism toward the possibility of knowing truth. In the social sciences, ethnographies and case studies began to appear alongside more traditional quantitative studies, and personal essays began to be published with more frequency in journals in the humanities. In their recent text examining *Narrative Inquiry*, Clandinin and Connelly point out that while a narrative approach is appropriate to education research because it grants a human dimension to studying how humans think and learn, this approach is employed across disciplines, and they have consulted "other social sciences and humanities for insights" into how narrative inquiries can work (5).

Tacit Topic Sentence

About 10 years ago, ethnographies and case studies began to appear alongside more traditional quantitative studies in the social sciences, and personal essays began to be published with more frequency in journals in the humanities. In their recent text examining *Narrative Inquiry*, Clandinin and Connelly point out that while a narrative approach is appropriate to education research because it grants a human dimension to studying how humans think and learn, they recognize that this approach has an interdisciplinary appeal, for they have consulted "other social sciences and humanities for insights" into how narrative inquiries can work (5).

Note: The above paragraph cites material from D. Jean Clandinin and F. Michael Connelly, *Narrative Inquiry: Experience and Story in Qualitative Research* (San Francisco: Jossey-Bass, 2000), 5.

You also need to consider that sometimes complex topic sentences are multi-layered and control several paragraphs. To demonstrate the topic idea that narrative inquiry is being used in many disciplines, a writer might decide to use three paragraphs to explore how there is evidence of this in the humanities, the social sciences, and, finally, the sciences.

Completeness

There is no formula to govern the length of a complete paragraph. You may find it helpful, however, to remember that for a paragraph to develop an idea fully usually requires a blend of general and specific information. On a general level, you state your topic sentence or paragraph point. More specific-level information follows this, serving as evidence to demonstrate your general point. For example, after an assertion, you might offer examples, facts and/or statistics as supporting detail.

While there are no tests for paragraph completeness, many undergraduate writers struggle with the problem of leaving their ideas underdeveloped. It can sometimes help to remind yourself that two examples are probably more convincing than one and that readers expect you to explain or interpret the way in which an example demonstrates your point. Moreover, it is also a good strategy to use a variety of evidence, so that you can strengthen the effect of an example or observation from experience by giving it alongside a relevant statistic or a supportive quotation from an expert. In the sample paragraph demonstrating the use of a direct topic sentence, the writer's observations and interpretations gain resonance because they are echoed in "the expert testimony" of Clandinin and Connelly.

■ EXERCISE

Look over several readings in Chapter 9, "Canadian Identities," to find examples of support paragraphs with overt and tacit topic sentences. Is it easier to read a paragraph when the topic sentence is directly stated? Could an author overdo this approach?

2

Representing Sources: Summary, Paraphrase, Quotation, and Documentation

THE ROLE OF REPRESENTING SOURCES

If asked to name the most important issues in essay writing, many writers would say "thesis" or "representing my own perspective on the topic," or, more elaborately, "developing an idea that's powerful enough to account for the topic in all its complexity." All of these answers emphasize the creative activity of the mind working to invent an argument that makes sense of a challenging topic: "What accounts for the popularity of social conservatism in some provinces and not others?" "What should be done to protect the City of Winnipeg from the next flooding of the Red River?" "To what extent can Margaret Atwood's *The Handmaid's Tale* be read as a logical prediction based on current social trends?" And the thesis that guides the writer through an adequate response to such questions is, without doubt, the heart and soul of an essay.

All intellectual work is a form of the human mind trying to understand the universe. In the course of doing this, the mind ventures a great many opinions, theories, hunches, claims, theses, some of them dead ends, others of them well worth following through on, but they are worth nothing if they are not grounded in an attempt to get it right—to see accurately and to represent what we see accurately. Without accurate representation of others' work on the subject, an essay is, at best, an intriguing rant, a series of unsupported claims that have not been tested against the phenomena they describe (a Mars launch, a short story, a three-toed sloth) or the studies of those phenomena done by other scholars. It is in fact by representing the work of other scholars that academic writing distinguishes itself from other kinds of writing. By situating our own perspectives in the existing body of scholarly work on the topic, rather than speaking as one—possibly brilliant—individual thinker, we work collaboratively toward the best possible understandings of our topic. (And by documenting our representations of others as shown toward the end of this chapter, we make sure that our representations of others can be checked for accuracy by our readers; in this way scholarly writing provides a system of quality assurance that is quite unique in the publishing world.)

The work that is represented can be one of two kinds: One might be a primary source that constitutes the topic of your paper (such as Leonard Cohen's

Beautiful Losers or Virginia Woolf's *A Room of One's Own*); the other might be a secondary source chosen from the existing body of scholarship on the topic (such as a critic's interpretation of *Beautiful Losers*). Whether the work is primary or secondary, it can be represented in three forms—summary, paraphrase, and quotation. The three forms cover a wide range, from complete fidelity to the original, quoting it word for word, to drastic changes to the original, summarizing a whole book in a few sentences. Nevertheless, all three are forms of the original version and a faithful *re*-presentation of it. Though summarizing is the most ethically demanding of the three since it undertakes such a radical transformation of the original, all three require that writers put themselves completely and conscientiously at the service of the source they undertake to represent.

Together, summary, paraphrase, and quotation can occupy 50 percent or more of a research essay. For examples of the extent of representation in scholarly writing, look at the student essay "A Vote for Wal-Mart" (pp. 126–129). Even though it has a strong thesis that clearly controls the development of the argument, a large portion of the essay consists of representations of others' work on the topic. But representing others is not just a humble rite of passage demanded of students: Scan the pages of any scholarly journal for the tell-tale footnote numbers or in-text citations that signify a representation of someone else's work and you will see how seriously professional scholars take this aspect of academic writing. The methods used vary with the disciplines—psychologists mainly use summary and paraphrase rather than quotation, and literary scholars mainly use quotation for primary sources and paraphrase for secondary ones—but all scholars use some form of representation in order to test their claims and integrate their work with that of others.

WHAT IS A SUMMARY?

The best way to demonstrate that you understand the information and the ideas in any piece of writing is to compose an accurate and clearly written summary of that piece. By a *summary* we mean a *brief restatement, in your own words, of the content of a passage* (in a group of paragraphs, a chapter, an article, a book). This restatement should focus on the *central idea* or thesis of the passage. The briefest of all summaries (one or two sentences) will do no more than this. A longer, more complete summary will indicate, in condensed form, the main points in the passage that support or explain the central idea. It will reflect the order in which these points are presented and the emphasis given to them. It may even include some important examples from the passage. But it will not include minor details. It will not repeat points simply for the purpose of emphasis. And it will not contain any of your own opinions or conclusions. It will simply extract the main line of argument of the passage.

A good summary, therefore, has three central qualities: *brevity, completeness*, and *objectivity*. Although summarizing seems a humble task in comparison to criticizing, representing a source accurately without letting your judgments surface is tough intellectual work that calls for extreme attentiveness and self-control.

Can a Summary Be Objective?

Consider, for example, how difficult objectivity might be to achieve in a summary. By definition, writing a summary requires you to select some aspects of the original and to leave out others. Since deciding what to select and what to leave out calls for your personal judgment, your summary is really a work of *interpretation*. And, certainly, your interpretation of a passage may differ from another person's. One factor affecting the nature and quality of your interpretation is your *prior knowledge* of the subject. For example, if you're attempting to summarize an anthropological article and you're a novice in the field, then your summary of the article might be quite different from that of your professor, who has spent 20 years studying this particular area and whose judgment about what is more significant and what is less significant is undoubtedly more reliable than your own. By the same token, your personal or professional *frame of reference* may also affect your interpretation. A union representative and a management representative attempting to summarize the latest management offer would probably come up with two very different accounts. Still, we believe that in most cases it's possible to produce a reasonably objective summary of a passage if you make a conscious, good-faith effort not to allow your own feelings on the subject to distort your account of the text.

Form of Summary

Writing a summary is sometimes required as an assignment in itself. For example,

- Find 10 books and articles on the topic of lesbian and gay rights legislation in Canada and produce a 100-word summary of each. (This is a form of annotated bibliography.)
- Write a 200-word summary of your research essay and insert it between the title page and page 1 of your essay. (This is an abstract.)
- Write a five-page summary of Michel Foucault's "The Discourse on Language."

A summary shows up in scholarly writing by professors, too:

- as an abstract of a proposed conference presentation
- as an abstract of a journal article, inserted between the title and first paragraph of the article.

But a summary is most common as an element of a larger piece of work, the research essay that requires the writer to synthesize many outside sources. A summary allows writers to do this efficiently without sacrificing accuracy.

Using the Summary

In some quarters, the summary has a bad reputation—and with reason. Summaries often are provided by writers as substitutes for analyses. As students, many of us have summarized books that we were supposed to *review* critically. The point is that the summary does have an important place in respectable university work. First, writing a summary is an excellent way to understand what you read, because it forces you to put the text into your own words. Practice with writing summaries also develops your general writing habits, since a good summary, like any other piece of good writing, is clear, coherent, and accurate.

Second, summaries are useful to your readers. Suppose you're writing a paper about the rise of Nazism in German villages in the 1930s, and in part of that paper you want to discuss Ursula Hegi's *Stones from the River* as a fictional treatment of the subject. A summary of the plot would be helpful to a reader who hasn't read—or who doesn't remember—the novel. (Of course, if the novel is on the reading list your professor gave you, you can safely omit the plot summary.) Or perhaps you're writing a paper about the creation of the territory of Nunavut in Canada's Arctic. If your reader isn't familiar with the acts of Parliament by which the territory was created, it would be a good idea to summarize these provisions at some early point in the paper. In many cases (a test, for instance), you can use a summary to demonstrate *your* knowledge of what your professor already knows; when writing a paper, you can use a summary to inform your professor about a source that may be unfamiliar.

Underestimating the Summary

It may seem to you that being able to tell (or to retell) exactly what a passage says is a skill that ought to be taken for granted in anyone who can read at the high-school level. Unfortunately, people don't always read carefully. Either they read so inattentively that they skip over words, phrases, or even whole sentences or they see the words in front of them but without registering their significance.

When a reader fails to pick up the meaning and the implications of a sentence or two, usually there's no real harm done. (An exception: You could lose credit on an exam or paper because you failed to read carefully a crucial instruction from your instructor.) But over longer stretches—the paragraph, the section, the article, or the chapter—inattentive or haphazard reading creates problems, for it will thwart your efforts to perceive the shape of the argument, to grasp the central idea, to determine the main points that compose it, to relate the parts of the whole, and to note key examples. This kind of reading takes more energy and determination than casual reading. But, in the long run, it's an energy-saving method because it enables you to retain the content of the material and to use that content as a basis for your own responses.

How to Write Summaries

Every article you read will present a different challenge as you work to summarize it. As you'll discover, saying in a few words what has taken someone else a great many can be difficult. But, like any other skill, the ability to summarize improves with practice. Here are a few pointers to get you started. They represent possible stages, or steps, in the process of writing a summary. These pointers are not meant to be ironclad rules; rather, they are designed to encourage habits of thinking that will allow you to vary your technique as the situation demands. Overall, the goal is to read carefully and extract the thesis and line of argument from the original text.

HOW TO WRITE SUMMARIES

- *Read* the passage carefully. Start looking for its structure of claims and support: the thesis and the main points (or, in a longer passage, stages of thought) used to advance that thesis.
- *Reread.* This time, divide the passage into sections or stages of thought. If you are summarizing a very short article, you might consider each paragraph to be a "stage of thought." If you are summarizing a longer article or a book, you will need to treat whole groups of paragraphs as stages of thought. In social science writing, the commencement of a new stage of thought is often indicated by a subtitle; in other forms of writing, you can often identify where one stage ends and another begins by asking, "Where could a subtitle be inserted?" *Label*, on the passage itself, each section or stage of thought. *Underline* key ideas and terms.
- On a separate sheet of paper, write *one-sentence summaries* of each stage of thought.
- *Write a thesis: a one- or two-sentence summary of the entire passage.* The thesis should express the central idea of the passage, as you have determined it from the preceding steps. You may find it useful to keep in mind the information contained in the lead sentence or paragraph of most newspaper stories—the *what, who, why, where, when,* and *how* of the matter. For persuasive passages, summarize in a sentence the author's conclusion. For descriptive passages, indicate the subject of the description and its key feature(s). *Note:* In some cases, especially in scholarly writing, *a suitable thesis may already be in the original passage.* If so, you may want to quote it directly in your summary.

- *Write the first draft of your summary* by (1) combining the thesis with your list of one-sentence summaries or (2) combining the thesis with one-sentence summaries *plus* significant details from the passage. In either case, eliminate repetition and less important information. Disregard minor details or generalize them (e.g., Mulroney and Chrétien might be generalized as "recent prime ministers"). Use as few words as possible to convey the main ideas.
- *Check your summary against the original passage* and make whatever adjustments are necessary for accuracy and completeness.
- *Revise your summary,* inserting transitional words and phrases where necessary to ensure coherence. *Avoid a series of short, choppy sentences.* Combine sentences for a smooth, logical flow of ideas.

Demonstration: Summary

To demonstrate these points at work, let's go through the process of summarizing a passage of expository material. Read the following passage carefully. Try to identify its four parts and to understand how these parts work together to create a single, compelling idea.

For the Infertile, a High-Tech Treadmill

SHERYL GAY STOLBERG

On a frigid Sunday morning in February 1995, Nancy Alisberg and Michael   1
Albano took a stroll on a windswept beach. They had fled their Brooklyn apartment for the Hamptons, holing up in a quaint bed-and-breakfast for the weekend. But this was no ordinary getaway.

It was, rather, a funeral of sorts. After three unsuccessful attempts at con-   2
ceiving a test-tube baby, the Brooklyn couple had come to the seashore to bury their dream of having a biological child.

Bundled up in their heavy winter coats, they settled in near a log to pro-   3
tect themselves from the wind. There, Ms. Alisberg and Mr. Albano, both lawyers, both in their early 40's, pulled lists from their pockets on which each had written characteristics of the other that they would miss in not having a baby from their own eggs and sperm. They read the lists aloud and then, because it was too windy to burn them, as they had planned, they buried them in the sand.

The ceremony, Ms. Alisberg said recently, "was to say goodbye and then   4
to try to work on the moving on." But moving on was easier said than done.

The couple began investigating adoption as soon as they returned home,   5
and they are now the parents of a 2-year-old girl from Korea. But at the same

time they plunged back into the seductive, emotionally wrenching world of reproductive medicine, signing up for egg donation, in which Ms. Alisberg might become pregnant using another woman's eggs.

"The technology," Mr. Albano said, "has given us so many options that   6
it is hard to say no."

For infertile couples, saying no to reproductive technology has become a   7
vexing problem. Every month, it seems, there is another stride in the science
of making babies. And while public attention inevitably focuses on the latest
accomplishment—the McCaughey septuplets, the California woman who
gave birth at 63 and other recent feats—the reality is that the high-tech path
to parenthood yields failure far more often than success, about three out of
four times.

Thousands of couples are riding the infertility merry-go-round, many   8
unable to get off for fear that the next expensive procedure is the one that will
finally work.

"My patients are always saying to me, 'How can I stop?'" said Dr. Alice   9
Domar, who directs the behavioral medicine program for infertility at the
Beth Israel Deaconess Medical Center in Boston. "I've got this 42-year-old
woman in my group who is just about at the end. She says they are ready to
move on, and then she hears about this cytoplasm stuff," in which doctors
mingle the core genetic blueprint of one egg with the surrounding fluid, or
cytoplasm, from another.

"Where," Dr. Domar asked, "do you get to the point where you say, 'I   10
can't do this anymore?'"

The question carries as much angst for infertility specialists as it does for 11
their patients. "This is the hardest part of my job," said Dr. Jamie A. Grifo,
director of the division of reproductive endocrinology at New York University
Medical Center. "I have patients whom I tell, point blank, 'You should stop,'
and they say to me, 'Well, I want to give it one more try.' I say: 'Here, look
at the data. Your chance is one percent.' And they say, 'Well, I'm going to be
that one, Doc.'"

The National Center for Health Statistics says that in 1995, the most   12
recent year for available figures, the United States had 60.2 million women of
reproductive age, and that 10 percent—or 6.1 million of them—were infertile.
Of these, about 600,000 had at some point tried assisted reproductive technology, participating in what Pamela Madsen, who runs a New York support
group for infertile women, calls "the ovarian Olympics."

New terms are entering the popular lexicon, from "assisted hatching," in   13
which researchers slit open the shells of embryos, to a veritable alphabet
soup of techniques. There is IVF, for in vitro fertilization, in which sperm and
egg are combined in a laboratory dish and then implanted into the uterus as
embryos. There is GIFT, for gamete intrafallopian transfer, in which eggs and
sperm are inserted into the fallopian tubes in the hope they will unite into
embryos. There is ZIFT, for zygote intrafallopian transfer, in which fertilized
embryos are transferred to the tubes. There is ICSI, for intracytoplasmic

sperm injection, in which male infertility is treated by sifting through a man's sperm and injecting a single strong one into a woman's egg. And of course, there is egg donation.

The procedures take place over the course of a month and are therefore   14
called cycles. The American Society for Reproductive Medicine estimates that in 1994, the most recent year for which figures are available, infertility clinics attempted 42,509 cycles of high-tech conception, resulting in 9,573 births, some multiple, for an overall success rate of 22.5 percent. A couple's chances of success depend on a variety of factors, including the woman's age and the quality of her eggs, as well as her husband's sperm count.

For in vitro fertilization, the most common technique, the success rate   15
was 20.7 percent. Egg donation has a much higher success rate—46.8 percent—but it means that a woman must give up a genetic connection to her child. Some, like Mr. Albano, have a difficult time with that. "It didn't sit well with me that I wouldn't have a pairing of my genetic material with hers," he said. "But Nancy was very much desirous of wanting to experience pregnancy and birth."

Critics have suggested that there is an element of subtle coercion in all   16
this state-of-the-art medicine, with infertility clinics making emotional appeals to couples at a particularly vulnerable point in their lives. Moreover, they fear that couples in their baby-making fervor are not thinking through the moral implications of having children whose genetic roots are different from their own.

"This is not just a science problem; it's a marketing problem," said   17
Barbara Katz Rothman, professor of sociology at City University of New York. "Once you are buying these services, there is a never-ending next service."

The treatments are expensive. In vitro fertilization costs, on average,   18
$7,800 per cycle. And some patients are going heavily in debt to pay for them, taking second and even third mortgages on their homes. While doctors who treat fertility consider it a disease, only 12 states require insurance companies to cover the treatments, which often can drag on for years.

"We pay $550 a month for our own insurance," said Heather Higgins,   19
28, of Billerica, Mass., a small town near the New Hampshire border. She and her husband, Eric, who drives a canteen truck, have spent more than six years trying to have a baby. "I would have the cheapo accident insurance if it weren't for the infertility. With $8,000 a cycle, I could never do it."

By her own estimation, Mrs. Higgins has attempted in vitro fertilization   20
more than 20 times. "I lost count at 21," she said.

Her physician, Dr. Vito Cardone of the Fertility Center of New England   21
in Reading, Mass., says the multiple attempts are necessary because Mrs. Higgins is a "poor producer," meaning the fertility drugs he gives her prompt her body to create only one or two eggs at a time, and sometimes none at all. He is pressing her to try egg donation, but Mrs. Higgins is not ready.

"I'm going to exhaust all efforts," she said, "emotionally, physically and   22
financially, until I can't."

She works part time as a medical assistant, but her days are governed by   23
the rhythm of her in vitro fertilization cycles: 16 days of fertility drugs, which
her husband injects into her buttocks (he practiced on an orange); vaginal
ultrasound probes to check egg development; egg retrieval, in which doctors
remove her eggs, mix them with sperm in a laboratory dish to create embryos
that will be inserted into her uterus when they are no bigger than eight cells,
and then 10 days of anxious waiting to find out if she is pregnant. She spends
much of her time at the computer, chatting electronically with infertile friends
in far-flung places.

"I probably sign on five or six times a day," she said. "Some of the mes-   24
sages are very sad."

Indeed, experts have long suspected that infertility causes depression,   25
and while there is little research on the topic, they are just beginning to learn
that depression can also contribute to infertility.

Dr. Domar, the counselor, said infertile women were twice as likely to be   26
depressed as those who are fertile. In 1993, she published research that found
women with infertility had the same levels of depression as those with cancer,
heart disease or the virus that causes AIDS.

But she said the last time anyone examined the link between treatment   27
failure and depression was 1984, when a study showed that 64 percent of
women who had undergone an unsuccessful in vitro fertilization cycle demonstrated symptoms of clinical depression. The results did not surprise her.

"Unsuccessful treatment is going to cause depression," she said. "That's   28
just common sense. The problem is that women who have the resources or
insurance bounce right back and do more cycles."

Indeed, Nancy Alisberg and Michael Albano said they would have con-   29
tinued their attempts at in vitro fertilization had it not been for genetic screening that showed Ms. Alisberg's eggs contained chromosomal anomalies,
meaning the infant would be born with birth defects.

The discovery, which prompted their trip to the Hamptons, came after   30
three emotionally grueling years of trying to conceive, including an unsuccessful effort to correct Mr. Albano's low sperm count by removing an
enlarged vein in his scrotum; two artificial inseminations, and three in vitro
fertilizations, including one that resulted in a "biochemical pregnancy," in
which a blood test suggested that Ms. Alisberg was pregnant. But the embryo
failed to implant.

The discovery of the genetic defects left the couple with a difficult deci-   31
sion: Would they move on to egg donation, which might enable Ms. Alisberg
to fulfill her desire to carry a baby? Or would they choose adoption, which
would virtually guarantee a child? Cost was an issue; while their health insurance covered in vitro fertilization, it did not cover egg donation. If they spent
$15,000 for donated eggs, the couple reasoned, they might lose the money
they had saved for adoption. While adoption agencies discourage it, they
decided to push ahead on both fronts.

Jumping back on the infertility merry-go-round was no picnic. To test the   32
likelihood that she would get pregnant with a donated egg, Ms. Alisberg had
to go through a "mock cycle" in which she took fertility drugs, underwent

blood tests, ultrasound scans and biopsies, all the while knowing that no embryos would be transferred into her uterus.

"Everybody I know who has gone through IVF and then started doing 33 donor eggs has a real visceral reaction to being back in that waiting room," Ms. Alisberg said. "You don't want to feel those things again."

On Dec. 27, 1995, Sophie Sang Ah Albano-Alisberg arrived from Korea, 34 4 months old, long and lean, with fuzzy black hair and beautiful clear skin. Her new parents met her at LaGuardia Airport, after two months of gazing at her picture. "I recognized her immediately," Mr. Albano said.

Not quite two weeks later, he and his wife received a call from their infer- 35 tility clinic, which had matched them with an egg donor. They spent a few days considering the offer, but finally rejected it. "It was not fair to Sophie," Ms. Alisberg said. "She had just arrived."

But she and her husband cannot bring themselves to eliminate the possi- 36 bility of egg donation entirely. Today, two years later, their names remain on the donor candidate list.

■   ■   ■

Reread, Divide into Stages of Thought, Underline

Let's consider our recommended pointers for writing a summary.

As you reread the passage, consider its significance as a whole and its stages of thought. What does it say? How is it organized? How does each part of the passage fit into the whole?

Many of the selections you read for your courses will use subheadings to identify their main sections for you. When a passage has no subheadings, as is the case with Stolberg's article, you must read carefully enough to identify the author's main stages of thought.

How do you determine where one stage of thought ends and the next one begins? Assuming that what you have read is unified and coherent, this should not be difficult. (When a selection is unified, all of its parts pertain to the main subject; when a selection is coherent, the parts follow one another in logical order.) Look, particularly, for transitional sentences at the beginning of paragraphs. Such sentences generally work in one or both of the following ways: (1) they summarize what has come before; (2) they set the stage for what is to follow.

For example, look at the sentence that opens paragraph 16: "Critics have suggested that there is an element of subtle coercion in all this state-of-the-art medicine, with infertility clinics making emotional appeals to couples at a particularly vulnerable point in their lives." Notice how the first part of this sentence, with its reference to "*this* state-of-the-art medicine" (italics added), asks the reader to recall information from the preceding section. The second part of the transitional sentence announces the topic of the upcoming section: 13 paragraphs devoted to the emotional vulnerability of couples involved in assisted reproductive technology.

Each section of an article will take several paragraphs to develop. Often between paragraphs, and almost certainly between sections of an article, you will find transitions that help you understand what you have just read and what you are about to read. For articles that have no subheadings, try writing your own section headings in the margins as you take notes. Then proceed with your summary.

The sections of Stolberg's article may be described as follows:

Section 1: Introduction—the difficulty of stepping off the high-tech tread-mill of fertility medicine, with a lead-in example (paragraphs 1–10).

Section 2: The technology—a brief review of the statistics and techniques associated with assisted reproductive technology (paragraphs 11–15).

Section 3: Emotional vulnerability—the lengths, financial and emotional, to which some will go in order to conceive, with an extended example (paragraphs 16–28).

Section 4: Difficult decision—based on genetic diagnosis and the choice to adopt rather than conceive, with the introductory example continued (paragraphs 29–36).

Here is how the first of these sections might look after you had marked the main ideas, by underlining and by marginal notations:

Example: Emotional difficulty of failed ART,[1] no biological children

On a frigid Sunday morning in February 1995, Nancy Alisberg and Michael Albano took a stroll on a windswept beach. They had fled their Brooklyn apartment for the Hamptons, holing up in a quaint bed-and-breakfast for the weekend. But this was no ordinary getaway. 1

It was, rather, a funeral of sorts. After three unsuccessful attempts at conceiving a test-tube baby, the Brooklyn couple had come to the seashore to bury their dream of having a biological child. 2

Bundled up in their heavy winter coats, they settled in near a log to protect themselves from the wind. There, Ms. Alisberg and Mr. Albano, both lawyers, both in their early 40's, pulled lists from their pockets on which each had written characteristics of the other that they would miss in not having a baby from their own eggs and sperm. They read the lists aloud and then, because it was too windy to burn them, as they had planned, they buried them in the sand. 3

---

[1] "ART," used in marginal notes on this and subsequent pages, is an abbreviation for "assisted reproductive technology."

The ceremony, Ms. Alisberg said recently, "was to say goodbye and then to try to work on the moving on." But moving on was easier said than done. 4

The couple began investigating adoption as soon as they returned home, and they are now the parents of a 2-year-old girl from Korea. But at the same time they plunged back into the seductive, emotionally wrenching world of reproductive medicine, signing up for egg donation, in which Ms. Alisberg might become pregnant using another woman's eggs. 5

Main Pt. of Article: Hard to say no to ART

"The technology," Mr. Albano said, "has given us so many options that it is hard to say no." 6

For infertile couples, saying no to reproductive technology has become a vexing problem. Every month, it seems, there is another stride in the science of making babies. And while public attention inevitably focuses on the latest accomplishment—the McCaughey septuplets, the California woman who gave birth at 63 and other recent feats—the reality is that the high-tech path to parenthood yields <u>failure</u> far more often than success, <u>about three out of four times.</u> 7

High-publicity success, but most often failure

Only 25% success rate

The "treadmill" of title

Thousands of couples are <u>riding the infertility merry-go-round,</u> many unable to get off for fear that the next expensive procedure is the one that will finally work. 8

Not even multiple failures can keep patients from hope

"My patients are always saying to me, 'How can I stop?'" said Dr. Alice Domar, who directs the behavioral medicine program for infertility at the Beth Israel Deaconess Medical Center in Boston. "I've got this 42-year-old woman in my group who is just about at the end. She says they are ready to move on, and then she hears about this cytoplasm stuff," in which doctors mingle the core genetic blueprint of one egg with the surrounding fluid, or cytoplasm, from another. 9

It's always the next new procedure that will work (finally)

For patients, when to quit is very hard

<u>"Where," Dr. Domar asked, "do you get to the point where you say, 'I can't do this anymore?'"</u> 10

Write a One-Sentence Summary of Each Stage of Thought

The purpose of this step is to wean you from the language of the original passage, so that you are not tied to it when writing the summary. Here are one-sentence summaries for each stage of thought in the four sections of Stolberg's article:

> *Section 1:* Introduction—the difficulty of stepping off the high-tech treadmill of fertility medicine, with a lead-in example (paragraphs 1–10).

Infertile couples face difficult emotional problems as they consider abandoning their efforts to become pregnant through assisted reproductive technologies (ART).

> *Section 2:* The technology—a brief review of the statistics and techniques associated with assisted reproductive technology (paragraphs 11–15).

ART is a broad term describing a set of complex laboratory procedures in which eggs are fertilized outside the body and then implanted in women who otherwise have been unable to become pregnant.

> *Section 3:* Emotional vulnerability—the lengths, financial and emotional, to which some will go in order to conceive, with an extended example (paragraphs 16–28).

The costs of these treatments are high both financially (roughly $8000 per attempted pregnancy) and emotionally (couples trying to conceive ride a roller coaster of hope with each ART attempt and despair with each ART failure; failures occur three out of every four attempts).

> *Section 4:* Difficult decision—based on genetic diagnosis and the choice to adopt rather than conceive, with the introductory example continued (paragraphs 29–36).

After three ART failures, Nancy Alisberg and Michael Albano chose to adopt a child but still hope to undergo yet another ART procedure.

Write a Thesis: A One- or Two-Sentence Summary of the Entire Passage

To ensure clarity for the reader, the first sentence of your summary should begin with the author's thesis, regardless of where it appears in the article itself.

A thesis consists of a subject and an assertion about that subject. How can we go about fashioning an adequate thesis for "For the Infertile, a High-Tech Treadmill"? Probably no two proposed thesis statements for this article would be worded identically, but it is fair to say that any reasonable thesis will indicate that the subject is assisted reproductive technology (ART) and the emotionally difficult decision of whether or not to continue fertility clinic treatments. What issues, specifically, does Stolberg believe are raised by ART? For a clue, look at the beginning of paragraph 7: "For infertile couples, saying no to reproductive technology has become a vexing problem." As Stolberg's title suggests, ART can be a "high-tech treadmill" that couples find difficult to leave. Mindful of Stolberg's subject and the assertion she makes about it, we can write a thesis statement *in our own words* and arrive at the following:

> Infertile couples face emotional difficulties as they consider abandoning their efforts to become pregnant through assisted reproductive technologies (ART).

To clarify for our readers the fact that this idea is Stolberg's and not ours, we'll frame the thesis as follows:

> In her article "For the Infertile, a High-Tech Treadmill," Sheryl Gay Stolberg reports that infertile couples face emotional difficulties as they consider abandoning their efforts to become pregnant through assisted reproductive technologies (ART).

The first sentence of a summary is crucially important, for it orients readers by letting them know what to expect in the coming paragraphs. The preceding example sentence provides the reader with both a direct reference to an article and a thesis for the upcoming summary. And lest you become frustrated too quickly, realize that writing an acceptable thesis for a summary takes time—in this case, three drafts, or roughly seven minutes of effort spent on one sentence and another few minutes of fine-tuning after a draft of the entire summary was completed. That is, the first draft of the thesis was too vague; the second draft was too cumbersome; and the third draft needed refinements.

Draft 1:   Sheryl Gay Stolberg reports on the emotional and

(Too vague—what   financial costs associated with assisted
about the costs?)

reproductive technologies.

Draft 2:   Sheryl Gay Stolberg reports that when *^infertile* couples

(cumbersome)

~~who want biological children~~ give up on efforts to

become pregnant through measures associated

with assisted reproductive technologies (ART),

the couples face emotional difficulties.

Draft 3:   In her article "For the Infertile, a High-Tech

Treadmill," Sheryl Gay Stolberg reports that ~~for~~

as they consider abandoning
their attempts to become   infertile couples ~~the decision to end attempts at~~

                                 pregnan~~cy~~*t* through assisted reproductive *face*

                                 technologies (ART)~~/is~~ ⟨emotional~~ly~~⟩ difficult. *ies*

Final: In her article "For the Infertile, a High-Tech

Treadmill," Sheryl Gay Stolberg reports that infertile

couples face emotional difficulties as they consider

abandoning their efforts to become pregnant

through assisted reproductive technologies (ART).

Write the First Draft of the Summary

Let's consider two possible summaries of the example passage: (1) a short summary, combining a thesis with one-sentence section summaries; and (2) a longer summary, combining thesis, one-sentence section summaries, and some carefully chosen details. Again, realize that you are reading final versions; each of the following summaries is the result of at least two full drafts.

(1) Short Summary: Combine Thesis Sentence with One-Sentence Section Summaries

In her article "For the Infertile, a High-Tech Treadmill," Sheryl Gay Stolberg reports that infertile couples face emotional difficulties as they consider abandoning their efforts to become pregnant through assisted reproductive technologies (ART). ART is a broad term describing a set of complex laboratory procedures in which eggs are fertilized outside the body and then implanted in women who otherwise have been unable to become pregnant. The treatments, which fail three out of every four attempts, are expensive, costing roughly $8000 per attempted pregnancy. Emotionally, the costs are high as well, as couples trying to conceive ride a roller coaster of hope with each ART attempt and despair with each ART failure. Stolberg illustrates this emotional turmoil with the story of a couple who adopted an infant from Korea after three ART failures but who still hope for a biological child by undergoing yet another ART procedure. Many who use ART become frustrated and depressed; still, they're eager to try again, hoping to beat the odds and give birth.

Discussion

This summary consists essentially of a restatement of Stolberg's thesis plus the section summaries, altered or expanded a little for stylistic purposes. The first sentence encompasses the summary of section 1 and is followed by the summaries of sections 2, 3, and 4. Notice in the summary of section 4 the decision to refer to Alisberg and Albano as "a couple" and to conclude with a sentence that uses the general outline of their story to re-emphasize the article's main point: that, despite the failures, couples want to continue high-tech efforts to conceive.

(2) Longer Summary: Combine Thesis Sentence, Section Summaries, and Carefully Chosen Details

The thesis and one-sentence section summaries also can be used as the outline for a more detailed summary. Most of the details in the passage, however, won't be necessary in a summary. It isn't *necessary* even in a longer summary of this passage to discuss either of Stolberg's examples—Higgins or Alisberg and Albano; it would be *appropriate*, though, to provide a bit more detail about Alisberg/Albano and, perhaps, about Higgins (who isn't mentioned in the first summary). In a more extended summary, concentrate on a few carefully selected details that might be desirable for clarity. For example, in "For the Infertile, a High-Tech Treadmill" you could mention that 600 000 women visit fertility clinics each year, and you could name a few of the ART procedures. You might also develop the notion that stepping off the "treadmill" of ART is difficult.

How do you know which details may be safely ignored and which ones may be advisable to include? The answer is that you won't always know. Developing good judgment in comprehending and summarizing texts is largely a matter of reading skill and prior knowledge. Consider the analogy of the chess player who can plot three separate winning strategies from a board position that to a novice looks like a hopeless jumble. In the same way, the more practised a reader you are, the more knowledgeable you become about the subject, and the better able you will be to make critical distinctions between elements of greater and lesser importance. In the meantime, read as carefully as you can and use your own best judgments as to how to present your material.

Here's one version of a completed summary, with carefully chosen details. Note that we have highlighted phrases and sentences added to the original, briefer summary.

Thesis

Section 1

Summary of

¶s 1–10

Section 2

Summary of

¶s 11–15

Section 3

Summary of

¶s 16–28

In her article "For the Infertile, a High-Tech Treadmill," Sheryl Gay Stolberg reports that infertile couples face emotional difficulties as they consider abandoning their efforts to become pregnant through assisted reproductive technologies (ART). ART is a broad term describing a set of complex laboratory procedures in which eggs are fertilized outside the body and then implanted in women who otherwise have been unable to become pregnant. These techniques include in vitro fertilization, gamete intrafallopian transfer, and intracytoplasmic sperm injection. Some 600 000 infertile women a year (as of 1995) visit fertility specialists in an effort to become pregnant. The treatments are expensive, costing roughly $8000 per attempted pregnancy. Emotionally, the costs are high as well, as couples attempting to conceive ride a roller coaster of hope with each ART attempt and despair with each ART failure. Unfortunately, disappointment is all too common since ART fails roughly in three out of every four attempts. Still, couples persist. One woman, who "lost count" of the number of procedures she had after 21 attempts, claimed that she would exhaust herself "emotionally, physically and financially" before resigning herself to never having a biological child. Fuelled by their intense emotional need and by rapidly evolving techniques that promise improved results, infertile couples feel justified in staying on the "high-tech [reproductive] treadmill," even after multiple failures. Stolberg illustrates the emotional difficulties of life on the treadmill through

Section 4
Summary of
¶s 29–36

the story of a couple who adopted an infant from Korea after three ART failures and the discovery that the woman's eggs were genetically flawed. Two years after adoption, the couple still hopes for a biological child, this time through a procedure that would allow the wife to become pregnant using another woman's eggs. The successes of complex procedures such as egg donation, when they occur, are dazzling. But a great many infertile couples who turn to ART become frustrated and depressed; even so, they're eager to try again, hoping to beat the odds and give birth.

Discussion

The structure of this summary generally reflects the structure of the original—with one notable departure. Stolberg splits her discussion of Alisberg and Albano between the beginning and end of the article, a useful strategy for bracketing the piece with a related introduction and conclusion. After the thesis, this summary omits reference to the Alisberg/Albano example in favour of defining assisted reproductive technology in terms that the reader can understand. The definition is followed with a section that lays out the emotional difficulties of infertile couples—the main point of Stolberg's article—and only then introduces Alisberg/Albano, to help make the point. For the sake of efficiency, the Alisberg/Albano example is discussed in only one place—at the end of the summary piece.

Compared to the first, briefer summary, this effort adds details about Stolberg's second example, Ms. Higgins; adds a figure for the number of women who visit fertility clinics annually; identifies three ART techniques; and adds one sentence on why infertile couples feel justified in continuing to seek ART even after multiple failures.

Just a note: Remember as you read student examples in this text that, along with the strengths, there are also writing weaknesses, which could be improved by some revision. For example, this passage is relatively long without paragraph division; as a reader, you may have wondered about how ideas could be subdivided, or wondered, more on a gut level, where to pause and rest.

Summary Length

How long should a summary be? This depends on the length of the original passage. A good rule of thumb is that a summary should be no longer than one-fourth of the original passage. Of course, if you were summarizing an entire chapter or even an entire book, it would have to be much shorter than that. The summary above is about one-fifth the length of the original passage. Although it shouldn't be very much longer, you have seen (pp. 36–37) that it could be quite a bit shorter.

The length of a summary, as well as the content of the summary, also depends on its *purpose*. Suppose you decided to use Stolberg's piece in a paper that dealt with the motivation of couples who persist with assisted reproductive technologies in the face of overwhelming odds. In this case, you might summarize *only* Stolberg's two examples—Higgins and Alisberg/Albano—to provide your paper with some poignant material. If, instead, you were writing a paper in which you argued against ART on the grounds that it was expensive and too prone to failure, you might omit reference to the examples and focus, instead, on Stolberg's use of statistics and basic information about ART. Thus, depending on your purpose, you would summarize either selected portions of a source or an entire source, as we will see more fully in the discussions of research essays in Chapter 4.

▓ EXERCISE

Read the following summary written by a student to convey the main ideas and some of the most important details of Stanley Milgram's "The Perils of Obedience," a fairly long and complex article that appears in Chapter 6 of this book (pp. 221).

Consider the ways in which this summary both follows and adapts the guidelines set out here explaining how to write a summary. For example, can you tell what Milgram's thesis is from reading the first sentences of the summary? Does paragraph two convey enough detail to allow you to comprehend the design of Milgram's experiment (which he explains in detail in his paragraphs 4–11)? Do the final sentences of the summary represent Milgram's conclusions about the ways modern society cultivates a dangerous climate of conformity?

Longer Summary: "The Perils of Obedience"

In "Perils of Obedience" (1974), credited Yale psychologist Stanley Milgram writes of an experiment he performed in the 60's, which tested human obedience under authority. Subjects were evaluated as to whether they followed instruction from the experimenter, the authority figure, to inflict pain on another person, who resists and protests. Surprisingly, results showed that most people were obedient. Through a few alterations in the experiment, Milgram draws the conclusion that many people are obedient in a social setting when they feel that others are in charge. Over-obedience is a danger, for individuals risk losing self-control and the capacity to think for themselves.

The experiment involved an authority figure, a hired actor playing the role of a student, and the subject, who thinks he is hired as a teacher for an experiment to test memory. The "teacher" is to administer simple word association questions to the student, and is directed by the authority figure to punish the learner with increasing intensity of electric shock for each wrong answer. The real experiment is to test the teacher's willingness to go against his or her own will to obey the experimenter by punishing (and presumably hurting) the student. Prior to the experiment, Milgram, along with various experts, predicted that most of the subjects would refuse to obey the instructions. In the first group of subjects, Yale undergraduates, 60% were obedient to the end. This number proved to be consistent for all subject groups. Milgram recounts a specific case at length, reproducing the dialogue, to convey how subjects attempt to resist the orders of the experimenter, but go on when the experimenter claims he will assume responsibility. Feeling panicked when his student pretends to have a heart condition, the subject nonetheless continues the experiment to the highest level of punishment.

With the data indicating surprising levels of compliance, Milgram attempted to find out why people responded the way they did. He made a slight adjustment to the procedure, allowing the subject to choose the level of punishment. This would clarify whether there were aggressive instincts within humans that were waiting for this "institutional justification, for the release of these impulses." Most subjects used low levels of punishment, which led to the conclusion that regular people do not enjoy inflicting pain but can be convinced to be cruel under orders. Choosing for themselves, they applied the smallest shock to ease their conscience and make the situation seem less harmful.

Another alteration was made to the experiment where the authority gave instructions over the phone, and only a third as many people were obedient in this situation. Milgram notes that the subjects take pleasure in being loyal to the experimenter. Since they are only following instructions, they proceed as if the burden of the deed is lifted off their shoulders. There were a few more alterations to the experiment, which produced the following results: (1) The experimenter's physical presence yields more obedient subjects. (2) Conflicting orders given by two different authorities are less successful than one direct command. (3) Peers can pressure one another into disobedience.

In a final alteration in the experiment, there are two subjects, one to ask the questions and the other to administer the punishment; here, Milgram wanted to examine how responsibility diminishes when people see themselves as part of a larger process. In this case, 37 out of 40 pairs were obedient. Neither subject took responsibility because they were only "an intermediate link in the chain." A final comparison is made to soldiers in a concentration camp following orders and being obedient to the authority. There is no one to assume responsibility and dangerous actions go unaccounted for. Milgram sees this lack of accountability, rife in modern society, as a relevant issue that must be addressed.

SUMMARIZING A NARRATIVE

A narrative is a story, a retelling of a person's experiences. That person and those experiences may be imaginary, as is the case with fiction, or they may be real, as in biography. Summarizing a narrative presents special challenges. You have seen that an author of an argument (such as Stolberg's "For the Infertile, a High-Tech Treadmill") follows assertions with examples and statements of support. Narrative presentations, however, usually are less direct. The author relates a story—event follows event—the point of which may never be stated directly. The charm, the force, and the very point of the narrative lies in the telling.

Because narratives generally do not exhibit the same logical development as does writing designed to convey information or present an argument, they do not lend themselves to summary in quite the same way. Narratives do have a logic (the poet Samuel Taylor Coleridge [1772–1834] once wrote that poetry has "a logic of its own, as severe as that of science"), but that logic may be emotional, imaginative, or plot-bound. The writer who summarizes a narrative is obliged to represent that logic through an overview—a synopsis—of the story's events and an account of how these events affect the central character(s).

When you summarize a narrative, bear in mind the principles that follow, as well as those listed in the box.

HOW TO SUMMARIZE NARRATIVES

- Your summary will *not* be a narrative, but rather the synopsis of a narrative. Your summary will likely be a paragraph at most.
- You will want to name and describe the principal characters of the narrative and describe the narrative's main actions or events.

- You should seek to connect the narrative's characters and events—describe the significance of events for (or the impact of events on) the character: What is the "logic" of the story?
- Don't offer mere plot summary when you should be analyzing; your summary should be a platform for your critical observations, not a substitute for them.

To summarize events, reread the narrative and make a marginal note each time you see that an action advances the story from one moment to the next. The key here is to recall that narratives take place *in time*. In your summary, be sure to re-create for your reader a sense of time flowing. Name and describe the characters as well. (For our purposes, *characters* refer to the persons, real or fictional, about whom the narrative is written.)

Earlier we made the point that summarizing any selection involves a degree of interpretation, and this is especially true of summarizing narratives. As you read the short summary of "The Lottery" that follows, notice how it emphasizes the impact of the events, rather than the details surrounding their unfolding. Yet deciding how to represent the significance of the events is tricky, for five readers would probably interpret the narrative's significance in five distinct ways, would they not? Yes and no: yes, in the sense that these readers, given their separate experiences, will read from different points of view; no, in the sense that readers should be able to distinguish between the impact of events as seen from the main characters' (i.e., townspeople's) points of view and the impact of these same events as seen from their (i.e., the readers') points of view. Whereas the townspeople submit, with varying levels of enthusiasm, to carrying out the ritual task, most readers probably agree that the narrative is about the human cruelty that can result from following outmoded rituals.

How Summarizing Narrative Differs from Summarizing Argument

At times, you will have to infer from clues in a narrative the significance of the events; at other times, the writer will be more direct. In the case of "The Lottery," Jackson never makes the point outright that the lottery is a cruel and outmoded ritual, but the details of her story, whose characters carry out a heinous act as if it is normal and necessary, make this case. Following are short summaries of Shirley Jackson's "The Lottery" (p. 280) and Doris Lessing's "Group Minds" (p. 210), both by Andrae Braun. Both original pieces—Jackson's fictional narrative and Lessing's article—appear in Chapter 6 and comment on the dangers of blind obedience. Whereas the point of the narrative is indirect and requires interpretation, the point of the article is relatively straightforward, and can be found stated in the text itself. To summarize the narrative, the writer has to convey not only what happened to whom, but also what the actions mean in relation to the theme of human obedience; to summarize the article, the writer needs only to present Lessing's main idea or thesis as well as the most outstanding points of support.

Short Summary of the Narrative "The Lottery"

The Winner Loses: A Summary of Shirley Jackson's "The Lottery"

> With a feeling of expectation in the early summer air, Shirley Jackson introduces unsuspecting readers, in her provocative "The Lottery," to an agrarian village casually gathering to hold its annual ritual of a lottery. An atmosphere of nervousness arises late in the assembly, and quickly infiltrates the attitudes and conversations of the villagers by the time the family representatives begin retrieving slips of paper from the black lottery box. Eventually, the one dotted slip of paper is pulled by Joe Hutchinson—in spite of his wife Tessie's opposition to the process as having been faulty and "unfair." As though her pleas were unknowingly against her own impending doom, the subsequent lottery within Mrs. Hutchinson's family unveils her as the one with the dotted slip of paper. Curiously, the only strong objection to this annual ritual is from this lone victim who stands in opposition to *how* the slip of paper was pulled, rather than the shocking consummation of it: to stone her as a human sacrifice. Villagers quietly carry out this horror with only the mildest debate simply because the lottery is a time-worn harvest ritual, easier to continue than to resist or reform.

Short Summary of the Argument "Group Minds"

Freedom from the Group Will: A Summary of "Group Minds" by Doris Lessing

> With a prolific career to amplify her message, Doris Lessing—in "Group Minds"—broadly challenges people living in the free countries of the West to activate the solid body of information on social laws that govern groups, in order improve society. In spite of the West's reputation for self-governing individualism, Lessing points out that its people, like the rest of the human race, appear to be innately obedient to the will of a group, or collective, of

individuals. Although she admits with empathy that going against the current of conformity is not easy, she is quick to point out that according to renowned experiments on obedience, there are too few individuals who will go against the flow. Lessing insists on the need to progress from the gathering and verifying of such information, to the application of it, by carefully instructing future generations to be able to demonstrate assertive free-thinking that will liberate individuals from following authority, unquestioningly, in group environments.

SUMMARIZING FIGURES AND TABLES

In your reading in the sciences and social sciences, often you will find data and concepts presented in non-text forms—as figures and tables. Such visual devices offer a snapshot, a pictorial overview, of material that is more quickly and clearly communicated in graphic form than as a series of (often complicated) sentences. The writer uses a numbered "figure" to present the quantitative results of research as points on a line or a bar, or as sections ("slices") of a pie. Pie charts show relative proportions, or percentages. Graphs, especially effective in showing patterns, relate one variable to another: for instance, income to years of education or a university student's grade point average to hours of studying.

HOW TO SUMMARIZE FIGURES AND TABLES

- Study the figure to identify its logic and main claims, including general trends and striking results. (Even though the data are not presented in sentence form, figures, like paragraphs, do make claims.)
- If the summary will be included in an essay, focus on the claims that relate to your topic, even if they do not support your perspective.
- Write the summary and check it against the figure for fairness and accuracy.
- Revise the summary for logical flow. Frame it properly by naming the source either in the summary itself or in a citation.

The figures and tables that follow appeared in a study on assisted reproductive technology (ART), conducted by the U.S. federal government's Centers for Disease Control, located in Atlanta, Georgia, and based on data collected from 281 fertility clinics in 1995.

In Figure 2.1, a *pie chart* relates the percentage of ART pregnancies (from fresh—non-frozen—embryos resulting from non-donor eggs) that led to the live births of a single child or multiple children. Study this pie chart to identify its main claims.

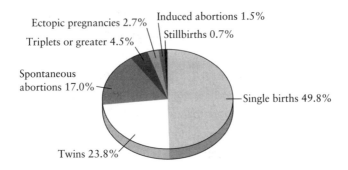

Ectopic pregnancies 2.7%

Induced abortions 1.5%

Triplets or greater 4.5%

Stillbirths 0.7%

Spontaneous
abortions 17.0%

Single births 49.8%

Twins 23.8%

FIGURE 2.1   Outcomes of Clinical Pregnancies Resulting from
ART, 1995

Here is a summary of the information presented:

By far, the most common outcome of a pregnancy that results from ART using
fresh embryos and non-donor eggs is a single birth (roughly 50 percent of live
births). Twins are born nearly one quarter of the time and triplets (or greater)
only 4.5 percent. Roughly 22 percent of such ART pregnancies do not lead to
a live birth.

The points on the *graph* in the next figure, 2.2, relate the age of women
undergoing ART and the success rates of their procedures, as measured by live
births. ("Cycle" refers to a specific attempt at pregnancy, using ART.) Here is
the summary that accompanied the graph in the national report:

A woman's age is the most important factor affecting the chances of a live
birth when the woman's own eggs are used. Figure [2.2] shows the live birth
rate for women of a given age who had an ART procedure in 1995. Rates
were relatively constant at about 25 percent among women aged 34 years and
younger but declined with age after 34. Success rates were zero among women
aged 47 years and older.

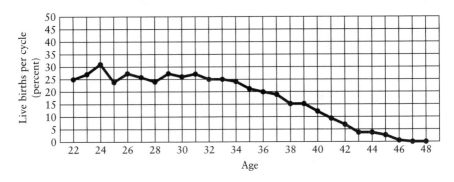

FIGURE 2.2   ART Live Birth Rates by Age of Woman, 1995

Sometimes a single graph will present information on two populations, or data sets, both of which are tracked with the same measurements. In Figure 2.3, the graph tracks the live birth rate of (1) ART for women whose own eggs are fertilized outside their bodies and implanted (that is, transferred from the test tube to the patient), and (2) women who receive *another* woman's (a donor's) egg that has been fertilized. Here is the summary that accompanied the graph in the national report:

> Figure [2.3] shows that the age of the woman undergoing ART treatment does not affect success rates for cycles using embryos formed from donor eggs as it affects success rates for cycles using embryos from a woman's own eggs. The likelihood of a fertilized egg implanting is related to the age of the woman who produced the egg. As a result, the success rate for cycles using donor embryos is nearly constant (around 30 percent) across all age groups from 25 to 50. This graph illustrates that women age 36 and older are more likely to have success with ART using donor eggs.

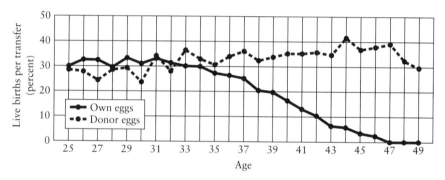

FIGURE 2.3 Live Births per Transfer for Fresh Embryos from Own and Donor Eggs by Age of Recipient, 1995

A *table* presents numerical data in rows and columns for quick reference. Tabular information can be incorporated into graphs, if the writer chooses. Graphs are preferable when the writer wants to emphasize a pattern or relationship; tables are used when the writer wants to emphasize numbers. Table 2.1 provides an overview of the entire 1995 national summary on assisted reproductive technologies.

An explanation of some terms and symbols will be useful in understanding this table. The mathematical symbols for "less than" (<) and "greater than" (>) indicate the age brackets of women in the study: younger than 35; 35 through 39; and older than 39. A "cycle" is a single attempt at pregnancy, using ART. Eggs fertilized in a laboratory—via in vitro fertilization (IVF)—can be transferred immediately into a woman's uterus or fallopian tubes (a so-called fresh embryo transfer) or can be frozen for later implantation (a "frozen" transfer). A woman can have her own fertilized egg transferred from the test tube to her uterus, or the egg of a donor. A "retrieval" is a collection

TABLE 2.1   1995 ART Pregnancy Success Rates

	AGE OF WOMEN			
	<35	35–39	>39	TOTAL
CYCLES USING FRESH EMBRYOS FROM NONDONOR EGGS				
Number of Cycles	21,019	16,728	8,159	45,906
Pregnancies per cycle (%)	29.7	23.4	13.2	24.4
Live births per cycle[a] (%)	25.3	18.2	8.0	19.6
Live births per retrieval[a] (%)	28.0	21.5	10.2	22.8
Live births per transfer[a] (%)	30.6	23.6	11.6	25.1
Cancellations (%)	9.1	14.8	21.5	13.6
Avg. number embryos transferred	4.0	4.0	4.1	4.0
Multiple birth rate per transfer				
Twins	9.8	6.6	1.9	7.4
Triplets or greater	2.6	1.2	0.3	1.7
CYCLES USING FROZEN EMBRYOS FROM NONDONOR EGGS				
Number of transfers	3,724	2,433	1,001	7,465
Live births per transfer[a] (%)	16.4	14.8	11.0	15.1
Avg. number embryos transferred	3.5	3.4	3.4	3.4
CYCLES USING DONOR EGGS				
Number of fresh transfers	572	668	2,112	3,352
Live births per transfer[a] (%)	30.8	35.8	36.7	35.5
Avg. number embryos transferred	4.0	4.0	4.2	4.1

[a] Pregnancies resulting in one or more children born alive; therefore, multiple births are counted as one.

From: Centers for Disease Control. *1995 Assisted Reproductive Technology Success Rates: National Summary and Fertility Clinic Reports.*

of eggs contained in the ovaries and then fertilized for implantation. A "cancellation" is an ART cycle that is stopped before eggs are retrieved or a frozen embryo is implanted.

A summary of such a comprehensive table will necessarily be selective, depending on which information from the table is pertinent to the task:

- In writing a paper on ART, you could draw on the data in this table to report on the number of women undergoing treatment.
- You could compare numbers of women receiving their own fertilized eggs for transplantation as opposed to donor eggs, noting that the non-donor transfer is by far the more common (53 371 transfers of non-donor eggs versus 3352 transfers of donor eggs).
- You could report on the high success rate of cycles using donor eggs as compared to the success rate of a woman's attempting pregnancy using her own eggs.
- From the numbers in the table you could infer that women seeking ART vastly prefer to have their own biological offspring.

- You might be interested in summarizing the age breakdown of women undergoing IVF and in noting that older women have higher success rates with donor eggs than do younger women. But for non-donor cycles, the younger the ART recipient, the better the likelihood of success.

You could glean other information from this table as well, depending on your research needs.

▧ EXERCISE

In Chapter 4, find the chart "Wal-Mart Takes Off" (p. 115). Summarize it, using the advice and consulting the models in this section.

PARAPHRASE

In certain cases, you may want to *paraphrase* rather than to summarize material. Writing a paraphrase is similar to writing a summary: It involves recasting a passage into your own words, and so it requires your complete understanding of the material. The difference is that while a summary is a shortened version of the original, the paraphrase is approximately the same length as the original.

Why write a paraphrase when you can quote the original? The main reason is to keep your own voice in control of the essay. Research essays typically involve so many representations of outside sources that always quoting instead of paraphrasing would result in the reader's hearing more from your sources than from you, resulting in jarring, confusing shifts of tone and terminology. The result could be chaotic, especially if the quotations do not share a common set of key terms with you, or do assume a familiarity with specialized terms that is inappropriate for your own purpose and audience.

You may decide, then, to paraphrase material written in language that is dense, abstract, archaic, or possibly confusing. For example, suppose you were writing a paper on some aspect of Canadian identity and you came across the following passage by Northrop Frye, a Canadian scholar and critic whose views helped to shape our thinking about the arts in Canada over the last half of the twentieth century:

> It is not much wonder if Canada developed with the bewilderment of a neglected child, preoccupied with trying to define its own identity, alternately bumptious and diffident about its own achievements. Adolescent dreams of glory haunt the Canadian consciousness (and unconsciousness), some naïve and some sophisticated. In the naïve area are the predictions that the twentieth century belongs to Canada, that our cities will become much bigger than they ought to be, or like Edmonton and Vancouver, "gateways" to somewhere else, reconstructed Northwest passages. The more sophisticated usually take the

form of a Messianic complex about Canadian culture, for Canadian culture, no less than Alberta, has always been "next year country." The myth of the hero brought up in the forest retreat, awaiting the moment when his giant strength will be fully grown and he can emerge into the world, informs a good deal of Canadian criticism down to our time. (221)

(From: Northrop Frye, *The Bush Garden: Essays on the Canadian Imagination*, Toronto: Anansi, 1971.)

You would like to introduce Frye's idea about how dreams of glory permeate the Canadian imagination, but you also don't want to slow down your essay with this somewhat abstract quotation. You may decide to attempt a paraphrase, as follows:

> Northrop Frye believes that the Canadian sense of identity lacks full maturity, so that we vacillate between thinking of ourselves in modest or in grandiose terms. Moreover, the images we use to define ourselves are immature in differing degrees. For example, in the popular imagination our dreams of glory hold that the future belongs to us or that our cities are gateways to great places. Taking a Messianic twist, a more sophisticated version of this dream holds that we have much to offer the world. Many of our critics write from the position that our superior strength is soon to be revealed to others.

Each sentence in the paraphrase corresponds to a sentence in the original. The paraphrase is somewhat shorter, yet the main difference is that we have replaced the language of the original with our own language.

When you come across a difficult or complex passage, sometimes the temptation is to skip over it. Resist this temptation! Use a paraphrase as a tool for explaining to yourself the main ideas of a difficult passage. By translating another writer's language into your own, you can clarify what you understand and pinpoint what you don't. The paraphrase therefore becomes a tool for learning the subject.

The following pointers will help you write paraphrases.

HOW TO WRITE PARAPHRASES

- Make sure that you understand the source passage.
- Substitute your own words for those of the source passage; look for synonyms that carry the same meaning as the original words.
- Use a different sentence pattern from that of the source; avoid using the source as a fill-in-the-blanks template for your paraphrase.
- Rearrange and connect your own sentences so that they read smoothly.

- *Note*: Don't paraphrase passages that you analyze closely, such as lines of poetry or parts of a speech. Quote them directly instead.
- *Always* provide a citation so that the reader knows what is being paraphrased. See the paragraph on citing sources at the end of this chapter for more information.

Let's consider some other examples. If you were investigating the ethical concerns relating to the practice of in vitro fertilization, you might conclude that you should read some medical literature. You might reasonably want to hear from the doctors themselves who are developing, performing, and questioning the procedures that you are researching. In professional journals and bulletins, physicians write to one another, not to the general public. They use specialized language. If you wanted to refer to a technically complex selection, as in the following excerpt from an article by Dietmar Mieth, you might need to write a paraphrase.

IN VITRO FERTILIZATION: FROM MEDICAL REPRODUCTION TO GENETIC DIAGNOSIS

DIETMAR MIETH

[I]t is not only an improvement in the success-rate that participating research scientists hope for but rather, developments in new fields of research in in-vitro gene diagnosis and in certain circumstances gene therapy. In view of this, the French expert J. F. Mattei has asked the following question: "Are we forced to accept that in vitro fertilization will become one of the most compelling methods of genetic diagnosis?" Evidently, by the introduction of a new law in France and Sweden (1994), this acceptance (albeit with certain restrictions) has already occurred prior to the application of in vitro fertilization reaching a technically mature and clinically applicable phase. This may seem astonishing in view of the question placed by the above-quoted French expert: the idea of embryo production so as to withhold one or two embryos before implantation presupposes a definite "attitude towards eugenics." And to destroy an embryo merely because of its genetic characteristics could signify the reduction of a human life to the sum of its genes. Mattei asks: "In face of a molecular judgment on our lives, is there no possibility for appeal? Will the diagnosis of inherited monogenetic illnesses soon be extended to genetic predisposition for multi-factorial illnesses?"

(From: *Biomedical Ethics: Newsletter of the European Network for Biomedical Ethics,* Vol. 1, No. 1 (1996).)

Like most literature intended for physicians, the language of this selection is somewhat forbidding to an audience of non-specialists, who have trouble with phrases such as "predisposition for multi-factorial illnesses." As a courtesy to your readers and in an effort to maintain a consistent tone and level in your essay, you could paraphrase this paragraph of the medical newsletter. First, of course, you must understand the meaning of the passage, perhaps no small task. But, having read the material carefully (and perhaps consulting a dictionary), you might eventually prepare a paraphrase such as this one:

> Writing in the *Newsletter of the European Network for Biomedical Ethics,* Dietmar Mieth (1996) reports that fertility specialists today want not only to improve the success rates of their procedures but also to diagnose and repair genetic problems before they implant fertilized eggs. Since the in vitro process often produces more fertilized eggs than can be used in a procedure, doctors may examine test-tube embryos for genetic defects and "withhold one or two" before implanting them. The practice of selectively implanting embryos raises concerns about eugenics and the rights of rejected embryos. On what genetic grounds will specialists distinguish flawed from healthy embryos and make a decision whether or not to implant? The appearance of single genes linked directly to specific, or "monogenetic," illnesses could be grounds for destroying an embryo. More complicated would be genes that predispose people to an illness but in no way guarantee the onset of that illness. Would these genes, which are only one factor in "multi-factorial illnesses," also be labelled undesirable and lead to embryo destruction? Advances in fertility science raise difficult questions. Already, even before techniques of genetic diagnosis are fully developed, nations are writing laws governing the practices of fertility clinics.

We begin our paraphrase with the same "not only/but also" logic of the original's first sentence, introducing the concepts of genetic diagnosis and therapy. The next four sentences in the original introduce concerns of a "French expert." Rather than quoting Mieth quoting the expert and immediately mentioning new laws in France and Sweden, we decided (first) to explain that in vitro fertilization procedures can give rise to more embryos than needed. We reasoned that non-medical readers would appreciate our making explicit the background knowledge that the author assumes of other physicians. Then we quote Mieth briefly ("withhold one or two" embryos) to provide some flavour of the original. We maintain focus on the ethical questions and wait until the end of the paraphrase before mentioning the laws to which Mieth refers. Our paraphrase is roughly the same length as the original, and it conveys the author's concerns about eugenics. As you can see, the paraphrase requires a writer to make some decisions about the presentation of material. In many, if not most, cases, you will need to do more than simply "translate" from the original, sentence-by-sentence, to write your paraphrase.

Our paraphrases have been somewhat shorter than the original, but this is not always the case. For example, suppose you wanted to paraphrase this statement by Sigmund Freud (the first sentence in the Tenth Lecture of his *General Introduction to Psychoanalysis,* published in 1920):

> We have found out that the distortion in dreams which hinders our understanding of them is due to the activities of a censorship, directed against the unacceptable, unconscious wish-impulses.

If you were to paraphrase this statement, you might come up with something like this:

> It is difficult to understand dreams because they contain distortions. Freud
>
> believed that these distortions arise from our internal censor, which
>
> attempts to suppress unconscious and forbidden desires.

Essentially, this paraphrase does little more than break up one sentence into two and somewhat rearrange the sentence structure for clarity.

WHEN TO SUMMARIZE/WHEN TO PARAPHRASE

Like summaries, then, *paraphrases* are useful devices, both in helping you to understand source material and in enabling you to convey the essence of this source material to your readers. When would you choose to write a summary instead of a paraphrase (or vice versa)? The answer to this question depends on your purpose in presenting your source material. As we've said, summaries are generally based on articles (or sections of articles) or books. Paraphrases are generally based on particularly difficult (or important) paragraphs or sentences. You would seldom paraphrase a long passage, or summarize a short one, unless there were particularly good reasons for doing so. (For example, a lawyer might want to paraphrase several pages of legal language so that his or her client, who is not a lawyer, could understand it.) The purpose of a summary is generally to save your reader time by presenting him or her with a brief and quickly readable version of a lengthy source. The purpose of a paraphrase is generally to clarify a short passage that might otherwise be unclear, or to integrate a writer's point into your own essay without shifting voice. Whether you summarize or paraphrase may also depend on the importance of your source. A particularly important source—if it is not too long—may rate a paraphrase. If it is less important, or peripheral to your central argument, you may choose to write a summary instead. And, of course, you may choose to summarize or paraphrase only part of your source—the part that is most relevant to the point you are making.

QUOTATIONS

A *quotation* records the exact language used by someone in speech or in writing. A *summary*, in contrast, is a brief restatement in your own words of what someone else has said or written. And a *paraphrase* also is a restatement, although one that is often as long as the original source. Any paper in which you draw upon sources will rely heavily on quotation, summary, and paraphrase. How do you choose among the three?

Remember that the papers you write should be your own—for the most part: your own language and certainly your own thesis, your own inferences, and your own conclusion. It follows that references to your source materials should be written primarily as summaries and paraphrases, both of which are built on restatement, not quotation. You will use summaries when you need a *brief* restatement, and paraphrases, which provide more explicit detail than summaries, when you need to follow the development of a source closely. When you quote too much, you risk losing ownership of your work: More easily than you might think, your voice can be drowned out by the voices of those you've quoted.

Nevertheless, quoting just the right source at the right time can significantly improve your papers. The trick is to know when and how to use quotations.

WHEN TO QUOTE

- Use quotations when another writer's language is particularly memorable and will add interest and liveliness to your paper.
- Use quotations when another writer's language is so clear and economical that to make the same point in your own words would, by comparison, be ineffective.
- Use quotations when you want the solid reputation of a source to lend authority and credibility to your own writing.
- Note: Literary analysis, such as an essay on a poem or play, calls for much more frequent use of direct quotations—from the poem or play itself, *not* from critics of the poem or play.

Quoting Memorable Language

Assume you're writing a paper on Napoleon Bonaparte's relationship with the celebrated Josephine. Through research you learn that two days after his marriage, Napoleon, given command of an army, left his bride for what was to be a brilliant military campaign in Italy. How did the young general respond to leaving his wife so soon after their wedding? You come across the following, written from the field of battle by Napoleon on April 3, 1796:

I have received all your letters, but none has such an impact on me as the last. Do you have any idea, darling, what you are doing, writing to me in those terms? Do you not think my situation cruel enough without intensifying my longing for you, overwhelming my soul? What a style! What emotions you evoke! Written in fire, they burn my poor heart! (96)

(From: Francis Mossiker, trans., *Napoleon and Josephine*, New York: Simon and Schuster, 1964.)

A summary of this passage might read as follows:

On April 3, 1796, Napoleon wrote to Josephine, expressing how sorely he missed her and how passionately he responded to her letters.

You might write the following as a paraphrase of the passage:

On April 3, 1796, Napoleon wrote to Josephine that he had received her letters and that one among all others had had a special impact, over-whelming his soul with fiery emotions and longing.

How feeble this summary and paraphrase are when compared with the original! Use the vivid language that your sources give you. In this case, quote Napoleon in your paper to make your subject come alive with memorable detail:

On April 3, 1796, a passionate, lovesick Napoleon responded to a letter from Josephine; she had written longingly to her husband, who, on a military campaign, acutely felt her absence. "Do you have any idea, darling, what you are doing, writing to me in those terms? . . . What emotions you evoke!" he said of her letters. "Written in fire, they burn my poor heart!"

You must credit your sources for all quotations, naming them either in (or at the end of) the sentence that includes the quotation or in a footnote.

Quoting Clear and Concise Language

You should quote a source when its language is particularly clear and economical—when your language, by contrast, would be wordy. Read this passage from a text on biology by Patricia Curtis:

The honeybee colony, which usually has a population of 30,000 to 40,000 workers, differs from that of the bumblebee and many other social bees or wasps in that it survives the winter. This means that the bees must stay warm despite the cold. Like other bees, the isolated honeybee cannot fly if the temperature falls below 10°C (50°F) and cannot walk if the temperature is below

7°C (45°F). Within the wintering hive, bees maintain their temperature by clustering together in a dense ball; the lower the temperature, the denser the cluster.
The clustered bees produce heat by constant muscular movements of their
wings, legs, and abdomens. In very cold weather, the bees on the outside of the
cluster keep moving toward the center, while those in the core of the cluster
move to the colder outside periphery. The entire cluster moves slowly about on
the combs, eating the stored honey from the combs as it moves. (822–23)

(From: "Winter Organization" in Patricia Curtis, *Biology*, 2nd ed., New York: Worth,
1976.)

A summary of this paragraph might read as follows:

Honeybees, unlike many other varieties of bee, are able to live through
the winter by "clustering together in a dense ball" for body warmth (Curtis
822–23).

A paraphrase of the same passage would be considerably more detailed:

According to Patricia Curtis, honeybees, unlike many other varieties of
bee (such as bumblebees), are able to live through the winter. The 30 000
to 40 000 bees within a honeybee hive could not, individually, move about
in cold winter temperatures. But when "clustering together in a dense
ball," the bees generate heat by constantly moving their body parts. The
cluster also moves slowly about the hive, eating honey stored in the
combs. This nutrition, in addition to the heat generated by the cluster,
enables the honeybee to survive the cold winter months. (822–23)

(To clarify the extent of the paraphrased material, Curtis's name is moved
from the citation to the beginning, and the page numbers are given at the end.)
    In both the summary and the paraphrase, we've quoted Curtis's "cluster-
ing together in a dense ball," a phrase that lies at the heart of her description
of wintering honeybees. For us to describe this clustering in any language
other than Curtis's would be pointless since her description is admirably brief
and precise.

Quoting Authoritative Language

You will also want to use quotations that lend authority to your work. When
quoting an expert or some prominent political, artistic, or historical figure, you
elevate your own work by placing it in esteemed company. Quote respected figures to establish background information in a paper, and your readers will
tend to perceive that information as reliable. Quote the opinions of respected fig-

ures to endorse some statement that you've made, and your statement becomes more credible to your readers. For example, in an essay on the importance of reading well, you could make use of a passage from Thoreau's *Walden:*

> Reading well is hard work and requires great skill and training. It "is a noble exercise," writes Henry David Thoreau in *Walden,* "and one that will task the reader more than any exercise which the customs of the day esteem. It requires a training such as the athletes underwent . . . . Books must be read as deliberately and reservedly as they were written." (72)

By quoting a famous philosopher and essayist on the subject of reading, you add legitimacy to your discussion. Not only do *you* regard reading to be a skill that is both difficult and important, so too does Henry David Thoreau, a highly influential thinker. In essays as in the larger world, you are known by the company you keep.

Incorporating Quotations into Your Sentences

Quoting Only the Part You Need

We've said that a writer selects passages for quotation that are especially *vivid and memorable, concise,* or *authoritative.* Now put these principles into practice. Suppose that while conducting research on Canadian history you've come across the following, written by Gordon Laird, in his book *Slumming It at the Rodeo: The Cultural Roots of Canada's Right-Wing Revolution:*

> Cabot may not have discovered Canada but his main method of exploration, getting lost, is a persistent national theme. Even the nation's moniker has its beginnings in the missteps of early explorers. In 1535 two Indian youths told Jacques Cartier about the route to *kanata.* They were referring to the Huron village of Stadacona; *kanata* was simply the word for "village" or "settlement." Cartier assumed Kanata referred to an entire region, soon to be annexed by Europe's imperial powers. His initial mistake compounded as France and England made themselves at home. By 1547 maps designated everything north of the St. Lawrence River as "Canada." (8)

(From: Gordon Laird, *Slumming It at the Rodeo,* Vancouver: Douglas and McIntyre, 1998.)

Suppose that in this entire paragraph you find a gem, a sentence with quotable words that will enliven your discussion. You may want to quote part of the following sentence:

> Cabot may not have discovered Canada but his main method of exploration, getting lost, is a persistent national theme.

Using Phrase, Sentence, or Block Quotations

Once you've selected the passage you want to quote, work the material into your paper in as natural and fluid a manner as possible. You can select a phrase and build it into your own sentence, making sure that it makes grammatical sense:

> Gordon Laird, taking an ironic view of Canadian settlement patterns, points out that "getting lost . . . is a persistent national theme" (8).

> Or

> Gordon Laird refers with disparagement to Cabot's main method of exploration, "getting lost," referring to indirection as a Canadian theme (8).

If including a longer quotation helps to make your case, you can choose to quote an entire sentence:

> Gordon Laird, in an ironic analysis of Canadian settlement patterns, notes that indirection is part of our history: "Cabot may not have discovered Canada but his main method of exploration, getting lost, is a persistent national theme" (8).

Finally, there are times when you need to include a longer quotation sometimes spanning several sentences.

> Gordon Laird's style of writing about our history engages the reader, since he finds humour in the way long-ago events nudge current-day life. Here he refers to Cabot's misadventures and wrong turns as thematic in the Canadian imagination:

>> Cabot may not have discovered Canada but his main method of exploration, getting lost, is a persistent national theme. Even the nation's moniker has its beginnings in the missteps of early explorers. In 1535 two Indian youths told Jacques Cartier about the route to *kanata*. They were referring to the Huron village of Stadacona; *kanata* was simply the word for "village" or "settlement." Cartier assumed Kanata referred to an entire region, soon to be annexed by Europe's imperial powers. His initial mistake compounded as France and England made themselves at home. By 1547 maps designated everything north of the St. Lawrence River as "Canada." (8)

Using a block quotation is often necessary when you are analyzing the style of a passage, but remember that too many block quotations can prevent your voice from being heard and create a choppy or "strung-together" effect.

Avoiding Freestanding Quotations

A quoted sentence should never stand by itself—as in the following example:

> Canadian settlement history has influenced how we think about being
> Canadian today. "Cabot may not have discovered Canada but his main
> method of exploration, getting lost, is a persistent national theme" (Laird 8).
> Many of the explorers contributed to our national character.

Even if it includes a parenthetical citation, a freestanding quotation would have the problem of being jarring to the reader. It is often helpful to introduce a quotation with a "signal phrase" that attributes the source not in a parenthetical citation, but in some other part of the sentence—beginning, middle, or end. Thus, you could write:

> According to cultural analyst Gordon Laird, "Cabot may not have discov-
> ered Canada but his main method of exploration, getting lost, is a persis-
> tent national theme" (Laird 8).

An alternative is to introduce a sentence-long quotation with a colon, but make sure that the signal statement stands on its own as a complete sentence:

> Writer Gordon Laird forms an ironic link between John Cabot's loss of
> direction and the Canadian preoccupation with losing our sense of place:
> "Cabot may not have discovered Canada but his main method of explo-
> ration, getting lost, is a persistent national theme" (8).

Use colons also to introduce block (indented) quotations (as in the examples above).

When attributing sources, try to vary the standard "states," "writes," "says," and so on. Other, stronger verbs you might consider include the following: "asserts," "argues," "maintains," "insists," "asks," and even "wonders." Your writing will be more dynamic if you are as precise in your choice of verbs to denote speech acts as you are in choosing verbs to denote physical acts.

Using Ellipses

Using quotations is made somewhat complicated when you want to quote the beginning and end of a passage but not its middle—as was the case when we quoted Henry David Thoreau. Here's part of the paragraph in *Walden* from which we quoted a few sentences:

> To read well, that is to read true books in a true spirit, is a noble exercise, and
> one that will task the reader more than any exercise which the customs of the

day esteem. It requires a training such as the athletes underwent, the steady intention almost of the whole life to this object. Books must be read as deliberately and reservedly as they were written. (72)

(From: "Reading," in *Walden*, New York: Signet Classic, 1960.)

And here is how we used this material:

Reading well is hard work and requires great skill and training. It "is a noble exercise," writes Henry David Thoreau in *Walden*, "and one that will task the reader more than any exercise which the customs of the day esteem. It requires a training such as the athletes underwent. . . . Books must be read as deliberately and reservedly as they were written" (72).

Whenever you quote a sentence but delete words from it, as we have done, indicate to the reader this deletion by placing an ellipsis mark—three spaced periods—in the sentence at the point of deletion. The rationale for using an ellipsis mark is that a direct quotation must be reproduced exactly as it was written or spoken. When writers delete or change any part of the quoted material, readers must be alerted so they don't think the changes were part of the original. Ellipsis marks and square brackets serve this purpose.

If you are deleting the middle of a single sentence, use an ellipsis in place of the deleted words:

"To read well . . . is a noble exercise, and one that will task the reader more than any exercise which the customs of the day esteem" (72).

If you are deleting the end of a quoted sentence, or if you are deleting entire sentences of a paragraph before continuing a quotation, include a period with the ellipsis, to make four instead of three dots:

"It requires a training such as the athletes underwent. . . . Books must be read as deliberately and reservedly as they were written" (72).

You should not use ellipses to indicate deleted words at the beginning or end of a quotation, only in the middle.

Using Square Brackets

Use square brackets whenever you need to add or substitute words in a quoted sentence. The brackets indicate to the reader a word or phrase that does not appear in the original passage but that you have inserted to avoid confusion. For example, when a pronoun's antecedent would be unclear to readers, delete the pronoun from the sentences and substitute an identifying word or phrase in brackets. When you make such a substitution, no ellipsis marks are needed. Assume that you wish to quote the third sentence in the following passage:

The short story has also been the form that, before the present era, most often crossed borders to bring international success to Canadian authors. Thomas Chandler Haliburton, revered by the American story-teller Mark Twain among others, was Canada's first writer to be widely recognized abroad. So immense was his popularity that more than a hundred editions of his Clockmaker sketches were printed in Canada, the United States, England, and, in translation, in France and Germany. (6)

(From: Russell Brown and Donna Bennett, "Introduction," in *Canadian Short Stories,* Toronto: Penguin, 2005.)

In quoting this sentence, you would need to identify whom the pronoun "his" refers to. You can do this inside the quotation by using brackets:

Haliburton's stories were widely printed and read not only in Canada but also beyond our borders: "So immense was his [Haliburton's] popularity that more than a hundred editions of his Clockmaker sketches were printed in Canada, the United States, England, and, in translation, in France and Germany" (6).

When the pronoun you want to identify occurs in the middle of the sentence to be quoted, as it does above, you need to use brackets.

WHEN TO SUMMARIZE, PARAPHRASE, AND QUOTE

Summarize:
- To present main points of a lengthy passage (article or book)
- To condense supporting points necessary to discussion

Paraphrase:
- To clarify a short passage
- To emphasize main points

Quote:
- To capture another writer's particularly memorable language
- To capture another writer's clearly and economically stated language
- To lend authority and credibility to your own writing
- To support a textual analysis with excerpts from the work under discussion

DOCUMENTING SOURCES

Documentation of outside sources is the most immediately identifiable footprint of scholarly work. Commonly understood as a courtesy or perhaps legality by which we acknowledge our indebtedness to other writers, documentation is actually far more important than that: It is the system by which we anchor our claims in the existing body of worldwide scholarship on the topic. By making use of other scholars' work, we ensure that our own work builds from where we are now rather than reinventing the wheel. By documenting our use of others' work, we provide assurance to our own readers that we have drawn on sources that followed sound scholarly method, and we give them the means to trace our research back to our original sources. Documentation is a scholar's way of saying, "You can trust my claims. I didn't just make this stuff up." Acknowledging debts is the least we are doing in that gesture—it's the scholarly equivalent of putting your shoes on before you leave the house. However, it is also completely compulsory.

AVOIDING PLAGIARISM

Plagiarism generally is defined as the attempt to pass off the work of another as one's own. Whether born out of calculation or desperation, plagiarism is the least tolerated offence in the academic world. The fact that most plagiarism is unintentional—arising from ignorance of conventions rather than deceitfulness—makes no difference to many professors.

You can avoid plagiarism and charges of plagiarism by following the basic rules below.

RULES TO AVOID PLAGIARISM

- Cite (a) *all* quoted material and (b) *all* summarized and paraphrased material, even if it is just information and not opinion, unless the information is common knowledge (e.g., Pierre Elliott Trudeau was Prime Minister of Canada during the 1970s).
- Make sure that both the *wording* and the *sentence structure* of your summaries and paraphrases are substantially your own.

The following passage of text about how to approach summarizing a narrative or story is reproduced from earlier in this chapter:

> Because narratives generally do not exhibit the same logical development as does writing designed to convey information or present an argument, they do not lend themselves to summary in quite the same way. Narratives do have a logic (the poet Samuel Taylor Coleridge [1772–1834] once wrote that poetry has "a logic of its own, as severe as that of science"), but that logic may be emotional, imaginative, or plot-bound. The writer who summarizes a narrative is obliged to represent that logic through an overview—a synopsis—of the story's events and an account of how these events affect the central character(s).

A student version of this passage might read as follows:

> Narratives usually do not exhibit the same logic as does writing designed to present information or an argument, so they do not lend themselves to summary in quite the same way. Narratives do have a logic, as the poet Samuel Taylor Coleridge noted when he wrote that poetry has "a logic of its own, as severe as that of science"; he meant that the logic may be emotional, imaginative, or plot-bound. To summarize a narrative, the writer is obliged to represent that logic through an overview of the story's events and an account of how these events touch the main character(s).

Clearly, this is intentional plagiarism. The student has copied the original passage almost word for word.

Here is another version of the same passage:

> Narratives usually do not exhibit the same logic as does writing designed to inform or argue, so they do not lend themselves to summary in quite the same way. The poet Samuel Taylor Coleridge wrote that poetry has "a logic of its own, as severe as that of science," by which he means that the logic may be emotional, imaginative, or plot-bound. To summarize a narrative, the writer represents that logic through an overview of the story's events and how these events touch the character(s).

This student has attempted to put the ideas into her own words, but both the wording and the sentence structure still are so heavily dependent on the original passage that even if it *were* cited, most professors would consider it plagiarism.

In the following version, the student has sufficiently changed the wording and sentence structure, and she properly credits the information to this Behrens text, so that there is no question of plagiarism:

> According to the authors of *Writing and Reading Across the Disciplines,* because stories have a different logic than that of writing designed to inform or argue, the conventions for summarizing them are different too. Rather than appealing to reason, the logic may be emotional, imaginative, or plot-bound, and the writer represents that logic in summary by giving an overview of the story's events in relation to the characters.

Remember, too, that quite apart from questions of plagiarism, it is essential to quote accurately. You are not permitted to change or omit any part of a quotation without using brackets or ellipses.

CITING SOURCES

When you refer to or quote the work of another, you are obligated to credit or cite your source properly. If you are writing a paper in the humanities, you probably will be expected to use the Modern Language Association (MLA) format for citation. This format is fully described in the *MLA Handbook for Writers of Research Papers.* A paper in the social sciences will probably use the American Psychological Association (APA) format. This format is fully described in the *Publication Manual of the American Psychological Association.*

■ EXERCISES

1. Read ahead to the essays at the end of Chapter 3, "Roll Back the Red Carpet for Boys" (p. 97) and "Our Daughters, Ourselves" (p. 98). Choose one and write a "short" summary of the article, following the directions in this chapter for dividing the article into sections, writing a one-sentence summary of each section, and then joining section summaries with a thesis. Prepare for the summary by making notes in the margins. Your finished product should be the result of two or more drafts.

2. Summarize the article "Group Minds" by Doris Lessing (p. 210) using the shorter method of summary—that is, your summary should capture the thesis statement and the main points of the article, but not the details (see pp. 38–39). Remember to "frame" the summary so that the author and title of the article are acknowledged early on and it remains clear that Lessing, not you, is the author of the material being summarized. Your summary should be one paragraph about 150 words long. Once you have completed your version, compare it to the student version that appears earlier in this chapter (pp. 46–47).

3. Summarize and properly frame Shirley Jackson's famous short story, "The Lottery" (pp. 280–288). This summary should be one paragraph about 150 words long that captures the main storyline and theme and refrains from personal judgment. Once you have completed your version, compare it to the student-written version that appears earlier in this chapter and be prepared to discuss the differences in class.

4. Write a short (one- or two-paragraph) essay about Lessing's article (p. 210) *and/or* Jackson's (p. 280) or Atwood's (p. 273) narratives in which you use all the different techniques of paraphrasing and quoting presented in this chapter. Do not worry about making profound comments: In this exercise, what counts is the accuracy of representation only. Specifically, your little essay should include the following elements:
   - a long quotation in block form
   - a sentence-length quotation
   - a short phrase-length quotation

Use each of the following techniques at least once:
- square brackets to signify an alteration of the original
- ellipsis marks to omit unnecessary words

Make sure that you provide a citation in either MLA or APA form for each quotation and punctuate it correctly.

Finally, make sure that each quotation is somehow embedded into your own prose—never leave a quotation free-standing (see p. 61).

Critiquing Sources: Textual Analysis and Response

CRITICAL READING

When writing papers in university, you are often called on to respond critically to source materials. Critical reading requires the ability to both summarize and evaluate a presentation. As you have seen, a *summary* is a brief restatement in your own words of the content of a passage. An *evaluation* is a more difficult matter, however. In your university work, you read to gain and *use* new information; but because sources are not equally valid or equally useful, you must learn to distinguish critically among sources by evaluating them.

There is no ready-made formula for determining validity. Critical reading and its written analogue—the *critique*—require discernment, sensitivity, imagination, and, above all, a willingness to become involved in what you read. These skills cannot be taken for granted and are developed only through repeated practice. You must begin somewhere, though, and we recommend that you start by posing two broad categories of questions about passages, articles, and books that you read. The first can be thought of as internal since it focuses closely on the text, the second as external since it involves stepping back from the text to consider it as one possible approach to the topic out of many: (1) What is the author's purpose in writing? Does he or she succeed in this purpose? (2) To what extent do you agree with the author? Whose interests are served by the text?

Question Category 1: Close Reading—What Is the Author's Purpose in Writing? Does He or She Succeed in This Purpose?

All critical reading *begins with an accurate summary*. Before attempting an evaluation, you must be able to locate an author's thesis and identify the selection's content and structure. You must understand the author's *purpose*. Authors write to inform, to entertain, and to persuade. A given piece may be *primarily informative* (a summary of the research on cloning), *primarily entertaining* (a play about the frustrations of young lovers), or *primarily persuasive* (an argument on why the government must do something to alleviate homelessness), or it may be all three (as in Timothy Findley's *The Wars*, about Canadian soldiers in World War I). Sometimes authors are not fully conscious of their purposes. Sometimes their purposes change as they write. But if the finished piece is coherent, it will have a primary reason for having been written, and it should be apparent that the author is attempting primarily to inform, entertain, or persuade a particular audience. To identify this primary reason—this purpose—is your first job as a critical reader. Your next job is to determine how successful the author has been. As a critical reader, you bring different criteria, or standards of judgment, to bear when you read pieces intended to inform, to entertain, and to persuade.

Writing to Inform

A piece intended to inform will provide definitions, describe or report on a process, recount a story, give historical background, and/or provide facts and figures. An informational piece responds to questions such as the following:

What (or who) is _____ ?
How does _____ work?
What is the controversy or problem about?
What happened?
How and why did it happen?
What were the results?
What are the arguments for and against _____ ?

To the extent that an author answers these and related questions and that the answers are a matter of verifiable record (i.e., you could check for accuracy if you had the time and inclination), the selection is intended to inform. Having determined this, you can organize your response by considering three other criteria: accuracy, significance, and fair interpretation of information.

Accuracy of Information

If you are going to use any of the information presented, you must be satisfied that it is trustworthy. One of your responsibilities as a critical reader is to find out if it is accurate.

Significance of Information

One useful question that you can put to a reading is "So what?" In the case of selections that attempt to inform, you may reasonably wonder whether the information makes a difference. What can the person who is reading gain from this information? How is knowledge advanced by the publication of this material? Is the information of importance to you or to others in a particular audience? Why or why not?

Fair Interpretation of Information

At times you will read reports, the sole function of which is to relate raw data or information. In these cases, you will build your response on the two questions in question category 1: What is the author's purpose in writing? Does she or he succeed in this purpose? More frequently, once an author has presented information, she or he will attempt to evaluate or interpret it—which is only reasonable, since information that has not been evaluated or interpreted is of little use. One of your tasks as a critical reader is to make a distinction between the author's presentation of facts and figures and his or her attempts to evaluate them. You may find that the information is valuable but the interpretation is not. Perhaps the author's conclusions are not justified. Could you offer a contrary explanation for the same facts? Does more information need to be gathered before conclusions can be drawn? Why?

Writing to Entertain

An author's purpose in writing may be to entertain. One response to entertainment is a hearty laugh, but it is not the only response: A good book (or play or poem) may prompt you to ruminate, or grow wistful, elated, angry. You read a piece (or view a work) and react with sadness, surprise, exhilaration, disbelief, horror, boredom. As with a response to an informative piece or an argument, your response to an essay, poem, story, play, novel, or film should be precisely stated and carefully developed. Ask yourself some of the following questions (you won't have space to explore all of them, but try to consider some of the most important):

- Did I care for the portrayal of a certain character?
- Did that character seem too sentimentalized, for example, or heroic?
- Did his adversaries seem too villainous or stupid?
- Were the situations believable? Was the action interesting or merely formulaic?
- Was the theme developed subtly, powerfully, or did the work come across as preachy or shrill?
- Did the action at the end of the work follow plausibly from what had come before?
- Was the language fresh and incisive or stale and predictable?

Explain as specifically as possible what elements of the work seemed effective or ineffective and why. Offer an overall assessment, elaborating on your views.

Writing to Persuade

Writing is frequently intended to persuade—that is, to influence the reader's thinking. To make a persuasive case, the writer must begin with an assertion that is arguable, some statement about which reasonable people could disagree. Such an assertion, when it serves as the essential organizing principle of the article or book, is called a *thesis* (see Chapter 1). Examples:

> Because they do not speak English, many children in this affluent land are being denied their fundamental right to equal educational opportunity.

> Bilingual education, which has been stridently promoted by a small group of activists with their own agenda, is detrimental to the very students it is supposed to serve.

Thesis statements such as these—and the subsidiary assertions used to help support them—represent conclusions that authors have drawn as a result of researching and thinking about the issue. You go through the same process yourself when you write persuasive papers or critiques. And just as you are entitled to critically evaluate the assertions of authors you read, so your professors—and other students—are entitled to evaluate *your* assertions, whether they are encountered as written arguments or as comments made in class discussion.

Keep in mind that writers organize arguments by arranging evidence to support one conclusion and oppose (or dismiss) another. You can assess the persuasiveness of the argument and the conclusion by determining whether the author has (1) clearly defined key terms, (2) used information fairly, (3) argued logically, and not fallaciously, and (4) appealed appropriately to emotion and ethics.

We will illustrate our discussion by referring to two articles. Glastonbury and LaMendola's "The Nature and Meaning of Data" is reproduced below, and Virginia Postrel's "Fatalist Attraction: The Dubious Case against Fooling Mother Nature" appears in Chapter 8 (pp. 416–420).

The Nature and Meaning of Data

BRYAN GLASTONBURY AND WALTER LAMENDOLA

Collecting Data about You

Have you purchased a new home appliance lately? Let's pretend that what you really need is a new vacuum cleaner. You buy one. As you unpack your new appliance, you carefully put aside the enclosed product information and warranty registration. The machine works well the next morning, so you have extra time to fill out and return your product registration card. It asks for your name, address, and telephone number. It asks where you made the purchase—their name, address, and telephone number. It probably goes on to ask for your age, gender, income group, number of members in household, and whether or not you own your own home. How much a year do you spend on appliances? What prompted you to buy the cleaner? Where will it be used? Why did you purchase this brand? Was it purchased for a specific member of your family? Was the decision to buy this cleaner made by a man, woman, or jointly? Have you ever owned a similar product? What was it? What brand? Do you own another cleaner? What model? Such questions are always posed with courtesy, without any sense of compulsion, and with an

explanation that your answers will help the company to a better understand-   2
ing of its customers' needs.

When you fill out and return your card, perhaps wondering what it has
to do with your purchase of the cleaner, you might be surprised to know that
it usually goes to a company that has paid the manufacturer for the rights to
the data. In due course the data will be computerized and resold to other companies, and you have unwittingly become a participant in a wide network,
without your knowledge and outside your control. For example, your data
may turn up being sold to a firm which markets carpets. As a result, you may
start receiving any number of unwanted mailings and telephone calls. In one
case reported in a national news service, a data company sold material
obtained from a national weight loss association to a chocolate company,
which reported a rise in sales as a consequence of using it.

Most of us probably consider the mailing label as the type of data that is   3
commonly bought and sold in the marketplace. That is just the tip of the ice-
berg, but we can start there. A typical mailing label will contain a name and
address. Some of the data companies (also called list brokers) may also want
your telephone number. It may be that they can buy a list of names and telephone numbers already on computer, or they have to go through the directory.
It is also possible to obtain lists of names linked to job, place of employment
and business phone number. By using a computer program these separate
sources of data can be merged to build up a comprehensive route for con-
tacting families, at home and work. The computer can cross-reference and
link in any other material that is available, like court records of debts or criminal convictions, or the age and income profile you provided with your
vacuum cleaner registration.

This type of collection and work with data represents the fastest growing   4
use of computerized data today, and list selling between businesses and industries has become a major activity. For example, credit bureau income from
selling data lists to marketing firms or list brokers, presently at about one
third of total revenue, may exceed their income from providing credit references within the next few years. Data is a big business for everyone. But
what type of data is collected? Is it just the basic factual background material
that we have considered so far, or is it more involved?

If we start with the example of a high school student, age 15, in the   5
U.S.A., we may be able to trace some of the major sources of data collection.
As high school students enter their second year, their names will start to find
a place on computerized lists, especially if they have been selected for any specific recognition or honours. A student of high academic accomplishments
will begin to receive mailings from colleges and universities, encouraging the
student to consider them. A little later the student may fill out an application
for automobile insurance, and this data will be entered into a database and
matched with criminal and credit files before the insurance application will be
considered for approval. The student will not know the results of the application check or whether due data is bought and sold in the marketplace.

The student may now want a vacation job, and when applying may be   6
asked questions about medical history, brushes with the police, home life,

what parents do, and performance in school. If the company is large, the job application will be stored on computer and another check of the applicant will occur. The check may include credit and criminal checks as well as checks of driving record and personal references. Again none of the outcomes will be known to the student. Our student passes the checks and is employed. On receiving the first pay cheque, he or she goes to the bank and opens an account. Here is another application form to fill in, and if the student wants an overdraft facility, some material about the parents' financial viability may be requested.

While the student is working, playing, studying, and becoming a pro-   7
ductive citizen, the marketing of personal data is leading to mailings about subscriptions to periodicals, cassette tape and compact disc buying clubs, and hosts of other consumer items aimed at teenagers. At the point of leaving school the mailings increase. Depending upon social and economic status, the contents of databases, and some further screening by a credit reporting bureau, the mail could bring an invitation to apply for a credit card. Our student still has not left the family home or gone to college, but look at the data already gathered. The computerized files have material on:

Insurance
Driving record
Criminal record
Employment
Medical history and condition
Educational record
Credit
Banking
Home life
Family relationships
Own and family finances
Lifestyle
Preferences and ideologies
Leisure activities
Shopping and consumption patterns
Travel and communications

So far we have shown how personal profiles are established as part of   8
massive data systems. How else can we use the material? To return to vacuum cleaners, as well as using those questionnaires to assemble personal profiles, we can use them compositely to build a model of the way groups of people act to purchase such appliances. We might analyze the data statistically, and find that people with medium family incomes say they spend the most money on appliances, and that in those families the woman makes the buying deci-sion for herself, usually at Acme Hardware Stores. The commercial value of this information is significant.

But what if we take it a step further. As a data company, I have product   9
registration data for vacuum cleaners, but I have also bought hundreds of other such databases. By performing operations upon the data, such as match-ing, selecting, relating, and modelling, I am now able to offer a comprehensive

marketing tool to others. One such tool, developed by Lotus and Equifax, is a piece of personal computer based marketing software called MarketPlace which, using a compact disc that contains data on about 120 million people in 80 million households in the U.S., allows the user to type in consumer profiles and print out mailing labels for the people who match the profile. The data about each person includes name, address, age, gender, estimated annual income, marital status, and shopping habits.

Such types of data collection, facilitated by computing and communica-   10
tion systems, are commonplace in a modern industrialized society, though the public presentation of MarketPlace led to opposition and its temporary withdrawal in 1990. It is certainly true that many of the valued services that we receive depend upon the systematic and orderly collection of data about us. What this example begins to outline is the pervasiveness of the data collection and the underlying ability to match and model pieces of data for the purpose of creating information which can be used to influence our decision making. Even more to the point, these data are the basis for others to make decisions about us and therefore control and manipulate our everyday life. And yet, as large and wide scale as these data systems are, they must be considered *personal* information systems because they hold data which relates to specific, identifiable individuals.

The Personal in Data Systems

Laws in different countries generally hold that storing data which relates to   11
specific, identifiable individuals constitutes a personal database, but they often do not go a stage further, to distinguish between differing types of data. While a computer system that collects your buying habits may be intrusive, for example, by sending you mail you do not want, a system which contains data about your mental health or political activities may be used in ways that can cause you serious harm, for example, by releasing your past history of depression to a potential employer. There is some data which people consider to be more personal than others, or that we consider to be intimate and do not want to be shared. Alternatively, there is data which we share, but only in confidence. In some situations, not limited to conversations with a lawyer or doctor, people expect that what is shared will be protected in some way by confidentiality. But how do we know that other people share our view of what is personal?

In a most interesting demonstration of defining personal data, Wacks   12
(1989, pp. 226–238) created an index. This is based upon the extent to which the exposure of data could potentially cause harm to a person. The data is rated by the degrees of sensitivity, low, medium or high. He defines *low sensitivity* as biographical data, and puts in this category basic facts about home, job and educational record. *Medium sensitivity* he describes as judgmental, including reports on us (school, employment) and matters involving a judgment or opinion of another person. Data which is *high sensitivity* is intimate, like our mental health record, where "there is a persuasive case for maintaining that at least some ... should not be collected at all" (p. 229).[1]

[1] Wacks, R. (1989). *Personal Information*. Clarendon Press, Oxford.

Generally, people are highly sensitive to health, ideological, criminal jus-   13
tice, and sexual data. It is true that sensitivity is difficult to define, and may
change not only from culture to culture, but from time to time. However, the
combination of the ability to identify a particular individual, the potential to
cause that individual harm, and the sensitivity of the data being collected are
personal considerations which surely need to be, in almost all cases, under the
control of the individual.

It is true that many of the services we need, such as health or social secu-   14
rity services, rely on us to furnish accurate and truthful data to them. One
might also argue that much of this data could be seen as trivial, as opposed to
private or sensitive. Indeed, in some countries (all of Scandinavia, for example),
data has been categorized to account for differences in sensitivity. It is also possible to argue that some data is of such import to society, and perhaps being
HIV positive presently fits this description, that it must not only be collected
but also related to specific individuals. Despite these arguments, the ultimate
concern needs to be framed within the context of protecting the individual in
everyday life. We can do this by honouring the right of the individual to advise
and consent. Not only should consent be the cornerstone of all approaches, but
also people need to have the right to be informed when and where data about
them is collected or stored. They need to give their specific consent to any activity which accesses, operates upon and uses this data. They need to be able to
access and correct data without risking vulnerability or expense.

The location and correction of data is not as simple as it may sound. It is   15
easiest to understand if we assume that the data is stored in one computer, but
of course it is not. The fact that it is traded means that it has passed to many
computers, possibly linked in a network, but just as possibly quite separate.
Leaving aside the complex practicalities, what is the value of a fight to view,
correct and sanction the use of our personal data, without a parallel right to
be informed of all computers on which it is held?

In order to illustrate these difficulties we can continue the example of our   16
student, who is now a high achieving university student nearing graduation,
but needing support, advice, and counselling about moving into a career.
Though a hard worker, the student has got involved in other activities, and is
worried about a number of matters. Can a campus counsellor help? The
counsellor, a psychologist, administers a number of tests which hint at a
rather unbalanced character. Consequently, in their discussions, they cover
the student's uncertainty about sexuality, disgust with war and government,
experimentation with alcohol and drugs, and concerns about the future of the
world. These discussions are very helpful to the student. They not only relieve
anxiety, but they contribute to a number of healthy decisions to change living
patterns. Things feel a lot more balanced, and, as the lifestyle changes, so
uncertainties disappear.

The future our student desires is a good beginning position in a large firm   17
of stockbrokers. After interviews for a number of positions, none of the
applications succeeds. The student's father has a close friend in one of the

firms, so makes a discreet enquiry. The friend reveals the reasons why no job was offered. Apparently, there are some damaging psychological test results which come up in the employment check. In addition, there is a psychological report which describes the student as confused, possibly sexually maladjusted, with occasional depression, marginally psychotic, and a potential non-conformist who may be addicted to drugs and alcohol. After calming down, the student recalls talks with the university counsellor, and also remembers in the first job application agreeing to a recruitment firm seeking a report from that source.

The student is able to find out that the firm is a subsidiary of Greater 18 Data. They admit to having the files in their main computer in Taiwan and agree to a formal request to review them for errors and corrections. In talking to a supervisor at Greater Data, the student finds that they have sold the files to others, and probably those have sent them to others again. In addition, the supervisor explains that while the student has the right to correct erroneous or incorrect data, the incorrect data will not be removed.

The student has now encountered a number of the major problems we 19 can expect in data collection and retention. The counsellor may have professional values about confidentiality, but does not ensure that they are extended to the computer system. Old data has been retained, with subjective interpretations which, while useful at the time of counselling, were later damaging to the interests of the student. No one, least of all the student, had been given the opportunity to assess whether old test results and notes were relevant to the present search for employment. Most critically, the student had no knowledge that the data was being kept, no knowledge of the use to which the data would be put, and had not been asked to consent to the use of the data.

■ ■ ■

Close Reading of an Essay

(1) Find Clearly Defined Terms

The validity of an argument depends to some degree on how carefully key terms have been defined. Take the assertion, for example, that North American society must be grounded in "family values." Just what do people who use this phrase mean by it? The validity of their argument depends on whether they and their readers agree on a definition of "family values"—as well as what it means to be "grounded in" family values. So, in responding to an argument, be sure you (and the author) are clear on what exactly is being argued. Only then can you respond to the logic of the argument, to the author's use of evidence, and to the author's conclusions.

In the article by Glastonbury and LaMendola, "personal data" is a key concept. Not only do they define what they mean by giving examples, but in paragraph 12 they round out their definition by exploring how Wacks created an index "based upon the extent to which the exposure of data could potentially cause harm to a person." By contrast, in her article that argues against those who want to slow down the process of developing and marketing of biomedical advances, Virginia Postrel (pp. 416–420) never defines the key term "biomedicine." Nor does she explain the people who might make up the "set of experts" whose interference she warns against; in the question section following her article (Discussion and Writing Suggestions, #6), the authors of this textbook begin to do this work when they talk about "genetic intervention being made *not* by individuals but by broader cultural authorities—governments, say, or international bodies of scientists." Because several of her key terms remain unspecified and unclear, it is sometimes difficult to be certain of her argument and thus to respond with confidence to all its parts.

(2) Test Fair Use of Information

Information is used as evidence in support of arguments. When presented with such evidence, ask yourself two questions: The *first:* "Is the information accurate and up-to-date?" At least a portion of an argument is rendered invalid if the information used to support it is inaccurate or out-of-date. The *second:* "Has the author cited *representative* information?" The evidence used in an argument must be presented in a spirit of fair play. An author is less than ethical who presents only evidence favouring his views when he is well aware that contrary evidence exists. For instance, it would be dishonest to argue that an economic recession is imminent and to cite as evidence only those indicators of economic well-being that have taken a decided turn for the worse while ignoring and failing to cite contrary (positive) evidence.

Virginia Postrel's essay (pp. 416–420) provides several examples of unfair use of information. In paragraph 11, for example, she refers to philosopher John Gray's reminder that death is as natural as the fatalism of a "biotechnophobe." She also quotes his reference to "macabre high-tech medicine involving organ transplantation," without providing a sense of context that might help us to understand the highly invasive and experimental procedures he may be discussing. Instead, Postrel follows up this brief quote with painting Gray as one opposed to helping suffering humanity ease its pain: "Suffering is the human condition, he suggested: We should just lie back and accept it."

(3) Assess Logical Argumentation

Logos—the appeal to reason—is central to scholarly writing. If they expect to persuade their audiences, speakers must argue logically and must supply appropriate evidence to support their case. Logical arguments are commonly of two types (often combined). The *deductive* argument begins with a generalization, then cites a specific case related to that generalization, from which follows a conclusion. A familiar example of deductive reasoning, used by Aristotle himself, is the following:

> All men are mortal. (*generalization*)
> Socrates is a man. (*specific case*)
> Socrates is mortal. (*conclusion about the specific case*)

In the terms we've just been discussing, this deduction may be restated as follows:

Socrates is mortal. (*claim*)
Socrates is a man. (*support*)
All men are mortal. (*assumption*)

An example of a more contemporary deductive argument may be seen in President John F. Kennedy's address to the American nation in June 1963 on the need for sweeping civil rights legislation. Kennedy begins with the generalizations that it "ought to be possible . . . for American students of any color to attend any public institution they select without having to be backed up by troops" and that "it ought to be possible for American citizens of any color to register and vote in a free election without interference or fear of reprisal." Kennedy then provides several specific examples (primarily recent events in Birmingham, Alabama) and statistics to show that this was not the case. He concludes:

> We face, therefore, a moral crisis as a country and a people. It cannot be met by repressive police action. It cannot be left to increased demonstrations in the streets. It cannot be quieted by token moves or talk. It is time to act in the Congress, in your state and local legislative body, and, above all, in all of our daily lives.

Underlying Kennedy's argument is the following reasoning:

All Americans should enjoy certain rights.
Some Americans do not enjoy these rights.
We must take action to ensure that all Americans enjoy these rights.

Another form of logical argumentation is *inductive* reasoning. A speaker or writer who argues inductively begins not with a generalization, but with several pieces of specific evidence. The speaker then draws a conclusion from this evidence. For example, during the Confederation debates in the 1860s, D'Arcy McGee of Lower Canada supported Canadian union and cautioned his countrymen to recognize the threat of American takeover. He begins this passage by citing situations in which the Americans have asserted their dominance and builds to his conclusion that in its current divided state, Canada is completely dependent on Britain for protection against American aggression:

> There has always been a desire amongst them for the acquisition of new territory, and the inexorable law of democratic existence seems to be its absorption. They coveted Florida, and seized it; they coveted Louisiana, and purchased it; they coveted Texas, and stole it; and then they picked a quarrel with Mexico, which ended by their getting California. They sometimes pretend to despise these our colonies as prizes beneath their ambition; but had we not had the strong arm of England over us we should not now have had a separate existence.

(From: Watkin, Edward William, *Canada and the States: Recollections 1851 to 1886*, Available online http://www.literaturemania.com/cnstr10/page56.asp.)

Statistical evidence was used by U.S. Senator Edward M. Kennedy (Democrat, Massachusetts) in arguing for passage of the *Racial Justice Act* of 1990, designed to ensure that minorities were not disproportionately singled out for the death penalty. Kennedy points out that 17 defendants in Fulton County, Georgia, between 1973 and 1980 were charged with killing police officers, but the only defendant who received the death sentence was a black man. Kennedy also cites statistics to show that "those who killed whites were 4.3 times more likely to receive the death penalty than were killers of blacks," and that "in Georgia, blacks who killed whites received the death penalty 16.7 percent of the time, while whites who killed received the death penalty only 4.2 percent of the time."

Of course, the mere piling up of evidence does not in itself make the speaker's case. Statistics can be selected and manipulated to prove anything, as demonstrated in Darrell Huff's landmark book *How to Lie with Statistics* (1954). Moreover, what appears to be a logical argument may, in fact, be fundamentally flawed. On the other hand, the fact that evidence can be distorted, statistics misused, and logic fractured does not mean that these tools of reason can be dispensed with or should be dismissed. It means only that audiences have to listen and read critically—perceptively, knowledgeably, and skeptically (though not necessarily cynically).

Avoiding Logical Fallacies

At some point, you will need to respond to the logic of the argument itself. To be convincing, an argument should be governed by principles of logic—clear and orderly thinking. This does *not* mean that an argument should not be biased. A biased argument—that is, an argument weighted toward one point of view and against others—may be valid as long as it is logically sound.

Here are several examples of faulty thinking and logical fallacies to watch for:

Emotionally Loaded Terms. Writers sometimes attempt to sway readers by using emotionally charged words: words with positive connotations to sway readers to their own point of view; words with negative connotations to sway readers away from the opposing point of view. The fact that an author uses emotionally loaded terms does not necessarily invalidate the argument. Emotional appeals are perfectly legitimate and time-honoured modes of persuasion. But in academic writing, which is grounded in logical argumentation, they should not be the *only* means of persuasion. You should be sensitive to *how* emotionally loaded terms are being used. In particular, are they being used deceptively or to hide the essential facts?

When we looked over the issue of using information unfairly and examined a passage from Postrel earlier, we might also have pointed out that in using the phrase "lie back and accept it" she is using an emotionally weighted phrase that is often used to taint victims as participants in their suffering. Thus, some readers might object not only that she is unfair in presenting Gray's position shorn of its original context, but also that she uses emotionally laden terms under the pretense of providing an accurate gloss.

Ad Hominem Argument. In an *ad hominem* argument, the writer rejects opposing views by attacking the person who holds them. By calling opponents names, an author avoids the issue:

> I could more easily accept my opponent's plan to increase revenues by collecting on delinquent tax bills if he had paid more than a hundred dollars in state taxes in each of the past three years. But the fact is, he's a millionaire with a millionaire's tax shelters. This man hasn't paid a wooden nickel for the state services he and his family depend on. So I ask you: Is *he* the one to be talking about taxes to *us*?

It could well be that the opponent has paid virtually no state taxes for three years; but this fact has nothing to do with, and is a ploy to divert attention from, the merits of a specific proposal for increasing revenues. The proposal is lost in the attack against the man himself, an attack that violates the principles of logic. Writers (and speakers) must make their points by citing evidence in support of their views and by challenging contrary evidence.

Postrel uses an *ad hominem* argument against German Research Minister Juergen Ruettgers toward the end of her essay (pp. 416–420) to make her point that we should be free to choose our own medicine. First, she quotes a statement of his that opposes cloning: "The cloned human would be an attack on the dignity and integrity of every single person on this earth." She goes on to deride him for taking this stance by saying that he is "wildly overreacting" before finally attacking his character: "We should not let the arrogant likes of Ruettgers block . . . future hopes."

Faulty Cause and Effect. The fact that one event precedes another in time does not mean that the first event has caused the second. An example: Fish begin dying by the thousands in a lake near your hometown. An environmental group immediately cites chemical dumping by several manufacturing plants as the cause. But other causes are possible: A disease might have affected the fish; the growth of algae might have contributed to the deaths; or acid rain might be a factor. The origins of an event are usually complex and are not always traceable to a single cause. So you must carefully examine cause-and-effect reasoning when you find a writer using it. In Latin, this fallacy is known as *post hoc, ergo propter hoc* ("after this, therefore because of this").

Either/Or Reasoning. Either/or reasoning also results from an unwillingness to recognize complexity. If an author analyzes a problem and offers only two explanations, one of which he or she refutes, then you are entitled to object that the other is not thereby proved true, since several other explanations (at the very least) are usually possible. For whatever reason, the author has chosen to overlook them. As an example, suppose you are reading a selection on genetic engineering and the author builds an argument on the basis of the following:

> Research in gene splicing is at a crossroads: Either scientists will be carefully monitored by civil authorities and their efforts limited to acceptable applications, such as disease control; or, lacking regulatory guidelines, sci-

entists will set their own ethical standards and begin programs in embryonic manipulation that, however well intended, exceed the proper limits of human knowledge.

Certainly, other possibilities for genetic engineering exist beyond the two mentioned here. But the author limits debate by establishing an either/or choice. Such limitation is artificial and does not allow for complexity. As a critical reader, be on the alert for either/or reasoning.

Hasty Generalization. Writers are guilty of hasty generalization when they draw their conclusions from too little evidence or from unrepresentative evidence. To argue that scientists should not proceed with the human genome project because a recent editorial urged that the project be abandoned is to make a hasty generalization. This lone editorial may be unrepresentative of the views of most people—both scientists and laypeople—who have studied and written about the matter. To argue that one should never obey authority because the Milgram experiment shows the dangers of obeying authority is to ignore the fact that Milgram's experiment was concerned primarily with obedience to *immoral* authority. Thus, the experimental situation was unrepresentative of most routine demands for obedience—for example, to obey a parental rule or to comply with a summons for jury duty—and a conclusion about the malevolence of all authority would be a hasty generalization.

In "The Nature and Meaning of Data," Glastonbury and LaMendola rely on an extended example that depicts the plight of a hypothetical individual who falls prey to out-of-control data-collection operations. This may encourage some readers to object that a single example is not convincing. Moreover, in this case the fact that the example is hypothetical further weakens its ability to serve as evidence.

False Analogy. Comparing one person, event, or issue to another may be illuminating, but it also may be confusing or misleading. The differences between the two may be more significant than the similarities, and the conclusions drawn from the one may not necessarily apply to the other. A writer who argues that it is reasonable to quarantine people with AIDS because quarantine has been effective in preventing the spread of smallpox is assuming an analogy between AIDS and smallpox that (because of the differences between the two diseases) is not valid.

Begging the Question. To beg the question is to assume as a proven fact the very thesis being argued. To assert, for example, that Canada is not in decline because it is as strong and prosperous as ever is not to prove anything: It is merely to repeat the claim in different words. This fallacy is also known as circular reasoning.

There is an example of question-begging in paragraph 14 of "The Nature and Meaning of Data." After arguing that individuals should be able to have control over their personal data, the authors cite several areas that might be exempt from such a rule of privacy. Rather than considering the implications for breaches of privacy arising from the creation of these exemptions, the authors return directly to their point that protecting individual rights should be the ultimate goal.

Non Sequitur. *Non sequitur* is Latin for "it does not follow"; the term is used to describe a conclusion that does not logically follow from a premise. "Since minorities have made such great strides in the last few decades," a writer may argue, "we no longer need affirmative action programs." Aside from the fact that the premise itself is arguable (*have* minorities made such great strides?), it does not follow that because minorities *may* have made great strides, there is no further need for affirmative action programs.

Oversimplification. Be alert for writers who offer easy solutions to complicated problems. "Canada's economy will be strong again if we all 'buy Canadian,'" a politician may argue. But the problems of our economy are complex and cannot be solved by a slogan or a simple change in buying habits. Likewise, a writer who argues that we should ban genetic engineering assumes that simple solutions ("just say 'no'") will be sufficient to deal with the complex moral dilemmas raised by this new technology.

It can be said that Glastonbury and LaMendola's argument partakes of similar oversimplification. After making the case that we are often unaware of how our personal data is being stored and moved through data banks, they recommend that individuals should control the dissemination of personal information, which seems an expression of hope for something that can no longer be.

(4) Examine Appeals to Ethics and Emotion

Speakers and writers have never relied upon logic alone to advance and support their claims. Over 2000 years ago, the Athenian philosopher and rhetorician Aristotle explained how speakers attempting to persuade others to their point of view could achieve their purpose not only by presenting a rational argument— what he called an appeal to *logos*—but also by relying on appeals to *ethos* and *pathos*.

Since we frequently find these three appeals employed in political argument, we have used many political examples in our discussion of logical argumentation and in the discussion of *ethos* and *pathos* that follows. But keep in mind that these appeals are also used extensively in advertising, in legal cases, in business plans, and in many other types of argument, with the balance among the three shifting from scholarly texts, where *logos* is paramount, to, say, advertising, where logic may be lacking but strong appeals are made to *pathos*.

Ethos

Ethos, or the ethical appeal, is an appeal based not on the ethical rationale for the subject under discussion, but rather on the ethical nature of the person making the appeal. A person making an argument must have a certain degree of credibility: That person must be of good character, be of sound sense, and be qualified to hold the office or recommend policy.

For example, in attempting to appeal to the public as a man of the people whose common sense and family values equipped him to serve as Prime Minister, Jean Chrétien often referred to having grown up in a big family in small-town Quebec. To draw this self-portrait, he sometimes referred to himself as "the little guy from Shawinigan," making an appeal to ethos that suggests that a "regular guy," rather than somebody larger than life, is best suited to lead our country.

L. A. Kauffman is not running for office but rather writing an article arguing against socialism as a viable ideology for the future ("Socialism: No." *Progressive*, April 1, 1993). To defuse objections that he is simply a tool of capitalism, Kauffman begins with an appeal to *ethos*: "Until recently, I was executive editor of the journal *Socialist Review*. Before that I worked for the Marxist magazine, *Monthly Review*. My bookshelves are filled with books of Marxist theory, and I even have a picture of Karl Marx up on my wall." Thus, Kauffman establishes his credentials to argue knowledgeably about Marxist ideology.

Pathos

Speakers and writers also may appeal to their audiences by the use of *pathos*, the appeal to the emotions. There is nothing inherently wrong with using an emotional appeal. Indeed, since emotions often move people far more powerfully than reason alone, speakers and writers would be foolish not to use emotion. And it would be a drab, humourless world if human beings were not subject to the sway of feeling, as well as reason. The emotional appeal becomes problematic only if it is the *sole or primary* basis of the argument. This is the kind of situation that led, for example, to the internment of Japanese Canadians during World War II or that leads to periodic calls for the return of the national anthem and "God Save the Queen" in schools.

U.S. President Ronald Reagan was a master of emotional appeal. He closed his first inaugural address with a reference to the view from the Capitol of Arlington National Cemetery, where lie thousands of markers of "heroes":

> Under one such marker lies a young man, Martin Treptow, who left his job in a small-town barbershop in 1917 to go to France with the famed Rainbow Division. There, on the western front, he was killed trying to carry a message between battalions under heavy artillery fire. We're told that on his body was found a diary. On the flyleaf under the heading, "My Pledge," he had written these words: "America must win this war. Therefore, I will work, I will save, I will sacrifice, I will endure, I will fight cheerfully and do my utmost, as if the issue of the whole struggle depended on me alone." The crisis we are facing today does not require of us the kind of sacrifice that Martin Treptow and so many thousands of others were called upon to make. It does require, however, our best effort and our willingness to believe in ourselves and to believe in our capacity to perform great deeds, to believe that together with God's help we can and will resolve the problems which now confront us.

Surely, Reagan implies, if Martin Treptow can act so courageously and so selflessly, we can do the same. The logic is somewhat unclear, since the connection between Martin Treptow and ordinary Americans of 1981 is rather tenuous (as Reagan concedes); but the emotional power of Martin Treptow, whom reporters were sent scurrying to research, carries the argument.

A more recent American president, Bill Clinton, also used pathos. Addressing an audience of the nation's governors on his welfare plan, Clinton closed his remarks by referring to a conversation he had held with a welfare mother who had gone through the kind of training program Clinton was advocating. Asked by Clinton whether she thought that such training programs should be mandatory, the mother said, "I sure do." When Clinton asked her why, she said:

> "Well, because if it wasn't, there would be a lot of people like me home watching the soaps because we don't believe we can make anything of ourselves anymore. So you've got to make it mandatory." And I said, "What's the best thing about having a job?" She said, "When my boy goes to school, and they say, 'What does your mama do for a living?' he can give an answer."

Clinton uses the emotional power he counts on in that anecdote to set up his conclusion: "We must end poverty for Americans who want to work. And we must do it on terms that dignify all of the rest of us, as well as help our country to work better. I need your help, and I think we can do it."

In a speech at his trial for treason in 1885, Louis Riel made a poetic appeal to the emotions of jurors and listeners when he compared his country to his mother and claimed to expect equal protection from harm at the hands of both:

> The day of my birth I was helpless and my mother took care of me. Today I am a man, but I am as helpless before this court in the Dominion of Canada as I was the day of my birth. The Northwest is also my mother; it is my mother country. Although my mother country is sick, some people have come from Lower Canada to help her take care of me. I am sure my mother country will not kill me any more than my mother did.

In a sense, this passage also constitutes an appeal to *ethos*, since in it Riel claims to be rooted in the soil of the Northwest and motivated by his desire to serve and protect it.

Question Category 2: Stepping Back—To What Extent Do You Agree with the Author?

When formulating a critical response to a source, try to distinguish your evaluation of the author's purpose and success at achieving that purpose from your agreement or disagreement with the author's views. The distinction allows you to respond to a piece of writing on its merits. As an unbiased, evenhanded critic, you evaluate an author's clarity of presentation, definition of terms, fair use of evidence, adherence to principles of logic, and appeals to ethics and emotion. To what extent has the author succeeded in achieving his or her purpose? Still withholding judgment, offer your assessment and give the author (in effect) a grade. Significantly, your assessment of the presentation may not coincide with your views of the author's conclusions: You may agree with an author entirely but feel that the presentation is superficial; you may find the author's logic and use of evidence to be rock solid but at the same time may resist certain conclusions. A critical evaluation works well when it is conducted in two parts. After evaluating the author's purpose and design for achieving that purpose, respond to the author's main assertions. In doing so, you'll want to (1) identify points of agreement and disagreement; (2) evaluate assumptions; and (3) ask whose interests are served by the text.

(1) Identify Points of Agreement and Disagreement

Be precise in identifying points of agreement and disagreement with an author. You should state as clearly as possible what *you* believe, and an effective way of doing this is to define your position in relation to that presented in the piece. Whether you agree enthusiastically, disagree, or agree with reservations, you can organize your reactions in two parts: First, summarize the author's position; second, state your own position and elaborate on your reasons for holding it. The elaboration, in effect, becomes an argument itself, and this is true regardless of the position you take. An opinion is effective when you support it by supplying evidence. Without such evidence, opinions cannot be authoritative. "I thought the article on inflation was lousy." Why? "I just thought so, that's all." This opinion is worthless because the criticism is imprecise: The critic has taken neither the time to read the article carefully nor the time to explore his own reactions carefully.

(2) Explore the Reasons for Agreement and Disagreement: Evaluate Assumptions

One way of elaborating your reactions to a reading is to explore the underlying *reasons* for agreement and disagreement. Your reactions are based largely on assumptions that you hold and how these assumptions compare with the author's. An *assumption* is a fundamental statement about the world and its operations that you take to be true. A writer's assumptions may be explicitly stated; but, just as often, assumptions are implicit and you will have to "ferret them out"—that is, to infer them. Consider an example:

> *In vitro* fertilization and embryo transfer are brought about outside the bodies of the couple through actions of third parties whose competence and technical activity determine the success of the procedure. Such fertilization entrusts the life and identity of the embryo into the power of doctors and biologists and establishes the domination of technology over the origin and destiny of the human person. Such

a relationship of domination is in itself contrary to the dignity and equality that must be common to parents and children.

(From: the Vatican document *Instruction on Respect for Human Life in Its Origin and on the Dignity of Procreation*, given at Rome, from the Congregation for the Doctrine of the Faith, February 22, 1987, as presented in *Origins: N.C. Documentary Service* 16 (40), March 19, 1987, 707.)

This paragraph is quoted from the February 1987 Vatican document on artificial procreation. Cardinal Joseph Ratzinger, principal author of the document, makes an implicit assumption in this paragraph: that no good can come of the domination of technology over conception. The use of technology to bring about conception is morally wrong. Yet there are thousands of childless couples, Roman Catholics included, who reject this assumption in favour of its opposite: that conception technology is an aid to the barren couple; far from creating a relationship of unequals, the technology brings children into the world who will be welcomed with joy and love.

Assumptions provide the foundation on which entire presentations are built. If you find an author's assumptions invalid, you may well disagree with conclusions that follow from these assumptions. The author of a book on developing nations may include a section outlining the resources and time that will be required to industrialize a particular country and so upgrade its general welfare. His assumption—that industrialization in that particular country will ensure or even affect the general welfare—may or may not be valid. If you do not share the assumption, in your eyes the rationale for the entire book may be undermined.

How do you determine the validity of assumptions once you have identified them? In the absence of more scientific criteria, validity may mean how well the author's assumptions stack up against your own experience, observations, and reading. A caution, however: The overall value of an article or book may depend only to a small degree on the validity of the author's assumptions. For instance, a sociologist may do a fine job of gathering statistical data about the incidence of crime in urban areas along the eastern seaboard. The sociologist also might be a Marxist, and you may disagree with her subsequent analysis of the data. Yet you may find the data extremely valuable for your own work.

(3) Ask "Whose Interests Are Served by the Text?"

Students sometimes feel that the text they are asked to evaluate for book reviews and other critical essays is so logically airtight, so solidly supported with scholarly references and impeccable logic, that they can find nothing to take issue with, reducing them to the role of appreciative readers who can do little but point out the various strengths of the text. Such a reaction is understandable, given that the text was produced by an expert on the topic, and by the time it was published had been revised many times and reviewed by other similarly expert specialists. While it is theoretically appropriate to write an entirely positive critique in cases where the text offers no reasonable grounds for disagreement, more often the appreciative stance suggests an inadequate critical stance from which to identify problems, or at least, omissions in the text: after all, no single book or article can possibly have considered its topic from every conceivable angle, and what a text doesn't do can be worthy of discussion. Sometimes it is possible to develop a critical perspective on a text by stepping back to ask what it actually does and doesn't do instead of asking how well it does what the author evidently meant it to do.

In any case, the question of authorial intention can be seen as irrelevant, since authors can die, change their minds, or have ulterior motives we can't know about; further, their texts can have effects very different from what they intended, and these effects can differ in different reading contexts.

For example, Erich Fromm's purpose in writing his article, "Disobedience as a Psychological and Moral Problem" (pp. 267–272) might have been to convince people of the time that they were obeying themselves to death and needed to practise civil disobedience in order to avoid destroying the world. But Fromm wrote his essay more than 40 years ago, in the context of the Cuban Missile Crisis, when it seemed as though the world had come within a hair's breadth of nuclear annihilation. Whatever Fromm's purpose in writing his essay, the world has undergone significant changes in the distribution of military power since that time, and the intervening years have seen the development of major social change movements—Aboriginal self-government, Black civil rights, feminism, and gay and lesbian rights, among others—that call into question his thesis of humanity's blind obedience to power. Because the world has changed, the effects of his text may be quite different, too. From this point of view, it might be more productive to ask what Fromm's text does than to ask how well it serves his purpose.

Scholars in the field of critical literacy point out that focusing on the author's purpose can be intellectually conservative since the terms of discussion are largely established by the author rather than by the critic. Even if we shift our definition of purpose from "author's intention" to the "thesis of the text," our frame of reference is pre-established. Critical analysis that focuses on purpose mostly works "within the box"—first the big box of all scholarly writing on the subject, then the smaller box of the text itself.

To address the former (i.e., all scholarly writing), traditional critical thinkers check to see if the author provides references to other trustworthy studies (i.e., scholarly research) in which any unproved statements *are* proved. To address the latter (i.e., the text itself), they ask pertinent questions that focus directly on the internal strength of the document:

- Does one claim lead logically to another? Are logical flaws avoided? (*logos*)
- Are appropriate methods used (e.g., statistical analysis, large enough sample size), and are they properly executed? (*logos*)
- Are all the claims backed up with solid evidence? (*logos*)
- Does the author ever try to get away with using emotion or personal experience instead of logic and objective evidence? (*pathos*)

- Does the author have the authority or credentials to speak on the subject? Does he or she seem trustworthy? (*ethos*)

In short, critical thinking works in a limited context. It identifies an object of analysis (a text, an idea, an argument) and assesses its internal logic.

This method of critical thinking, the one most popular in universities, is "critical" in the sense of being necessary to find the "truth" by exposing and avoiding the mistakes of everyday common sense. As such, it is tremendously important to rigorous intellectual work and nothing is likely to get published in the scholarly press if it fails the test of critical thinking. However, traditional critical thinking is not a perfect method and, in itself, can tend to be intellectually conservative rather than conducive to new perspectives. The following statements reflect mainstream beliefs that have passed the test of traditional critical thinking either in our own or earlier times; they have all been fiercely defended as true by scholars using traditional critical thinking:

- Women should not attend university because studying diverts energy from the uterus.
- Women should not be allowed to vote or hold political office because they lack the rational capacities of men.
- It is acceptable to enslave people of other races because slavery helps the white race to prosper and spread Christianity worldwide in accordance with God's plan.
- It is in everyone's best interests to annihilate Aboriginal languages, religions, and traditions and to assimilate Aboriginal people into Canadian culture.
- Human beings are the only living creatures that are conscious and have emotions.
- We are all completely free to think and do as we want in a Western democracy like Canada. If we are poor, it's our own fault.

These statements, most of them generally rejected now as blatantly unjust constructions of reality designed to serve the interests of those in power, were produced by powerful social institutions such as universities, dominant religions, law, and medicine. Recognizing that to some extent (the exact extent is the subject of fervent debate between constructionist and modernist intellectuals) traditional critical thinking has historically tended to serve the interests of the status quo, scholars in the field of critical literacy have developed a parallel method of critical thinking that is designed to open up new perspectives by asking "whose interests are served" by the text. This method is "critical" in the sense of "critical social theory": its focus is primarily on power rather than on "truth," and it looks for signs that a particular text is premised on versions of "truth" that serve the interests of dominant culture. These questions are pertinent when reading the articles in the chapter on Canadian identity, for example, where the texts offer competing definitions of Canadian identity and national purpose that serve the interests of some groups (say, advocates of multiculturalism) at the expense of others (say, middle-class conservative defenders of the status quo).

CRITICAL LITERACY

Critical literacy involves becoming aware of the "box" constructed by the text itself (sometimes called "reading against the grain" of a text), by exposing its politics and drawing attention to its oppressive effects; and developing alternate texts, for example, alternate ways of understanding the topic of civil disobedience. In order to get at what texts do, we can ask impertinent questions—ones the author doesn't invite—such as the following:

- Whose interests are served by this text? Whose interests are harmed?
- Who benefits from the way this problem is analyzed? Who is hurt by the way this problem is analyzed?
- What is treated as a root cause? What difference does this make?
- Who's telling the story? What difference does that make?
- Whose voices are heard in this text? Whose are left out? What difference does this make?
- What relevant factors are not considered?
- What kind of evidence is used? What kind of evidence could have been used? What difference would that make?
- What political actions would this text support?

  And finally,

- How else could this story have been told/this problem have been analyzed?

We have included later in this chapter a student essay that critiques Fromm's article by focusing on such questions.

CRITIQUE

A *critique* is a *formalized, critical reading of a passage*. It also is a personal response; but writing a critique is considerably more rigorous than saying that a movie is "great," or a book is "fascinating," or "I didn't like it." These are all responses, and, as such, they're a valid, even essential, part of your understanding of what you see and read. But such responses don't help illuminate the subject for anyone—even you—if you haven't explained how you arrived at your conclusions.

Your task in writing a critique is to turn your critical reading of a passage into a systematic evaluation to deepen your reader's (and your own) understanding of that passage. Among other things, you're interested in determining what an author says, how well the points are made, what assumptions underlie the argument, what issues are overlooked, and what implications can be drawn from such an analysis. Critiques, positive or negative, should include a fair and accurate summary of the passage; they also should include a statement of your own assumptions. It is important to remember that you bring to bear an entire set of assumptions about the world. Stated or not, these assumptions underlie every evaluative comment you make; you therefore have an obligation, both to the reader and to yourself, to clarify your standards. Not only do your readers stand to gain by your forthrightness, but you do as well: In the process of writing a critical assessment, you are forced to examine your own knowledge, beliefs, and assumptions. Ultimately, the critique is a way of learning about yourself.

How to Write Critiques

You may find it useful to organize your critiques in five sections: introduction, summary, analysis of the presentation, your response to the presentation, and conclusion.

The box below contains some guidelines for writing critiques. Note that they are guidelines, not a rigid formula. Thousands of authors write critiques that do not follow the structure outlined here. Until you are more confident and practised in writing critiques, however, we suggest you follow these guidelines. They are meant not to restrict you, but rather to provide you with a workable method of writing critical analyses that incorporates a logical sequence of development.

HOW TO WRITE CRITIQUES

- *Introduction.* Introduce both the passage under analysis and the author. State the author's main argument and the point(s) you intend to make about it. Provide background material to help your readers understand the relevance or appeal of the passage. This background material might include one or more of the following: an explanation of why the subject is of current interest; a reference to a possible controversy surrounding the subject of the passage or the passage itself; biographical information about the author; an account of the circumstances under which the passage was written; or a reference to the intended audience of the passage.

- *Summary.* Summarize the author's main points, making sure to state the author's purpose for writing.

- *Analysis of the presentation.* Evaluate the validity of the author's presentation, as distinct from your points of agreement or disagreement. Comment on the author's success in achieving his or her purpose by reviewing three or four specific points. You might base your review on one (or more) of the following criteria:

  Is the information accurate?

  Is the information significant?

  Has the author defined terms clearly?

  Has the author used and interpreted information fairly?

  Has the author argued logically?

> - *Your response to the presentation.* Now it is your turn to respond to the author's views. With which views do you agree? With which do you disagree? Whose interests are served by the text? Discuss your reasons for agreement and disagreement, tying these reasons, when possible, to assumptions—both the author's and your own.
> - *Conclusion.* State your conclusions about the overall validity of the piece—your assessment of the author's success at achieving his or her aims and your reactions to the author's views. Remind the reader of the weaknesses and strengths of the passage.

When you write a critique based on an essay in this text, you'll find it helpful to first read the Discussion and Writing Suggestions following that essay. These suggestions will lead you to some of the more fruitful areas of inquiry. Beware of simply responding mechanically to them, however, or your essay could degenerate into a series of short, disjointed responses. You need to organize your reactions into a coherent whole: The critique should be informed by a consistent point of view.

Demonstration: Critique

The selections you will likely be inclined to critique are those that argue a specific position. Indeed, every argument you read is an invitation to agreement or disagreement. It remains only for you to speak up and justify your position.

We start our demonstration with Colleen Still's critique of Fromm's "Disobedience as a Psychological and Moral Problem" (pp. 267–272). Still bases her critique on identifying what Fromm *doesn't* do in his analysis of the problem, arguing that we no longer need to be convinced that disobedience is not a sin. Following Still's essay is a critique of John Stackhouse's article, "I'm Tired of Being a Slave to the Church Floor" (pp. 155–160) by Josh Grummett, which demonstrates one approach to writing a positive but insightful critique.

A Critique of "Disobedience as a Psychological and Moral Problem"

COLLEEN STILL

Erich Fromm's essay, "Disobedience as a Psychological and Moral Problem," 1
was published in 1963 in the wake of the Cuban missile crisis and the consequent fears of nuclear annihilation. Fromm has been described as a psychoanalyst, philosopher, historian and sociologist searching for solutions to personal and ideological conflicts (267). His essay is a call to wake up before

we are blown up: to not leave the decision of whether humans should continue to exist solely in the hands of a few morally unqualified leaders. Fromm meticulously defines the psychological and moral qualities of an effective protester, but offers no indication of what it is that his psychologically mature, morally strong protester might actually *do*. In the early sixties Fromm's readers may have needed to hear his message that disobedience is not inherently immoral. Today, if we fail to stop the reckless behaviour of those in power, I think it is not because we are afraid to be bad or afraid of what the neighbours will say, but because we do not know what we can *do* that might have an effect.

Fromm begins with a reminder that for centuries those with power have   2
taught that good people are obedient. Fromm contrasts this view with his thesis: "human history began with an act of disobedience, and it is not unlikely that it will be terminated by an act of obedience" (267). That an "act of disobedience" initiated our history is explained in this way: when Adam and Eve disobey and have to leave their garden, humankind separates from nature to develop its own powers the way a young child begins to develop its separate identity when it learns to say "no." Fromm argues that spiritual and intellectual developments require disobedience to conservative authorities and habits of thought. He explains that obedience to rational authority poses no problem. Obedience to irrational (exploitive) authority involves disobeying our own consciences and "the laws of humanity and of reason" (269). This requires the use of force or persuasion. Historically, the minority in power has found it more convenient to rule the majority by training them to want to obey, rather than by using force. This inculcation is one reason Fromm gives for our reluctance to resist irrational authority: another is that it is comforting and safe to be on the side of the powerful. Fromm reminds us of the long struggle in pre-nineteenth-century Europe of workers, philosophers and scientists who, with faith in reason and mistrust of tradition, cultivated the skills and the freedom to question and to disobey traditional authorities. In contrast to them, contemporary citizens are as irresponsible in their blind obedience as Adolph Eichmann, Fromm says. Unless we can disobey our leaders, Fromm warns, their emotional immaturity could lead to the destruction of our world.

I assume Fromm's argument that history started with the disobedience of   3
Adam and Eve is a response to people who use religious texts to justify their demands for obedience. As someone not familiar with Biblical studies, I felt left out of the beginning of human history, and had to join humanity later on as we continued to evolve spiritually and intellectually, all the while needing to disobey established norms of thought and behaviour before we could innovate new ones.

Fromm goes to lengths to make clear what kind of disobedience is con-   4
structive: about one-third of his essay is definitions of types of obedience, conscience and authority. He establishes that he is not advocating compulsive disobedience, but that he considers disobedience to exploitive powers to be a responsibility that can be carried out only by someone who is psychologically independent, is guided by principles, and is brave enough to risk being wrong (270).

If Fromm's intention is to persuade us to say "no" to nuclear annihila- 5
tion, his analysis of what discourages us (i.e., our lack of psychological
strength to stand apart from the powers that be, and our manipulation by
these powers), might be more effective if he identified contemporary powers
and their means of manipulation. Instead Fromm points out that what we
need to do now has been done before: he holds up as models the people of
pre-Industrial Europe. The essay's ending, following an "Eichmann is us"
argument, hits the reader with an accusation: "he would do it again. And so
would we—and so do we" (271), that shocks us out of the contemplation of
the past and into the urgency of the imminent threat to existence.

Fromm leaves us impressed with the urgent need for action, but with a lot 6
of unanswered questions about what that action might be. How did his historical models develop the character and skills to resist exploitive authority,
and how much of what they did is relevant to our situation today? For example, can the faith in reason, which in the past was a revolutionary force,
really save us from following the exploitive leader? It seems to me that the
choice of what is "reasonable" involves not only the acknowledgement of the
provable facts, but also includes an intuitive component, such as Fromm
mentions in his definition of the humanistic conscience: "an intuitive knowledge of what is human and inhuman" (269), of what is healthy or destructive.
By transferring our faith from kings and church leaders to science, we escaped
adherence to a lot of oppressive irrational ideas, but confidence in our own
intuition is one baby that was thrown out with the bathwater. People's trust
in their own judgment is overwhelmed by our ever-expanding body of scientific information, largely the property of "experts." We might know what is
right, but it is hard to debate "experts" in their own territory. If we do trust
our own voices, can we make them heard without large amounts of money to
hire professional lobbyists or to buy television commercials? Are we as helpless as we feel?

To develop the "capacity to disobey" (270), we need more than the 7
courage of our convictions, and more than faith in rational thought. We need
to learn methods of protest that work for our times. Without practical knowledge, skills and resources to make our views heard, we will continue to sit by,
helplessly watching governments fan the flames of international conflicts,
watching the rich get richer and the poor get poorer, and watching the
destruction of our natural environment. Forty years after Fromm's writing we
are less in need of convincing that it is not a sin to disobey, but we need as
much as ever to know *how* to disobey.

Work Cited

Fromm, Erich. "Disobedience as a Psychological and Moral Problem." *Writing and
Reading Across the Disciplines*, Can. ed. Ed. Laurence Behrens et al. Toronto: Pearson
Education Canada Inc., 2007. 259–264.

■ ■ ■

Portrait of the Drifter as a Real Person: John Stackhouse Demonstrates the Power of New Journalism

JOSH GRUMMETT

When the Sally Ann truck finally pulls up on Queen Street, shortly after 7 a.m., we join the lineup at its open window. A man in the truck offers coffee to a half-dozen people waiting, stamping their feet to stay warm. (157)

For his 1999 *The Globe and Mail* article on the Toronto homeless, titled "I'm   1
Tired of Being a Slave to the Church Floor," John Stackhouse was not content
to sit at his desk, pulling up research reports and phoning in some interviews.
He chose instead the method of 'new journalism'—going in and being a part
of what he was writing about, a style of writing pioneered by the late Hunter
S. Thompson as 'gonzo journalism.' He lived homeless for a week, going from
shelter to shelter, panhandling, and talking to other drifters. A powerful
piece, it vividly demonstrates the need for an alternative system of sheltering
the homeless and getting them back on their feet, and for stemming the tide
of drugs that flows through the shelters. Stackhouse's use of the new journalism method and style not only creates a graphic and provocative piece, but
also serves as a goad and example to all people who would otherwise be content with swivel chairs and monitor screens.

The first two questions to ask of Stackhouse's article are about its verac-   2
ity and its effectiveness—both extremely key, given the fact that it *is* a journalistic piece. Stackhouse relegates all opinion and conclusion to the piece's
epilogue, leaving his experiences and the words of other drifters to stand
alone in the article itself. This produces an audible ring of truth to the piece,
especially when he refers to his home as "a luxury I always knew I had"
(160)—it paints the image of Stackhouse as an unbiased reporter, leaving all
personal opinion until the moment he arrives in his home, research complete. Its effectiveness is only enhanced by its truth and veracity; by letting that
ring of truth echo in the reader's mind, Stackhouse enhances the rest of his
article, creating a strong desire to read the article over again—even if only to
read such brilliant turns of phrase as the following:

> I say goodbye to B. J. in front of the Eaton Centre and head inside,
> watching him one more time through the glass, holding his hand out in
> the night, as though he were reaching for salmon in a big-city river of
> shoppers. (159)

Stackhouse's thesis can be found succinctly stated at the very end of the   3
article:

> Perhaps when we stop talking about the "homeless" as though theirs
> were a separate world, when we start seeing people . . . as integral pieces

of our society, maybe then we can do more than just get them through the night. (160)

He concentrates on a few main points to drive his thesis home, points that run throughout the article itself. Giving the example of Billy Jack, a big-hearted Mi'kmaq man who "likes to call himself one of the originals, one of the grand old native [sic] drunks who has been on the Toronto streets since the sixties" (156), Stackhouse asserts that there are several drifters who remain drifting out of "pride and sense of place" (157)—noting in passing that in the day prior to his writing, Billy Jack received two bottles of wine and a pack of cigarettes, which the drifter considered a good day.

Another point that Stackhouse never overtly states himself—but can be deduced from Jack Layton's blustering rebuttal—is that the roots of the "problem" are not monetary. He cites the example of a drifter he met early in the morning of day 7,

> . . . one of the overnight guests [who] walks instead to the church park-ing lot to warm up his car. He's off for another day hauling scrap metal to dumps, a business that earns him $600 to $700 a week.

> "I know I shouldn't be here," he says, stamping out his cigarette before heading off for the day. "I shouldn't be in a shelter, but whenever I get some money, I spend it all partying with the ladies." (160)

By letting the drifter speak for himself, Stackhouse is implicitly saying that the roots of the problem may be partially psychological, and not entirely monetary.

Stackhouse also vividly shows that there *is* indeed money that goes to homeless shelters, in the example of the Blythwood Road Baptist Church, a place he refers to as his "last resort" (159)—leaving it ambiguous as to whether he's referring to desperation or beachside hotels. He begins the epi-logue with the following:

> When I had set out a week earlier to live homeless, I did not expect to be eating pancakes and sausage before breakfast and pastries before bed, or to earn $20 an hour simply by sitting on the ground with a cardboard sign in front of me. (160)

Later on he states how he didn't expect to find "the isolation and belit-tlement that make the street so much more a psychological challenge than a physical one" (160). By drawing these conclusions, Stackhouse furthers his thesis—that the key to doing more than just "getting [the homeless] through the night" lies in seeing that they are people, and not just something that throwing money at will fix.

As far as I am concerned, Stackhouse's presentation of his article is bril-liant. It has a very clear logical flow: it's the stream of his experience, broken up by headings delineating which day he writes about. This is also key to its emotional appeal; the article comes across less like your standard, boring inverted-pyramid Associated Press blurb, and more like a series of personal journals, written just before he tucked in for the night—something I can appreciate more emotionally. Indeed, it is difficult to determine whether he left anything out; by strictly limiting his article to seat-of-the-pants new journalism and separating his conclusions out into the epilogue, Stackhouse allows his audience to draw its own conclusions regarding the issue of drifters and homelessness in Toronto. The reader can easily buy into new journalism—we've all written diaries and journals of our own, even if the exercise was abortive in most cases.

Stackhouse, in writing in a new journalistic style, has created a graphic   7 and provocative, yet also rational and stunningly researched, article and statement on the homeless in Toronto. After reading "I'm Tired of Being a Slave to the Church Floor," it's easy to see how Jack Layton could watch "most people [he] know[s] . . . reading and talking about the series ever since" (162).

Works Cited

Layton, Jack. "The Homeless: Are We Part of the Problem?" *Writing and Reading Across the Disciplines*, Cdn. ed., Ed. Laurence Behrens et al. Toronto: Pearson Education Canada Inc., 2007. 155–158.

Stackhouse, John. "I'm Tired of Being a Slave to the Church Floor." *Writing and Reading Across the Disciplines*, Cdn. ed., Laurence Behrens et al. Toronto: Pearson Education Canada Inc., 2007. 149–155.

■ ■ ■

■ EXERCISE

Read the following two articles that address the issue of how gender difference influences the experiences of boys and girls in Canada, and then select one on which to write a critique, using the techniques introduced in this chapter. Donna Laframboise argues that boys have been disadvantaged by the recent efforts to improve the treatment and expectations of girls. Stevie Cameron's article points out that the problem for girls and women goes beyond legislating gender equity and resides in changing ingrained and dangerous misogynistic attitudes. We provide two arguments from which to choose because each will help you to think critically about the issues. Use (and give credit to) one author in critiquing the other. Your critique should be the result of several drafts.

Roll Back the Red Carpet for Boys

DONNA LAFRAMBOISE

Every now and again, in random bits and pieces, we run up against the fact   1
that being male isn't the red-carpet experience much of recent feminism would
have us believe. Young males are more likely to be physically abused by their
parents, to drop out of school, and to face unemployment than their female
counterparts. Between the ages of 15 and 24, they take their own lives five
times as often. As adults, males are more likely to be homeless, more prone to
alcohol and gambling addictions, twice as likely to be robbed or murdered,
nine times more likely to be killed in an occupational accident, and [on average, they] go to their graves six years earlier than their sisters.

Yet, so attached are we to the view that the patriarchy has designed the   2
world for the benefit of males that these truths fail to sink in. Although headlines would scream and alarm bells would ring if the opposite were the case,
inequality isn't an important social issue when males are being shortchanged.
Talk about youth suicide, for instance, and you'll be informed that what
really deserves attention is not the appalling number of dead male bodies, but
the fact that girls say they *attempt* suicide more often than do boys.

The latest examples of this "who cares, they're only guys" mentality are   3
reports that girls are outperforming boys in school. In 1996, six out of ten
high-school honours graduates in Ontario and British Columbia were female.
Even though girls were besting boys a decade earlier (in 1986, 53 per cent of
Ontario honours grads and 57 per cent of . . . B.C. [graduates] were girls),
the 1990s have been replete with media commentary telling us it's girls who
merit our concern. In 1994, Myra and David Sadker's book *Failing at
Fairness: How Our Schools Cheat Girls* appeared. A year later, Michele
Landsberg wrote a column in *The Toronto Star* [headed] "School sexism so
routine it's almost invisible." A news story, also in *The Star,* about the higher-
than-average Montreal dropout rate implied we should be concerned about
this phenomenon partly because "45 per cent of dropouts are young women."
Despite being in the majority, the boys weren't worth mentioning.

When girls do worse in math and science, when they don't sign up for   4
skilled trades or engineering, it's the system's fault. Their parents aren't
encouraging them; the schools are male-oriented and unwelcoming; the boys
are harassing them; and society is sending them traditional-role-model messages, but when the boys do poorly, it's their own fault. Even though they're
children, the responsibility gets loaded directly onto their meagre shoulders.
In a recent *Globe* article, "Where the Boys Aren't: At the Top of the Class,"
educators tell the media that "too many boys don't seem to be even trying,"
and blame "a boy culture that celebrates bravado, lassitude, and stupidity."
Rather than ask boys for their input, the reporter interviewed girls who criticized the boys' study habits.

The fact that masculinity and intellectualism have always been an uneasy   5
fit (football players get dates, bookworms don't) doesn't even make it into the
conversation. The idea that boys may be confused about whether or not they
should excel, since feminism has drawn a straight line between female oppression and male achievement, isn't discussed. The fact that elementary schools
are dominated by female teachers who scold and punish boys more frequently
than they do girls, and that boys suffer from more learning disabilities, isn't
mentioned. The notion that educators, parents, and governments have spent
the past 15 years ignoring boys, so it's little wonder that they themselves have
become complacent about their performance, isn't considered.

Girls are victims of circumstance and boys are masters of their own fate.   6
Girls are moulded and manipulated by social pressures; boys make conscious
choices. Girls get to blame everyone but themselves; everyone gets to blame
boys. Wasn't feminism supposed to be about abolishing double standards?

■ ■ ■

Our Daughters, Ourselves

STEVIE CAMERON

They are so precious to us, our daughters. When they are born we see their   1
futures as unlimited, and as they grow and learn we try so hard to protect
them: This is how we cross the street, hold my hand, wear your boots, don't
talk to strangers, run to the neighbors if a man tries to get you in his car.

We tell our bright, shining girls that they can be anything: firefighters,   2
doctors, policewomen, lawyers, scientists, soldiers, athletes, artists. What we
don't tell them, yet, is how hard it will be. Maybe, we say to ourselves, by the
time they're older it will be easier for them than it was for us.

But as they grow and learn, with aching hearts we have to start dealing   3
with their bewilderment about injustice. Why do the boys get the best gyms,
the best equipment and the best times on the field? Most of the school sports
budget? Why does football matter more than gymnastics? Why are most of
the teachers women and most of the principals men? Why do the boys make
more money at their part-time jobs than we do?

And as they grow and learn we have to go on trying to protect them: 4
We'll pick you up at the subway, we'll fetch you from the movie, stay with the
group, make sure the parents drive you home from baby-sitting, don't walk
across the park alone, lock the house if we're not there.

It's not fair, they say. Boys can walk where they want, come in when they   5
want, work where they want. Not really, we say; boys get attacked too. But
boys are not targets for men the way girls are, so girls have to be more careful.

Sometimes our girls don't make it. Sometimes, despite our best efforts   6
and all our love, they go on drugs, drop out, screw up. On the whole, however, our daughters turn into interesting, delightful people. They plan for
college and university, and with wonder and pride we see them competing
with the boys for spaces in engineering schools, medical schools, law schools,
business schools. For them we dream of Rhodes scholarships, Harvard graduate school, gold medals; sometimes, we even dare to say these words out
loud and our daughters reward us with indulgent hugs. Our message is that
anything is possible.

We bite back the cautions that we feel we should give them; maybe by the   7
time they've graduated, things will have changed, we say to ourselves.
Probably by the time they're out, they will make partner when the men do, be
asked to join the same clubs, run for political office. Perhaps they'll even be
able to tee off at the same time men do at the golf club.

But we still warn them: park close to the movie, get a deadbolt for your   8
apartment, check your windows, tell your roommates where you are. Call me.
Call me.

And then with aching hearts we take our precious daughters to lunch and   9
listen to them talk about their friends: the one who was beaten by her boy
friend and then shunned by his friends when she asked for help from the dean;
the one who was attacked in the parking lot; the one who gets obscene and
threatening calls from a boy in her residence; the one who gets raped on a
date; the one who was mocked by the male students in the public meeting.

They tell us about the sexism they're discovering in the adult world at   10
university. Women professors who can't get jobs, who can't get tenure. Male
professors who cannot comprehend women's stony silence after sexist jokes.
An administration that only pays lip service to women's issues and refuses to
accept the reality of physical danger to women on campus.

They tell us they're talking among themselves about how men are   11
demanding rights over unborn children; it's not old dinosaurs who go to
court to prevent a woman's abortion, it's young men. It's young men, they say
with disbelief, their own generation, their own buddies with good education,
from "nice" families, who are abusive.

What can we say to our bright and shining daughters? How can we tell   12
them how much we hurt to see them developing the same scars we've carried?
How much we wanted it to be different for them? It's all about power, we say
to them. Sharing power is not easy for anyone and men do not find it easy to
share among themselves, much less with a group of equally talented, able
women. So men make all those stupid cracks about needing a sex-change
operation to get a job or a promotion and they wind up believing it.

Now our daughters have been shocked to the core, as we all have, by the   13
violence in Montreal. They hear the women were separated from the men and
meticulously slaughtered by a man who blamed feminists for his troubles.
They ask themselves why nobody was able to help the terrified women, to
somehow stop the hunter as he roamed the engineering building.

So now our daughters are truly frightened and it makes their mothers   14
furious that they are frightened. They survived all the childhood dangers, they
were careful as we trained them to be, they worked hard. Anything was possible and our daughters proved it. And now they are more scared than they
were when they were little girls.

Fourteen of our bright and shining daughters won places in engineering   15
schools, doing things we, their mothers, only dreamed of. That we lost them
has broken our hearts; what is worse is that we are not surprised.

■   ■   ■

4

Incorporating Sources into a Research Essay

Your ability to draw on two or more sources in an essay depends on your ability to infer relationships among sources—essays, articles, fiction, and also non-written sources, such as lectures, interviews, and observations. You infer relationships all the time—say, between something you've read in the newspaper and something you've seen for yourself, or between the teaching styles of your favourite and least favourite instructors. In a research essay, you make explicit the relationships that you have inferred among separate sources.

The skills you've already learned and practised from the previous three chapters will be vital in writing research essays. Clearly, before you're in a position to draw relationships between two or more sources, you must understand what those sources say; in other words, you must be able to *summarize* these sources. It will frequently be helpful for your readers if you provide at least partial summaries of sources in your synthesis essays. At the same time, you must go beyond summary to make judgments—judgments based, of course, on your *critical reading* of your sources. You should already have drawn some conclusions about the quality and validity of these sources; and you should know how much you agree or disagree with the points made in your sources and the reasons for your agreement or disagreement.

Further, you must go beyond the critique of individual sources to determine the relationship among them. Is the information in source B, for example, an extended illustration of the generalizations in source A? Would it be useful to compare and contrast source C with source B? Having read and considered sources A, B, and C, can you infer something else—D (not a source, but your own idea)?

Because a research essay is based on two or more sources, you will need to be selective when choosing information from each. It would be neither possible nor desirable, for instance, to discuss in a 10-page paper on the stability of the Canadian dollar every point that the authors of two books make about their subject. What you as a writer must do is select from each source the ideas and information that best allow you to achieve your purpose.

Your purpose in reading source materials and then in drawing on them to write your own material is often reflected in the wording of an assignment. For instance, consider the following assignments on Atlantic Coast hunting and fishing issues:

Canadian History:	Evaluate an author's treatment of the origins of the East Coast seal hunt.
Economics:	Argue the following proposition, in light of your readings: "The East Coast seal hunt was stopped not for reasons of moral principle but for reasons of economic necessity."
Government:	Prepare a report on the effects of the seal hunt moratorium on Atlantic politics.
Mass Communications:	Discuss how the use of film and photography of the hunt may have affected the perceptions of wealthy consumers living in industrial cities.
Literature:	Select two twentieth-century writers whose work you believe was influenced by the Greenpeace protests. Discuss the ways this influence is apparent in a novel or a group of short stories written by each author. The works should not be *about* actual protest episodes.
Applied Technology:	Compare and contrast the technology of the modern seal hunt with the technology available a century earlier.

Each of these assignments creates a particular purpose for writing. Having located sources relevant to your topic, you would select, for possible use in a paper, only those parts that helped you in fulfilling this purpose. And how you used those parts, how you related them to other material from other sources, would also depend on your purpose. For instance, if you were working on the government assignment, you might possibly draw on the same source as another student working on the literature assignment by referring to well-known author Farley Mowat's *A Whale for the Killing*, which puts pressure on the animal harvest industry. But because the purposes of these assignments are different, you and the other student would make different uses of this source. Parts or aspects of the book that you find worthy of detailed analysis might be mentioned only in passing (or not at all) by the other student.

ASSESSING THE SCHOLARLY STRENGTH OF YOUR SOURCES

Some professors ask that you draw exclusively on recent articles and books from scholarly journals and publishers as the research base of your essays. In such cases, the sources have been "peer reviewed" or screened by scholarly specialists, meaning that you can be fairly confident that those sources will be considered strong enough for use in an essay. But sometimes professors allow you more latitude in the use of sources, allowing some to be drawn from magazines or the web. In such cases, you must assess the scholarly strength of the sources yourself to determine whether they are appropriate for use. This can be done using the following criteria:

ASSESSING THE SCHOLARLY STRENGTH OF SOURCES

- Currency—is the author as up-to-date as the subject demands? What has happened since the source was published? Has scholarly thinking on the subject changed? Has the world changed? An article published five years ago might be satisfactory for a history essay but not for an essay on genetic engineering, for example.
- Accuracy—to the best of your knowledge, does the author present the situation accurately?
- Authority—does the author have reliable credentials to write on the subject?

  Why should you believe him or her? Look for evidence of academic credentials such as a Ph.D., affiliation with a university such as a professorial or research position, and other scholarly publications.

  In the absence of academic affiliation, look for other professional credentials such as Professional Engineer or Clinical Psychologist.

  Authority is also borrowed from the journal or scholarly press that published the source; how much or how little authority does the place of publication have?

  Also look for the use of personal experience as the main authority for the work, which might lessen the scholarly strength of the source but allow for its use as an example of the perspective of someone directly affected by the issue under discussion.
- Objectivity—does the author seem biased in any way? Or does she acknowledge opposing perspectives and treat them seriously, carefully explaining why her own perspective is superior?
- Coverage—does the author cover the topic thoroughly within its own limits, or are important factors/aspects left out?

USING YOUR SOURCES

Your purpose determines not only what parts of your sources you will use but also how you will relate them to one another. Notice that the mass communications assignment requires you to draw a *cause-and-effect* relationship between films and photographs and perceptions of seal hunt cruelty. The applied technology assignment requires you to *compare and contrast* recent to early seal hunt technology. The economics assignment requires you to *argue* a proposition. In each case, *your purpose will determine how you relate your source materials to one another.*

Consider some other examples. You may be asked on an exam question or in instructions for a paper to *describe* two or three approaches to prison reform during the past decade. You may be asked to *compare and contrast* one country's approach to imprisonment with another's. You may be asked to develop an *argument* of your own on this subject, based on your reading. Sometimes (when you are not given a specific assignment) you determine your own purpose: You are interested in exploring a particular subject; you are interested in making a case for one approach or another. In any event, your purpose shapes your essay. Your purpose determines which sources you research, which ones you use, which parts of them you use, at which points in your essay you use them, and in what manner you relate them to one another.

HOW TO WRITE RESEARCH ESSAYS

Although writing research essays can't be reduced to a lockstep method, it should help you to follow the guidelines listed in the following box.

We emphasize the *research-based argument* in this chapter—the essay that synthesizes a range of source material in order to develop an argument— because it is by far the most common type of research essay. We'll also consider developing essays using *explanatory* and *comparison-contrast* techniques as well as personal essays that use no outside sources at all.

HOW TO WRITE RESEARCH ESSAYS

- **Consider your purpose in writing.** What are you trying to accomplish in your essay? How will this purpose shape the way you approach your sources?
- **Select and carefully read your sources,** according to your purpose and your assessment of the scholarly strength of each source. Then reread the passages, mentally summarizing each. Identify those aspects or parts of your sources that will help you fulfill your purpose. When rereading the sources, *label* or *underline* the main ideas, key terms, and any details you want to use in the essay.
- **Formulate a thesis.** Your thesis is the main idea that you want to present in your essay. It should be expressed as a complete sentence. Sometimes the thesis is the first sentence, but more often it is *the final sentence of the first paragraph*. If you are writing an *inductively arranged* essay (see p. 123), the thesis sentence may not appear until the final paragraphs. (See Chapter 1 for more information on writing an effective thesis.)
- **Decide how you will use your source material.** How will the information and the ideas in the passages help you fulfill your purpose?

- **Develop an organizational plan,** according to your thesis. How will you arrange your material? It is not necessary to prepare a formal outline. But you should have some plan that will indicate the order in which you will present your material and that will indicate the relationships among your sources. As an optional step, draft the topic sentences for main sections. This can be a helpful transition from organizational plan to first draft.

- **Write the first draft** of your research essay, following your organizational plan. Be flexible with your plan, however. Frequently, you will use an outline to get started. As you write, you may discover new ideas and make room for them by adjusting the outline. When this happens, reread your work frequently, making sure that your thesis still accounts for what follows and that what follows still logically supports your thesis.

- **Document your sources.** You may do this by crediting them within the body of the essay or by having a list of "Works Cited" at the end.

- **Revise your essay,** inserting transitional words and phrases where necessary. Make sure that the essay reads smoothly, logically, and clearly from beginning to end. Check for grammatical correctness, punctuation, spelling.

Note: Writing is a recursive process, and you should accept a certain amount of backtracking and reformulating as inevitable. For instance, in developing an organizational plan (the fifth step in the procedures outlined in this box), you may discover a gap in your presentation that will send you scrambling for another source—back to the second step outlined here. You may find that formulating a thesis and making inferences among sources occur simultaneously; indeed, inferences often are made before a thesis is formulated. Our recommendations for writing research essays will give you a structure; they will get you started. But be flexible in your approach; expect discontinuity and, if possible, be comforted that through backtracking and reformulating you will eventually produce a coherent, well-crafted essay.

THE RESEARCH ARGUMENT

An argumentative thesis is *persuasive in purpose*. Writers working with the same source materials might conceive of and support other, opposite theses. So the thesis for a research argument is a claim about which reasonable people could disagree. It is a claim about which—given the right arguments—your audience might be persuaded to agree. The strategy of your research argument is therefore to find and use convincing *support* for your *claim*.

For the most part, arguments should be constructed logically, or rationally, so that claims are supported by logical explanation or evidence in the form of facts or expert opinions. However, keep in mind the discussion of *ethos* and *pathos* in Chapter 3. It is always important to establish your own credibility by presenting your work in a professional style appropriate to the disciplinary context in which you are writing. It is also important to be aware of the emotional dimensions of your topic. On one end of the scale of appealing to pathos is merely avoiding disrespectful language that makes you seem callous or flippant, on the other end is describing a situation in deliberately emotive terms in order to help win the reader's support of your argument. Be careful, though. In more scientific disciplines such as psychology, any such appeal to the emotions may be seen as an inappropriate departure from rigorous thought, and whatever the disciplinary context of the assignment, appeals to emotion must always be offered in support of logic, never in place of it.

Developing a Research-based Argument

The Wal-Mart Controversy

To demonstrate how to plan and draft a research-based argument, let's consider the subject of controversies surrounding the development of Wal-Mart. If you were taking an economics or business economics course, you would probably at some point consider the functioning of the market economy. For consumers, one of the most striking trends in this economy in recent times has been the rise of superstores such as Wal-Mart, Home Depot, Costco, and Staples. Most consumers find these vast shopping outlets convenient and economical. Others find them an abomination, contending that these ugly and predatory outlets drive out of business the mom-and-pop stores that were the staple of small-town life.

For a major research paper of several thousand words, your instructor might ask you to submit an "annotated bibliography" for approval before proceeding with the work of writing the essay. An annotated bibliography looks like a regular works cited list except that it includes a note about each source. Typically, the note consists of a brief summary of its contents, and perhaps an explanation of its relevance to your purpose and its suitability as a source for an academic essay. For example, the entry for the first source reproduced below might look like this:

> Ortega, Bob. "Ban the Bargains." *The Wall Street Journal* 11 Oct. 1994: 1+.
>
> Ortega describes various protests against Wal-Mart across the U.S. and provides quotations from anti–Wal-Mart activists. I could use this source to demonstrate the extent of the opposition to Wal-Mart. The *WSJ* is not a scholarly source, but it is a highly reputable paper, and one unlikely to be biased against big business. However, I would like to find a more recent source.

The bibliography is presented in alphabetical order. Since it is a working document meant to assist in the planning stage, it may contain sources that you ultimately decide not to cite in your essay (and it therefore should not be called a "Works Cited" or "References" list).

Suppose, in preparing to write a short paper on Wal-Mart, you came up with the following sources. Read them carefully, noting as you do the kinds of information and ideas you could draw upon to develop a research-based argument.

Note: To save space and for the purpose of demonstration, the following passages are brief excerpts only. In preparing your paper, naturally you would draw upon entire articles from which these extracts were taken.

Ban the Bargains

BOB ORTEGA

"Ultimate Predator"

To denizens of the counterculture, Wal-Mart stands for everything they dis-   1
like about American society—mindless consumerism, paved landscapes and homogenization of community identity.

"We've lost a sense of taste, of refinement—we're destroying our culture   2
and replacing it with . . . Wal-Mart," says Allan B. Wolf, a Kent State University alumnus now trying to keep Wal-Mart out of Cleveland Heights, Ohio, where he is a high-school teacher.

"We'd never have fought another business as hard as we've fought Wal-   3
Mart," says Alice Doyle, of Cottage Grove, Ore., who calls the giant discounter "the ultimate predator."

At Wal-Mart headquarters in Bentonville, Ark., company officials char-   4
acterize all opponents, ex-hippie and otherwise, as "a vocal minority." They deny that their store has become, for some activists, a kind of successor to Vietnam.

Don Shinkle, a Wal-Mart vice president, says "there are maybe eight to   5
10 sites where there is opposition." However, there are at least 40 organized groups actively opposing proposed or anticipated Wal-Mart stores in communities such as Oceanside, Calif.; Gaithersburg, Md.; Quincy, Mass.; East Lampeter, Penn.; Lake Placid, N.Y.; and Gallatin, Tenn.

Local opposition has delayed some stores and led the company to drop its   6
plans in Greenfield, Mass., and two other towns in that state; as well as in Bath, Maine; Simi Valley, Calif.; and Ross and West Hempfield, Pa.

Protest March

The residents of Cleveland Heights hope to join that list. On a recent Monday   7
there, a large crowd, including some people who had been tear-gassed at Kent State 24 years ago for protesting the war, led a march on city hall and chanted, "One, two, three, four—we don't want your Wal-Mart store." Says Jordan Yin, a leader of the anti–Wal-Mart coalition, "Old hippies describes the whole town."

In Fort Collins, Colo., Shelby Robinson, a former Vietnam War protester   8
and member of the George McGovern campaign, has little success these days
persuading her old companions to join her lobbying for solar power, animal
rights or vegetarianism. But when Wal-Mart proposed coming to town, the
activist impulses of her old friends came alive, and many joined her in fighting the store.

"I really hate Wal-Mart," says Ms. Robinson, a self-employed clothing   9
designer. "Everything's starting to look the same, everybody buys all the
same things—a lot of small-town character is being lost. They disrupt local
communities, they hurt small businesses, they add to our sprawl and pollution
because everybody drives farther, they don't pay a living wage—and visually,
they're atrocious."

In Boulder, Colo., Wal-Mart real-estate manager Steven P. Lane tried   10
appeasing the city's ex-hippies by proposing a "green store" that he said would
be environmentally friendly, right up to the solar-powered sign out front. But
when city council member Spencer Havlick, who helped organize the first Earth
Day in 1970, suggested that the whole store be solar-powered, Mr. Lane fell
silent. Dr. Havlick, professor of environmental design at the University of
Colorado, says, "Their proposal wasn't as green as they thought it was."

These activists have hardly slowed Wal-Mart's overall expansion—it   11
expects to add 125 stores next year to its existing 2,504. But even so, some
Wal-Mart sympathizers find them irritating. William W. Whyte, who bid
good riddance to hippies when he graduated from Kent State in 1970, now
finds himself annoyed by them again, as an analyst following Wal-Mart for
Stephens Inc.

"The same types of people demonstrating then are demonstrating now,"   12
grumbles Mr. Whyte. "If they had to worry about putting food on the table,
they'd probably be working for Wal-Mart instead of protesting them."

Some Wal-Mart supporters call the protesters elitists for opposing a pur-   13
veyor of low-priced goods. But Tim Allen, who at age 26 has been active in
the development of a "green" housing co-op and an organizer of the Wal-
Mart protest movement in Ithaca, replies that "people aren't poor because
they're paying 15 cents more for a pair of underwear."

■   ■   ■

Eight Ways to Stop the Store

ALBERT NORMAN

Last week I received another red-white-and-blue invitation to a Wal-Mart   1
grand opening in Rindge, New Hampshire. I say "another" because Wal-
Mart has already invited me to its new store in Hinsdale, New Hampshire,
just twenty miles away. With over $67 billion in annual sales, and more than

2,000 stores, Wal-Mart holds a grand opening somewhere in America almost every other day. But it will never invite me to its new store in Greenfield, Massachusetts, my home town, because Greenfield voters recently rejected Wal-Mart at the ballot box.

The Arkansas mega-retailer has emerged as the main threat to Main   2
Street, U.S.A. Economic impact studies in Iowa, Massachusetts, and elsewhere suggest that Wal-Mart's gains are largely captured from other merchants. Within two years of a grand opening, Wal-Mart stores in an average-size Iowa town generated $10 million in annual sales—by "stealing" $8.3 million from other businesses.

Since our victory in Greenfield, we have received dozens of letters from   3
"Stop the WAL" activists in towns like East Aurora, New York; Palatine, Illinois; Mountville, Pennsylvania; Williston, Vermont; Branford, Connecticut—small communities fighting the battle of Jericho. If these towns follow a few simple rules of engagement, they will find that the WAL *will* come tumbling down:

Quote scripture: Wal-Mart founder Sam Walton said it best in his auto-   4
biography: "If some community, for whatever reason, doesn't want us in there, we aren't interested in going in and creating a fuss." Or, as one company V.P. stated, "We have so many opportunities for building in communities that want Wal-Marts, it would be foolish of us to pursue construction in communities that don't want us." The greater the fuss raised by local citizens, the more foolish Wal-Mart becomes.

Learn Wal-Math: Wal-Mathematicians only know how to add. They   5
never talk about the jobs they destroy, the vacant retail space they create or their impact on commercial property values. In our town, the company agreed to pay for an impact study that gave enough data to kill three Wal-Marts. Dollars merely shifted from cash registers on one side of town to Wal-Mart registers on the other side of town. Except for one high school scholarship per year, Wal-Mart gives very little back to the community.

Exploit their errors: Wal-Mart always makes plenty of mistakes. In our   6
community, the company tried to push its way onto industrially zoned land. It needed a variance not only to rezone land to commercial use but also to permit buildings larger than 40,000 square feet. This was the "hook" we needed to trip the company up. Rezoning required a Town Council vote (which it won), but our town charter allowed voters to seek reconsideration of the vote, and ultimately, a referendum. All we needed was the opportunity to bring this to the general public—and we won. Wal-Mart also violated state law by mailing an anonymous flier to voters.

Fight capital with capital: In our town (pop. 20,000) Wal-Mart spent   7
more than $30,000 trying to influence the outcome of a general referendum. It even created a citizen group as a front. But Greenfield residents raised $17,000 to stop the store—roughly half of which came from local businesses. A media campaign and grass-roots organizing costs money. If Wal-Mart is willing to spend liberally to get into your town, its competitors should be willing to come forward with cash also.

Beat them at the grass roots: Wal-Mart can buy public relations firms and   8
telemarketers but it can't find bodies willing to leaflet at supermarkets, write
dozens of letters to the editor, organize a press conference or make calls in the
precincts. Local coalitions can draw opinion-makers from the business community (department, hardware and grocery stores, pharmacies, sporting
goods stores), environmentalists, political activists and homeowners. Treat
this effort like a political campaign: The Citizens versus the WAL.

Get out your vote: Our largest expenditure was on a local telemarketing   9
company that polled 4,000 voters to identify their leanings on Wal-Mart. Our
volunteers then called those voters leaning against the WAL two days before
the election. On election day, we had poll-watchers at all nine precincts. If our
voters weren't at the polls by 5 p.m., we reminded them to get up from the
dinner table and stop the mega-store.

Appeal to the heart as well as the head: One theme the Wal-Mart culture   10
has a hard time responding to is the loss of small-town quality of life. You
can't buy rural life style on any Wal-Mart shelf—once you lose it, Wal-Mart
can't sell it back to you. Wal-Mart's impact on small-town ethos is enormous.
We had graphs and bar charts on job loss and retail growth—but we also
communicated with people on an emotional level. Wal-Mart became the
WAL—an unwanted shove into urbanization, with all the negatives that
threaten small-town folks.

Hire a professional: The greatest mistake most citizen groups make is   11
trying to fight the world's largest retailer with a mimeo-machine mentality.
Most communities have a political consultant nearby, someone who can
develop a media campaign and understand how to get a floppy disk of town
voters with phone numbers. Wal-Mart uses hired guns; so should anti–Wal-
Mart forces.

"Your real mission," a Wal-Mart executive recently wrote to a commu-   12
nity activist, "is to be blindly obstructionist." On the contrary, we found it
was Wal-Mart that would blindly say anything and do anything to bulldoze
its way toward another grand opening in America. But if community coalitions organize early, bring their case directly to the public and trumpet the
downside of mega-store development, the WALs will fall in Jericho.

■ ■ ■

Wal-Mart's War on Main Street

SARAH ANDERSON

Across the country, thousands of rural people are battling to save their local   1
downtowns. Many of these fights have taken the form of anti–Wal-Mart campaigns. In Vermont, citizens' groups allowed Wal-Mart to enter the state only
after the company agreed to a long list of demands regarding the size and oper-

ation of the stores. Three Massachusetts towns and another in Maine have defeated bids by Wal-Mart to build in their communities. In Arkansas, three independent drugstore owners won a suit charging that Wal-Mart had used "predatory pricing," or selling below cost, to drive out competitors. Canadian citizens are asking Wal-Mart to sign a "Pledge of Corporate Responsibility" before opening in their towns. In at least a dozen other U.S. communities, groups have fought to keep Wal-Mart out or to restrict the firm's activities.

2   By attacking Wal-Mart, these campaigns have helped raise awareness of the value of locally owned independent stores on Main Street. Their concerns generally fall in five areas:

3   • *Sprawl Mart*—Wal-Mart nearly always builds along a highway outside town to take advantage of cheap, often unzoned land. This usually attracts additional commercial development, forcing the community to extend services (telephone and power lines, water and sewage services, and so forth) to that area, despite sufficient existing infrastructure downtown.

4   • *Wal-Mart channels resources out of a community*—studies have shown that a dollar spent on a local business has four or five times the economic spin-off of a dollar spent at a Wal-Mart, since a large share of Wal-Mart's profit returns to its Arkansas headquarters or is pumped into national advertising campaigns.

5   • *Wal-Mart destroys jobs in locally owned stores*—a Wal-Mart–funded community impact study debunked the retailer's claim that it would create a lot of jobs in Greenfield, Massachusetts. Although Wal-Mart planned to hire 274 people at its Greenfield store, the community could expect to gain only eight net jobs, because of projected losses at other businesses that would have to compete with Wal-Mart.

6   • *Citizen Wal-Mart?*—in at least one town—Hearne, Texas—Wal-Mart destroyed its Main Street competitors and then deserted the town in search of higher returns elsewhere. Unable to attract new businesses to the devastated Main Street, local residents have no choice but to drive long distances to buy basic goods.

7   • *One-stop shopping culture*—in Greenfield, where citizens voted to keep Wal-Mart out, anti–Wal-Mart campaign manager Al Norman said he saw a resurgence of appreciation for Main Street. "People realized there's one thing you can't buy at Wal-Mart, and that's small-town quality of life," Norman explains. "This community decided it was not ready to die for a cheap pair of underwear."

8   Small towns cannot return to the past, when families did all their shopping and socializing in their hometown. Rural life is changing and there's no use denying it. The most important question is, who will define the future? Will it be Wal-Mart, whose narrow corporate interests have little to do with building healthy communities? Will it be the department of transportation, whose purpose is to move cars faster? Will it be the banks and suppliers primarily interested in doing business with the big guys? Or will it be the people who live in small towns, whose hard work and support are essential to any effort to revitalize Main Street?

■ ■ ■

Who's Really the Villain?

JO-ANN JOHNSTON

Cheap underwear. That's all Wal-Mart Corp. contributes as it squeezes the   1
life out of a community's downtown, according to Albert Norman, an outspoken Wal-Mart critic. His sentiment—and talent for rousing support—led
folks in rural Greenfield, Massachusetts, to block the company's plans to
build a store there. It also established the political consultant as one of the best
known opponents to "Sprawl-mart" in the country. But fighting off Wal-
Mart hasn't done much for the 18,845 residents of Greenfield.

As in numerous other communities during the past ten years, Wal-Mart   2
simply found a site just a short distance away from its original target. In this
case, it's in Orange, a smaller town located up the road about twenty-five
minutes from downtown Greenfield. Meanwhile, this area ranks as the state's
second poorest in per capita income. And in January, it posted an unemployment rate of 6.1 percent—attributable partly to the recent closings of a paper
plant, a container factory, and a large store that sold liquidated merchandise.
Wal-Mart would have brought to Greenfield 240 tax-paying jobs and
increased retail traffic.

Set to open later this year, the store in Orange will be yet another exam-   3
ple of how saying "go away" to the likes of Wal-Mart overlooks a much
deeper problem facing small-town America: the need to change a way of
doing business while maintaining, or improving, a deeply valued way of life.
An increasing number of people are beginning to realize that small-town
merchants need to adapt to changes in their communities, the economy, and
their industries instead of chastising an outside company. That means accepting the fact that a Wal-Mart, or a similar retailer, may become a neighbor.

Such thinking is hogwash as far as anti–Wal-Marters are concerned.   4
Consumerism has run amok if a town figures it needs a Wal-Mart, says
Norman [see "Eight Ways to Stop the Store," pp. 108–110], who today
works with people in Illinois, Ohio, New England, and other regions to stop
Wal-Marts and other large discount retailers from setting up shop. His list of
reasons to fight such chain stores is lengthy, with perhaps one of the most
popular being the potential loss of small-town quality of life. People move to
small towns from urban or suburban America in part to escape from mall and
shopping strip development, he says, not to see it duplicated.

That emotional argument carries weight, especially in New England,   5
where twelve cities and one state, Vermont, have fought Wal-Mart. A current
battle is taking place in Sturbridge, a historic town in eastern Massachusetts
where community activists are fighting to keep Wal-Mart out. The town
draws 60 percent of its general business from tourism-related trade, says
local Wal-Mart opponent Carol Goodwin. "We market history," she says.
The town and its re-creation of an early American village are the state's

second largest tourist attraction. A big cookie-cutter mart off the freeway could obscure this town of eight thousand's special appeal, she says.

Sturbridge may want to take a lesson from its neighbor to the northwest, however. Merchants in Greenfield face the possible loss of business due to the fact that Wal-Mart found a location "just over the hill" from where it was first looking to build. Kenneth Stone, an economist at Iowa State University and the country's leading researcher on the economic impacts of Wal-Marts, found that towns in the Midwest and East suffered a "retail leakage" of shoppers who instead drove to the closest regional shopping center with a discount store.   6

Does that mean Greenfield shoppers will now drive to Orange? Well, several of the town's shoppers complained during the Wal-Mart battle that area merchants could use competition because of their poor selection, high prices, limited hours, and lackluster service. Meanwhile, Wal-Mart has a good reputation for service. A *Consumer Reports* reader poll in late 1994 found that fifty thousand people rated Wal-Mart the highest in customer satisfaction of "value-oriented chains."   7

In many ways, what is happening to small-town retail corridors is similar to how mom-and-pop corporations were caught off guard during the takeover frenzy of the 1980s. Survivors became more efficient to avoid being picked off by raiders looking to maximize shareholder profits. With Wal-Mart, it's a matter of maximizing retailing opportunities for consumers.   8

By the time a community knows the demographically astute Wal-Mart has its eye on an area, it's virtually too late to stop *somebody* from coming into town, says Bill Sakelarios, president of the Concord-based Retail Merchants Association of New Hampshire. In Greenfield, for instance, the threat of competition to that town's small retailers didn't disappear with the Wal-Mart vote. BJ's Wholesale club is considering the town for a store.   9

Wal-Mart is viewed as a threat, though, because it uses bulk buying, discount pricing, and tight inventory and distribution management that smaller retailers can't keep up with. It also has the competitive advantage of size: The company's sales surged 22 percent to more than $82 billion, while net income climbed 15 percent to more than $2.6 billion in the year ended January 31, 1995, compared with year-earlier results.   10

Because it's so huge, the best defense against Wal-Mart for small-town retailers is to adapt, evolve, and create some stronghold that will make them viable and worth keeping, even in the face of new competition, says Robert Kahn, a Lafayette, California, management consultant who has worked with the chain and publishes a newsletter called *Retailing Today*. All kinds of stores have found ways to survive in the shadow of Wal-Mart, he says. Grocery stores have maintained check cashing, hardware stores and nurseries have offered classes, women's clothing retailers have filled in the gaps in the Wal-Mart line. Others point to pharmacies that have been able to compete with Wal-Marts. Stone met one druggist who kept a loyal clientele of shut-ins   11 who spent $200 to $300 a month individually on prescriptions by offering home delivery, something Wal-Mart didn't do in his market.

The argument that self-improvement and change for small retailers may   12
be the answer is definitely scorned in some circles. But stores that balk at such notions may not get much sympathy from customers who have had to change jobs or learn new skills—all because of shifts in the structure of the economies in the fields in which they work.

"You read stories about how towns don't want Wal-Mart, but in many   13
cases that's a very few people getting a lot of publicity. And I may have on my desk a petition signed by fifteen thousand people saying, 'Please come, ignore the one hundred people who are trying to block the store,'" Wal-Mart President and CEO David Glass told a press gathering in December. "In retailing, you have a very simple answer to all that. Any community that didn't want a Wal-Mart store—all they've got to do is not shop there. And I guarantee a store, even if it's [just] built, won't be there long."

Another thing to consider is what happens if Wal-Mart, or a store like it,   14
comes into town, stays for ten years, and then leaves. Where that's happened, retailers who found ways to adapt to Wal-Mart's presence still believe they're much better as a result. In Nowata, Oklahoma, Wal-Mart pulled up stakes last year and deserted a town of 3,900 people who had come to depend on it as their second largest tax payer, as well as their major retailing center. But several local merchants survived Wal-Mart's stay of fourteen years because they learned to adjust their business practices. Wayne Clark, whose father opened Clark's Sentry Hardware in 1938, says he survived Wal-Mart's presence by providing better service and a more specialized inventory.

Nowata also brings up another interesting question on the Wal-Mart   15
controversy: Could it be that old-time downtowns simply are obsolete and an impediment to efficient retailing? Many retailers have probably been in a precarious position for a long time, for a number of reasons, and then place the blame for problems or eventual demise on the highly visible Wal-Mart, says Sakelarios. "Wal-Mart is being singled out. Small-town business districts brought a lot of this on themselves," agrees Iowa State's Stone.

As cars have drawn shopping to other locales, downtown districts haven't   16
worked hard enough to remain competitive and efficient, data suggest. "Small retailers often believe that the community *owes them* rather than *they owe* the community," Kahn wrote in his December newsletter.

He cites as evidence a recent survey of more than 1,500 Illinois retailers   17
conducted by the state's merchant association. Kahn found it stunning that 54 percent reorder inventory for their stores only when they're already out of stock. That translates into poor selection and service, Kahn says, because small retailers often can't get priority shipments from vendors and most often wait for five to fifteen days to get fresh stock in, leaving customers without that selection in the interim. "That's not providing any service. If it's not in stock, eventually the customer is going to go somewhere else," Kahn points out.

Kahn also criticized the 63 percent of the retailers surveyed who claimed   18
to know what their customers want, even though they didn't track customer
purchases.

Apart from self-inflicted injuries, retailers are also pressured on other   19
fronts, says John Donnellan, a member of the Consumer Studies faculty at the
University of Massachusetts in Ames. The growth of the mail-order catalogs,
cable TV shopping networks, specialized category stores such as Toys 'R' Us,
and now, possibly, shopping via on-line computer services, all present more
competition for small merchants that draw from local markets.

The only difference with Wal-Mart is that it's the biggest, most identifi-   20
able source of that new and increasing competition. As a result, it has become
a lightning rod for all the angst and anxiety of struggling shop keepers—
deserved or not.

■ ■ ■

Wal-Mart Takes Off

JAMES F. MOORE

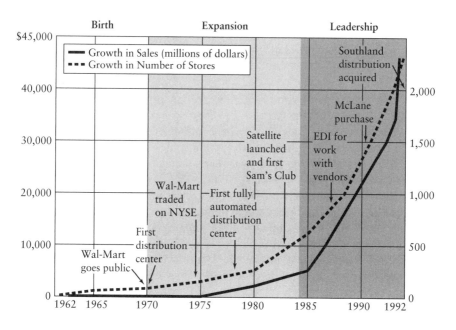

Source: James F. Moore. Chart: "Wal-Mart Takes Off" in "Predators and Prey," *Harvard Business Review*, May–June 1993, p. 82.

■ ■ ■

Mall Owners Vent Anger at Wal-Mart

DAVID O'BRIEN

A plan by Wal-Mart to abandon two Winnipeg shopping centres has sparked   1
a mud-slinging feud between the retail empire and two prominent businessmen.

David Asper and Bob Akman, partners in a company that owns the   2
affected malls, accused Wal-Mart of being a poor corporate citizen and a
major cause of urban sprawl.

"Wal-Mart does nothing for our community," Bob Akman, president of   3
Creswin Properties Ltd., told a public hearing at city hall. "We need to send
a message to Wal-Mart that instead of exporting its profits, the quid pro quo
for doing business here is to be a good corporate citizen at a level commen-
surate with its ability to give."

A spokesman for Wal-Mart's Canadian operations called the remarks   4
"absurd and completely untrue."

"I feel sorry for them," said Andrew Pelletier, Wal-Mart's director of   5
public affairs. "They're using our good name as a political platform (and)
that's outrageous."

Creswin owns several properties in Winnipeg, including Garden City   6
Square, which Wal-Mart is planning to abandon for undeveloped land further
north. The company also has an interest in Grant Park Shopping Centre,
which Wal-Mart also plans to quit.

Asper, a partner in Creswin and son of media mogul Izzy Asper, also   7
expressed disappointment that Wal-Mart wasn't pulling its weight in the
community.

"They're not doing a whole lot for the city," Asper said.   8

Added Akman: "As one peruses the programs of the symphony, ballet,   9
theatre centre, Theatre for Young People, folk festival, Folklorama, West
End Cultural Centre, Assiniboine Park Pavilion and so on, there is a deafen-
ing silence from Wal-Mart." Wal-Mart earns about $350 million in sales
from its six Winnipeg stores, he said.

Akman's comments were made at a public hearing on proposed amend-   10
ments to Plan Winnipeg, the city's development blueprint.

Wal-Mart wants to vacate its 130 000-square-foot location in Garden   11
City Square and build a new store about two kilometres to the north.

However, the land is designated rural and Wal-Mart's developer has   12
asked the city to change it to a classification that permits residential and
commercial development.

Akman and Asper said if Wal-Mart is allowed to open a store in an   13
undeveloped part of Winnipeg, it will fuel urban sprawl and increase the
city's costs for transit, schools and maintenance of streets, sewer and water.

And if Wal-Mart moves from Garden City Square, they said, it will   14
weaken the remaining businesses.

The two businessmen conceded in interviews they had an obvious self-   15
interest in opposing Wal-Mart's relocation.

Meanwhile, Pelletier said Wal-Mart is a generous and responsible cor- 16
porate citizen. Since opening in Canada six years ago, Pelletier said, Wal-Mart
has raised and donated $8 million to local charities.

He said he couldn't say how much the chain contributes to charities in 17
Manitoba, but each store in the chain is responsible for identifying local
causes and raising money to support them.

The retailer was a major contributor to flood relief in Manitoba follow- 18
ing the 1997 flood of the century and it has donated 7 000 bottles of water to
Walkerton, Ont., following the tainted-water scandal that devastated the
town.

Pelletier also dismissed the idea that Wal-Mart contributes to urban 19
sprawl, calling it "a fear tactic that won't work any more."

The issue is expected to generate fierce debate in council, where the new 20
Plan Winnipeg document must be approved June 21.

■ ■ ■

Wal-Mart's Cheer: My Short Life as an Associate

MARY MCALISTER

I didn't like it. Wal-Mart's application form asked me to agree to drug test- 1
ing and to permit access to my medical records. But after two months of looking for work in my small B.C. town, I was getting desperate. I clenched my
teeth and signed.

I was granted an interview with the manager. He didn't ask me to pee in 2
a cup after all. He didn't ask me about my work experience either. But he was
very curious about what I thought of the Wal-Mart cheer. I'd heard about this
cheer, chanted by employees each morning before the store opens. "Sounds
like fun!" I said.

He was pleased to tell me that, although most people start off in part- 3
time positions, everyone at Wal-Mart is "equal." When a full-time position
comes up, he informed me, "the newest person stands the same chance as
someone who's been around for years."

Next I was asked to fill out a questionnaire on my opinions. In fact, it 4
was a morality test: 55 questions on theft, tardiness and other ethical dilemmas. Seven questions focused on the use of pot.

Q. John goes outside for his coffee break and takes one puff from a mar- 5
ijuana cigarette. He believes that a small amount will not affect his job performance." Agree or disagree?

Six months later, I was called for a job as a Wal-Mart "associate." 6

I started right away at what my manager affectionately called "Wal-   7
Mart School." I learned that in 1950 Mr. Sam Walton opened his first five-
and-dime store in Bentonville, Arkansas, and now there are over 2,400
Wal-Mart stores in the U.S. and Canada. Every page of my handbook was
emblazoned with a huge, red Canadian flag. Canadian, eh?

I was shown how to lift, carry, climb and cut safely. "Accidents cut into   8
company profits," said my trainer. I was encouraged to take my full (unpaid)
lunch breaks and to avoid clocking overtime hours. "Because," said my trainer,
"your work is not worth time and a half."

I learned the emergency code word for a bomb threat (code blue), a gun   9
(code orange), a hostage-taking (code red) and a tornado warning (code
black)—events perhaps more likely to occur in Bentonville, Arkansas.

Finally I got my bright blue vest and hit the floor. My section was domes-   10
tics: bedding, towels, furniture, picture frames. There I witnessed the gore of
consumption: people ripped open plastic bags to see if the sheets were the
right size; they unrolled carpets in the aisles to see how they felt underfoot;
they stuffed nearly empty Orange Julius cups between pillows; they got upset
if we ran out of 97-cent Venetian blinds.

As I walked up the aisles, tidying up, I was soon affected with consumer   11
mania myself. I began scribbling down shopping lists on the palm of my
hand: clock radio, photo album, free weights, cat treats! By the end of two
weeks, I had spent my whole first pay cheque: $238. My mania quickly sub-
sided.

On breaks in the lunch room, I was happy to discover a bunch of dis-   12
gruntled workers; I liked listening to their fantasies. One said, "On my last
day here I'm going to get on the intercom and say, 'Would the duty manager
please come to till no. 5 to kiss my ass!'" I had a fantasy, too: in the middle
of a busy Saturday afternoon, I would announce over the intercom "code
black in bedding" and then start spinning around like a whirling dervish.

For weeks there was no mention of the Wal-Mart cheer. I began to think   13
the folks at my store had thought better of it. But I was wrong. One day I was
standing in front at a morning meeting. The manager finished giving us the
sales goal for the day, week and month, and then turned to the woman beside
me, saying, "Hey Cath! How about leading us in a cheer?" It was too late for
me to move to the back.

My co-worker started clapping and everyone joined in except me. She   14
spoke so fast that I couldn't hear what she was saying. Then she started
spelling it out: W-A-L . . . . I waited to see the wiggling of the hips that I had
been told accompanied the "squiggly" in the middle of the Wal-Mart name.
If it happened, I missed it. It was all over and everyone was laughing—from
embarrassment, I think.

Wal-Mart laid me off after the Christmas rush. They gave me a baseball   15
hat and a hand-shake. I wiggled my hips as I walked out the door.

■   ■   ■

The Last Retailer in Canada?

KEVIN LIBIN

In eight years, Wal-Mart has become our biggest retailer. Now it's expected to get into grocery. But if its growth in other markets is any indication, it won't stop there.

It's 6 a.m. on a Saturday in late February and, as everyone else in Bentonville, Ark., snoozes, Wal-Mart's Home Office is buzzing. Even finding a parking spot outside the unimpressive brown low-rise is tough—but it's nothing compared with the challenge of snagging a seat in the huge auditorium inside. In no time, it's standing room only for hundreds of Wal-Mart associates (they're never called employees) and their kin. But they're used to it. The meetings are a weekly fixture at Wal-Mart—and everyone is bursting with enthusiasm. 1

This particular morning, employees are revved up more than ever—even during a two-hour review of weekly sales figures. Today is the annual meeting where Wal-Mart executives announce their personal VPI—or "volume producing item"—some underdeveloped high-margin product they think they'll be able to turn into a moneymaker using good old-fashioned merchandising skills pioneered by founder Sam Walton—or, as the folks here in Bentonville call him, "Mr. Sam!" Virtually everyone in the company—from cashiers to the CEO—gets to pick a pet product. And with 10 senior execs sitting onstage in their weekend jeans and T-shirts, the VPI program takes on a fever pitch of collegial competitiveness. Walls are plastered with posters featuring the world's most powerful retail moguls pushing sandals, detergents, lip balm and duct tape. 2

As the show gets under way, execs begin taunting one another's selections—much to the crowd's delight. Some show short films touting their product's profit potential, while good-naturedly trash-talking those of their colleagues. In one, a manager squashes competing VPI products with a steamroller. H. Lee Scott, Wal-Mart's president and CEO, has somehow convinced *Today Show* cohost Katie Couric to make a video promoting his. Someone else has invited Mr. T to the event; he bolts from backstage punching the air to the theme from Rocky, accompanied by giant Ritz Bits and a shadowboxing Mr. Peanut. "I pity the fool who don't support Bob and Tom's VPI," he barks. "I pity the fool who don't support it with a four-way display." The crowd goes wild. 3

Not many retailers can get this kind of enthusiasm out of their staff—especially this early on a weekend. But if you ask any of the cheery people here what gets them out of bed for this, they'll tell you with utmost sincerity that it's all part of Wal-Mart's "culture." 4

Whatever that is, it's working. The world's largest retailer—which rang up a staggering US$217.7 billion in worldwide sales last year—has now surpassed ExxonMobil as the top moneymaker in history. In the US, Wal-Mart 5

Stores Inc. (NYSE: WMT) is not only the biggest retailer, but it is also the biggest grocer and private employer, and it has the highest return on equity of any retailer. If estimates are correct, it is on track for yet another 18% bump in earnings this year.

In newer markets such as Canada, Wal-Mart's work has only just begun. In eight short years, it has easily surpassed the Hudson Bay Co. and its Zellers chain (TSE: HBC) to become Canada's No. 1 retailer—it has an estimated $8.75 billion in revenue with only a fraction of the stores. If, or rather when, Wal-Mart decides to shift into high gear, some predict the same fate for Zellers that recently befell the doomed Kmart chain in the US. But Canadian discounters are not the only ones who should be worried. Stores like Sears (TSE: SCC), the Bay and Canadian Tire (TSE: CTR) have also felt the heat, as Wal-Mart expands onto their turf, adding upscale, lifestyle-oriented goods to its stable of discount items. Investors have been buzzing with anticipation that Wal-Mart may soon bring groceries into Canada—either on its own, or by gobbling up an existing grocer such as Loblaw Cos. Ltd. (TSE: L)—and finally add the missing element that has become as strong as its general merchandise business in other parts of the world.

In fact, despite its successes, Wal-Mart's move into Canada has so far been one of its least aggressive. To understand in which direction Wal-Mart may be heading here, you need only look further afield. In China, South Korea, the UK, Germany, Argentina, Mexico and particularly the US, the company has shown it can do much more than open a few dozen discount stores and handily grab market share from domestic retailers. What Wal-Mart has managed to do is create what may be the perfect retail operation—one that satisfies almost every kind of shopper. If it ever decides to wallop Canada with everything it's got, we may find we'll never need to shop anywhere else again.

There's no better place to witness Wal-Mart "culture" up close than in Bentonville, where Mr. T fires up the crowd. But the man with the mohawk isn't just pumping snack foods for the benefit of the locals. The event is beamed live via satellite into staff rooms across the US, courtesy of Wal-Mart's own closed-circuit TV network—a key part of an incredible technological infrastructure that has fueled the retailer's growth.

Step inside Wal-Mart's studios on any given weekday and you'll find one executive or another hosting a show targeted at a particular region or job function—and taking calls from around the US while keeping tabs on stores. (Occasionally associates, and even customers, are treated to more entertaining fare, such as the FWL bass fishing championships or live concerts featuring the likes of Britney Spears and the Bee Gees.) In addition to TV, Wal-Mart also operates the world's largest radio network, which broadcasts four channels of shopping-friendly music into all stores and features special programming, such as the "Midnight Cafe," for overnight staff.

But more important than what's being transmitted into Wal-Mart stores is the high-tech data constantly beaming out of them. Every single item is constantly tracked by a monstrous digital infrastructure. Sam Walton believed the secret to retail success was keeping a close eye on his stores—what they were selling, what they weren't, and why. Before his death in 1992, he used to fly around in his own planes, personally visiting several each day. Today, the company keeps a fleet of 18 planes at its US headquarters (and two in Toronto)—and regional managers spend four days a week humping around their territories.

When Walton started the Wal-Mart chain from the five-and-dime in Rogers, Ark., bearing his name in 1962, the same year US discounters Kmart and Target were founded—he had little more than a bunch of easily duplicated bargain-barn concepts. His mantra—Stack it deep/Sell it cheap/Stack it high and watch it fly/Hear those downtown merchants cry!—smacks of the oldest of old economies. But what has emerged is, in fact, an unmistakably New Economy phenomenon. While investors tripped over themselves in the late '90s hunting for cutting-edge high-tech retail concepts, they may have missed the biggest e-commerce opportunity of all. Since Wal-Mart went public in 1970 at US$16.50, it has split 10 times; its stock now trades for about US$62. A hundred shares bought back in '70 would be worth US$6.3 million today. **11**

As ubiquitous as Wal-Mart has become, there are serious misconceptions about the place—particularly here in Canada—where remodeled Woolco outlets, acquired in 1994, pale in comparison to some of its majestic US stores. Some of the myths may stem from the rather tense relationship the retailer has had with the media. When it burst onto the Canadian scene with its initial acquisition of 122 faltering Woolco stores, for example, it got a rather chilly reception. "Remember the headlines?" says Mario Pilozzi, president and CEO of Wal-Mart Canada. "'American company takes over company in Canada.' Frankly, I still don't understand it." **12**

Neither does Carole Foote. "What's Canadian anymore?" she asks. "Even Tim Hortons is American." Far from opposing a Wal-Mart incursion, last year the 46-year-old grandmother from Miramichi, NB, sent the company a petition with more than 11,000 signatures imploring it to open a store in her area. "We've got one Zellers and a Bargain Giant and there's a Canadian Tire—but you can't get clothes there," she says. Most townspeople, she adds, drive an hour or two to Moncton or Bathurst to shop—at a Wal-Mart, of course. Miramichi is but one of 68 small towns clamoring for a Wal-Mart of their own, says Pilozzi **13**

With so much potential here, Wal-Mart's incursion into Canada's grocery market is a question of when, not if. And when Wal-Mart does make its move, you can be sure of one thing: it will happen quickly. "We only have one competitive advantage, and that's speed," says Menzer. "We have to be first and move first. We are now the largest company in the world. Everybody has a 'Beat Wal-Mart' strategy." Maybe. But it's more likely that many of its Canadian competitors aren't thinking nearly that big. Because when Wal-Mart really gets rolling here, some of them may just be too busy fighting for their lives. **14**

■ ■ ■

Consider Your Purpose

Determining your specific purpose in writing a research argument is crucial. What, exactly, you want to do will affect your claim, the evidence you select to support your claim, and the way you organize the evidence. Your purpose may be clear to you before you begin research, may emerge during the course of research, or may not emerge until after you have completed your research. Of course, the sooner your purpose is clear to you, the fewer wasted motions you will make. On the other hand, the more you approach research as an exploratory process, the likelier it is that your conclusions will emerge from the sources themselves, rather than from preconceived ideas.

Let's say that while reading these sources, your own encounters with Wal-Mart influence your thinking on the subject and you find yourself agreeing more with the supporters than with the detractors of Wal-Mart. Perhaps you didn't grow up in a small town, so you don't have much experience with or knowledge of the kind of retail stores that the megastores have been displacing.

On the one hand, you can understand and even sympathize with the viewpoints of critics such as Norman and Anderson. (You may have shopped in the smaller stores in towns you have visited, or seen them portrayed in movies, or perhaps even visited reconstructed small-town stores in heritage museums.) On the other hand, it seems to you unrealistic in this day and age to expect that stores like Wal-Mart can be stopped or should be. For you, the prices and the convenience are a big plus. Your purpose, then, is formed from this kind of response to the source material.

Making a Claim: Formulate a Thesis

One useful way of approaching an argument is to see it as making a *claim*. A claim is a proposition, a conclusion that you are trying to prove or demonstrate. If your purpose is to demonstrate that it is neither possible nor desirable to stop the spread of Wal-Mart, then that is the claim at the heart of your argument. The claim is generally expressed in one-sentence form as a *thesis* (see Chapter 1). Your thesis usually reflects the view you have come to adopt on the basis of reading and thinking about an issue or topic.

To develop a "working" or provisional thesis about Y, it is often useful to complete a "starter" phrase like this: About topic Y, I believe that _____. If you want to position your view in the context of opposing claims, you might try a "starter" phrase like this: Although some people believe _____ (and others believe _____), I believe that _____. These phrases can initiate the drafting process by nudging you into expressing a position that you have come to hold on the basis of reading and reflecting. As you continue the drafting process, you will of course refine your views and the way you state your claim.

You may not want to divulge your thesis until the end of the paper, to draw the reader along toward your conclusion, allowing the thesis to flow naturally out of the argument and the evidence on which it is based. If you do this, you are working *inductively*. Or, you may wish to be more direct and *begin* with your thesis in your opening paragraph, following the thesis statement with evidence to support it. If you do this, you are working *deductively*. In academic papers, deductive arguments are far more common than inductive arguments.

Based on your reactions to reading the sources, you decide to concede that the case against Wal-Mart has some merit and certainly some homespun appeal, but that opponents of such megastores are being unrealistic in expecting most people to sacrifice convenience and economy for the sake of retaining a vanishing way of life. After a few tries, you arrive at the following provisional thesis:

> Opponents of the giant discount chains have made powerful arguments against them, and it's too bad that these megastores are helping to make a way of life extinct; but opponents should realize that stores such as Wal-Mart are so successful because most people prefer bargains and convenience to tradition and small-town charm.

Decide How You Will Use Your Source Material

To support your claim, you use information found in sources. You can also use appeals to *ethos* and *pathos* in these sources. Of course, not every piece of information in a source is useful for supporting a claim. By the same token, you may draw support for your own claim from sources that make entirely different claims. For example, if you want to support the claim that Wal-Mart's growth is alarming, then you might use selective data from the store's website annual report, even though the overall purpose of the website report is to claim the exact opposite: that Wal-Mart's growth is good for both customers and stockholders.

Similarly, you might use one source as part of a counter-argument—an argument opposite to your own—so that you can demonstrate its weaknesses and, in the process, strengthen your own claim. On the other hand, the author of one of your sources may be so convincing in supporting a claim that you adopt it yourself, either partially or entirely. The point is that the argument is in your hands; you must devise it yourself and must use your sources in ways that will support the claim expressed in your thesis.

Your thesis commits you to (1) recognize the arguments made by opponents of Wal-Mart, and (2) argue that Wal-Marts will prevail because they offer people advantages that the traditional retail shops can't match. The sources provide plenty of information and ideas—that is, evidence—that will allow you to support your thesis. Norman and Anderson sum up the anti–Wal-Mart case, one that is also described more objectively by Ortega.

Johnston offers the primary argument for Wal-Mart, and other data showing the growth of the chain are provided by Wal-Mart itself (on its website).

Develop an Organizational Plan

Having developed a provisional thesis, and having decided how to use your source materials, how do you logically organize your essay? In many cases, a well-written thesis will suggest an overall organization. Thus, the first part of your essay will address the powerful arguments made by opponents of Wal-Mart. The second part will cover the even more powerful case (in your judgment) to be made on the other side. Sorting through your material and categorizing it by topic and subtopic, you might arrive at the following outline:

    I. Introduction. The emotional anti–Wal-Mart case; conflict of values: consumerism vs. small-town North America. *Thesis*.

    II. Spectacular growth of Wal-Mart.

    III. The case against Wal-Mart.

      1. Arguments against Wal-Mart.

      2. Al Norman's crusade.

    IV. Transition: the case for Wal-Mart.

    V. Concession: charm of small-town stores. But—problems with small-town stores.

    VI. Changes in North American economy and lifestyle and their effect on Main Street.

    VII. How traditionalists and store owners can deal with Wal-Mart.

      1. Fight it.

      2. Adjust by competing in ways that Wal-Mart can't.

    VIII. Conclusion. Wal-Mart is not a "villain" because it offers what people want.

At this point you may be ready to begin writing the essay. Some writers, though, find it useful to flesh out the plan into a sentence-style outline that clearly displays the structure of claims and supporting source material by which the essay will develop its thesis. Such an outline might look like this:

Thesis: Opponents of the giant discount chains have made powerful arguments against them, and it's too bad that these megastores are helping to make a way of life extinct; but opponents should realize that stores such as Wal-Mart are so successful because most people prefer bargains and convenience to tradition and small-town charm.

I. Introduction. The case against Wal-Mart is highly emotional because it is based on conflicting values: consumerism vs. small-town North America.

II. Wal-Mart has had spectacular growth.

    a. Stats from "Wal-Mart Stores"

III. Critics see Wal-Mart as the worst of North American culture.

    a. Arguments against Wal-Mart by Anderson, Ortega.

    b. Al Norman has organized a crusade against Wal-Mart—in Anderson.

IV. Transition: These critics miss the point that people want the bargains and convenience Wal-Mart offers.

V. Concession: Small-town stores are charming, but they have problems too.

    a. Poor service, selection, etc.—see Johnston.

    b. Wal-mart is a symptom of change, not the cause.

VI. Changes in the North American economy and lifestyle, not just "Wal-Mart," have had a major effect on Main Street (Johnston).

VII. Traditionalists and store owners can fight Wal-Mart or compete.

    a. Fight it (Norman)—but be aware of the costs.

    b. Adjust by competing in ways that Wal-Mart can't (Johnston).

VIII. Conclusion. Wal-Mart is not a "villain" because it offers what people want.

Argument Strategy

The argument represented by this outline deals with a claim of *value*, rather than a claim of *fact*. In other words, this is not an argument over whether Wal-Marts *are* better, according to some objective standard, than Main Street variety stores, since there is no such standard about which most people would agree. (Of course, if "better" were defined as more profitable, then this argument *would* become one of fact and would, in fact, be easily disposed of, since numbers would provide sufficient support for the claim.) Rather, it is an argument based on values which have a different priority for different people—convenience and economy *versus* charm and traditional small-town life. Your thesis, therefore, is based not only upon the *supporting evidence*, but also upon your assumptions about the relative value of convenience and economy, on the one hand, and charm and traditional small-town life, on the other. Accordingly, while some of the claims introduced are based upon an appeal to *logos*, most are based upon the appeal to *pathos*. Some are even based upon *ethos*, since the writer will occasionally imply that her view has the authority of being representative of that of most people.

To *support* her claims, the writer will rely upon a combination of summary, paraphrase, and quotation—much of it *testimony* from either "average" customers or from proponents of one side or the other of the debate. Note that despite her own essentially pro–Wal-Mart position, the writer provides *counter-arguments* and *concessions*, indicating that she is not afraid to fairly represent the views of the other side, and even to give them some credit (the concession) before she responds and reinforces her own argument.

Draft and Revise

The final draft of a completed essay, based upon the above outline, follows. Following the essay, the argument strategy is discussed in paragraph-by-paragraph detail. In addition, thesis, transitional, and topic sentences are highlighted throughout the essay. Modern Language Association (MLA) style is used for documentation. The Works Cited list provides original publication information so that it can be used as a model for producing your own documentation pages. Note that some of the sources cited are included in the set of readings in this chapter, and that for ease of use, in-text citations for those sources are to pages in *Writing and Reading Across the Disciplines*.

Demonstration Essay

A Vote for Wal-Mart

According to one critic, Wal-Mart is waging a "War on Main Street." 1
Anti–Wal-Mart activists think that we should "Ban the Bargains." A pro–Wal-Mart writer asks "Who's Really the Villain?" Obviously, the ever-expanding Wal-Mart brings some people's emotions to the boiling point. This seems strange. After all, Wal-Mart doesn't seem one of those hot-button issues like abortion or capital punishment. But for many, this is not just about discount department stores; it's about conflicting values: the values of small-town North America versus the values of "mindless consumerism" (Ortega 107). I don't consider myself a mindless consumerist, but I happen to like Wal-Marts. Opponents of the giant discount chains have made powerful arguments against them, and it's too bad that these megastores are helping to make a way of life extinct; but opponents should realize that stores like Wal-Mart are so successful because most people prefer bargains and convenience to tradition and small-town charm.

Wal-Mart's growth has been spectacular. Launched in 1962, by 1997 2
Wal-Mart had over 2900 stores, including 502 "Supercenters" ("Wal-Mart Stores"). Al Norman, one of Wal-Mart's most vocal critics, reported that in 1994 Wal-Mart had over $67 billion in sales ("Eight Ways" 108). Four years

later, Wal-Mart's annual sales climbed to almost $118 billion ("Wal-Mart Stores"). Wal-Mart also owns Sam's Club, another discount chain, which opened in early 1983 (chart: "Wal-Mart Takes Off" 115), and now numbers 483 stores ("Wal-Mart Stores").

To its critics, Wal-Mart seems to represent everything that's wrong with modern North American society. Sarah Anderson, an economist and the daughter of a small-town retailer, argues that Wal-Mart encourages urban sprawl, drains money from local economies, kills downtowns and local jobs, and destroys the quality of small-town life (111). Others blame Wal-Mart for the "homogenization of community identity" (Ortega 107). One local resident complains, "Everything's starting to look the same, everybody buys all the same things—a lot of small-town character is being lost." She adds, "Visually, [Wal-Marts] are atrocious" (qtd. in Ortega 108). 3

Activist Al Norman has helped organize local communities to fight the spread of Wal-Mart. His website, "Sprawl-Busters," proudly lists 248 communities that have succeeded in beating back a big-box store's advance on their town ("Victorious Secret"). (He also lists communities that have rejected other large discounters like Home Depot, Costco, and Kmart.) Norman argues that "Wal-Mart's gains are largely captured from other merchants" ("Eight Ways" 109). His rallying cry is that communities are "not ready to die for a cheap pair of underwear" (qtd. in Anderson 111). 4

But rhetoric like this is overkill. Norman might as well blame computer makers for the death of typewriters or automakers for the death of horse-and-buggy rigs. Horses and buggies may be more picturesque and romantic than cars, but most North Americans drive cars these days because they're a lot faster and more convenient. If customers choose to buy underwear at Wal-Mart instead of the mom-and-pop store downtown, that's because it's easier to get to Wal-Mart—and to park there—and because cheapness is a quality that matters to them. 5

I agree that Wal-Marts are unattractive and "charmless." They just don't have the warmth or individuality of some of the small shops you find in downtown areas, especially if they've been in business for generations. But like most people, I'm willing to sacrifice warmth and individuality if I can get just what I want at a price I can afford. As Jo-Ann Johnston points out, mom-and-pop stores have brought on a lot of their own problems by not being sufficiently responsive to what their customers need. She notes, "several of the town's shoppers complained during the Wal-Mart battle that area 6 merchants could use competition because of their poor selection, high prices, limited hours, and lackluster service" (113). Johnston points out that if customers can't find what they want at the price they want at local stores, it's not surprising that they go to Wal-Mart.

As even opponents of Wal-Mart admit, North American downtowns were in trouble long before Wal-Mart arrived on the scene. Changes in the economy and in the North American lifestyle have contributed to the end of a traditional way of life. In other words, stores such as Wal-Mart are a symptom rather than a cause of the changes in Main Street. Blaming Wal-Mart "overlooks a much deeper problem facing small-town America," writes Jo-Ann Johnston: "the need to change a way of doing business while main-   7 taining, or improving, a deeply valued way of life" (112). As Sarah Anderson admits, "Small towns cannot return to the past, when families did all their shopping and socializing in their hometown. Rural life is changing and there's no use denying it" (111).

In "Eight Ways to Stop the Store," Norman provides tips for community activists on how to fight Wal-Mart. I agree that if most people don't want Wal-Mart in their community, they should campaign against it and keep it out. I even think that the community might be a more pleasant place to live without the huge discount chains. But I also believe that residents of these communities should be aware of the price they will pay, both financially and in convenience, for maintaining their traditional way of doing business. Even   8 without Wal-Mart, local downtowns will have trouble holding on to their customers. A better plan than keeping the big discounters out would be for local retailers to adapt to the changing times and to the competition. Some store owners have found ways of offering their customers what Wal-Mart can't provide: personalized services, such as home delivery or special orders, along with merchandise not available in the chain stores (Johnston 113–114).

Wal-Mart did not become the huge success it is by forcing its products on an unwilling public. People shop there because they want to. They want to save money and they want to find what they're looking for. Who can blame them? Wal-Mart may not be pretty, but it's also not "the villain."

Works Cited

Anderson, Sarah. "Wal-Mart's War on Main Street." *Progressive* Nov. 1994: 19–21.

Johnston, Jo-Ann. "Who's Really the Villain?" *Business Ethics* May–June 1995: 16–18.

Moore, James F. Chart: "Wal-Mart Takes Off." "Predators and Prey." *Harvard Business Review* May–June 1993: 82.

Norman, Albert. "Eight Ways to Stop the Store." *The Nation* 28 Mar. 1994: 418.

——. "Victorious Secret." *Sprawl-Busters*. [n.d.]. 29 June 2005 http://www.sprawl-busters.com/victoryz.html.

Ortega, Bob. "Ban the Bargains." *The Wall Street Journal* 11 Oct. 1994: 1+.

"Wal-Mart Stores, Inc." *Hoover's Handbook of American Business*. Austin, TX: Business Press, 1998.

■ ■ ■

Discussion

The writer of this research-based argument attempts to support a *claim*—one that essentially favours Wal-Mart—by offering *support* in the form of facts (examples and statistics) and opinions (testimony of experts and "average" customers). However, since the writer's claim is one of *value*, as opposed to fact, its effectiveness depends partially upon the extent to which we, as readers, agree with the *assumptions* underlying the argument. An assumption (sometimes called a *warrant*) is a generalization or principle about how the world works or should work—a fundamental statement of belief about facts or values. In this particular case, the underlying assumption is that the values of cheapness and convenience are preferable, as a rule, to the values of charm and small-town tradition. Assumptions often are deeply rooted in people's psyches, sometimes deriving from lifelong experiences and observations, and are not easily changed, even by the most logical arguments. People who grew up in small-town America and remember it fondly are therefore far less likely to be persuaded by the support offered for this writer's claim than are those who have lived in urban and suburban areas.

- In the *introductory paragraph*, the writer summarizes some of the most heated arguments against Wal-Mart by citing some of the titles of recent articles about the store. The writer goes on to explain the intensity of emotion generated by stores such as Wal-Mart by linking it to a larger conflict of values: the values of small-town North America vs. the values of consumerism. The writer then states her own preference for Wal-Mart, which leads to her *claim* (represented in the *thesis* at the end of the first paragraph).

Argument strategy: The writer sets up the argument as one of conflicting *values*, relying here upon summary and quotations that support an appeal to *pathos* (emotions of the reader). The writer also provides the beginning of an appeal to *ethos* (establishing herself as credible) by stating, in the sentence before the thesis, her own views as a consumer.

- In the *second paragraph*, the writer discusses the spectacular growth of Wal-Mart. This growth is indirectly, rather than directly, relevant to the debate itself, since it is this apparently unstoppable growth that has caused Wal-Mart to be perceived as such a threat by opponents.

  Argument strategy: This paragraph relies primarily upon the appeal to *logos* (logic) since its main purpose is to establish Wal-Mart's spectacular success. The argument here is supported primarily with statistics.

- In the *third and fourth paragraphs*, the writer discusses the case against Wal-Mart. The third paragraph covers the objections most commonly advanced by Wal-Mart critics. Three sources (Anderson, Ortega, and "Shopping with the Enemy") provide the source material for this paragraph. In the next paragraph, the writer focuses on Al Norman, one of the most prominent anti–Wal-Mart activists, who has helped localities organize campaigns against new Wal-Marts, some of them successful.

  Argument strategy: The third paragraph, part of the *counter-argument*, attempts to support claims of value (that is, *pathos*) with a combination of summary (topic sentence), paraphrase (second sentence), and quotation (following sentences). The fourth paragraph, a continuation of the counter-argument, relies on a combination of appeals to *logos* (the numbers of communities that, according to Norman, have rejected Wal-Mart) and *pathos* (the quotation in the final sentence of the paragraph).

- The *fifth paragraph* begins the transition to the opposite side. The writer begins advancing her own claim—that people aren't willing to sacrifice convenience and price to charm and tradition. She also suggests that the small-town North American Main Street that Wal-Mart is replacing was dying anyway.

  Argument strategy: This paragraph makes a transition from the counter-argument to the writer's own argument. Initially, the appeal is to *logos:* She draws an analogy between the passing of traditional Main Street stores and the passing of typewriters and horses and buggies. This is followed by another appeal to *pathos*—the importance of efficiency, convenience, and cheapness.

- In the *sixth paragraph*, the writer admits that Wal-Marts are not pretty, charming, or unique, but argues that the mom-and-pop stores have their own problems: small selection, non-responsiveness to customer needs, indifferent service, and relatively high prices.

> **Argument strategy:** In this paragraph, the writer makes an important *concession* (part of the counter-argument) that charm is important; but she continues to use the appeal to *pathos* to support the primary claim. Note that in the middle of the paragraph, the writer makes an appeal to *ethos* (" . . . like most people, I'm willing to sacrifice warmth and individuality if I can get just what I want at a price I can afford"). This statement aligns the writer with what most people want from their shopping experiences. After all, the writer implies, this is a matter of good sense—a quality the reader is likely to think valuable, a quality that she or he appears to share with the writer.

- *Paragraph seven* deals more explicitly than the fifth paragraph with the passing away of traditional small-town North America, owing to changes in the economy and in lifestyle.

  Argument strategy: In this paragraph the writer follows through with her strategy of relying upon a combination of *logos* and *pathos* to support her claim. Beginning by summarizing the reasons for the decline of Main Street, she concludes the paragraph with quotations focusing on the sad but inevitable passing of a way of life.

- In *paragraph eight*, the writer concedes that people are free to fight Wal-Mart coming to their town if they don't want the giant store; but a better course of action might be for local merchants to adjust to Wal-Mart by offering goods and services that the giant store is unwilling or unable to, such as home delivery and specialty merchandise.

  Argument strategy: At this point, the writer focuses almost all her attention on the appeal to logic: She summarizes both the essential nature of the conflict and suggestions offered by one source for counteracting the Wal-Mart threat.

- In *paragraph nine*, the writer concludes by reemphasizing her claim: Wal-Mart is successful because it gives customers what they want.

  Argument strategy: The writer wraps up her argument by re-emphasizing the reasons offered for Wal-Mart's success. She rounds off her discussion by repeating, in quotation marks, the "villain" epithet with which the paper begins. The final sentence again combines the appeal to *pathos* (we admittedly cannot call Wal-Mart "pretty") and *logos* (in view of the evidence offered as support, it makes no sense to label Wal-Mart a "villain").

Of course, many other approaches to a research argument would be possible based on the sources provided here. One, obviously, would be the opposite argument: that in embracing Wal-Marts and other giant chains, North America is losing part of its soul—or, at a less profound level, small towns are losing part of their charm and distinctive character. Another might be to assess the quality of the various positions according, for example, to the nature of the evidence provided or the type of logic employed. Another might be to de-emphasize the more concrete issue of stores such as Wal-Mart and to focus on the broader issue of changes in small-town life. Whatever your approach to the subject, in first *analyzing* the various sources and then *synthesizing* them to support your argument, you are engaging in the kind of critical thinking that is essential to success in a good deal of academic and professional work.

DEVELOPING AND ORGANIZING THE SUPPORT FOR YOUR ARGUMENT

Experienced writers seem to have an intuitive sense of how to develop and present the supporting evidence for their claims. Less experienced writers wonder what to say first, and having decided on that, wonder what to say next. There is no single method of presentation. But the techniques of even the most experienced writers often boil down to a few tried and tested arrangements.

As we've seen in the demonstration essay in this chapter, the key to devising effective arguments is to find and use those kinds of support that most persuasively strengthen your claim. Some writers categorize support into two broad types: *evidence* and *motivational appeals*. Evidence, in the form of facts, statistics, and expert testimony, helps make the appeal to *logos* or reason. Motivational appeals—appeals to *pathos* and to *ethos*—are employed to get people to change their minds, to agree with the writer or speaker, or to decide upon a plan of activity.

Following are some of the most common principles for using and organizing support for your claims.

Summarize, Paraphrase, and Quote Supporting Evidence

In most of the papers and reports you will write in college and the professional world, evidence and motivational appeals derive from summarizing, paraphrasing, and quoting material in the sources either that have been provided to you or that you have independently researched. (See Chapter 2 on when to summarize, paraphrase, and quote material from sources.) As we noted above, the third paragraph of the Wal-Mart essay offers all three treatments of evidence: In the first sentence, the writer *summarizes* anti–Wal-Mart sentiment in the sources; in the second sentence, she *paraphrases* Sarah Anderson; in the third sentence, she *quotes* Bob Ortega.

Provide Various Types of Evidence and Motivational Appeals

Keep in mind the appeals to both *logos* and *pathos*. As we've discussed, the appeal to *logos* is based on evidence that consists of a combination of *facts, statistics*, and *expert testimony*. In the Wal-Mart essay, the writer uses all of these varieties of evidence: facts (the economic decline of small-town North America, as discussed in paragraph 7), statistics (the growth of Wal-Mart, as documented in paragraph 2), and testimony (the quotations in paragraph 3). The appeal to *pathos* is based on the appeal to the needs and values of the audience. In the Wal-Mart essay, this appeal is exemplified in the use of support (for example, the quotations in paragraph 6 about the limitations of mom-and-pop stores) that are likely to make readers upset or dissatisfied because they feel that they need greater selection, efficiency, and economy than the smaller stores can offer them.

Use Climactic Order

Organize by climactic order when you plan to offer a number of different categories or elements of support for your claim. Recognize, however, that some are more important—that is, are likely to be more persuasive—than others. The basic principle here is that you should *save the most important evidence for the end*, since whatever you have said last is what readers are likely to most remember. A secondary principle is that whatever you say first is what they are *next* most likely to remember. Therefore, when you have several reasons to support your claim, an effective argument strategy is to present the second most important, then one or more additional reasons, and finally, the most important reason.

Use Logical or Conventional Order

Using logical or conventional order means that you use as a template a pre-established pattern or plan for arguing your case.

- One common pattern is describing or arguing a *problem/solution*. Using this pattern, you begin with an introduction in which you typically define the problem, then perhaps explain its origins, then offer one or more solutions, then conclude. The article in Chapter 3, "The Nature and Meaning of Data" (pp. 71–76), followed this pattern: First the writers provide an extended example of the problem, then they define it and establish its significance and forms, and then toward the conclusion they offer several recommendations for change (if not all-out solutions).
- Another common pattern is presenting *two sides of a controversy*. Using this pattern, you introduce the controversy and (if a research-based argument) your own point of view or claim, then explain each side's arguments, providing reasons that your point of view should prevail. This is the pattern of our demonstration essay. After an introduction to the controversy, the writer defines the problem by establishing the spectacular growth of Wal-Mart, then presents both sides of the controversy—taking care, because of the principle of climactic order, to present the pro-Wal-Mart side last.

- Another common pattern is *comparison-contrast*. In fact, this pattern is so important that we will discuss it separately in the next section.
- The order in which you present elements of an argument is sometimes dictated by the conventions of the discipline in which you are writing. For example, lab reports and experiments in the sciences and social sciences often follow this pattern: *Opening* or *Introduction, Methods and Materials* [of the experiment], *Results, Discussion.* Legal arguments often follow the IRAC format: *Issue, Rule, Application, Conclusion.*

Present and Respond to Counter-Arguments

As we have seen in the Wal-Mart essay, people who develop arguments on a controversial topic can effectively use *counter-argument* to help support their claims. When you use counter-argument, you present an argument *against* your claim, but then show that this argument is weak or flawed. The advantage of this technique is that you demonstrate that you are aware of the other side of the argument and that you are prepared to answer it.

Here is how a counter-argument typically is developed:

A. Introduction and claim
B. Main opposing argument
C. Refutation of opposing argument
D. Main positive argument

In the Wal-Mart essay, the writer gives a fair representation—using summary, paraphrase, and quotation—of the anti–Wal-Mart case for the purpose of showing that it is weaker than the pro–Wal-Mart case.

Use Concession

Concession is a variation of counter-argument. As in counter-argument, you present the opposing viewpoint, but instead of demolishing that argument, you concede that it does have some validity and even some appeal, although your own argument is the stronger one. This bolsters your own standing—your own *ethos*—as a fair-minded person who is not blind to the virtues of the other side.

Here is an outline for a concession argument:

A. Introduction and claim
B. Important opposing argument
C. Concession that this argument has some validity
D. Positive argument(s)

Sometimes, when you are developing a *counter-argument* or *concession argument*, you may become convinced of the validity of the opposing point of view and change your own views. Don't be afraid of this happening. Writing is a tool for learning. To change your mind because of new evidence is a sign of flexibility and maturity, and your writing can only be the better for it.

Avoid Common Fallacies in Developing and Using Support

In Chapter 3, in the section on critical reading, we considered some of the criteria that you, as a reader, may use for evaluating informative and persuasive writing. We discussed how you can assess the accuracy, the significance, and the author's interpretation of the information presented. We also considered the importance in good argument of clearly defined key terms and the pitfalls of emotionally loaded language. Finally, we saw how to recognize such logical fallacies as either/or reasoning, faulty cause-and-effect reasoning, hasty generalization, and false analogy. As a writer, no less than as a critical reader, be aware of these common problems and try to avoid them.

■ EXERCISE

Write a research-based argument that draws on the full range of sources in this chapter (including, if you wish, the student demonstration essay) and reflects the Canadian context of the Wal-Mart issue. Begin by reading the sources and developing an outline. Remember that an argument requires a strong thesis. Your essay should be approximately 1500 words long.

THE EXPLANATORY RESEARCH ESSAY

Your job in writing an explanatory paper—or in writing the explanatory portion of an argumentative paper—is not to argue a particular point, but rather to *present the facts in a reasonably objective manner*. Of course, explanatory papers, like other academic papers, should be based on a thesis. But the purpose of a thesis in an explanatory paper is less to advance a particular opinion than to focus the various facts contained in the paper. Whereas an argument has a strong thesis that proposes a debatable claim about the topic, the explanatory essay has a mild thesis that does not enter into debatable concepts but instead offers an organizational principle for the essay.

Explanatory writing is fairly modest in purpose. It emphasizes the materials in the sources themselves, not your own interpretation. Since your reader is not always in a position to read your sources, this kind of essay, if done well, can be very informative. But the main characteristic of the explanatory essay is that it is designed more to *inform* than to *persuade*. The thesis in the explanatory essay is less a device for arguing a particular point than a device for providing focus and direction to an objective presentation of facts or opinions. As the writer of an explanatory essay, you remain, for the most part, a detached observer.

You may disagree with this, contending that a thesis for an explanatory essay still represents a particular point of view. For example, the following thesis for an explanatory essay on the Wal-Mart problem might be seen as taking a position:

In debating the economic, social, and cultural impact of Wal-Mart, writers on both sides raise compelling arguments grounded in concerns about quality of life.

By acknowledging that the debate is significant rather than trivial and claiming that the writers are concerned with the quality of our lives, even this balanced and mostly informative thesis represents a particular point of view. Note, however, that explanatory writing does NOT focus on advancing a particular claim, and that it is unlikely that either the sources or discussion included in the essay will encourage the reader to draw conclusions. In this sense, this version of the Wal-Mart thesis is not debatable; it serves to focus and organize the discussion that follows rather than to advance an argument.

Some of the papers you write in class will be more or less explanatory in nature. An explanation helps readers understand a topic. Writers explain by dividing a subject into its component parts and presenting them to the reader in a clear and orderly fashion. Explanations may entail descriptions that re-create in words some object, place, emotion, event, sequence of events, or state of affairs. As a student reporter, you may need to explain an event—to relate when, where, and how it took place. In a science lab, you would observe the conditions and results of an experiment and record them for review by others. In a political science course, you might review research on a particular subject—say, the complexities underlying the debate over welfare—and then present the results of your research to your professor.

Consider Your Purpose

First remember that before considering the *how*, you must consider the *why*. In other words, what is your *purpose* in incorporating your sources? You might use them for a paper dealing with a broad issue, such as, for example, the dangers of relying too heavily upon computers. If this were your purpose, your sources would be used to advance an *argument* for a particular viewpoint about the dangers of technology. Or, for a course dealing with the social impact of technology, you might be studying how the development of new programming languages and the decline of old ones can create unforeseen trouble in the years to come. Or, moving out of the academic world and into the commercial one, you might be a computer consultant preparing a brochure for potential clients who, you hope, will hire you to fix problems with their computers. In this brochure, you want to spell out the nature of the problems that can occur and how serious each one is.

Formulate a Thesis

The difference between a purpose and a thesis is a difference primarily of focus. Your purpose provides direction to your research and focus to your paper. Your thesis sharpens this focus by narrowing it and formulating it in words of a declarative statement.

When writing an explanatory thesis with the simple purpose of presenting source material with little or no comment, the thesis would be the most obvious statement you could make about the relationship among the passages. By "obvious," we mean a statement based on an idea that is clearly supported in all the passages. Using the Wal-Mart sources, for example, an explanatory thesis could emphasize the fact that there are different ways to look at the store.

> *Draft:* Those who write about Wal-Mart are divided in their assessment of whether its impact is positive or negative.

This thesis could be focused more narrowly (for example, which group of writers will be examined?). It can use more specific diction (its impact on what?).

> *Redrafted:* Those who report on consumer trends and habits are divided on their assessment of Wal-Mart's economic impact and social influence.

Decide How You Will Use Your Source Material

The easiest way to deal with sources is to summarize them. But because you are incorporating *ideas* rather than whole sources, you will have to be more selective than if you were writing a simple summary. You don't have to treat *all* the ideas in your sources, just the ones related to your thesis. Some sources might be summarized in their entirety; others, only in part. Using the techniques of summary, determine section by section the main topics of each source, focusing only on those topics related to your thesis. Write brief phrases in the margin, underline key phrases or sentences, or take notes on a separate sheet of paper or in a word processing file or electronic data filing program. Decide how your sources can help you achieve your purpose and support your thesis.

Develop an Organizational Plan

An organizational plan is your plan for presenting material to the reader. What material will you present? To find out, examine your thesis. Do the content and structure of the thesis (that is, the number and order of assertions) suggest an organizational plan for the paper? Expect to devote at least one paragraph of your paper to developing each section of this plan. Having identified likely sections, think through the possibilities of arrangement. Ask yourself: What information does the reader need to understand first? How do I build on this first section—what block of information will follow? Think of each section in relation to others until you have placed them all and have worked your way through to a plan for the whole paper.

Study your thesis, and let it help suggest an organization. Bear in mind that any one paper can be written—successfully—according to a variety of plans. Your job before beginning your first draft is to explore possibilities. Sketch a series of rough outlines: Arrange and rearrange your paper's likely sections until you sketch a plan that both facilitates the reader's understanding and achieves your objectives as writer. Your final paper may well deviate from your final sketch, since in the act of writing you may discover the need to explore new material, to omit planned material, or to refocus your entire presentation. Just the same, a well-conceived organizational plan will encourage you to begin writing a draft.

Based on the working thesis developed above—about the range of views Wal-Mart elicits from commentators—we could develop a six-point plan, including introduction and conclusion:

A. Introduction: explanation of the two divergent views about Wal-Mart's economic and social impact and identification of those who tend to hold these views.

B. Social Impact: jobs: Costs—too many "McJobs" (low pay, low security). Advantages—availability of "on-the-job" training jobs.

C. Social Impact: neighbourhoods: Costs—rushing through concrete exteriors and landscapes. Advantages—all-in-one store and mall shopping.

D. Social Impact: aesthetics: Costs—interior as "box." Advantages— pressure on small business to become more competitive.

E. Economic Impact: Costs—loss of small Canadian-owned business. Advantages—pressure on small business to become more competitive.

F. Conclusion—summing up.

As an optional step to strengthen your sense of how to arrange main points, you may want to write draft versions of topic sentences; these will get you started on each main section of your essay and will help give you the sense of direction you need to proceed. When read in a sequence following the thesis, topic sentences, even in draft form, can give an idea of the logical progression of the essay as a whole.

THE COMPARISON-AND-CONTRAST RESEARCH ESSAY

Comparison-and-contrast techniques enable you to examine two subjects (or two sources) in terms of one another. When you compare, you consider *similarities*. When you contrast, you consider *differences*. By comparing and contrasting, you perform a multi-faceted analysis that often suggests subtleties that otherwise might not have come to your (or the reader's) attention.

Comparison and contrast can serve several purposes. You may want to show differences and similarities, or to place emphasis on one or the other. Or you might compare and contrast to recommend a choice, moving into the territory of argument by making the claim that A is better than B.

To organize a comparison-and-contrast argument, you must carefully read sources to discover *significant criteria for analysis*. A *criterion* is a specific point to which both of your authors refer and about which they may agree or disagree. (For example, in a comparative report on compact cars, criteria for *comparison and contrast* might be road handling, fuel economy, and comfort of ride.) The best criteria are those that allow you not only to account for obvious similarities and differences between sources but also to plumb deeper, to more subtle and significant similarities and differences.

There are two basic approaches to organizing a comparison-and-contrast analysis: organization by *subject* or *source* and organization by *criteria*.

1. Demonstration: *Organizing by subject or by source*

You can organize a comparative essay as two separate presentations or summaries of your subjects, followed by a discussion in which you point out significant similarities and differences.

If you are working with two subjects, describe each, and then discuss both the obvious and subtle similarities and differences, focusing on the most significant:

   I. Introduce the essay; lead to thesis.
   II. Describe subject A by discussing its significant features.
   III. Describe subject B by discussing its significant features.
   IV. Write a paragraph (or two) in which you discuss the significant points of comparison and contrast between subjects A and B.
   V. End with a conclusion in which you summarize your points and, perhaps, raise and respond to pertinent questions.

The above outline works equally well for essays structured by source: Summarize each, and then compare them.

Organization by source is best saved for passages that are briefly summarized. If the summary of your source becomes too long, your audience might forget the remarks you made in the first summary as they are reading the second. A comparison-and-contrast essay organized by source might proceed like this:

  I. Introduce the essay; lead to thesis.
  II. Summarize passage A by discussing its significant features.
  III. Summarize passage B by discussing its significant features.
  IV. Write a paragraph (or two) in which you discuss the significant points of comparison and contrast between passages A and B.
  V. End with a conclusion in which you summarize your points and, perhaps, raise and respond to pertinent questions.

Using examples from the Wal-Mart sources included in this chapter, we might set out to compare Norman's position against the store to Johnston's defence of it:

  I. Introduce the two writers and their ideas; point out that they are different.
  II. Summarize Norman's views.
  III. Summarize Johnston's views.
  IV. Write a paragraph (or two) in which you discuss the significant points of comparison and contrast between Norman and Johnston.
  V. End with a conclusion to summarize the main points and, perhaps, to raise and respond to pertinent questions.

This outline could be developed into the following draft of an essay structured by source. Note that this essay and the next one are meant to illustrate the basic pattern of comparison essays and they are shorter than any you would likely be assigned. MLA citation and documentation style are used in this draft, and sources are treated as "Selections from an Edited Collection or Anthology."

Demonstration Essay: Organizing by Source

Wal-Mart, Inc.: Two Approaches to Facing the Giant

Since Sam Walton founded Wal-Mart in 1962, it has grown from a single   1
store to a retail empire earning over US$82 billion in annual sales and
encompassing well over 2000 stores in North America (Johnston 112). This
enormous level of success has come, say many critics, at significant
expense, and the corporation has been criticized for blocking the unioniza-
tion of its workforce, driving smaller retailers out of business, and even
damaging the quality of life in small towns. One of its most vocal critics is Al

Norman, a "political consultant" (Johnston 112) who works with communities to fight Wal-Mart openings. Whereas Norman sees Wal-Mart as overwhelmingly destructive in its impact and focuses on strategies for stopping its growth, Jo-Ann Johnston makes a case that Wal-Mart is merely a discount store that obviously appeals to customers, and that it is the responsibility of retailers to do a better job of competing with it instead of just complaining about it (Johnston 114).

Norman's article, "Eight Ways to Stop the Store," begins with the story of Wal-Mart's economic growth and ends by arguing that "Wal-Mart would . . . do anything and say anything to bulldoze its way toward another grand opening" (110). Norman argues that, far from contributing to the economy as Wal-Mart claims, its success has come at the expense of other retailers: in Norman's words, "[d]ollars merely [shift] from cash registers on one side of town to Wal-Mart registers on the other side of town" (109). In the process of suggesting his eight strategies for stopping the store, he argues that communities can be successful in their fight against Wal-Mart if they appeal to the public, beginning as soon as plans to open a store are revealed, and expose the negative impact of Wal-Mart stores (110).

Johnston's essay, in contrast, asks "Who's Really the Villain?" After offering the story of a small town that has suffered economically by turning down the hundreds of jobs that would have come with a new Wal-Mart, she launches her argument that retailers in such towns are at fault for merely "chastising" Wal-Mart when they should be focused on "adapt[ing] to changes in their communities, the economy, and their industries" (112). Johnston ends by explaining that Wal-Mart may be the biggest source of competition for small-town retailers, but it is only one among many, including shopping channels on television, web-based retailers and big box specialty stores (115).

Overall, Johnston presents a more complex view of the Wal-Mart issue than does Norman, one that acknowledges the positive reasons for its success. Norman's pitch to community organizing and sentimentality about small-town life gives his argument an emotional appeal that Johnston's sober prescription of hard work and innovative business practices lacks. Both paint Wal-Mart as an economic juggernaut that presents a formidable threat to small-town retailers, but in the end it is Johnston's approach that seems the more practical one to meeting that challenge.

Works Cited

Johnston, Jo-Ann. "Who's Really the Villain?" *Writing and Reading Across the Disciplines*. Eds. Laurence Behrens et al. Toronto: Pearson, 2007. 112–15.

Norman, Albert. "Eight Ways to Stop the Store." *Writing and Reading Across the Disciplines*. Eds. Laurence Behrens et al. Toronto: Pearson, 2007. 108–10.

■ ■ ■

2. Demonstration: *Organizing by criteria*

Instead of summarizing entire passages one at a time with the intention of comparing them later, you could discuss two passages simultaneously, examining the views of each author point by point (criterion by criterion), comparing and contrasting these views in the process. The criterion approach is best used when you have a number of points to discuss or when passages are long and/or complex. A comparison-and-contrast essay organized by criteria might look like this:

I. Introduce the essay; lead to thesis.
II. Criterion 1
    A. Discuss what author A says about this point.
    B. Discuss what author B says about this point, comparing and contrasting B's treatment of the point with A's.
III. Criterion 2
    A. Discuss what author A says about this point.
    B. Discuss what author B says about this point, comparing and contrasting B's treatment of the point with A's.

And so on. Proceed criterion by criterion until you have completed your discussion. Be sure to arrange criteria with a clear method; knowing how the discussion of one criterion leads to the next will ensure smooth transitions throughout your paper. End with a conclusion in which you summarize your points and, perhaps, raise and respond to pertinent questions.

Here is an example of a criterion-based outline that compares Norman's and Johnston's views on Wal-Mart:

I. Introduce the two writers and their views on the economic and cultural effects of the store and the solutions they propose for small-town retailers.
II. Criterion 1: economic results
    A. Discuss what Norman says about economic troubles.
    B. Discuss what Johnston says about economic gains, comparing and contrasting her treatment of the point with Norman's.
III. Criterion 2: cultural results
    A. Discuss what Norman says about the way Wal-Mart destroys North-American culture.

      B. Discuss what Johnston says about the impact on culture, comparing and contrasting her treatment of the point with Norman's.

  IV. Criterion 3: proposed course of action

      A. Discuss Norman's approach to combatting Wal-Mart.

      B. Discuss Johnston's approach, comparing and contrasting her approach with Norman's.

This outline could be developed into the following essay structured by criterion. For this example, we are using APA style citations and reference list:

Demonstration Essay: Organizing by Criteria

Wal-Mart, Inc.: Two Approaches to Facing the Giant

Since Sam Walton founded Wal-Mart in 1962, it has grown from a single   1 store to a retail empire earning over US$82 billion in annual sales and encompassing well over 2000 stores in North America (Johnston, 2007, p. 113). This enormous level of success has come, say many critics, at significant expense, and the corporation has been criticized for blocking the unionization of its workforce, driving smaller retailers out of business, and even damaging the quality of life in small towns. One of its most vocal critics is Al Norman, a "political consultant" (Johnston, 2007, p. 112) who works with communities to fight Wal-Mart openings. Whereas Norman (2007) sees Wal-Mart as overwhelmingly destructive in its impact and focuses on strategies for stopping its growth (pp. 108–110), Jo-Ann Johnston (2007) makes a case that Wal-Mart is merely a discount store that obviously appeals to customers, and that it is the responsibility of retailers to learn to compete with it instead of just complaining about it (p. 112).

    Norman (2007) characterizes Wal-Mart's economic impact as uniformly   2 negative. Its success, he argues, comes at the expense of other merchants: not only does it put smaller retailers out of business, he claims, but it is "stealing" from them (p. 109). Additionally, Wal-Marts destroy jobs, hurt property values, and result in "vacant retail space" (p. 109). To Norman, the positive economic impact of Wal-Mart is negligible, being limited, he claims, to sponsoring one annual scholarship (p. 109). In contrast to Norman's focus on the negative impact of Wal-Mart on existing businesses, Johnston (2007) points to the record of job creation and "increased retail traffic" when Wal-Mart opens in a community (p. 113). Although Norman does not

acknowledge it, his own figures support Johnston's claim of increased economic activity: when Wal-Mart opened in a small Iowa town, sales went from
US$8.3 million to US$10 million (Norman, 2007, p. 109). Significantly,
Johnston (2007) also warns Wal-Mart's opponents of the record of job loss
and a "'retail leakage' of shoppers . . . to the closest regional shopping
center with a discount store" (p. 113).

   Norman's argument does not rest only on economic impact but also on   3
the cultural one, and his appeal is more emotional than logical. His basic
claim is that when a Wal-Mart opens, small towns get "an unwanted shove
into urbanization" that destroys their quality of life (2007, p. 110), that quality of life being implicitly defined as the experience of dealing with small businesses instead of large discounters. Although she refers to Norman's work
several times, Johnston (2007) seems neutral on the issue of Wal-Mart's
damage to small-town culture. She concedes that small-town retailers are
indeed losing business to Wal-Mart, and that small towns are concerned
about losing "a deeply valued way of life" (2007, p. 112). However, she
argues very strongly that small-town merchants are the authors of their
own misfortune because they complain about Wal-Mart instead of figuring
out why their former customers are opting to shop there and changing their
business practices to become more competitive (2007, p. 113).

   Both Norman and Johnston see that Wal-Mart threatens small-town   4
retailers and, insofar as those retailers are integral to small-town culture,
threatens small towns themselves. But they differ sharply in their views of
Wal-Mart and of how people ought to respond to that threat. Whereas
Norman (2007) paints Wal-Mart as the "villain" in a story of economic
damage, the answer Johnston (2007) gives to the question posed in her
title, though she does not state it explicitly, is that the suffering retailers are
themselves to blame. Her argument makes Norman's seem simplistic and
even naive, not only because she takes more economic factors into account
than he does, but because of the persuasiveness of her argument that Wal-
Mart is only one aspect of huge economic changes that must be adapted to
because they cannot, and even should not, be stopped (Johnston, 2007,
p. 115). Where Norman (2007) gives us "Eight Ways to Stop the Store" and
go back to the way things were, Johnston (2007) encourages small retailers
to learn from the lessons of lost business and start providing their customers with the levels of service, pricing, and availability that they find in

Wal-Mart—or provide them with something else such as free home delivery or specialized goods that Wal-Mart does not (pp. 113–114).

Apart from agreeing that small retailers are losing business to Wal- 5
Mart, Norman and Johnston are radically different in their perspectives on the issue. They differ in their assessment of the economic and cultural impact of Wal-Mart, but more significantly, in their assessment of "Who's Really the Villain" in this story of business lost and what should be done about it. Although Norman (2007) appeals to the nostalgia some may feel for "Main Street, USA" (p. 109), Johnston's much more thorough analysis of the situation makes it clear that efforts to "Stop the Store" (Norman, 2007, p. 108) are a risky distraction from the need to learn to compete with it.

References

Johnston, J. (2007). Who's really the villain? In L. Behrens, L.J. Rosen, J. McLeod Rogers and C. Taylor (Eds.), *Writing and reading across the disciplines* (pp. 112–15). Toronto: Pearson.

Norman, Albert. (2007). Eight ways to stop the store. In L. Behrens, L.J. Rosen, J. McLeod Rogers and C. Taylor (Eds.), *Writing and reading across the disciplines* (pp. 108–10). Toronto: Pearson.

■ ■ ■

THE PERSONAL ARGUMENT

The personal argument often uses no academic sources and relies mainly on the writer's personal experiences. Although the research argument is a mainstay of academic writing in the humanities and many social science disciplines, the personal argument is a form preferred by many professional writers. Some, like Douglas Coupland in "End: Zed" (pp. 491–493), base their insight and reasoning on life experiences, while others, like Pat Capponi in the excerpt from *The War at Home* (pp. 193–200), stake a position based on experience coupled with careful observation.

By the time you get to university—and then for as long as you live—you develop opinions and insights on the basis of experience and observations. To write a personal argument essay, you are usually asked to reflect on a particular area of your experience—how you developed your writing or reading skills, for example, or how you have developed a religious faith—in order to share your insight with readers. Many first-year composition courses begin with a personal writing assignment, inviting students to write with confidence about something they already know well. Increasingly, other courses that emphasize self-reflection as an important component of intellectual work also assign personal arguments. For example, an education student might be asked to reflect on her own experience of the power structures of school culture, or a communications student might be asked to write about his own social location with reference to race, gender, and sexuality.

Usually, you don't have to do research to discover what others have said about your topic, since this form of writing privileges your voice and perspective. Yet this form of writing is not really a holiday from other forms of scholarly writing, for even if it does not involve research and textual analysis strictly speaking, it does prompt you to evaluate the "text" of your own life: your life history is the text you consult and evaluate, in order to determine claim and support. And, as always, you need to make decisions about what to include and emphasize, and to how to organize an effective beginning, middle and end.

Perhaps most important, you need to ensure that your story makes a point. Of course, because you are dealing with the realm of experience, you do not need to set out to prove or conclude anything, but somewhere your experience should resonate with others, moving beyond recording events in detail in order to make a broader point about life. You will probably find it helpful to think about the Personal Argument as having twin components, as its name suggests—it is about a personal experience (or about several experiences, depending on the approach you pick) *and* it also makes an argument. In this way, the personal essay has a thesis—the details of the story support the point the story makes about human experience.

Since personal stories come in many varieties, there is no one formula to follow prescribing just where you tell the story and where you stop to make your point. An important decision for you as the writer is whether to state your argument at the beginning, the end, or even in both places. Stronger writers may even decide that the story itself conveys the argument, so that the thesis is tacit, rather than stated overtly or directly.

While the personal argument does not provide definitive evidence, it sometimes has the power to strike an emotional chord of response in readers in ways facts and generalizations cannot. It also provides a particular epistemic perspective in enabling an understanding of particular things, as writer Marjorie Kinnan Rawlings points out: "Thoreau went off to live in the woods alone, to find out what the world was like. Now a man may learn a great deal of the general from studying the specific, whereas it's impossible to know the specific by studying the general."[1]

Following is a sample of a personal argument essay by a student asked to reflect on literacy experiences, in order to make a broader point about the value of writing. Notice how he reaches out to the reader in the opening paragraph by speaking in broad terms about the expressive difficulties of shy people, who suffer setbacks because they are disinclined to speak up. He states his thesis directly at paragraph end: "Thankfully, for those of us in quiet

[1]Marjorie Kinnan Rawlings, *Cross Creek* (Toronto: Thomas Saunders, 1942), 359.

corners, there is the written word. Sometimes it's our only voice, the only way we can ever be heard."

Paragraph two shifts focus to the personal story, beginning the presentation of an extended example on which the writer bases his argument that quiet people are at a disadvantage in life, even if they have powerful written voices. He restates his thesis idea in the concluding paragraph, directly linking it to the story he has told when he refers to preferring writing to speaking in a world that privileges the outspoken.

Demonstration Essay

If a Tree Falls but Nobody's Listening

We all have something to say. Even the most stoic among us has an inner voice that craves recognition or, at the very least, acknowledgement. For most, this craving is satisfied through the most natural means—we simply speak up. It would seem to be the most natural of processes, and it also seems to be a prerequisite to public and social success. It is rare that the quiet child in the corner will be elected class president, or that the shy bookworm will rise through the ranks in a corporation. I'm sure it happens, just not all that often. Where then do those of us with a quieter nature find our voice? We have as much to say as our more vocal peers, if not more. The need to be heard may be more subdued and contemplative, but it still nags at us. Thankfully, for those of us in quiet corners, there is the written word. Sometimes it's our only voice, the only way we can ever be heard. 1

I was always painfully shy, and usually spoke only when I was first spoken to. It annoyed me that this always seemed to be treated as a shortcoming. There always seemed to be someone trying to "get me out of my shell" or push me to "open up." This, of course, pushed me further and further into my shell. Why couldn't people understand that I liked who I was, quiet nature and all? On those occasions when I was dragged out, I was like a goldfish that had fallen from its bowl. As a rule, I generally felt that most people talked too much and said too little. My meandering, methodical mind found the world a noisy, intrusive place. As a result, being anywhere near the centre of attention was to me like being in the centre of Hiroshima in the summer of 1945. 2

My refuge was in books. As luck would have it, I learned to read before starting school so, from that moment on, I had a place of peace—a place where I was master of my time and destiny. As a youngster, I immersed 3 myself in tales of humour and adventure. Indeed, I spent as much time reading as I did playing! After starting school, another side of my nature began to emerge. A thirst for knowledge! If Jupiter was said to be big, I wanted to know how big. If the dog could happily eat cat food, I wanted to know why. As a result, I gradually began to gravitate toward non-fiction and reference books: biographies, history texts, atlases. If it explained something, I wanted to hear it. I would discover in later years that this propensity was part of a larger facet of my personality—a continuous search for the absolute, molecular level truth about virtually everything. My personality, therefore, inspired me to read and, subsequently, decided what I would read. As well, it seemed that, with my nose in a book, I didn't have to face a troubled home life or being treated as a "nerd" at school.

It may have been my personality that drove my love of reading, but it   4
was my chosen venues of reading that spawned my love of writing. My hunger for knowledge seemed to lead to a sort of saturation. It was as if there was a need for an outlet—a valve to release some of the swirling currents and storms of thought. And so I began to write. At first it was lists: lists of countries and their populations, lists of prime ministers and their terms in office. Such lists were, of course, intended for no one's eyes but mine. It was as if this was my way of organizing and making sense of an ocean of information. I found a similar release in poetry and great prose. I was in awe of great writers, from Ralph Waldo Emerson to Bob Dylan, who could say so much with so few words. Their depth and breadth were so wonderfully, polarly different from the facts and data I'd always found comfort in.

And so, a writing style was born. I enjoy writing, although I rarely have   5
time to indulge. I find my prose to be a mixture of pointed information, swimming in pools of adjectives and analogies. In school, my teachers seemed amazed that such a quiet, studious boy could write with depth and feeling. It seems strange now that they should have found it curious. Just because a person is silent doesn't mean they lack a voice. On paper, I could laugh and scream—as I never could verbally. I could rail against injustice, wink at life's subtle ironies, and spit in the eye of thick-headed bullies and oppressive fathers.

Later experiences would drag me (to some extent) from my shell, much   6
to my benefit. As I began to learn to express myself in the "loud" world, I also became aware of the loss that accompanied the change. Although I still had

a vast appreciation for great writers, and an ongoing infatuation with facts and data, I no longer seemed to have the time to dance with them directly. Gone were the poetry and useless lists. It was as if, as my outer voice grew bolder, my inner voice became more and more subdued. Today, it appears only in vague echoes.

Is it always this way? Must there always be something lost with every gain? Today, I find myself in the role of a manager in industry where whatever boldness and volume I have achieved are, once again, below the expected norms. It is a world of fast, confident decisions and brash politics. I am proud of my achievements but somehow dissatisfied. I do find, however, that, when my pen does meet paper, it still seeks and speaks the truth. I had found my voice when I was young. Unfortunately, I let myself be convinced that that voice wasn't strong enough, wasn't good enough. I suppose it could be said that I "sold my soul" many years ago for material success. Or lost it while wandering around dark corners in my late teens. Either way, it's as if I haven't time to be myself anymore. I only hope that the voice is not lost, but resting. Someday I hope to retrieve it, to hear my own voice again.

7

■ ■ ■

SUMMARY

In this chapter, we've considered the personal essay that involves no outside sources, and the three main types of essay that involve incorporating outside sources: the research-based *argument*, the *explanatory* research essay, and the *comparison-contrast* research essay. Although for ease of comprehension we've placed them into separate categories, these types are not, of course, mutually exclusive. Both argument essays and explanatory essays often involve elements of one another, and comparison-contrast essays can fall into either of the previous categories. Similarly, the personal argument can be centred in experience but enriched by quotations and references to sources that help the writer explore the significance of the experience. Which format you choose will depend upon your *purpose* and the method that you decide is best suited to achieve this purpose.

If your main purpose is to persuade your readers to agree with your viewpoint on a subject, or to change their minds, or to decide upon a particular course of action, then you will be composing an argument essay. If your main purpose, on the other hand, is to help your audience understand a particular subject, and in particular to help them understand the essential elements or significance of this subject, then you will be composing an explanatory essay.

If one effective technique of making your case is to establish similarities or differences between your subject and another one, then you will compose a comparison-contrast essay—which may well be just *part* of a larger essay topic.

In planning and drafting these essays, you can draw upon a variety of strategies: supporting your claims by summarizing, paraphrasing, and quoting from your sources, handling opposing points by refuting, minimizing, or conceding to them, and choosing from among formats such as climactic or conventional order that will best help you to achieve your purpose.

5

Homeless in the "Just Society"

If it is true that "the poor are always with us," it is also true that people have different ideas about the causes of poverty and about the ways we might solve or respond to it. Part of the enduring legacy of Liberal Prime Minister Pierre Trudeau is the *Canadian Charter of Rights and Freedoms,* which attempts to enshrine conditions for citizenry in a "just society." As he imagined it, this society would ensure equal opportunities for advancement by providing those in need with the means to prosper: "The Just Society will be one in which all of our people will have the means and motivation to participate. . . . The just society will be one in which those regions and groups which have not fully shared in the country's affluence will be given a better opportunity. The just society will be one in which such urban problems as housing and pollution will be attacked through the application of new knowledge and new techniques."[1]

Even though we like to believe that ours is a just society of equal opportunity, the number of people without sustaining jobs and permanent housing continues to grow in Canada. Among those who have written about homelessness in Canada, there is some disagreement about what causes people to become entrapped in poverty. Despite paying lip service to the idea that the homeless deserve assistance, John Stackhouse (pp. 155–160) seems to believe that individuals are responsible for attaining a level of self-sufficiency; he describes many of the homeless as reckless freeloaders and generally presents the experience of homelessness as something individuals choose. On the other hand, Jack Layton (pp. 161–163) espouses liberal views when he insists it is the role of government to provide affordable housing alternatives. He points out that the homeless are often trapped by a series of circumstances, and cannot function on their own to find alternatives to improve their situation.

Leaving aside political questions about the cause of and cure for poverty and homelessness, the final articles in this chapter describe the situation of people struggling on the street. In common, authors in these pieces avoid broad generalizations, providing instead case studies that describe individual lives and struggles. In "Life on the Streets," a chapter excerpted from a well-researched academic study by Thomas O'Reilly-Fleming, the author describes some of the realities facing the homeless, drawing a specific picture through a case-study approach. The excerpt from Tom C. Allen's book, *Someone to Talk To,* looks at experiences of homeless people in Vancouver, as seen through the eyes of someone engaged in a helping profession. The excerpt

[1] Pierre Elliott Trudeau, "The Just Society," in *The Essential Trudeau,* ed. Ron Graham (Toronto: McClelland and Stewart, 1998), 18–19.

from Pat Capponi's book *The War at Home* examines homeless activists in Montreal from the perspective of a writer who is herself an activist who has experienced poverty first-hand. Thus the three writers bring different expertise and experience to writing about poverty.

Canadian Charter of Rights and Freedoms

The Canadian Charter of Rights and Freedoms *was part of the* Constitution Act *of 1982, which was a modernization of the original* British North America Act *of 1867. Passing this Act required the British Parliament to act on a joint address from the Canadian Senate and the House of Commons. As Dickerson and Flanagan point out in their book* An Introduction to Canadian Politics, *the Act "not only lists and confirms the pre-existing parts of the written constitution but also introduces important new substance, particularly in the first thirty-four sections, known as the Canadian Charter of Rights and Freedoms."[2]*

The sections that we have reproduced are those that speak to civil liberties and to issues of equality rights.

Whereas Canada is founded upon principles that recognize the supremacy of God and the rule of law:

Guarantee of Rights and Freedoms

Rights and freedoms in Canada

1. The *Canadian Charter of Rights and Freedoms* guarantees the rights and freedoms set out in it subject only to such reasonable limits prescribed by law as can be demonstrably justified in a free and democratic society.

Fundamental freedoms

Fundamental Freedoms

2. Everyone has the following fundamental freedoms:

a) freedom of conscience and religion;
b) freedom of thought, belief, opinion and expression, including freedom of the press and other media of communication;
c) freedom of peaceful assembly; and
d) freedom of association.

Mobility of citizens

Mobility Rights

6. (1) Every citizen of Canada has the right to enter, remain in and leave Canada.

[2] Mark O. Dickerson and Thomas Flanagan, *An Introduction to Canadian Politics: A Conceptual Approach* (Toronto: Nelson, 1998), 70.

Rights to move and gain livelihood

(2) Every citizen of Canada and every person who has the status of a permanent resident of Canada has the right

a) to move to and take up residence in any province; and

b) to pursue the gaining of a livelihood in any province.

Limitation

(3) The rights specified in subsection (2) are subject to

a) any laws or practices of general application in force in a province other than those that discriminate among persons primarily on the basis of province of present or previous residence; and

b) any laws providing for reasonable residency requirements as a qualification for the receipt of publicly provided social services.

Affirmative action programs

(4) Subsections (2) and (3) do not preclude any law, program or activity that has as its object the amelioration in a province of conditions of individuals in that province who are socially or economically disadvantaged if the rate of employment in that province is below the rate of employment in Canada.

Legal Rights

Life, liberty and security of person

7. Everyone has the right to life, liberty and security of the person and the right not to be deprived thereof except in accordance with the principles of fundamental justice.

Search or seizure

8. Everyone has the right to be secure against unreasonable search or seizure.

Detention or imprisonment

9. Everyone has the right not to be arbitrarily detained or imprisoned.

Arrest or detention

10. Everyone has the right on arrest or detention

a) to be informed promptly of the reasons therefor;

b) to retain and instruct counsel without delay and to be informed of that right; and

c) to have the validity of the detention determined by way of *habeas corpus* and to be released if the detention is not lawful.

Proceedings in criminal and penal matters

11. Any person charged with an offence has the right

a) to be informed without unreasonable delay of the specific offence;

b) to be tried within a reasonable time;

c) not to be compelled to be a witness in proceedings against that person in respect of the offence;

d) to be presumed innocent until proven guilty according to law in a fair and public hearing by an independent and impartial tribunal;

e) not to be denied reasonable bail without just cause;

f) except in the case of an offence under military law tried before a military tribunal, to the benefit of trial by jury where the maximum punishment for the offence is imprisonment for five years or a more severe punishment;

g) not to be found guilty on account of any act or omission unless, at the time of the act or omission, it constituted an offence under Canadian or international law or was criminal according to the general principles of law recognized by the community of nations;

h) if finally acquitted of the offence, not to be tried for it again and, if finally found guilty and punished for the offence, not to be tried or punished for it again; and

i) if found guilty of the offence and if the punishment for the offence has been varied between the time of commission and the time of sentencing, to the benefit of the lesser punishment.

Treatment or punishment

12. Everyone has the right not to be subjected to any cruel and unusual treatment or punishment.

Self-crimination

13. A witness who testifies in any proceedings has the right not to have any incriminating evidence so given used to incriminate that witness in any other proceedings, except in a prosecution for perjury or for the giving of contradictory evidence.

Interpreter

14. A party or witness in any proceedings who does not understand or speak the language in which the proceedings are conducted or who is deaf has the right to the assistance of an interpreter.

Equality Rights

Equality before and under law and equal protection and benefit of law

15. (1) Every individual is equal before and under the law and has the right to the equal protection and equal benefit of the law without discrimination and, in particular, without discrimination based on race, national or ethnic origin, colour, religion, sex, age or mental or physical disability.

Affirmative action programs

(2) Subsection (1) does not preclude any law, program or activity that has as its object the amelioration of conditions of disadvantaged individuals or groups including those that are disadvantaged because of race, national or ethnic origin, colour, religion, sex, age or mental or physical disability.

■ ■ ■

Discussion and Writing Suggestions

1. Do these points guarantee that Canadian citizens have the right to expect a degree of economic security, or is the Charter vague about this?
2. Develop an argument that refers to the Charter to defend the point that everyone deserves a basic level of comfort and safety in our society.

"I'm Tired of Being a Slave to the Church Floor"

JOHN STACKHOUSE

John Stackhouse is now the Report on Business *editor of* The Globe and Mail. *Previously, he was the newspaper's correspondent-at-large, based in Toronto, and for seven years its Third-World correspondent based in New Delhi. He has also worked as a senior writer for* Report on Business Magazine, *and as a reporter for the* Financial Times, London Free Press *and* Toronto Star. *He was educated at Queen's University in Kingston, Ontario, and lives in Toronto.*

He has won five National Newspaper Awards, a National Magazine Award
and an Amnesty International Award for human rights reporting. Understood in
this context, his article can be regarded as his attempt to take a sympathetic view
of the homeless as individuals making choices. As the response by Jack Layton (in
the article that follows this one) brings to light, however, Stackhouse's article had
an incendiary effect on those who argue for social and political action to bring an
end to suffering caused by inequality. In the article that follows (excerpted from
a longer series), Stackhouse reports on the last two days of his week-long experi-
ence of pretending to be homeless in downtown Toronto.

In Toronto—Day 6
Billy Jack: A Foot in Both Worlds

The wind is still whipping across Toronto's Nathan Phillips Square when a   1
clock tower strikes six and I wake up to find that most of my cardboard shelter has blown away in the night. Someone has also come by and laid an
extra sleeping bag on top of me.

The others sleeping in the square, huddled in cardboard boxes, under-   2
neath walkways like me, are also slowly rising, stooped, shivering, searching
for the Sally Ann coffee truck that does not come for another hour.

All the money I made the day before—$223 panhandling on Toronto's   3
streets—provides little comfort to my numb joints and sore back, and it
won't get me into a toilet within blocks of here. I join a few others behind a
wall, the only place downtown at this hour where we can go.

Across the square, however, one man seems to stand above it all. Alone,   4
he looks as though he has lived this way for a thousand years, which, as Billy
Jack tells it, is what he's done.

B. J. has just come down from the walkway above me, where he slept   5
with no blanket and two bottles of wine in his system. It was, he says, a fairly
restrained night. It was also so cold he tried to stay awake all night, wandering from one coffee shop to the next before he eventually found a wind-
break.

I give B. J. my extra sleeping bag and suggest he hide it between a pillar   6
and the wall. He gives me a cigarette as thanks. It's been only weeks since he
got out of Collins Bay penitentiary near Kingston, Ont.—five years this time
for busting up a couple of guys in a bar—and he's forgotten some of the
details of street life.

At 58, with 20 years of jail time behind him, B. J. is still a big bear of a   7
man who looks and sounds like Wolfman Jack. In many ways he is from
another age. He likes to call himself one of the originals, one of the grand old
native drunks who has been on Toronto streets since the sixties.

For years, he and his wife worked part of the year, in Toronto and out-   8
side the city. Sometimes they had their own home, or they stayed in shelters.
They had two kids. And they drank, right up till the days when his wife was
dying, in his arms, from bone cancer.

That was 12 years ago.   9

Street life now is not what it used to be, not with all the drugs, tough new   10
laws and the politics of homelessness. B. J.'s daughter, a nurse at a major
Toronto hospital, keeps pleading with him to come off the street and live with
her and her husband and family. His grandchildren need him, she says. They
need his epic Mi'kmaq tales, his big, thick chest to rest on, and his baritone
voice to lull them to sleep.

They need a hero, which is what B. J. tries to be every now and then,   11
when he's not in prison and shows up at his daughter's house for a night. He
chokes up as he speaks of what she's done with her life. But he can't stay, not
with his pride and sense of place.

B. J.'s voice perks up when he talks of his other home, the one out here.   12
Last night, a complete stranger gave him a pack of cigarettes when he asked
for only one. A man who passes him every day gave him two bottles of wine.

"I drink to forget my troubles," B. J. says. "But you know, every morn-   13
ing I wake up and they're still there."

He could go back to his two-room house in the bush in western   14
Newfoundland, where he was born. A salmon river runs through the property,
he says, and the fish jump so high you can almost catch them with your
hands. But the Newfoundland coast is a lonely place, with few jobs and no
one to throw toonies your way.

We both cough from the cold, prompting B. J. to pull out a bottle of   15
mouthwash. He takes a gulp for a morning kick and buckles over to keep
from regurgitating it.

"The loneliness is the hardest part out here," he says.   16

So why does he stay?   17

"I believe God has put me here for a reason. I have no idea what that   18
reason is. I could have walked by it a thousand times. But I gotta keep lookin'.
One day, God will show me His reason."

When the Sally Ann truck finally pulls up on Queen Street, shortly after   19
7 a.m., we join the lineup at its open window. A man in the truck offers coffee
and porridge with brown sugar, as well as new underwear, tuques and gloves
to a half-dozen people waiting, stamping their feet to stay warm.

B. J. does not remember so many people on the street a decade ago, or a   20
decade before that. "It was never like this," he says. "I don't know what's
happened to this city."

He thanks me again for the sleeping bag and goes to find a spot to pan-   21
handle and then a place to drink.

I take a streetcar west, to the Parkdale recreation centre, a smoky store-   22
front room that looks like an old pool hall. I hope to find people who might
be more needful than the panhandlers who get so much public attention
when poverty is the subject.

On a Saturday afternoon, with a light snow starting to swirl in the wind,   23
the centre is filled with people, at least 50 of them who have homes, big needs
and little attention. Packaged up here, a half hour's haul from Yonge Street,
they are not seen as the "homeless" are.

I sit down at a card table with a group of men who are smoking cigarettes 24
and drinking 30-cent cups of coffee. At the end of the table, a man stands and
waves to no one in particular. Another keeps saying, "motherfucker," gur-
gling in between. After a free lunch is served, a third man talks to his plate of
chicken-fried rice, telling each forkful: "You are from Mars."

The confusion does not faze Jim, a middle-aged man who works at a 25
bakery for below minimum wage, to supplement his disability insurance. The
company he gets at the centre is important but not as important as his job, an
occupation that he says is more valuable than a roof or free meal.

"In a constitutional democracy, employment is a fundamental right, but 26
that's not working here," he says earnestly.

He thinks Canada should tie all social assistance to employment. When 27
I mention workfare, he cringes. "'Make them work for it' is the old capitalist idea," he says.

His idea is no different in the end, only justified differently. "I take the 28
view of medical science. According to medical science, working makes people
healthier."

"It's much better than sitting around watching TV and drinking coffee. 29
Look at all the money we would save on health care. In other countries, you
have to take a job. It may not be the right job but you have to take the one the
government gives you or finds for you, if you want assistance."

When the recreation centre closes and I return to Yonge Street, I find 30
myself begging again. I don't need the money any more, or the added experience, but the desire has become insatiable—a desire, as Jim said, to be occupied.

Waiting at a streetcar stop, I sit down on the pavement and hold out my 31
cap. Two dollars, thank you.

Before I buy myself dinner, I feel a need to work for it, so I take a spot in 32
a subway station. I set my target at $5, enough for a McDonald's Value
Meal, but when I reach that in a few minutes, I can't resist shooting for $10
and then $15. As I'm packing up, an elderly woman stops and hands me a
$10 bill. I have to tell myself again to stop, to concede my space to another
panhandler who is sitting beyond the doors. Only when I'm walking upstairs
to the street do I realize that I'm telling myself to do this out loud.

Two Saturdays before Christmas, Yonge Street is jammed with people, 33
festive music and a neon rainbow of lights on every corner. In the middle of
the crush, I spot B. J. on the sidewalk, sorting through coins in his palm to
give to another panhandler, beggar to beggar, on the pavement.

"I can't do business if you're just standin' there," the panhandler com- 34
plains to B. J.

"Fuck off," B. J. says. 35

"No, you fuck off," the other man says, and so B. J. leaves with his fist- 36
ful of change.

As we walk down the crowded street together, I notice after a few steps 37
how drunk he is. He has been in bars all day and can barely keep himself from
falling into the traffic.

I say goodbye to B. J. in front of the Eaton Centre and head inside,   38
watching him one more time through the glass, holding his hand out in the
night, as though he were reaching for salmon in a big-city river of shoppers.

Day 7
A Shelter Amid Affluence

On the coldest night so far in December, every downtown shelter was beyond   39
capacity, so I took a subway token from Out of the Cold, plus a plate of stir-
fried chicken, and headed uptown to my last resort, a shelter in Blythwood
Road Baptist Church in affluent north Toronto.

Set on a tony street between three-storey detached houses, each festooned   40
with Christmas lights, the church and its Saturday-night shelter are at the high
end of the homeless universe. When I find the basement, the mattresses are
already laid out, and they're not the slit and stained ones I had at the
Salvation Army. These are firm, thick foam, covered with clean plastic.

Lying on the floor, against the far wall, a squeegee girl gives her boyfriend   41
a back rub, his shoulder tattoos exposed to the gym air. Next to them, a cat
sleeps, chained to a backpack. There are the usual people with troubles, talking to the night, and the regular natives whom I dined with a few nights
before at another church, already passed out on their mats.

Before I can find my own place, a woman says I'm still in time for dinner   42
and suggests I take a plate of shepherd's pie and vegetables, or some hot soup.
I say I'm stuffed, though I can't resist the dessert table, laced with cakes, a gin-
gerbread house and freshly brewed coffee, which the staff made when a
woman complained the old pot was watery.

I take a mug of coffee outside to sit on the front steps with Gary, a big,   43
bearded man I had met at another shelter. Up and down the street there are
Christmas lights to stare at, and above us a sky full of stars not visible downtown. Gary points to some of the intricate brick design in a neighbouring
house.

"This is a real traditional neighbourhood," he says, comparing it with his   44
own life now sleeping in a different place every night. "I bet these people
never have to go anywhere."

Gary has driven taxis and worked in the building trade as a draftsman,   45
but lately he hasn't been able to sit still, not since he "met a witch," a woman
who fleeced him of his money, he says. He's been on the move for three
years now, from shelter to shelter, saving what he can to get back on his feet.

"I'm tired of being a slave to the church floor," he says as we head   46
inside. He plans to have his own place by New Year's.

I nod appreciatively. There are the B. J.s, the people who will always live   47
on the street because of its freedoms. And then there are the Garys, who quietly have a plan to get off the street, if only they can manage their addictions
and illnesses.

In the morning, we're served fried eggs, hash browns, toast, Danish pas-   48
tries, cold cereal, orange juice and coffee as the church volunteers pick up our

mats and wash the floors. I realize that in the past week of free beds and free meals, I have not once been asked to do a thing, not even clean the dishes.

At 7:30 in the morning, we're thrown back on the street, where a van   49
waits to ferry people downtown. One of the overnight guests walks instead to the church parking lot to warm up his car. He's off for another day hauling scrap metal to dumps, a business that earns him $600 to $700 a week.

"I know I shouldn't be here," he says, stamping out his cigarette before   50
heading off for the day. "I shouldn't be in a shelter, but whenever I get money, I spend it all partying with the ladies."

As soon as we're off church property, just before 8 a.m., a couple of the   51
guys I'm with pull out bottles of Labatt Ice stowed in their jackets. A third pours whiskey from a flask into a plastic jug, mixing it with orange juice he took from the church basement in one of their ceramic mugs, which he chucks in a hedge.

This is my last day on the street, and I say goodbye to the others on the   52
bus, which we have pretty much to ourselves since a couple of middle-aged women moved to sit next to the driver, driven away by our noise. One of the men tells me to go to Blessed Sacrament Church tonight, up Yonge Street. The food is always good.

"Hey, man," he says, as I head for the door. "Have a good day."   53

Epilogue

When I had set out a week earlier to live homeless, I did not expect to be   54
eating pancakes and sausage for breakfast and pastries before bed, or to earn $20 an hour simply by sitting on the ground with a cardboard sign in front of me. Nor did I expect to see so much crack flowing through the shelters whose very names have, for years, been the representation of public goodwill.

When I stepped into the shadows of homelessness, for admittedly a fleet-   55
ing moment, I also did not expect to find the isolation and belittlement that make the street so much more a psychological challenge than a physical one.

I was surprised by the enormous public compassion and desire to see that   56
no one in our society live this way. And I was taken by the large social infra-structure for the homeless, at least to get them through the night—the shelters, meal centres and emergency vans—as much as it needs to better weed out the freeloaders.

But what struck me most when I headed home (a luxury I always knew   57
I had), was the large public desire to find a "solution," as though homeless-ness was a disease and a cure could be discovered.

I could only think of how diverse were the people I met—from Dexter,   58
the hard-working ex-con, to Peter, the dry-waller and inveterate gambler, to Dwight, the crack-head guitarist—and how each has problems, often unre-lated to shelter, that are far different from the other.

Perhaps when we stop talking about the "homeless" as though theirs   59
were a separate world, when we start seeing people such as Dexter, Peter and Dwight as integral pieces of our society, maybe then we can do more than just get them through the night.

■   ■   ■

Discussion and Writing Suggestions

1. If you could ask the author a question about his experience living the life of a homeless person, what would it be? In doing this sort of research or journalism, there are ethical concerns. How long does one need to adopt a role in order to begin to "fit in" and gain insight into a way of life? Can such "impersonation" be ethical?

2. How would you characterize the tone of this article? Does Stackhouse seem to like or respect the homeless people he describes? Does he seem to be fair-minded in presenting the evidence?

3. Compare the way in which Stackhouse presents the experience of being homeless to the way in which it is treated by Thomas O'Reilly-Fleming. Consider how the conventions of journalism and academic writing are apparent, respectively, in each writer's approach.

The Homeless: Are We Part of the Problem?

JACK LAYTON

Jack Layton, leader of the NDP, served as the president of the Federation of Canadian Municipalities and chaired its National Housing Policy Options team. His work at the Federation led to the creation of a coalition of municipalities from across Canada that work together for a renewed federal housing policy. As a member of Toronto's council he co-chaired the Homeless Advisory Committee, which provided a vital policy link to front-line workers and people who have experienced homelessness. He is the author of Homelessness: The Making and Unmaking of a Crisis. *Layton has taught urban studies at all of Toronto's universities and is now adjunct professor in the planning program of the geography department at the University of Toronto.*

In the following article that appeared in The Globe and Mail *in December of 1999, written specifically to rebut John Stackhouse's article "'I'm Tired of Being a Slave to the Church Floor,'" Layton calls for action to solve the "looming housing crisis" in Canada. He is critical of Stackhouse's field-research approach to homelessness, saying that trying to understand the problem by spending seven days on the street requires "ignoring years of research in favour of a week outdoors."*

It couldn't have been worse timed.   1

Just when we thought we had broken through the Canadian conscious-   2
ness and begun to forge a national consensus on the problem of homelessness, along came *Globe and Mail* reporter John Stackhouse and his pretense of life on the street.

The day after Claudette Bradshaw, the federal co-ordinator for home-   3
lessness, announced in Toronto that the government would contribute
$753-million to build housing and shelters, Mr. Stackhouse, ignoring years of
research in favour of a week outdoors, told us that public resources are used
by crack dealers, that beggars earn professional wages and that "there is
more free food than the homeless can eat."

Most people I know have been reading and talking about the series ever   4
since, but for many of the wrong reasons. I could hear the cynical "I told you
so" reverberating over morning coffee.

Mr. Stackhouse's seven-day masquerade among the thousands of legiti-   5
mately homeless on Toronto's streets has done a great disservice to these
people.

This is not to say that there was nothing valuable in the three-part series.   6
Reading all the diaries allowed us to reach the conclusions where Mr.
Stackhouse offers wisdom. He suggests that simply expanding emergency
services month after month will not solve the problems that the homeless face.
More government money, he says, will solve the problem only if it gets to the
root of the high cost of urban housing and addresses crack and alcohol abuse.
In these solid conclusions, the author is repeating fragments of the compre-
hensive plans developed by those who devoted years to the study of the issue.

The problem is that, in getting to these conclusions, he fans the flames of   7
the "blame the victim" psychology that motivates those who deny any social
responsibility for the homeless crisis.

Now, anyone who spent eight years reporting on the affairs of countries   8
with average per-capita incomes measured in hundreds of dollars would have
a unique perspective on homelessness in Toronto. To someone who watched
as meagre grains of rice were distributed to outstretched hands in wartorn
refugee camps, a church basement breakfast served up by volunteers complete
with eggs, fruit and hot coffee would seem luxurious.

But does that warrant calling people who go to these breakfasts "free-   9
loaders"?

In a way, still, the series had the surreal feel of a report from the front   10
lines by a journalist dropped into a foreign land by parachute. This journalist was, fortunately, secure in knowing he'd be brought back to home base
after the seven-day assignment. His security made his situation fundamentally different than the people he was trying to mimic.

And therein lies the problem. Pretending not to have a home can never be   11
the same as not having one at all.

Knowing you have a home means you are not without hope. Many on   12
the street are, literally, without hope or home. The bravado we saw some
homeless people express to the newcomer on the streets is only one expression
of that hopelessness—carving out an identity, masking the reality with display.

When the entrepreneurship that beggars illustrated as they ganged up to   13
protect their turf forced small fry such as Mr. Stackhouse out of the subway

station, the actions were implicitly criticized. Yet the same entrepreneurship exercised upstairs in the bank towers is celebrated. The more takeovers, mergers and market share, the better! Panhandlers were merely replicating the titans of business.

The reportage was best in its accounts of how ordinary Torontonians 14 reacted to the homeless: "I've seen women give money and kind words 10 times more often than men."

Mr. Stackhouse's successful days of panhandling suggest that 15 Torontonians are generous people and do not blame others for the conditions in which they find themselves.

Let's suppose that the series about seven days in the lives of a city's 16 homeless had been written by people who had been homeless themselves but had found a way out. How would it have been different?

The daily struggles to find housing would have played a more prominent 17 part in the narrative. Thousands of people calling the homelessness hotline trying desperately to find a place. Those who have escaped from the cycle of homelessness invariably focus on the importance of having their own safe and affordable place. A home has often been the starting point for recovery.

In Toronto, a homeless addict finishing a treatment program is tossed 18 back out into the street and emergency environment. There's no home in which to carry out a long-term recovery. A person struggling with a mental-health challenge, complete with a medication regime, is left on the streets with no secure place to be well. A convict is released from prison, again to the streets, only to be recycled through the system once again. Emergency wards and hospitals discharge people to the streets and hostels when what they really need is a healthy house and some personal support so they can recuperate.

The diary of the truly homeless would also see the simple desire to be 19 treated with respect rising powerfully to the surface. Whatever the pathway to homelessness might have been, support and respect have to characterize the way out.

Success stories can be found amongst the emergency programs. These are 20 the ones that have been founded on these three key principles: The housing must be secure so you do not have to line up night after night in the cold for a mat or cot; respect, encouragement and careful support for the wounds and personal challenges faced by each homeless individual must be present; and, in the best programs, homeless people themselves actually have some say about what happens to them.

Emergency shelters alone are not the answer, that's for sure. The old 21 slogan "homes not hostels" still applies. Besides, shelters are terribly expensive compared to permanent housing. At $25 000 to $40 000 a shelter bed a year, we could house five people in long-term housing for the same price. The taxpayer would win and so would those facing homelessness. Do we really want more hostels when we could have positive supportive programs such as Homes First, an operation in the city centre? Homes First focuses on providing permanent housing while addressing the individual needs of each resident. It's all done in a climate of respect.

Mr. Stackhouse acknowledges the effects of the loss of respect he felt as   22
a homeless person on our streets. Even though his homelessness was temporary, he knew in his gut what could happen to his humanity, stripped of an
identity, of his own place in our city. Re-establishing his place, and the place
of all those facing the looming housing crisis, requires housing, respect and
support, all of which will take dollars. But they will be well spent.

Discussion and Writing Suggestions

1. If you could interview this author about his response to Stackhouse, what
   would you ask him?
2. Layton addresses the issue of the homeless in Toronto. For those of us who
   live outside Toronto, do you think any of his observations are still pertinent?
3. As national leader of the NDP, has Jack Layton been able to put any of his
   approaches or solutions to solving homelessness into practice?

■ ■ ■

Life on the Streets

THOMAS O'REILLY-FLEMING

This is a chapter excerpt from Down and Out in Canada, *a scholarly book published in 1993 that helped to set the tone for much of the Canadian debate about
the plight of the homeless. Dr. O'Reilly-Fleming, then a professor at the University
of Windsor, lived with the homeless for about a year in order to conduct his
ethnography.*

One of the central problems of our attempts to understand the homeless   1
resides in explaining why they have been cast off by the mainstream of society. When I interviewed homeless people throughout this country, two questions were the focus of much of the discussion that took place. First, why do
people become trapped within the cycles of homelessness for months or even
years? Secondly, what is it about the life course of these individuals that has
locked them into a cycle of despair? The answers to both these questions were
neither simple nor easily explored with homeless people. In a sense one is
asking how a person constructs reality, and to reflect more deeply upon the
forces, both personal and structural, that have brought them to this position
as a social pariah. While it is not possible in the constraints of a book such as
this to record every life story of homeless persons, it is possible to provide
accounts of lives that reflect broader themes in the construction of a homeless
identity in Canadian society. From these accounts, it has been possible to construct images of the process of being homeless and the role played by the

homeless and various social service agencies in ameliorating and/or perpetuating the homeless condition.

While no single explanation of either the causes or the realities of homeless existence would be fair to the variety of individual life courses developed by homeless people, there are commonalities which link their experiences. Further, this chapter will proceed first to present the experience of homelessness from the viewpoint of various homeless "groups" and social service personnel and then move on to an analysis of the core problems that predominate in relegating, and keeping, homeless people in the position of societal misfits. Finally, the lifeworks of the homeless will be put into perspective by a critical examination of the various forms of legal control that regulate their lives, from municipal by-laws through to welfare regulations.

Just Getting By

To the average observer, Joe is a typical 24-year-old. He is well groomed and dressed in neat blue jeans, a striped clean shirt, running shoes and a pale blue windbreaker. He has a pleasant personality and a direct manner of speaking. He talks in an animated style, is intelligent and able to contemplate his life with insight and directness. Joe is homeless. Joe has not always been homeless. Neither is he a victim of a child welfare system that cannot cope with its all too many charges. He does not have a problem with alcohol or drugs, although he has used "coke." His behaviour is not pathological. Joe's story is one that tells us much about the series of contingencies that can move one from full status in our society to its farthest margins. As we begin our interview, I tell him what we will be exploring. He immediately blurted out the following summary of his life, "I left home at 16, got myself a job working for a cleaner, pretty soon I had my own contacts and started a company. I got married at 18, had two kids, and had a house and a mortgage. My wife left me and after that I couldn't take it and started using cocaine. Pretty soon I couldn't pay the bills and I didn't care anymore. I lost everything and now I'm here."

Joe is used to telling his story to social workers and has developed a one minute travelogue to guide them through his life. It is a symptom that is prevalent amongst the homeless, tired of talking about the same "sad" story to worker after worker who is either looking for the root cause of their homelessness or simply going through the motions of filling out the forms. Front line workers and those that do intakes with the homeless at shelters and hostels often explain the behaviour of the homeless in terms of one overriding problem. For teens this is most often abuse, whether physical or sexual; for men it is frequently a problem with booze or drugs; for families the problem is one characterized by social dependency handed down from generation to generation. The real dimensions of the problems of the homeless like Joe may lie hidden in much more complex contingencies that affect their life, but are less amenable to quick diagnoses and quick fixes. In this, workers fall prey to the process of labelling people, an approach that sociologists have long explored. Labels, while they may simplify the world, are often constructed at the expense of some loss to those labelled. Howard Becker, a well-known sociologist, instructs us that, "Deviance is behavior that is so labelled." In other words, the labelling of a person as "someone with a booze problem" or "the product of an abused home" has the effect of transforming them into a deviant individual. In this characterization their current position in society as a homeless person reflects some personal failing, inadequacy or lack of effort.[1] Persons in our society who are so labelled are therefore seen as being the authors of their own problems. Although on one level we may have some sympathy for the homeless person, the refusal to look more deeply into the roots of homelessness as a structural problem in society has had immediate consequences both for the treatment of the homeless person as a dependant in the social welfare network, and in their view of themselves. One feature of labelling is that persons may, after countless interactions in which this label is reaffirmed, begin to self-label themselves as having a problem that is largely beyond their control.[2] At the same time they are constantly confronted with it by social workers and other agency staff. The homeless person develops what has been termed a **master status**, which means that once one learns about their problem, one knows all one needs to in order to interact with the individual.

Joe is viewed as a young man with intelligence and potential by the staff.   5 In his own words, "I can do the job of the staff when you come right down to it. They all know it. I had my own business for several years, so this is nothing." Joe is also seen as a man whose homelessness is related to his "drug problem." A further analysis of Joe's story is instructive in terms of both the factors that lead to homelessness and the reasons that persons often remain stuck in a homeless situation for long periods of time.

During his marriage, relations with his wife were good according to Joe.   6 He and his wife were well off financially and enjoyed each other's company. Joe enjoyed drinking occasionally at a local bar, and there a young woman, a friend of his brother's, became infatuated with him. She often joined him, his brother and his brother's girlfriend for a drink. She asked Joe to have sex with her on several occasions but he refused, telling her he was happily married with children. One evening Joe returned to his home to find that his wife was extremely upset and was packing to leave with the children. Apparently, the young woman who desired his sexual attention had gone to his home and told his wife that she had been having an affair with her husband, "and went into all of the details of having sex and how I didn't love her anymore." His wife did not believe his story regarding the other woman despite the support of others who had seen him interact with her. His wife left him and soon after he "slumped into a deep, deep depression." As Joe describes it, "Nothing meant anything to me anymore. I loved my wife and children and it just didn't make any sense. I hadn't done anything and here I was being punished." Soon Joe was drinking constantly and began to take cocaine to dull the pain of the loss of his family. "I just didn't care about anything anymore, like if the world can be that cruel when you're a good guy, work hard, give your family a good life, what's the point?" In the end Joe lost his business, then his house, and within a few months of his wife's departure he was homeless.

Now after almost a year in various homeless shelters in several cities he is able to reflect on his fall from "normalcy." "A lot of the staff think my problem is cocaine, but I haven't done any since I became homeless. My problem is I get overwhelmed by thinking about starting out again. I guess I've earned some time off to think and get a new start. I don't want to get back into the mainstream of society right away, I've got to get my head straight. I can do it again easily, that's not the hard part (getting a job) it's knowing that I've found out what I need, then I'll be outta here." So for Joe, homelessness presents somewhat of a resting place from some of the pressures of society. What he is as a person cannot be taken away from him; he is one of the small number of homeless who can understand the label accorded them, but has the personal resources to reject this label and remain optimistic about the future. Joe observes, "Look, just because a guy loses some money that doesn't mean he's stupid. Look at Donald Trump. He lost millions. Do you hear anyone saying he's stupid, that he won't climb back again? It's all relative to where you are in society and how much you can afford to lose without sinking into a hole. I'll be back, but when it's right for me." Far from being simple bragging, Joe's comments are based in his belief in his own abilities and his assessment of his current state of mind. Like many homeless interviewed, Joe had lost his connections or bonds to society when, as a good citizen doing what he felt were the right things, his world was wrongfully demolished. This was a world, then, that he could no longer simply continue to invest in. His adaptations through alcohol and cocaine resulted in his demise as a person with a stake in society, but it was precisely because he did not want a stake in a society that he saw as having betrayed him.

Going Down Slow

Jake is a native Canadian who is 26 years of age. Born on a Saskatchewan farm, he is currently living in a men's shelter in Vancouver. He is immaculately dressed in clean deep blue jogging shorts, running shoes and a crisp white shirt. He does not have a dishevelled appearance traditionally, and mistakenly today, accorded to the homeless. Jake has short neat black hair that is clean. He is well groomed and could easily be mistaken for one of the social workers in the local shelter. He is pleasant and his perceptions of his own situation are clear and unwashed. Jake left the family farm when he was 16 years old. He had been adopted from the reserve into a white farm family, and completed a high school education. "After that I met my wife. I married her when she was 16; I was 19 at the time. That was the bad thing, at that time coming off of the farm and I guess the stress of a new child in the family. I guess if I looked hard enough . . . it was wham, bam thank you ma'am and you find yourself in a predicament that you totally don't need to." He describes his adoptive parents as "the most supportive people I know. See, in Saskatchewan they distinguish between the Indian and white people whatever." Jake loved school and said in the interview, "I'd've loved to go back to school."

Jake finally got work just before the birth of his first child. He feels that   9 his daughter "changed his life quite a bit." He was employed as a farm labourer, and had a natural knack with engines. "I could run anything, I still can run any tractor and combine, you name it I can run it. I know how to weld . . . ."

What happened in Jake's life to bring him to the margins of existence?   10 "Everything was going great like before I came out here in February of last year. I was incarcerated for 18 months. At that time I was drinking and it was a violent crime you know. Took a baseball bat, fought with a guy over a hundred dollars, took his knees out, it's just as simple as that, and obviously the courts didn't think too much of it." Previously he had spent five years in prison in Saskatchewan for committing an armed robbery. "I guess, I don't know maybe I wanted to prove something. I don't know what it was. I could see that upsetting the marriage, I mean, wouldn't you?"

Jake spent the time after prison working in a well-known restaurant bar.   11 "It's great. The thing that happened to me I got burnt out, burn out syndrome . . . like six days a week and when you're on a management team and you're working on salary it doesn't matter how many hours you put in." Jake made $500 a week at the job take home pay and had an apartment that cost $460 a month. "I just don't know what went wrong really." Jake had no savings when he quit his job in July of 1991. "I don't know, I bought a lot of things. I don't know, I'm a material person. I like to buy a t.v., everything, you see, you know that you may want later . . . like I've still got all of this in storage." Jake had worked for almost 18 months full time six days a week in a progressively more responsible position, finally achieving the status of kitchen manager. He suddenly found one day that his will to work had left him. For him, homelessness was an oasis away from the responsibilities he was being asked to perform to survive. "It's not that I'm lazy or anything. I just want to get my head clear. I've only been off work for a couple of months." Although he is entitled to unemployment he does not collect it, a view of welfare support that is widely espoused by homeless people. Welfare of any kind places a person in a position of perceived dependency. As psychopaths I researched in a hospital in Britain put it, "Don't give me a gift, then I'm in debt to you." The homeless do not want to accumulate any more social debts than possible and often view various forms of welfare above the minimum required to survive with a jaundiced eye. As Jake put it, "Yes, I'm entitled to it but if I wanted to abuse the system I could go ahead and abuse the system up and down and left and centre and without paying anything but I don't want to do it. That's not what I'm after. I just want to get my head cleared."

The Loner

Dave is 27 years old and comes from a foster parent background. He left 12
home at 16 and has been living in the shelter system and on the street ever
since. He displays the signs of complete dependence on the system and has
resigned himself to shelter life. He rarely breaks the cycle of dependency:

I'll meet somebody like a friend or a girl. I may stay there for a couple of 13
weeks just for the hell of it depending on the situation. I'm basically here
though because I don't like livin' with other people ... it's not right, I'm not
used to it. Well, it's a matter of pride and dignity you know, you feel weird
you know like, I'm just not used to it. I don't like the idea, I'm uh, like a loner.

Dave is indeed an outcast from society. He has no friends and his only 14
forms of social communication come with social workers and drinking buddies in the parks. He lives hedonistically enjoying the moment since the future
is unreal for him:

Some people have their own style of living, my style just happens to be 15
have a good time ... you're limited to the amount of friends you have (in the
shelter). The hostel's full of all kinds of people, grubby people, ignorant
people, people who have no brains, ignorant people, people who have no
ambition, people who drink and they can't do anything like they're idiots so
I meet the odd person I can get along with.

While he accepts his own limitations as a fully functioning human being, 16
he does not place blame for the predicament which besets homeless people on
the system. He voices a common view that the homeless are the source of their
own problems:

Yah either drugs or they just screwed up ... (Is it the system that screwed 17
up?) No, no I don't believe that for one minute. Well okay, it's hard to get
work but there's a lot of people here that complain about work but they don't
even try to get up and look. They don't even know how to comb their hair.
They don't even know how to present themselves so how are they gonna get
a job? They stay out all night drinkin', they wake up with a hangover, it's just
that they're abusing the system.

For Dave, his current homeless condition is explained as a temporary 18
state of affairs though it has lasted over six months now:

I'm not rushin nothin'. I'm just gonna reconstruct my life slowly. I'm not 19
gonna rush nothin' cause I've got enough grey hair. I'm just gonna do it, but
do it slowly and casually, and be happy that's all. I wanna take care of the
mind. No stress, no nothin'.

While Dave portrays his homelessness as being relatively free of stress, in 20
actual fact he is constantly under pressure by the front line workers to seek
employment, is constantly searching for a place to stay, and is subject to the
rigours of street life. While being interviewed he sported deep healing cuts on
his face, the result of a brawl in a local bar. Such wounds are common in the
sample interviewed for this book, as violence in many forms is endemic to
homeless life.

Dave, in concert with many of his fellow homeless, views his current state   21
of affairs as a form of relative freedom, having exchanged the pressures of the
workplace for the problems of the street. He sees himself as having: 22

Lots of freedom . . . in respect of somebody telling me where to go, how
to do it, or you know, what to do.

Fighting Docility: Social Control Agencies Versus the Homeless

For homeless Canadians, social service, welfare, and helping agencies are   23
often viewed in a negative context as more likely to hurt them than help them.
Despite the best and worst intentions of each of these types of agencies,
homeless people have instinctively and through numerous encounters with the
therapeutic enterprise come to realize that they are often better off with a minimum of recourse to the state for assistance. Sociologists, like Stan Cohen,
have described the "net" of control that extends throughout society.[3] He
argues that all social service functions are either implicitly themselves, or are
tied to institutions that control the behaviour of those considered "different"
in society. Canadian civil rights activist Alan Borovoy has written about our
society's limited ability to tolerate behaviour of others that we find even
mildly irritating.[4] Whether it is a group of picketers trying to protest to protect their jobs, or a homeless person asking for assistance, we often expect
someone to remove them from view, in essence, to control them.

The homeless do not have a single identity in the world of helping agen-   24
cies. As I argued earlier, homeless persons are often assigned a master status
that helps social service personnel to "get a fix" on them, and explain their
present and previous behaviours. Various agencies assign the homeless to
differing categories to fit the mandate of their organization. A homeless
person may be an alcohol abuser for one agency, an unemployable person for
another group, and a person with mental problems at another facility.
Although these may form either significant or minor facets of their personality, the point is that they face a constant stripping down of self and categorization into multiple deviant selves as they move from agency to agency. The
homeless also become "known" on their trek through various shelters and
hostels. Their thick accumulating files become less of an aid to assisting them
and more of a means of denigrating their lack of success in altering their life
circumstances, and of providing material for cutting personal criticisms. At
the same time, the homeless represent fodder for the various agencies' struggle to assert "ownership" over the homeless problem. The homeless, like
other marginalized groups, such as criminals, make possible the existence of
a wide variety of "helping" agencies who, besides assisting the homeless,
"help" themselves to substantial salaries.

The homeless sense, and are the victims of, this interconnectedness of   25
agencies. The homeless are reduced to a state of childlike dependency. Critics
of the welfare system have long been aware of the inadequacies of a system of
assistance that is characterized by over-bureaucratization, inhumanity and
mistrust. Ben Carniol, a professor and social worker at Ryerson Polytechnic,

has written scathingly of this system. He writes what we commonly understand but is often disputed: "It has become commonplace for people in need to desperately try to avoid getting into the welfare system in the first place."[5] Tied in with this concept of attempting to remain above the dark and forbidding waters of the welfare ocean is the recurring myth of capitalist culture, "the belief that each individual has both the responsibility and the opportunity to 'make it.'" Echoing the words of persons interviewed across Canada for this book, Carniol's sample of welfare recipients found that there was "most often a debilitating sense of dehumanization in being on welfare."[6] In fact, most homeless persons, as with the overwhelming majority of welfare recipients, go to great lengths to avoid being on welfare. Being "on the pogey" even for the homeless means that one has hit bottom, has sunk to a state of total dependency with no resources left to draw upon. Many, on contemplating the status of welfare recipients, will starve themselves, commit petty crimes, beg, take the most menial of underpaid jobs or even prostitute themselves, to stay off the dole.

The medicalization of the problems of the homeless is a common approach taken by social agencies in Canada. Although all homeless are subject to categorization as somehow being slightly less than whole, women are far more commonly the brunt of such approaches. While viewing the homeless problem as emanating most centrally from some form of "sickness" in the form of depression or some other form of mental malady has a certain appeal in that ill health may be attacked by medical intervention; a more sinister interpretation is that the illness is chronic. Again, by shifting the blame onto the victim, in this case often of family violence, or of oppression by a male partner, and in the wider realms of society, as well as by asserting that the problem is largely psychological, the burden for recovery lands once again in the lap of the downtrodden. These strategic interventions put social workers in the position of reinforcing and adding to the negative images of their supposed clients. The woman is now not only homeless, but suffering from some form of mental illness! How reassuring to be a single mother thrust out from the security of one's home only to be declared essentially insane by a helpful social worker! One woman interviewed in Vancouver put it this way, "My husband left and it was a couple of months until everything fell apart. No one could help me anymore or they didn't want to, and so I had to go on welfare. Jesus, the first thing they told me was that I was sick and needed help, as if I didn't have enough worries. So I told the worker, 'Who the fuck wouldn't be depressed, no husband, no money, no place to live, no job and now I have to listen to this.'" Helen Levine wrote compellingly about the impotency of women in modern social relations who are encouraged to be the authors of their own destruction. Levine wrote it "is an insidious tool used to contain women's rage and despair to invalidate our experience of the world." Eventually, usually sooner than later, it results in "guilt, anxiety and depression" keeping women "docile and fearful, unable to act on our own behalf."[7] More destructive than this process, Levine argues, and more damnable, is the collusion that is exercised by the so-called helping professions who "in practice as in theory, collude with and reinforce the self-destruct mechanism in women."[8]

Through 20 years of reports on welfare by federal and provincial governments, two constant themes have emerged. One is that of alienation of the recipients within the process who feel lessened by the treatment they receive attempting to collect what is essentially a social right. Secondly, those who look after the welfare system, and its many manifestations through the shelters and hostels of the country, are disenchanted with the system and its recipients. Throughout the system of social services across this country, humanity is in short supply as recipients of any form of benefit are forced to act as beggars in order to receive their due, supplicating at the altar of the welfare agent. Doyle and Visano's report on social welfare services underscores the constant barrage of intimidation and humiliation that awaits those who must queue in the lengthening welfare lines in this country, the longest now in history.[9] The very position that the homeless find themselves in, asking for assistance, provides reinforcement that these are people who are not part of the "deserving poor," that is, those who are not personally responsible for their own sorrows. The systematic inferiorization of the homeless, the constant reminding of this status, and its continual reaffirmation in consultations between agents and agencies informs the homeless person that they are branded and stigmatized wherever they turn.

Little wonder that in a few months the homeless person has often slid into a state of dependency unable to see any means of altering their station in life. Workers that are in a position to assist them are also in an equal position to withhold services, finances, shelter, and advice. My overwhelming impression of the interviews between social workers and the homeless during some four years of research was that the worker has certain ideas about the character and problems of the individual. The worker ideally is supposed to work with the client on strategies for achieving certain goals, most generally, obtaining employment. However, the worker generally winds up lecturing the client on his/her inadequacies and lack of personal effort. The exchange is not one of equals working to solve a problem but is more accurately characterized as an exercise in control on the part of the worker. Workers often do not consciously realize that they are engaged in this process. Many genuinely wish to help their clients. A greater number, however, have grown tired of "the whining" and "laziness" of their charges. With staggering caseloads and the demand for shelter space constant, and growing, they are faced with an unending stream of anxious would-be shelter residents throughout the day. As a young female worker at one shelter put it, "I see 15 or more every day here wanting to get in. They've usually got files several inches thick and they're hopeless. You go through the same routine you did last time and they still don't do a thing to help themselves. I'm leaving this job in two months and going to . . . . After two years in welfare and two years here I've had it. You tell these people, 'Yes there's welfare, but you've got to do something for yourself.' They have no idea, no idea at all." The homeless person is not in a position to seek other alternatives if they don't like the service they are receiving. The immediate concerns of getting a place to stay are paramount, and realistically they understand that they are without the power to complain. Who would listen to a complaint by a homeless person? The homeless made their complaints over and over again to the writer in the course of interviews and conversations, but they remain secret and whispered for fear of losing even the little they have managed to wrangle from the welfare system.

Few homeless people will admit to ever being physically ill, ill enough,   29 that is, to require medical treatment. Few of the homeless trust doctors or hospitals to treat them without some other obligation on their part being involved. Many fear that seeking treatment for an illness or injury will result in their being institutionalized as mentally ill. As one 25-year-old put it, "If you go to an emergency room looking this bad they'll think you've lost your marbles and try to lock you up as crazy." Medical personnel are also viewed as having links to the police and other social agencies, which they certainly do. Many of the homeless do not want any involvement with the police and so avoid doctors. Going to a physician also requires that a person give their name, address if available, and a health insurance number. There are many homeless who do not want to make this kind of information available to others, whether they are inmates on parole seeking to avoid possible trouble, persons who do not want to be found for a variety of reasons, or simply those who harbour unfounded fears. Some shelters have developed a relationship with a local doctor and/or nurse to provide on-site treatment on a weekly basis without the necessity for patients to divulge information they would not be comfortable giving. In Toronto, two nurses run a drop-in clinic where homeless men and women can have their afflictions tended to without giving any information on themselves. Most commonly they are treated for ailments related to their feet or hands—exposure, hypothermia—and breathing disorders. Their clinic has been operating successfully for over two years and has been able to avoid the intrusion of the medical establishment and the paraphernalia of paranoia that over-formalization seems to bring in the minds of the homeless.

"Laws Are for Rich People"

Laws have particular functions in our society. The homeless, being both with-   30 out accommodation and hence visible on the street, are subject to an inordinate amount of attention on the part of the police and other agents of control in our society. Previously in this chapter it was argued that society organizes its control institutions into a form of network. The social analyst Michel Foucault referred to the ability of these institutions to exert power over the lives of individuals in society, to make them into docile citizens, as the "micropolitics of control."[10] Of any group in Canada, the homeless are most subject to the ministrations of these control measures, and their lives are largely circumscribed by both formal and informal regulation by welfare rules, by-laws and criminal laws. In this section, the impact of these various legal sanctions on the lives of homeless people will be explored.

Welfare Regulation: The Politics of Exclusion

While social assistance is intended as a safety net for those who become most vulnerable in society, the rules surrounding the acquisition of entitlement to welfare are questionable at best.[11] It may reasonably be argued that the current welfare system does much to perpetuate the problems of the homeless by short-circuiting their attempts to re-establish themselves in the mainstream of society. The first and most significant problem with the welfare system is the ridiculous requirement that persons must have a place of residence in order to receive a welfare cheque. Without a place to stay that has an identifiable address, a homeless person is not permitted any form of assistance. Many of the homeless do not, and will perhaps never, have any address other than an abandoned car, a neglected dumpster, or a park bench. Are they any less deserving of help? Obviously, it is these individuals who are most in need of sustenance, but are rendered ineligible because they do not have a place to stay. It is the great Catch-22 of homelessness: in order to get a home you have to have welfare; if you don't have a home you can't collect welfare. Although some jurisdictions, most notably in Montreal, have developed innovative schemes to counter this inequity in our welfare system, few homeless people in this country can collect assistance without first getting enmeshed in the social control system. In other words, most homeless have to seek residence at a shelter or hostel, which then becomes their address for the purposes of welfare. 31

In many provinces, persons are entitled to "emergency" welfare cheques when they first present themselves to a shelter. In Ontario, they may collect slightly more than $300 under this scheme. However, one of the further problems with the residence requirements is the transient nature of the homeless population. There are, again, a not insignificant number of homeless persons who leave the shelter before a cheque can arrive. While this behaviour strikes the uninformed as incredible, one must put it in the context of life in degrading, threatening, and sometimes violent lodgings. Whether one is threatened, gets fed up with being treated badly or simply wanders off because of a lack of investment in life, cheques are often undeliverable because the intended recipient has left the address given. 32

While there are many critics of public assistance for the needy, few would want to change places with the homeless despite their criticisms of them as lazy and shiftless. This attitude was expressed by Mike Harris, the leader of the Ontario Progressive Conservative party. Harris argued before a business luncheon at The Canadian Club that welfare recipients abuse the system. He stated, "I'm suggesting that we should not be paying out all that money to stay home and do nothing."[12] While Harris argues that the majority on welfare can be trained or educated for jobs, and suggests tying welfare payments to compliance with these initiatives, he demonstrated a complete ignorance of 33 the plight of homeless Canadians. If one considers a single mother of one child as a homeless person who will collect social assistance, then how will she accomplish retraining? If she has a preschool child it is expected that some-how she will arrange for the care of the child during her retraining. While this may seem a practical idea, any cursory examination of child care in this country leads one to the simple conclusion that it is in short supply and high demand. Even if the mother were to be able to secure a place in a childcare setting for her child, it is unlikely she will be able to afford it while retraining herself for employment that is going to yield a wage insufficient to meet her childcare expenses. The alternative is to leave her child in suspect care, spend-ing her working days worrying constantly about her child's welfare. Women with children suffer more greatly than any other group amongst our homeless population for there is little societal comprehension of the impossibilities associated with trying to provide a decent life on a meagre allowance while juggling several disparate roles. Welfare remains for the most part as a form of indentured pauperism.

Endnotes

[1] See Howard S. Becker, *Outsiders*, New York: Free Press, 1963. Ostensibly the argument is that no behaviour is deviant until it is so labelled by society. The use of LSD, for example, was not illegal in the U.S.A. until the late 1960s when its use became criminalized. Before that point it was one of the "tolerable" deviances in our society, as Robert Stebbins pointed out in his work *Deviance: Tolerable Differences*, Toronto: Prentice-Hall, 1988. This process is referred to as labelling. While some labels have little effect on those to whom they are applied, others may carry significant weight in terms of evoking negative societal reactions. The label "ex-criminal" has moral, legal and social implications, while the label "lazy" car-ries with it more limited sanctions.

[2] Richard Ericson's early study of released delinquents in Britain, *Young Offenders and Their Social Work*, Farnborough: Gower, 1975, is one of the finest examples of field research on a group that engaged in self-labelling. For an exhaustive analysis of labelling theory see R. Ericson, *Criminal Reactions: The Labelling Perspective*, Farnborough: Gower, 1975.

[3] Stan Cohen, "The Punitive City: Notes on the Dispersal of Social Control," *Contemporary Crises*, Vol. 3, 1979: 339–363, and Stan Cohen, *Visions of Social Control: Crime, Punishment and Classification*, Cambridge: Polity Press, 1985. According to Cohen, the net of control is growing progressively wider in contem-porary society and the mesh is becoming increasingly smaller, trapping persons who were formerly of no interest to social control agencies in its web. This is, in essence, an outgrowth of the increasing size of control agencies like the police and the progress in technological invasion into privacy. This argument is very similar to that produced by Emile Durkheim on the boundary maintenance functions of deviance; that is, as the system of control swallows up all of the most visible and severe forms of deviance, new more marginal types of deviance will be scanned for

infractions and be subject to criminalization. See my earlier article, "The Bawdy House Boys: Some Notes on Media, Sporadic Moral Crusades and Selective Law Enforcement," *Canadian Criminology Forum*, Vol. 3, No. 3, 1981.

[4] Borovoy, *ibid.*

[5] Ben Carniol, *Case Critical: Challenging Social Work in Canada*, Second Edition, Toronto: Between the Lines, 1990–91.

[6] *Ibid.*, 92.

[7] Helen Levine, "The Personal Is Political: Feminism and the Helping Professions," in A. Miles and G. Finn (eds.), *Feminism in Canada: From Pressure to Politics*, Montreal: Black Rose, 1982.

[8] *Ibid.*, 91.

[9] Robert Doyle and L. Visano, *A Time for Action!—Access to Health and Social Services for Members of Diverse Cultural and Racial Groups in Metropolitan Toronto* (Report 1), Toronto: Social Planning Council of Metropolitan Toronto, 1987.

[10] M. Foucault, *ibid.*

[11] For a feminist analysis see J. Dale and P. Foster, *Feminists and State Welfare*, London: RKP, 1986. See also *The General Welfare Assistance Act*, Sec 1 (i) (i) Chapter 188, R.S.C. Statutes of Canada; The Special Senate Subcommittee on Poverty, Poverty in Canada, Ottawa: Information Canada, 1971: 83 found that the welfare process was degrading to all parties involved in it: "It repels both the people who depend on the hand-outs and those who administer them. Alienation on the part of welfare recipients and disenchantment on the part of welfare administrators was evident. . . ." In Ontario, short-term benefits known as general welfare assistance typically are allocated to the jobless and those with temporary illnesses. Family benefits is a longer term form of aid and goes mainly to sole-support parents and disabled people. See also Richard Titmuss, *Commitment to Welfare*, London: Unwin, 1970.

[12] *The Windsor Star*, April 1990.

■ ■ ■

Discussion and Writing Suggestions

1. Compare the experience of homelessness as it is depicted in two or more case-study situations.
2. On the basis of O'Reilly-Fleming's presentation, is it possible to say if he has a liberal or conservative orientation in relation to the problem of homelessness?
3. Compare this writer's tone to that of Stackhouse and Layton. Does he strike a more objective stance?
4. What do the endnotes contribute to the ethos of this presentation?

Someone To Talk To:
Care and Control of the Homeless

TOM C. ALLEN

This excerpt comes from Tom C. Allen's book-length study of the homeless in Vancouver's Downtown Eastside (2000), which chronicles the cycle of poverty, marginalization and despair that moves people from homes to streets and shelters.

Tom C. Allen has worked in community services and teaches criminology at Kwantlen University College. He claims conflict resolution and peace making as among his research interests, and continues to study concepts of social control.

Getting By

The homeless are subject to processes of marginalization in their quest for safety, security and recognition. For these persons a lack of political power and social resources contributes to isolation, anxiety, frustration and rejection. Subsequently, the homeless person may engage in various strategies to get by:

> The survival strategies of homeless people may be regarded as spontaneous, random, contradictory, illogical, ill-conceived or even bizarre. But judgments of this sort, exposing the contents of mainstream society's cultural baggage and the need to hold the irksome other at arm's length, fail to comprehend the imperative of adaptation and change in a world which does not conform to dominant conceptions of "reality." . . . Life on the streets requires adherence to a different set of organizing principles, an alternate reality. (Daly 1996:11)

Needing to belong somewhere

The social isolation and disaffiliation that usually accompany homelessness can contribute to ill health, anxiety and depression, as well as intensify and aggravate individual problems, for "a sense of belonging is as important as the physical shelter in making a 'home'" (Grigsby et al. 1990:142). In order to cope with disaffiliation and the lack of social bonds and sustenance previously provided by family, friends or job, the homeless person may seek material assistance and emotional support from other homeless persons and networks. These ties may help the person to avoid isolation and thereby function outside traditional social roles, while at the same time contributing to an entrenchment of the homeless condition:

> The street offers . . . the spectacle of society without integration into its values: proximity, but not participation. It becomes symbolic of their distress . . . . It belongs to everybody and nobody, and puts everyone on the same footing. It cancels out the past and makes the future uncertain: only the present moment counts. (Agnelli, cited in Daly 1996:136)

Brian pictured the street scene as a place to escape and feel accepted,   3
regardless of one's condition:

> It's not just the drugs and alcohol, it's definitely the lifestyle that I'm
> attracted to. . . . Nobody cares, I guess. Attitude too. . . . You can pretty
> well do anything. You could still walk down the street and find someone
> to talk to, even though you haven't had a shower for a month. Even
> though that doesn't include myself but, you know what I mean, you
> don't even have to worry about nothing like, to care for yourself, your
> personal hygiene. I know a lot of people do that.

Jason, a twenty-eight-year-old male with a grade-three education, had   4
been at Triage for three days at the time of the interview. Jason had a long history of foster homes, alcohol or other drug treatment agencies, prisons and
jails (totaling over fifteen years when juvenile as well as adult incarceration is
included) and mental health facilities. At the time of the interview he had not
worked for more than four years, saying what prevented him from getting
employment was his criminal record and his disabled status, including dyslexia.
Jason, fearful of being by himself and needing to be around other people no
matter how tenuous the relationship, romanticized living in the downtown
hotels as providing a sense of belonging and companionship:

> When you go into a hotel . . . the reason why people usually do that is
> 'cause often they've left a shelter. They're used to communicating and
> living with a lot of people. A hotel will give that. There's always people
> around you. Even though . . . it's a negative influence, they're looking
> for that support, that family setting which they can find in a hotel. 'Cause
> there's a lot of people. You talk, you drink, you're around people con-
> stantly. You're never lonely. You always got someone to talk to.

Sally provided insight into Jason's idyllic perception of life in the rooms   5
when she referred to the underlying disconnection of those who end up
cycling between shelter and hotel and back again: "I find that the people that
do go from here to the hotels in the area are back here because they don't
have any companionship. And loneliness is probably the worst thing that can
happen to a person."

Desperate lives

Homelessness contributes to a criminogenic situation where crimes are com-   6
mitted to deal with social and economic strains, and otherwise unmotivated
people are enticed to break the law (McCarthy and Hagen 1991; Snow et al.
1989). The conditions of deprivation and destitution that characterize homelessness may result in coping mechanisms and survival strategies that are not
in the interests of the community. Rather than endure an apparently pointless
existence, a person may resort to unlawful activities in order to get by. When
life is solitary, poor, nasty, brutish and short, it is each for him/herself, as Sally
explained: "I've gone to people that I thought were supportive friends and I've

been hurt by them. I've been ripped off, because they're down here, they're sick, they're dying and they're so desperate."

Recently arrived from Manitoba, Jason said he had come to British   7
Columbia for his personal safety; he would not reveal what he was running from, except that it involved the police, the community and previous criminal activities. He had tried to get into Lookout but said he was barred. Jason revealed he suffers from mood swings and is HIV positive. At the time of the interview Jason maintained his main support mechanisms were the staff at shelters and drop-ins. I asked Jason what Triage does for him and he replied: "A lot of homeless people will break the law just to provide shelter, three square meals a day. . . . They will go out and hurt somebody or take out their frustration 'cause they don't know where to go for help." For Jason, Triage is a place of temporary assistance where he can get help to sort out his problems.

The longer one is on the street homeless, the higher the probability of   8
engaging in criminal acts; this reflects the processes of survival and adaptation (Snow et al. 1989). As detailed in Table 6, the leading sources of income for the participants in the month previous to the interview were welfare, underground activities and the sale of personal belongings. The underground activities included drug dealing, shoplifting, breaking and entering, fencing stolen goods and prostitution. Mark commented: "A lot of the faces I see are workin' the streets, until their bodies give out and they can't do it anymore."

Donna pictured a life of desperation in which human life is devalued, and   9
violence and victimization are just another way to get by:

> You'll be out on the streets, you have nowhere to go, you'll be stealing. You'll be selling yourself. You'll constantly do anything to survive. Even if that means taking somebody's life, you will. . . . I know a lot of girls beat up people, to get money and change, you name it, cigarettes. You see people getting beat up, elderly ladies getting beat up.

A place to stay for the night
Virtually all the research participants said there was no need to go hungry   10
downtown. What was harder to find was suitable shelter. This may be because food is essential for survival, whereas shelter is not.

On the Downtown Eastside there are various places where one can camp   11
out for the night. Particular places attract particular people. Christine explained that

> Oppenheimer Park actually is the best park. But up around where we were, Lakewood and Dundas, it's a bunch of jonesing. People that would sell their brother for a toke. Except there, not too many people fix; they smoke, which is worse.

Brian had previously been staying in a downtown hotel but had to leave   12
because he could not pay his rent. In the last year he said he had been assaulted

three times, once by a friend, once by an acquaintance and once by the police. Brian reiterated Jason's statement when he said that the shelter

> keeps us off the street. Keeps us out of trouble. Like most of us, if this shelter wasn't here, we'd be resorting to other ways to survive. . . . If you couldn't get into another shelter, you'd either be sleeping outside or you'd be robbing or stealing to survive.

When one is homeless certain facilities are used for purposes for which   13
they were originally unintended. Shelter had been sought in a hospital, jail or detox centre for fourteen of the respondents. Reynaldo, who had failed to make a court appearance, sought shelter at the city jail:

> I had a "did not appear" charge, and it wasn't like an outstanding warrant. I went down [to the police station]. I was hoping to have a place to stay 'cause I had no place to stay. I could have stayed at my brother-in-law's place, but there's too much stuff happening there. So I turned myself in. I didn't know what to do.

Women often attach themselves to men to avoid the risk of homelessness   14
(Snow et al. 1986). Sally had been sharing a room with a male friend who, when he got his pension cheque, would drink too much and become abusive. The binges would last for a few days and she would clear out of his way or join in. She was at Triage because it was one of those times for exiting the scene:

> I would hate to be in a position that I see a lot of women my age where they essentially are like pets to old men. . . . They go and live with older men, with old pensioners, because the older pensioners have a little money, and it's not necessarily a sexual thing, it's a companionship thing. I see this happen with a lot of women. And I view that as being just another step towards being more and more dependent.

Somewhere to go

John, a visitor on the night of our interview, lived in a downtown hotel a   15
short walking distance from Triage. John had been in a foster home as a child and in mental health facilities as both a child and an adult. Twenty-eight years old, he had worked for two and a half years as a gas station attendant and for five days at telemarketing, from which he was fired because of poor sales. In his lifetime John said that he had been assaulted over a hundred times. He said he appreciated "the visiting hours, and the meals, and the sandwiches, someone to talk to when in crisis." John's account shows the indispensability of shelters such as Triage in the daily survival strategies of many people who live on Vancouver's Downtown Eastside:

> It's a place to go to. . . . I would dare say, if it wasn't for a place like Triage, visiting hours, or the drop-in, and I had nowhere to go, forgive me for the way it sounds, I would probably be dead. That's how much these

places mean to me. If I didn't have, I'd be dead, because I could not stand the loneliness. I could not stand being in a hotel room from day till night. I could not stand it.

Homeless and near-homeless persons use multiple resources and possess 16 skills that they are often presumed to lack in their quest for daily sustenance; their strategies for "getting by" show them to be quite resourceful (Koegel, Burnam and Parr 1990; Robertson 1993). Tony, who often slept outside, described how he used the services available on the Downtown Eastside:

> I would go down and have a shower at the Forty Four and shave there. And then I would leave my backpack at one of the lockers at the Carnegie Centre and I would leave it there all day so I don't have to carry it around with me. And I would just go from soup line to soup line. There's a lot of places to eat around here. A person never has to go hungry, that's for sure. A lot of freebies. People are very generous, you know. There's a lot of good, a lot of kindness.

Removal activities

The homeless suffer higher rates of victimization than the general population 17 (Snow et al. 1989). Survival strategies and adaptational processes involve hardening to the violence of the urban area and turning away from threatening incidents, muggings and assaults. Christine explained why she avoided involved relationships:

> If you show somebody down here that you care, they take advantage of it. They use you like you've never been used. So, sure I had five friends brutally murdered last year. I cared, I cried. I guess maybe I done that because I could never show them how much I cared in case they took advantage of it.

In order to survive, a process of disengagement takes place, as Allan described:

> I admit that I just choose not to see a lot of it. Mainly because it doesn't have anything to do with who I am or what I'm about. Yes, I still see some of it, but I tend to block a lot of it out. . . . I just tend to ignore it all. Not because I'm ignorant but just because it has nothing to do with who I am. . . . So if you're asking about drugs and hookers and that sort of thing I really don't notice it. I don't just because that's not where I'm at, so I tend to block those things out.

Hardening to violence and turning a blind eye is a process of removal in 18 the pretence that it is not really happening. Rather than get involved in someone else's trouble, it is safer to look downwards at the pavement and withdraw into a veil of self-deception. David explained that it makes sense to pretend one does not see:

> Sometimes we go down there and we see things, but we don't see 'em 'cause it's bad. . . . We do it all the time, man, I know I do. I see things I

don't want to see, and wished I hadn't seen 'em, 'cause I don't know what, it stagnates me, man, it makes me feel down.

Bruce described how he would walk by an unsettling event and entrench his position of studied disinvolvement in the events going on around him:

> I see people, the drunks. They lay on the sidewalk and then guys pick them up and go through their pockets. And I see it, there's not much I can do about it. I don't want to get over and help the guy and then end up getting stabbed or something. So you just kinda turn your head like you didn't see it. And you're disgusted, right. And the next two people come by and they try and do the same thing but his pockets are empty. It's happening all the time. Especially if it's just around welfare day.

Jim talked about seeing muggings on the Downtown Eastside and how he learned to mind his own business:

> I was shocked at first, because I'd actually seen that. But the unspoken law of keep your mouth shut is the way it is around here. It's so funny how I fit right in, no problem. . . . Being able to keep my mouth shut.

Beth agreed that "if you get involved in somebody else's violence . . . I   19
mean if I was to jump in and interfere not knowing the situation at all, that would definitely cause a lot of bullshit. So I just pass by." This committed disattachment to what many of us would term public trouble is also characteristic of relations in prisons, jails and other places of subcultural adaptation. As Barak (1990:7) explains: 20

> The violent nature of homelessness and the victimization of the homeless is captured in the experiences of those persons who had previously endured lives of poverty, domestic abuse, and/or neglect, only to eventually "escape" into the world of homelessness.

Putting up a front

Simon explained that a person on skid row learns how to cope with the   21
everyday threats of physical and psychic assault by putting up a front: "On the street, it's nobody's gonna fuck with you because they know if they do that you're in that position of power. That you don't have to do anything yourself, it's just gonna be done. Power, it's a strong word." Simon told how he deals with threats from law enforcement personnel:

> When a cop grabs me for something, the first thing I say is I got syringes in my pocket, I'm HIV positive. And that just takes the edge off whatever situation right away. . . . And you just draw on different situations. Even though I got dope on me, I've always carried syringes. I've always had syringes on me. So when the situation ever arises, that's the first thing that comes out of my mouth. I'm HIV positive, I've got syringes, I don't know if the caps are on them or not. I don't have any weapons. I'll open my jacket, you can check if you want or I'll take them out. I'd rather me

take 'em out, you know. It just relaxes the whole situation, instead of fuckin' mouthin' off. If you're gonna mouth off, if I call you a fuckin' piece of shit, well, you're gonna react.

Tony said one develops a new personality "in order to survive. You have   22
to sort of act tougher than what you really are. Especially if you're not that sort of personality, you better get it."

The contradictions of these strategies of survival are that they help people   23
to survive the challenges of the street but simultaneously contribute to the conditions of their privation. Acceptance and resignation become the norm, and control is left to those of authority.

Control of the Poor, the Homeless and the Near-homeless

The function of status degradation is social control (Goffman 1963). Social   24
welfare regulates and maintains market discipline by retaining the eighteenth-century concept of less eligibility (Culhane 1996; Piven and Cloward 1993). State assistance is meant to be a less eligible, or less desirable, alternative to disciplined activity, as welfare clients are degraded by having to ask for hand-outs. Luke expressed this ignominy: "I've felt degraded going in [to welfare]. Belittled might be the right word."

The contradiction in the stigma of the selective transfer of welfare—   25
which has the effect of lowering self-esteem so that the politicization of the group becomes almost impossible (Armitage 1975)—is that being on social assistance and living downtown can contribute to resignation and hopeless-ness. As Phil explained, "The longer I stay here the more l lose the impetus to get out of that system."

The control effect of the shelter is to contain the non-productive for a   26
brief interval, during which time clients are disciplined before being returned to the outlying community, perhaps more ordered than when they first arrived. But the community to which they are returned is the same one that contributed to their needing shelter in the first place. As Christie (1994:197) asks:

> Are inner cities places where those with no aspirations choose to flock together, or are they dumping grounds for those not given an even share of the benefits of modern societies? Meaning given to certain phenomena has consequences for the measures chosen, just as the measures give meaning back.

The shelter has instrumental ends, but often the practices are expressive   27
of something else: defining moral careers and creating hierarchies of identifi-cation and separation. Its instrumental purpose is to house, stabilize or treat, but its expressive course may be to attach stigma to those of lost status. The shelter creates "occasions of hazard" (Harré 1993:205) against or through which the client works and the process is defined.

Limits to help

Control involves getting residents back out onto the street and into their own   28
housing. In practice this usually means moving into a hotel room in the area
or into shared accommodation. Edward explained that shelters promote a
migratory lifestyle among their users,

> because the way these shelters operate, the staff's hands are tied accord-
> ing to certain rules and regulations, and the demand for a large number
> of people for a place, so they have to move people on. . . . The demand
> for people needing shelter all the time creates a situation where you can't
> stay here. It's not a long-term solution. It's a temporary solution. It doesn't
> deal with the long-term problems. 'Cause it's not set up for that. It
> doesn't have the capacity to go beyond that, so there's a limit for the help
> that you can get.

When Simon was not staying at Triage, he would sometimes come in for   29
a meal, to use the clothing room, or just to talk. Occasionally, as a technique
for controlling interpersonal space, the shelter staff would close down visiting
hours. In commenting on this practice, Simon revealed how important the
shelter is in some people's lives: "It's like a slap in the head actually when the
sign says there's no visiting tonight. A lot of people really count on just that.
And it's a letdown. So you turn away downtown."

Another resident, Mark, communicated that he would get angry when he   30
needed a time of stability and the sign said no visiting.

Becoming a file

The public welfare apparatus depends on a "reified clientele" (Friedenberg   31
1975:1)—those who are conscripted from among the poor and destitute for
the purpose of administering services and who provide the *raison d'être* of its
existence. "Conscript clienteles" (Friedenberg 1975:2) are those pressed into
the service of caregivers, professionals and agencies and who are not free to
refuse the service. This reification of clientele produces an "institutional sym-
biosis" (Friedenberg 1975:18) in which the institutions and agencies come to
depend on one another for referrals and in which the individual is bounced
around like a ping-pong ball. Daly (1996:9) observes:

> Because they lack a collective voice and are not organized, individuals on
> the street are represented by proxies whose interests may be self-serving.
> A self-perpetuating network, characterized by common interests, mutual
> dependencies and benefits, it has fashioned a web of interdependent com-
> munities based on self-interest. It includes government agencies and
> bureaucrats, not-for-profit and voluntary organizations, professional
> caregivers and shelter operators. While most are well-intentioned, they,
> nevertheless, are motivated by a desire to exercise power and a need for
> control: the power of the purse strings, the ability to set policy, to allocate
> resources, to plan and design programs, to decide who will be helped and
> who will not, to determine whose interests will be represented, and to
> sanction or condemn certain practices, values or beliefs.

Triage is defined and accepted as a place for marginalized persons. A 32 large sign outside tells passersby and those who enter that this is so. But when a person spends most of her or his time in formally identified places of marginalization, identity solidifies. Like homosexuals in a gay bar, like addicts in a shooting gallery, like mental patients in a drop-in centre, they entrench their identity in the place (Goffman 1963). When persons are disoriented because of stressful situations and when there is a lack of connection to normalizing structure, they are more amenable to an exceptional category, such as homeless misfit.

I once heard a woman at Triage say in a loud voice that she was not a 33 mental patient, she was a drug addict. It may be that in an effort to define an apparently more acceptable identity, she was letting us know that her personhood was not of a psychiatric origin but of an alternative culture of her own choosing.

The term "client" is descriptive of a relationship, not a person (Simpkin 34 1979). I asked the participants what this term meant to them. Linda had a long history of being a client:

> I really don't like that term, because all my life I've been labeled as just a number, a file number. A client of the children's aid. A client of the hospital. I have a hard time with that label. I would rather be called a person in need rather than a client.

Mark, with previous practice in social work, had direct knowledge of being both a provider and a consumer of social service:

> Client ... usually denotes that you're the person that's getting something from somebody else. They're giving it to you. It's a power thing. Structure. You have this, and I'm going to get it from you. Instead of a team sort of a thing which I would much rather see. People as being part of it, part of the process. Information. We keep information from people as well in social work and that sort of thing. Because it keeps them from having the power. And I don't know if that's a conscious thing or what that is, but that's there.

Institutions depend on written information for their existence. This 35 process of categorization and differentiation of "problem populations" contributes to an ideology of order, discipline and punitive regulation rather than social liberation (Cohen 1979). The official write-up is entered into a computer database that becomes a permanent record of who the person is and what she or he is about. Acting out can result in a negative notation, which then becomes a concrete exposition of identity. Selective attributions and events can be used to support the idea that the person was always like that. These designations are often based on superficial observation with limited awareness of the subjective meaning of the persons being classified in interaction with events and structure. Lofland (1969:144) recognized that:

> Models of deviant categories are founded precisely upon the assumption that particular classes of people are more likely to perform deviant acts

and to be particular types of deviant persons. . . . Imputations of actors as deviant can have as much or more to do with who is coding with what category under what circumstances than with simple discernment of specially differentiated deviant persons.

When a person is given a room at Triage, she or he is assigned a file   36
number and an intake is done. In a process of categorization, the homeless person is "socially identified" and the responses are organized accordingly. In an essentialist endeavour to separate and classify, "pivotal categories," such as alcoholic, drug addict or mental patient, are advanced (Lofland 1969). This nosological endeavour facilitates classification of people in order to predict, organize and discipline them (Foucault 1980). "The fundamental need of social man *(sic)* [is] to participate in a system of meaning—a system of action possibilities" (Lofland 1969:277). However, categorical definitions of homelessness fail to address the interrelated needs that pertain to physical, emotional and material conditions (Fabricant 1988). "The descriptions used become labels which can pigeonhole individuals in negative ways . . . those who are down and out are seen by many as hopeless, a latter-day version of the 'undeserving poor'" (Daly 1996:7).

I asked the participants what they thought of the file system at Triage,   37
that is, what they thought of having written biographies created when they enter as a resident. Some participants did not know of the file system and were surprised when I informed them of this practice. Mark perceived the relation of subject/object when he observed:

> I think files tend to be like baggage that people start carrying around with them, and you become your file. It could be a real bad thing. You know, that they been draggin' this baggage around with them for a long time. You literally get a plastic bag and a file folder. This is who this person is, and I don't think it tells the whole story, any file, any subjective type of recording of one person's opinion about the other person. . . . What goes in that file is gonna be what the next person sees and it doesn't always tell the picture.

Beth, however, argued that client file documents facilitate institutional   38
efficiency in that the person is catalogued for future identification: "You know, if you come back they have to be able to find you somehow, and that's what the file is for. . . . They have to be able to find my file. We've got to be filed somewhere."

Hierarchical relationships

The Triage shelter depends on volunteers from the community who come in   39
and help with everyday domestic tasks such as bed-making, laundry and kitchen chores. In return the volunteer might get cigarettes, a meal or first choice at clothing donations. The shelter justifies this activity as offering the volunteer a sense of accomplishment and purpose as well as providing a valuable service to the facility. Jim was a volunteer at Triage and commented that,

"we've been here a while, so we call ourselves the senior clients. . . it makes us feel good that we earned that sort of respect. . . . . Something that you've earned."

However, the line between volunteer and staff is clearly demarcated in a   40
process of rational, professional distancing that contributes to the client's isolation (Fabricant 1988). Limits are organized around the apparent full acceptance of the client, and the relationship is constrained by hierarchy in order to avoid embarrassment. Occasionally a helper would cross the line and staff would remark that "so and so" was becoming "pseudo-staff." The volunteer would be brought back into line with a warning to respect the boundaries between staff and client. In turn, this would contribute to the client's powerlessness and entrench her or his identity, erecting a barrier to empowerment and collective agency. "Charity is scraps from the table and justice is being invited to the table itself" (Tiernan 1992:655).

Triage decision-making is top-down or hierarchical, moving from the   41
executive director to the coordinator, the shift supervisors, and the community workers. Decision-making excludes the residents themselves. Allan expressed resentment against the bureaucratic structure of a shelter system that allows no space for the voices of the clients to be heard: "And that's what bothers me about this place. Is that we're not asked, we're just sort of shuffled along."

Controlling space

Triage has a day program in which those who live in hotel rooms nearby can   42
come in for meals, get their medication dispensed or have other needs attended to. For many of these people the shelter is their primary resource. This is a good service, but it does little to alleviate the conditions in which the people live. Rather, it leads to dependency and regimentation, with the marginalized being hidden from public view. As Brian observed, institutionalization is "more or less relying on someone to have your food there, washing your clothes, whatever."

In January 1996, a day client who depended on Triage for his meals and   43
medication was found dead in his nearby hotel room. This client was a regular at Triage; he loved to talk with the staff and hang around drinking coffee and smoking cigarettes. Sometimes, when his coping mechanisms broke down, he would check into the shelter for two or three days to repair. He loved to talk of when he was much younger and of the cars he had—when he was a professional musician and the effects of his medications for schizophrenia had not yet caused his tongue to swell and his head to permanently tilt at forty-five degrees to his body. This client was sometimes asked to leave after getting his medications and having his customary cup of coffee, because of his taking up limited space. The shelter needed to place control over care.

Clients at Triage often have to wait in line for toothpaste, a towel or their   44
medications. Most of us do not particularly enjoy standing in lineups, but if we are dissatisfied with the service we have a choice of going to another place. A resident of the shelter system lacks this choice. The client can

sometimes go to another facility, but this is not necessarily a viable option. The client endures the wait for a comb or a cigarette paper, sometimes expressing resistance to this humbling ritual through impatience and frustration. As Edward remarked, "seeking a place like this is not a choice. It's not much of a choice, and that's why it contradicts the word 'client.'"

Allan expressed anger and resentment at having his life organized accord-   45
ing to someone else's schedule:

> I can't take my meds when I want to. . . . And so that is really demeaning, having to stand there, shove the medication in and have them watch. . . . I wouldn't want to be dependent on this place for a meal once a week, or twice a week for that matter, or even for my hour of TV everyday. I wouldn't want to have someone telling me that I could come in during these times. To use this type of facility during this time and go down to the clothing room. I wouldn't want my life orchestrated that way.

As Barak (1991) notes, many homeless persons choose alternatives to the   46
shelter because of its structure of containment and order. Donna compared the shelter to a jail:

> So-called group homes and shelters, some of the people don't like that word. . . . I know some people don't like to go into shelters. They'd rather stay out on the street than go to shelters 'cause they don't really like being, most people I know, it's being locked up. A lot of people like their freedom. . . . 'Cause it seems like you go to jail or something like that.

Regulating behaviour

Control is infused within the stigma of being poor and homeless. For a time   47
the homeless person is contained behind a locked door (locked to outsiders, not to insiders) of a structure organized around the fundamental principles of asylum. However, it is not just the shelter that contains—it is the urban core where bodies are bought and sold, targets are beaten and robbed, and a safe place for the night is highly regarded.

At Triage, in exchange for the provision of a few days' shelter, clients are   48
expected to follow certain basic rules. The possession of illicit drugs or unauthorized medications, the leaving of a syringe around the premises, or the assault of anyone in the shelter results in immediate eviction. However, the rules are in direct opposition to the everyday activities happening right outside the shelter doors—on the street outside, drugs and violence are everywhere.

Control is organized around a discourse of defending selves against out-   49
side forces, of holding the wolves at bay. Jason supported the idea that the activities happening outside the shelter doors are out of bounds at Triage:

> Without control in the shelter, fuck, it would be chaos. It would be stealing, drugs coming in, booze coming in, hookers coming in, people would be getting diseases left, right and centre. So you got to have control in a shelter. No control you got problems.

Triage has a medication room reserved for the storage and dispensation   50
of various pharmaceuticals, including sedative/hypnotics, antidepressants,
anti-psychotics, analgesics, antibiotics, anti-virals and synthetic narcotics.
The use or possession of any drug that is not prescribed by a physician and
listed on the resident's medication sheet is prohibited; a client's infraction of
this rule usually results in immediate eviction. Brian declared:

> I notice the people that come in drinking. The drugs are probably toler-
> ated more than the alcohol. That probably discriminates against the alco-
> holic. But it's probably harder to deal with someone on alcohol than it is
> to deal with someone on drugs.

Many of those who access the shelter service have drug problems but   51
avoid staff when using for fear of losing their bed. This produces a cat and
mouse game where the skillful are able to avoid detection and the careless get
caught. Donna explained:

> Like take this other shelter. They think that if some of you got red eyes
> or if you're tired and things like that, they put you down as, oh, proba-
> bly she came in so on and so on and this time she was high or it looks like
> she was drunk. Things like that they put down on the, what do you call
> it, in the books every night when they write things down. And some of the
> things aren't true that they put down. And you feel very insecure about
> things like that. And you really don't want to tell your problems to them,
> some of these places.

The need for order and discipline at the shelter creates situations in   52
which a client engages in denial and pretence. I have seen residents so obviously under the influence of alcohol or some other drug that they could
hardly stand up, but who would vehemently deny their condition. They knew
that if they admitted to such use they would be asked to leave the building for
a period of time and wait outside until they are not so visibly high. So it was
in their interests to deny the reality. As Brian observed:

> How honest can we be with you here? Say if I was out using, I'd been
> using, whatever, on the street everyday and I came and talked to you and
> told you that I'd been using and I feel like I'm abusing this place, would
> that necessarily mean that you're gonna lose your bed?

Sally illustrated that the very activities that the shelter seeks to prohibit   53
are topics of everyday conversation, cultivating illicit desire, "because there
are so many people with drug addictions here, that everybody sits around and
talks about drugs, and this creates craving, invisible cravings. It's caused me
to crave drugs, and I'm a very casual user."

Bruce suggested that those persons who use the shelter as a detoxification   54
centre should have their liberties restricted as well as their use of prescribed
medications:

> I think if people are going to come in here to straighten up . . . the first
> seven days they shouldn't be allowed out. Getting straight. Like one girl

here she's on the methadone program, I don't think that should be allowed. From my point of view. 'Cause other people see that. The people that are straight. She's kind of miserable now. She was sick for a few days there, now she's ready to go hustling.

A contradiction in Bruce's statement is that the medical use of methadone   55
as a substitute for heroin may be of personal benefit to the addict, but a problem for others in the same social milieu. It is not so much the use of methadone that is problematic but the visible effects of the opiate synthetic. On August 7, 1997, I counted eighty prescribed drugs between twenty-eight residents in the Triage medication room. One resident had sixteen different medications.

Stress and high physiological arousal are interactive with social isolation,   56
urban environments, racial and ethnic discrimination, and low social position. Homelessness and vulnerability to homelessness are associated with structural factors and situations that produce arousal, and coping mechanisms seeking to reduce this arousal may be aggressive, independent of psychological/biological factors (Bernard 1990). Homelessness and the threat of homelessness can be a traumatic event resulting in negative coping strategies situated within cultural values and social structure (Hoff 1989). Mark described an incident in which a person had to be physically removed from Triage:

> Although it was diffused, they were dragging her out of the building, and it just escalates. I think that could have been avoided altogether. If she would have got the pants. She's all wet. She's pregnant or whatever. She's got her story. Those are her needs at that time. At least some way of being able to put her on hold. But putting somebody on hold that's already been on hold for a long period of time, I can see where that's coming from. So I don't know exactly how that could have been handled differently, but I know that it could have been alleviated, probably.

Emergency shelters for the homeless and near-homeless lack a client   57
advocate for those discharged on procedural grounds and denied admittance (Culhane 1992). As Mark went on to observe, disruptive behaviour at Triage can result in the person's being barred,

> and they end up losing it because they don't have the skills to say, hey look, I do have needs too. So in some ways people, like this lady tonight who was venting, she was really empowering herself. Though she probably wouldn't see it as that, and she's now had something, one of her last bastions of, you know, anything that she can handle [removed]. So that now, when these people like that, barred for a month or two months, or whatever it is, now where do they go?

A three-fold division of interests exists in social services: the public at   58
large, the providers of service and the consumers of the service. The tension between the three interests increases with the amount of regulatory activity,

so that maximum regulation, as in criminal captivity, results in maximum dissension between groups about what constitutes social assistance (Armitage 1975).

In a minimalist welfare state, the poor and the homeless are managed   59
through deviance processing. Deviance and identity are constructed by those in the system and defined and constructed through interaction with others (Harré 1993; Lofland 1969). Those perceived as a threat to socially accepted definitions are subjected to some kind of control. The homeless make ambiguous the social division of work and family as they threaten the social order— they need to be responded to through control and exclusion. "The homeless are dangerous to the ruling class because in their struggle to survive they must demand changes that cannot take place without creating a new system of distribution of food and shelter on the basis of need" (Aulette and Aulette 1987:253).

In the shelter, practices of control are often cloaked in a rhetoric of care.   60
The subtlety of control-based practices is difficult to detect; the clients in this study were so grateful to have a safe and secure place to stay that issues of power were located, for them, around the regulation of disruptive behaviour. I asked the participants what control meant to them and how it connected with the practice of care at Triage. Beth stated: "Being able to handle the outbursts and the personalities, just the personalities of each individual client, that's care and control in itself."

Like all institutions Triage is tightly controlled as to its internal structure   61
and the discipline of its bodies. Rules and boundaries are enforced with the threat of ejection back out into the street. However, embedded within these control-based techniques there is also a practice of care. Control interacts with care in a balancing act in which care is contingent on discipline and orderly presentation. Morris summarized this dialectic: "They control the shelter, so people like, to protect people, and like that shows that they care right there. They're both linked, you know."

References

Armitage, A. 1975. *Social Welfare in Canada: Ideals and Realities*. Toronto: McClelland & Stewart.

Aulette, J., and A. Aulette. 1987. "Police Harassment of the Homeless: The Political Purpose of the Criminalization of Homelessness." *Humanity and Society* 11(2).

Barak, G. 1990. "The Violent Nature of Homelessness." *Critical Criminologist* 2(2).

Barak, G. and R. M. Bohm. 1989. "The Crimes of the Homeless or the Crime of Homelessness?" On the Dialectics of Criminalization, Decriminalization, and Victimization." *Contemporary Crises* 13.

Bernard, T. J. 1990. "Angry Aggression Among the 'Truly Disadvantaged.'" *Criminology* 28(1).

Christie, N. 1994. *Crime Control as Industry: Towards GULAGS, Western Style*. Second edition. London: Routledge.

Cohen, S. 1979. "The Punitive City: Notes on the Dispersal of Social Control." *Contemporary Crises* 3.

Culhane, D. 1996. "The Homeless Shelter and the Nineteenth-Century Poorhouse: Comparing Notes from Two Eras of 'Indoor Relief.'" In M.B. Lykes, A. Banuazizi, R. Liem and M. Morris (eds.), *Myths about the Powerless: Contesting Social Inequalities.* Philadelphia: Temple University Press.

Daly, G., 1996. *Homeless: Policies, Strategies, and Lives on the Street.* London: Routledge.

Fabricant, M. 1988. "Empowering the Homeless." *Social Policy* 18.

Foucault, M. 1980. *Power/Knowledge: Selected Interviews and Other Writings, 1972–1977.* New York: Pantheon Books.

Friedenberg, E. Z. 1975. *The Disposal of Liberty and Other Industrial Wastes.* New York: Doubleday.

Goffman, E. 1963. *Stigma: Notes on the Management of Spoiled Identity.* New York: Simon & Schuster.

Grigsby, C., D. Baumann, S.E. Gregorich and C. Roberts-Gray. 1990. "Disaffiliation to Entrenchment: A Model for Understanding Homelessness." *Journal of Social Issues* 46(4).

Harre, R. 1993. *Social Being.* Second edition. Oxford: Blackwell.

Hoff, L. A. 1989. *People in Crisis: Understanding and Helping.* Third edition. Redwood City, Calif.: Addison-Wesley.

Koegal, P., M. A. Burnam and R. K. Farr. 1990. "Subsistence Adaptation among Homeless Adults in the Inner City of Los Angeles." *Journal of Social Issues* 46(4).

Lofland, J. 1969. *Deviance and Identity.* Englewood Cliffs, N.J.: Prentice-Hall.

McCarthy, B., and J. Hagen. 1991. "Homelessness: A Criminogenic Situation?" *British Journal of Crimininology* 31 (4).

Piven, F. F., and R. A. Cloward. 1993. *Regulating the Poor: The Functions of Public Welfare.* Revised edition. New York: Vintage.

Robertson, B. 1993. "Streets of Kamloops: An Ethnography." Unpublished master's thesis, Simon Fraser University. Burnaby, B.C.

Snow, D. A., S. G. Baker and L. Anderson. 1989. "Criminality and Homeless Men: An Empirical Assessment." *Social Problems* 36(5).

Snow, D. A., S. G. Baker, L. Anderson and M. Martin. 1986. "The Myth of Pervasive Mental Illness among the Homeless." *Social Problems* 33(5).

Tiernan, K. 1992. "Homelessness: The Politics of Accommodation." *New England Journal of Public Policy* 8(1).

■ ■ ■

Discussion and Writing Suggestions

1. Does Allen attempt to offer solutions? Is he fashioning generalizations about the plight of the homeless, or does he emphasize the need to look at individual cases?
2. Does he strike a pose of objectivity? How would you describe the author's ethos?

■ ■ ■

The War at Home: An Intimate Portrait of Canada's Poor

PAT CAPPONI

In this excerpt from her book, The War at Home: An Intimate Portrait of Canada's Poor, *Pat Capponi looks at the poor in Montreal, specifically at those who take activist positions on the need for welfare reform. The book as a whole profiles her experiences across Canada, allowing her to sketch some of the similarities and differences in the situations faced by the homeless in different regions.*

Capponi is the author of several critically acclaimed books that take an insider's look at various social issues in Canada. She has taken on an active role in the psychiatric survivor community, and has been awarded the Order of Ontario.

Leadership in the Underclass is perhaps the most challenging kind of activism.   1
Communication between activists across the country is incredibly difficult, since phones are often a luxury and long-distance calls far too expensive to be a possibility. Fax machines are the property of funded agencies, not of individuals on welfare. The cost of stamps and envelopes, the cost of reproducing documents to send out, the transportation costs to get people to meetings, are all prohibitive.

There is often no safe base to organize from, the activist himself being   2
constantly bombarded by the consequences of prolonged poverty: ill health, hunger, fear of eviction, and that generalized moment-to-moment fearful awareness that things can always get worse. Activists themselves become divided up, the same way we divide up the assistance offered, and get trapped and isolated in their own little worlds. The big picture becomes elusive, connections don't get made.

The building housing this anti-poverty group in Notre-Dame-de-Grâce   3
(NDG) is empty except for three people. The donations of clothing smell of mould.

"If we give up, there will be no dissenting voice," says Annette, who runs   4
this operation. "That's what happened in Nazi Germany, no dissenting voices.

We are the ones, in various progressive movements, who say: this is wrong, this isn't true. We're on a train hurtling towards an abyss. It's only if there are enough people standing in front of the train, building an alternative track, that we might all be saved. Otherwise, humanity is doomed."

Those who choose to act as champions of the poor and disenfranchised are themselves trapped and demoralized: by the enormity of the problems, the lack of solutions, and, for people like Annette, now fifty-three years old, by poverty itself.   5

Annette has lived on the fringes of society most of her adult life. Born in England, she grew up in Norway. She still remembers the lingering effects of war, the presence of unexploded bombs in the back yards of neat little houses.   6

Her parents travelled a lot, and she went from Norway to Holland, to Newfoundland, then Montreal. "Before I even reached adolescence," she says, "I'd lived in four different countries."   7

Her father worked in aviation, as a mechanic. He was originally from a small island in Norway, and he served in the merchant marine and the military. Annette describes her mother as a "victim of the patriarchy, male domination and privilege." Her parents divorced when she was seventeen, a good thing for both of them, she feels.   8

What does she have, if anything, to look forward to?   9

"I made it this far, so if I get to fifty-five, I'll be moved from welfare onto pension. I'll be better off. You receive $712 if you live alone."   10

"Not much of a goal," I say softly. "Do you ever wish things had turned out differently for you?"   11

"Sure, I have regrets. I've worked really hard, and there's never anything comes out of it, not for me personally. I guess I've gone through two-thirds of my life, I've experienced rage, anger and despair: it's all still there in some respects. I'm not even sure I've been able to effect immediate change, or if I'll see the effects of the efforts of people like me in my lifetime. I think the first time I became politically aware was during the Cuban missile crisis, you know, the sirens going off all the time. I realized then that the people who are in control of this planet are insane."   12

Poison pools at the bottom, where the ladder turns into a chute, slick and without footholds. Diseases like AIDS, tuberculosis and Hepatitis C; drugs—new and old—ranging from smack to crack; prostitution—foulness spreads in ever-widening circles.   13

Things are coming unglued. Where once we stepped over one drunk passed out and snoring on the sidewalk, we now step over children huddled in sleeping bags: angry, defiant, dangerous children we refuse to recognize as our own. They seem to gather in clumps at Metro stations, packs of kids in leather and denim, hair shorn or up in spikes. They all have a patina of road dust and dirt, and an aura of danger. There is no one able or willing to speak to me in English, and, of course, being raised in Montreal and "learning French" in every grade, I have no command of the language.   14

According to the executive director of Dans La Rue, a shelter, drop-in and medical facility dedicated to street kids, the children who can speak   15

English just keep running, out to places like Vancouver. The rest are trapped here. "Pops," a.k.a. Father Emmett Johns, the founder of Dans La Rue, is responsible for the Metro station gatherings. Almost a decade ago, he started handing out hot dogs to street kids. In 1997, 40,000 hot dogs were distributed from a van belonging to the organization to the children in the streets, making the first "helping connection" the kids have seen for a while.

The staff at Dans La Rue, on Ontario Street East, see children as young   16
as twelve and up to twenty-five. Most have run away from small towns outside of the city, escaping physical or sexual abuse in their families, for life on the street. Here, they fall prey to street drugs, prostitution and crime. Staff try a variety of ways to snag the children, hot dogs being the least complicated. There's education upgrading available, nursing care, a food and clothing distribution area, even a place with large metal rings drilled into the concrete floor, for the children to tie up the "drug dogs" that are their frequent companions, protecting dealers from ripoffs and stalling police.

In 1996, Dans La Rue handled 30,000 visits to the van, received 15,612   17
daytime visits at the emergency shelter, helped 740 kids find housing, another 573 fight drug addiction, 452 children return to their families, and provided help and friends/mentors to 567 street kids looking for work. As well, 28,000 bags of groceries were distributed.

This whole organization grew out of Pops's efforts, including the Bunker,   18
a shelter that can house twenty kids a night. They have an arrangement with the people responsible for children's services, a postponing of the legal requirement to report underage children for three days, which means the kids can have short vacations from the street without being hauled away. There are few rules here, aside from respecting people and property.

While I'm in Montreal, they are preparing for a fundraising dinner that   19
Mila Mulroney is backing. I raise my eyebrows under my hat when I see the television promo, since I'm not her biggest fan, but I keep my opinions to myself.

It's crowded and noisy in the Ontario Street offices. A makeshift band is   20
practising head-banger music. A nurse is talking to a young woman while examining her feet. The donations room is spilling over with sanitary napkins, boxes of Kraft Dinner, tinned goods and a variety of clothing.

It's difficult, walking through here, feeling the hostility radiating from   21
some of the drop-ins, not to see this as the devolution of our societal efforts at child rescue. I flash back to the orderly, middle-class group home environment of Couvrette House, the home I ran for Summerhill Homes here in the city, in which seven teenage boys were given another chance at life.

It's nice for Mila of course, and her efforts at rehabilitating her public   22
image as a caring, maternal person. It's even nice for the staff and volunteers who are engaged in worthwhile efforts. But—it's so little, and so late. . . .

Clifford and Alexandra are two young people also trying to make it. She   23
studies social work at McGill University, and he is on welfare.

I met Alexandra, an attractive, intelligent, thoughtful young woman,   24
when she was enlisted as a French-language interpreter for an interview I was

trying to conduct at a legal rights organization. If she's learned anything here, it's that: "I never, never, never want to be on welfare."

She cast her lot early: "When I was fifteen, I worked at a designer cloth- 25
ing store. I wouldn't ever say that things looked good on someone when they didn't. I decided I won't be a big person taking from little people: that's what business seems to be doing to people today."

Now, to support herself through school, she works at a designer coffee 26
store. She stays on while others quit in disgust.

"I'm learning a lot about life. These bosses know how badly you need the 27
money. So they have a free hand when it comes to treating you badly: yelling and being as unpleasant as possible with the little power they have."

When she told him what she's been putting up with, her boyfriend, 28
Clifford, told her that she should have quit on the first day.

"Maybe I should have." 29

Clifford admires her, especially her single-minded pursuit of her goal. He 30
hasn't been able to find steady work, and being on welfare is demoralizing, even though, as he tells me, he's seen much worse in his young life, especially in his early days in Haiti.

"Here at least there are people to help you. The poverty in Haiti, you 31
can't compare it. You see someone living on the street in Montreal, and you go, oh that poor person, but in Haiti, most people are on the streets, and there is no one to intervene."

His mother lived in New York, and had a good job cleaning office build- 32
ings. He stayed with his aunt in Haiti, who was a nurse married to a doctor. They ran a clinic out of their home. There were always a lot of children around.

"A lot of parents couldn't afford to raise their kids, so they'd send them 33
to my aunt's. They weren't treated like maids or anything, but they'd help out with cleaning, cooking. I grew up not having to do anything for myself."

He attended elementary school in Haiti, and it was strict. 34

"The teachers were allowed to whip you if you did anything bad. Then 35
the parents would have a go when you got home."

He was sent to Montreal to live with yet another aunt. He went to school 36
in Montreal North, starting in grade five.

"I didn't like the teachers. Then another kid in my class stole something 37
and they blamed it on me. I got suspended."

To his aunt, this was a very big thing. She put him on a bus and sent him 38
to his mother in New York.

"I couldn't speak English, just French and Creole, so I was put back to 39
grade three in order to learn the language. I would have been totally lost if it weren't for a couple of Haitian kids I found."

And he loved his other new discovery: television. In about six months, 40
he'd learned enough of the English language from his favourite programs to jump ahead to grade six.

His mother cleaned offices and mopped floors—heavy, hard work— 41
while his stepfather stayed home and criticized him. He was relieved to return

with his mother to Montreal, leaving behind his stepfather, and it was in high school that he met Alexandra.

They didn't encounter much trouble as an interracial couple, although some of the black female students weren't too happy with his choice. They both shrugged that off.   42

Clifford took computer training at a privately run, for-profit school his uncle recommended. It was hard, he confesses, very condensed. He could have used more time to thoroughly understand what he was expected to learn. He gets short-term jobs now—two, three months at a time—but then he's back on social assistance.   43

"We want to live here, it's our city. We may not have a house with a white picket fence, but we're a stable couple, and we want to make it."   44

Alexandra has known that she wanted to work with people since she was five years old. At first, I thought I'd become a cop. I had this distorted view that they actually help people." She sighs for innocence lost.   45

She wonders sometimes what keeps her going to school, knowing that only service jobs will be waiting when she graduates. "Everything is being cut, everything. It seems the jobs of the future are the jobs at the bottom."   46

Her father, who left the family home when she was five, encourages her to stick it out: "He tells me to visualize my goal everyday, and I'll achieve it."   47

She considers herself relatively fortunate in that by the time she completes her B.A., her student debt will be only $10,000.   48

Alexandra told me about Laurent Prud'homme, a fifty-three-year-old Montrealer to whom fate and the mindless search for profits dealt a considerable blow. He's a thoughtful, kind, newly politicized individual who cares enough to step outside his own experience and reach out to others. Laurent describes himself as "kind of a square guy." His hair used to be dark blond, now it's greying.   49

"I'm pretty ordinary looking, always clean-shaven and dressed conservatively. I don't like heavy metal music, I still enjoy the Big Band sound, soft and classical music."   50

He's been thinking a lot about society and where it's heading.   51

"Three years ago, I was vice-president and director of a branch of a publishing company, pulling down $75,000 a year. We started it, my friend and I. He was the marketing manager. We got financial backing from three guys in Toronto. I'd spent about eighteen years in the city working in advertising, first as a translator, then as a junior copywriter, then as an account executive."   52

He and his friend started an annual publication, listing all the manufacturers of computers and computer parts and software in the market. It was the right idea at the right time, and they soon expanded their endeavours to the extent that revenues were at the $4.5-million mark.   53

They were in prolonged negotiations with their financial backers about company profit-sharing and stocks when they were called in, asked to hand over the keys to their office and their company cars: the company had been sold to an American firm. And that was it.   54

"Maybe we should have suspected, but we were naïve. My partner got 55 really depressed. At our age, late forties, jobs in Montreal are hard to come by, even those at a lower level than we were used to. I sold my house in Dorval and my wife's car, bought an old Chevette. A big dip in your standard of living. I figured, better to make even $200 a week than to use up our savings."

He got minimum-wage jobs: telemarketing, polling. It was pretty awful, 56 demoralizing. They would time him on bathroom breaks, listen in to his calls.

"But I was pretty lucky. I already had a sense that I was not my job. Not 57 what I owned or what I made. That's what made the difference between me and my partner."

For eight years Laurent had used his spare time to work as a volunteer for 58 a non-profit group, giving personal development courses to adults in the community from all walks of life. This effort to help others eventually helped him to handle the stress of losing what he'd worked so hard for.

"My partner had been a real health freak, he exercised regularly, took 59 natural food supplements. Took good care of himself. His depression stopped all that—within a year he'd lost his house. His wife took his daughter and left, telling him he was not the same man she'd married eighteen years ago. And then he died, just a year after they sold the company out from under us. Cancer. He was a professional, a good, good man—to die so tragically. And just because of a crazy lust for more and more money."

Laurent was raised in a middle-class family. His dad worked at General 60 Motors, and his mother, though she stayed home, was very ambitious. They would buy a house, live in it while renovating it, then sell and start again.

"I was painting walls and repairing holes when I was eight years old," he 61 remembers.

"I had friends telling me, and they were right, that I was losing my lan- 62 guage living in Toronto." It was suggested to him that he find a nice French girl, and he did. He met his wife in Toronto, where she was part of an exchange program involving civil servants from Quebec and Ontario.

His wife is no longer able to work; arthritis cripples her hands. And she 63 is now sometimes alarmed at how "radical" her husband is becoming.

"I see so many miserable, penniless people who have no idea of the pos- 64 sibilities out there," Laurent tells me. "Maybe it's time that people with wider vision tried to help them."

Laurent believes all the current political parties constitute an *ancien* 65 *régime,* a blend of old, self-serving ideas and irrelevancies. He talks with his friends about starting a new political party, a party of relevance that would concentrate on job creation, not separation.

• • •

Philip Amsel is making it. He calls himself an aristocrat of welfare, the 66 Cadillac even.

We arrange to meet at the Network Café, opposite the Snowdon Metro 67 station. He's been recommended to me by a McGill social work professor,

Eric Shragge, who, along with the Ashers, has provided me with an extensive list of contacts.

Philip's already at a smoking table when I arrive, a pleasant-looking   68
man nursing a coffee, just a bit rumpled. I'm interrupting his two-week vacation, but he doesn't seem to mind at all.

He's on a lot of medication, I can see it in his eyes and in the evident dry-   69
ness of his lips and mouth. He was diagnosed with paranoid schizophrenia in the 1970s, but has since been rediagnosed as manic depressive. (It often happens that the first label undergoes re-examination and "correction" as the diagnostic flavour of the month changes.)

He takes: Nozanan, 100 milligrams in the evening; three pills of lithium   70
a day; and tops it off with Serax as required. He's been hospitalized four times.

He grew up in a normal middle-class home in Ville St. Laurent, and his   71
childhood was happy enough, he remembers. He liked to write, had good friends. Life was filled with possibilities.

"Sometimes I think it would have been nice to have kids and a marriage,   72
but I had a very action-filled youth, with lots of partying."

If he regrets anything, and he tries not to, it's his experimentation with   73
"pollutants."

As soon as I hear that word, I have a crystal-clear mental picture of a   74
transparent plastic bag filled to overflowing with oddly shaped pink pills: little amphetamine wonders that made people feel like Superman. Friends of mine, in Dawson College, had a pharmaceutical connection that made them as available as candy, and we swallowed them as if they were.

You never got hungry, you could stay up round the clock, you could out-   75
race the fastest car—or at least you felt you could. The downs were unpleasant, leaving you strung-out and paranoid, so the trick was to stay up, postpone the crash as long as possible, or mellow it out with pot or beer.

I remember feeling the pills were making me a little too crazy, and going   76
off them cold turkey after months. I was walking down a school corridor when I started sweating buckets. It drenched my clothes, and I had to hide in the bathroom till that, and the shaking, stopped.

Philip thought they gave him an edge, made him smarter, cleverer. What   77
they actually made him was psychotic, resulting in his original misdiagnosis, and of course treatment with medications inappropriate to the "disease."

"When people I'd gone to school with were building their careers, I was   78
in a mental hospital."

He struggled his way back into the normal work world—he has a busi-   79
ness background in real estate. He smiles at me, wondering if I can visualize him in his former office on de Maisonneuve, wearing, he assures me, a suit.

He's been an activist for it seems like forever. He used to be president of   80
the Notre-Dame-de-Grâce (NDG) anti-poverty group I visited earlier, but now he's involved in an Urban Issues Program, funded by a grant from the Bronfmans. If you work for a community program while on welfare, you can get about $800 a month.

He divides his time between the NDG community council food bank,   81
putting out a newsletter in which he sometimes writes editorials, and community theatre. In the last play he was involved in, he played the welfare
agent.

"It's okay for rich people to go to movies and plays just to be entertained,   82
but the poor have to go to an 'education,'" he muses. Still, it's a good learning tool. "We always have a hero or heroine with a problem, like a single
mom trying to go back to school. We stop the action, say the landlord or the
welfare worker is yelling at her, 'You just don't want to work,'"—and, he adds
thoughtfully, some people are like that, but it may be because they're afraid
of failing again—"we'll stop the action and ask the audience—most of whom
have been in similar circumstances—what she should say or do."

He's lucky to have been able to rent from an elderly couple in Snowdon   83
who appreciate their quiet tenant enough to charge him only $400. Philip
thought it wise to leave NDG, where he could never get away from his work.
He was constantly running into people in need, or who wanted to discuss this
and that. You have to develop survival mechanisms if you want to last as an
activist.

There is so much to do, and so few resources, personal and otherwise, to   84
call on to get things done. He's closer to the ground than Annette, without a
trace of ideology, and perhaps he finds it easier to communicate with his peers
than she does.

As our conversation winds down, a man comes in with his child and   85
stops, after an instant of surprised recognition, to chat with Philip. They
used to sell real estate out of the same office, and it's an awkward conversation, both participants pretty self-conscious.

I can't help but wonder how many similar encounters between the main-   86
stream employed and their disappeared former colleagues occur every day in
the city.

■ ■ ■

Discussion and Writing Suggestions

1. How is Capponi's approach similar to that of Stackhouse? of Allen? of
   O'Reilly-Fleming?
2. Capponi is clearly sympathetic to the plight of the poor and homeless
   people she profiles. Does this constitute bias that taints her findings, or is
   she identifying her experiences and beliefs to establish the nature of her
   credibility?

■ WRITING ACTIVITIES

1. Write an article for a newsmagazine about the current political landscape in Canada, in relation to poverty issues. Focus on the difference between Liberals and Conservatives, but include other political ideologies, such as those of the NDP, the Green Party, or the Bloc, indicating where ideological boundaries sometimes seem to blur. Don't take sides, but do your best to give an objective account of some of the key political debates and the kinds of arguments they have generated.

2. Choose whether to fashion your article in the style of (1) an objective newsmagazine article or (2) an editorial or argumentative article. If you choose the first option for this assignment, your paper should be relatively objective. If you choose the second, explain why you advocate one set of positions and oppose the other. In developing your argument, you must do more than simply express your opinion; try to support your opinion with solid evidence and logical reasoning.

3. Select two or three authors represented in this chapter and compare and contrast their use of argument. Compare selections that have some common denominator—for example, subject matter, or position on the political spectrum, or type of argument, or use of language. For instance, you might look at articles that do not draw on outside sources, like those by Stackhouse and Layton, to compare and contrast the kinds of evidence and logic each author uses. Or you might look at articles that use a case-study approach to profile the lives of individuals, comparing the length and details of the portraits, and the way authors move from case to point. Discuss the strategies that the authors use in advancing their cases and the effectiveness of their arguments.

4. Write a speech, either for the Prime Minister, a provincial premier, or a social advocacy representative, recommending a course of action on an aspect of responding to homelessness. Draw upon the relevant selections in the chapter to obtain evidence and also to determine key points of ideological contention on the issue. Be careful to acknowledge and then respond to opposing points of view.

5. Some have observed that the media and intellectuals in Canada are generally soft on liberals and harder on conservatives. Journalists and scholars are sometimes stereotyped as ex-protesters—bleeding hearts who have championed left-wing causes—who use their writing to salve their own consciences and, perhaps, do some social good. Do the articles we have selected contain this sort of left-wing slant? If so, is it obvious or covert, and what forms of evidence can you cite to demonstrate your point? If you want to evaluate another source, you might look instead at your local newspaper(s) over a period of time (say a full week) to see if you can identify the presence—subtle or obvious—of a political perspective in the articles. Alternatively, with the same question in mind, you might consider whether a newsmagazine like *Maclean's* can be identified with a particular political perspective.

■ RESEARCH ACTIVITIES

1. Write an article of five pages for a newsmagazine on the ideological debate surrounding poverty and homelessness, representing views across the political spectrum. Try to be as objective as possible. Your job is to inform your readers of the nature of the debate, not to argue one side or another on any particular issue.

2. Prepare an *annotated bibliography* of sources, drawn from across the political spectrum, that address the issue of poverty. Write at least eight bibliographical entries: Include at least one magazine or newspaper article or editorial and one book or monograph report from left-wing publishers; include one article or editorial or book report from right-wing publishers. Use APA or MLA format for citations. Instead of arranging these citations alphabetically, however, arrange them into a political spectrum going from far right to far left—or vice versa. Thus, your bibliography could provide a detailed plan—in terms of both content and organization—for an actual paper dealing with the range of political positions and political rhetoric. Each entry should be one-half page to one page long.

   Identify each author's political position, if it is evident. Give enough quotations to support your identification. In cases for which the author is not arguing from an identifiable position but only reporting facts, indicate which position the reported facts support, and explain how. (*Note:* Some newspapers or magazines have an identifiable political viewpoint in general, in their news and op-ed orientation, but also attempt to present other views at least some of the time. For example, *The Globe and Mail* is predominantly liberal, but often carries conservative op-ed columns, letters, etc. So you shouldn't assume that any article appearing in such a periodical will automatically have its predominant viewpoint; look for other identifying clues.)

3. As a member of a group of three or four, select one of the following scenarios:
   - You are a member of an election (or re-election) campaign staff for a political candidate.
   - You are a member of a citizen action group that is working to pass a voter referendum.
   - Some other comparable scenario of your own choosing.

   Focus your efforts on the interaction of poverty with a particular controversial *domestic issue*—for example, affirmative action, immigration policy, abortion, education, law and order, health care, or drug policy. (If you are working for a political candidate, recognize that there may be other issues in the campaign, but imagine that this particular issue is the crucial one at this particular time.)

   Produce *three reports* for the benefit of your candidate or your group:

- A background survey of the issue. What is the history of this issue, both in a social context and as it has affected recent political events and campaigns? (4–5 pages)
- A survey and analysis of the *pro* and *con* arguments on the issue, as they have been articulated by recent commentators and political figures. Organize your discussion of these arguments and positions *along a political spectrum*, ranging from *extreme left* (or *right*) to *moderate* to *extreme right* (or *left*). If you have already prepared the annotated bibliography called for in the previous assignment, you may wish to use it as a basis for this section. (6–7 pages)
- A set of *recommendations for strategy*, based on your assignment, of the most effective ways to proceed and for your side to prevail. Suggest effective *rhetorical* ways of promoting your side and attacking the other side. Suggest ways of using *language* for maximum effect. At the same time, suggest ways to avoid coming across as extreme in your position, and ways by which your position might be perceived as the most reasonable one. (4–5 pages)

4. Examine the record of the federal government in response to homelessness and write a report on its philosophy and political activities in the past decade or so. Or research the Canadian Communist party. Check major newspaper and magazine indexes; check government documents; write to the parties themselves, asking for information. Who have been some of their candidates? What were their programs? How well have they done at election time? Has their popularity been increasing or decreasing?

5. Examine two or three successive issues of a magazine or journal at the left or right ends of the political spectrum and write an analysis of the kinds of positions authors of articles in these periodicals take on various issues, as well as the type of rhetorical devices they use to persuade their readers.

Obedience to Authority

Would you obey an order to inflict pain on another person? Most of us, if confronted with this question, would probably be quick to answer: "Never!" Yet if the conclusions of researchers are to be trusted, it is not psychopaths who kill non-combatant civilians in wartime and torture victims in prisons around the world but rather ordinary people following orders. People obey. This is a basic, necessary fact of human society. As Stanley Milgram, an author of one of the readings in this chapter, put it, "Obedience is as basic an element in the structure of social life as one can point to. Some system of authority is a requirement of all communal living" (p. 213).

The question, then, is not, "Should we obey the orders of an authority figure?" but rather, "To what *extent* should we obey?" Each generation seems to give new meaning to these questions. When senior Nazi officers were charged at Nuremberg with responsibility for crimes committed under their charge in concentration camps, they offered the defence that they were only following orders. During the Vietnam War, a number of American soldiers followed a commander's orders and murdered civilians in the hamlet of My Lai. In the 1990s the world was horrified by genocidal violence in Rwanda and in the former nation of Yugoslavia. These were civil wars, in which people who had been living for generations as neighbours suddenly, upon the instigation and orders of their leaders, turned upon and slaughtered one another.

Sadly, this phenomenon of brutal behaviour associated with group mentality is seen not only in wartime. In less dramatic ways, conflicts over the extent to which we obey orders surface in everyday life. How often have you read of people who claim they were just going along with the gang when they assaulted a teenager or terrorized an elderly person in the course of a home invasion? Perhaps you have found yourself going against your own better judgment in your school years to tease or bully a classmate because everyone else in your group of friends was doing it; if not, you almost certainly observed such behaviour. There may not have been any explicit order—the group may not even have had a leader—but it had sufficient authority nonetheless to command obedience. At one point or another, you may face a moral dilemma at work. Perhaps it will take this form: The boss tells you to overlook File X in preparing a report for a certain client. But you're sure that File X pertains directly to the report and contains information that will alarm the client. What should you do? The dilemmas of obedience also emerge on some campuses with the rite of fraternity hazing. Psychologists Janice Gibson and Mika

Haritos-Fatouros have made the startling observation that whether the obedience in question involves a pledge's joining a fraternity or a torturer's joining an elite military corps, the *process* by which one acquiesces to a superior's order (and thereby becomes a member of the group) is remarkably the same:

> There are several ways to teach people to do the unthinkable, and we have developed a model to explain how they are used. We have also found that college fraternities, although they are far removed from the grim world of torture and violent combat, use similar methods for initiating new members to ensure their faithfulness to the fraternity's rules and values. However, this unthinking loyalty can sometimes lead to dangerous actions: Over the past 10 years, there have been countless injuries during fraternity initiations and 39 deaths. These training techniques are designed to instill obedience in people, but they can easily be a guide for an intensive course in torture.
>
> 1. *Screening to find the best prospects:* Normal, well-adjusted people with the physical, intellectual and, in some cases, political attributes necessary for the task.
> 2. *Techniques to increase binding among these prospects:* Initiation rites to isolate people from society and introduce them to a new social order, with different rules and values.
>
>   Elitist attitudes and "in-group" language, which highlight the differences between the group and the rest of society.
> 3. *Techniques to reduce the strain of obedience:* Blaming and dehumanizing the victims, so it is less disturbing to harm them.
>
>   Harassment, the constant physical and psychological intimidation that prevents logical thinking and promotes the instinctive responses needed for acts of inhuman cruelty.
>
>   Rewards for obedience and punishments for not cooperating.
>
>   Social modelling by watching other group members commit violent acts and then receive rewards.
>
>   Systematic desensitization to repugnant acts by gradual exposure to them, so they appear routine and normal despite conflicts with previous moral standards.

(From: Janice T. Gibson and Mika Haritos-Fatouros, "The Education of a Torturer," *Psychology Today* (November 1986). Reprinted with permission from *Psychology Today* Magazine. Copyright 1986 Sussex Publishers, Inc.)

In this chapter, you will explore the dilemmas inherent in obeying the orders of an authority. The chapter begins with Isaiah Berlin's "Notes on Prejudice," in which he looks toward the nationalistic qualities of group mentality to account for the phenomenon behind so much of the violence of history. Next, in a brief essay adapted from a lecture, British novelist Doris Lessing helps set a context for the discussion by questioning the manner in which we call ourselves individualists yet fail to understand how groups define and exert influence over us. Next, psychologist Solomon Asch describes an experiment he devised to demonstrate the powerful influence of group pressure upon individual judgment. Psychologist Stanley Milgram then reports on his own landmark study in which he set out to determine the extent to which ordinary individuals would obey the clearly immoral orders of an authority figure. The results were shocking, not only to the psychiatrists who predicted that few people would follow such orders but also to many other social scientists and laypeople—some of whom applauded Milgram for his fiendishly ingenious design, some of whom bitterly attacked him for unethical procedures. We include one of these attacks, a scathing review by psychologist Diana Baumrind.

Karen Messing then takes up another aspect of the motive for obedience demonstrated by Milgram's work: the unquestioning respect that people have for science and scientists. Next, Philip Zimbardo reports on his famous (and controversial) Stanford Prison Experiment, in which volunteers exhibited astonishingly convincing authoritarian and obedient attitudes as they play-acted at being prisoners and guards. An essay and two pieces of chillingly realistic fiction follow. In "Disobedience as a Psychological and Moral Problem," psychoanalyst and philosopher Erich Fromm discusses the comforts of obedient behaviour. In a passage from *The Handmaid's Tale*, Margaret Atwood shows how individual behaviour can be controlled by group participation in ritualized violence. In "The Lottery," Shirley Jackson tells the story of a community that faithfully meets its yearly obligation.

Notes on Prejudice

ISAIAH BERLIN

Isaiah Berlin was a social historian and philosopher best known as an opponent of authoritarianism and defender of liberal pluralism through his brilliant philosophical essays. His "Notes" were introduced this way when they were first published in The New York Review of Books:

> *Isaiah Berlin liked to allude to a passage in Bertrand Russell's History of Western Philosophy where Russell says that, if we are to understand a philosopher's views, we must "apprehend their imaginative background," [1] or the philosopher's "inner citadel," as Berlin calls it [2]. The character of one of the main rooms in Berlin's own citadel is vividly expressed in some hurried notes Berlin wrote for a friend (who does not wish to be identified) in 1981. His friend was due to give a lecture, and wrote to Berlin to ask for suggestions about how he might treat his theme. Berlin had to go abroad early on the day after he received the request, and wrote the notes quickly, in his own hand, without time for revision or expansion. The result is somewhat breathless and telegraphic, no doubt, but it conveys with great immediacy Berlin's opposition to intolerance and prejudice, especially fanatical monism, stereotypes, and aggressive nationalism. Its relevance to the events of September 11, 2001, hardly needs stressing.*
>
> *Berlin's manuscript is reproduced here in a direct transcript, with only a few adjustments to make it easier to read. I have omitted material relevant only to the specific occasion.*
>
> —*Henry Hardy*, New York Review of Books

1.

Few things have done more harm than the belief on the part of individu-   1
als or groups (or tribes or states or nations or churches) that he or she or they
are in sole possession of the truth: especially about how to live, what to be &
do—& that those who differ from them are not merely mistaken, but wicked
or mad: & need restraining or suppressing. It is a terrible and dangerous arrogance to believe that you alone are right: have a magical eye which sees the
truth: & that others cannot be right if they disagree.

This makes one certain that there is one goal & one only for one's nation   2
or church or the whole of humanity, & that it is worth any amount of suffering (particularly on the part of other people) if only the goal is attained—
"through an ocean of blood to the Kingdom of Love" (or something like this)
said Robespierre[3]: & Hitler, Lenin, Stalin, & I daresay leaders in the religious wars of Christian v. Moslem or Catholics v. Protestants sincerely
believed this: the belief that there is one & only one true answer to the central questions which have agonized mankind & that one has it oneself—or
one's leader has it—was responsible for the oceans of blood: but no Kingdom
of Love sprang from it—or could: there are many ways of living, believing,
behaving: mere knowledge provided by history, anthropology, literature, art,
law makes clear that the differences of cultures & characters are as deep as the
similarities (which make men human) & that we are none the poorer for this
rich variety: knowledge of it opens the windows of the mind (and soul) and
makes people wiser, nicer, & more civilized: absence of it breeds irrational
prejudice, hatreds, ghastly extermination of heretics and those who are different: if the two great wars plus Hitler's genocides haven't taught us that, we
are incurable.

The most valuable—or one of the most valuable—elements in the British   3
tradition is precisely the relative freedom from political, racial, religious
fanaticism & monomania. Compromising with people with whom you don't
sympathize or altogether understand is indispensable to any decent society:
nothing is more destructive than a happy sense of one's own—or one's
nation's—infallibility, which lets you destroy others with a quiet conscience
because you are doing God's (e.g. the Spanish Inquisition or the Ayatollas) or
the superior race's (e.g. Hitler) or History's (e.g. Lenin–Stalin) work.

The only cure is understanding how other societies—in space or time—   4
live: and that it is possible to lead lives different from one's own, & yet to be
fully human, worthy of love, respect or at least curiosity. Jesus, Socrates, John
Hus of Bohemia, the great chemist Lavoisier, socialists and liberals (as well as
conservatives) in Russia, Jews in Germany, all perished at the hands of "infallible" ideologues: intuitive certainty is no substitute for carefully tested empirical knowledge based on observation and experiment and free discussion
between men: the first people totalitarians destroy or silence are men of ideas
& free minds.

2.

Another source of avoidable conflict is stereotypes. Tribes hate neigh-   5
bouring tribes by whom they feel threatened, & then rationalize their fears by

representing them as wicked or inferior, or absurd or despicable in some way. Yet these stereotypes alter sometimes quite rapidly. Take the nineteenth century alone: in, say, 1840 the French are thought of as swashbuckling, gallant, immoral, militarized, men with curly moustachios, dangerous to women, likely to invade England in revenge for Waterloo; & the Germans are beer drinking, rather ludicrous provincials, musical, full of misty metaphysics, harmless but somewhat absurd. By 1871 the Germans are Uhlans storming through France, invited by the terrible Bismarck—terrifying Prussian militarists filled with national pride, etc. France is a poor, crushed, civilized land, in need of protection from all good men, lest its art & literature are crushed underheel by the terrible invaders.

The Russians in the nineteenth century are crushed serfs, darkly brooding semi-religious Slav mystics who write deep novels, a huge horde of cossacks loyal to the Tsar, who sing beautifully. In our times all this has dramatically altered: crushed population, yes, but technology, tanks, godless materialism, crusade against capitalism, etc. The English are ruthless imperialists lording it over fuzzy wuzzies, looking down their long noses at the rest of the world—& then impoverished, liberal, decent welfare state beneficiaries in need of allies. And so on. All these stereotypes are substitutes for real knowledge—which is ever of anything so simple or permanent as a particular generalized image of foreigners—and are stimuli to national self satisfaction & disdain of other nations. It is a prop to nationalism.

3.

Nationalism—which everybody in the nineteenth century thought was ebbing—is the strongest & most dangerous force at large to-day. It is usually the product of a wound inflicted by one nation on the pride or territory of another: if Louis XIV had not attacked & devastated the Germans, & humiliated them for years—the Sun King whose state gave laws to everybody, in politics, warfare, art, philosophy, science—then the Germans would not, perhaps, have become quite so aggressive by, say, the early nineteenth century when they became fiercely nationalistic against Napoleon. If the Russians, similarly, had not been treated as a barbarous mass by the West in the nineteenth century, or the Chinese had not been humiliated by opium wars or general exploitation, neither would have fallen so easily to a doctrine which promised they would inherit the earth after they had, with the help of historic forces which none may stop, crushed all the capitalist unbelievers. If the Indians had not been patronized, etc., etc. Conquest, enslavement of peoples, imperialism etc. are not fed just by greed or desire for glory, but have to justify themselves to themselves by some central idea: French as the only true culture; the white man's burden; communism: & the stereotypes of others as inferior or wicked. Only knowledge, carefully acquired & not by short cuts, can dispel this: even that won't dispel human aggressiveness or dislike for the dissimilar (in skin, culture, religion) by itself: still, education in history, anthropology, law (especially if they are "comparative" & not just of one's own country as they usually are) helps.

■　■　■

Notes

[1] *History of Western Philosophy* (Simon and Schuster, 1945), p. 226.

[2] For example, in *Four Essays on Liberty* (Oxford University Press, 1969), p. 135.

[3] Berlin may be referring to the passage where Robespierre writes that "en scellant notre ouvrage de notre sang, nous puissons voir au moins briller l'aurore de la félicité universelle" ("by sealing our work with our blood, we may see at least the bright dawn of universal happiness"). Rapport sur les principes de morale politique qui doivent guider la Convention nationale dans l'administration intérieure de la République [Paris, 1794], p. 4.

■ ■ ■

Discussion and Writing Suggestions

1. Berlin's thesis is that nationalism is dangerous because of the assumptions of superiority imbedded in it. Why would a belief in the superiority of one's group (nation, religion, etc.) become dangerous? Can you think of any examples of supremacist thinking that do not necessarily have an aggressive phase in which the group sets out to convert or oppress non-members?
2. How could the State promote love for one's country without fostering supremacist thinking?
3. Is Canada a supremacist nation? Is the United States?

Group Minds

DORIS LESSING

Doris Lessing sets a context for the discussion on obedience by illuminating a fundamental conflict: We in the Western world celebrate our individualism, but we're naive in understanding the ways that groups largely undercut our individuality. "We are group animals still," says Lessing, "and there is nothing wrong with that. But what is dangerous is . . . not understanding the social laws that govern groups and govern us." This chapter is largely devoted to an exploration of these tendencies. As you read selections by Milgram and the other authors here, bear in mind Lessing's troubling question: If we know that individuals will violate their own good common sense and moral codes in order to become accepted members of a group, why then can't we put this knowledge to use and teach people to be wary of group pressures?

Doris Lessing, the daughter of farmers, was born in Persia, now Iran, in 1919. She attended a Roman Catholic convent and a girls' high school in southern Rhodesia (now Zimbabwe). From 1959 through to the present, Lessing has written more than 20 works of fiction and has been called "the best woman novelist" of the post-war era. Her work has received a great deal of scholarly attention. She is, perhaps, best known for her Five Short Novels *(1954),* The Golden Notebook *(1962), and* Briefing for a Descent into Hell *(1971). The jury that awarded her the Asturias Prize for literature in 2001 described her as "an impassioned freedom fighter, who has spared no effort in her commitment to Third World causes, through literature and the personal experience of a hazardous biography."*[1]

People living in the West, in societies that we describe as Western, or as the free world, may be educated in many different ways, but they will all emerge with an idea about themselves that goes something like this: I am a citizen of a free society, and that means I am an individual, making individual choices. My mind is my own, my opinions are chosen by me, I am free to do as I will, and at the worst the pressures on me are economic, that is, I may be too poor to do as I want.   1

This set of ideas may sound something like a caricature, but it is not so far off how we see ourselves. It is a portrait that may not have been acquired consciously, but is part of a general atmosphere or set of assumptions that influence our ideas about ourselves.   2

People in the West therefore may go through their entire lives never thinking to analyze this very flattering picture, and as a result are helpless against all kinds of pressures on them to conform in many kinds of ways.   3

The fact is that we all live our lives in groups—the family, work groups, social, religious and political groups. Very few people indeed are happy as solitaries, and they tend to be seen by their neighbors as peculiar or selfish or worse. Most people cannot stand being alone for long. They are always seeking groups to belong to, and if one group dissolves, they look for another. We are group animals still, and there is nothing wrong with that. But what is dangerous is not the belonging to a group, or groups, but not understanding the social laws that govern groups and govern us.   4

When we're in a group, we tend to think as that group does: we may even have joined the group to find "like-minded" people. But we also find our thinking changing because we belong to a group. It is the hardest thing in the world to maintain an individual dissident opinion, as a member of a group.   5

It seems to me that this is something we have all experienced—something we take for granted, may never have thought about it. But a great deal of experiment has gone on among psychologists and sociologists on this very theme. If I describe an experiment or two, then anyone listening who may be a sociologist or psychologist will groan, oh God not *again*—for they will have heard of these classic experiments far too often. My guess is that the rest of the people will never have heard of these experiments, never have had these ideas presented to them. If my guess is true, then it aptly illustrates my general thesis, and the general idea behind these talks, that we (the human race) are now in possession of a great deal of hard information about ourselves, but we do not use it to improve our institutions and therefore our lives.   6

[1] Associated Press, "Top Literary Prize for 'Freedom Fighter' Lessing," *Winnipeg Free Press* (9 June 2001): B7.

A typical test, or experiment, on this theme goes like this. A group of   7
people are taken into the researcher's confidence. A minority of one or two
are left in the dark. Some situation demanding measurement or assessment is
chosen. For instance, comparing lengths of wood that differ only a little from
each other, but enough to be perceptible, or shapes that are almost the same
size. The majority in the group—according to instruction—will assert stubbornly that these two shapes or lengths are the same length, or size, while the
solitary individual, or the couple, who have not been so instructed will assert
that the pieces of wood or whatever are different. But the majority will continue to insist—speaking metaphorically—that black is white, and after a
period of exasperation, irritation, even anger, certainly incomprehension, the
minority will fall into line. Not always, but nearly always. There are indeed
glorious individuals who stubbornly insist on telling the truth as they see it,
but most give in to the majority opinion, obey the atmosphere.

When put as badly, as unflatteringly, as this, reactions tend to be incred-   8
ulous: "I certainly wouldn't give in, I speak my mind. . . ." But would you?

People who have experienced a lot of groups, who perhaps have observed   9
their own behavior, may agree that the hardest thing in the world is to stand
out against one's group, a group of one's peers. Many agree that among our
most shameful memories is this, how often we said black was white because
other people were saying it.

In other words, we know that this is true of human behavior, but how do   10
we know it? It is one thing to admit it, in a vague uncomfortable sort of way
(which probably includes the hope that one will never again be in such a testing situation) but quite another to make that cool step into a kind of objectivity, where one may say, "Right, if that's what human beings are like,
myself included, then let's admit it, examine and organize our attitudes
accordingly."

This mechanism, of obedience to the group, does not only mean obedi-   11
ence or submission to a small group, or one that is sharply determined, like a
religion or political party. It means, too, conforming to those large, vague, ill-
defined collections of people who may never think of themselves as having a
collective mind because they are aware of differences of opinion—but which,
to people from outside, from another culture, seem very minor. The underlying assumptions and assertions that govern the group are never discussed,
never challenged, probably never noticed, the main one being precisely this:
that it *is* a group mind, intensely resistant to change, equipped with sacred
assumptions about which there can be no discussion.

But suppose this kind of thing were taught in schools?   12

Let us just suppose it, for a moment. . . . But at once the nub of the prob-   13
lem is laid bare.

Imagine us saying to children, "In the last fifty or so years, the human   14
race has become aware of a great deal of information about its mechanisms;
how it behaves, how it must behave under certain circumstances. If this is to
be useful, you must learn to contemplate these rules calmly, dispassionately,

disinterestedly, without emotion. It is information that will set people free from blind loyalties, obedience to slogans, rhetoric, leaders, group emotions." Well, there it is.

■　■　■

Review Questions

1. What is the flattering portrait Lessing paints of people living in the West?
2. Lessing believes that individuals in the West are "helpless against all kinds of pressures on them to conform in many kinds of ways." Why?
3. Lessing refers to a class of experiments on obedience. Summarize the "typical" experiment.

Discussion and Writing Suggestions

1. Lessing writes that "what is dangerous is not the belonging to a group, or groups, but not understanding the social laws that govern groups and govern us." What is the danger Lessing is speaking of here?
2. Lessing states that "we (the human race) are now in possession of a great deal of hard information about ourselves, but we do not use it to improve our institutions and therefore our lives." First, do you agree with Lessing? Can you cite other examples (aside from information on obedience to authority) in which we do not use our knowledge to better humankind?
3. Explore some of the difficulties in applying this "hard information" about humankind that Lessing speaks of. Assume she's correct in claiming that we don't incorporate our knowledge of human nature into the running of our institutions. Why don't we? What are the difficulties of *acting* on information?
4. Lessing speaks of "people who remember how they acted in school" and of their guilt in recalling how they succumbed to group pressures. Can you recall such an event? What feelings do you have about it now?

Opinions and Social Pressure

SOLOMON E. ASCH

In the early 1950s, Solomon Asch (b. 1907), a social psychologist at Rutgers University in New Brunswick, New Jersey, conducted a series of simple but inge- nious experiments on the influence of group pressure upon the individual. Essentially, he discovered, individuals can be influenced by groups to deny the evi- dence of their own senses. Together with the Milgram experiments of the follow- ing decade (see the following selections), these studies provide powerful evidence of the degree to which individuals can surrender their own judgment to others, even when those others are clearly in the wrong. The results of these experiments have implications far beyond the laboratory: They can explain a good deal of the normal human behaviour we see every day—at school, at work, at home.

That social influences shape every person's practices, judgments and beliefs is   1
a truism to which anyone will readily assent. A child masters his "native" dialect down to the finest nuances; a member of a tribe of cannibals accepts cannibalism as altogether fitting and proper. All the social sciences take their departure from the observation of the profound effects that groups exert on their members. For psychologists, group pressure upon the minds of individuals raises a host of questions they would like to investigate in detail.

How, and to what extent, do social forces constrain people's opinions   2
and attitudes? This question is especially pertinent in our day. The same epoch that has witnessed the unprecedented technical extension of communication has also brought into existence the deliberate manipulation of opinion and the "engineering of consent." There are many good reasons why, as citizens and as scientists, we should be concerned with studying the ways in which human beings form their opinions and the role that social conditions play.

Studies of these questions began with the interest in hypnosis aroused by   3
the French physician Jean Martin Charcot (a teacher of Sigmund Freud) toward the end of the 19th century. Charcot believed that only hysterical patients could be fully hypnotized, but this view was soon challenged by two other physicians, Hyppolyte Bernheim and A. A. Liébault, who demonstrated that they could put most people under the hypnotic spell. Bernheim proposed that hypnosis was but an extreme form of a normal psychological process which became known as "suggestibility." It was shown that monotonous reiteration of instructions could induce in normal persons in the waking state involuntary bodily changes such as swaying or rigidity of the arms, and sensations such as warmth and odor.

It was not long before social thinkers seized upon these discoveries as a   4
basis for explaining numerous social phenomena, from the spread of opinion to the formation of crowds and the following of leaders. The sociologist Gabriel Tarde summed it all up in the aphorism: "Social man is a somnambulist."

When the new discipline of social psychology was born at the beginning   5
of this century, its first experiments were essentially adaptations of the suggestion demonstration. The technique generally followed a simple plan. The subjects, usually college students, were asked to give their opinions or preferences concerning various matters; some time later they were again asked to state their choices, but now they were also informed of the opinions held by authorities or large groups of their peers on the same matters. (Often the alleged consensus was fictitious.) Most of these studies had substantially the same result: confronted with opinions contrary to their own, many subjects

apparently shifted their judgments in the direction of the views of the majorities or the experts. The late psychologist Edward L. Thorndike reported that he had succeeded in modifying the esthetic preferences of adults by this procedure. Other psychologists reported that people's evaluations of the merit of a literary passage could be raised or lowered by ascribing the passage to different authors. Apparently the sheer weight of numbers or authority sufficed to change opinions, even when no arguments for the opinions themselves were provided.

Now the very ease of success in these experiments arouses suspicion.   6
Did the subjects actually change their opinions, or were the experimental victories scored only on paper? On grounds of common sense, one must question whether opinions are generally as watery as these studies indicate. There is some reason to wonder whether it was not the investigators who, in their enthusiasm for a theory, were suggestible, and whether the ostensibly gullible subjects were not providing answers which they thought good subjects were expected to give.

The investigations were guided by certain underlying assumptions, which   7
today are common currency and account for much that is thought and said about the operations of propaganda and public opinion. The assumptions are that people submit uncritically and painlessly to external manipulation by suggestion or prestige, and that any given idea or value can be "sold" or "unsold" without reference to its merits. We should be skeptical, however, of the supposition that the power of social pressure necessarily implies uncritical submission to it: independence and the capacity to rise above group passion are also open to human beings. Further, one may question on psychological grounds whether it is possible as a rule to change a person's judgment of a situation or an object without first changing his knowledge or assumptions about it.

In what follows I shall describe some experiments in an investigation of   8
the effects of group pressure which was carried out recently with the help of a number of my associates. The tests not only demonstrate the operations of group pressure upon individuals but also illustrate a new kind of attack on the problem and some of the more subtle questions that it raises.

A group of seven to nine young men, all college students, are assembled   9
in a classroom for a "psychological experiment" in visual judgment. The experimenter informs them that they will be comparing the lengths of lines. He shows two large white cards [see Figure 1]. On one is a single vertical black line—the standard whose length is to be matched. On the other card are three vertical lines of various lengths. The subjects are to choose the one that is of the same length as the line on the other card. One of the three actually is of the same length; the other two are substantially different, the difference ranging from three quarters of an inch to an inch and three quarters.

The experiment opens uneventfully. The subjects announce their answers   10
in the order in which they have been seated in the room, and on the first round every person chooses the same matching line. Then a second set of

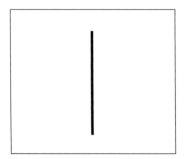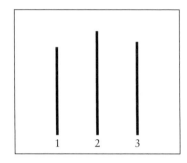

FIGURE 1

Subjects were shown two cards. One bore a standard line. The other bore three lines, one of which was the same length as the standard. The subjects were asked to choose this line.

cards is exposed; again the group is unanimous. The members appear ready to endure politely another boring experiment. On the third trial there is an unexpected disturbance. One person near the end of the group disagrees with all the others in his selection of the matching line. He looks surprised, indeed incredulous, about the disagreement. On the following trial he disagrees again, while the others remain unanimous in their choice. The dissenter becomes more and more worried and hesitant as the disagreement continues in succeeding trials; he may pause before announcing his answer and speak in a low voice, or he may smile in an embarrassed way.

What the dissenter does not know is that all the other members of the   11
group were instructed by the experimenter beforehand to give incorrect answers in unanimity at certain points. The single individual who is not a party to this prearrangement is the focal subject of our experiment. He is placed in a position in which, while he is actually giving the correct answers, he finds himself unexpectedly in a minority of one, opposed by a unanimous and arbitrary majority with respect to a clear and simple fact. Upon him we have brought to bear two opposed forces: the evidence of his senses and the unanimous opinion of a group of his peers. Also, he must declare his judgments in public, before a majority which has also stated its position publicly.

The instructed majority occasionally reports correctly in order to reduce   12
the possibility that the naive subject will suspect collusion against him. (In only a few cases did the subject actually show suspicion; when this happened, the experiment was stopped and the results were not counted.) There are 18 trials in each series, and on 12 of these the majority responds erroneously.

How do people respond to group pressure in this situation? I shall report   13
first the statistical results of a series in which a total of 123 subjects from three institutions of higher learning (not including my own Swarthmore College) were placed in the minority situation described above.

Two alternatives were open to the subject: he could act independently, repudiating the majority, or he could go along with the majority, repudiating the evidence of his senses. Of the 123 put to the test, a considerable percentage yielded to the majority. Whereas in ordinary circumstances individuals matching the lines will make mistakes less than 1 per cent of the time, under group pressure the minority subjects swung to acceptance of the misleading majority's wrong judgments in 36.8 per cent of the selections.

Of course individuals differed in response. At one extreme, about one quarter of the subjects were completely independent and never agreed with the erroneous judgments of the majority. At the other extreme, some individuals went with the majority nearly all the time. The performances of individuals in this experiment tend to be highly consistent. Those who strike out on the path of independence do not, as a rule, succumb to the majority even over an extended series of trials, while those who choose the path of compliance are unable to free themselves as the ordeal is prolonged.

The reasons for the startling individual differences have not yet been investigated in detail. At this point we can only report some tentative generalizations from talks with the subjects, each of whom was interviewed at the end of the experiment. Among the independent individuals were many who held fast because of staunch confidence in their own judgment. The most significant fact about them was not absence of responsiveness to the majority but a capacity to recover from doubt and to reestablish their equilibrium. Others who acted independently came to believe that the majority was correct in its answers, but they continued their dissent on the simple ground that it was their obligation to call the play as they saw it.

Among the extremely yielding persons we found a group who quickly reached the conclusion: "I am wrong, they are right." Others yielded in order "not to spoil your results." Many of the individuals who went along suspected that the majority were "sheep" following the first responder, or that the majority were victims of an optical illusion; nevertheless, these suspicions failed to free them at the moment of decision. More disquieting were the reactions of subjects who construed their difference from the majority as a sign of some general deficiency in themselves, which at all costs they must hide. On this basis they desperately tried to merge with the majority, not realizing the longer-range consequences to themselves. All the yielding subjects underestimated the frequency with which they conformed.

Which aspect of the influence of a majority is more important—the size of the majority or its unanimity? The experiment was modified to examine this question. In one series the size of the opposition was varied from one to 15 persons. The results showed a clear trend. When a subject was confronted with only a single individual who contradicted his answers, he was swayed little: he continued to answer independently and correctly in nearly all trials. When the opposition was increased to two, the pressure became substantial: minority subjects now accepted the wrong answer 13.6 per cent of the time. Under the pressure of a majority of three, the subjects' errors jumped to 31.8 per cent. But further increases in the size of the majority apparently did not

14

15

16

17

18

increase the weight of the pressure substantially. Clearly the size of the opposition is important only up to a point.

Disturbance of the majority's unanimity had a striking effect. In this   19
experiment the subject was given the support of a truthful partner—either another individual who did not know of the prearranged agreement among the rest of the group, or a person who was instructed to give correct answers throughout.

The presence of a supporting partner depleted the majority of much of its   20
power. Its pressure on the dissenting individual was reduced to one fourth: that is, subjects answered incorrectly only one fourth as often as under the pressure of a unanimous majority. The weakest persons did not yield as readily. Most interesting were the reactions to the partner. Generally the feeling toward him was one of warmth and closeness; he was credited with inspiring confidence. However, the subjects repudiated the suggestion that the partner decided them to be independent.

Was the partner's effect a consequence of his dissent, or was it related to   21
his accuracy? We now introduced into the experimental group a person who was instructed to dissent from the majority but also to disagree with the subject. In some experiments the majority was always to choose the worst of the comparison lines and the instructed dissenter to pick the line that was closer to the length of the standard one; in others the majority was consistently intermediate and the dissenter most in error. In this manner we were able to study the relative influence of "compromising" and "extremist" dissenters.

Again the results are clear. When a moderate dissenter is present the   22
effect of the majority on the subject decreases by approximately one third, and extremes of yielding disappear. Moreover, most of the errors the subjects do make are moderate, rather than flagrant. In short, the dissenter largely controls the choice of errors. To this extent the subjects broke away from the majority even while bending to it.

On the other hand, when the dissenter always chose the line that was   23
more flagrantly different from the standard, the results were of quite a different kind. The extremist dissenter produced a remarkable freeing of the subjects; their errors dropped to only 9 per cent. Furthermore, all the errors were of the moderate variety. We were able to conclude that dissents *per se* increased independence and moderated the errors that occurred, and that the direction of dissent exerted consistent effects.

In all the foregoing experiments each subject was observed only in a   24
single setting. We now turned to studying the effects upon a given individual of a change in the situation to which he was exposed. The first experiment examined the consequences of losing or gaining a partner. The instructed partner began by answering correctly on the first six trials. With his support the subject usually resisted pressure from the majority: 18 of 27 subjects were completely independent. But after six trials the partner joined the majority. As soon as he did so, there was an abrupt rise in the subjects' errors. Their submission to the majority was just about as frequent as when the minority subject was opposed by a unanimous majority throughout.

It was surprising to find that the experience of having had a partner and 25 of having braved the majority opposition with him had failed to strengthen the individuals' independence. Questioning at the conclusion of the experiment suggested that we had overlooked an important circumstance; namely, the strong specific effect of "desertion" by the partner to the other side. We therefore changed the conditions so that the partner would simply leave the group at the proper point. (To allay suspicion it was announced in advance that he had an appointment with the dean.) In this form of the experiment, the partner's effect outlasted his presence. The errors increased after his departure, but less markedly than after a partner switched to the majority.

In a variant of this procedure the trials began with the majority unani- 26 mously giving correct answers. Then they gradually broke away until on the sixth trial the naive subject was alone and the group unanimously against him. As long as the subject had anyone on his side, he was almost invariably independent, but as soon as he found himself alone, the tendency to conform to the majority rose abruptly.

As might be expected, an individual's resistance to group pressure in 27 these experiments depends to a considerable degree on how wrong the majority is. We varied the discrepancy between the standard line and the other lines systematically, with the hope of reaching a point where the error of the majority would be so glaring that every subject would repudiate it and choose independently. In this we regretfully did not succeed. Even when the difference between the lines was seven inches, there were still some who yielded to the error of the majority.

The study provides clear answers to a few relatively simple questions, and 28 it raises many others that await investigation. We would like to know the degree of consistency of persons in situations which differ in content and structure. If consistency of independence or conformity in behavior is shown to be a fact, how is it functionally related to qualities of character and personality? In what ways is independence related to sociological or cultural conditions? Are leaders more independent than other people, or are they adept at following their followers? These and many other questions may perhaps be answerable by investigations of the type described here.

Life in society requires consensus as an indispensable condition. But con- 29 sensus, to be productive, requires that each individual contribute independently out of his experience and insight. When consensus comes under the dominance of conformity, the social process is polluted and the individual at the same time surrenders the powers on which his functioning as a feeling and thinking being depends. That we have found the tendency to conformity in our society so strong that reasonably intelligent and well-meaning young people are willing to call white black is a matter of concern. It raises questions about our ways of education and about the values that guide our conduct.

Yet anyone inclined to draw too pessimistic conclusions from this report 30 would do well to remind himself that the capacities for independence are not to be underestimated. He may also draw some consolation from a further observation: those who participated in this challenging experiment agreed nearly without exception that independence was preferable to conformity.

■ ■ ■

Review Questions

1. What is "suggestibility"? How is this phenomenon related to social pressure?
2. Summarize the procedure and results of the Asch experiment. What conclusions does Asch draw from these results?
3. To what extent did varying the size of the majority and its unanimity affect the experimental results?
4. What distinction does Asch draw between consensus and conformity?

Discussion and Writing Suggestions

1. Before discussing the experiment, Asch considers how easily people's opinions or attitudes may be shaped by social pressure. To what extent do you agree with this conclusion? Write a short paper on this subject, drawing upon examples from your own experience or observation or from your reading.
2. Do the results of this experiment surprise you? Or do they confirm facts about human behaviour that you had already suspected, observed, or experienced? Explain, in two or three paragraphs. Provide examples, relating these examples to features of the Asch experiment.
3. Frequently, the conclusions drawn from a researcher's experimental results are challenged on the basis that laboratory conditions do not accurately reflect the complexity of human behaviour. Asch draws certain conclusions about the degree to which individuals are affected by group pressures based on an experiment involving subjects choosing matching line lengths. To what extent, if any, do you believe that these conclusions lack validity because the behaviour at the heart of the experiment is too dissimilar to real-life situations of group pressure on the individual? Support your opinions with examples.
4. We are all familiar with the phenomenon of "peer pressure." To what extent do Asch's experiments demonstrate the power of peer pressure? To what extent do you think that other factors may be at work? Explain, providing examples.
5. Asch's experiments, conducted in the early 1950s, involved groups of "seven to nine young men, all college students." To what extent do you believe that the results of a similar experiment would be different today? To what extent might they be different if the subjects had included women, as well, and subjects of various ages, from children, to middle-aged people, to older people? To what extent do you believe that the social class or culture of the subjects might have an impact upon the experimental results? Support your opinions with examples and logical reasoning. (Beware, however, of overgeneralizing, based upon insufficient evidence.)

The Perils of Obedience

STANLEY MILGRAM

In 1963, a Yale psychologist conducted one of the classic studies on obedience that Doris Lessing refers to in "Group Minds." Stanley Milgram designed an experiment that forced participants either to violate their conscience by obeying the immoral demands of an authority figure or to refuse those demands. Surprisingly, Milgram found that few participants could resist the authority's orders, even when the participants knew that following these orders would result in another person's pain. Were the participants in these experiments incipient mass murderers? No, said Milgram. They were "ordinary people, simply doing their jobs." The implications of Milgram's conclusions are immense.

Consider: Where does evil reside? What sort of people were responsible for the Holocaust, and for the long list of other atrocities that seem to blight the human record in every generation? Is it a lunatic fringe, a few sick but powerful people who are responsible for atrocities? If so, then we decent folk needn't ever look inside ourselves to understand evil since (by our definition) evil lurks out there, in "those sick ones." Milgram's study suggested otherwise: that under a special set of circumstances the obedience we naturally show authority figures can transform us into agents of terror.

The article that follows is one of the longest in this text, and it may help you to know in advance the author's organization. In paragraphs 1–11, Milgram discusses the larger significance and the history of dilemmas involving obedience to authority; he then summarizes his basic experimental design and follows with a report of one experiment. Milgram organizes the remainder of his article into sections, which he has subtitled "An Unexpected Outcome," "Peculiar Reactions," "The Etiquette of Submission," and "Duty without Conflict." He begins his conclusion in paragraph 108. If you find the article too long to complete in a single sitting, then plan to read sections at a time, taking notes on each until you're done. Anticipate the article immediately following Milgram's: It reviews his work and concerns itself mainly about the ethics of his experimental design. Consider these ethics as you read so that you, in turn, can respond to Milgram's critics.

Stanley Milgram (1933–1984) taught and conducted research at Yale and Harvard universities and at the Graduate Center, City University of New York. He was named Guggenheim Fellow in 1972–1973 and a year later was nominated for the National Book Award for Obedience to Authority. *His other books include* Television and Antisocial Behavior *(1973),* The City and the Self *(1974),* Human Aggression *(1976), and* The Individual in the Social World *(1977).*

Obedience is as basic an element in the structure of social life as one can point   1
to. Some system of authority is a requirement of all communal living, and it is only the person dwelling in isolation who is not forced to respond, with defiance or submission, to the commands of others. For many people, obedience is a deeply ingrained behavior tendency, indeed a potent impulse overriding training in ethics, sympathy, and moral conduct.

The dilemma inherent in submission to authority is ancient, as old as the   2
story of Abraham, and the question of whether one should obey when commands conflict with conscience has been argued by Plato, dramatized in
Antigone, and treated to philosophic analysis in almost every historical epoch.
Conservative philosophers argue that the very fabric of society is threatened
by disobedience, while humanists stress the primacy of the individual conscience.

The legal and philosophic aspects of obedience are of enormous import,   3
but they say very little about how most people behave in concrete situations.
I set up a simple experiment at Yale University to test how much pain an ordinary citizen would inflict on another person simply because he was ordered to
by an experimental scientist. Stark authority was pitted against the subjects'
strongest moral imperatives against hurting others, and, with the subjects' ears
ringing with the screams of the victims, authority won more often than not.
The extreme willingness of adults to go to almost any lengths on the command of an authority constitutes the chief finding of the study and the fact
most urgently demanding explanation.

In the basic experimental design, two people come to a psychology lab-   4
oratory to take part in a study of memory and learning. One of them is designated as a "teacher" and the other a "learner." The experimenter explains
that the study is concerned with the effects of punishment on learning. The
learner is conducted into a room, seated in a kind of miniature electric chair;
his arms are strapped to prevent excessive movement, and an electrode is
attached to his wrist. He is told that he will be read lists of simple word pairs,
and that he will then be tested on his ability to remember the second word of
a pair when he hears the first one again. Whenever he makes an error, he will
receive electric shocks of increasing intensity.

The real focus of the experiment is the teacher. After watching the learner   5
being strapped into place, he is seated before an impressive shock generator.
The instrument panel consists of thirty level switches set in a horizontal line.
Each switch is clearly labeled with a voltage designation ranging from 15 to
450 volts. The following designations are clearly indicated for groups of four
switches, going from left to right: Slight Shock, Moderate Shock, Strong Shock,
Very Strong Shock, Intense Shock, Extreme Intensity Shock, Danger: Severe
Shock. (Two switches after this last designation are simply marked XXX.)

When a switch is depressed, a pilot light corresponding to each switch is   6
illuminated in bright red; an electric buzzing is heard; a blue light, labeled
"voltage energizer," flashes; the dial on the voltage meter swings to the right;
and various relay clicks sound off.

The upper left-hand corner of the generator is labeled SHOCK GENER-   7
ATOR, TYPE ZLB, DYSON INSTRUMENT COMPANY, WALTHAM,
MASS. OUTPUT 15 VOLTS–450 VOLTS.

Each subject is given a sample 45-volt shock from the generator before   8
his run as teacher, and the jolt strengthens his belief in the authenticity of the
machine.

The teacher is a genuinely naïve subject who has come to the laboratory 9
for the experiment. The learner, or victim, is actually an actor who receives no
shock at all. The point of the experiment is to see how far a person will proceed in a concrete and measurable situation in which he is ordered to inflict
increasing pain on a protesting victim.

Conflict arises when the man receiving the shock begins to show that he 10
is experiencing discomfort. At 75 volts, he grunts; at 120 volts, he complains
loudly; at 150, he demands to be released from the experiment. As the voltage increases, his protests become more vehement and emotional. At 285
volts, his response can be described only as an agonized scream. Soon thereafter, he makes no sound at all.

For the teacher, the situation quickly becomes one of gripping tension. It 11
is not a game for him; conflict is intense and obvious. The manifest suffering
of the learner presses him to quit; but each time he hesitates to administer a
shock, the experimenter orders him to continue. To extricate himself from this
plight, the subject must make a clear break with authority.[1]

The subject, Gretchen Brandt,[2] is an attractive thirty-one-year-old med- 12
ical technician who works at the Yale Medical School. She had emigrated
from Germany five years before.

On several occasions when the learner complains, she turns to the exper- 13
imenter coolly and inquires, "Shall I continue?" She promptly returns to her
task when the experimenter asks her to do so. At the administration of 210
volts, she turns to the experimenter, remarking firmly, "Well, I'm sorry, I
don't think we should continue."

EXPERIMENTER: The experiment requires that you go on until he has learned 14
    all the word pairs correctly.
BRANDT: He has a heart condition. I'm sorry. He told you that before. 15
EXPERIMENTER: The shocks may be painful but they are not dangerous. 16
BRANDT: Well, I'm sorry, I think when shocks continue like this, they *are* dan- 17
    gerous. You ask him if he wants to get out. It's his free will.
EXPERIMENTER: It is absolutely essential that we continue. . . . 18
BRANDT: I'd like you to ask him. We came here of our free will. If he wants to 19
    continue I'll go ahead. He told you he had a heart condition. I'm sorry.
    I don't want to be responsible for anything happening to him. I wouldn't
    like it for me either.
EXPERIMENTER: You have no other choice. 20
BRANDT: I think we are here on our own free will. I don't want to be respon- 21
    sible if anything happens to him. Please understand that.

She refuses to go further and the experiment is terminated. 22

The woman is firm and resolute throughout. She indicates in the inter- 23
view that she was in no way tense or nervous, and this corresponds to her

---

[1] The ethical problems of carrying out an experiment of this sort are too complex to be dealt
with here, but they receive extended treatment in the book from which this article is adapted.
[2] Names of subjects described in this piece have been changed.

controlled appearance during the experiment. She feels that the last shock she administered to the learner was extremely painful and reiterates that she "did not want to be responsible for any harm to him."

The woman's straightforward, courteous behavior in the experiment,   24 lack of tension, and total control of her own action seem to make disobedience a simple and rational deed. Her behavior is the very embodiment of what I envisioned would be true for almost all subjects.

An Unexpected Outcome

Before the experiments, I sought predictions about the outcome from various   25 kinds of people—psychiatrists, college sophomores, middle-class adults, graduate students and faculty in the behavioral sciences. With remarkable similarity, they predicted that virtually all subjects would refuse to obey the experimenter. The psychiatrists, specifically, predicted that most subjects would not go beyond 150 volts, when the victim makes his first explicit demand to be freed. They expected that only 4 percent would reach 300 volts, and that only a pathological fringe of about one in a thousand would administer the highest shock on the board.

These predictions were unequivocally wrong. Of the forty subjects in the   26 first experiment, twenty-five obeyed the orders of the experimenter to the end, punishing the victim until they reached the most potent shock available on the generator. After 450 volts were administered three times, the experimenter called a halt to the session. Many obedient subjects then heaved sighs of relief, mopped their brows, rubbed their fingers over their eyes, or nervously fumbled cigarettes. Others displayed only minimal signs of tension from beginning to end.

When the very first experiments were carried out, Yale undergraduates   27 were used as subjects, and about 60 percent of them were fully obedient. A colleague of mine immediately dismissed these findings as having no relevance to "ordinary" people, asserting that Yale undergraduates are a highly aggressive, competitive bunch who step on each other's necks on the slightest provocation. He assured me that when "ordinary" people were tested, the results would be quite different. As we moved from the pilot studies to the regular experimental series, people drawn from every stratum of New Haven life came to be employed in the experiment: professionals, white-collar workers, unemployed persons, and industrial workers. *The experiment's total outcome was the same as we had observed among the students.*

Moreover, when the experiments were repeated in Princeton, Munich,   28 Rome, South Africa, and Australia, the level of obedience was invariably somewhat *higher* than found in the investigation reported in this article. Thus one scientist in Munich found 85 percent of his subjects to be obedient.

Fred Prozi's reactions, if more dramatic than most, illuminate the con-   29 flicts experienced by others in less visible form. About fifty years old and unemployed at the time of the experiment, he has a good-natured, if slightly dissolute, appearance, and he strikes people as a rather ordinary fellow. He begins the session calmly but becomes tense as it proceeds. After delivering the 180-volt shock, he pivots around in his chair and, shaking his head, addresses the experimenter in agitated tones:

PROZI: I can't stand it. I'm not going to kill that man in there. You hear him hollering? | 30

EXPERIMENTER: As I told you before, the shocks may be painful, but . . . | 31

PROZI: But he's hollering. He can't stand it. What's going to happen to him? | 32

EXPERIMENTER (*HIS VOICE IS PATIENT, MATTER-OF-FACT*): The experiment requires that you continue, Teacher. | 33

PROZI: Aaah, but unh, I'm not going to get that man sick in there—know what I mean? | 34

EXPERIMENTER: Whether the learner likes it or not, we must go on, through all the word pairs. | 35

PROZI: I refuse to take the responsibility. He's in there hollering! | 36

EXPERIMENTER: It's absolutely essential that you continue, Prozi. | 37

PROZI (*INDICATING THE UNUSED QUESTIONS*): There's too many left here. I mean, Jeez, if he gets them wrong, there's too many of them left. I mean, who's going to take the responsibility if anything happens to that gentleman? | 38

EXPERIMENTER: I'm responsible for anything that happens to him. Continue, please. | 39

PROZI: All right. (*Consults list of words.*) The next one's "Slow—walk, truck, dance, music." Answer, please. (*A buzzing sound indicates the learner has signaled his answer.*) Wrong. A hundred and ninety-five volts. "Dance." (*Zzumph!*) | 40

LEARNER (*YELLING*): Let me out of here! My heart's bothering me! (*Teacher looks at experimenter.*) | 41

EXPERIMENTER: Continue, please. | 42

LEARNER (*SCREAMING*): Let me out of here! You have no right to keep me here! Let me out of here, my heart's bothering me, let me out! | 43

PROZI (*SHAKES HEAD, PATS THE TABLE NERVOUSLY*): You see, he's hollering. Hear that? Gee, I don't know. | 44

EXPERIMENTER: The experiment requires . . . | 45

PROZI (*INTERRUPTING*): I know it does, sir, but I mean—hunh! He don't know what he's getting in for. He's up to 195 volts! (*Experiment continues, through 210 volts, 225 volts, 240 volts, 255 volts, 270 volts, at which point Prozi, with evident relief, runs out of word-pair questions.*) | 46

EXPERIMENTER: You'll have to go back to the beginning of that page and go through them again until he's learned them all correctly. | 47

PROZI: Aw, no. I'm not going to kill that man. You mean I've got to keep going up with the scale? No sir. He's hollering in there. I'm not going to give him 450 volts. | 48

EXPERIMENTER: The experiment requires that you go on. | 49

LEARNER: Ohhh. I absolutely refuse to answer anymore. (*Shouting urgently now.*) Let me out of here! You can't hold me here! Get me out. Get-me-out-of-here! | 50

EXPERIMENTER: Continue. The next word is "Green," please.   51

PROZI: "Green—grass, hat, ink, apple." (*Nothing happens. No answering*   52
buzz. Just gloomy silence.)

PROZI: I don't think he is going to answer.   53

EXPERIMENTER: If the learner doesn't answer in a reasonable time, about four   54
or five seconds, consider the answer wrong. And follow the same procedures you have been doing for wrong answers. Say, "Wrong," tell him
the number of volts, give him the punishment, read him the correct
answer. Continue, please.

PROZI: "Green—grass, hat, ink, apple." Answer, please. (*More silence. Subject*   55
just sits there.)

EXPERIMENTER: Go on with the procedure, please.   56

PROZI: Three hundred and fifteen volts. The answer is "ink." (*Zzumph!*)   57

LEARNER: Ohh. Ooohh.   58

PROZI: (*RELIEVED TO HEAR RESPONSE*): Next one . . .   59

LEARNER: I absolutely refuse to answer.   60

PROZI: You got to. You get a shock if you don't answer. (*Experiment con-*   61
tinues with learner refusing to answer, and finally, failing even to grunt
or groan. At 375 volts, the subject stands up.)

Prozi: I think something's happened to that fellow in there. I don't get no   62
answer. He was hollering at less voltage. Can't you check in and see if
he's all right, please?

EXPERIMENTER (*WITH SAME DETACHED CALM*): Not once we've started. Please   63
continue, Teacher.

PROZI (*SITS DOWN, SIGHS DEEPLY*): "Cool—day, shade, water, paint." Answer,   64
please. Are you all right in there? Are you all right?

EXPERIMENTER: Please continue, Teacher. Continue, please. (*Subject pushes*   65
lever. Zzumph!)

PROZI (*SWIVELING AROUND IN HIS CHAIR*): Something's happened to that man   66
in there. (*Swiveling back.*) Next one. "Low—dollar, necklace, moon,
paint." (*Turning around again.*) Something's happened to that man in
there. You better check in on him, sir. He won't answer or nothing.

EXPERIMENTER: Continue. Go on, please.   67

PROZI: You accept all responsibility?   68

EXPERIMENTER: The responsibility is mine. Correct. Please go on. (*Subject*   69
returns to his list, starts running through words as rapidly as he can
read them, works through to 450 volts.)

PROZI: That's that.   70

EXPERIMENTER: Continue using the 450 switch for each wrong answer.   71
Continue, please.

PROZI: But I don't get anything!   72

EXPERIMENTER: Please continue. The next word is "white."   73

PROZI: Don't you think you should look in on him, please?   74

EXPERIMENTER: Not once we've started the experiment.   75

PROZI: What if he's dead in there? (*Gestures toward the room with the elec-* 76
tric chair.) I mean, he told me he can't stand the shock, sir. I don't mean
to be rude, but I think you should look in on him. All you have to do is
look in on him. All you have to do is look in the door. I don't get no
answer, no noise. Something might have happened to the gentleman in
there, sir.

EXPERIMENTER: We must continue. Go on, please. 77

PROZI: You mean keep giving him what? Four-hundred-fifty volts, what he's 78
got now?

EXPERIMENTER: That's correct. Continue. The next word is "white." 79

PROZI (*NOW AT A FURIOUS PACE*): "White—cloud, horse, rock, house." 80
Answer, please. The answer is "horse." Four hundred and fifty volts.
(*Zzumph!*) Next word, "Bag—paint, music, clown, girl." The answer is
"paint." Four hundred and fifty volts. (*Zzumph!*) Next word is "Short—
sentence, movie . . . "

EXPERIMENTER: Excuse me, Teacher. We'll have to discontinue the experi- 81
ment.

Peculiar Reactions

Morris Braverman, another subject, is a thirty-nine-year-old social worker. He 82
looks older than his years because of his bald head and serious demeanor. His
brow is furrowed, as if all the world's burdens were carried on his face. He
appears intelligent and concerned.

When the learner refuses to answer and the experimenter instructs 83
Braverman to treat the absence of an answer as equivalent to a wrong answer,
he takes his instruction to heart. Before administering 300 volts he asserts offi-
ciously to the victim, "Mr. Wallace, your silence has to be considered as a
wrong answer." Then he administers the shock. He offers half-heartedly to
change places with the learner, then asks the experimenter, "Do I have to
follow these instructions literally?" He is satisfied with the experimenter's
answer that he does. His very refined and authoritative manner of speaking is
increasingly broken up by wheezing laughter.

The experimenter's notes on Mr. Braverman at the last few shocks are: 84

Almost breaking up now each time gives shock. Rubbing face to hide
laughter. Squinting, trying to hide face with hand, still laughing. Cannot
control his laughter at this point no matter what he does. Clenching fist,
pushing it onto table.

In an interview after the session, Mr. Braverman summarizes the exper- 85
iment with impressive fluency and intelligence. He feels the experiment may
have been designed also to "test the effects on the teacher of being in an essentially sadistic role, as well as the reactions of a student to a learning situation
that was authoritative and punitive." When asked how painful the last few
shocks administered to the learner were, he indicates that the most extreme

category on the scale is not adequate (it read EXTREMELY PAINFUL) and places his mark at the edge of the scale with an arrow carrying it beyond the scale.

It is almost impossible to convey the greatly relaxed, sedate quality of his   86
conversation in the interview. In the most relaxed terms, he speaks about his severe inner tension.

EXPERIMENTER: At what point were you most tense or nervous?   87
MR. BRAVERMAN: Well, when he first began to cry out in pain, and I realized   88
    this was hurting him. This got worse when he just blocked and refused to
    answer. There was I. I'm a nice person, I think, hurting somebody, and
    caught up in what seemed a mad situation . . . and in the interest of sci-
    ence, one goes through with it.

When the interviewer pursues the general question of tension, Mr.   89
Braverman spontaneously mentions his laughter.

"My reactions were awfully peculiar. I don't know if you were watching   90
me, but my reactions were giggly, and trying to stifle laughter. This isn't the
way I usually am. This was a sheer reaction to a totally impossible situation.
And my reaction was to the situation of having to hurt somebody. And being
totally helpless and caught up in a set of circumstances where I just couldn't
deviate and I couldn't try to help. This is what got me."

Mr. Braverman, like all subjects, was told the actual nature and purpose   91
of the experiment, and a year later he affirmed in a questionnaire that he had
learned something of personal importance: "What appalled me was that I
could possess this capacity for obedience and compliance to a central idea,
i.e., the value of a memory experiment, even after it became clear that continued adherence to this value was at the expense of violation of another
value, i.e., don't hurt someone who is helpless and not hurting you. As my
wife said, 'You can call yourself Eichmann.'[3] I hope I deal more effectively
with any future conflicts of values I encounter."

The Etiquette of Submission

One theoretical interpretation of this behavior holds that all people harbor 92
deeply aggressive instincts continually pressing for expression, and that the
experiment provides institutional justification for the release of these impulses.
According to this view, if a person is placed in a situation in which he has
complete power over another individual, whom he may punish as much as he
likes, all that is sadistic and bestial in man comes to the fore. The impulse to
shock the victim is seen to flow from the potent aggressive tendencies, which
are part of the motivational life of the individual, and the experiment, because
it provides social legitimacy, simply opens the door to their expression.

---

[3] *Adolf Eichmann* (1906–1962), the Nazi official responsible for implementing Hitler's
"Final Solution" to exterminate the Jews, escaped to Argentina after World War II. In 1960,
Israeli agents captured him and brought him to Israel, where he was tried as a war criminal
and sentenced to death. At his trial, Eichmann maintained that he was merely following
orders in arranging murders of his victims.

It becomes vital, therefore, to compare the subject's performance when he is under orders and when he is allowed to choose the shock level. [93]

The procedure was identical to our standard experiment, except that the teacher was told that he was free to select any shock level on any of the trials. (The experimenter took pains to point out that the teacher could use the highest levels on the generator, the lowest, any in between, or any combination of levels.) Each subject proceeded for thirty critical trials. The learner's protests were coordinated to standard shock levels, his first grunt coming at 75 volts, his first vehement protest at 150 volts. [94]

The average shock used during the thirty critical trials was less than 60 volts—lower than the point at which the victim showed the first signs of discomfort. Three of the forty subjects did not go beyond the very lowest level on the board, twenty-eight went no higher than 75 volts, and thirty-eight did not go beyond the first loud protest at 150 volts. Two subjects provided the exception, administering up to 325 and 450 volts, but the overall result was that the great majority of people delivered very low, usually painless, shocks when the choice was explicitly up to them. [95]

This condition of the experiment undermines another commonly offered explanation of the subjects' behavior—that those who shocked the victim at the most severe levels came only from the sadistic fringe of society. If one considers that almost two-thirds of the participants fall into the category of "obedient" subjects, and that they represented ordinary people drawn from working, managerial, and professional classes, the argument becomes very shaky. Indeed, it is highly reminiscent of the issue that arose in connection with Hannah Arendt's 1963 book, *Eichmann in Jerusalem.* Arendt contended that the prosecution's effort to depict Eichmann as a sadistic monster was fundamentally wrong, that he came closer to being an uninspired bureaucrat who simply sat at his desk and did his job. For asserting her views, Arendt became the object of considerable scorn, even calumny. Somehow, it was felt that the monstrous deeds carried out by Eichmann required a brutal, twisted personality, evil incarnate. After witnessing hundreds of ordinary persons submit to the authority in our own experiments, I must conclude that Arendt's conception of the banality of evil comes closer to the truth than one might dare imagine. The ordinary person who shocked the victim did so out of a sense of obligation—an impression of his duties as a subject—and not from any peculiarly aggressive tendencies. [96]

This is, perhaps, the most fundamental lesson of our study: ordinary people, simply doing their jobs, and without any particular hostility on their part, can become agents in a terrible destructive process. Moreover, even when the destructive effects of their work become patently clear, and they are asked to carry out actions incompatible with fundamental standards of morality, relatively few people have the resources needed to resist authority. [97]

Many of the people were in some sense against what they did to the learner, and many protested even while they obeyed. Some were totally convinced of the wrongness of their actions but could not bring themselves to [98] make an open break with authority. They often derived satisfaction from their thoughts and felt that—within themselves, at least—they had been on the side of the angels. They tried to reduce strain by obeying the experimenter but "only slightly," encouraging the learner, touching the generator switches gingerly. When interviewed, such a subject would stress that he had "asserted my humanity" by administering the briefest shock possible. Handling the conflict in this manner was easier than defiance.

The situation is constructed so that there is no way the subject can stop   99
shocking the learner without violating the experimenter's definitions of his own competence. The subject fears that he will appear arrogant, untoward, and rude if he breaks off. Although these inhibiting emotions appear small in scope alongside the violence being done to the learner, they suffuse the mind and feelings of the subject, who is miserable at the prospect of having to repudiate the authority to his face. (When the experiment was altered so that the experimenter gave his instructions by telephone instead of in person, only a third as many people were fully obedient through 450 volts.) It is a curious thing that a measure of compassion on the part of the subject—an unwillingness to "hurt" the experimenter's feelings—is part of those binding forces inhibiting his disobedience. The withdrawal of such deference may be as painful to the subject as to the authority he defies.

Duty without Conflict

The subjects do not derive satisfaction from inflicting pain, but they often like   100
the feeling they get from pleasing the experimenter. They are proud of doing a good job, obeying the experimenter under difficult circumstances. While the subjects administered only mild shocks on their own initiative, one experimental variation showed that, under orders, 30 percent of them were willing to deliver 450 volts even when they had to forcibly push the learner's hand down on the electrode.

Bruno Batta is a thirty-seven-year-old welder who took part in the vari-   101
ation requiring the use of force. He was born in New Haven, his parents in Italy. He has a rough-hewn face that conveys a conspicuous lack of alertness. He has some difficulty in mastering the experimental procedure and needs to be corrected by the experimenter several times. He shows appreciation for the help and willingness to do what is required. After the 150-volt level, Batta has to force the learner's hand down on the shock plate, since the learner himself refuses to touch it.

When the learner first complains, Mr. Batta pays no attention to him. His   102
face remains impassive, as if to dissociate himself from the learner's disruptive behavior. When the experimenter instructs him to force the learner's hand down, he adopts a rigid, mechanical procedure. He tests the generator switch. When it fails to function, he immediately forces the learner's hand onto the shock plate. All the while he maintains the same rigid mask. The learner, seated alongside him, begs him to stop, but with robotic impassivity he continues the procedure.

What is extraordinary is his apparent total indifference to the learner; he   103
hardly takes cognizance of him as a human being. Meanwhile, he relates to
the experimenter in a submissive and courteous fashion.

At the 330-volt level, the learner refuses not only to touch the shock plate   104
but also to provide any answers. Annoyed, Batta turns to him, and chastises
him: "You better answer and get it over with. We can't stay here all night."
These are the only words he directs to the learner in the course of an hour.
Never again does he speak to him. The scene is brutal and depressing, his
hard, impassive face showing total indifference as he subdues the screaming
learner and gives him shocks. He seems to derive no pleasure from the act
itself, only quiet satisfaction at doing his job properly.

When he administers 450 volts, he turns to the experimenter and asks,   105
"Where do we go from here, Professor?" His tone is deferential and expresses
his willingness to be a cooperative subject, in contrast to the learner's obsti-
nacy.

At the end of the session he tells the experimenter how honored he has   106
been to help him, and in a moment of contrition, remarks, "Sir, sorry it
couldn't have been a full experiment."

He has done his honest best. It is only the deficient behavior of the learn-   107
er that has denied the experimenter full satisfaction.

The essence of obedience is that a person comes to view himself as the   108
instrument for carrying out another person's wishes, and he therefore no
longer regards himself as responsible for his actions. Once this critical shift of
viewpoint has occurred, all of the essential features of obedience follow. The
most far-reaching consequence is that the person feels responsible *to* the
authority directing him but feels no responsibility *for* the content of the
actions that the authority prescribes. Morality does not disappear—it acquires
a radically different focus: the subordinate person feels shame or pride
depending on how adequately he has performed the actions called for by
authority.

Language provides numerous terms to pinpoint this type of morality: *loy-*   109
alty, *duty*, *discipline* all are terms heavily saturated with moral meaning and
refer to the degree to which a person fulfills his obligations to authority. They
refer not to the "goodness" of the person per se but to the adequacy with
which a subordinate fulfills his socially defined role. The most frequent defense
of the individual who has performed a heinous act under command of authority is that he has simply done his duty. In asserting this defense, the individual
is not introducing an alibi concocted for the moment but is reporting honestly
on the psychological attitude induced by submission to authority.

For a person to feel responsible for his actions, he must sense that the   110
behavior has flowed from "the self." In the situation we have studied, subjects
have precisely the opposite view of their actions—namely, they see them as
originating in the motives of some other person. Subjects in the experiment
frequently said, "If it were up to me, I would not have administered shocks to
the learner."

Once authority has been isolated as the cause of the subject's behavior, it   111
is legitimate to inquire into the necessary elements of authority and how it
must be perceived in order to gain his compliance. We conducted some investigations into the kinds of changes that would cause the experimenter to lose
his power and to be disobeyed by the subject. Some of the variations revealed
that:

- *The experimenter's physical presence has a marked impact on his author-*   112
  ity. As cited earlier, obedience dropped off sharply when orders were given
  by telephone. The experimenter could often induce a disobedient subject to
  go on by returning to the laboratory.

- *Conflicting authority severely paralyzes action.* When two experimenters   113
  of equal status, both seated at the command desk, gave incompatible
  orders, no shocks were delivered past the point of their disagreement.

- *The rebellious action of others severely undermines authority.* In one vari-   114
  ation, three teachers (two actors and a real subject) administered a test and
  shocks. When the two actors disobeyed the experimenter and refused to go
  beyond a certain shock level, thirty-six of forty subjects joined their disobedient peers and refused as well.

Although the experimenter's authority was fragile in some respects, it is   115
also true that he had almost none of the tools used in ordinary command
structures. For example, the experimenter did not threaten the subjects with
punishment—such as loss of income, community ostracism, or jail—for failure to obey. Neither could he offer incentives. Indeed, we should expect the
experimenter's authority to be much less than that of someone like a general,
since the experimenter has no power to enforce his imperatives, and since participation in a psychological experiment scarcely evokes the sense of urgency
and dedication found in warfare. Despite these limitations, he still managed
to command a dismaying degree of obedience.

I will cite one final variation of the experiment that depicts a dilemma   116
that is more common in everyday life. The subject was not ordered to pull the
lever that shocked the victim, but merely to perform a subsidiary task (administering the word-pair test) while another person administered the shock. In
this situation, thirty-seven of forty adults continued to the highest level on the
shock generator. Predictably, they excused their behavior by saying that the
responsibility belonged to the man who actually pulled the switch. This may
illustrate a dangerously typical arrangement in a complex society: it is easy to
ignore responsibility when one is only an intermediate link in a chain of
action.

The problem of obedience is not wholly psychological. The form and   117
shape of society and the way it is developing have much to do with it. There
was a time, perhaps, when people were able to give a fully human response to
any situation because they were fully absorbed in it as human beings. But as
soon as there was a division of labor things changed. Beyond a certain point,
the breaking up of society into people carrying out narrow and very special
jobs takes away from the human quality of work and life. A person does not

get to see the whole situation but only a small part of it, and is thus unable to act without some kind of overall direction. He yields to authority but in doing so is alienated from his own actions.

Even Eichmann was sickened when he toured the concentration camps,   118 but he had only to sit at a desk and shuffle papers. At the same time the man in the camp who actually dropped Cyclon-b into the gas chambers was able to justify *his* behavior on the ground that he was only following orders from above. Thus there is a fragmentation of the total human act; no one is confronted with the consequences of his decision to carry out the evil act. The person who assumes responsibility has evaporated. Perhaps this is the most common characteristic of socially organized evil in modern society.

■ ■ ■

Review Questions

1. Milgram states that obedience is a basic element in the structure of social life. How so?
2. What is the dilemma inherent in obedience to authority?
3. Summarize the obedience experiments.
4. What predictions did experts and laypeople make about the experiments before they were conducted? How did these predictions compare with the experimental results?
5. What are Milgram's views regarding the two assumptions bearing on his experiment that (1) people are naturally aggressive and (2) a lunatic, sadistic fringe is responsible for shocking learners to the maximum limit?
6. How do Milgram's findings corroborate Hannah Arendt's thesis about the "banality of evil"?
7. What, according to Milgram, is the "essence of obedience"?
8. How did being an intermediate link in a chain of action affect a subject's willingness to continue with the experiment?
9. In the article's final two paragraphs, Milgram speaks of a "fragmentation of the total human act." To what is he referring?

Discussion and Writing Suggestions

1. "Conservative philosophers argue that the very fabric of society is threatened by disobedience, while humanists stress the primacy of the individual conscience." Develop the arguments of both the conservative and the humanist regarding obedience to authority. Be prepared to debate the ethics of obedience by defending one position or the other.
2. Would you have been glad to participate in the Milgram experiments? Why or why not?
3. The ethics of Milgram's experimental design came under sharp attack. Diana Baumrind's review of the experiment typifies the criticism; but before you read her work, try to anticipate the objections she raises.

4. Given the general outcome of the experiments, why do you suppose Milgram gives as his first example of a subject's response the German émigré's refusal to continue the electrical shocks?

5. Does the outcome of the experiment upset you in any way? Do you feel the experiment teaches us anything new about human nature?

6. Comment on Milgram's skill as a writer of description. How effectively does he portray his subjects when introducing them? When recreating their tension in the experiment?

7. Mrs. Braverman said to her husband: "You can call yourself Eichmann." Do you agree with Mrs. Braverman? Explain.

8. Reread paragraphs 29 through 81, the transcript of the experiment in which Mr. Prozi participated. Appreciating that Prozi was debriefed—that is, was assured that no harm came to the learner—imagine what Prozi might have been thinking as he drove home after the experiment. Develop your thoughts into a monologue, written in the first person, with Prozi at the wheel of his car.

Review of Stanley Milgram's Experiments on Obedience

DIANA BAUMRIND

Many of Milgram's colleagues saluted him for providing that "hard information" about human nature that Doris Lessing speaks of. Others attacked him for violating the rights of his subjects. Still others faulted his experimental design and claimed he could not, with any validity, speculate on life outside the laboratory based on the behaviour of his subjects within.

In the following review excerpt, psychologist Diana Baumrind severely criticizes Milgram for "entrapping" his subjects and potentially harming their "self-image or ability to trust adult authorities in the future." In the discussion on p. 239, we summarize Milgram's response to Baumrind's critique.

Diana Baumrind is a psychologist who, when writing this review, worked at the Institute of Human Development, University of California, Berkeley. The review appeared in American Psychologist *shortly after Milgram published the results of his first experiments in 1963.*

. . . The dependent, obedient attitude assumed by most subjects in the experimental setting is appropriate to that situation. The "game" is defined by the experimenter and he makes the rules. By volunteering, the subject agrees implicitly to assume a posture of trust and obedience. While the experimental conditions leave him exposed, the subject has the right to assume that his security and self-esteem will be protected.   1

There are other professional situations in which one member—the patient   2
or client—expects help and protection from the other—the physician or psychologist. But the interpersonal relationship between experimenter and subject additionally has unique features which are likely to provoke initial anxiety
in the subject. The laboratory is unfamiliar as a setting and the rules of behavior ambiguous compared to a clinician's office. Because of the anxiety and
passivity generated by the setting, the subject is more prone to behave in an
obedient, suggestible manner in the laboratory than elsewhere. Therefore, the
laboratory is not the place to study degree of obedience or suggestibility, as a
function of a particular experimental condition, since the base line for these
phenomena as found in the laboratory is probably much higher than in most
other settings. Thus experiments in which the relationship to the experimenter as an authority is used as an independent condition are imperfectly
designed for the same reason that they are prone to injure the subjects
involved. They disregard the special quality of trust and obedience with which
the subject appropriately regards the experimenter.

Other phenomena which present ethical decisions, unlike those men-   3
tioned above, *can* be reproduced successfully in the laboratory. Failure experience, conformity to peer judgment, and isolation are among such
phenomena. In these cases we can expect the experimenter to take whatever
measures are necessary to prevent the subject from leaving the laboratory
more humiliated, insecure, alienated, or hostile than when he arrived. To
guarantee that an especially sensitive subject leaves a stressful experimental
experience in the proper state sometimes requires special clinical training. But
usually an attitude of compassion, respect, gratitude, and common sense will
suffice, and no amount of clinical training will substitute. The subject has the
right to expect that the psychologist with whom he is interacting has some
concern for his welfare, and the personal attributes and professional skill to
express his good will effectively.

Unfortunately, the subject is not always treated with the respect he   4
deserves. It has become more commonplace in sociopsychological laboratory
studies to manipulate, embarrass, and discomfort subjects. At times the insult
to the subject's sensibilities extends to the journal reader when the results are
reported. Milgram's (1963) study is a case in point. The following is
Milgram's abstract of his experiment:

> This article describes a procedure for the study of destructive obedience
> in the laboratory. It consists of ordering a naive S to administer increas-
> ingly more severe punishment to a victim in the context of a learning
> experiment.[1] Punishment is administered by means of a shock generator
> with 30 graded switches ranging from Slight Shock to Danger: Severe
> Shock. The victim is a confederate of E. The primary dependent variable
> is the maximum shock the S is willing to administer before he refuses to

[1] In psychological experiments, *S* is an abbreviation for *subject; E* is an abbreviation for
experimenter.

continue further.[2] 26 Ss obeyed the experimental commands fully, and administered the highest shock on the generator. 14 Ss broke off the experiment at some point after the victim protested and refused to provide further answers. The procedure created extreme levels of nervous tension in some Ss. Profuse sweating, trembling, and stuttering were typical expressions of this emotional disturbance. One unexpected sign of tension—yet to be explained—was the regular occurrence of nervous laughter, which in some Ss developed into uncontrollable seizures. The variety of interesting behavioral dynamics observed in the experiment, the reality of the situation for the S, and the possibility of parametric variation[3] within the framework of the procedure point to the fruitfulness of further study [p. 371].

The detached, objective manner in which Milgram reports the emotional   5
disturbance suffered by his subjects contrasts sharply with his graphic account of that disturbance. Following are two other quotes describing the effects on his subjects of the experimental conditions:

> I observed a mature and initially poised businessman enter the laboratory smiling and confident. Within 20 minutes he was reduced to a twitching, stuttering wreck, who was rapidly approaching a point of nervous collapse. He constantly pulled on his earlobe, and twisted his hands. At one point he pushed his fist into his forehead and muttered: "Oh God, let's stop it." And yet he continued to respond to every word of the experimenter, and obeyed to the end [p. 377].
>
> In a large number of cases the degree of tension reached extremes that are rarely seen in sociopsychological laboratory studies. Subjects were observed to sweat, tremble, stutter, bite their lips, groan, and dig their fingernails into their flesh. These were characteristic rather than exceptional responses to the experiment.
>
> One sign of tension was the regular occurrence of nervous laughing fits. Fourteen of the 40 subjects showed definite signs of nervous laughter and smiling. The laughter seemed entirely out of place, even bizarre. Full-blown, uncontrollable seizures were observed for 3 subjects. On one occasion we observed a seizure so violently convulsive that it was necessary to call a halt to the experiment . . . [p. 375].

Milgram does state that,

> After the interview, procedures were undertaken to assure that the subject would leave the laboratory in a state of well being. A friendly reconciliation was arranged between the subject and the victim, and an effort was made to reduce any tensions that arose as a result of the experiment [p. 374].

---

[2] In the context of a psychological experiment, a *dependent variable* is a behavior that is expected to change as a result of changes in the experimental procedure.

[3] *Parametric variation* is a statistical term that describes the degree to which information based on data for one experiment can be applied to data for a slightly different experiment.

It would be interesting to know what sort of procedures could dissipate the type of emotional disturbance just described. In view of the effects on subjects, traumatic to a degree which Milgram himself considers nearly unprecedented in sociopsychological experiments, his casual assurance that these tensions were dissipated before the subject left the laboratory is unconvincing.

What could be the rational basis for such a posture of indifference?   6
Perhaps Milgram supplies the answer himself when he partially explains the subject's destructive obedience as follows, "Thus they assume that the discomfort caused the victim is momentary, while the scientific gains resulting from the experiment are enduring [p. 378]." Indeed such a rationale might suffice to justify the means used to achieve his end if that end were of inestimable value to humanity or were not itself transformed by the means by which it was attained.

The behavioral psychologist is not in as good a position to objectify his   7
faith in the significance of his work as medical colleagues at points of breakthrough. His experimental situations are not sufficiently accurate models of real-life experience; his sampling techniques are seldom of a scope which would justify the meaning with which he would like to endow his results; and these results are hard to reproduce by colleagues with opposing theoretical views. Unlike the Sabin vaccine,[4] for example, the concrete benefit to humanity of his particular piece of work, no matter how competently handled, cannot justify the risk that real harm will be done to the subject. I am not speaking of physical discomfort, inconvenience, or experimental deception per se, but of permanent harm, however slight. I do regard the emotional disturbance described by Milgram as potentially harmful because it could easily effect an alteration in the subject's self-image or ability to trust adult authorities in the future. It is potentially harmful to a subject to commit, in the course of an experiment, acts which he himself considers unworthy, particularly when he has been entrapped into committing such acts by an individual he has reason to trust. The subject's personal responsibility for his actions is not erased because the experimenter reveals to him the means which he used to stimulate these actions. The subject realizes that he would have hurt the victim if the current were on. The realization that he also made a fool of himself by accepting the experimental set results in additional loss of self-esteem. Moreover, the subject finds it difficult to express his anger outwardly after the experimenter in a self-acceptant but friendly manner reveals the hoax.

A fairly intense corrective interpersonal experience is indicated wherein   8
the subject admits and accepts his responsibility for his own actions, and at the same time gives vent to his hurt and anger at being fooled. Perhaps an experience as distressing as the one described by Milgram can be integrated by the subject, provided that careful thought is given to the matter. The propriety of such experimentation is still in question even if such a reparational experience were forthcoming. Without it I would expect a naive, sensitive subject to remain deeply hurt and anxious for some time, and a sophisticated, cynical subject to become even more alienated and distrustful.

[4] The Sabin vaccine provides immunization against polio.

In addition the experimental procedure used by Milgram does not appear   9
suited to the objectives of the study because it does not take into account the
special quality of the set which the subject has in the experimental situation.
Milgram is concerned with a very important problem, namely, the social
consequences of destructive obedience. He says,

> Gas chambers were built, death camps were guarded, daily quotas of
> corpses were produced with the same efficiency as the manufacture of
> appliances. These inhumane policies may have originated in the mind of
> a single person, but they could only be carried out on a massive scale if
> a very large number of persons obeyed orders [p. 371].

But the parallel between authority-subordinate relationships in Hitler's   10
Germany and in Milgram's laboratory is unclear. In the former situation the
SS man or member of the German Officer Corps, when obeying orders to
slaughter, had no reason to think of his superior officer as benignly disposed
towards himself or their victims. The victims were perceived as subhuman and
not worthy of consideration. The subordinate officer was an agent in a great
cause. He did not need to feel guilt or conflict because within his frame of reference he was acting rightly.

It is obvious from Milgram's own descriptions that most of his subjects   11
were concerned about their victims and did trust the experimenter, and that
their distressful conflict was generated in part by the consequences of these
two disparate but appropriate attitudes. Their distress may have resulted
from shock at what the experimenter was doing to them as well as from what
they thought they were doing to their victims. In any case there is not a convincing parallel between the phenomena studied by Milgram and destructive
obedience as the concept would apply to the subordinate-authority relationship demonstrated in Hitler's Germany. If the experiments were conducted
"outside of New Haven and without any visible ties to the university," I
would still question their validity on similar although not identical grounds.
In addition, I would question the representativeness of a sample of subjects
who would voluntarily participate within a noninstitutional setting.

In summary, the experimental objectives of the psychologist are seldom   12
incompatible with the subject's ongoing state of well being, provided that the
experimenter is willing to take the subject's motives and interests into consideration when planning his methods and correctives. Section 4b in *Ethical
Standards of Psychologists* (APA, undated) reads in part:

> Only when a problem is significant and can be investigated in no other way
> is the psychologist justified in exposing human subjects to emotional stress
> or other possible harm. In conducting such research, the psychologist
> must seriously consider the possibility of harmful aftereffects, and should
> be prepared to remove them as soon as permitted by the design of the
> experiment. Where the danger of serious aftereffects exists, research should
> be conducted only when the subjects or their responsible agents are fully
> informed of this possibility and volunteer nevertheless [p. 12].

From the subject's point of view procedures which involve loss of dignity, self-esteem and trust in rational authority are probably most harmful in the long run and require the most thoughtfully planned reparations, if engaged in at all. The public image of psychology as a profession is highly related to our own actions, and some of these actions are changeworthy. It is important that as research psychologists we protect our ethical sensibilities rather than adapt our personal standards to include as appropriate the kind of indignities to which Milgram's subjects were exposed. I would not like to see experiments such as Milgram's proceed unless the subjects were fully informed of the dangers of serious aftereffects and his correctives were clearly shown to be effective in restoring their state of well being.

■ ■ ■

References

American Psychological Association. Ethical standards of psychologists: A summary of ethical principles. Washington, D.C.: APA, undated.

Milgram, S. Behavioral study of obedience. *Journal of Abnormal and Social Psychology* 67, 1963, pp. 371–378.

Discussion

Stanley Milgram replied to Baumrind's critique in a lengthy critique of his own [From Stanley Milgram, "Issues in the Study of Obedience: A Reply to Baumrind," *American Psychologist* 19 (1964): 848–851]. Following are his principal points:

- Milgram believed that the experimental findings were in large part responsible for Baumrind's criticism. He writes:

    Is not Baumrind's criticism based as much on the unanticipated findings as on the method? The findings were that some subjects performed in what appeared to be a shockingly immoral way. If, instead, every one of the subjects had broken off at "slight shock," or at the first sign of the learner's discomfort, the results would have been pleasant, and reassuring, and who would protest?

- Milgram objected to Baumrind's assertion that those who participated in the experiment would have trouble justifying their behaviour. Milgram conducted follow-up questionnaires. The results, summarized in Table 1, indicate that 84 percent of the subjects claimed they were pleased to have been a part of the experiment.

TABLE 1 Excerpt from Questionnaire Used in a Follow-up Study of the Obedience Research

NOW THAT I HAVE READ THE REPORT, AND ALL THINGS CONSIDERED ...	DEFIANT	OBEDIENT	ALL
1. I am very glad to have been in the experiment	40.0%	47.8%	43.5%
2. I am glad to have been in the experiment	43.8%	35.7%	40.2%
3. I am neither sorry nor glad to have been in the experiment	15.3%	14.8%	15.1%
4. I am sorry to have been in the experiment	0.8%	0.7%	0.8%
5. I am very sorry to have been in the experiment	0.0%	1.0%	0.5%

Note—Ninety-two percent of the subjects returned the questionnaire. The characteristics of the nonrespondents were checked against the respondents. They differed from the respondents only with regard to age; younger people were overrepresented in the nonresponding group.

- Baumrind objected that studies of obedience cannot meaningfully be carried out in a laboratory setting, since the obedience occurred in a context where it was appropriate. Milgram's response: "I reject Baumrind's argument that the observed obedience does not count because it occurred where it is appropriate. That is precisely why it *does* count. A soldier's obedience is no less meaningful because it occurs in a pertinent military context."
- Milgram concludes his critique in this way: "If there is a moral to be learned from the obedience study, it is that every man must be responsible for his own actions. This author accepts full responsibility for the design and execution of the study. Some people may feel it should not have been done. I disagree and accept the burden of their judgment."

Review Questions

1. Why might a subject volunteer for an experiment? Why do subjects typically assume a dependent, obedient attitude?
2. Why is a laboratory not a suitable setting for a study of obedience?
3. For what reasons does Baumrind feel that the Milgram experiment was potentially harmful?
4. For what reasons does Baumrind question the relationship between Milgram's findings and the obedient behaviour of subordinates in Nazi Germany?

Discussion and Writing Suggestions

1. Baumrind contends that the Milgram experiment is imperfectly designed for two reasons: (1) The laboratory is not the place to test obedience; (2) Milgram disregarded the trust that subjects usually show an experimenter. Do you agree with Baumrind's objections? Do you find them equally valid?
2. Baumrind states that the ethical procedures of the experiment keep it from having significant value. Do you agree?

3. Do you agree with Baumrind that the subjects were "entrapped" into committing unworthy acts?

4. Assume the identity of a participant in Milgram's experiment who obeyed the experimenter by shocking the learner with the maximum voltage. You have just returned from the lab, and your spouse asks you about your day. Compose the conversation that follows.

The Scientific Mystique: Can a White Lab Coat Guarantee Purity in the Search for Knowledge about the Nature of Women?

KAREN MESSING

Karen Messing is the director of Centre d'études des interactions biologiques santé/environnement (CINBOISE) and professor of biological sciences at the University of Quebec in Montreal. In this article, the author brings the issue of "blind obedience" into the realm of medical research, where, she argues, highly specialized scientists with a vested interest in pursuing their own research have inappropriate influence over other researchers and the general public. Note: Superscript numbers within the article refer to Karen Messing's list of references.

In the 1950s and 1960s, Yale professor Stanley Milgram reported results from a series of experiments that shocked many academics.[1] In these experiments he asked his subjects to press a button which they believed delivered painful electric shocks to people, in an ostensible attempt to find out how much electricity the human body could stand. The "victims" were confederates of the experimenter and simulated increasing pain and anguish as the subjects thought they were intensifying the shocks. To Milgram's surprise, 20 per cent of the subjects could be induced to administer "shocks" that they believed were lethal, when told by the experimenter that the study required it. And if the investigator wore a lab coat, the percentage of "killer" subjects who would do this increased to 65 per cent. These experiments were commonly interpreted as showing that people are very obedient to authority. It is clear that they also demonstrate the tremendous respect lay people have for the authority of scientists and for scientific experiments.

Part of this scientific mystique comes from the image of science as the search for objective truth, a pursuit of knowledge carried out in neutral surroundings by disinterested observers. This view is based on a romanticism that most scientists do not actively discourage, but which has, as all of us engaged in science know, very little to do with reality.

In the present chapter I will show that the scientific community is in fact moulded by the society of which it is a part. Scientists, and the data we

produce, are not and cannot be free from the prejudices, ideologies, or interests of the larger society. This lack of objectivity is manifested in the ways scientists are selected and in the scientific results themselves. The examples I use
will relate primarily to the treatment of women[2] by the scientific community,
but similar mechanisms affect working-class people, blacks, or other groups
that are under-represented in the scientific establishment.

It will be useful to look at several components of the scientific process;   4
they can be divided roughly into those relating to the scientists themselves and
those pertaining to the process.

The scientist
1. The selection of scientists
2. Their access to facilities for scientific work.

I will show that research scientists are a highly selected group whose interests
are not typical of a cross section of society. This situation has a strong influence on the scientific process.

The process
3. The choice of research topic
4. The wording of the hypothesis
5. The choice of experimental subjects
6. The choice of appropriate controls
7. The method of observation
8. Data analysis
9. The interpretation of data
10. The publication of results
11. The popularization of results

For each of these components, I will give examples of how the ideology and
background of the researcher can influence the results, and how these results
then become accepted scientific truth.

The Selection of the Scientist

Many articles have been written lately on the difficulties facing women who   5
want to be scientists. These barriers have been of various kinds: exploitation
of women scientists,[3] undervaluing of their contributions,[4] and exclusion of
them from "old-boy" communication networks.[5]

In addition, many women are cut off at the start by the forced choice   6
between child bearing and graduate studies.[6] It usually takes eight to nine
years of post-secondary education to get a PhD in the sciences. For a person
to get through this, he or she must have a great deal of persistence and confidence and either a good supply of money or the time to earn it. Financial
needs go up and available time, of course, goes down when child care is
involved. The demands of research can produce major conflicts for those of
us with children. Chemical reactions, physical phenomena, and cell behaviour
do not fit neatly into an eight-hour day. Therefore, the laboratory scientist

must be available at all hours and often on weekends. The same is true of field work in ecology or geology, for example.

For this reason, conciliation of research schedules with child bearing and child raising is nearly impossible to do well. At 5 p.m. just as one has finally got conditions for an experiment right, it is time to pick up the children. One has the unacceptable choices of rushing off to the day-care centre, thereby wasting the day's work, or making the phone calls to the day-care centre, arranging a sitter, changing the arrangements for supper, and staying to do the experiment, afterward facing one's own guilt and the eventual revenge of children and mate. The total exhaustion associated with this period is not conducive to creative work of any kind.[7] One of my graduate students supports her two children, aged 1 and 2, by taking part-time jobs. By the time she gets to the lab in the morning, she feels she has already put in a full work day.

The scientific community does not tolerate the temporary lowering of productivity associated with child raising, although the years of graduate studies are also those in which most people have children. The Canadian NSERC fellowships for gifted students have an absolute limit of two years in which to obtain the Master of Sciences degree. While maternity leave (unpaid) is granted, no provision is made for a slower rhythm of work once the mother returns to the laboratory or field. If she takes longer than two years for the MSc, she can get no PhD support.

These conditions make it equally difficult for anyone to hold a part-time job, so that the student who must earn money in order to stay in school faces the same problem as someone with family responsibilities.

Access to Facilities for Scientific Work

Doing science requires space, equipment, and infrastructure. While some world-shaking results have been obtained using minimal facilities, most modern biological endeavours, for example, are facilitated by the latest models of spectrophotometers, computer-assisted chromatography, scintillation counters, ultracentrifuges, and so on. Plenty of these machines are found in the top-rated universities, where up-and-coming scientists are hired to tenure track positions if they have been superstars in graduate school. Less successful scientists are found in underequipped universities and in less secure jobs, where even access to a laboratory may be a problem.

In the United States, female PhDs are more than four times as likely as males to be unemployed and constitute only 6.6% of tenured PhD faculty in the sciences. Most of the scientific community is now white and male.[8] This is not to say that blacks or females necessarily would do neutral, non-sexist research, but that science is done primarily by only certain people, who seek recognition from peers who are similar to them.

The Choice of Research Topic

The choice of topic is influenced by several factors: the interest of the scientist, that of his or her present and future employers, and the ability to get funding for the work. Because of their sex and class, the large majority of scientists are less likely than the general population to be interested in such topics as the occupational exposures that present a risk to the nursing mother, alternate (non-hormonal) treatments for the discomforts of menopause, how a woman can give herself a safe (and, where necessary, secret) abortion, what work postures increase the likelihood of menstrual cramps, and how a low-income family can provide itself with nutritious meals. On the other hand, there is plenty of research, supported by drug companies, on drug therapy for menopausal women,[9] by government on what racial and income groups have the most abortions,[10] by employers on the relationship between women's physiological cycles and productivity,[11] and by private charity on how to prevent a rich, fat-laden diet from causing heart disease.[12]

The Wording of the Research Hypothesis

Articulating the hypothesis is crucial to the scientific method. Research is done   13
in order to find an answer to a specific question, and the way the question is posed often determines the way the research will be carried out and how the eventual data will be interpreted. John Money and Anke Ehrhardt, for example, have done a good deal of research on whether prenatal hormone exposures explain sex-specific behaviours. In one study[13] they looked at children who have only one sex chromosome, an x, rather than the usual two (xx for girls, xy for boys), a condition that is called Turner's syndrome and is symbolized xo. Money and Ehrhardt hypothesized that since xo children, like normal girls, are less exposed than males to prenatal androgens (so-called male hormones) they should be "feminine," just as normal xx girls are. They defined "femininity" as not being a tomboy, preferring "girls' toys," wearing dresses rather than pants, being marriage-oriented rather than career-oriented in early adolescence, and so forth. By these criteria, their xo subjects were indeed found to be even more feminine than normal xx girls. It is unlikely that an investigator who was less accepting of present-day sex role stereotypes would have shaped the hypothesis this way, since she or he would consider "femininity" an inappropriate variable on which to study individuals with Turner's syndrome, who, though they have a vulva and not a penis, in fact lack most primary and all secondary female sexual characteristics. They are further distinguished by being unusually short, and many have a webbed neck and are mentally retarded. Hence, they probably have quite different social and biological experiences than most ordinary girls. A more critical investigator might also question the criteria of "femininity" chosen by these authors.

The controversy surrounding xyy males a few years ago is a similar   14
example of a hypothesis that was based on a socially-defined point of view, this time involving prejudice about males. Early investigators, finding a large number of men with an extra male (y) chromosome in prisons, formulated the hypothesis that people who have an extra y chromosome (xyy) must be "supermales," which they took to mean that these people would be especially prone to violence. They failed to consider the fact that xyy males are

unusually large, slow, and somewhat retarded. Thus, it was only after much money and time had been wasted that another hypothesis, that *xyy* males had the same chance as other retarded males of being in prison, was tested and confirmed.[14]

The Choice of Experimental Subjects

The clearest example of bias in the choice of a study population is the simple and extremely common exclusion of *women* from studies in which one wishes to obtain information about *people*. In a study of occupational cancers in the lead industry, all 950 women (but not blacks or short people) were excluded in order to keep the sample uniform.[15] In another study, as reported by Jeanne Stellman, 370 599 males were studied by the National Institutes of Health, in order to identify risk factors for heart disease.[16] Heart disease is also the leading cause of death in women, but women's risk factors were not studied. In reporting the results of such studies, authors rarely state clearly that they apply only to men.

Another way that a poor image of women (especially poor Third World women) conditions research strategies is by a callous disregard for the welfare of female subjects. For example, the birth control pill, though developed in Massachusetts, was first tested in Puerto Rico. And in 1971, long after its efficacy had been established, Dr. Joseph Goldzieher decided to test the Pill once more at his clinic. *Without their knowledge,* eighty of his 398 patients were given placebos (pills that looked and tasted like the Pill but were ineffective) instead of the Pill. All of the women chosen for this study had proven themselves fertile by having at least three previous children. Within a few months, 10 of the women who were receiving the fake pills had become pregnant with unwanted fetuses.[17] Legal abortion was not available for these women.

The Choice of Appropriate Controls

The choice of controls is probably the factor that has the most influence on research results. Our research group was recently confronted with this issue when trying to determine whether rates of congenital malformations were higher than usual among the offspring of men occupationally exposed to a radioactive dust. These men lived near the factory, which discharged its untreated effluent into the air. If we used neighbours as controls, we would underestimate the effects of *factory*-caused exposures, since both groups would have some exposure to the dust. If we used as controls people who lived elsewhere, the measured effect might be greater, but we would be unable to identify the proportion due to specifically occupational exposures. Yet the usefulness of the results in bargaining with employers might be enhanced, because of the greater difference between the workers and the unexposed control population.

A glaring example of a poor choice of control group comes from a study of the effects of occupational exposure to radium.[18] Sharpe examined the incidence of stillbirths and miscarriages among female workers exposed to radium and compared them to pregnancy outcomes of the wives of their male co-workers, calling this "a not unreasonable control group." Not unreasonable, that is, if one forgets that males can also suffer genetic damage from radium exposure and pass it on to their children. The common idea that child bearing is an exclusively female province may account for Sharpe's forgetfulness.

Another example of the selection of a control group by sex-biased   19 assumptions occurred at a seminar given in 1977 at the Université du Québec by an ethologist from the Université de Rennes in France. The speaker described a study of the mating behaviour of large mammals, in which three female goats, sheep, or cows were tethered in separate stalls and offered serially to 100 males. The subsequent pawing, sniffing, and copulatory behaviour of the males was recorded. When asked why 100 males were necessary, the speaker replied that it was necessary to observe the full range of behaviour. When asked why, in that case, there were only three females, he answered, "To keep the conditions standard." In studying the most bilateral of behaviours, sexual intercourse, a feminist would find it less reasonable to select females to represent "standard conditions" and males to study the "range of behaviour." She would assume that results would be as skewed by the choice of a limited number of individuals of one sex as of the other.

The Method of Observation

The data an investigator collects are affected by the choice of tools (ques-   20 tionnaires, interview schedules, observations, biochemical tests) and the data that are considered valid and relevant. Ideology can affect all of these.

For example, in their study of the prevalence of warts among poultry   21 slaughter-house workers, Mergler, Vezina and Beauvais[19] recorded the incidence by asking workers on a questionnaire how many warts they had. The study showed that workers who reported that they worked with saws, that their workplace was humid, and/or that their protective gloves did not fit correctly had a significantly higher incidence of warts. During a presentation of these results at a scientific meeting, the study was criticized on the basis that the workers were incompetent to count their warts and that counting should be done by a qualified medical practitioner. This criticism ignored the fact that doctors are in general less familiar with these warts than are the affected workers, some of whom had upwards of a hundred warts on their hands.

Crucial data can also be ignored because of ideological bias. In a 1963   22 study of the effect of work on pregnancy outcome by the U.S. Public Health Service, the worker's *husband's* occupation was recorded, but that of the pregnant worker herself was not.[20] This expensive study was thus useless for identifying working conditions that pose a risk to pregnant women and their fetuses, and the absence of such data has rendered protection very difficult.[21] Nevertheless, a recent (1980) study of the causes of premature delivery did not even include in its parameters the question of *whether* the mother was employed, let alone her particular occupation.[22] The bias that blinds investigators to the fact that many married women work outside the home prevents research results from helping employed women.

A methodological weakness found in many studies of sex-specific behaviour is the reliance on a single observer who is aware of the hypothesis being tested, and who may therefore be biased. The Money and Ehrhardt studies,[23] for example, compared girls of various hormonal statuses with respect to "femininity" on the basis of an interview with a single counsellor who knew the girl's history. Another example of a single-observer study comes from sociobiology. David Barash formulated the hypothesis that male ducks rape females because the males need to ensure a maximal number of descendants to maximize their own "reproductive success." Based on this, he predicted that a female who had been raped by a strange male would be re-raped as soon as possible by her usual consort (ducks live in couples). To test this complex hypothesis, Barash (alone) observed mallards for 558 hours, decided (alone) which male ducks were "husbands" and which were "strangers," and also which copulations were rape and which were mutually desired; he found, unsurprisingly, that his observations squared with his hypothesis.[24]

Even when experiments are performed under controlled laboratory conditions, observers may be biased by their political or social interests. A technical study of the chromosomes (hereditary material) of people exposed to industrial pollutants ran into this problem. For many years, the Hooker Chemical company discharged waste products into Love Canal, New York. Residents noticed a high rate of congenital malformations and illness among their children and pets and asked the Environmental Protection Agency to do a study. Eleven of 37 residents were found to have abnormal-looking chromosomes. When the residents demanded to be evaluated, a review panel was set up to look at the chromosomes. The panel did not see the same abnormalities as the EPA.[25] Thus started a long exchange in the pages of scientific journals. Each side has its scientists, but the scientists on the two sides did not perceive the chromosomes on the microscope slides in the same way.

Data Analysis

There is a large literature on "demand characteristics" of experimental situations; that is, the tendency of experimenters, their subjects, and their research assistants to produce by unconscious manipulations the data desired by the investigator.[26] Steven Gould has illustrated this point in his re-analysis of data on cranial capacity of different races, showing how a distinguished 19th century investigator manipulated his data to prove (incorrectly) that blacks had smaller brains than whites.[27] Another study of experimenter bias showed that research assistants made three times as many errors in arithmetic that favoured the chief's hypothesis as errors that went against it.[28]

Few non-scientists are aware of how many simple errors can be found in the scientific literature and in well-known, respected journals. For instance, the previously cited Money and Ehrhardt article used a statistical (chi-square) test under conditions where the use of this test is forbidden by elementary statistics texts (too many expected values were less than five). The Barash study contained an arithmetic error that rendered results statistically significant, in

that the probability of the situation occurring by chance is given as less than
.001, when the data in fact yield a probability of its occurring through chance
alone as greater than .05.

There are also instances of intentional mis-analyses of data. A case that   27
has recently come to light is that of Sir Cyril Burt, a prominent British psychologist and educational planner, who is now known to have manipulated
data supposedly collected from twins reared apart so as to demonstrate a
strong genetic component in IQ.[29] The fact that it took nearly 50 years for
Burt's deceptions to be revealed is perhaps evidence that his conclusions,
used for many years to argue for racial and class differences in intelligence,
agreed so closely with widely held prejudices that a critical eye was never cast
on the data.

The Interpretation of Data

One of the major questions in the occupational health and safety field, as well   28
as in the anti-nuclear movement, is the degree of genetic damage induced by
low levels of ionizing radiation. In Quebec, a case is under arbitration in
which a radiodiagnostic technician applied for leave with pay during her
pregnancy in accordance with a contract clause that provides for such leave
if working conditions endanger a fetus. The employer argued that radiation
below a certain threshold level poses no problem for the fetus; the union
argued that there is no threshold, and that any exposure is associated with
some probability of damage.[30] Scientists were found to testify on both sides,
since the argument turns on the extrapolation of a particular dose-responsive
curve, for which it is prohibitively time-consuming and expensive to obtain
complete data to the lowest possible doses.[31,32] Scientists testifying on behalf
of the union or the employer interpreted the same data in opposite ways; each
found that the data supported the contention of her or his side.

There are many such cases where interpretation of data depends on one's   29
point of view; the controversies about race and IQ,[33] about male "genes" for
mathematical ability,[34] and about the effectiveness of chemical spraying in
insect control[35] are examples of areas where all intensive research effort has
not succeeded in settling a scientific question, owing to the involvement of
opposing groups with a vested economic or social interest in opposite conclusions.

The Publication of Results

After writing up the research results, the scientist submits a paper to a jour-   30
nal, which sends it to a few people working in the same field for review. This
process is meant to guarantee that no slipshod work is published, that errors
will be corrected, and that worthy articles find an audience. In practice the
system is far from ideal. Once a scientist has made a name, he or she (though,
of course, usually he) can often get an article published quickly after only perfunctory review. Less well-known scientists can have considerably more difficulty, especially if their results depart from accepted dogma.

Results that reinforce prevalent biases are often accepted without question. For example, recently, the anthropologist C. O. Lovejoy published an article in *Science* with the ambitious title "The Origin of Man."[36] Some weeks later, he informed the journalists that he had played a little joke. He had stated in his discussion that "the human female is continually sexually receptive." As authority for this statement he cited not research results, but "D. C. Johannsen, personal communication." This is the learned equivalent of saying, "My buddy told me in the locker room." Presumably because the original statement did not seem unreasonable to the reviewers, none of them picked up the faulty citation. A feminist reviewer might have, of course.

The Popularization of Results

Many research papers have been published on the cause of superior male performance on mathematics tests in high school.[37] Some papers support the hypothesis that males have superior genes, others that they have an environmentally conferred advantage. Therefore, it is hard to find a scientific basis for the fuss and furor that followed the publication of a recent study by Benbow and Stanley showing that one proposed environmental determinant—number of mathematics courses taken—could be eliminated from consideration.[38] There was no attempt by the authors to eliminate all environmental influences, and no evidence for genetic determination was offered. Yet the paper elicited editorial comment in the issue of *Science* magazine in which it appeared, and within a few weeks of publication *Time, Newsweek,* and local newspapers were publishing articles with titles like "Sex differences in achievement in and attitudes toward mathematics result from superior mathematical ability."[39] No similar publicity had accompanied Elizabeth Fennema's article of a few years earlier,[40] in which, based on the same data, she had argued for an environmental determination. The ideology of the media greatly influences which scientific results enter into the popular culture.

Some results lend themselves to use in political and social battles. Money and Ehrhardt's research on hormonal determination of sex-typical behaviour has slipped into the givens of popular science. They are quoted extensively in the sexology courses at the Université du Québec and in popular magazine articles.[41]

And David Barash, after studying rape in birds, wrote a widely read *Psychology Today* article in which he suggested that the double standard of sexual behaviour among humans follows the bird pattern, owing to men's biologically based need to inject their sperm into as many women as possible.[42] This view was also quickly picked up and published by *Playboy* under the title, "Do Men Need to Cheat on Their Women? A New Science Says Yes."[43]

On the other hand, ideology and special interests may prevent some research results from becoming publicized. In 1979, Dr. David Horrobin was fired from the Clinical Research Institute of Montreal for having "prematurely" publicized research results suggesting that the tranquilizer Valium may promote cancer of the breast in women. These results, subsequently confirmed by other investigators, were certainly of immediate practical value for women since one woman in eleven gets breast cancer and Valium is the most commonly used prescription drug on the market.[44] No such censorship has been practised on Benbow's and Stanley's results or interpretations, which are prejudicial to women's education, on those of Barash, which justify rape, or on those of Burt, which support racism, although Horrobin's studies were based on much more data than any of these.

In fact, as we have seen in the preceding examples, scientists, protected by   36 their image as zealous seekers after truth, have been allowed to say the most outrageous things about women with impunity. Such statements have been used to limit women's access to educational and occupational opportunities and have damaged our health. And, of course, scientists have also done damage to minority and working-class men. The problem of scientific objectivity is therefore not simply an academic one.

It is about time that scientists be regarded with the same skepticism as   37 other members of the establishment. If and when we achieve an egalitarian society, we may hope for a science more in touch with people's needs. Industrial hygienists will listen to workers when they look for risks associated with working conditions. Biologists will consult with, rather than experiment on, women who want contraceptive devices, and psychologists will search for the basis of co-operative rather than aggressive behaviour. Until that time, since we still have a long struggle ahead of us, we would be wise to examine closely, even belligerently, what scientists have to say about the nature of women.

References

Acknowledgements—I would like to thank Lesley Lee for bringing the methodological issues in the mathematics and sex research to my attention, and Jean-Pierre Reveret and Luc Desnovers for reading the manuscript.

1. Stanley Milgram, *Obedience to Authority* (New York: Harper & Row, 1973).

2. The treatment of women is more specifically covered in Ruth Hubbard, Mary Sue Henifin and Barbara Fried, eds., *Biological Woman—The Convenient Myth* (Cambridge, MA: Schenkman Publishing Co., 1982). This book contains an extensive bibliography.

3. Naomi Weisstein, "Adventures of a Woman in Science," *Fed. Proc.* 35 (1976): 2226–2231.

4. Anne Sayre, *Rosalind Franklin and DNA: A Vivid View of What It Is Like to Be a Gifted Woman in an Especially Male Profession* (New York: W. W. Norton and Co., 1975).

5. Nancy Hopkins, "The High Price of Success in Science," *Radcliffe Quarterly* 62 (June 1976): 16–18.

6. Liliane Stehelin, "Science, Women and Ideology," in *Ideology of / in the National Sciences*, H. Rose and S. Rose, eds. (Cambridge, MA: Schenkman Publishing Co., 1979).

7. I speak from my own experience and that of my graduate students.

8. Betty Vetter, "Degree Completion by Women and Minorities in Science Increases," *Science* 214 (1982): 1313–1321; Betty M. Vetter and Elinor L. Babco, "New Data Show Slow Changes in Science Labour Force," *Science* 216 (1982): 1094–1095.

9. M. Whitehead et al., "Synthetic Absorption from Premarin Vaginal Cream" in I. D. Cooke, ed., *The Role of Estrogen / Progesterone in the Management of the Menopause* (Baltimore, MD: University Park Press, 1978).

10. Centre for Disease Control, *Abortion Surveillance*, 1978. (Issued November 1980. U.S. Department of Health and Human Services.)

11. F. S. Preston et al., "Effects of Flying and of Time Changes on Menstrual Cycle Length and on Performance in Airline Stewardesses," *Aerospace Medicine* 44 (1973): 438–443.

12. A. Kurkis et al., "Effect of Saturated and Unsaturated Fat Diets on Lipid Profiles of Plasma Lipoproteins," *Atherosclerosis* 41 (1982): 221–241.

13. Anke Ehrhardt, Nancy Greenberg, and John Money, "Female Gender Identity and Absence of Fetal Gonadal Hormones: Turner's Syndrome," *Johns Hopkins Medical Journal* 126 (1970): 237–248.

14. Herman A. Witkin et al., "Criminality in XYY and XXY Men," *Science* 193 (1976): 547–555.

15. W. Clarke Cooker, "Cancer Mortality Patterns in the Lead Industry," *Annals N. Y. Acad. Sci.* 271 (1976): 2250–2259.

16. Jeanne M. Stellman, *Women's Work, Women's Health: Myths and Realities* (New York: Pantheon Books, 1977), pp. 32–33.

17. Gena Corea, *The Hidden Malpractice* (New York: HBJ. Books, 1977), p. 16.

18. William D. Sharpe, "Chronic Radium Intoxication: Clinical and Autopsy Findings in Long-term New Jersey Survivors," *Environmental Research* 8 (1974): 243–383, 310.

19. Donna Mergler, Nicole Vezina, and Annette Beauvais, "Warts Amongst Workers in Poultry Slaughter-houses," *Scand. J. of Work, Envi. and Health* 8, suppl. 1 (1982): 180–184.

20. U.S. Department of Health, Education and Welfare, *Employment During Pregnancy: Legitimate Live Births 1963* (Washington, D.C: U.S. Government Printing Office, 1963).

21. Karen Messing, "Est-ce que la travailleuse enceinte est protegée au Quebec?" *Union Médicale* (February, 1982).

22. Gertrud S. Berkowitz, "All Epidemiologic Study of Preterm Delivery," *Am. J. Epidemiol.* 113 (1981): 81–92.

23. Anke A. Ehrhardt, Ralph Epstein, and John Money, "Fetal Androgens and Female Gender Identity in the Early-treated Adrenogenital Syndrome," *Johns Hopkins Med. Journal* 122 (1968): 160–168; see also study in note 13.

24. David Barash, "Sociobiology of Rape in Mallards (*Arias platyrynchos*): Responses of the Mated Male," *Science* 197 (1977): 788–789.

25. Gina B. Kolata, "Love Canal: False Alarm Caused by Botched Study," *Science* 208 (1980): 1239–1240.

26. Robert Rosenthal, *Experimenter Effects in Behavioural Research* (New York: Appleton-Century-Crofts, 1966).

27. Steven J. Gould, "Morton's Ranking of Races by Cranial Capacity," *Science* 200 (1978): 503–509.

28. J. L. Kennedy and H. P. Uhoff, "Experiments on the Nature of Extrasensory Perception, III. Recording Error Criticizer of Extra-chance Scores," *J. Parapsychol.* 3 (1939): 226–245.

29. D. D. Dorfman, "The Cyril Burt Question: New Findings," *Science* 201 (1978): 1177–1180.

30. Arbitration hearing on the case of Mme. Adrienne Robichaud, before Judge Jean-Jacques Turcotte, Quebec, 1980–82.

31. Charles E. Land, "Estimating Cancer Risks from Low Doses of Ionizing Radiation," *Science* 209 (1980): 1197–1203.

32. John W. Gofman, *Radiation and Human Health* (San Francisco: Sierra Club Books, 1981).

33. Joanna J. Ryan, "I.Q.—The Illusion of Objectivity," in Ken Richardson and David Spears, eds., *Race and Intelligence* (Baltimore, MD: Penguin Books, 1972): 36–55.

34. Jon Beckwith and John Durkin, "Girls, Boys and Math," *Science for the People* 13, No. 5 (Sept./Oct. 1981): 6–9; 32–35.

35. Robert Van den Bosch, *The Pesticide Conspiracy* (New York: Doubleday, 1978).

36. C. Owen Lovejoy, "The Origin of Man," *Science* 211 (1981): 341–350.

37. Lynn H. Fox et al., eds., *Women and the Mathematical Mystique* (Baltimore, MD: Johns Hopkins University Press, 1980).

38. Camilla P. Benbow and Julian C. Stanley, "Sex Differences in Math Ability: Fact or Artifact," *Science* 210 (1980): 1262–1264.

39. D. A. Williams and P. King, "Sex Differences in Achievement in and Attitudes toward Mathematics Result from Superior Mathematical Ability," *Newsweek* (December 15, 1980): 73.

40. Elizabeth Fennema, "Sex-Related Differences in Mathematical Achievement: Where and Why?" in L. H. Fox et al., eds., *Women and the Mathematical Mystique* (Baltimore, MD: Johns Hopkins University Press, 1980).

41. For example, Pierre Sormany, "Le cerveau a-t-il un sexe?" *L'Actualité* (November 1980): 35 ff.

42. David Barash, "Sexual Selection in Birdland," *Psychology Today* (March 1978): 81–86.

43. Scot Morris, "Do Men *Need* to Cheat on Their Women? A New Science Says Yes: Darwin and the Double Standard," *Playboy* (May 1978): 109 ff.

44. Francie F. Pelletier, "La belle au bois dormant se meurt: le valium et le cancer du sein," *La Vie en Rose* (Juin, Juillet, Août 1981): 33–37.

■ ■ ■

Discussion and Writing Suggestions

1. Do you agree with Messing's basic point that science is not objective? Do you think it is possible to achieve a completely unbiased scientific method to ensure that the kinds of biases Messing identifies are filtered out of science?

2. Even if there is scientific bias against women and other non-dominant cultural groups, does it do any real harm? Or is Messing overdramatizing the case? Should we be worried or not? What kinds of harm might be done by the unquestioning acceptance of biased science?

3. Messing refers to science as having a "mystique" that protects it from public scrutiny. Are the sciences alone among academic disciplines in cultivating this aura of untouchable authority? Thinking about your experience of college or university so far, can you identify any ways in which academics present their knowledge as unquestionable? Or is it your experience that critical scrutiny is encouraged?

The Stanford Prison Experiment

PHILIP K. ZIMBARDO

As well known—and as controversial—as the Milgram obedience experiments, the Stanford Prison Experiment (1973) raises troubling questions about the ability of individuals to resist authoritarian or obedient roles, if the social setting requires these roles. Philip K. Zimbardo, professor of psychology at Stanford University, set out to study the process by which prisoners and guards "learn" to become compliant and authoritarian, respectively. To find subjects for the experiment, Zimbardo placed an advertisement in a local newspaper:

> Male college students needed for psychological study of prison life. $15 per day for 1–2 weeks beginning Aug. 14. For further information & applications, come to Room 248, Jordan Hall, Stanford U.

The ad drew 75 responses. From these Zimbardo and his colleagues selected 21 university-age men, half of whom would become "prisoners" in the experiment, the other half "guards." The elaborate role-playing scenario, planned for two weeks, had to be cut short due to the intensity of subjects' responses. This article first appeared in the New York Times Magazine *(April 8, 1973).*

*In prison, those things withheld from and denied to the prisoner become
precisely what he wants most of all.*
                          —Eldridge Cleaver, "Soul on Ice"

*Our sense of power is more vivid when we break a man's spirit than when
we win his heart.*
                    —Eric Hoffer, "The Passionate State of Mind"

*Every prison that men build is built with bricks of shame, / and bound
with bars lest Christ should see how men their brothers maim.*
                    —Oscar Wilde, "The Ballad of Reading Gaol"

Wherever anyone is against his will that is to him a prison.
                                —Epictetus, "Discourses"

The quiet of a summer morning in Palo Alto, Calif., was shattered by a   1
screeching squad car siren as police swept through the city picking up college
students in a surprise mass arrest. Each suspect was charged with a felony,
warned of his constitutional rights, spread-eagled against the car, searched,
handcuffed and carted off in the back seat of the squad car to the police station for booking.

After fingerprinting and the preparation of identification forms for his   2
"jacket" (central information file), each prisoner was left isolated in a detention cell to wonder what he had done to get himself into this mess. After a
while, he was blindfolded and transported to the "Stanford County Prison."
Here he began the process of becoming a prisoner—stripped naked, skin-
searched, deloused and issued a uniform, bedding, soup and towel.

The warden offered an impromptu welcome: 3

"As you probably know, I'm your warden. All of you have shown that   4
you are unable to function outside in the real world for one reason or another—
that somehow you lack the responsibility of good citizens of this great country. We of this prison, your correctional staff, are going to help you learn
what your responsibilities as citizens of this country are. Here are the rules.
Sometime in the near future there will be a copy of the rules posted in each of
the cells. We expect you to know them and to be able to recite them by
number. If you follow all of these rules and keep your hands clean, repent for
your misdeeds and show a proper attitude of penitence, you and I will get
along just fine."

There followed a reading of the 16 basic rules of prisoner conduct, "Rule   5
Number One: Prisoners must remain silent during rest periods, after lights are
out, during meals and whenever they are outside the prison yard. Two:
Prisoners must eat at mealtimes and only at mealtimes. Three: Prisoners must
not move, tamper, deface or damage walls, ceilings, windows, doors, or other
prison property . . . . Seven: Prisoners must address each other by their ID
number only. Eight: Prisoners must address the guards as 'Mr. Correctional

Officer.' . . . Sixteen: Failure to obey any of the above rules may result in punishment."

By late afternoon these youthful "first offenders" sat in dazed silence on the cots in their barren cells trying to make sense of the events that had transformed their lives so dramatically.

If the police arrests and processing were executed with customary detachment, however, there were some things that didn't fit. For these men were now part of a very unusual kind of prison, an experimental mock prison, created by social psychologists to study the effects of imprisonment upon volunteer research subjects. When we planned our two-week-long simulation of prison life, we sought to understand more about the process by which people called "prisoners" lose their liberty, civil rights, independence and privacy, while those called "guards" gain social power by accepting the responsibility for controlling and managing the lives of their dependent charges.

Why didn't we pursue this research in a real prison? First, prison systems are fortresses of secrecy, closed to impartial observation, and thereby immune to critical analysis from anyone not already part of the correctional authority. Second, in any real prison, it is impossible to separate what each individual brings into the prison from what the prison brings out in each person.

We populated our mock prison with a homogeneous group of people who could be considered "normal-average" on the basis of clinical interviews and personality tests. Our participants (10 prisoners and 11 guards) were selected from more than 75 volunteers recruited through ads in the city and campus newspapers. The applicants were mostly college students from all over the United States and Canada who happened to be in the Stanford area during the summer and were attracted by the lure of earning $15 a day for participating in a study of prison life. We selected only those judged to be emotionally stable, physically healthy, mature, law-abiding citizens.

The sample of average, middle-class, Caucasian, college-age males (plus one Oriental student) was arbitrarily divided by the flip of a coin. Half were randomly assigned to play the role of guards, the others of prisoners. There were no measurable differences between the guards and the prisoners at the start of the experiment. Although initially warned that as prisoners their privacy and other civil rights would be violated and that they might be subjected to harassment, every subject was completely confident of his ability to endure whatever the prison had to offer for the full two-week experimental period. Each subject unhesitatingly agreed to give his "informed consent" to participate.

The prison was constructed in the basement of Stanford University's psychology building, which was deserted after the end of the summer-school session. A long corridor was converted into the prison "yard" by partitioning off both ends. Three small laboratory rooms opening onto this corridor were made into cells by installing metal barred doors and replacing existing furniture with cots, three to a cell. Adjacent offices were refurnished as guards' quarters, interview-testing rooms and bedrooms for the "warden" (Jaffe) and

the "superintendent" (Zimbardo). A concealed video camera and hidden
microphones recorded much of the activity and conversation of guards and
prisoners. The physical environment was one in which prisoners could always
be observed by the staff, the only exception being when they were secluded in
solitary confinement (a small, dark storage closet, labeled "The Hole").

Our mock prison represented an attempt to simulate the psychological 12
state of imprisonment in certain ways. We based our experiment on an in-
depth analysis of the prison situation, developed after hundreds of hours of
discussion with Carlo Prescott (our ex-con consultant), parole officers and
correctional personnel, and after reviewing much of the existing literature on
prisons and concentration camps.

"Real" prisoners typically report feeling powerless, arbitrarily controlled, 13
dependent, frustrated, hopeless, anonymous, dehumanized and emasculated.
It was not possible, pragmatically or ethically, to create such chronic states in
volunteer subjects who realize that they are in an experiment for only a short
time. Racism, physical brutality, indefinite confinement and enforced homosexuality were not features of our mock prison. But we did try to reproduce
those elements of the prison experience that seemed most fundamental.

We promoted anonymity by seeking to minimize each prisoner's sense of 14
uniqueness and prior identity. The prisoners wore smocks and nylon stocking
caps; they had to use their ID numbers; their personal effects were removed
and they were housed in barren cells. All of this made them appear similar to
each other and indistinguishable to observers. Their smocks, which were like
dresses, were worn without undergarments, causing the prisoners to be
restrained in their physical actions and to move in ways that were more feminine than masculine. The prisoners were forced to obtain permission from the
guard for routine and simple activities such as writing letters, smoking a cigarette or even going to the toilet; this elicited from them a childlike dependency.

Their quarters, though clean and neat, were small, stark and without 15
esthetic appeal. The lack of windows resulted in poor air circulation, and per-
sistent odors arose from the unwashed bodies of the prisoners. After 10 p.m.
lockup, toilet privileges were denied, so prisoners who had to relieve themselves would have to urinate and defecate in buckets provided by the guards.
Sometimes the guards refused permission to have them cleaned out, and this
made the prison smell.

Above all, "real" prisons are machines for playing tricks with the human 16
conception of time. In our windowless prison, the prisoners often did not even
know whether it was day or night. A few hours after falling asleep, they
were roused by shrill whistles for their "count." The ostensible purpose of the
count was to provide a public test of the prisoners' knowledge of the rules and
of their ID numbers. But more important, the count, which occurred at least
once on each of the three different guard shifts, provided a regular occasion
for the guards to relate to the prisoners. Over the course of the study, the
duration of the counts was spontaneously increased by the guards from their

initial perfunctory 10 minutes to a seemingly interminable several hours. During these confrontations, guards who were bored could find ways to amuse themselves, ridiculing recalcitrant prisoners, enforcing arbitrary rules and openly exaggerating any dissension among the prisoners.

The guards were also "deindividualized": They wore identical khaki uniforms and silver reflector sunglasses that made eye contact with them impossible. Their symbols of power were billy clubs, whistles, handcuffs and the keys to the cells and the "main gate." Although our guards received no formal training from us in how to be guards, for the most part they moved with apparent ease into their roles. The media had already provided them with ample models of prison guards to emulate. 17

Because we were as interested in the guards' behavior as in the prisoners', they were given considerable latitude to improvise and to develop strategies and tactics of prisoner management. Our guards were told that they must maintain "law and order" in this prison, that they were responsible for handling any trouble that might break out, and they were cautioned about the seriousness and potential dangers of the situation they were about to enter. Surprisingly, in most prison systems, "real" guards are not given much more psychological preparation or adequate training than this for what is one of the most complex, demanding and dangerous jobs our society has to offer. They are expected to learn how to adjust to their new employment mostly from on-the-job experience, and from contacts with the "old bulls" during a survival-of-the-fittest orientation period. According to an orientation manual for correctional officers at San Quentin, "the only way you really get to know San Quentin is through experience and time. Some of us take more time and must go through more experiences than others to accomplish this; some really never do get there." 18

You cannot be a prisoner if no one will be your guard, and you cannot be a prison guard if no one takes you or your prison seriously. Therefore, over time a perverted symbiotic relationship developed. As the guards became more aggressive, prisoners became more passive; assertion by the guards led to dependency in the prisoners; self-aggrandizement was met with self-deprecation, authority with helplessness, and the counterpart of the guards' sense of mastery and control was the depression and hopelessness witnessed in the prisoners. As these differences in behavior, mood and perception became more evident to all, the need for the now "righteously" powerful guards to rule the obviously inferior and powerless inmates became a sufficient reason to support almost any further indignity of man against man: 19

Guard K: "During the inspection, I went to cell 2 to mess up a bed which the prisoner had made and he grabbed me, screaming that he had just made it, and he wasn't going to let me mess it up. He grabbed my throat, and although he was laughing I was pretty scared. . . . I lashed out with my stick and hit him in the chin (although not very hard), and when I freed myself I became angry. I wanted to get back in the cell and have a go with him, since he attacked me when I was not ready." 20

Guard M: "I was surprised at myself . . . I made them call each other   21
names and clean the toilets out with their bare hands. I practically considered
the prisoners cattle, and I kept thinking: 'I have to watch out for them in case
they try something.'"

Guard A: "I was tired of seeing the prisoners in their rags and smelling   22
the strong odors of their bodies that filled the cells. I watched them tear at
each other on orders given by us. They didn't see it as an experiment. It was
real and they were fighting to keep their identity. But we were always there to
show them who was boss."

Because the first day passed without incident, we were surprised and   23
totally unprepared for the rebellion that broke out on the morning of the
second day. The prisoners removed their stocking caps, ripped off their numbers and barricaded themselves inside the cells by putting their beds against
the doors. What should we do? The guards were very much upset because the
prisoners also began to taunt and curse them to their faces. When the morning shift of guards came on, they were upset at the night shift who, they felt,
must have been too permissive and too lenient. The guards had to handle the
rebellion themselves, and what they did was startling to behold.

At first they insisted that reinforcements be called in. The two guards   24
who were waiting on stand-by call at home came in, and the night shift of
guards voluntarily remained on duty (without extra pay) to bolster the morning shift. The guards met and decided to treat force with force. They got a fire
extinguisher that shot a stream of skin-chilling carbon dioxide and forced the
prisoners away from the doors; they broke into each cell, stripped the prisoners naked, took the beds out, forced the prisoners who were the ringleaders into solitary confinement and generally began to harass and intimidate the
prisoners.

After crushing the riot, the guards decided to head off further unrest by   25
creating a privileged cell for those who were "good prisoners" and then,
without explanation, switching some of the troublemakers into it and some of
the good prisoners out into the other cells. The prisoner ringleaders could not
trust these new cellmates because they had not joined in the riot and might
even be "snitches." The prisoners never again acted in unity against the
system. One of the leaders of the prisoner revolt later confided:

"If we had gotten together then, I think we could have taken over the   26
place. But when I saw the revolt wasn't working, I decided to toe the line.
Everyone settled into the same pattern. From then on, we were really controlled by the guards."

It was after this episode that the guards really began to demonstrate   27
their inventiveness in the application of arbitrary power. They made the prisoners obey petty, meaningless and often inconsistent rules, forced them to
engage in tedious, useless work, such as moving cartons back and forth
between closets and picking thorns out of their blankets for hours on end.
(The guards had previously dragged the blankets through thorny bushes to
create this disagreeable task.) Not only did the prisoners have to sing songs or

laugh or refrain from smiling on command; they were also encouraged to curse and vilify each other publicly during some of the counts. They sounded off their numbers endlessly and were repeatedly made to do pushups, on occasion with a guard stepping on them or a prisoner sitting on them.

Slowly the prisoners became resigned to their fate and even behaved in ways that actually helped to justify their dehumanizing treatment at the hands of the guards. Analysis of the tape-recorded private conversations between prisoners and of remarks made by them to interviewers revealed that fully half could be classified as nonsupportive of other prisoners. More dramatic, 85 percent of the evaluative statements by prisoners about their fellow prisoners were uncomplimentary and deprecating. 28

This should be taken in the context of an even more surprising result. What do you imagine the prisoners talked about when they were alone in their cells with each other, given a temporary respite from the continual harassment and surveillance by the guards? Girl friends, career plans, hobbies or politics? 29

No, their concerns were almost exclusively riveted to prison topics. Their monitored conversations revealed that only 10 percent of the time was devoted to "outside" topics, while 90 percent of the time they discussed escape plans, the awful food, grievances or ingratiating tactics to use with specific guards in order to get a cigarette, permission to go to the toilet or some other favor. Their obsession with these immediate survival concerns made talk about the past and future an idle luxury. 30

And this was not a minor point. So long as the prisoners did not get to know each other as people, they only extended the oppressiveness and reality of their life as prisoners. For the most part, each prisoner observed his fellow prisoners allowing the guards to humiliate them, acting like compliant sheep, carrying out mindless orders with total obedience and even being cursed by fellow prisoners (at a guard's command). Under such circumstances, how could a prisoner have respect for his fellows, or any self-respect for what *he* obviously was becoming in the eyes of all those evaluating him? 31

The combination of realism and symbolism in this experiment had fused to create a vivid illusion of imprisonment. The illusion merged inextricably with reality for at least some of the time for every individual in the situation. It was remarkable how readily we all slipped into our roles, temporarily gave up our identities and allowed these assigned roles and the social forces in the situation to guide, shape and eventually to control our freedom of thought and action. 32

But precisely where does one's "identity" end and one's "role" begin? When the private self and the public role behavior clash, what direction will attempts to impose consistency take? Consider the reactions of the parents, relatives and friends of the prisoners who visited their forlorn sons, brothers and lovers during two scheduled visitors' hours. They were taught in short order that they were our guests, allowed the privilege of visiting only by complying with the regulations of the institution. They had to register, were 33 made to wait half an hour, were told that only two visitors could see any one prisoner; the total visiting time was cut from an hour to only 10 minutes, they had to be under the surveillance of a guard, and before any parents could enter the visiting area, they had to discuss their son's case with the warden. Of course they complained about these arbitrary rules, but their conditioned, middle-class reaction was to work within the system to appeal privately to the superintendent to make conditions better for their prisoners.

In less than 36 hours, we were forced to release prisoner 8612 because of   34
extreme depression, disorganized thinking, uncontrollable crying and fits of rage. We did so reluctantly because we believed he was trying to "con" us— it was unimaginable that a volunteer prisoner in a mock prison could legitimately be suffering and disturbed to that extent. But then on each of the next three days another prisoner reacted with similar anxiety symptoms, and we were forced to terminate them, too. In a fifth case, a prisoner was released after developing a psychosomatic rash over his entire body (triggered by rejection of his parole appeal by the mock parole board). These men were simply unable to make an adequate adjustment to prison life. Those who endured the prison experience to the end could be distinguished from those who broke down and were released early in only one dimension—authoritarianism. On a psychological test designed to reveal a person's authoritarianism, those prisoners who had the highest scores were best able to function in this authoritarian prison environment.

If the authoritarian situation became a serious matter for the prisoners, it   35
became even more serious—and sinister—for the guards. Typically, the guards insulted the prisoners, threatened them, were physically aggressive, used instruments (night sticks, fire extinguishers, etc.) to keep the prisoners in line and referred to them in impersonal, anonymous, deprecating ways: "Hey, you," or "You [obscenity], 5401, come here." From the first to the last day, there was a significant increase in the guards' use of most of these domineering, abusive tactics.

Everyone and everything in the prison was defined by power. To be a   36
guard who did not take advantage of this institutionally sanctioned use of power was to appear "weak," "out of it," "wired up by the prisoners," or simply a deviant from the established norms of appropriate guard behavior. Using Erich Fromm's definition of sadism, as "the wish for absolute control over another living being," all of the mock guards at one time or another during this study behaved sadistically toward the prisoners. Many of them reported—in their diaries, on critical-incident report forms and during postexperimental interviews—being delighted in the new-found power and control they exercised and sorry to see it relinquished at the end of the study.

Some of the guards reacted to the situation in the extreme and behaved   37
with great hostility and cruelty in the forms of degradation they invented for the prisoners. But others were kinder; they occasionally did little favors for the prisoners, were reluctant to punish them, and avoided situations where prisoners were being harassed. The torment experienced by one of these good

guards is obvious in his perceptive analysis of what it felt like to be responded to as a "guard":

"What made the experience most depressing for me was the fact that we were continually called upon to act in a way that just was contrary to what I really feel inside. I don't feel like I'm the type of person that would be a guard, just constantly giving out [orders] . . . and forcing people to do things, and pushing and lying—it just didn't seem like me, and to continually keep up and put on a face like that is just really one of the most oppressive things you can do. It's almost like a prison that you create yourself—you get into it, and it becomes almost the definition you make of yourself, it almost becomes like walls, and you want to break out and you want just to be able to tell everyone that 'this isn't really me at all, and I'm not the person that's confined in there—I'm a person who wants to get out and show you that I am free, and I do have my own will, and I'm not the sadistic type of person that enjoys this kind of thing.'"

Still, the behavior of these good guards seemed more motivated by a desire to be liked by everyone in the system than by a concern for the inmates' welfare. No guard ever intervened in any direct way on behalf of the prisoners, ever interfered with the orders of the cruelest guards or ever openly complained about the subhuman quality of life that characterized this prison.

Perhaps the most devastating impact of the more hostile guards was their creation of a capricious, arbitrary environment. Over time the prisoners began to react passively. When our mock prisoners asked questions, they got answers about half the time, but the rest of the time they were insulted and punished—and it was not possible for them to predict which would be the outcome. As they began to "toe the line," they stopped resisting, questioning and, indeed, almost ceased responding altogether. There was a general decrease in all categories of response as they learned the safest strategy to use in an unpredictable, threatening environment from which there is no physical escape—do nothing, except what is required. Act not, want not, feel not and you will not get into trouble in prisonlike situations.

Can it really be, you wonder, that intelligent, educated volunteers could have lost sight of the reality that they were merely acting a part in an elaborate game that would eventually end? There are many indications not only that they did, but that, in addition, so did we and so did other apparently sensible, responsible adults.

Prisoner 819, who had gone into an uncontrollable crying fit, was about to be prematurely released from the prison when a guard lined up the prisoners and had them chant in unison, "819 is a bad prisoner. Because of what 819 did to prison property we all must suffer. 819 is a bad prisoner." Over and over again. When we realized 819 might be overhearing this, we rushed into the room where 819 was supposed to be resting, only to find him in tears, prepared to go back into the prison because he could not leave as long as the others thought he was a "bad prisoner." Sick as he felt, he had to prove to them he was not a "bad" prisoner. He had to be persuaded that he was not a prisoner at all, that the others were also just students, that this was just an experiment and not a prison and the prison staff were only research psychologists. A report from the warden notes, "While I believe that it was necessary for *staff* [me] to enact the warden role, at least some of the time, I am startled by the ease with which I could turn off my sensitivity and concern for others for 'a good cause.'"

Consider our overreaction to the rumor of a mass escape plot that one of   43
the guards claimed to have overheard. It went as follows: Prisoner 8612, previously released for emotional disturbance, was only faking. He was going to round up a bunch of his friends, and they would storm the prison right after visiting hours. Instead of collecting data on the pattern of rumor transmission, we made plans to maintain the security of our institution. After putting a confederate informer into the cell 8612 had occupied to get specific information about the escape plans, the superintendent went back to the Palo Alto Police Department to request transfer of our prisoners to the old city jail. His impassioned plea was only turned down at the last minute when the problem of insurance and city liability for our prisoners was raised by a city official. Angered at this lack of cooperation, the staff formulated another plan. Our jail was dismantled, the prisoners, chained and blindfolded, were carted off to a remote storage room. When the conspirators arrived, they would be told the study was over, their friends had been sent home, there was nothing left to liberate. After they left, we would redouble the security features of our prison making any future escape attempts futile. We even planned to lure ex-prisoner 8612 back on some pretext and imprison him again, because he had been released on false pretenses! The rumor turned out to be just that—a full day had passed in which we collected little or no data, worked incredibly hard to tear down and then rebuild our prison. Our reaction, however, was as much one of relief and joy as of exhaustion and frustration.

When a former prison chaplain was invited to talk with the prisoners (the   44
grievance committee had requested church services), he puzzled everyone by disparaging each inmate for not having taken any constructive action in order to get released. "Don't you know you must have a lawyer in order to get bail, or to appeal the charges against you?" Several of them accepted his invitation to contact their parents in order to secure the services of an attorney. The next night one of the parents stopped at the superintendent's office before visiting time and handed him the name and phone number of her cousin who was a public defender. She said that a priest had called her and suggested the need for a lawyer's services! We called the lawyer. He came, interviewed the prisoners, discussed sources of bail money and promised to return again after the weekend.

But perhaps the most telling account of the insidious development of this   45
new reality, of the gradual Kafkaesque metamorphosis of good into evil, appears in excerpts from the diary of one of the guards, Guard A:

Prior to start of experiment: "As I am a pacifist and nonaggressive indi-   46
vidual I cannot see a time when I might guard and/or maltreat other living things."

After an orientation meeting: "Buying uniforms at the end of the meeting   47
confirms the gamelike atmosphere of this thing. I doubt whether many of us
share the expectations of 'seriousness' that the experimenters seem to have."

First Day: "Feel sure that the prisoners will make fun of my appearance   48
and I evolve my first basic strategy—mainly not to smile at anything they say
or do which would be admitting it's all only a game. . . . At cell 3 I stop and
setting my voice hard and low say to 5486, 'What are you smiling at?'
'Nothing, Mr. Correctional Officer.' 'Well, see that you don't.' (As I walk off
I feel stupid.)"

Second Day: "5704 asked for a cigarette and I ignored him—because I   49
am a non-smoker and could not empathize. . . . Meanwhile since I was feeling empathetic towards 1037, I determined not to talk with him . . . after we
had count and lights out [Guard D] and I held a loud conversation about
going home to our girl friends and what we were going to do to them."

Third Day (preparing for the first visitors' night): "After warning the   50
prisoners not to make any complaints unless they wanted the visit terminated fast, we finally brought in the first parents. I made sure I was one of the
guards on the yard, because this was my first chance for the type of manipu-
lative power that I really like—being a very noticed figure with almost complete control over what is said or not. While the parents and prisoners sat in
chairs, I sat on the end of the table dangling my feet and contradicting anything I felt like. This was the first part of the experiment I was really enjoying. . . . 817 is being obnoxious and bears watching."

Fourth Day: " . . . The psychologist rebukes me for handcuffing and   51
blindfolding a prisoner before leaving the [counseling] office, and I resentfully
reply that it is both necessary security and my business anyway."

Fifth Day: "I harass 'Sarge' who continues to stubbornly overrespond to   52
all commands. I have singled him out for special abuse both because he begs
for it and because I simply don't like him. The real trouble starts at dinner.
The new prisoner (416) refuses to eat his sausage. . . we throw him into the
Hole ordering him to hold sausages in each hand. We have a crisis of authority; this rebellious conduct potentially undermines the complete control we
have over the others. We decide to play upon prisoner solidarity and tell the
new one that all the others will be deprived of visitors if he does not eat his
dinner. . . . I walk by and slam my stick into the Hole door. . . . I am very
angry at this prisoner for causing discomfort and trouble for the others. I
decided to force-feed him, but he wouldn't eat. I let the food slide down his
face. I didn't believe it was me doing it. I hated myself for making him eat but
I hated him more for not eating."

Sixth Day: "The experiment is over. I feel elated but am shocked to find   53
some other guards disappointed somewhat because of the loss of money and
some because they are enjoying themselves."

We were no longer dealing with an intellectual exercise in which a   54
hypothesis was being evaluated in the dispassionate manner dictated by the
canons of the scientific method. We were caught up in the passion of the

present, the suffering, the need to control people, not variables, the escalation
of power and all of the unexpected things that were erupting around and
within us. We had to end this experiment: So our planned two-week simulation was aborted after only six (was it only six?) days and nights.

Was it worth all the suffering just to prove what everybody knows—that   55
some people are sadistic, others weak and prisons are not beds of roses? If
that is all we demonstrated in this research, then it was certainly not worth the
anguish. We believe there are many significant implications to be derived
from this experience, only a few of which can be suggested here.

The potential social value of this study derives precisely from the fact that   56
normal, healthy, educated young men could be so radically transformed
under the institutional pressures of a "prison environment." If this could
happen in so short a time, without the excesses that are possible in real prisons, and if it could happen to the "cream-of-the-crop of American youth,"
then one can only shudder to imagine what society is doing both to the actual
guards and prisoners who are at this very moment participating in that unnatural "social experiment."

The pathology observed in this study cannot be reasonably attributed in   57
pre-existing personality differences of the subjects, that option being eliminated by our selection procedures and random assignment. Rather, the subjects' abnormal social and personal reactions are best seen as a product of
their transaction with an environment that supported the behavior that would
be pathological in other settings, but was "appropriate" in this prison. Had
we observed comparable reactions in a real prison, the psychiatrist undoubtedly would have been able to attribute any prisoner's behavior to character
defects or personality maladjustment, while critics of the prison system would
have been quick to label the guards as "psychopathic." This tendency to
locate the source of behavior disorders inside a particular person or group
underestimates the power of situational forces.

Our colleague, David Rosenhan, has very convincingly shown that once   58
a sane person (pretending to be insane) gets labeled as insane and committed
to a mental hospital, it is the label that is the reality which is treated and not
the person. This dehumanizing tendency to respond to other people according to socially determined labels and often arbitrarily assigned roles is also
apparent in a recent "mock hospital" study designed by Norma Jean Orlando
to extend the ideas in our research.

Personnel from the staff of Elgin State Hospital in Illinois role-played   59
either mental patients or staff in a weekend simulation on a ward in the hospital. The mock mental patients soon displayed behavior indistinguishable
from that we usually associate with the chronic pathological syndromes of
acute mental patients: Incessant pacing, uncontrollable weeping, depression,
hostility, fights, stealing from each other, complaining. Many of the "mock
staff" took advantage of their power to act in ways comparable to our mock
guards by dehumanizing their powerless victims.

During a series of encounter debriefing sessions immediately after our 60 experiment, we all had an opportunity to vent our strong feelings and to reflect upon the moral and ethical issues each of us faced, and we considered how we might react more morally in future "real-life" analogues to this situation. Year-long follow-ups with our subjects via questionnaires, personal interviews and group reunions indicate that their mental anguish was transient and situationally specific, but the self-knowledge gained has persisted.

By far the most disturbing implication of our research comes from the 61 parallels between what occurred in that basement mock prison and daily experiences in our own lives—and we presume yours. The physical institution of prison is but a concrete and steel metaphor for the existence of more pervasive, albeit less obvious, prisons of the mind that all of us daily create, populate and perpetuate. We speak here of the prisons of racism, sexism, despair, shyness, "neurotic hang-ups" and the like. The social convention of marriage, as one example, becomes for many couples a state of imprisonment in which one partner agrees to be prisoner or guard, forcing or allowing the other to play the reciprocal role—invariably without making the contract explicit.

To what extent do we allow ourselves to become imprisoned by docilely 62 accepting the roles others assign us or, indeed, choose to remain prisoners because being passive and dependent frees us from the need to act and be responsible for our actions? The prison of fear constructed in the delusions of the paranoid is no less confining or less real than the cell that every shy person erects to limit his own freedom in anxious anticipation of being ridiculed and rejected by his guards—often guards of his own making.

■ ■ ■

Review Questions

1. What was Zimbardo's primary goal in undertaking the prison experiment?
2. What was the profile of subjects in the experiments? Why is this profile significant?
3. Zimbardo claims that there is a "process" (paragraphs 2, 7) of becoming a prisoner. What is this process?
4. What inverse psychological relationships developed between prisoners and guards?
5. What was the result of the prison "riot"?
6. Why did prisoners have no respect for each other or for themselves?
7. How does the journal of Guard A illustrate what Zimbardo calls the "gradual Kafkaesque metamorphosis of good into evil"? See paragraphs 45–54.
8. What are the reasons people would voluntarily become prisoners?
9. How can the mind keep people in jail?

Discussion and Writing Suggestions

1. Reread the four epigraphs to this article. Write a paragraph of response to any one of them, in light of Zimbardo's discussion of the prison experiment.

2. You may have thought, before reading this article, that being a prisoner is a physical fact, not a psychological state. What are the differences between these two views?

3. In paragraph 8, Zimbardo explains his reasons for not pursuing his research in a real prison. He writes that "it is impossible to separate what each individual brings into the prison from what the prison brings out in each person." What does he mean? And how does this distinction prove important later in the article (see paragraph 57)?

4. Zimbardo reports that, at the beginning of the experiment, each of the "prisoner" subjects "was completely confident of his ability to endure whatever the prison had to offer for the full two-week experimental period" (paragraph 10). Had you been a subject, would you have been so confident, prior to the experiment? Given what you've learned of the experiment, do you think you would have psychologically "become" a prisoner or guard if you had been selected for these roles? (And if not, what makes you so sure?)

5. Identify two passages in this article: one that surprised you relating to the prisoners; and one that surprised you relating to the guards. Write a paragraph explaining your response to each. Now read the two passages in light of each other. Do you see any patterns underlying your responses?

6. Zimbardo claims that the implications of his research matter deeply—that the mock prison he created is a metaphor for prisons of the mind "that all of us daily create, populate and perpetuate" (paragraph 61). Zimbardo mentions the prisons of "racism, sexism, despair, [and] shyness." Choose any one of these and discuss how it is a mental prison.

7. Reread paragraphs 61 and 62. Zimbardo makes a metaphorical jump from his experiment to the psychological realities of your daily life. Prisons—the artificial one he created and actual prisons—stand for something: social systems in which there are those who give orders and those who obey. All metaphors break down at some point. Where does this one break down?

8. Zimbardo suggests that we might "choose to remain prisoners because being passive and dependent frees us from the need to act and be responsible for our actions" (paragraph 62). Do you agree? What are the burdens of being disobedient?

Disobedience as a Psychological and Moral Problem

ERICH FROMM

Erich Fromm (1900–1980) was one of this century's most distinguished writers and thinkers. Psychoanalyst and philosopher, historian and sociologist, he ranged widely in his interests and defied easy characterization. Fromm studied the works of Freud and Marx closely, and published on them both, but he was not aligned strictly with either. In much of his voluminous writing, he struggled to articulate a view that could help bridge ideological and personal conflicts and bring dignity to those who struggled with isolation in the industrial world. Author of more than 30 books and contributor to numerous edited collections and journals, Fromm is best known for Escape from Freedom *(1941),* The Art of Loving *(1956), and* To Have or to Be? *(1976).*

In the essay that follows, first published in 1963, Fromm discusses the seductive comforts of obedience, and he makes distinctions among varieties of obedience, some of which he believes are destructive, and others, life affirming. His thoughts on nuclear annihilation may seem dated in these days of post–Cold War co-operation, but it is worth remembering that Fromm wrote his essay just after the Cuban missile crisis, when fears of a third world war ran high. (We might note that despite the welcomed reductions of nuclear stockpiles, the United States and Russia still possess, and retain battle plans for, thousands of warheads; many other countries have since developed nuclear missiles.) On the major points of his essay, concerning the psychological and moral problems of obedience, Fromm remains as pertinent today as when he wrote 40 years ago.

For centuries kings, priests, feudal lords, industrial bosses and parents have   1
insisted that *obedience is a virtue* and that *disobedience is a vice*. In order to
introduce another point of view, let us set against this position the following
statement: *human history began with an act of disobedience, and it is not
unlikely that it will be terminated by an act of obedience.*

Human history was ushered in by an act of disobedience according to the   2
Hebrew and Greek myths. Adam and Eve, living in the Garden of Eden,
were part of nature; they were in harmony with it, yet did not transcend it.
They were in nature as the fetus is in the womb of the mother. They were
human, and at the same time not yet human. All this changed when they disobeyed an order. By breaking the ties with earth and mother, by cutting the
umbilical cord, man emerged from a prehuman harmony and was able to take
the first step into independence and freedom. The act of disobedience set
Adam and Eve free and opened their eyes. They recognized each other as
strangers and the world outside them as strange and even hostile. Their act of
disobedience broke the primary bond with nature and made them individuals.
"Original sin," far from corrupting man, set him free; it was the beginning of

history. Man had to leave the Garden of Eden in order to learn to rely on his own powers and to become fully human.

The prophets, in their messianic concept, confirmed the idea that man   3
had been right in disobeying; that he had not been corrupted by his "sin," but freed from the fetters of pre-human harmony. For the prophets, *history* is the place where man becomes human; during its unfolding he develops his powers of reason and of love until he creates a new harmony between himself, his fellow man and nature. This new harmony is described as "the end of days," that period of history in which there is peace between man and man, between man and nature. It is a "new" paradise created by man himself, and one which he alone could create because he was forced to leave the "old" paradise as a result of his disobedience.

Just as the Hebrew myth of Adam and Eve, so the Greek myth of   4
Prometheus sees all of human civilization based on an act of disobedience. Prometheus, in stealing the fire from the gods, lays the foundation for the evolution of man. There would be no human history were it not for Prometheus' "crime." He, like Adam and Eve, is punished for his disobedience. But he does not repent and ask for forgiveness. On the contrary, he proudly says: "I would rather be chained to this rock than be the obedient servant of the gods."

Man has continued to evolve by acts of disobedience. Not only was his   5
spiritual development possible only because there were men who dared to say no to the powers that be in the name of their conscience or their faith, but also his intellectual development was dependent on the capacity for being disobedient—disobedient to authorities who tried to muzzle new thoughts and to the authority of long-established opinions which declared a change to be nonsense.

If the capacity for disobedience constituted the beginning of human his-   6
tory, obedience might very well, as I have said, cause the end of human history. I am not speaking symbolically or poetically. There is the possibility, or even the probability, that the human race will destroy civilization and even all life upon earth within the next five to ten years. There is no rationality or sense in it. But the fact is that, while we are living technically in the Atomic Age, the majority of men—including most of those who are in power—still live emotionally in the Stone Age; that while our mathematics, astronomy, and the natural sciences are of the twentieth century, most of our ideas about politics, the state, and society lag far behind the age of science. If mankind commits suicide it will be because people will obey those who command them to push the deadly buttons; because they will obey the archaic passions of fear, hate, and greed; because they will obey obsolete clichés of State sovereignty and national honor. The Soviet leaders talk much about revolutions, and we in the "free world" talk much about freedom. Yet they and we discourage disobedience—in the Soviet Union explicitly and by force, in the free world implicitly and by the more subtle methods of persuasion.

But I do not mean to say that all disobedience is a virtue and all obedi-   7
ence a vice. Such a view would ignore the dialectical relationship between obedience and disobedience. Whenever the principles which are obeyed and those
which are disobeyed are irreconcilable, an act of obedience to one principle is
necessarily an act of disobedience to its counterpart and vice versa. Antigone
is the classic example of this dichotomy. By obeying the inhuman laws of the
State, Antigone necessarily would disobey the laws of humanity. By obeying
the latter, she must disobey the former. All martyrs of religious faiths, of freedom and of science have had to disobey those who wanted to muzzle them in
order to obey their own consciences, the laws of humanity and of reason. If
a man can only obey and not disobey, he is a slave; if he can only disobey and
not obey, he is a rebel (not a revolutionary); he acts out of anger, disappointment, resentment, yet not in the name of a conviction or a principle.

However, in order to prevent a confusion of terms an important qualifi-   8
cation must be made. Obedience to a person, institution or power (heteronomous obedience) is submission; it implies the abdication of my
autonomy and the acceptance of a foreign will or judgment in place of my
own. Obedience to my own reason or conviction (autonomous obedience) is
not an act of submission but one of affirmation. My conviction and my judgment, if authentically mine, are part of me. If I follow them rather than the
judgment of others, I am being myself; hence the word *obey* can be applied
only in a metaphorical sense and with a meaning which is fundamentally different from the one in the case of "heteronomous obedience."

But this distinction still needs two further qualifications, one with regard   9
to the concept of conscience and the other with regard to the concept of
authority.

The word *conscience* is used to express two phenomena which are quite   10
distinct from each other. One is the "authoritarian conscience" which is the
internalized voice of an authority whom we are eager to please and afraid of
displeasing. This authoritarian conscience is what most people experience
when they obey their conscience. It is also the conscience which Freud speaks
of, and which he called "Super-Ego." This Super-Ego represents the internalized commands and prohibitions of father, accepted by the son out of fear.
Different from the authoritarian conscience is the "humanistic conscience";
this is the voice present in every human being and independent from external
sanctions and rewards. Humanistic conscience is based on the fact that as
human beings we have an intuitive knowledge of what is human and inhuman, what is conducive of life and what is destructive of life. This conscience
serves our functioning as human beings. It is the voice which calls us back to
ourselves, to our humanity.

Authoritarian conscience (Super-Ego) is still obedience to a power outside   11
of myself, even though this power has been internalized. Consciously I believe
that I am following *my* conscience; in effect, however, I have swallowed the
principles of *power*; just because of the illusion that humanistic conscience
and Super-Ego are identical, internalized authority is so much more effective

than the authority which is clearly experienced as not being part of me. Obedience to the "authoritarian conscience," like all obedience to outside thoughts and power, tends to debilitate "humanistic conscience," the ability to be and to judge oneself.

The statement, on the other hand, that obedience to another person is   12 *ipso facto* submission needs also to be qualified by distinguishing "irrational" from "rational" authority. An example of rational authority is to be found in the relationship between student and teacher; one of irrational authority in the relationship between slave and master. Both relationships are based on the fact that the authority of the person in command is accepted. Dynamically, however, they are of a different nature. The interests of the teacher and the student, in the ideal case, lie in the same direction. The teacher is satisfied if he succeeds in furthering the student; if he has failed to do so, the failure is his and the student's. The slave owner, on the other hand, wants to exploit the slave as much as possible. The more he gets out of him the more satisfied he is. At the same time, the slave tries to defend as best he can his claims for a minimum of happiness. The interests of slave and master are antagonistic, because what is advantageous to the one is detrimental to the other. The superiority of the one over the other has a different function in each case; in the first it is the condition for the furtherance of the person subjected to the authority, and in the second it is the condition for his exploitation. Another distinction runs parallel to this: rational authority is rational because the authority, whether it is held by a teacher or a captain of a ship giving orders in an emergency, acts in the name of reason which, being universal, I can accept without submitting. Irrational authority has to use force or suggestion, because no one would let himself be exploited if he were free to prevent it.

Why is man so prone to obey and why is it so difficult for him to dis-   13 obey? As long as I am obedient to the power of the State, the Church, or public opinion, I feel safe and protected. In fact it makes little difference what power it is that I am obedient to. It is always an institution, or men, who use force in one form or another and who fraudulently claim omniscience and omnipotence. My obedience makes me part of the power I worship, and hence I feel strong. I can make no error, since it decides for me; I cannot be alone, because it watches over me; I cannot commit a sin, because it does not let me do so, and even if I do sin, the punishment is only the way of returning to the almighty power.

In order to disobey, one must have the courage to be alone, to err and to   14 sin. But courage is not enough. The capacity for courage depends on a person's state of development. Only if a person has emerged from mother's lap and father's commands, only if he has emerged as a fully developed individual and thus has acquired the capacity to think and feel for himself, only then can he have the courage to say "no" to power, to disobey.

A person can become free through acts of disobedience by learning to say   15 no to power. But not only is the capacity for disobedience the condition for freedom; freedom is also the condition for disobedience. If I am afraid of freedom, I cannot dare to say "no," I cannot have the courage to be disobedient. Indeed, freedom and the capacity for disobedience are inseparable; hence any social, political, and religious system which proclaims freedom, yet stamps out disobedience, cannot speak the truth.

There is another reason why it is so difficult to dare to disobey, to say "no" to power. During most of human history obedience has been identified with virtue and disobedience with sin. The reason is simple: thus far throughout most of history a minority has ruled over the majority. This rule was made necessary by the fact that there was only enough of the good things of life for the few, and only the crumbs remained for the many. If the few wanted to enjoy the good things and, beyond that, to have the many serve them and work for them, one condition was necessary: the many had to learn obedience. To be sure, obedience can be established by sheer force. But this method has many disadvantages. It constitutes a constant threat that one day the many might have the means to overthrow the few by force; furthermore there are many kinds of work which cannot be done properly if nothing but fear is behind the obedience. Hence the obedience which is only rooted in the fear of force must be transformed into one rooted in man's heart. Man must want and even need to obey, instead of only fearing to disobey. If this is to be achieved, power must assume the qualities of the All Good, of the All Wise; it must become All Knowing. If this happens, power can proclaim that disobedience is sin and obedience virtue; and once this has been proclaimed, the many can accept obedience because it is good and detest disobedience because it is bad, rather than to detest themselves for being cowards. From Luther to the nineteenth century one was concerned with overt and explicit authorities. Luther, the pope, the princes, wanted to uphold it; the middle class, the workers, the philosophers, tried to uproot it. The fight against authority in the State as well as in the family was often the very basis for the development of an independent and daring person. The fight against authority was inseparable from the intellectual mood which characterized the philosophers of the enlightenment and the scientists. This "critical mood" was one of faith in reason, and at the same time of doubt in everything which is said or thought, inasmuch as it is based on tradition, superstition, custom, power. The principles *sapere aude* and *de omnibus est dubitandum*—"dare to be wise" and "of all one must doubt"—were characteristic of the attitude which permitted and furthered the capacity to say "no."

The case of Adolf Eichmann is symbolic of our situation and has a significance far beyond the one in which his accusers in the courtroom in Jerusalem were concerned with. Eichmann is a symbol of the organization man, of the alienated bureaucrat for whom men, women and children have become numbers. He is a symbol of all of us. We can see ourselves in Eichmann. But the most frightening thing about him is that after the entire story was told in terms of his own admissions, he was able in perfect good faith to plead his innocence. It is clear that if he were once more in the same situation he would do it again. And so would we—and so do we.

The organization man has lost the capacity to disobey, he is not even   18
aware of the fact that he obeys. At this point in history the capacity to doubt,
to criticize and to disobey may be all that stands between a future for
mankind and the end of civilization.

■ ■ ■

Review Questions

1. What does Fromm mean when he writes that disobedience is "the first
   step into independence and freedom"?
2. Fromm writes that history began with an act of disobedience and will
   likely end with an act of obedience. What does he mean?
3. What is the difference between "heteronomous obedience" and
   "autonomous obedience"?
4. How does Fromm distinguish between "authoritarian conscience" and
   "humanistic conscience"?
5. When is obedience to another person *not* submission?
6. What are the psychological comforts of obedience, and why would
   authorities rather have people obey out of love than out of fear?

Discussion and Writing Suggestions

1. Fromm suggests that scientifically we live in the twentieth century but that
   politically and emotionally we live in the Stone Age. As you observe events
   in the world, both near and far, would you agree? Why?
2. Fromm writes: "If a man can only obey and not disobey, he is a slave; if he
   can only disobey and not obey, he is a rebel (not a revolutionary) . . . ."
   Explain Fromm's meaning here. Explain, as well, the implication that to be
   fully human one must have the freedom to both obey and disobey.
3. Fromm writes that "obedience makes me part of the power I worship, and
   hence I feel strong." Does this statement ring true for you? Discuss, in writing, an occasion in which you felt powerful because you obeyed a group
   norm.
4. In paragraph 16, Fromm equates obedience with cowardice. Can you identify a situation in which you were obedient but, now that you reflect on it,
   also were cowardly? That is, can you recall a time when you caved in to a
   group but now wish you hadn't? Explain.
5. Fromm says that we can see ourselves in Adolf Eichmann—that as an organization man he "has lost the capacity to disobey, he is not even aware of
   the fact that he obeys." To what extent do you recognize yourself in this
   portrait?

The Handmaid's Tale

MARGARET ATWOOD

In The Handmaid's Tale, *Canada's most prolific novelist tells the story of a not-too-distant future society where a patriarchal form of fundamentalist Christianity has taken over political power in the United States, totally controlling the lives of everyone in the society. Women are acutely oppressed, having been stripped of their freedoms practically overnight—even their ATM cards were invalidated to cut off access to money—with nary a word of protest from men. As extreme as the depiction is, the roots of Atwood's sexist society can perhaps be found not only in the history of Puritan theocracy in New England, but in contemporary Canada as well, and many readers of this novel have found it a frighteningly imaginable forecast of the future, should the country become swept up in right-wing religious political trends. In the chapters excerpted here, people have gathered to participate in the public executions of several people who have violated the laws of Gilead. As you read these chapters, think about how the authorities win assent for punishing political dissidents under the guise of protecting the population.*

Atwood is an internationally renowned writer of poetry, essays, literary criticism, children's books, short stories, and, most famously, novels. Among the most well known are The Edible Woman, Surfacing, The Journals of Susannah Moodie, Cat's Eye, The Robber Bride, Alias Grace, The Blind Assassin, *and* The Handmaid's Tale. *She has won numerous literary awards for her works, among them the Governor General's Award, the* Ms Magazine's Woman of the Year, *the Ida Nudel Humanitarian Award from the Canadian Jewish Congress, the American Humanist of the Year Award, the Commonwealth Writers Prize, and the* Sunday Times *Prize, the Booker Prize, the Giller Prize, the* Sunday Times *Award for Literary Excellence, and Le Chevalier dans l'Ordre des Arts et des Lettres in France. Born in Ottawa in 1939, she has lived in many cities in Canada, Europe, and the United States and has resided in Toronto since 1992, where she maintains an active presence as a writer and social activist. She is a Companion of the Order of Canada.*

Chapter Forty-Two

The bell is tolling; we can hear it from a long way off. It's morning, and today   1
we've had no breakfast. When we reach the main gate we file through it, two
by two. There's a heavy contingent of guards, special-detail Angels, with riot
gear—the helmets with the bulging dark plexiglass visors that make them look
like beetles, the long clubs, the gas-canister guns—in cordon around the outside of the Wall. That's in case of hysteria. The hooks on the Wall are empty.

This is a district Salvaging, for women only. Salvagings are always seg-   2
regated. It was announced yesterday. They tell you only the day before. It's
not enough time, to get used to it.

To the tolling of the bell we walk along the paths once used by students,   3
past buildings that were once lecture halls and dormitories. It's very strange
to be in here again. From the outside you can't tell that anything's changed,
except that the blinds on most of the windows are drawn down. These buildings belong to the Eyes now.

We file onto the wide lawn in front of what used to be the library. The   4
white steps going up are still the same, the main entrance is unaltered. There's
a wooden stage erected on the lawn, something like the one they used every
spring, for Commencement, in the time before. I think of hats, pastel hats
worn by some of the mothers, and of the black gowns the students would put
on, and the red ones. But this stage is not the same after all, because of the
three wooden posts that stand on it, with the loops of rope.

At the front of the stage there is a microphone; the television camera is   5
discreetly off to the side.

I've only been to one of these before, two years ago. Women's Salvagings   6
are not frequent. There is less need for them. These days we are so well
behaved.

I don't want to be telling this story.   7

We take our places in the standard order: Wives and daughters on the   8
folding wooden chairs placed towards the back, Econo-wives and Marthas
around the edges and on the library steps, and Handmaids at the front, where
everyone can keep an eye on us. We don't sit on chairs, but kneel, and this
time we have cushions, small red velvet ones with nothing written on them,
not even *Faith*.

Luckily the weather is all right: not too hot, cloudy-bright. It would be   9
miserable kneeling here in the rain. Maybe that's why they leave it so late to
tell us: so they'll know what the weather will be like. That's as good a reason
as any.

I kneel on my red velvet cushion. I try to think about tonight, about   10
making love, in the dark, in the light reflected off the white walls. I remember
being held.

There's a long piece of rope which winds like a snake in front of the first   11
row of cushions, along the second, and back through the lines of chairs,
bending like a very old, very slow river viewed from the air, down to the back.
The rope is thick and brown and smells of tar. The front end of the rope runs
up onto the stage. It's like a fuse, or the string of a balloon.

On stage, to the left, are those who are to be salvaged: two Handmaids,   12
one Wife. Wives are unusual, and despite myself I look at this one with interest. I want to know what she has done.

They have been placed here before the gates were opened. All of them sit   13
on folding wooden chairs, like graduating students who are about to be given
prizes. Their hands rest in their laps, looking as if they are folded sedately.
They sway a little, they've probably been given injections or pills, so they
won't make a fuss. It's better if things go smoothly. Are they attached to their
chairs? Impossible to say, under all that drapery.

Now the official procession is approaching the stage, mounting the steps 14
at the right: three women, one Aunt in front, two Salvagers in their black
hoods and cloaks a pace behind her. Behind them are the other Aunts. The
whisperings among us hush. The three arrange themselves, turn towards us,
the Aunt flanked by the two black-robed Salvagers.

It's Aunt Lydia. How many years since I've seen her? I'd begun to think 15
she existed only in my head, but here she is, a little older. I have a good view,
I can see the deepening furrows to either side of her nose, the engraved frown.
Her eyes blink, she smiles nervously, peering to left and right, checking out the
audience, and lifts a hand to fidget with her headdress. An odd strangling
sound comes over the P.A. system: she is clearing her throat.

I've begun to shiver. Hatred fills my mouth like spit. 16

The sun comes out, and the stage and its occupants light up like a 17
Christmas crèche. I can see the wrinkles under Aunt Lydia's eyes, the pallor
of the seated women, the hairs on the rope in front of me on the grass, the
blades of grass. There is a dandelion, right in front of me, the colour of egg
yolk. I feel hungry. The bell stops tolling.

Aunt Lydia stands up, smooths down her skirt with both hands, and 18
steps forward to the mike. "Good afternoon, ladies," she says, and there is an
instant and ear-splitting feedback whine from the P.A. system. From among
us, incredibly, there is laughter. It's hard not to laugh, it's the tension, and the
look of irritation on Aunt Lydia's face as she adjusts the sound. This is supposed to be dignified.

"Good afternoon, ladies," she says again, her voice now tinny and flat- 19
tened. It's *ladies* instead of *girls* because of the Wives. "I'm sure we are all
aware of the unfortunate circumstances that bring us all here together on this
beautiful morning, when I am certain we would all rather be doing something
else, at least I speak for myself, but duty is a hard taskmaster, or may I say on
this occasion taskmistress, and it is in the name of duty that we are here
today."

She goes on like this for some minutes, but I don't listen. I've heard this 20
speech, or one like it, often enough before: the same platitudes, the same slogans, the same phrases: the torch of the future, the cradle of the race, the task
before us. It's hard to believe there will not be polite clapping after this
speech, and tea and cookies served on the lawn.

That was the prologue, I think. Now she'll get down to it. 21

Aunt Lydia rummages in her pocket, produces a crumpled piece of paper. 22
This she takes an undue length of time to unfold and scan. She's rubbing our
noses in it, letting us know exactly who she is, making us watch her as she
silently reads, flaunting her prerogative. Obscene, I think. Let's get this over
with.

"In the past," says Aunt Lydia, "it has been the custom to precede the 23
actual Salvagings with a detailed account of the crimes of which the prisoners stand convicted. However, we have found that such a public account,
especially when televised, is invariably followed by a rash, if I may call it that,

an outbreak I should say, of exactly similar crimes. So we have decided in the best interests of all to discontinue this practice. The Salvagings will proceed without further ado."

A collective murmur goes up from us. The crimes of others are a secret   24
language among us. Through them we show ourselves what we might be capable of, after all. This is not a popular announcement. But you would never know it from Aunt Lydia, who smiles and blinks as if washed in applause. Now we are left to our own devices, our own speculations. The first one, the one they're now raising from her chair, black-gloved hands on her upper arms: reading? No, that's only a hand cut off, on the third conviction. Unchastity, or an attempt on the life of her Commander? Or the Commander's Wife, more likely. That's what we're thinking. As for the Wife, there's mostly just one thing they get salvaged for. They can do almost anything to us, but they aren't allowed to kill us, not legally. Not with knitting needles or garden shears, or knives purloined from the kitchen, and especially not when we are pregnant. It could be adultery, of course. It could always be that.

Or attempted escape.   25

"Ofcharles," Aunt Lydia announces. No one I know. The woman is   26
brought forward; she walks as if she's really concentrating on it, one foot, the other foot, she's definitely drugged. There's a groggy off-centre smile on her mouth. One side of her face contracts, an uncoordinated wink, aimed at the camera. They'll never show it, of course, this isn't live. The two Salvagers tie her hands, behind her back.

From behind me there's a sound of retching.   27

That's why we don't get breakfast.   28

"Janine, most likely," Ofglen whispers.   29

I've seen it before, the white bag placed over the head, the woman helped   30
up onto the high stool as if she's being helped up the steps of a bus, steadied there, the noose adjusted delicately around the neck, like a vestment, the stool kicked away. I've heard the long sigh go up, from around me, the sigh like air coming out of an air mattress, I've seen Aunt Lydia place her hand over the mike, to stifle the other sounds coming from behind her, I've leaned forward to touch the rope in front of me, in time with the others, both hands on it, the rope hairy, sticky with tar in the hot sun, then placed my hand on my heart to show my unity with the Salvagers and my consent, and my complicity in the death of this woman. I have seen the kicking feet and the two in black who now seize hold of them and drag downwards with all their weight. I don't want to see it any more. I look at the grass instead. I describe the rope.

Chapter Forty-Three

The three bodies hang there, even with the white sacks over their heads look-   31
ing curiously stretched, like chickens strung up by the necks in a meatshop window; like birds with their wings clipped, like flightless birds, wrecked angels. It's hard to take your eyes off them. Beneath the hems of the dresses

the feet dangle, two pairs of red shoes, one pair of blue. If it weren't for the ropes and the sacks it could be a kind of dance, a ballet, caught by flash-camera: mid-air. They look arranged. They look like showbiz. It must have been Aunt Lydia who put the blue one in the middle.

"Today's Salvaging is now concluded," Aunt Lydia announces into the mike. "But . . . " 32

We turn to her, listen to her, watch her. She has always known how to space her pauses. A ripple runs over us, a stir. Something else, perhaps, is going to happen. 33

"But you may stand up, and form a circle." She smiles down upon us, generous, munificent. She is about to give us something. *Bestow.* "Orderly, now." 34

She is talking to us, to the Handmaids. Some of the Wives are leaving now, some of the daughters. Most of them stay, but they stay behind, out of the way, they watch merely. They are not part of the circle. 35

Two Guardians have moved forward and are coiling up the thick rope, getting it out of the way. Others move the cushions. We are milling around now, on the grass space in front of the stage, some jockeying for position at the front, next to the centre, many pushing just as hard to work their way to the middle where they will be shielded. It's a mistake to hang back too obviously in any group like this; it stamps you as lukewarm, lacking in zeal. There's an energy building here, a murmur, a tremor of readiness and anger. The bodies tense, the eyes are brighter, as if aiming. 36

I don't want to be at the front, or at the back either. I'm not sure what's coming, though I sense it won't be anything I want to see up close. But Ofglen has hold of my arm, she tugs me with her, and now we're in the second line, with only a thin hedge of bodies in front of us. I don't want to see, yet I don't pull back either. I've heard rumours, which I only half believed. Despite everything I already know, I say to myself: they wouldn't go that far. 37

"You know the rules for a Particicution," Aunt Lydia says. "You will wait until I blow the whistle. After that, what you do is up to you, until I blow the whistle again. Understood?" 38

A noise comes from among us, a formless assent. 39

"Well then," says Aunt Lydia. She nods. Two Guardians, not the same ones that have taken away the rope, come forward now from behind the stage. Between them they half-carry, half-drag a third man. He too is in a Guardian's uniform, but he has no hat on and the uniform is dirty and torn. His face is cut and bruised, deep reddish-brown bruises; the flesh is swollen and knobby, stubbled with unshaven beard. This doesn't look like a face but like an unknown vegetable, a mangled bulb or tuber, something that's grown wrong. Even from where I'm standing I can smell him: he smells of shit and vomit. His hair is blond and falls over his face, spiky with what? Dried sweat? 40

I stare at him with revulsion. He looks drunk. He looks like a drunk that's been in a fight. Why have they brought a drunk in here? 41

"This man," says Aunt Lydia, "has been convicted of rape." Her voice   42
trembles with rage, and a kind of triumph. "He was once a Guardian. He has
disgraced his uniform. He has abused his position of trust. His partner in
viciousness has already been shot. The penalty for rape, as you know, is
death. Deuteronomy 22:23–29. I might add that this crime involved two of
you and took place at gunpoint. It was also brutal. I will not offend your ears
with any details, except to say that one woman was pregnant and the baby
died."

A sigh goes up from us; despite myself I feel my hands clench. It is too   43
much, this violation. The baby too, after what we go through. It's true, there
is a bloodlust; I want to tear, gouge, rend.

We jostle forward, our heads turn from side to side, our nostrils flare,   44
sniffing death, we look at one another, seeing the hatred. Shooting was too
good. The man's head swivels groggily around: has he even heard her?

Aunt Lydia waits a moment; then she gives a little smile and raises her   45
whistle to her lips. We hear it, shrill and silver, an echo from a volleyball game
of long ago.

The two Guardians let go of the third man's arms and step back. He stag-   46
gers—is he drugged?—and falls to his knees. His eyes are shrivelled up inside
the puffy flesh of his face, as if the light is too bright for him. They've kept
him in darkness. He raises one hand to his cheek, as though to feel if he is still
there. All of this happens quickly, but it seems to be slowly.

Nobody moves forward. The women are looking at him with horror; as   47
if he's a half-dead rat dragging itself across a kitchen floor. He's squinting
around at us, the circle of red women. One corner of his mouth moves up,
incredible—a smile?

I try to look inside him, inside the trashed face, see what he must really   48
look like. I think he's about thirty. It isn't Luke.

But it could have been, I know that. It could be Nick. I know that what-   49
ever he's done I can't touch him.

He says something. It comes out thick, as if his throat is bruised, his   50
tongue huge in his mouth, but I hear it anyway. He says, "I didn't . . . "

There's a surge forward, like a crowd at a rock concert in the former   51
time, when the doors opened, that urgency coming like a wave through us.
The air is bright with adrenalin, we are permitted anything and this is freedom, in my body also, I'm reeling, red spreads everywhere, but before that
tide of cloth and bodies hits him Ofglen is shoving through the women in
front of us, propelling herself with her elbows, left, right, and running
towards him. She pushes him down, sideways, then kicks his head viciously,
one, two, three times, sharp painful jabs with the foot, well-aimed. Now
there are sounds, gasps, a low noise like growling, yells, and the red bodies
tumble forward and I can no longer see, he's obscured by arms, fists, feet. A
high scream comes from somewhere, like a horse in terror.

I keep back, try to stay on my feet. Something hits me from behind. I   52
stagger. When I regain my balance and look around, I see the Wives and

daughters leaning forward in their chairs, the Aunts on the platform gazing down with interest. They must have a better view from up there.

He has become an *it*.   53

Ofglen is back beside me. Her face is tight, expressionless.   54

"I saw what you did," I say to her. Now I'm beginning to feel again: 55
shock, outrage, nausea. Barbarism. "Why did you do that? You! I thought you . . ."

"Don't look at me," she says. "They're watching."   56

"I don't care," I say. My voice is rising, I can't help it.   57

"Get control of yourself," she says. She pretends to brush me off, my arm   58
and shoulder, bringing her face close to my ear. "Don't be stupid. He wasn't a rapist at all, he was a political. He was one of ours. I knocked him out. Put him out of his misery. Don't you know what they're doing to him?"

One of ours, I think. A Guardian. It seems impossible.   59

Aunt Lydia blows her whistle again, but they don't stop at once. The two   60
Guardians move in, pulling them off, from what's left. Some lie on the grass where they've been hit or kicked by accident. Some have fainted. They straggle away, in twos and threes or by themselves. They seem dazed.

"You will find your partners and re-form your line," Aunt Lydia says   61
into the mike. Few pay attention to her. A woman comes towards us, walking as if she's feeling her way with her feet, in the dark: Janine. There's a smear of blood across her cheek, and more of it on the white of her headdress. She's smiling, a bright diminutive smile. Her eyes have come loose.

"Hi there," she says. "How are you doing?" She's holding something,   62
tightly, in her right hand. It's a clump of blond hair. She gives a small giggle.

"Janine," I say. But she's let go, totally now, she's in free fall, she's in   63
withdrawal.

"You have a nice day," she says, and walks on past us, towards the   64
gate.

I look after her. Easy out, is what I think. I don't even feel sorry for her,   65
although I should. I feel angry. I'm not proud of myself for this, or for any of it. But then, that's the point.

My hands smell of warm tar. I want to go back to the house and up to   66
the bathroom and scrub and scrub, with the harsh soap and the pumice, to get every trace of this smell off my skin. The smell makes me feel sick.

But also I'm hungry. This is monstrous, but nevertheless it's true. Death   67
makes me hungry. Maybe it's because I've been emptied; or maybe it's the body's way of seeing to it that I remain alive, continue to repeat its bedrock prayer: *I am, I am*. I am, still.

I want to go to bed, make love, right now.   68

I think of the word *relish*.   69

I could eat a horse.   70

■ ■ ■

Discussion and Writing Suggestions

1. As we noted when introducing Atwood's story, many readers have found the events depicted chillingly realistic, just "certain tendencies now in existence carried to their logical conclusion," as the hardcover dustjacket notes. What is your response to Atwood's story? Is it totally far-fetched? Or do you, too, find the society she depicts all too easy to imagine? Why or why not?

2. Some of the women have joined enthusiastically in the "particicution" of the tortured Guardian, but the narrator reveals a very conflicted set of emotions and motivations as she watches the executions. In what ways does she find herself drawn into participating, outwardly and inwardly, despite her distaste for the proceedings?

3. How does it serve the interests of the Gilead authorities to have the women believe the executed man was a rapist?

4. Most Canadian women have had the right to vote for at least 50 years (status Indians did not win the right to vote until 1960), depending on their province of residence, and there has been significant progress achieved in the struggle for women's equality before the law. But at current rates, it will be another 500 years before women are equally represented in influential sectors such as government, academia, business management, and the professions. What insights does Atwood offer into the psychological impact of authority that might account for women's resigned attitude to this extremely slow progress?

5. Do you think that you and an equally talented, determined, educated, prosperous female classmate (if you are a man, or a male classmate, if you are a woman) have the same chance of becoming Prime Minister of Canada? How would group mentality affect your ambitions and your chances?

The Lottery

SHIRLEY JACKSON

On the morning of June 28, 1948, I walked down to the post office in our little Vermont town to pick up the mail. I was quite casual about it, as I recall—I opened the box, took out a couple of bills and a letter or two, talked to the postmaster for a few minutes, and left, never supposing that it was the last time for months that I was to pick up the mail without an active feeling of panic. By the next week I had to change my mailbox to the largest one in the post office, and casual conversation with the postmaster was out of the question, because he wasn't speaking to me. June 28, 1948, was the day *The New Yorker* came out with a story of mine in it. It was not my first published story, nor my last, but I have been assured over and over that if it had been the only story I ever wrote or published, there would be people who would not forget my name.[1]

So begins Shirley Jackson's "biography" of her short story "The Lottery." The New Yorker published the story in the summer of 1948 and some months later, having been besieged with letters, acknowledged that the piece had generated "more mail than any . . . fiction they had ever published"—the great majority of it negative. In 1960, Jackson wrote that "millions of people, and my mother, had taken a pronounced dislike to me" for having written the story—which, over the years, proved to be Jackson's most widely anthologized one. If you've read "The Lottery," you will have some idea of why it was so controversial. If you haven't, we don't want to spoil the effect by discussing what happens.

Shirley Jackson (1919–1965), short-story writer and novelist, was born in San Francisco and raised in California and New York. She began her post-secondary education at the University of Rochester and completed it at Syracuse University. She married Stanley Edgar Hyman (writer and teacher) and with him had four children. In her brief career, Jackson wrote six novels and two works of non-fiction. She won the Edgar Allen Poe Award (1961) as well as a Syracuse University Arents Pioneer Medal for Outstanding Achievement (1965).

The morning of June 27th was clear and sunny, with the fresh warmth of a full-summer day; the flowers were blossoming profusely and the grass was richly green. The people of the village began to gather in the square, between the post office and the bank, around ten o'clock; in some towns there were so many people that the lottery took two days and had to be started on June 26th, but in this village, where there were only about three hundred people, the whole lottery took less than two hours, so it could begin at ten o'clock in the morning and still be through in time to allow the villagers to get home for noon dinner.   1

The children assembled first, of course. School was recently over for the summer, and the feeling of liberty sat uneasily on most of them; they tended to gather together quietly for a while before they broke into boisterous play, and their talk was still of the classroom and the teacher, of books and reprimands. Bobby Martin had already stuffed his pockets full of stones, and the other boys soon followed his example, selecting the smoothest and roundest stones; Bobby and Harry Jones and Dickie Delacroix—the villagers pronounced this "Dellacroy"—eventually made a great pile of stones in one corner of the square and guarded it against the raids of the other boys. The girls stood aside, talking among themselves, looking over their shoulders at the boys, and the very small children rolled in the dust or clung to the hands of their older brothers or sisters.   2

---

[1] "Biography of a Story," from *Come Along With Me*, by Shirley Jackson. Copyright 1948, 1952, © 1960 by Shirley Jackson. Used by permission of Viking Penguin, a division of Penguin Books USA Inc. 1st paragraph, p. 211 + selected quotations, pp. 214–221.

Soon the men began to gather, surveying their own children, speaking of   3
planting and rain, tractors and taxes. They stood together, away from the pile
of stones in the corner, and their jokes were quiet and they smiled rather than
laughed. The women, wearing faded house dresses and sweaters, came shortly
after their menfolk. They greeted one another and exchanged bits of gossip as
they went to join their husbands. Soon the women, standing by their husbands, began to call to their children, and the children came reluctantly,
having to be called four or five times. Bobby Martin ducked under his
mother's grasping hand and ran, laughing, back to the pile of stones. His
father spoke up sharply, and Bobby came quickly and took his place between
his father and his oldest brother.

The lottery was conducted—as were the square dances, the teenage club,   4
the Halloween program—by Mr. Summers, who had time and energy to
devote to civic activities. He was a round-faced, jovial man and he ran the
coal business, and people were sorry for him, because he had no children and
his wife was a scold. When he arrived in the square, carrying the wooden
black box, there was a murmur of conversation among the villagers, and he
waved and called, "Little late today, folks." The postmaster, Mr. Graves, followed him, carrying a three-legged stool, and the stool was put in the center
of the square and Mr. Summers set the black box down on it. The villagers
kept their distance, leaving a space between themselves and the stool, and
when Mr. Summers said, "Some of you fellows want to give me a hand?"
there was a hesitation before two men, Mr. Martin and his oldest son, Baxter,
came forward to hold the box steady on the stool while Mr. Summers stirred
up the papers inside it.

The original paraphernalia for the lottery had been lost long ago, and the   5
black box now resting on the stool had been put into use even before Old
Man Warner, the oldest man in town, was born. Mr. Summers spoke frequently to the villagers about making a new box, but no one liked to upset
even as much tradition as was represented by the black box. There was a story
that the present box had been made with some pieces of the box that had pre-
ceded it, the one that had been constructed when the first people settled
down to make a village here. Every year, after the lottery, Mr. Summers
began talking again about a new box, but every year the subject was allowed
to fade off without anything's being done. The black box grew shabbier each
year; by now it was no longer completely black but splintered badly along one
side to show the original wood color, and in some places faded or stained.

Mr. Martin and his oldest son, Baxter, held the black box securely on the   6
stool until Mr. Summers had stirred the papers thoroughly with his hand.
Because so much of the ritual had been forgotten or discarded, Mr. Summers
had been successful in having slips of paper substituted for the chips of wood
that had been used for generations. Chips of wood, Mr. Summers had argued,
had been all very well when the village was tiny, but now that the population
was more than three hundred and likely to keep on growing, it was necessary
to use something that would fit more easily into the black box. The night

before the lottery, Mr. Summers and Mr. Graves made up the slips of paper and put them in the box, and it was then taken to the safe of Mr. Summers' coal company and locked up until Mr. Summers was ready to take it to the square next morning. The rest of the year, the box was put away, sometimes one place, sometimes another; it had spent one year in Mr. Graves's barn and another year underfoot in the post office, and sometimes it was set on a shelf in the Martin grocery and left there.

There was a great deal of fussing to be done before Mr. Summers declared the lottery open. There were the lists to make up—of heads of families, heads of households in each family, members of each household in each family. There was the proper swearing-in of Mr. Summers by the postmaster, as the official of the lottery; at one time, some people remembered, there had been a recital of some sort, performed by the official of the lottery, a perfunctory, tuneless chant that had been rattled off duly each year; some people believed that the official of the lottery used to stand just so when he said or sang it, others believed that he was supposed to walk among the people, but years and years ago this part of the ritual had been allowed to lapse. There had been, also, a ritual salute, which the official of the lottery had had to use in addressing each person who came up to draw from the box, but this also had changed with time, until now, it was felt necessary only for the official to speak to each person approaching. Mr. Summers was very good at all this; in his clean white shirt and blue jeans, with one hand resting carelessly on the black box, he seemed very proper and important as he talked interminably to Mr. Graves and the Martins.

Just as Mr. Summers finally left off talking and turned to the assembled villagers, Mrs. Hutchinson came hurriedly along the path to the square, her sweater thrown over her shoulders, and slid into place in the back of the crowd. "Clean forgot what day it was," she said to Mrs. Delacroix, who stood next to her, and they both laughed softly. "Thought my old man was out back stacking wood," Mrs. Hutchinson went on, "and then I looked out the window and the kids was gone, and then I remembered it was the twenty-seventh and came a-running." She dried her hands on her apron, and Mrs. Delacroix said, "You're in time, though. They're still talking away up there."

Mrs. Hutchinson craned her neck to see through the crowd and found her husband and children standing near the front. She tapped Mrs. Delacroix on the arm as a farewell and began to make her way through the crowd. The people separated good-humoredly to let her through; two or three people said, in voices just loud enough to be heard across the crowd, "Here comes your Missus, Hutchinson," and "Bill, she made it after all." Mrs. Hutchinson reached her husband, and Mr. Summers, who had been waiting, said cheerfully, "Thought we were going to have to get on without you, Tessie." Mrs. Hutchinson said, grinning, "Wouldn't have me leave m'dishes in the sink, now, would you, Joe?," and soft laughter ran through the crowd as the people stirred back into position after Mrs. Hutchinson's arrival.

"Well, now," Mr. Summers said soberly, "guess we better get started, get   10
this over with, so's we can go back to work. Anybody ain't here?"

"Dunbar," several people said. "Dunbar, Dunbar."   11

Mr. Summers consulted his list. "Clyde Dunbar," he said. "That's right.   12
He's broke his leg, hasn't he? Who's drawing for him?"

"Me, I guess," a woman said, and Mr. Summers turned to look at her.   13
"Wife draws for her husband," Mr. Summers said. "Don't you have a grown
boy to do it for you, Janey?" Although Mr. Summers and everyone else in the
village knew the answer perfectly well, it was the business of the official of the
lottery to ask such questions formally. Mr. Summers waited with an expression of polite interest while Mrs. Dunbar answered.

"Horace's not but sixteen yet," Mrs. Dunbar said regretfully. "Guess I   14
gotta fill in for the old man this year."

"Right," Mr. Summers said. He made a note on the list he was holding.   15
Then he asked, "Watson boy drawing this year?"

A tall boy in the crowd raised his hand. "Here," he said. "I'm drawing   16
for m'mother and me." He blinked his eyes nervously and ducked his head as
several voices in the crowd said things like "Good fellow, Jack," and "Glad
to see your mother's got a man to do it."

"Well," Mr. Summers said, "guess that's everyone. Old Man Warner   17
make it?"

"Here," a voice said, and Mr. Summers nodded.   18

A sudden hush fell on the crowd as Mr. Summers cleared his throat and   19
looked at the list. "All ready?" he called. "Now, I'll read the names—heads
of families first—and the men come up and take a paper out of the box. Keep
the paper folded in your hand without looking at it until everyone has had a
turn. Everything clear?"

The people had done it so many times that they only half listened to the   20
directions; most of them were quiet, wetting their lips, not looking around.
Then Mr. Summers raised one hand high and said, "Adams." A man disengaged himself from the crowd and came forward. "Hi, Steve," Mr. Summers
said, and Mr. Adams said, "Hi, Joe." They grinned at one another humor-
ously and nervously. Then Mr. Adams reached into the black box and took
out a folded paper. He held it firmly by one corner as he turned and went
hastily back to his place in the crowd, where he stood a little apart from his
family, not looking down at his hand.

"Allen," Mr. Summers said. "Anderson. . . . Bentham."   21

"Seems like there's no time at all between lotteries any more," Mrs.   22
Delacroix said to Mrs. Graves in the back row. "Seems like we got through
with the last one only last week."

"Time sure goes fast," Mrs. Graves said.   23

"Clark. . . . Delacroix."   24

"There goes my old man," Mrs. Delacroix said. She held her breath   25
while her husband went forward.

"Dunbar," Mr. Summers said, and Mrs. Dunbar went steadily to the box   26
while one of the women said, "Go on, Janey," and another said, "There she
goes."

"We're next," Mrs. Graves said. She watched while Mr. Graves came   27
around from the side of the box, greeted Mr. Summers gravely, and selected
a slip of paper from the box. By now, all through the crowd there were men
holding the small folded papers in their large hands, turning them over and
over nervously. Mrs. Dunbar and her two sons stood together, Mrs. Dunbar
holding the slip of paper.

"Harburt. . . . Hutchinson."   28

"Get up there, Bill," Mrs. Hutchinson said, and the people near her   29
laughed.

"Jones."   30

"They do say," Mr. Adams said to Old Man Warner, who stood next to   31
him, "that over in the north village they're talking of giving up the lottery."

Old Man Warner snorted. "Pack of crazy fools," he said. "Listening to   32
the young folks, nothing's good enough for *them*. Next thing you know,
they'll be wanting to go back to living in caves, nobody work any more, live
that way for a while. Used to be a saying about 'Lottery in June, corn be
heavy soon.' First thing you know, we'd all be eating stewed chickweed and
acorns. There's *always* been a lottery," he added petulantly. "Bad enough to
see young Joe Summers up there joking with everybody."

"Some places have already quit lotteries," Mrs. Adams said.   33

"Nothing but trouble in *that*," Old Man Warner said stoutly. "Pack of   34
young fools."

"Martin." And Bobby Martin watched his father go forward.   35
"Overdyke. . . . Percy."

"I wish they'd hurry," Mrs. Dunbar said to her older son. "I wish they'd   36
hurry."

"They're almost through," her son said.   37

"You get ready to run tell Dad," Mrs. Dunbar said.   38

Mr. Summers called his own name and then stepped forward precisely   39
and selected a slip from the box. Then he called, "Warner."

"Seventy-seventh year I been in the lottery," Old Man Warner said as he   40
went through the crowd. "Seventy-seventh time."

"Watson." The tall boy came awkwardly through the crowd. Someone   41
said, "Don't be nervous, Jack," and Mr. Summers said, "Take your time,
son."

"Zanini."   42

After that, there was a long pause, a breathless pause, until Mr. Summers,   43
holding his slip of paper in the air, said, "All right, fellows." For a minute, no
one moved, and then all the slips of paper were opened. Suddenly, all the
women began to speak at once, saying, "Who is it?," "Who's got it?," "Is it
the Dunbars?," "Is it the Watsons?" Then the voices began to say, "It's
Hutchinson. It's Bill," "Bill Hutchinson's got it."

"Go tell your father," Mrs. Dunbar said to her older son.   44

People began to look around to see the Hutchinsons. Bill Hutchinson was   45
standing quiet, staring down at the paper in his hand. Suddenly, Tessie
Hutchinson shouted to Mr. Summers, "You didn't give him time enough to
take any paper he wanted. I saw you. It wasn't fair!"

"Be a good sport, Tessie," Mrs. Delacroix called, and Mrs. Graves said,   46
"All of us took the same chance."

"Shut up, Tessie," Bill Hutchinson said.   47

"Well, everyone," Mr. Summers said, "that was done pretty fast, and   48
now we've got to be hurrying a little more to get done in time." He consulted his next list. "Bill," he said, "you draw for the Hutchinson family. You got
any other households in the Hutchinsons?"

"There's Don and Eva," Mrs. Hutchinson yelled. "Make *them* take their   49
chance!"

"Daughters draw with their husbands' families, Tessie," Mr. Summers   50
said gently. "You know that as well as anyone else."

"It wasn't *fair*," Tessie said.   51

"I guess not, Joe," Bill Hutchinson said regretfully. "My daughter draws   52
with her husband's family, that's only fair. And I've got no other family
except the kids."

"Then, as far as drawing for families is concerned, it's you," Mr.   53
Summers said in explanation, "and as far as drawing for households is concerned, that's you, too. Right?"

"Right," Bill Hutchinson said.   54

"How many kids, Bill?" Mr. Summers asked formally.   55

"Three," Bill Hutchinson said. "There's Bill, Jr., and Nancy, and little   56
Dave. And Tessie and me."

"All right, then," Mr. Summers said. "Harry, you got their tickets back?"   57

Mr. Graves nodded and held up the slips of paper. "Put them in the box,   58
then," Mr. Summers directed. "Take Bill's and put it in."

"I think we ought to start over," Mrs. Hutchinson said, as quietly as she   59
could. "I tell you it wasn't *fair*. You didn't give him enough time to choose.
Everybody saw that."

Mr. Graves had selected the five slips and put them in the box, and he   60
dropped all the papers but those onto the ground, where the breeze caught
them and lifted them off.

"Listen, everybody," Mrs. Hutchinson was saying to the people around   61
her.

"Ready, Bill?" Mr. Summers asked, and Bill Hutchinson, with one quick   62
glance around at his wife and children, nodded.

"Remember," Mr. Summers said, "take the slips and keep them folded   63
until each person has taken one. Harry, you help little Dave." Mr. Graves
took the hand of the little boy, who came willingly with him up to the box.
"Take a paper out of the box, Davy," Mr. Summers said. Davy put his hand
into the box and laughed. "Take just *one* paper," Mrs. Summers said.

"Harry, you hold it for him." Mr. Graves took the child's hand and removed the folded paper from the tight fist and held it while little Dave stood next to him and looked up at him wonderingly.

"Nancy next," Mr. Summers said. Nancy was twelve and her school 64 friends breathed heavily as she went forward, switching her skirt, and took a slip daintily from the box. "Bill, Jr.," Mr. Summers said, and Billy, his face red and his feet overlarge, nearly knocked the box over as he got a paper out. "Tessie," Mr. Summers said. She hesitated for a minute, looking around defiantly, and then set her lips and went up to the box. She snatched a paper out and held it behind her.

"Bill," Mr. Summers said, and Bill Hutchinson reached into the box and 65 felt around, bringing his hand out at last with the slip of paper in it.

The crowd was quiet. A girl whispered, "I hope it's not Nancy," and the 66 sound of the whisper reached the edges of the crowd.

"It's not the way it used to be," Old Man Warner said clearly. "People 67 ain't the way they used to be."

"All right," Mr. Summers said. "Open the papers, Harry, you open little 68 Dave's."

Mr. Graves opened the slip of paper and there was a general sigh through 69 the crowd as he held it up and everyone could see that it was blank. Nancy and Bill, Jr., opened theirs at the same time, and both beamed and laughed, turning around to the crowd and holding their slips of paper above their heads.

"Tessie," Mr. Summers said. There was a pause, and then Mr. Summers 70 looked at Bill Hutchinson, and Bill unfolded his paper and showed it. It was blank.

"It's Tessie," Mr. Summers said, and his voice was hushed. "Show us her 71 paper, Bill."

Bill Hutchinson went over to his wife and forced the slip of paper out of 72 her hand. It had a black spot on it, the black spot Mr. Summers had made the night before with the heavy pencil in the coal-company office. Bill Hutchinson held it up, and there was a stir in the crowd.

"All right, folks," Mr. Summers said. "Let's finish quickly." 73

Although the villagers had forgotten the ritual and lost the original black 74 box, they still remembered to use stones. The pile of stones the boys had made earlier was ready; there were stones on the ground with the blowing scraps of paper that had come out of the box. Mrs. Delacroix selected a stone so large she had to pick it up with both hands and turned to Mrs. Dunbar. "Come on," she said. "Hurry up."

Mrs. Dunbar had small stones in both hands, and she said, gasping for 75 breath, "I can't run at all. You'll have to go ahead and I'll catch up with you."

The children had stones already, and someone gave little Davy 76 Hutchinson a few pebbles.

Tessie Hutchinson was in the center of a cleared space by now, and she 77 held her hands out desperately as the villagers moved in on her. "It isn't fair," she said. A stone hit her on the side of the head.

Old Man Warner was saying, "Come on, come on, everyone." Steve   78
Adams was in front of the crowd of villagers, with Mrs. Graves beside him.

"It isn't fair, it isn't right," Mrs. Hutchinson screamed, and then they   79
were upon her.

■ ■ ■

Discussion and Writing Suggestions

1. Many readers believed that the events depicted in "The Lottery" actually
   happened. A sampling of the letters that Jackson received in response to the
   story:

   (Kansas) Will you please tell me the locale and the year of that custom?
   (Oregon) Where in heaven's name does there exist such barbarity as
   described in the story?
   (New York) Do such tribunal rituals still exist and if so where?
   (New York) To a reader who has only a fleeting knowledge of traditional rites in various parts of the country (I presume the plot was laid
   in the United States) I found the cruelty of the ceremony outrageous, if
   not unbelievable. It may be just a custom or ritual which I am not
   familiar with.
   (New York) Would you please explain whether such improbable rituals
   occur in our Middle Western states, and what their origin and purpose
   are?
   (Nevada) Although we recognize the story to be fiction is it possible
   that it is based on fact?

   What is your response to comments such as these that suggest surprise, certainly, but also acceptance of the violence committed in the story?

2. One reader of "The Lottery," from Missouri, wrote to *The New Yorker*
   and accused it of "publishing a story that reached a new low in human
   viciousness." Do you feel that Jackson has reached this "new low"? Explain
   your answer.

3. Several more letter writers attempted to get at the meaning of the story:
   (Illinois) If it is simply a fictitious example of man's innate cruelty, it isn't
   a very good one. Man, stupid and cruel as he is, has always had sense
   enough to imagine or invent a charge against the objects of his persecu-
   tion: the Christian martyrs, the New England witches, the Jews and
   Negroes. But nobody had anything against Mrs. Hutchinson, and they
   only wanted to get through quickly so they could go home for lunch.
   (California) I missed something here. Perhaps there was some facet of
   the victim's character which made her unpopular with the other villagers. I expected the people to evince a feeling of dread and terror, or
   else sadistic pleasure, but perhaps they were laconic, unemotional New
   Englanders.
   (Indiana) When I first read the story in my issue, I felt that there was
   no moral significance present, that the story was just terrifying, and

that was all. However, there has to be a reason why it is so alarming to so many people. I feel that the only solution, the only reason it bothered so many people is that it shows the power of society over the individual. We saw the ease with which society can crush any single one of us. At the same time, we saw that society need have no rational reason for crushing the one, or the few, or sometimes the many.

Take any one of these readings of the story and respond to it by writing a brief essay or, perhaps, a letter.

4. What does the story suggest to you about authority and obedience to authority? Who—or what—holds authority in the village? Why do people continue with the annual killing, despite the fact that "some places have already quit lotteries"?

■ WRITING ACTIVITIES

1. Compare and contrast the Asch and the Milgram experiments, considering their separate (1) objectives, (2) experimental designs and procedures, (3) results, and (4) conclusions. To what extent do the findings of these two experiments reinforce one another? To what extent do they highlight different, if related, social phenomena? To what extent do their results reinforce those of Zimbardo's prison experiment?

2. Assume for the moment you agree with Doris Lessing: Children need to be taught how to disobey so they can recognize and avoid situations that give rise to harmful obedience. If you were the curriculum co-ordinator for your local school system, how would you teach children to disobey? What would be your curriculum? What homework would you assign? What class projects? What field trips? One complicated part of your job would be to train children to understand the difference between *responsible* disobedience and anarchy. What is the difference?

   Take up these questions in an essay that draws both on your experiences as a student and on your understanding of the selections in this chapter. Points that you might want to consider in developing the essay: defining overly obedient children; appropriate classroom behaviour for responsibly disobedient children (as opposed to inappropriate behaviour); reading lists (would "The Lottery" and *The Handmaid's Tale* be included?); homework assignments; field trips; class projects.

3. A certain amount of obedience is a given in society, or so Stanley Milgram and others observe. Social order—indeed, civilization itself—would not be possible unless individuals were willing to surrender a portion of their autonomy to the state. Allowing that we all are obedient (and that, for the sake of civil order, we must be to an extent), define the point at which obedience to a figure of authority becomes dangerous.

   As you develop your definition, consider the ways you might use the work of authors in this chapter and their definitions of acceptable and unacceptable levels of obedience. Do you agree with the ways in which others have drawn the line between reasonable and dangerous obedience? What examples from current stories in the news or from your own experience can you draw on to test various definitions?

4. Describe a situation in which you were faced with a moral dilemma of whether to obey a figure of authority. After describing the situation and the action you took (or didn't take), discuss your behaviour in light of any two readings in this chapter. You might consider a straightforward, four-part structure for your essay: (1) your description; (2) your discussion, in light of source A; (3) your discussion, in light of source B; and (4) your conclusion—an overall appraisal of your behaviour.

5. At one point in his essay (paragraph 16), Erich Fromm equates obedience with cowardice. Earlier in the chapter, Doris Lessing (paragraph 9) observes that "among our most shameful memories is this, how often we said black was white because other people were saying it." Using the work of these authors as a point of departure, reconsider an act of obedience or disobedience in your own life. Describe pertinent circumstances for your reader. Based on what you have learned in this chapter, reassess your behaviour. Would you behave similarly if given a second chance in the same situation?

6. Reread "The Lottery" and/or our excerpt from *The Handmaid's Tale* and analyze the patterns of and reasons for obedience in the story(s). Base your analysis on two sources in this chapter: Erich Fromm's essay, especially paragraphs 13–16 on the psychological comforts of obedience; and Doris Lessing's speech on the dangers of "not understanding the social laws that govern groups."

7. In his response to Diana Baumrind, Stanley Milgram makes a point of insisting that follow-up interviews with subjects in his experiments show that a large majority were pleased, in the long run, to have participated. (See Table 1 in the discussion after Baumrind, page 240) Writing on his own post-experiment surveys and interviews, Philip Zimbardo writes that his subjects believed their "mental anguish was transient and situationally specific, but the self-knowledge gained has persisted" (paragraph 60). Why might they *and* the experimenters nonetheless have been eager to accept a positive, final judgment of the experiments? Develop an essay in response to this question, drawing on the selections by Milgram, Zimbardo, and Baumrind.

8. Develop a synthesis in which you extend Baumrind's critique of Milgram to the Stanford prison experiment. This assignment requires that you understand the core elements of Baumrind's critique; that you have a clear understanding of Zimbardo's experiment; and that you systematically apply elements of the critiques, as you see fit, to Zimbardo's work. In your conclusion, offer your overall assessment of the Stanford Prison Experiment. To do this, you might answer Zimbardo's own question in paragraph 55: "Was [the experiment] worth all the suffering . . . ?" Or

you might respond to another question: Do you agree that Zimbardo is warranted in extending the conclusions of his experiment to the general population?

9. In response to the question "Why is man so prone to obey and why is it so difficult for him to disobey?" Erich Fromm suggests that obedience lets people identify with the powerful and invites feelings of safety. Disobedience is psychologically more difficult and requires an act of courage. (See paragraphs 13 and 14.) Solomon Asch notes that the tendency to conformity is generally stronger than the tendency to independence. And in his final paragraph, Philip Zimbardo writes that a "prison of fear" keeps people compliant and frees them of the need to take responsibility for their own actions. In a synthesis that draws on these three sources, explore the interplay of *fear* and its opposite, *courage*, in relation to obedience. To prevent the essay from becoming too abstract, direct your attention repeatedly to a single case, the details of which will help to keep your focus. "The Lottery" could serve nicely as this case, as could a particular event from your own life.

■ RESEARCH ACTIVITIES

1. When Milgram's results were first published in book form in 1974, they generated heated controversy. The reaction reprinted here (by Baumrind) represents only a very small portion of that controversy. Research other reactions to the Milgram experiments and discuss your findings. Begin with the reviews listed and excerpted in the *Book Review Digest*; also use the *Social Science Index*, the *Readers' Guide to Periodical Literature*, and newspaper indexes to locate articles, editorials, and letters to the editor on the experiments (and any other general or social science periodical indexes in print or electronic form that cover material written as far back as 1974). (Note that editorials and letters are not always indexed. Letters appear within two to four weeks of the weekly magazine articles to which they refer, and within one to two weeks of newspaper articles.) What were the chief types of reactions? To what extent were the reactions favourable?

2. The purpose of Milgram's experiment, along with a great deal of other social science research in the years after World War II, was to help throw light on how the Nazi atrocities could have happened. Research the Nuremberg war crimes tribunals following World War II. Drawing specifically on the statements of those who testified at Nuremberg, as well as those who have written about it, show how Milgram's experiments do help explain the Holocaust and other Nazi crimes. In addition to relevant articles, see Telford Taylor, *Nuremberg and Vietnam: An American Tragedy* (1970); Hannah Arendt, *Eichmann in Jerusalem: A Report on the Banality of Evil* (1963); Richard A. Falk, Gabriel Kolko, and Robert J. Lifton (eds.), *Crimes of War* (1971).

3. Obtain a copy of the transcript of the trial of Adolf Eichmann—the Nazi official who carried out Hitler's "final solution" for the extermination of the Jews. Read also Hannah Arendt's *Eichmann in Jerusalem: A Report on the Banality of Evil,* along with the reviews of this book. Write a critique both of Arendt's book and of the reviews it received.

4. The My Lai massacre in Vietnam in 1969 was a particularly egregious case of overobedience to military authority in wartime. Show the connections between this event and Milgram's experiments. Note that Milgram himself dealt with the My Lai massacre in the epilogue to his *Obedience to Authority: An Experimental View* (1974).

5. Since feminism re-emerged as a strong activist movement in the early 1970s, it has been passionately resisted by social conservatives who argue that women are better off under a patriarchal system. Among them are the REAL Women of Canada ("Realistic Equal Active for Life"), an anti-feminist group largely composed of middle-class Catholic and Protestant fundamentalist women over the age of 40[2]; the group was originally connected with Conservative backbenchers in the House of Commons who opposed the extension of women's legal rights and protections. Use general and social science periodical indexes to find articles about REAL Women and other instances of women who are fighting to preserve social structures that feminists oppose as sexist. Also search your library catalogue for related books on the backlash against feminism, including Andrea Dworkin's *Right Wing Women.* Using these books and articles as sources of insight, write an essay that accounts for the political phenomenon of women who advocate obedience to patriarchal authority.

6. At the outset of his article, Stanley Milgram refers to imaginative works revolving around the issue of obedience to authority: the story of Abraham and Isaac; three of Plato's dialogues, "Apology," "Crito," and "Phaedo"; and the story of Antigone (dramatized by both the fifth-century B.C.E. Athenian Sophocles and the twentieth-century Frenchman Jean Anouilh). In this chapter, we have reprinted Shirley Jackson's "The Lottery," and an excerpt from Margaret Atwood's *The Handmaid's Tale,* which also can be read as stories about obedience to authority. And many other fictional works deal with obedience to authority—for example, Herman Wouk's novel *The Caine Mutiny* (and his subsequent play *The Caine Mutiny Court Martial*). Check with your instructor, with a librarian, and with such sources as the *Short Story Index* to locate other imaginative works on this theme. Write a paper discussing the various ways in which the subject has been treated in fiction and drama. To ensure coherence, draw comparisons and contrasts among works showing the connections and the variations on the theme of obedience to authority.

[2] L. K. Erwin, "REAL Women, Anti-Feminism, and the Welfare State," *Resources for Feminist Research/Documentation sur la Recherche Feministe* 17.3 (1988): 147–49.

Power and Privilege in School Culture

Whatever else schools might be, they have always operated as instruments of normalization, servants of the state whose primary responsibility is to take five-year-olds through a 10- or 12-year character-building process that will make them into citizens who share behaviours and values compatible with the smooth functioning of the state: loyalty, obedience, hard work, and self-reliance. Historically, this mission has been visible in such practices as reciting the Lord's Prayer and the national anthem, and most notoriously in the establishment of the residential school system, which was designed to assimilate Aboriginal children into mainstream culture by annihilating their own.

Canadians often think of excesses of citizenship as a U.S. phenomenon, and it is true that there are comparatively fewer proponents of the "My country, right or wrong" form of patriotism here. But while we may like to think that our school systems are now organized around dedication to all children's achieving their potential, there is a large body of scholarship that indicates otherwise. Studies in the sociology of education analyze the many ways (inappropriately standardized testing, greater resources for schools in prosperous neighbourhoods) in which schools effectively serve to reproduce the existing hierarchies of society, where social inequities are manifested along lines of race, gender, class, sexual orientation, and other differences. Ironically, as Doris Lessing argues in her essay "Group Minds" (pp. 210–213), education does this in part by teaching people that if they are poor or harshly treated it is their own fault, and not the result of any injustice in our social arrangements. Given the personal conflicts built into the school system, it should not be surprising, then, that individuals within it can be caught up in their own power struggles.

In this chapter, we bring together readings that approach various issues of power and privilege in school culture. One important perspective is signalled in the opening piece by Karen Mock: There are many teachers now in the school system who conceive good citizenship not as blind loyalty but as critical intelligence and a passion for justice that includes the courage to defy the group. This is followed by an article investigating the widespread phenomenon of bullying, perhaps the most pressing issue of power in schools today. Shocked into rethinking the significance of bullying after a string of retaliatory shootings across North America, most of us now agree that it is wrong to dismiss complaints of bullying with a "kids will be kids" attitude. Teachers and school officials who used to reply to the complaints of victimized students with the message that bullying was wrong, but that tattling was even worse, are now trying to learn how to recognize bullying and take responsibility for intervening in it. Some are wondering how the culture of schools participates in the production of bullying: Are children just showing they've learned their lessons well when they bully those who are somehow different from the norm?

In a related article, Catherine Taylor examines the persistence of homophobia as an enduring aspect of the power structures of school culture and argues that educators have an ethical and legal responsibility to help build inclusive communities that fully respect all the children in their care. Next we have two readings about the residential school system in which Aboriginal children were abused by white teachers who participated in the racist group mentality of colonial Canada. Judges Murray Sinclair and A. C. Hamilton and law professor Anne McGillivray analyze both state-sanctioned and systemic abuses of power in residential schools, and the traumatic effects of abuse that persist in Aboriginal communities today. Following these we offer an example of a defence of the residential school system and its employees in the form of a short article by a Sociology of Education professor. The chapter concludes with two articles that argue for implementing educational approaches to confronting differences that directly tackle the problem of producing a less violent future.

As you read the texts in this chapter, you may find yourself thinking back to Chapter 6, with its focus on the psychological roots and ramifications of obedience to authority and the value we place on it in our society.

Victims, Perpetrators, Bystanders, Activists: Who Are They? Who Are You?

KAREN R. MOCK

In this article, Karen Mock claims that if we are to work against the possibility of future holocausts, teachers need to help students develop their own sense of humanity so that when evil forces are at work, they will be prepared to be activists and risk takers rather than bystanders or perpetrators.

Dr. Mock is a registered psychologist and the National Director of the League for Human Rights of B'nai B'rith Canada, an agency committed to the struggle against racism and bigotry. She has worked as a human rights consultant, taught in the education faculties of the University of Toronto, Ryerson University, and York University, and served on many boards and committees related to race relations and multiculturalism.

I have just returned from leading the 1996 Holocaust and Hope Educators'   1
Study Tour to Germany, Poland, and Israel. Although it is the fourth time I
have conducted the program, I continue to be overwhelmed by images and
emotions of the trip, and even more overwhelmed by the challenges of raising
a generation to believe that the world can be a better place and that they can
acquire the skills and commitment to make it so. By the time you read this, we
will be well into another school year, implementing a curriculum that results
in our students' being able to rhyme off the names and deeds of evil murderers and perpetrators of wars far more readily than the stories and names of the
countless victims. Try it, and you'll see what I mean.

With our emphasis on skills and knowledge for outcomes-based learning,   2
how often do we reflect on the factors that lead to moral behaviour—to acts
of bravery, courage and altruism—rather than the more typical behaviours of
following the crowd, bullying, or scapegoating others to get our way, or
merely being spectators to world events, bystanders to unspeakable evil? As
Yehuda Bauer once said: "After the Holocaust, we live in a world where the
impossible became possible." How do we begin to understand this? Who
were the victims—as people, as individuals and not just as numbers? What
was it about the perpetrators that could lead them to commit such inhuman,
barbaric acts? How could so many stand by in silence? What differentiated
the rescuers, those few who took a stand and risked their lives to save others,
from the masses who aided and abetted the murderers? Who were they?
What would I have done in the same circumstances? What would I do today?
What would you do? And what relevance does all of this have for our lives in
Canada in the 1990s? These are the questions that haunt the educators who
took this difficult trip. The answers are crucial in shaping their teaching upon
their return, and are relevant to all our teaching, no matter what the subject
area. Perhaps Haim Ginott, in his open letter to teachers, said it best:

Dear Teacher,

I am a survivor of a concentration camp. My eyes saw what no man
should witness: Gas chambers built by learned engineers. Children poisoned by educated physicians. Infants killed by trained nurses. Women
and babies shot and burned by high school and college graduates. So I am
suspicious of education. My request is: Help your students become
human. Your efforts must never produce learned monsters, skilled psychopaths, educated Eichmanns. Reading, writing, arithmetic are important only if they serve to make our children more humane.

Haim Ginott,
Teacher and Child, 1972

Victims—Telling Their Story in Colour

I want to write first of the victims, because that is so rarely the case. Almost   3
all of our historical accounts over the centuries are told from the point of view
of those in power or of the conquerors, rarely of the people or the cultures
that were destroyed. The same is true today. We read of victorious Crusaders,
not of vanquished communities. We remember Marc Lepine, but how many
of his victims, young female engineering students, can we name? We call it the
Nerland Inquiry, when Carny Nerland was the white supremacist perpetrator
and Leo LaChance was the aboriginal man he murdered. It is as the African
proverb says: until the lions learn to speak and to write, tales of bravery and
courage will only be told of the hunters.

The voices of the victims are silent. It is we who must speak up for them,   4
to tell their stories so that the tremendous void they left is felt in our classrooms, and in the way that they would like to have been remembered—not as
emaciated victims or "lambs led to the slaughter" but as human beings who
lived colourful, vibrant lives and struggled valiantly to survive with dignity in
whatever way possible. As Rachel Maier Korazin (1996), a noted Holocaust
educator in Israel, has said:

> The only thing black and white in their lives was the photography of the
> era. We must put the colour back in their lives, not by showing Nazi
> photos of their victimization, but by teaching about the life and the cul-
> ture that was lost. It is OK to visit and to dance in Poland. Jews lived in
> there for over 800 years; they were murdered there for only six.

Once survivors began to speak about the unspeakable, extensive research   5
and writings indicate that many of the victims proved the human capacity to
rise above their horrifying circumstances. In the concentration camps every
event conspired to make the prisoner lose hold, but resistance took a variety
of forms. As Viktor Frankl (1959) explains: "Hunger, humiliation, fear and
deep anger at injustice are rendered tolerable by closely guarded images of
beloved persons, by religion, by a grim sense of humour—and glimpses of the
healing beauties of nature." But Frankl goes on to point out that these don't
establish the will to live unless the victim makes larger sense out of apparently
senseless suffering. Quoting Nietzsche, Frankl, who was himself a survivor
and near death several times during the war, believes that "he who has a
WHY to live can bear with almost any HOW." This, then, for Frankl is the
central theme of existentialism: to live is to suffer; to survive is to find meaning in the suffering; if there is a purpose in life at all, there must be a purpose
in suffering and in dying. But no one can tell another what this purpose is.
Each must find out for the self and must accept the responsibility that the
answer prescribes.

Elie Wiesel (1990) describes exactly this phenomenon in the remarkable   6
efforts of several victims who chronicled otherwise unbelievable events.
Prompted by the taunts of SS guards that even if some survived, no one
would ever believe them, victims such as Zalman Gradowski, Leib Langfuss

and Yankel Wiernik wrote testimonies, diaries, chronologies of events, and the personal stories of other victims. Why? Because, according to Wiesel just as the killer was determined to erase Jewish memory, his victims fought to maintain it. Wrote Gradowski: "The purpose of my writing is to make sure that something of the truth reaches the world and moves it to avenge our lives. This is the purpose of my life." In the final analysis, what alone remains is, as Frankl says, "the last of human freedoms—the ability to choose one's attitude in a given set of circumstances."

In the face of evil—of racial hatred, rape, child abuse—or even in the face   7
of senseless, inexplicable accidents or acts of God—one is cast in the role of victim, a powerless and helpless position over which the victim has no control. It is reported that many victims chanted the viddui, the prayer asking forgiveness, on their way to the gas chambers. Rape victims feel a tremendous sense of guilt and shame. Abused children apologize, beg forgiveness, convinced they are to blame for vicious beatings. But such events are never the fault of the victims or of innocent survivors, although overwhelming guilt and self-blame sometimes lead to suicide. The question "Why me?" becomes "Why not me?"—sometimes with tragic answers. There is, of course, another common reaction; that is, for the victim to become the victimizer, the abused become the abuser, the survivor become the perpetrator—leading to self-hatred and sometimes also to suicide. The cycle of victimhood cannot be broken unless there is an intervention—someone to show it is not the fault of the victim, someone to substitute other models of behaviour.

Perpetrators—Ordinary People or Willing Accomplices?

There are those who try to describe the architects and perpetrators of the   8
Holocaust as inhuman sadists who were aberrant, insane, or otherwise marginalized and unusual. Browning describes them as ordinary men, in his book about a Ukrainian police battalion who had rather mundane choices to make as to whether they would take on the railway deportation shifts and other tasks to facilitate the murder of Jews, instead of their regular policing duties. And the choices were often made for rather trivial reasons. On the other hand, Goldhagen describes them as Hitler's "willing executioners," living in a Europe ripe with anti-Semitism such that the majority of the population willingly and knowingly became accomplices to murder. The reality is that then, as now, the origin of the Holocaust—or of rape or hate crime or child abuse—is the story of the perpetrators and what was done to their psyches, not about the victims who were targets no matter what they did.

Perpetrators feel themselves to be victims, usually have low self-esteem,   9
and are looking for someone to blame for their problems. They have often been raised in abusive, authoritarian environments. They are easily swayed by propaganda, usually foisted on them by a hatemonger who is looking to increase his own power base by promising his audience more power, opportunity and self-reliance, all the while imposing increasing discipline and control, building on their anger and alienation, and stereotyping and scapegoating others who are less powerful. Perpetrators let themselves be

convinced that they are acting for the good of their own people, often believing that they are justified by religion. We should not forget that each SS officer's belt buckle bore the inscription "Gott Mit Uns," God Is With Us. We see the same pattern today in the so-called neo-Nazi movement, skinheads, Holocaust deniers, white supremacist groups, and even in the black Nation of Islam—charismatic leaders gathering adherents with religious and pseudo-religious fervour. Such hatemongers know how to manipulate a following who can be easily bullied into submission under the guise of strict discipline and who rarely think for themselves. Followers get further and further drawn in by the rhetoric until it's too late to get out, for the perpetrators inevitably use the same tactics to control their own ranks as they do to victimize others.

Are we all just ordinary people who, under the right circumstances, could   10
become willing accomplices? Could they be us if the right "hot buttons" were pressed? Before we too readily dismiss such a notion, think for a moment of some examples of modern perpetrators—people who put a lesser value on some human lives than others. Soldiers in Somalia who dehumanized a people until murder was the punishment for alleged theft of food. Officials who decided, for whatever reason, not to test blood for HIV, resulting in the deaths of thousands of innocent patients. Politicians who stir up anger and scapegoat immigrants and people of colour to garner votes. And what about those who blame the victims of harassment or even rape; or, worse still, those who turn a blind eye? Are bystanders who might have intervened to stop such inhuman acts not themselves perpetrators?

Bystanders—Passive Accomplices

"Bigotry and hatred are not the most urgent problems—the most important   11
and tragic problem is silence." These are the words of Rabbi Joachim Prinz who spoke just before Martin Luther King delivered his "I have a dream" speech at the March on Washington in 1963. Rabbi Prinz had been a rabbi in Berlin at the time of the Third Reich and knew all too well the tragic consequences when good people stand by and do nothing in the face of evil. It remains incomprehensible that the whole world stood by in silence, as in many cases it does today, as innocents continued to be murdered. The transcript of the Evian Conference of 1938 and the Bermuda Conference of 1943, when the nature and extent of the death factories were well documented, exposes the excuses given by the world powers—the Allies and neutral countries—and by major agencies such as the Red Cross and the Vatican for not intervening and for not taking refugees from Nazi-occupied Europe: we're drained by the war effort, poor economy, not enough room, and so on. It was the tiny Dominican Republic who agreed to take the most refugees while other doors remained closed.

It will interest readers to note that Canada refused to rescue any doomed   12
souls, and even refused to host the conference, which was originally supposed to be held in Ottawa, lest the local community and desperate relatives might bring too much pressure to bear on our government to do something. Bystanders all.

What do you do today when a friend or colleague reveals an incident of 13 abuse or harassment—turn a blind eye? Accuse the victim of being over-sensitive? Does your organization or department go into "cover-up" mode when a gross injustice or ethical breach is revealed? Does the "whistle blower" get marginalized and accused of not being a team player? Do the needs of the organization get put before the needs and lives of human beings? Do we think of the minor inconvenience to ourselves and families as more important than helping a friend in dire need, or even a stranger in mortal danger? Do we let the bullies abuse others and manipulate us without standing up? Where people are arbitrarily victimized, do we stand up or stand by? There are always choices to be made.

When you look at a map of Europe and examine the locations of all the 14 slave labour camps, concentration camps, and death camps (as we did with Dr. Racelle Weiman at the Ghetto Fighters Holocaust Education Centre near Haifa), you are immediately struck by the fact that while the majority were in Germany, Poland, and other parts of Eastern Europe, such camps existed in almost every country occupied by the Nazis, except for two: Denmark and Bulgaria. There was not one camp in either Denmark or Bulgaria because their populations said no. They would not build such camps nor subject their own citizens to slave labour or death, regardless of their religion. Their leaders, their governments, and their people refused to give up their Jews. They stood up to the Nazis, and the Nazis backed down. And we are faced with the stark realization that it didn't have to happen. The Nazis proceeded to implement the mass murder of innocents, the "final solution," in countries where the leadership and most of the population either stood by or collaborated, where there was no active, organized resistance to the war against the Jews.

But even there, in the darkness, there were some rays of light—the res- 15 cuers, the "righteous gentiles," truly the Righteous Among the Nations, as they are called by the State of Israel—people who saved Jews for absolutely no personal gain. Who are they? Who are those who made the moral choice to take action, to become "participants" as Wiesel calls them, rather than bystanders? What makes a person become an activist, to take a stand, often at great personal risk to themselves and their families? And what can we learn from them to teach others?

Activists, Participants, Risk-Takers—Rays of Light and Hope

Why does a person risk his or her life to save another, and what do such res- 16 cuers, true heroes, have in common? This was exactly what Oliner and Oliner (*The Altruistic Personality*, 1988) set out to discover in their exhaustive study of hundreds of righteous gentiles. Surprisingly, when asked why they risked their lives to save a Jew, most could give no specific reason, it was not that they saved friends—indeed, many rescued absolute strangers and even people they didn't like very much. They did it because it was the only human thing to do. There was no other reason, in Rabbi Joachim's words, again at the

March on Washington in 1963: "Neighbour is not a geographic term, it is a moral concept."

In an effort to determine what comprises the altruistic personality, Oliner   17
and Oliner conducted thorough interviews and personality assessments of several hundred rescuers. They found these activists had four factors in common—characteristics that speak volumes to educators about how we might teach to achieve our most important outcome, that of making our students more humane.

1. *Rescuers were and are critical thinkers.* These activists were self-   18
determining individuals who did not have a "follow the crowd" mentality; rather, they evaluated what they heard and saw with a strong sense of independence and autonomy. So they could reject the Nazi ideology and propaganda as irrational and simply not true, and even reject the laws, rather than blindly following along. Personality tests revealed that the ego was well-developed but not self-centred or narcissistic. They were "mavericks" in other aspects of their lives as well, people who marched to their own tune.

2. *Rescuers had role models who taught right from wrong.* Rescuers were   19
and are ordinary people from all walks of life—farmers, teachers, business people, rich, poor, parents, singles, Protestant, Catholic. And most had done nothing very dramatic or exceptional before the war. According to Oliner and Oliner, what most distinguished them were their connections with others in relationships of commitment and care, and their perception of who and what should be obeyed. Their rules and examples of conduct were learned from a parent, peer, teacher or mentor who helped them understand the way of determining right from wrong, and the importance of holding yourself accountable, regardless of what others say or do. The people I am calling activists, then, inevitably had a person who modelled for them a way of behaving differently, morally, and with a strong sense of social justice, regardless of the level of authority in the hierarchy of whoever is giving the orders to behave otherwise.

3. *Rescuers had a strong sense of self-worth.* It has often been said that   20
if you value yourself, you can give something to others. Psychological profiles revealed that rescuers of intended victims during the war had a positive sense of self-esteem. They were much more likely than bystanders, who were also interviewed, to have had the kind of approving, non-punitive early parenting that is associated with low ethnocentrism and high democratic potential. Their parents were described as warm people and models of caring behaviours, often with empathy for the underdog. They taught that one must perceive others as individuals, not as representatives of a type or group. Rescuers generally felt good about what they had done, and reflected on the rescuing experience as one of the high points in their lives, despite the tremendous additional strain and hardship placed on themselves and their families over and above the effects of the war. Bystanders, on the other hand, stressed their own

victimization during the war, compared their pain to the victims, blamed others for their situation, claimed they did not know, were angry that the people they turned away didn't appreciate their risk or offer them money or other forms of compensation, and generally described themselves as powerless in the situation.

4. *Rescuers had a sense of optimism and hope.* Almost all of the righteous 21 gentiles interviewed by the Oliners expressed a strong sense of feeling during the war that there had to be something better, that the world could and should be a better place, and that it was possible to achieve it. Rescuers refused to see Jews as guilty or beyond hope, and refused to see themselves as helpless, despite whatever evidence there was to the contrary. They believed that even one person could make a difference, and did not shrink from taking action in the direction of hope. Oliner and Oliner concluded their study as follows:

> If we persist in defining ourselves as doomed, human nature as beyond redemption, and social institutions beyond reform, then we shall create a future that will merely confirm this view. Rescuers made a choice that affirmed the value and meaningfulness of each life in the midst of a diabolical social order that denied it. Can we do otherwise?

Who Are You? And What Do We Want Our Students to Be?

What are the lessons to be drawn from all of this? The purpose of the 22 Holocaust and Hope Educators' Study Tour, and of my raising these issues, is not to enshrine Holocaust education as a memorial to the victims or as an anthropology or history lesson about a thousand years of European Jewish culture lost. Rather, the issues discussed here must have meaning for our own lives and the lives of our students. What do we want our students to learn? For those who understand oppression and have been hurt by prejudice, racism, sexism or exclusion, one lesson to be learned is never to allow yourself to be victimized again, and to develop skills and defence mechanisms to ensure that does not happen. But what about never allowing yourself to be the perpetrator? Victims must not become victimizers, and must learn to recognize totalitarian thinking and behaviour in themselves as well as in others. We must break the cycle of abuse and victimization, and ensure that the oppressed do not become the oppressors.

Whatever we teach about the Holocaust, we must make it very clear that 23 there was right and there was wrong, and we must not be afraid to set clear parameters. These are not issues of relativity. I do not believe that one person's terrorist is another's freedom fighter. This is not a matter of point of view. The murder of innocents is wrong, no matter what the cause, no matter what political or national side you are on. What is right is the dignity of human life, and the equality and indivisibility of human life. No life is worth less than another. Racelle Weiman captured it best when she warned that we should not be Holocaust educators, but Non-Holocaust educators; that is, we must teach towards creating a world without ethnic cleansing and genocide, without hate, racism, anti-Semitism, or human rights abuses.

We must also reach the point of accepting that we can never understand   24
what it means to be a victim—of the Holocaust, of rape, of abuse, of racism, of gay bashing—unless we were there, in that person's shoes. Who are we, then, to evaluate another's reaction? Or to argue about someone's personal interpretation of a traumatic experience? Or to judge and compare levels of grief or create a hierarchy of pain? As Rachel Maier Korazin so poignantly put it when our minds were still reeling from the images and sensations of the camps: "Say to the survivor, I will never understand the way you do—and, God forbid, you do not want me to. But I need to know. And we can start from here."

And so we have a starting point with our students: for learning about and   25
helping to heal the victim and the survivor; for becoming activists, risk-takers, critical thinkers, role models; for refusing to be perpetrators of, or bystanders to, evil or abuse of any kind. We have a starting point for teaching our students how to become humane, so that they will create a world where the impossible could not be possible again.

Author's Note: I want to thank two outstanding educators, colleagues and friends, Rachel Maier Korazin and Racelle Weiman, for their continuing contribution to the Holocaust and Hope Program, and for their inspiration for this article. It is dedicated to the memory of Richard Youngman.

References

Frankl, Viktor. *Man's Search for Meaning.* New York: Washington Square Press, 1985.
Ginott, Haim. *Teacher and Child.* New York: Pelican Books, 1972.
Korazin, Rachel. Personal Communication, 1996.
Oliner, S. P. and P. M. Oliner. *The Altruistic Personality.* New York: The Free Press, 1988.
Weiman, Racelle. "True Hero." *Jerusalem Post,* April 27, 1994.
Wiesel, E., L. Dawidowicz, D. Rabinowitz, and R. McAfee Brown. *Dimensions of the Holocaust* (2nd ed.). Evanston, IL: Northwestern University Press, 1990.

■ ■ ■

Discussion and Writing Suggestions

1. Think about your own knowledge of terrible events in human history. Do you know more about the perpetrators of the events than you do about the victims? What were your sources of information? What would Mock say is missing from your knowledge of these events?

2. Do you agree with Mock that the school curriculum should be changed to place much more emphasis on the production of the courage needed to defy unjust authority? Could this be done only in the context of history courses? Or could such lessons in humanity have a place in other subjects as well?

Bullying at School: A Canadian Perspective

ALICE CHARACH, DEBRA PEPLER, AND SUZANNE ZIEGLER

Children who terrorize others have been an element of school life for many   1
years. Such aggression in school-aged children has been the subject of wide
research in Europe, but bullying in schools has been largely unexplored in
North America. Scandinavian researchers have been investigating "mobbing"
or bully/victim problems since the early 1970s.[1] More recently, educators
and researchers in the United Kingdom have identified bullying as disturbingly
common in British schools.[2]

Bullying is generally acknowledged to be a form of childhood aggression   2
imbedded in an ongoing relationship between a bully or bullies and a victim
or victims. Olweus defines bullying as occurring when a person is "exposed,
repeatedly and over time, to negative actions on the part of one or more persons."[3] Bullies appear intent on causing distress for their own gain or gratifi-
cation, and the victim or victims are less powerful than the bully or bullies.[4]
Bullying can be direct physical or verbal aggression, or indirect, such as
threats and intimidation, exclusion or gossip.

Rates of bully-victim problems vary from country to country. In 1983,   3
Olweus and his colleagues used an anonymous self-report survey to study bullying among students aged 8–16 in the Norwegian comprehensive school
system. Fifteen per cent of students were involved in bully-victim problems
more than once or twice a term: 7% identified themselves as bullies and 9%
identified themselves as victims. Five per cent of students reported serious bullying, occurring weekly or more often, of these 2% were bullies and 3%
were victims.[5]

In Great Britain, a survey of young adolescents using Olweus' self-report   4
questionnaires, with minor changes to suit the British context, revealed higher
rates of bullying. Among 234 secondary school students, ages 13 and 15
years, 12% of students indicated they were bullies, and 22% indicated they
were victims more than once or twice a term.[6] Fourteen per cent of students

---

[1] D. Olweus, *Aggression in Schools: Bullies and Whipping Boys* (Washington, DC:
Hemisphere Publishing, 1978); D. Olweus, "Bully/Victim Problems Among School Children:
Basic Facts and Effects of a School-based Intervention Program," in D. Pepler and K. H.
Rubin (eds.) *The Development and Treatment of Childhood Aggression* (Hillsdale, NJ:
Erlbaum, 1991), pp. 411–448; and E. Roland, "Bullying: Scandinavian Research Tradition,"
in D. Tattum and D. Lane (eds.) *Bullying in Schools* (London: Trentham Books, 1989).
[2] M. Boulton and K. Underwood, "Bully/Victim Problems Among Middle School Children,"
British Journal of Educational Psychology 62 (1992), pp. 73–87; and C. Yates and P.
Smith, "Bullying in Two English Comprehensive Schools," in E. Roland and E. Munthe
(eds.) *Bullying: An International Perspective* (London: David Fulton, 1989), pp. 22–34.
[3] D. Olweus, "Bully/Victim Problems Among School Children," *op. cit.*, p. 413.
[4] V. E. Besag, *Bullies and Victims in Schools* (Milton Keynes, PA: Open University Press,
1989); and D. Olweus, *ibid*.
[5] D. Olweus, *ibid*.
[6] C. Yates and P. Smith, *op. cit.*

reported serious bullying, of these 4% were bullies and 10% were victims. In a similar survey at three middle schools, 296 younger children, ages 8–9 and 11–12, reported similarly high rates of bully-victim problems. Seventeen per cent of students reported bullying others, and 21% of students reported being victimized, more than once or twice a term.[7] Ten per cent of students reported bullying, weekly or more often, nearly 4% as bullies and 6% as victims.

To date no one has published a similar survey of bullying among students   5
in North American schools. Perry, Kusel and Perry[8] used a peer nomination scale to examine victimization among children in grades 3 to 6 (ages 8–12). In a survey of 165 students, 10% of children were reported to be severely vic-timized. Bully-victim problems are a major concern for educators because most bullying occurs on school grounds, rather than on the way to or from school.[9] In the Norwegian study, the prevalence of bullying on the schoolyard was inversely related to the number of teachers on yard duty. Students reported that teachers generally did little to stop bullying at school. The parents of both bullies and victims were generally unaware of bullying incidents at school and rarely discussed it with their children.[10]

Although the child's temperament and family environment are significant   6
factors in the personality development of individual bullies and victims,[11] the school environment also plays a role. Stephenson and Smith compared teacher attitudes in six schools where there were many bullying incidents with teacher attitudes in six schools where there were few bullying incidents. Teachers in five of the six schools with few bully-victim problems consis-tently expressed the importance of preventing bullying. In schools with high levels of bully-victim problems, teachers expressed a wide variety of opinions regarding what to do when students bully others.

In the late 1980s public concern arose in Toronto over the increasing vio-   7
lence seen in various communities. This coincided with the publication of reports describing the Norwegian bully-victim intervention program that suc-cessfully reduced the incidence of self-reported bully-victim problems by 50% over two years.[12] Educators at the City of Toronto Board of Education responded by sponsoring the survey reported here. The purpose of the survey was to investigate the extent of bully-victim problems within the City of Toronto schools; to inquire about students' ideas, attitudes, and experiences of bullying and victimization, and to gather information regarding parents' and teachers' perceptions of bully-victim problems.

---

[7] M. Boulton and K. Underwood, *op. cit.*
[8] D. G. Perry, S. J. Kusel and L. C. Perry, "Victims of Peer Aggression," *Developmental Psychology* 24:6 (1988), pp. 807–814.
[9] D. Olweus, "Bully/Victim Problems," *op. cit.*
[10] *Ibid.*
[11] D. Olweus, *Aggression in Schools, op. cit.*; P. Stephenson and D. Smith, "Bullying in the Junior School," in D. Tattum and D. Lane (eds.) *Bullying in Schools* (London: Trentham Books, 1989); and V. E. Besag, *op. cit.*
[12] D. Olweus, "Bully/Victim Problems," *op. cit.*

The Survey

Setting and Subjects

This study was conducted in schools in the City of Toronto. The population of the city and of the schools is extremely diverse and heavily immigrant. Twenty-two classrooms in 16 schools were selected to ensure students from a wide variety of backgrounds were included in the study. The classrooms ranged from junior kindergarten (JK) to grade 8 (ages 4–14). Six of the classrooms were for children with special needs. One day before distributing questionnaires, each classroom held a group discussion about bullying problems. This ensured that all students understood the concept of bullying.

Self-report Questionnaires

Three anonymous self-report questionnaires were distributed, one to students, one to school staff, and one to parents. The student questionnaire was an English translation of the self-report questionnaire developed by Olweus for use in schools in Scandinavia.[13] It was modified slightly for Canadian expressions. Similar questionnaires were developed for parents and school staff. All three surveys were distributed in May of the school year. The reference period for the questionnaire was "since the beginning of the term," and indicated since mid-March, a time of approximately two months.

Six questions, not derived from the Norwegian questionnaire, were also included in the survey: (1) Why do you think that some students bully other students? (2) Where does this happen? (3) What do you think students should do if they are bullied? (4) What do you think teachers can do to help? (5) What do you think parents can do to help? and (6) At your school, how often does it happen that children are bullied because of race?

The student self-report questionnaire was administered by teachers to 211 students, 106 females and 105 males in 14 classrooms from grades 4 to 8. Some grade 3 students were included if they were part of a split grade 3/4 classroom. The questionnaire was not suitable for students below grade 3.[14]

The staff survey was given to all teachers of the 22 classrooms involved in the research, and to all the other staff members (teachers, administrators, lunchroom supervisors, caretakers) in the 16 schools. The response rate for staff members completing the questionnaires was 60% (372 staff).

The questionnaire for parents was translated into 16 languages and distributed to parents of the students in the 22 classrooms in the study. It was completed by 172 parents, a response rate of 38%.

---

[13] D. Olweus, "Questionnaire for Students: Junior," unpublished document, University of Bergen, Norway, 1989.

[14] E. Roland, *op. cit.*

Results and Discussion

Prevalence of Bullying-Victim Problems

Bullying is a frequent occurrence according to students in Toronto: 49%   14
reported having been bullied at least once or twice during the term. Parents
appeared to be less aware than students of bullying; only 32% indicated that
their children had been bullied at least once or twice during the term. Twenty
per cent of students reported being bullied more than once or twice during the
term, and 14% of parents reported that their children experienced this level
of more frequent bullying. Eight per cent of students reported being bullied
regularly, weekly or more often. These rates are similar to rates of bullying in
Great Britain.[15] They are approximately twice those reported by students in
Norway.[16]

When asked whether they had bullied other students during the term,   15
61% of students indicated they had not bullied other students at all in the present term. Twenty-four per cent said they had done so only once or twice. The
remaining 15% of students admitted to more frequent bullying. Only 2% of
students admitted to a very high frequency of bullying (once a week or more).
This figure, however, may be an underestimate: when asked whether they had
bullied anyone in the last five school days, one-quarter of all students and one-
third of the self-reported bullies acknowledged that they had done so.

Corroborating evidence on the prevalence of bullying comes from reports   16
of the number of bullies per class. Thirty-eight per cent of students and 36%
of their teachers reported that there were at least three or four bullies in their
class. This represents at least one bully per ten students, suggesting that the
self-report rate of 15% of children involved in frequent bullying is not an
underestimate. Only 16% of students and 29% of teachers indicated that
there were no children in their class who had bullied during the term.

Age and Gender

The gender and age patterns in the Toronto data were similar to those in the   17
Norwegian and British surveys. The proportions of boys (20%) and girls
(21%) who reported being victimized were essentially the same; however,
three times as many boys (23%) as girls (8%) acknowledged bullying others
more than once or twice per term. Younger children (40% of 9-year-olds)
reported more victimization than did older children (8% of 13-year-olds and
5% of 14-year-olds). The 10-, 11-, and 12-year olds reported similar levels of
victimization (30%, 21% and 30%, respectively).

The highest proportion of children admitting to bullying was in grades 5   18
and 6, ages 11 to 12 years. When students, parents and staff were asked about
the relative ages of bullies and victims, they all indicated that bullies were
most often peers of the victim, the same age and in the same class or grade—
those children who spend the most time together.

---

[15] C. Yates and P. Smith, *op. cit.*; and M. Boulton and K. Underwood, *op. cit.*
[16] D. Olweus, "Bully/Victim Problems," *op. cit.*

Why Children Bully

All students, and the subset of bullies, cited the desire to feel powerful (68%   19
and 59%) followed by a desire to be "cool" (65% and 56%) as the primary
motives for bullying. Staff and parents also cited the desire for power as the
primary reason for bullying (75% and 71%), but they differed from the students by indicating that bullies were motivated by low self-esteem (55%,
41% and 17%, respectively).

Factors in Victimization

Race appeared to be a factor in victimization. Race-related bullying was   20
reported by 43% of students and 36% of the classroom teachers. Overall, one
in five students reported that race-related bullying happens often in their
school; one in two students from disadvantaged neighbourhoods reported
that race-related bullying happens often.

Compared to the other students, victims were more likely to describe   21
themselves as often alone at recess, often lonely at school, and feeling less
well-liked than others. In particular, students in self-contained classrooms for
children with special needs were more likely to report being victimized than
students in regular classes, 38% and 18%, respectively.

How Children Respond to Bullying

The present study documents children's emotional responses and actions in   22
bullying situations. Children were asked how they felt watching bullying incidents, even if they themselves were not the victims. Sixty-one per cent reported
feeling that bullying is very unpleasant. Twenty-nine per cent reported that
bullying is somewhat unpleasant and 10% expressed indifference to bullying.
The children who "did not feel much" were more likely to be bullies.

Forty-three per cent of children reported that they try to help when a   23
child is being bullied; 33% reported that they felt they should help but do not;
and 24% reported that bullying was none of their business. This pattern is
similar to that reported among British middle school students.[17] Thirty-two
per cent of the students said that peers frequently try to stop bullying incidents
at school, and 13% reported that peers intervene at least occasionally.

Taken together the data on children's feelings and actions in response to   24
seeing bullying indicate that a majority of students in grades 3 through 8 dislike bullying in their schools and want to help stop it. Only a third of the students (more often boys than girls) indicated they could join a bullying episode.

A major thrust of the Toronto survey was to collect information that   25
would help in customizing an intervention to address bullying and victimization in the schools. Students, school staff and parents were asked what students should do if bullied. With the exception of bullies, a majority of
respondents in all groups advised telling parents and teachers. Bullies were

---

[17] M. Boulton and K. Underwood, *op. cit.*

more likely to suggest fighting back than were either victims or students who were neither bullies nor victims. Victims' pattern of responses was also unique. They were more likely to suggest doing nothing if bullied. These responses suggest that any intervention designed to decrease bullying must involve adults as well as children.

The Role of Adults

When asked what teachers can do to help, a majority of each group of respondents thought teachers should talk to students. About half of each group thought a teacher should punish the bully. Students did not agree with school staff that teachers should get bully and victim to talk with each other. Students and school staff also suggested that parents talk to the students about bullying and victimization. 26

From the above responses, it is clear that most students, parents and school personnel see adults as having a major role to play in addressing bullying in schools. Yet when asked about where bullying occurs and what is done to stop it, discrepancies appear between the perspectives of children and adults. For example, students and parents differed on where they thought bullying occurred. Students reported that bullying happened at school in areas that parents may assume are supervised, such as playgrounds, school hallways, and classrooms. 27

Parents and students both indicated that the playground was the most common site for bullying; however, parents cited unsupervised routes on the way to and from school more frequently than did children. Parents and school staff were less aware of the bullying that happens in classrooms than were students. Apparently, adults assume that bullying seldom occurs where students are supervised. 28

The majority of students who had been victimized had talked to their parents and/or their teachers about it. Nevertheless, almost a third of the victims, many of those who were most frequently bullied, reported that they had not sought adult help. So even though teachers reported that many students come to them for help, this apparently does not include some children who are at highest risk. Many parents and teachers may be unaware that these particular children are being bullied. Boulton and Underwood, after interviewing victims, suggest that many victims do not report bullying incidents because they fear retaliation by the bully.[18] 29

The frequency of adult intervention to stop bullying was also seen quite differently by students and by teachers. Whereas nearly three-quarters of the teachers reported that they usually intervene if they see bullying going on, only one-quarter of the students reported that teachers typically intervene. Such a discrepancy may arise because students see a greater number of incidents than teachers, thus accounting for their impression that teachers rarely 30

---

[18] *Ibid.*

intervene. Craig and Pepler[19] observed aggressive children and socially competent children in schoolyards and found that teachers intervened in only 4% of bullying incidents.

The Role of Children

From the classroom group discussions about bullying, it was clear that younger children, in kindergarten to grade 4, look to adults for protection from bullying. By grade 6, however, students generally feel that bullying cannot be stopped. As children get older they retain the perception that adult intervention is both infrequent and ineffective. They develop a more sophisticated understanding of antisocial behaviour as originating in early childhood experiences in the family. In the classroom discussions, students in grades 5 and 6 openly acknowledged that bullying is fun, and blamed victims for being "wimps," "nerds," "weak" and "afraid to fight back." By contrast, older students, in grade 8 classrooms, described the bullies as troubled, and developed an image of a bully as the product of a violent and neglectful home.   31

How a child's increased understanding of bullying might influence his or her behaviour is not yet clear. The survey data reported here suggest that over time students relinquish their attempts to stop bullying: One out of two students aged 9–12 reported trying to help children who were being bullied, while only three out of ten students aged 13–14 reported doing so. One important component of an intervention, therefore, is to develop children's understanding of bullying and victimization in conjunction with strategies they can use to curtail the problem.   32

Intervention: An Ecological Approach

Bullying is best understood using an ecological perspective. The behaviours of the bullies, victims and peers are interrelated and unfold within the wider system of the school. The aggression of bullies is inextricably linked to the passivity of victims in a context where adults are generally unaware of the extent of the problem, and other children are unsure about whether or how to get involved. In fact, students advise each other to avoid bullies and stay with friends. Thus, victims, who described themselves as lonely and socially isolated, may indeed be left alone to fend for themselves against overwhelming odds.   33

The attitudes of parents, teachers, and school administrators may inadvertently perpetuate bully/victim problems. Canadian schools exist within a cultural context where violent acts often go unacknowledged, victims are blamed for their own fates, and a curtain of silence is maintained. Societal attitudes toward bullying in schools are similar to those about racism, family violence and child abuse. There appears to be a lack of understanding about   34

---

[19] W. M. Craig and D. J. Pepler, "Contextual Factors in Bullying and Victimization," paper presented at the Canadian Psychological Association Conference, Quebec City, June 1992.

the extent and seriousness of the problem and a feeling that outsiders should not get involved.

Numerous interventions to address aggressive behaviour in children have   35
been tried, most at the level of the individual child or family. Many of these have shown only partial success.[20] Interventions for aggressive behaviour problems include social skills, cognitive, and parent training programs, as well as experimental classrooms. Interventions designed to combat bully-victim problems in schools will need to address the complex issues at several different levels.

Olweus describes the optimal intervention as one that addresses bullying at   36
the whole school, classroom, and individual levels. The intervention must be a collaborative effort of teachers and parents and students. The first step in the intervention process is the development of a school policy with clearly stated rules against bullying. Classroom discussions are also an essential feature. Such discussions serve to sensitize children to the problem, engage them in establishing rules and consequences for bullying, and in developing strategies for assisting children who are victimized. The optimal intervention also includes increased adult supervision of playgrounds. These components were incorporated in the model intervention used in schools throughout Norway which significantly decreased the incidence of self-reported bully-victim problems.[21]

The current survey provides direction for further development of pro-   37
grams to address bully-victim problems. In particular, a whole school intervention should build on the students' desire for bullying to stop and their attempts to be helpful. Extra effort should be focused in grades 5 and 6 classrooms where students expressed attitudes blaming the victims. It is important to encourage children to continue their attempts to stop bullying and to give them strategies that will work in a context with adult support. Peers could be included by delegating positions of responsibility to "neutral" students. These students could help other children solve problems on the playground when teachers are not readily available. An example of this type of intervention is the Peacemakers program.[22]

In summary, the general findings in the Toronto survey match those in   38
the British and Scandinavian survey, where the same anonymous self-report questionnaires were used: boys were more involved than girls, young children were more victimized than older ones, and bullying was more common in school than outside. Many teachers and parents were unaware of individual

[20] For example, see J. D. Coie, M. Underwood, and J. E. Lochman, "Programmatic Intervention with Aggressive Children in the School Setting," in D. J. Pepler and K. H. Rubin (eds.) *The Development and Treatment of Childhood Aggression* (Hillsdale, NJ: Erlbaum, 1991), pp. 389–410; G. R. Patterson, D. Capaldi, and L. Bank, "An Early Starter Model for Predicting Delinquency," in D. J. Pepler and K. H. Rubin, *op. cit.*, pp. 139–168; and D. J. Pepler, G. King, and W. Byrd, "A Social-cognitively Based Social Skills Training Program for Aggressive Children," in D. J. Pepler and K. H. Rubin, *op. cit.*, pp. 361–379.
[21] D. Olweus, "Bully/Victim Problems," *op. cit.*
[22] Tom Roderick, "Johnny Can Learn to Negotiate," *Educational Leadership* 45:4 (1988), pp. 86–90.

children's involvement and children reported that teachers infrequently intervened in bullying. The number of students involved in bully-victim problems in this Toronto survey, one in three students, was similar to rates in Great Britain, but higher than in Scandinavia. Bullying is common among Canadian school children. Interventions designed to address the hidden violence of bullying in the schools must be ecological in design and comprehensive in scope.

■ ■ ■

Building Community through Anti-Homophobia Education

CATHERINE TAYLOR

Catherine Taylor is an associate professor in the Bachelor of Education Program and Centre for Academic Writing at The University of Winnipeg. She specializes in critical education as an approach to building community and empowering students who are marginalized within the school system. She has written chapters in a number of books and articles in the journals Ethnologies, Atlantis, *and* Intercultural Studies. *Her current research involves a community-based needs assessment of members of the transgender and Two Spirit community of Manitoba. In the following abridged article she argues that schools need to start living up to their legal and ethical responsibilities to all their students, not just the heterosexual ones.*

Every year, it's the same old song. Educators are disappointed and concerned   1
when bright students of obviously high academic potential attend classes sporadically and eventually stop coming to class altogether. Every year, we worry about students who underachieve and seem disengaged from the curriculum. We worry about the students who seem depressed, or isolated, or targeted by bullies, and often we wish they would confide in us. We are shocked when withdrawn, harried-looking students disappear from the back rows of our classrooms and appear a few days later in the obituary listings, described as "suddenly taken from us."

The reasons behind this sad litany vary. One consistently underestimated   2
cause, however, is a homophobic school culture that feeds a disproportionately high incidence of suicide, depression, dropping out, and underperformance among lesbian, gay, bisexual, and transgender (lgbt) students. Most of us want to do everything in our power to prevent such things from happening to our students. In reality, though, teachers are often a nonfactor in this ongoing story. They are seldom confided in by lgbt students in trouble, and they seldom intervene in cases of bullying. It is not being homosexual that destroys the lives of lgbt people, but the cultural terrorism that goes along

with not being heterosexual (or, in the case of transgender people, of being a feminine boy or a masculine girl). Given the levels of isolation and hostility experienced by lgbt students, it is a tribute to their courage that most manage to survive their educations with sufficient self-esteem to live to be adults.

In this chapter, I pose the questions: As inner-city educators, what can we   3 do to help our lgbt students develop the resilience to endure the insults to their dignity that they will almost certainly encounter in their school years? How can we help make our schools into inclusive communities that no longer participate in the process of dehumanizing lgbt students?

Anti-homophobia education is an umbrella term for a variety of   4 approaches used to challenge two quite distinct forms of discrimination faced by lgbt people: homophobia and heterosexism. *Homophobia* is an odd term— it implies that the problem is an irrational fear, which arises on its own from some ancient part of our brain, rather like arachnophobia or acrophobia. Homophobia can be experienced as a fear (fear of homosexuals molesting children, for example), but it is far from being irrational or innate. Instead, it is the inevitable product of the intense social pressure to condemn homosexuality in our society, and the absolute demand to do so in certain pockets of society such as fundamentalist religions and "hyper-masculine" sports such as football. Homophobia has traditionally been backed up by severe disciplinary practices: for example, lgbt people in North America were routinely subjected to shock treatment and aversion therapy until the American Psychological Association (1973) finally delisted homosexuality as a mental disorder. Homophobia should perhaps be thought of as a negative attitude to lgbt people, often quite intensely emotional, and often attached to religious or other moral codes. Homophobic attitudes provide the fuel and the justification for acts of prejudice against lgbt people, ranging from employment discrimination to name-calling and physical assault.

Heterosexism, in contrast, is more like sexism in that it does not rely on   5 negative emotions toward lgbt people. Many people who oppose full rights for lgbt people claim that they have no hard feelings toward them. The GLEE Project of educational initiatives on the subject defines heterosexism this way (2001):

> Heterosexism is the stigmatisation, denial or denigration of non-heterosexual relationships. It is the assumption that either everybody is or should be heterosexual, and is the belief that heterosexual relationships are the only valid and legitimate type of relationship. It is manifested in the exclusion by omission or design of non-heterosexual persons in policies, procedures or activities of societal institutions.

The "hidden curriculum" of most public schools can be described as   6 *heterosexist*—it ignores non-heterosexual content. While the message conveyed by this silence is not explicitly homophobic, since it does not involve negative content about lgbt people, it effectively teaches that lgbt people are not worthy of inclusion. Name-calling, threats, and assault are examples of directly *homophobic* constituents of school experience for lgbt students. Both homophobia and heterosexism poison the climate of school culture for lgbt students, and both are challenged under anti-homophobia education.

The use of the term *lgbt* is relatively recent. In the earliest days of anti-homophobia education, many people used the simpler term, *gay*. This usage gave way to *lesbian and gay*, and then to *lesbian/gay/bisexual* or *lgb* for the same reason that people stopped using the term *men* to mean "men, women, and children." While the issues of transgender people are not synonymous with lgb issues, they occupy similarly oppressed social locations in a hetero-sexist, homophobic culture, and *lgb* has largely given way to *lgbt*. Being transgender implies that one's identity violates gender codes, whereas lgb people might be perfectly in synch with every gender norm (apart from same-sex partner choice) that is culturally prescribed for their biological sex. A transgender person might be biologically male but identify as a female in self-concept, behaviour, clothing preferences, and so on; regardless of the sex of her preferred partner, she is so far outside the concept of heterosexuality in our society that she, too, is the target of homophobia and heterosexism. As McFarland (2001) notes:

> If traditional gender role behavior is breached, homophobic actions are taken to punish anyone—gay or straight, male or female—in the name of enforcing the standards of heterosexuality. Thus, students become victims of violence because of the connection between homophobia and rigid gender roles defined by heterosexism.

It is especially important for inner-city teachers to be aware of the presence of transgender students in their classes, given the increased visibility of transgender people in inner-city communities, particularly among Aboriginal adolescents who identify as "two-spirited." In Winnipeg, for example, a support group for lgbt youth offered at Nine Circles Community Centre draws mostly two-spirited boys—most of whom have dropped out of school. Aboriginal students are already at higher risk of suicide and dropping out (Gotowiec & Beiser, 1994; Kirmayer, Brass & Tait, 2000), and being transgender in a homophobic culture makes them particularly vulnerable (Clements-Nolle, Marx, Guzman & Katz, 2001).

The Ethical Case for Anti-homophobia Education

Although inner-city teachers have led the way, the vast majority of teachers (even in inner-city schools) do not consider anti-homophobia education to be part of their teaching responsibilities. Many offer no more than a quick rebuke when they witness taunting and bullying. Some do not even do that. The reason for inaction is rarely homophobia. More often it is a combination of not being aware of the presence of gay and lesbian students (many teachers mistakenly believe they have never encountered either a lgbt student or a student with lgbt parents), thinking homosexuality education belongs only in health class (if anywhere at all), underestimating the damage caused by homophobia, and fearing the professional repercussions of arousing the ire of homophobic parents. Teachers can feel especially vulnerable if they themselves are lesbian or gay, or if they teach for a school board or in a school with official or unofficial prohibitions against discussing homosexuality. Teachers, particularly those who follow fundamentalist Christian and Muslim faith traditions, may avoid anti-homophobia education on religious grounds. They can feel that they are violating religious teachings on sexual morality if they include gays and lesbians in the definition of who is entitled to human rights and actively defend those rights (Taylor, 2002).

The last twenty-five years have seen tremendous improvements in the life   10
possibilities for lgbt people in Canada. However, parts of Canadian society are still very homophobic, and it can be risky for teachers to practice anti-homophobia education in some schools. Although teachers in a few school divisions such as Winnipeg School Division #1 and the former Toronto Board of Education have the support of the school board (McCaskell, 1999; McCaskell & Russell 2000), superintendents in other divisions forbid teachers to come out or to discuss homosexuality in the classroom. In those places, perhaps all we can ask of teachers is that they watch for and intervene in incidents of homophobic harassment, and leave more proactive efforts to others.

That being said, there is clearly an enormous need for anti-homophobia   11
education. Researchers have found that homophobic school cultures are directly implicated in the disproportionately high rates of depression, dropping out, and suicide among lesbian and gay students (Bagley & D'Augelli, 2000; MYRBS, 1997; Siversten & Thames, 1995). We know something about the landscape of a homophobic school culture, as well. Schools are sites of homophobic assaults, both verbal and physical, and the vast majority of queer-bashing incidents on and off school property are committed by teenaged boys (Comstock, 1991; McFarland, 2001). We know, too, that the estimated "one in ten" of our students who are or will be lesbian or gay

> ... spen[d] a major portion of their school lives feeling isolated, fearful, and confused, forced to confront their emerging sexuality in settings that range, as they understood it, from ignorance of their existence, on the one hand, to open hostility, on the other (Ginsberg, 1996).

Adolescence is often a confusing, lonely time for heterosexual students,   12
and the cliquish social hierarchies of school culture are not always kind to them—even with the consolations of parental support, sympathetic school counsellors, a circle of friends at school, and a trillion-dollar music, television, and film industry directed to heterosexual youth. Imagine, then, the miseries of lgbt students. For them, any and all of these sources of potential support and affirmation are far more likely to be homophobic (McFarland, 2001). There is no social environment—schools, to our continuing shame, included—that is free from risk of harm (Pilkington & D'Augelli, 1995). As Plummer (1999) observed following his study of Australian boys,

> For kids who fit in, school days are halcyon days. For kids who are a bit different, school can be worse than prison because kids form gangs and

boys who get marginalised can't possibly win against a whole group. They are confined to the playground, they can't get away, even the trip on the school bus can be traumatic.

For example, the terms *gay* and *fag* are drearily common insults, fre- 13 quently hurled by students and rarely objected to by teachers. Our children learn that whatever gay is (and often the children using the term have no idea), it is clearly not a desirable identity in school culture (Human Rights Watch, 2001). A Toronto Board of Education survey found that one of the first words immigrant children who speak English as a second language learn at their new Canadian schools is *fag* (Galt, 1998).

Lessons in homophobia are underway in schoolyards around the world. 14 An Australian study found that boys learn to be homophobic in the primary school playground, and by their late teens they are using the word *poofter* twenty-five to fifty times a day (Edmunds, 1999). The same sort of statistic is reported in the United States, where "the typical high school student hears anti-gay slurs 25.5 times a day" (Carter, 1997, p.1). According to Calgary police Const. Doug Jones, co-chairman of a police liaison committee with the city's gay-lesbian community:

> There's very little done and very little support given by school staff . . . If someone yells across the hall from one student to another calling one a fag, it's overlooked, whereas if a student were to use a racist name, the teacher would be all over that person (Harrington, 2000).

We can only imagine the effect of such a poisonous atmosphere on the spirits of lgbt students, especially in the absence of any counteracting positive representations of lgbt people in the curriculum.

From our experience with inclusive education in areas such as gender and 15 ethnicity, we also know what needs to be done to counter this appalling situation. Educators can contribute to the process of social change by including gays and lesbians in the curriculum and by providing opportunities for critical reflection on homophobic cultural practices. Students who never see themselves represented, let alone represented positively, are taught that they are not worthy of inclusion. Other students, never having their prejudices challenged, learn that their prejudices are socially acceptable. By our silences, we teach students to have negative attitudes to homosexuality. The situation of lgbt students is comparable to that of students of colour who are exposed to racism outside the classroom and to a whites-only curriculum inside it (a situation that is compounded for lgbt students of colour, who endure both homophobia and racism).

Some people argue that anti-homophobia education should be left up to 16 parents, thereby leaving the school system uncontroversially neutral on the subject. This sidesteps responsibility—lgbt students usually conceal their sexual identities from their families and, sadly, often for very good reason. Their rate of running away from home and of being thrown out of home is as disproportionately high as their experiences of depression, dropping out of school, and suicide (Ryan & Futterman, 1998). In this respect, their situation is unlike that of students from other socially marginalized identities, such as students of colour and non-Christian religious students. These students can usually find safe haven at home with parents who share their struggles and can teach them to become resilient in the face of the everyday bigotry they encounter at school. The plight of lgbt students is unique in having a core aspect of their identity treated like a morally distasteful subject at home and at school.

Knowing what we do, I believe that it is incumbent on ethical educators   17
to act.

Inner-city Support for Anti-homophobia Education

Any educator involved in the struggle for social equality can expect to   18
encounter resistance from socially conservative quarters. However, it seems that Canadian young people in general are far from homophobic. This suggests that while we routinely underestimate the homophobia of school culture, we may be overestimating the resistance we are likely to encounter in the classroom and in the staff room. For example, a survey of 1003 Canadian teenagers between sixteen and eighteen years of age found that two-thirds (67 percent) endorse the legalization of same-sex marriage (Kiener, 2000).

Other surveys such as a Decima Research poll (2001) of Canadians eigh-   19
teen years and over show a steady increase in openness to same-sex rights in Canadian society, with higher support among people under thirty-five, residents of large urban centres, and women. Support was lower among people over fifty-five years, prairie residents, small-town residents, and men. We fit with the results of a study of 240 American college students (Bowen & Bourgeois, 2001), which found they consistently misperceive their peers as much less accepting than themselves of lgbt people. Canadian society has never been more open to the removal of this last socially acceptable form of discrimination, and the polls suggest that urban young people are even less entrenched in homophobic attitudes than the population in general. The problem, then, is not necessarily that a given culture is profoundly homophobic. Rather, the problem is that non-homophobic people rarely actively challenge the homophobic behaviour of their peers. Many even participate in homophobic taunting and derogation, thinking that little harm will come of it.

Many educators who are aware of the deadly toll of homophobia are   20
starting to take anti-homophobia education seriously. Television programs like *Ellen* and *Will and Grace* are not enough to turn the tide. Educators need to help lesbian and gay students develop the resilience to cope with the various assaults to their dignity that they encounter at school and in the larger culture. We also need to teach in ways that contribute to social change so that gay and lesbian students can hope for a freer future. To do that, we need to expand our pedagogical efforts from building resilience in lesbian and gay students (as important as that work is) to changing the conditions that oppress them in the first place. That means nourishing the capacity for anti-homophobic attitudes and actions among all students so that the ones doing the oppressing stop, and the ones passively standing by start challenging the

behaviour of homophobic people. As Beverley Daniel Tatum (1999) notes in connection with the struggle against racism, finding allies is crucial to the restoration of hope among oppressed people. Resilience without hope of social change is not empowerment but mere coping skills—an ability to tolerate the intolerable. We all want more than that for our students.

Many inner-city teachers find that students want to unlearn homophobia 21 when given the opportunity. There is some resistance, especially given the compulsory status of heterosexual masculinity in boys' culture (Plummer, 1999). Instances of strong resistance to anti-homophobia education do occur but are limited mainly to students and parents from exceptionally anti-homosexual religious backgrounds (Taylor, 2002). Teachers find that most students are much more open to the challenge than they had assumed.

Although lgbt students usually experience school as a hostile environ- 22 ment, they should not be thought of as bereft of resources. In fact, efforts to disrupt a homophobic school culture often begin with the students themselves. Gay-Straight Alliance clubs are typically formed by students, both lgbt and straight. Teacher involvement is very important but deliberately limited to two faculty advisors per club so as to maintain a student-centred environment. To avoid shifting the focus away from the work of alliance in common cause, everyone refrains from announcing their sexual orientation. By mid-2000, there were fifty such clubs in Canadian schools (mostly in British Columbia, Manitoba, Ontario, and Nova Scotia), and over 700 in the United States (Harrington, 2000). By late 2001, there were over 1000 clubs in the United States, or approximately one in every fifteen schools (GLSEN, 2001).

When inner-city teachers first start to think about building anti- 23 homophobia education into their work, they can usually find enthusiastic support in their own communities, whether through lesbian and gay parents or local advocacy organizations such as PFLAG and lgbt resource centres. These organizations are often willing to supply speakers and to suggest teaching resources. Teachers who have hesitated to be the first in their school to introduce anti-homophobia education are likely to come forward once someone else has tested the waters.

Our attempts to build capacity for inclusive respectful community can 24 often start with mobilizing the capacity that has already been developed in the inner city, and joining in struggles that have been going on without us.

Legal Support for Anti-homophobia Education

Further support for anti-homophobia education exists in the form of human 25 rights law at the federal and provincial levels that prohibits discrimination on the grounds of sexual orientation. While the law does not specifically address curriculum, such legislation can have a strong legitimizing effect for potential allies who might be wavering because of homophobic peer pressure.

Recently, the Supreme Court of Canada (EGALE, 2001) affirmed this 26 prohibition in the case of Trinity Western University. The school, a fundamentalist Christian college in Langley, British Columbia, required its students and teachers to pledge, in writing, to refrain from homosexual activity on the grounds that it is a "sexual sin" and "biblically condemned" (para. 4). In its decision, the Court ruled that the B.C. College of Teachers was unjustified in barring graduates of the college from candidacy for teaching positions and ruled that teachers, like everyone else, are entitled to hold "sexist, racist or homophobic beliefs" (para. 36). However, the Court also held that teachers are not entitled to act on such beliefs: "If a teacher in the public school system engages in discriminatory conduct, that teacher can be subject to disciplinary proceedings" (para. 37). In ruling that teachers can think what they like, but must treat every child equally and with respect, the Court referred to Section 15 of the Charter of Rights and Freedoms and the Human Rights Code of British Columbia, both of which guarantee equality and prohibit discrimination on the grounds of sexual orientation.

What, then, does it mean to uphold the law and treat everyone with   27 "respect"? To some, it means simply to refrain from attacking others, whether or not we agree with them. But the Supreme Court holds us to a more ambitious standard:

> The rights enshrined in s. 15(1) of the Charter are fundamental to Canada. They reflect the fondest dreams, the highest hopes and finest aspirations of Canadian society . . . Canada by the broad scope and fundamental fairness of the provisions of s. 15(1) has taken a further step in the recognition of the fundamental importance and the innate dignity of the individual. That it has done so is not only praiseworthy but essential to achieving the magnificent goal of equal dignity for all. . . . In order to achieve equality the intrinsic worthiness and importance of every individual must be recognized regardless of the age, sex, colour, origins, or other characteristics of the person. This in turn should lead to a sense of dignity and worthiness for every Canadian and the greatest possible pride and appreciation in being a part of a great nation. (para. 26)

This insistence on "equal dignity for all," on "a sense of dignity and wor-   28 thiness for every Canadian," jibes with the understanding of respect found in the literature of progressive education. In it, teachers cite the traditional curriculum as contributing to a poisoned atmosphere that robs marginalized groups of dignity by excluding them and remaining silent about their oppression. For anti-homophobia educators, this understanding of respect means teaching students that it is wrong to insult or assault gay and lesbian people. It also means changing the curriculum in ways that build students' capacity to enact the kind of respect that makes "a sense of dignity and worthiness" possible for everyone in the classroom. That includes lgbt students.

References

American Psychological Association. (1973). *Diagnostic and statistical manual*. Second Edition. Washington, DC: American Psychological Association.

Bagley, C., & D'Augelli, A. R. (2000). Suicidal behaviour in gay, lesbian, and bisexual youth. *British Medical Journal, 320*(7250), 1617–8.

Bowen, A. M., & Bourgeois, M. J. (2001). Attitudes toward lesbian, gay, and bisexual college students: The contribution of pluralistic ignorance, dynamic social impact, and contact theories. *Journal of American College Health*, 50, 91–96.

Carter, K. (1997, March 7). Gay slurs abound. *Des Moines Register*, p. 1.

Clements-Nolle, K., Marx, R., Guzman, R., & Katz, M. (2001). HIV prevalence, risk behaviors, health care use, and mental health status of transgender persons: Implications for public health intervention. *American Journal of Public Health*, 91(6), 915–21.

Comstock, G. D. (1991). *Violence against lesbians and gay men*. New York, Oxford: Columbia UP.

Decima Research. (2001, January 22). Canadians split on same sex marriages. Ottawa: Decima Research Incorporated. Retrieved November 22, 2001 from <http://www.decima.ca/research/WhatsNew/010122.asp>.

EGALE Canada. (2001, May 17). Supreme Court rules: Evangelical university teaching graduates can hold discriminatory beliefs—so long as they don't act upon them. Press Release. Retrieved November 25, 2001 from <http://www.islandnet.com/~egale/pressrel/010517.htm>.

Edmunds, M. (1999, December 27). Gay abuse starts at primary school. *Melbourne Herald Sun*. Retrieved December 11, 2001 from <http://www.youth.org/loco/PERSONProject/Alerts/International/abuse3.html>.

Galt, V. (1998, January 13). Hard lessons in Gay Tolerance 101: High-school workshop meets resistance from some students, some principals. *Globe and Mail*. Retrieved December 11, 2001 from < http://www.globe andmail.com>.

Ginsberg, R. W. (1996). *In the triangle/out of the circle: Gay/lesbian students' school experience*. (Abstract). ED.D., Thesis, DAI, Vol. 58-01A, p. 72, 163 pages. Retrieved December 18, 2001 from <http://www.virtualcity.com/youthsuicide/gbsuicide2.htm#105>.

GLEE. (2001). *GLEE project: A network of educational initiatives to combat homophobia and heterosexism*. Retrieved December 11, 2001 from <http://glee.oulu.fi/project.html>.

GLSEN tallies 1000 gay-straight alliances. (2001, November 21). *GLSEN News*. Gay Lesbian and Straight Education Network. Retrieved December 11, 2001 from <http://www.glsen.org/templates/news/>.

Gotowiec, A., & Beiser, M. (1994). Aboriginal children's mental health: Unique challenges. *Canada's Mental Health*, 41(4), 7–11.

Harrington, C. (2000, March 9). *The last frontier of social tolerance: Students combat homophobia by forming gay-straight clubs*. Canadian Press. Retrieved December 11, 2001 from <http://www.youth.org/loco/PERSONProject/Alerts/International/GSAs.html>.

Human Rights Watch. (2001). *Hatred in the hallways: Violence and discrimination against lesbian, gay, bisexual, and transgendered students in U.S. Schools*. Retrieved October 20, 2001 from <http://www.hrw.org/reports/2001/uslgbt/toc.html>.

Kiener, R. (2000, June). What teens really think. *Reader's Digest*. Retrieved October 30, 2001 from <http://www.readersdigest.ca/mag/2000/06/think_teens.html>.

Kirmayer, L. J., Brass, G. M., & Tait, C. L. (2000). The mental health of Aboriginal peoples: Transformations of identity and community. *Canadian Journal of Psychiatry, 45*(7), 607–16.

McCaskell, T. (1999). Homophobic violence in schools. *Orbit,* 29(4), 20–21.

McCaskell, T., & Russell, V. (2000). Anti-homophobia initiatives at the former Toronto Board of Education. In T. Goldstein & D. Selby (Eds.), *Weaving connections: Educating for peace, social and environmental justice.* (pp. 27–56). Toronto: Sumach Press.

McFarland, W. P. (2001). The legal duty to protect gay and lesbian students from violence in school. *Professional School Counseling, 4*(3), 171–79.

MYRBS. (1997). *Massachusetts Youth Risk Behavior Survey.* Massachusetts Department of Education.

Pilkington, N., & D'Augelli, A. R. (1995). Victimization of lesbian, gay, and bisexual youth in community settings. *Journal of Community Psychology* 23(1), 34–56.

Plummer, David. (1999). *One of the Boys: Masculinity and homophobia and modern manhood.* Binghamton, NY: Haworth/Harrington Press. [Publicity release retrieved December 18, 2001 from <http://www.une.edu.au/publicity/newsreleases/november99/111-99.html>.].

Ryan, C., & Futterman, D. (1998). *Lesbian and gay youth: Care and counselling.* Columbia University Press: New York.

Sivertsen, W. D., & Thames, T. B. (1995). Each child that dies: Gays and lesbians in your schools. In J. M. Novak & L. G. Denti, (Eds.), *Multicultures: Unity through diversity. A monograph of diversity in the field of education.* Volume 1. Retrieved December 15, 2001 from <http://www.outproud.org/article_each_child.html>.

Tatum, B. D. (1999). Teaching white students about racism: The search for white allies and the restoration of hope. In I. Shor and C. Pari (Eds.), *Critical literacy in action: Writing words, changing worlds* (pp. 53–67). Portsmouth, NH: Boynton/Cook.

Taylor, C. G. (2002). Beyond empathy: Confronting homophobia in critical education courses. *Journal of Lesbian Studies* 6, 3/4: 219–34. Also published in L. Cramer (Ed.), *Addressing homophobia on college campuses.* New York: Haworth Press.

Trinity Western University v. British Columbia College of Teachers, [2001] 1. S.C.R. Retrieved November 20, 2001 from <http://www.lexum.umontreal.ca/csc-scc/en/pub/2001/vol1/html/2001scr1_0772.html>.

■ ■ ■

Discussion and Writing Suggestions

1. Even though same-sex rights are protected by the Charter of Rights and Freedoms (page 152), the education system has been very slow to start integrating anti-homophobia education into the curriculum. Do you agree with Taylor that schools have a legal and ethical obligation to include anti-homophobia education in the curriculum alongside other instruction in diversity and human rights? If not, do you think that the Charter should be overridden in this regard?
2. It is difficult to know how many lgbt students there are in a particular classroom; but if we use the 10% estimate, and add to that the students who have an lgbt friend or family member, the number of students in the lgbt community is quite large. Were you aware of this sizable group of students in your high school? If so, what made you aware of their existence? If not, why do you suppose you were not aware of their presence?

The Residential School System

MURRAY SINCLAIR AND A. C. HAMILTON

Although Aboriginal people have long said that the justice system of Canada was racist, it was not until 1988, in the aftermath of high-profile cases involving the violent deaths of Aboriginal people, that the province of Manitoba instituted the Aboriginal Justice Inquiry (AJI). When the massive report was released in 1991, it included an analysis of the racist mentality behind the development of the residential school system, with its explicit goals of assimilating Aboriginal people by destroying their culture. The system, together with other aspects of European colonization of Canada, had disastrous effects, one of them being the over-representation of Aboriginal people in the courts and prisons. The entire report can be found at www.ajic.mb.ca/.

The two authors of the report are the Honourable Murray Sinclair and Associate Chief Justice A. C. Hamilton. Sinclair was appointed a Judge of the Manitoba Court of Queen's Bench in 2001, having served since 1988 as Associate Chief Judge of the Provincial Court of Manitoba, an appointment that made him Manitoba's first Aboriginal judge, and Canada's second. (At present there are 18 Aboriginal judges in Canada.) Hamilton was appointed to the Manitoba Court of Queen's Bench in 1971, and as Associate Chief Justice of the Family Division (Manitoba's new Unified Family Court) in 1983; he retired from the Bench in 1993 to focus on mediation work and Aboriginal issues.

Since the time of earliest contact, Aboriginal people and European settlers   1
have seen things from vastly divergent points of view, because their attitudes
and philosophies differed. The interaction of the two groups has been characterized as one of "cooperation and conflict but, more importantly, by

misconceptions and contradictions."[4] One of the first, and perhaps the most enduring, of these misconceptions was that:

> Europeans assumed the superiority of their culture over that of any Aboriginal peoples. Out of that misconception grew the European conviction that in order for the Indians to survive, they would have to be assimilated into the European social order.[5]

At first, these differences had minimal impact upon most Aboriginal   2 people. The missionaries tried to convert Aboriginal people and to mould them into their religious ideal, often with mixed results.

> The Indians . . . had no more idea of religious authority, as opposed to personal beliefs, than they had of a coercive political hierarchy. The individual freedom that was fundamental to Indian culture ruled out both the idea of heresy and of subordinating one's will to priestly guidance. The concept of authority and the respect for it that was inculcated into all civilized peoples provided the missionary and the civilized non-Christian with a common basis of understanding that was totally lacking between the missionary and the Indians of Eastern Canada. The fundamental problem that the Recollets saw impeding their work was that the Indians were too "primitive" to be converted. From this they drew the devastatingly simple conclusion that if they were to convert the Indians they had first to find ways of "civilizing" them.[6]

This was an impossible task as long as Aboriginal people continued to   3 live in vibrant, self-sufficient communities often far removed from the missionaries' influence. However, this did not prevent the missionaries from forming opinions about the ways Aboriginal people raised and taught their children, or from laying the foundation for future misconceptions of Aboriginal child-rearing methods. In view of current ideas about child-rearing, it is interesting to reflect that no aspect of behaviour shocked the French more than their refusal to use physical punishment to discipline their children. On general principles, the Huron considered it wrong to coerce or humiliate an individual publicly. To their own way of thinking, a child was an individual with his or her own needs and rights rather than something amorphous that must be moulded into shape. The Huron feared a child who was unduly humiliated, like an adult, might be driven to commit suicide.[7]

Aboriginal parents taught their children   4

> . . . to assume adult roles in an atmosphere of warmth and affection. Learning emphasized such values as respect for all living things, sharing, self-reliance, individual responsibility, and proper conduct. Children also had to learn how to utilize the environment most effectively for economic survival. Integral to all aspects of the education of the young was the spiritual, and events in the life-cycle from birth to death were marked with ceremonies stressing the individual's link to the spiritual and sacred. Cultural continuity was thus ensured.[8]

The early missionaries also condemned Aboriginal child-rearing methods   7
as being negligent, irresponsible and "uncivilized." This stereotype was to
endure even after Aboriginal people had lost much of their independence
and "in the point of view of the European, the Indian became irrelevant."[9]
From then on, the relationship between Aboriginal people and Europeans
became even more one-sided and paternalistic. Aboriginal people were
reduced to being "wards of the state."[10] All relevant decision-making power
on financial, social or political matters, and even education, came to rest in
the hands of the federal government. Eventually, the cause of "civilizing"
Aboriginal people to European cultures and values evolved into the government policy of "assimilation," and education became "the primary vehicle in
the civilization and advancement of the Indian race."[11]

The federal government had little previous experience in "civilizing"   6
Aboriginal people so it turned to the United States for an example. It sent
Nicholas F. Davin to study the Americans' "aggressive civilization policy,"[12]
based on sending Indian children to large, racially segregated, industrial
schools. Davin was convinced the Americans were correct in their approach
and the only way to "civilize" Aboriginal people was to remove them from
the disruptive influences of the parents and the community. His final comment in the report to Ottawa was representative of attitudes of the time that
" . . . if anything is to be done with the Indian, we must catch him very
young."[13]

The federal government delegated the job of "civilizing" and "educating"   7
Aboriginal people in Canada to religious organizations and churches. It
encouraged the opening of large, industrial residential schools far from
reserves and, later, of boarding schools for younger children nearer to their
homes. There, every aspect of European life, from dress and behaviour to religion and language, was impressed upon the Aboriginal children. The belief
was that Indians were a vanishing race and their only hope of surviving was
to assimilate. Their uncivilized and pagan ways would be replaced by good
Christian values.

The residential school system was a conscious, deliberate and often brutal   8
attempt to force Aboriginal people to assimilate into mainstream society,
mostly by forcing the children away from their languages, cultures and societies. In 1920, during debates in the House of Commons on planned changes
to the *Indian Act*, Duncan Campbell Scott, the Deputy Superintendent of
Indian Affairs, left no doubt about the federal government's aims: "Our
object is to continue until there is not a single Indian in Canada that has not
been absorbed into the body politic and there is no Indian question, and no
Indian department, that is the whole object of this Bill."[14]

The experience of residential schools is one shared by many Aboriginal   9
people all across Canada. That experience was marked by emotional, physical and sexual abuse, social and spiritual deprivation, and substandard education. "Even as assimilation was stated as the goal of education for Native
people," one researcher wrote, "the assimilation was to take place under
conditions which would cause no threat to the surrounding business and

farming community."[15] Few Aboriginal people achieved more than a grade five level of education.

The main goal of residential schools and the assimilation policy, however, was not further education, but, rather, to remove Aboriginal children from the influences of their parents and communities, and to rid them of their languages and cultures. The methods, as one former residential school student explained, often were brutally effective:

> The elimination of language has always been a primary stage in a process of cultural genocide. This was the primary function of the residential school. My father, who attended Alberni Indian Residential School for four years in the twenties, was physically tortured by his teachers for speaking Tseshaht: they pushed sewing needles through his tongue, a routine punishment for language offenders. . . . The needle tortures suffered by my father affected all my family (I have six brothers and six sisters). My Dad's attitude became "why teach my children Indian if they are going to be punished for speaking it?" so he would not allow my mother to speak Indian to us in his presence. I never learned how to speak my own language. I am now, therefore, truly a "dumb Indian."[16]

After the Second World War, the federal government began to reconsider its assimilation policy. It wanted a more effective means of accomplishing the ultimate aims of the policy. This coincided with yet another revamping of the *Indian Act* and another set of hearings at the House of Commons. This also allowed another famous Canadian, noted anthropologist Diamond Jenness, to unveil his "Plan for Liquidating Canada's Indian Problems Within 25 Years." Jenness proposed abolishing Indian reserves, scrapping the treaties and integrating Indian students into the public school system. For the time being, the federal government shelved most of Jenness' proposals. It did, however, heed his suggestion to change the *Indian Act* to allow Indian children to be enrolled in public schools. This event signalled "the beginning of the end for many residential schools."[17]

The effects upon Aboriginal societies of the federal government's residential school system, and its policy of assimilation, have been astounding. Residential schools denigrated Aboriginal cultures, customs and religions, and disrupted the traditional practices of Aboriginal child-rearing and education. They tore apart families and extended families, leaving the children straddling two worlds, the European one and that of their own Aboriginal societies, but belonging to neither. These policies have caused a wound to fester in Aboriginal communities that has left them diminished to this day. In testimony to our Inquiry, Janet Ross said:

> I'd like to begin at the boarding school. The boarding school is where the alienation began. Children were placed there, plucked out of their homes. The bond between parents and children was fragmented severely—some lost forever. Some searched for the love between parent and child endlessly, searching for it in other ways, never to be restored. The boarding schools

taught us violence. Violence was emphasized through physical, corporal punishment, strappings, beatings, bruising and control. We learned to understand that this was power and control. I remember being very confused when someone told me that my natural mother had died. Hence growing up for me not knowing whether my mother was really mine always created some more confusion. I searched for that love in [foster] parents, but that bond had been broken; you felt that it just wasn't there. The boarding schools were extremely influential towards our poor self-image and low self-esteem, because we were continuously put down by the use of text books portraying negative images of Indian people.

The loss of successive generations of children to residential schools, the   13
destruction of Aboriginal economic bases, the decimation of their populations through diseases and the increasing dependence on government welfare have led to social chaos. This manifests itself in Aboriginal communities through staggering poverty rates, high unemployment rates, high suicide rates, lower education levels, high rates of alcoholism and high rates of crime. In individuals, the legacy of the residential schools has been lowered self-esteem, confusion of self-identity and cultural identity, and a distrust of, and antagonism toward, authority.

The residential school experience also resulted in a breakdown in tradi-   14
tional Aboriginal methods of teaching child-rearing and parenting. Entire families once took part in the raising of children. Young parents, like young parents everywhere, learned how to raise their children from their own parents, by example. Traditionally, they also drew upon the examples and advice of their extended families, their grandparents, uncles, aunts and siblings. The residential schools made this impossible. Without that example, many Aboriginal parents today feel that they have never learned how to raise their own children.

Aboriginal communities have not yet recovered from the damage caused   15
by the residential schools. It is only in recent times that children are again being taught close to home. For the first time in over 100 years, many families are experiencing a generation of children who live with parents until their teens. The readjustment to this new situation has been difficult for both the parents and their children. The current generation of parents does not even have its own experiences as children growing up in a unified family upon which to draw.

The damage done by these schools is still evident today, as Aboriginal   16
people struggle to recapture their cultural practices and beliefs. The return of self-identity and self-esteem is a slow process.

Notes

4. Jean Barman, Yvonne Hebert and Don McCaskill, eds., *Indian Education in Canada, Vol. I: The Legacy* (Vancouver: University of British Columbia Press, 1986), p. 2.

5. *Ibid.*

6. Bruce G. Trigger, *The Children of Aataentsic: A History of the Huron People to 1660* (Montreal and Kingston: McGill-Queen's University Press, 1976), p. 378.

7. *Ibid.,* p. 47.

8. Barman, Hebert and McCaskill, *Indian Education in Canada,* p. 3.

9. E. P. Patterson, *The Canadian Indian: A History since 1500* (Don Mills: Collier-Macmillan, 1972), p. 72.

10. Kahn-Tineta Miller and George Lerchs, *The Historical Development of the Indian Act* (Ottawa: Treaties and Historical Research Branch, Department of Indian Affairs and Northern Development, 1978), p. 114.

11. Canada, Department of Indian Affairs and Northern Development, *Annual Report* (Ottawa, 1976), p. 6.

12. N. F. Davin, "Report on Industrial Schools for Indians and Halfbreeds" (Ottawa: Public Archives, 14 March 1879), PAC RG 10, Vol. 6001, File 1-1-1, Part 1.

13. *Ibid.*

14. Cited in J. R. Miller, *Skyscrapers Hide the Heavens: A History of Indian-White Relations in Canada* (Toronto: University of Toronto Press, 1989), pp. 206–7.

15. Celia Haig-Brown, *Resistance and Renewal: Surviving the Indian Residential School* (Vancouver: Tillacum Library, 1988), p. 67.

16. Randy Fred, "Introduction," in *Ibid.*, pp. 1–2.

17. Haig-Brown, *Resistance and Renewal,* p. 28.

■ ■ ■

Discussion and Writing Suggestions

1. What assumptions about the nature of civilization would have served to justify the Canadian government's decision to annihilate "Indian" culture?

2. Has mainstream Canadian society progressed from the clearly racist days in which the residential school system was implemented? Or are there still signs of old beliefs in the superiority of British culture?

3. Do you agree with this thesis statement? "The curriculum of modern-day public schools and private schools continues to serve the interests of dominant culture by marginalizing minority cultures." How could you support (or refute) this thesis based on your own experience?

Civilizing Childhood and *Education and Normalization: The Residential School*

ANNE MCGILLIVRAY

In this extract from a much longer work, Anne McGillivray examines the roots of the residential school program in a racist nineteenth-century concept of adult Indians as children and Indian children as needing to be civilized into Anglo-Canadian culture. McGillivray argues that "the residential schools were maintained far beyond their time, when child welfare policy had moved toward family-centred solutions and interventions were at least overtly based less on class and 'race' than apprehension of harm. The project 'failed dismally' due in large part to Indian resistance."

Dr. McGillivray is a law professor at the University of Manitoba, and the author of many book chapters and journal articles on a wide range of legal topics. Several of her publications address issues concerning the concepts, status, and treatment of children in the Canadian legal system, including Governing Childhood *(Aldershot Press, 1997). A complete list of her work can be found on the University website: www.umanitoba.ca/academic/faculties/law/faculty/ mcgillivray.html.*

Civilizing Childhood

Eighteenth-century utopian constructs of innocence uncontaminated by civi-   1
lization made the "noble savage" a cognate of childhood. As Sir Hector
Langevin observed during the 1876 *Indian Act* debates, "Indians were not in
the same position as white men . . . they were like children to a very great
extent. They, therefore, required a great deal more protection."[33] Nineteenth-
century assimilation policies infantilized the Indian, remaking the adult in the
image of childhood. Indians were in law state wards under the *Indian Act,*
confined to the reserve, subject to protectionist policies (Indian agents, pass
systems, liquor prohibitions),[34] forbidden religious and cultural practices,[35]
subjects of projects of improvement, objects of pity, finally welfare-dependent.

The equation of Aboriginal peoples with childhood and dependency in   2
English foreign policy was reflected in two reports: the 1834 *Report from His
Majesty's Commission for Inquiring into the Administration and Practical
Operation of the Poor Laws* and the 1837 House of Commons *Report of the
Select Committee on Aborigines.* The Select Committee was concerned with
"Native Inhabitants of Countries where British Settlements are made . . . to
promote the spread of civilization among them," while the Commission on
the Poor Laws was concerned with problems of the outcast closer to home.
Both reports provided for special overseers or protectors, proposed training
programs aimed at low-level employment and emphasized assimilation of

their respective target groups into the larger society. Both reports stressed childhood and the need to educate, civilize, and bring into Christianity the young pauper or Aborigine. As the Select Committee on Aborigines noted, "True civilization and Christianity are inseparable: the former has never been found, but as a fruit of the latter."

If the adult "Aborigine" was infantilized in the process of assimilation,   3
the child was literally to be pressed into its service. This arose from a series of changes in Anglo-Canadian ideas about the governance of childhood. This chapter introduces these ideas, taking as illustration two childsaving projects which shared the civilizing vision which came to centre on Aboriginal childhood: the English child migration movement and the Winnipeg Home of the Friendless.

Childhood is both focus and creation of civilization, a life stage dedicated   4
to the inculcation of a sociospecific citizenship. By the close of the 18th century, childhood had fully emerged as a legally and socially distinct life estate and numerous European constructs of childhood were extant.[36] By the last third of the 19th century, childhood was identified as both social problem and locus of charitable and state projects of citizenship. The health, welfare and rearing of children, as Rose observed, was "linked in thought and practice to the destiny of the nation and the responsibilities of the state,"[37] an association which was to make childhood "the most intensively governed sector of human existence." In the late 19th-century shift from government *of* the family to governance *through* the family,[38] the child became a symptom of relational problems within the family and between family and state, a major point of entry into the family for the new complex of family-oriented tutelary disciplines and agencies empowered to remove children from "abnormal" environments. Intervention and removal primarily affected families of marginal social status, while expert tutelage, being "voluntary," was to have a broader impact. Childhood was, in effect, colonized by the state.

The governance of childhood was aimed at the induction of a docile cit-   5
izenship, the creation of a disciplined soul. What motivated the "great project," Rose argues, was not the "repressive desire for surveillance and control" initially posited by Foucault. It was, rather,

> a profoundly humanistic and egalitarian project, one that searched for the causes of failure of citizenship and sought to provide the knowledge that was to ensure the extension of the benefits of society to all its members.[39]

Where the "members" had no perception of themselves as such, and no desire to join, this humanistic project of reform might well be perceived as "repressive surveillance."

The shift in relations between "childhood" and state was reflected in the   6
massive expansion of child welfare powers and programs in late 19th-century Canada.[40] The province of Manitoba, carved out of the North-West Territories in 1870, based its child welfare legislation on that of Ontario. The Ontario *Humane Societies Act* had been amended to give animal protection groups the power to remove children from the lawful custody of parents and

guardians for neglect or mistreatment (*qua* the New York *Mary Ellen* case) but the need for separate societies and legislation became apparent. Canadian child law reformer J. J. Kelso wrote in his diary 10 January, 1890, "The difficulty is cropping up of keeping the animals and children from clashing, the two having their separate and distinct friends."[41] Ontario legislation was appropriately amended and Manitoba followed suit, instituting a system of quasi-charitable Children's Aid Societies in 1891 and enacting its *Child Protection Act* in 1898. (The Children's Aid Society model is extant in Manitoba and Ontario but was never adopted by provinces further west.)

The spate of reform continued in Manitoba, as elsewhere, into the next ⁷ century. In place of a single statute based on the Tudor Poor Laws (the Manitoba *Apprentices and Minors Act, 1877*), there were by 1913 a multitude of statutory provisions in Manitoba empowering agencies to apprehend children for parental delict (neglect and abuse, immoral conduct) and delict of the child (vagrancy, truancy, expulsion from school, petty crime, exposure to immorality). The apprehended child would be placed in a normalizing environment, at first the industrial school; later, under the Kelso family model, in a foster family. By the 1920s, child welfare philosophy was moving away from child apprehension and institutional regimes, instead favouring family therapy and family-based settings.[42] Professional social workers and university-based experts were replacing the charitable amateur, to become the new "owners" of child welfare. To honour the new therapeutic commitment, "child protection" was renamed "child and family services."

The new childsaving, despite the renaming, shared much with the old. ⁸

> Despite the advancement of new ideas and procedures, the ultimate goal … remained unchanged from that of earlier generations of middle-class child-savers: to avoid present and future expenditures on public welfare and to guarantee social peace and stability by transforming dependent children into industrious, law-abiding workers.[43]

The new expertise legitimated the middle-class bias of child welfare estab- ⁹ lished by 19th-century moral crusaders and poor and non-anglophone families continued to be singled out. The new agencies and experts defined the normative family according to certain assumptions,

> first, that the natural, inevitable, and highest form of the family is a particular type of household arrangement—a nuclear unity comprising two adults in a monogamous, heterosexual, legal marriage, and their dependent children; second, that the family is premised on the biological or sexual division of labour that gives each member a different, but complementary, role with attendant obligations; third, the family is a private haven that operates on the basis of consensus as opposed to the public sphere of the marketplace where competition and conflict prevail.[44]

The construct has central implications for Aboriginal child welfare: it ¹⁰ omits the childcare networks of kith and kin which function in pre-industrial societies to intervene in times of difficulty and provide alternate caregiving[45] and it ignores the complex extended-family structure of original societies. It is a monolithic construct[46] tailored to justify state intervention in "abnormal" families.

Canadian child welfare philosophy prior to the Second World War was   11
imbricated in a social Darwinism which read into "survival of the fittest" a Canadian imperialism aspiring to equal partnership with England in the Empire.[47] The Canadian social purity movement embraced this vision of citizenship in its therapeutic focus on cleanliness and purity, medical and moral hygiene. The movement evangelicized a nativism which excised Aboriginal peoples from the Canadian landscape and viewed childhood as a blank slate upon which could be inscribed a chosen character. While the child might be irredeemably tainted by parental shortcomings, ethnicity or race, the enterprise, due to much confusion about eugenics and determinism, was nonetheless worth the try. Child welfare in the age of moral hygiene was characterized by an "unabashed" interventionism in which sociology and religion formed a seamless web: "the perfect sociology, perfectly applied, will realize the Kingdom of God on Earth."[48]

The English child migration movement exemplified the imperialist project   12
of citizenship and provides parallels to the "normalization" of Aboriginal children. Beginning in 1618 with a group of "orphaned and destitute" children sent from England to Virginia and lasting 350 years, 150 000 British children aged four to fourteen were exported to the colonies for apprenticeship as farm and household labourers.[49] Two out of three were sent to Canada, the "healthiest" colony, between 1870 and 1925 in the evangelical entrepreneurship of such Victorian childsavers as "Dr." Thomas Barnardo and the infamous Maria Rye. Under banners of Empire and child-saving, health and opportunity, children were exported to save public welfare costs and costs of future delinquency, and to fill colonial needs for cheap labour and English stock. Fear of uncivilized children was also a motive. A contemporary poem urged, perhaps tongue-in-cheek,[50]

> Take them away! Take them away!
> Out of the gutter, the ooze, and the slime,
> Where the little vermin paddle and crawl
> Till they grow and ripen in crime.

The conclusion reflects 19th-century beliefs in the restorative powers of the New World: "The new shall repair the wrongs of the old."

At least two-thirds of child migrants were not orphans, as the public and   13
the publicity supposed, but children placed in institutional care, primarily by parents and often on a temporary basis, and exported without consent. Many lost all contact with family. Despite sharing a language and "mother" culture with the colonies which received them, the children experienced cultural disorientation, discrimination as the "offal of the most depraved characters in the city of the old country," much physical and sexual abuse, emotional loss and inadequate and sometimes deadly living conditions. Moral panics circled about the child migrants. "Much crime, drunkenness and prostitution was

seen as a result," wrote a late 19th-century Winnipeg correspondent, although the *Winnipeg Free Press* observed that most of the "crimes" in question were committed by local children. Labour unions complained that the child migrants were driving the working man out of the workplace.[51] The children were morally and genetically unfit to associate with Canadian children, wrote the prestigious Dr. Kenneth Clarke after sharing a train with a new shipment. "In Canada we are deliberately adding to our population hundreds of children bearing all the stigmata of physical and mental degeneracy" and the government should be held criminally liable. The 1893 "Highways and Hedges" magazine of the English National Children's Homes Society was in accord.

> For some of them are of poor human material; their constitution—physical and mental—is of inferior texture; they are naturally deficient in force of character and moral stamina; their antecedents were once vicious or at least unpromising; the sad entail of hereditary weakness or wickedness makes these unfortunate juveniles peculiarly the objects of our compassionate and continuous care ... Canada is no place to shoot rubbish. It is a magnificent British colony waiting for development ...

The majority of children were sent to Ontario and Manitoba and were a common feature of rural life.[52] These provinces not being places "to shoot rubbish," restrictive legislation was enacted in 1897 which prohibited, under penalty of a fine of $100 or 3 months' imprisonment, immigration of any child 14

> who has been reared or who has resided amongst habitual criminals, or any child whose parents have been habitual criminals, lunatics or idiots, or weak-minded or defective constitutionally or confirmed paupers, or diseased ...

Canada stopped accepting the children in 1925 due to new and more expensive ideas about child welfare management (vetted placements and follow-up visits, for example) at the onset of the Depression.[53] These new ideas about child welfare were not without their opponents on the homefront. 15

The Winnipeg Home of the Friendless, an evangelical "Christian refuge of last resort" for "orphaned or destitute" children and unwed mothers, was founded and run by Kansas evangelist Laura Crouch from 1900 to 1929. The Home was exempted from child welfare legislation by certificate of incorporation in 1913, a timely move as provincial powers of investigation and apprehension were reaching a temporary zenith. Empowered to refuse direct access of any "person or agency" (including parents) to child inmates, and to apprentice or adopt out any child without consent of child or parent, the Home was privately funded by a wealthy grocer (Crouch testified she began operation with $5.00 and prayer provided the rest), held impressive rural and urban properties and operated two farms run on child labour.[54] Sixty-three former inmates testified before a provincial inquiry to beatings with straps, laths and switches—some "for cause," others ritual; to fear and intimidation, inadequate diet, isolation in cellars for up to four weeks at a time, 15 to 20 16 hour workdays, badly crowded dormitories, forced religious observance (Crouch evangelized a doomsday "holy roller" cult), lack of medical help and inadequate education. All complaints were dismissed.

Those who managed the Home were "extremely earnest Christian   17 people" while "retrospective recollections of happenings in youth are apt to be distorted, unduly favourable or the reverse," wrote Deputy Minister of Education Dr. Robert Fletcher in his 1927 report. The corporal punishment described by witnesses was deserved, exaggerated or fabricated. Fletcher mused on the religious benefits of such punishment.

> Notwithstanding that physical punishment is no remedy at all for the disease of mind and body complained of, we are further impressed with the religious possibilities in the matter. The strictest mentor is he or she who lives by the letter rather than by the spirit ... The true object of all punishment is to reform the mind of the victim.

Fletcher viewed the conflicting views expressed before his inquiry—   18 "Social investigators claim to have been refused admission to the premises, the Home officials say they have been spied upon"—as conflicts of ideology caused by a "fundamental difference in policy" between the new social work and the religious mandate of the Home.

> Social workers today have as objective the placing of every homeless child with a family in a home with adoptive or foster parents ... The Home of the Friendless is conducted on diametrically opposed lines. It is not only an institutional home for children but also it endeavours to absorb those children for life as workers ... and in the religious work [of the Home] ...

Fletcher was sufficiently impressed by Crouch and her staff that he rec-   19 ommended that the Home continue operation and be given a tax bailout by the province. This was not done. The Home was closed in 1929 for failure to pay taxes. Its huge property holdings—"The farm equipment alone is large even in western conception"—became the object of a series of disputed property grabs by city and province. The children were seized by provincial authorities. Crouch took the remainder of her flock to British Columbia, where her Burnaby operation was shut down 10 years later amid similar controversy.

The history of the Home of the Friendless illustrates the endurance and   20 sanctioning of the 19th-century institutional model well into the Progressive Era of professional childsaving and foster care. It further illustrates inadequacies of the new child welfare legislation and philosophy. Children's Aid Society workers had attempted over a 10-year period, without success, to gain access to Home records and child inmates. Questions were raised in the Manitoba legislature. Affidavits of former inmates were taken by Percy Paget, Chair of the Board of Welfare Supervision and it was these, together with the direct testimony of former inmates, which formed the basis of evidence before the inquiry. Claims of inadequate educational curriculum rather than of child maltreatment may have finally attracted government action, as child welfare and education were a single department at the time. The Fletcher report did recommend that "no new child-caring institution be permitted to commence operation in Manitoba until it shows itself willing to subscribe to … lawful Government requirements."

The Home's practices of isolation, corporal punishment, child labour,   21 minimal education, regimentation, evangelicism and cultural devaluation— many of its inmates were the children of immigrants—illustrate strategies for the governance of childhood which disabled distinctions between corporal punishment and abuse, child labour and exploitation, minimal education and inadequate education. These distinctions were unclear even to government policy-makers, as the competing views of Fletcher and Paget demonstrate.

Child migration and the residential schooling exemplified in the Home of   22 the Friendless were designed to normalize childhood by instilling values of Anglo-Canadian Christian citizenship in the children of the poor. The fact that they were challenged by the "new" childsaving of the first decades of the 20th century illustrates competing modes of child management—foster care and family support versus the orphanage, industrial school or reformatory; family model versus institutional model—rather than a fundamental dis- agreement with earlier technologies of transformation and normalization. The perishing child and the dangerous child were to be reformed by corporal punishment, regimentation and surveillance, isolation from kin and culture, cultural devaluation, religious indoctrination, education tailored to social status and child labour, whatever the model. These technologies were appro- priated for assimilating the Aboriginal child. Indian residential schools were closely modelled on mainstream 19th-century institutional regimes for nor- malizing childhood. Like the Home of the Friendless, Indian residential schools escaped the attentions of the new childsaving by virtue of an insulat- ing legal regime.

Education and Normalization: The Residential School

Aboriginal parenting practices shocked early observers. The Jesuit missionary   23 Le Jeune spent the winter of 1633–34 with the Montaignais, a Quebec Algonkian people linguistically and culturally related to the Plains Cree. His observations of Aboriginal childhood point to an unusual freedom to exper- iment, inclusion in the adult activities of the community and, worst of all, no corporal punishment but only a single reprimand as a last resort. Le Jeune concluded that removal from family and tribe was essential to the institution of a proper educational regime. In his imagined regime, the children would have a period of complete freedom to accustom them to the pleasures of European food and clothing such that "they will have a horror of Savages and their filth." A disciplinary regime, with appropriate corporal punishments, would then be introduced.[55] Le Jeune's was perhaps the earliest example of a normalization scheme for Aboriginal childhood based on residential school- ing and corporal punishment. This chapter is a brief survey of Indian resi- dential schooling in Canada.

The foundations of a mission school which would board Aboriginal chil-   24
dren at Red River were laid by Hudson's Bay Company chaplain John West
on his arrival at the trading post of York Factory in August 1820.[56] West was
immediately impressed with the need for his services. The "corrupt influence
and barter of spirituous liquors at a Trading Post" made it "peculiarly incumbent upon me to seek to ameliorate their sad condition, as degraded, emaciated, and wandering in ignorance." Further, "some spoke of impossibilities in
the way of teaching them Christianity or the first rudiments of settled and civilized life." West had a ready answer for this problem on his first contact with
the new world and its indigenous inhabitants. The answer was childhood.

> If little hope could be cherished of arresting the adult Indian in his wan-
> derings and unsettled habits of life, it appeared to me, that a wide and
> most extensive field, presented itself for cultivation in the instruction of
> the native children. With the aid of an interpreter, I spoke to an Indian
> called Withawee-capo, about taking two of his boys to the Red River
> Colony with me to educate and maintain. He yielded to my request; and
> I shall never forget the affectionate manner in which he brought the
> eldest in his arms, and placed him in the canoe on the morning of my
> departure . . . I considered that I bore a pledge from the Indian that many
> more children might be found, if an Establishment was formed in British
> Christian sympathy, and British liberality for their education and support
> (15 August, 1820).

West sought Hudson's Bay Company support for his "Establishment."   25
His argument was not based on Christian sympathy for the noble savage but,
more cleverly, on the threat to social order posed by deserted "Half Caste
children" who must "equally claim the attention of the Christian
Philanthropist with those who are of pure Aboriginal blood."

> I have suggested to the Committee of the H. B. Company the importance
> of collecting and educating the numerous Half Breed children, whose par-
> ents have died or deserted them, and who are found running about the dif-
> ferent Factories in ignorance and idleness. Neglected as they hitherto
> have been, they grow up in great depravity, and should they be led to
> "find their grounds" with the Indians, it cannot be a matter of surprise,
> if at any time collectively, or in parties they should threaten the peace of
> the country and the safety of the Trading Posts (12 August, 1822).

This was an astute appeal to the widespread fears of unmediated childhood
which propelled 19th-century evangelical childsaving.

Parents posed a problem. Like Le Jeune before him, West saw the need to   26
separate child from mother culture and from the mother.

> [T]he last two Indian Saulteaux boys have given us a little trouble in dis-
> ciplining them to the school, from the mother living constantly about the
> settlement, and occasionally visiting them, when they have run off with
> their sisters to the wigwam (20 April, 1823).

This convinced him that "it is far better to obtain the children from a distance, as those who are in the school and at a distance from their parents soon become reconciled to the restraint, and happy upon the Establishment."[57] West returned to England disappointed by the failure of the Hudson's Bay Company to support his efforts. His Mission, however, was not lost.

The 1842 Bagot Commission recognized the difficulty of assimilating Aboriginal children who remained in contact with families. The Commission recommended as antidote the establishment of farm-based boarding schools far away from parental influence and interference. Residential schooling was approved by the Upper Canada Chiefs gathered at Orillia in 1846 who agreed to pay one-fourth of their annuities for 25 years in support of the school, although they objected to its assimilationist agenda. The system was extended in Upper Canada in the 1850s and 1860s. The Indian Department sent lawyer-journalist Nicholas Davin to investigate the United States model of "aggressive civilization" which removed Plains Aboriginal youth "from the tribal way of life" for industrial school training. Davin's 1879 *Report on Industrial Schools for Indians and Half-breeds* reflected the Bagot Commission conclusion that the schools worked best when farm-based and church-run.   27

The Canadian system was designed for Indian Affairs by Egerton Ryerson, Chief Superintendent of Education for Upper Canada. Ryerson led the campaign in the latter half of the 19th century for the establishment of a system of free universal compulsory education which would, he believed, create social cohesion by inculcating a common morality. Ryerson objected in principle to industrial schooling, as it segregated the children of the poor, but conceded it would do for the "worst" children. These presumably included Aboriginal children. His "Indian industrial schools" "were to give [the Indian] a plain English education adapted to the working farmer and mechanic" and would include a strong Christian component because "nothing can be done to improve and elevate [the Indian's] character without the aid of religious feeling." The schools were to be joint undertakings of the federal Indian Department and major Christian denominations, supported by contributory child labour.   28

Although the precedent system of small mission schools like West's proposed "Establishment" continued, Indian Affairs policy shifted in favour of industrial and boarding schools (a distinction dropped in 1923 for the term "residential school"). Beginning in the 1880s in fulfilment of the Numbered Treaty obligations to educate Indian children, the residential school system expanded throughout the Northwest, the former territory of the Hudson's Bay Company and West's original mission. West's "Half-breed children" had no place in official Indian policy. In total, 80 schools were constructed, most in the Prairie region. Between 1901 and 1961, the percentage of registered Indian children enrolled in residential schools fluctuated between 12 per cent and 37 per cent. In 1936, 42 per cent of Manitoba Indian children were registered in a residential school. This compares with 3 per cent in Quebec, 36 per cent in Ontario, 77 per cent in Saskatchewan, and 98 per cent in Alberta.[58]   29

The schools were to be located as far as possible from the Indian bands.   30
As a member of Parliament explained in 1883,[59]

> [i]f these schools are to succeed, we must not have them too near the
> bands; in order to educate the children properly we must separate them
> from their families. Some people may say this is hard, but if we want to
> civilize them we must do that.

Children between the ages of three or four and 14 were taken from their   31
parents and "villages," by now "reserves," to schools hundreds of kilometres
away. Their hair was cut or shaved off, they were separated by age and
gender, denied sibling contact and given new names. The curriculum consisted
of morning classes, rarely above a grade 3–5 level, with field or house work
for the rest of the day. Only English speech was permitted, reflecting conscious assimilation and unconscious racial superiority. The poet Matthew
Arnold, then British Inspector of Schools, had written in 1852 of the link
between language and empire.[60]

> It must always be the desire of a government to render its dominions, as
> far as possible, homogenous. Sooner or later the difference of language
> . . . will probably be effaced . . . an event which is socially and politi-
> cally desirable.

A similar philosophy underlay residential school policy. Speaking an   32
Aboriginal language was prohibited or severely restricted and punishment for
infraction could be severe.[61] The efficacy of a residential school education
depended equally on removal from family and culture, and on "precept and
example." According to the 1889 Indian Affairs *Annual Report*,[62]

> The boarding school disassociates the Indian child from the deleterious
> home influences to which he would otherwise be subjected. It reclaims him
> from the uncivilized state in which he has been brought up. It brings him
> into contact from day to day with all that tends to effect a change in his
> views and habits of life. By precept and example he is taught to endeav-
> our to excel in what will be most useful to him.

Removal of children from "the demoralizing and degrading influence of   33
the tepees," as the *Calgary Herald* rather crudely put it in 1892, was necessary
to the program. But a Presbyterian missionary wrote home in 1903 that the
schools were no more than an attempt "to educate & colonize a people
against their will."[63]

Nineteenth-century imperialism was carried into 20th-century Indian   34
Affairs policy under the stewardship of Duncan Campbell Scott, whose service
lasted from 1878 to 1932. By 1909, assimilation was becoming less "aggressive" due to cost, tactical resistance and the successful marginalization of
Plains Indians. The path of Prairie settlement having been cleared, the path of
assimilation was less important and citizenship through protective segregation—a slower assimilation—now became the justification for continuing the

Indian Affairs policy of apartheid. Scott, mid-career as Indian Affairs Superintendent of Education, wrote of the change in 1909.[64]

> The government and the churches have abandoned, to a large extent, previous policies which attempted to "Canadianize" the Indians. Through a process of vocational, and to a smaller extent academic training, they are now attempting to make good Indians, rather than poor mixtures of Indians and whites. While the idea is still Christian citizenship, the government now hopes to move towards this end by continuing to segregate the Indian population, in large measure from the white races.

Despite a gradual relaxation of policy—newer schools were located closer to the bands; language restrictions were eased—resistance to schooling increased. In summer breaks, familial and cultural norms were confusingly reasserted. Some children had lost their Aboriginal language and skills but by summer's end had lost their English. Children resisted by speaking their own languages, playing truant or avoiding the Indian agent who collected children at summer's end. A few engaged in acts of violence or arson. Parents resisted, visiting against the rules (one Saskatchewan school built a sleeping porch for parents, to the consternation of the Bishop), withdrawing children because of corporal punishment practices, removing instructors for physical or sexual abuse, boycotting schools with overt assimilationist policies, fighting for the establishment of schools which would give their children a European education without Christian indoctrination, refusing to enrol their children without assurance of non-conversion. Although an "English" education was sought and valued by Aboriginal peoples who recognized the inevitability of change, assimilation was consistently rejected.

Some children may have been assimilated, depending on how success is here defined. Certainly the schools produced children who had learned enough for effective resistance and who became 20th-century social and political leaders—"the most promising pupils are found to have retrograded and to have become leaders in the pagan life of the reserves," Scott wrote in 1913. Up to one half of all children enrolled prior to 1914 never went home. Indian Affairs medical officer P. H. Bryce reported in 1912 that "It is quite within the mark to say that 50 per cent of the children who passed through these schools did not live to benefit from the education which they received therein."[65] There are rumours of unmarked graves behind residential schools, said to hold the infanticided offspring of nuns.[66] If such graves exist, it is probable that they hold the unclaimed bodies of child victims of tuberculosis. The disease was spread in the stifling conditions of crowded and airless dormitory life during the long harsh Prairie winters and by the English love of brass bands, the instruments being vectors of the disease. "TB" sanitariums still dot the Prairie landscape. These child deaths were an unforeseen example of resolving "the Indian problem" by extermination, not by war, genocide, starvation, ignorance or neglect, but by "doing good."

Other children graduated to a life which did not accommodate their skills   37
and whose skills they had lost. The non-nurturing attentions of instructors,
early and prolonged separation from parents and siblings and the experience
of institutional life did not teach residential school pupils either Aboriginal or
Euro/Anglo–Canadian parenting norms. Corporal punishment, a longstanding
feature of European education,[67] was an important part of the regime and
came to symbolize the cultural and social destruction of the residential school
experience. Some schools had a "discipline officer" whose rod required a certain number of weekly strokes.[68] William Clarence Thomas, Superintendent,
Peguis School Board, told the Kimelman Inquiry in 1985 that[69]

> [o]ne school principal in Brandon used to call us God's children three
> times on Sundays at the three services and the rest of the week call us dirty
> little Indians. No one ever told us they loved us. We were mere numbers.
> Strapping, beatings, hair cut to baldness, being tethered to the flag pole, half
> day school with unqualified tutors, and slave labour the other half . . .

Janet Ross told the 1991 Manitoba Aboriginal Justice Inquiry that

> [t]he boarding school is where the alienation began. Children were placed
> there, plucked out of their homes. The bond between parents and children
> was fragmented severely—some lost forever . . . The boarding schools
> taught us violence. Violence was emphasized through physical, corporal
> punishment, strapping, beatings, bruising and control. We learned to
> understand that this was power and control.

Many children were sexually abused by teachers and clerics or by older   38
children who had been similarly abused; most were controlled through abase-
ment, cultural devaluation, humiliation and corporal punishment. The
Aboriginal Justice Inquiry summarized the experience as one "marked by
emotional, physical and sexual abuse, social and spiritual deprivation, and
substandard education . . . Aboriginal communities have not yet recovered
from the damage."[70] Sexual use of children, corporal punishment and damaged parent-child bonds, recognized precursors of abuse, infiltrated reserve
childhood. Economic disintegration leading to apathy and substance abuse
provided the conditions of neglect and an environment in which child abuse
as defined by child welfare policy and legislation could flourish.

The residential schools were maintained far beyond their time, when   39
child welfare policy had moved toward family-centred solutions and interventions were at least overtly based less on class and "race" than apprehension of harm. The project "failed dismally" due in large part to Indian
resistance[71] and the last schools (excepting a few which were turned over to
First Nations management) were closed in the 1960s. The dream of empire
which fuelled the assimilation of Indian childhood, as it fuelled assimilation
of the children of poor and the marginalized through child migration and
19th-century child welfare, backfired. The imperialist mission of recon-
structing Indian childhood on an Anglo-Canadian model made residential

schooling an important symbol of assimilation and cultural destruction. A second system has emerged as an equally powerful symbol of cultural genocide: the 20th-century child protection system.

■ ■ ■

Notes

33. Miller, 1989, *supra note* 10 at 191.

34. The pass system was instituted to control movements during the summer of 1885 in the wake of the North-West Rebellion and was virtually unenforced by 1893 but the petty power it gave federal Indian Agents has long been a sore point. Control over band membership, reserve access and use of alcohol on-reserve are now governed by band by-law.

35. Delegitimation creates resistance. The custom of the potlatch, for example, died out as a cultural practice in Alaska, where it was not prohibited, long before it died out in Canada, where it was illegal.

36. Stone describes four views of the nature of the child which had emerged by the mid-19th century, "the adoption of each of which profoundly affects the way [the child] is treated": born in Original Sin and requiring total subordination of will to adult authority (the "religious" view); born *tabula rasa,* entirely malleable (the "environmental" view); born with character and potential predetermined but somewhat susceptible to improvement through education (the "biological" view); born good and corrupted by society (the "Utopian" view, crystallized in Rousseau's *Emile*). L. Stone, *The Family, Sex and Marriage in England 1500–1800* (Pelican, 1979) 254. These competing visions of childhood are all visible in 19th-century childhood discourse and protection policy.

37. N. Rose, *Governing the Soul: The Shaping of the Private Self* (Routledge, 1989) 257. See R. Dingwall *et al.,* "Childhood as a Social Problem: A Survey of the History of Legal Regulation" (1984) 11 J. *Law and Society;* M. D. A. Freeman, *The Rights and Wrongs of Children* (Pinter, 1983). The difference for late 19th-century child welfare is one of degree.

38. J. Donzelot, *The Policing of Families* (Hutchinson, 1980). Donzelot's observation that the changing governance of childhood improved conditions for children and women is not borne out to any great degree in this study of Aboriginal childhood.

39. Rose, *supra* note 37 at 186.

40. J. Ursel, *Private Lives, Public Policy: 100 Years of State Intervention in the Family* (Women's Press, 1992). The new interest in the regulation of childhood and the statutory augmentation of state powers is seen in England, France, and the United States, with remarkable similarities in provisions and justifications.

41. Kelso was a key figure in the development of the Canadian foster care system, Children's Aid Societies, statutory powers of apprehension and the juvenile

court. See J. Bullen, "J. J. Kelso and the 'New' Child-savers: The Genesis of the Children's Aid Movement in Ontario" (1990) 82 *Ontario History* 107. The need for new legislation was publicized in the New York "Mary Ellen" case, in which a child houseworker was removed from abusive guardians under animal protection legislation, there being no other legal grounds for her apprehension.

42. D. E. Chunn, *From Punishment to Doing Good: Family Courts and Socialized Justice in Ontario 1890–1940* (University of Toronto Press, 1992); Ursel, note 36; L. Gordon, *Heroes of Their Own Lives: The Politics and History of Family Violence, Boston 1880–1960* (Penguin, 1988); C. Hooper, "Child Sexual Abuse and the Regulation of Women: Variations on a Theme" in C. Smart, ed., *Regulating Womanhood: Historical Essays on Marriage, Motherhood and Sexuality* (Routledge, 1992).

43. Bullen, *supra* note 41 at 157–58. Children were placed on farms, given a bare education, subjected to "many obvious injustices" and "condemned to a working-class world that offered few opportunities for personal development and social mobility."

44. Chunn, *supra* note 42 at 36.

45. See J. Korbin, *Child Abuse and Neglect: Cross-Cultural Perspectives* (University of California Press, 1981). The "norm" is also heterosexually biased and omits family formations which do not include children.

46. M. Eichler, *Families in Canada Today: Recent Changes and Their Policy Consequences* (Gage, 1983). Eichler calls this the "monolithic bias." Closely linked is the "conservative bias" which includes "a tendency to either ignore children altogether, or to see them merely as objects to be acted upon, rather than as active participants in family life."

47. M. Valverde, *The Age of Light, Soap and Water: Moral Reform in English Canada, 1885–1925* (McClelland & Stewart, 1991). Valverde establishes linkages between hygiene (cleanliness, moral reform, social and racial purity); Canadian nativism (anglo-Protestant patriotism which sought to identify a "native" Canadian identity in the British Empire); and the "unabashed" interventionism of social work. "Nativism" was most strident on the Prairies, "fantastical" in view of the fact that Western Canada was neither administratively nor in its general population "white," until late in the 19th century (107–8).

48. *Ibid.* at 54, citing Canadian Methodist minister Samuel Dwight Chown, one of the first of the proto-professionals to attempt the reconciliation of social science and religious values.

49. An estimated 11 per cent of the Canadian population may be their descendants. The last group left England in 1967. See P. Bean and J. Melville, *Lost Children of the Empire: The Untold Story of Britain's Child Migrants* (Unwin Hyman, 1990). The movement was both "welfarist" and "instrumentalist" according to J. Eekalaar, "The Chief Glory: The Export of Children from the U.K." (1994) 4 J. *Law and Society* 487. For a Canadian perspective, see K. Bagnell, *The Little Immigrants* (Macmillan, 1980).

50. "The Departure of the Innocents" in Bean and Melville, *ibid.* at 59.

51. Untrue, given the children's farm or domestic placement and lack of skills, but effective in the enactment of Canadian child labour laws which tended to benefit adults rather than children.

52. For depictions of Manitoba "Barnardo boys" in fiction, see R.J.C. Stead, *The Bail Jumper* (Briggs, 1914) and E.A.W. Gill, *Love in Manitoba* (Musson, 1911). In both novels, the "Barnardo boys" are ill-treated, of problematic morals and all but nameless. Gill, a cleric with St. John's Cathedral Winnipeg on leave from England, also wrote *A Manitoba Chore Boy: Letters From an Emigrant* (London Religious Tract Society, 1908), a glowing account of a year on a Manitoba farm aimed at juvenile readers and overt propaganda for child migration.

53. The economic value of child labour was vitiated by child labour laws and by political and economic change. Exploitation of the "Home" children was apparent by the turn of the century and lack of follow-up by British child export agencies was strongly criticized by Canadian observers. Imperialism shaped child welfare until the "Great War" changed Canada's relations with England and ended colonialist aspirations. The Depression coincided with "The Dirty Thirties" of Prairie drought and deep poverty.

54. *Home of the Friendless Report of the Investigating Committee, 1926* (Manitoba Sessional Paper No. 47). The Home's purpose, according to its Articles of Incorporation, was "sheltering, relieving, assisting, reclaiming or otherwise dealing with the fallen, helpless, destitute and afflicted, or other person, whether male or female, needing help, protection or assistance including children." Its religious agenda was protected by the provision that "No person shall hold the office of directress or manager unless she shall be an Evangelical Protestant." The Home could contract for an "absolute and uninterrupted custody of and control" of children "which shall be upheld by all courts." Control of girls would cease at 18, of boys at 16. As the 1926 Report noted, the provisions were "in obvious conflict with both the spirit and the letter of general provisions of *The Child Welfare Act*" of 1922; s. 188 of that Act exempted the Home from its general provisions, permitting only a right of inspection. This was a "bare right" according to its Directress. The Articles were based on those of the Winnipeg Children's Home, incorporated in 1887. S. 188 was amended effective 23 April, 1926, in consultation with Crouch, to authorize the public inquiry. The evidence points strongly to a spy on the Fletcher committee, alerting Crouch to "surprise" Home inspections. I am grateful to Dr. Len Kaminski, University of Manitoba, for sharing this important archival research with me and for his helpful discussions on the implications and aftermath of the Report.

55. L.R. Bull, "Indian Residential Schooling: the Native Perspective" (1991) 18 (Supplement) *Canadian Journal of Native Education* 3 at 14–15. On residential schools, see also note 10 generally; J.R. Miller, "Owen Glendower, Hotspur, and Canadian Indian Policy" in Miller, 1991, note 10; Aboriginal Justice Inquiry, note 9; N.R. Ing, "The Effects of Residential Schools on Native Child-Rearing Practices" (1991) 18 (Supplement) *Canadian Journal of Native Education* 65; Cariboo Tribal Council and University of Guelph,

"Faith Misplaced: Lasting Effects of Abuse in a First Nations Community" (1991) 18 *Canadian Journal of Native Education* 161; J. Gresko, "White "Rites" and Indian "Rites": Indian Education and National Responses in the West, 1870–1910" in D.C. Jones *et al.*, *Shaping the Schools of the Canadian West* (Detsilig, 1979) at 84.

56. Reverend John West, First Priest of the Church of England in the Red River Settlement in the Years 1820 to 1823, *The British North West American Indians With Free Thoughts on the Red River Settlement* (typescript copy of the original diary manuscript, St. John College Library, University of Manitoba). "In my appointment as Chaplain to the [Hudson's Bay] Company, my instructions were to reside at the Red River Settlement; and under the encouragement and support of the Church Missionary Society, I was to seek the Instruction and to ameliorate the condition of the native Indians." West embarked 27 May, 1820 at Graves End on the company ship *Eddystone*. His diary records many instances of the care taken by Indian parents of their children "of whom they were passionately fond" (yet "they brutally lend their daughters of tender age, for a few beads, or a little tobacco"). He returned 10 September, 1823 with a disappointing letter from Governor Simpson which elicited the observation that "the resolves of Council in Hudson's Bay relative to the amelioration of the condition of the Indians, and promoting morality and religion in the country, were like the acts of the west Indian legislatures passed professedly with a view to the promoting of religion among the slaves: *worse than nullities.*" Costs of his "Establishment" must fall to Mission charity. I am grateful to Russell Smandych for bringing the manuscript to my attention.

57. The mother, a widow who refused to entrust her daughters to West, secretly took her sons away amid rumours that West would "cut off the ears of one of them for leaving the school without leave." West makes mention of the jealousy of "the Catholics" of his "Native Indian School Establishment," with the inference that this was the source of the rumours: "The attempt is made to prejudice the minds of the Indians against giving their children, insinuating that I wish to collect them, with the intention of taking them to England." The mother's decampment was occasioned by preparations of West's ally Chief Pigewis [Peguis] to make war on her people, the Sioux. West's hopes of addressing Peguis' tribe on educating their children were frustrated: "Oh! what faith, and patience, and perseverance are necessary lest the mind should grow weary in the arduous work of seeking to evangelize the Heathen" (*ibid.*, 30 March, 1823).

58. Based on Armitage, *supra* note 10 at 107 *et seq.*

59. Miller 1989, *supra* note 33 at 196.

60. Arnold referred to the "effacement" of the Welsh language, a unique branch of Gaelic. When English state education was enforced in Wales in 1880, Welsh was outlawed from the schools and children were punished for speaking it, a point of pride for many. The anglicization project backfired, leading to the late–19th-century renaissance of Welsh literature and culture. English schooling for Wales was fuelled by the Commissioners' horror at the lack of religious knowledge of children interviewed, who were probably pulling their collective leg. J. Morris, *The Matter of Wales* (Oxford, 1984) 239. The dif-

ference for Aboriginal children is most notably the removal from family and village systems of support and the imposition of a much more alien system. On the "invention" or "rediscovery" of Welsh culture (with parallels yet to be explored for Aboriginal cultural rediscovery), see P. Morgan, "From a Death to a View: The Hunt for the Welsh Past in the Romantic Period" in E. Hobsbawm and T. Ranger, *The Invention of Tradition* (Cambridge, 1983).

61. These included beating, head-shaving, isolation and ridicule. Restrictions were eventually relaxed. Children in later decades learned rudiments of their own languages from other students and were exposed to other Aboriginal cultures, an experience which later played a strong role in the pan-Indian movement (*supra* note 32) and the strategies of self-government.

62. Miller 1989, *supra* note 33 at 196.

63. J.R. Miller, "Owen Glendower," "Hotspur and Canadian Indian Policy" in J.R. Miller, ed. *Sweet Promises: A Reader on Indian-White Relations in Canada* (University of Toronto Press, 1991) at 332.

64. Bull, *supra* note 55.

65. Miller, 1989, *supra* note 33 at 213.

66. Conversation of the author with a Cree student, April 1994.

67. A. McGillivray, "*R. v. K.(M.)*: Legitimating Brutality" (1993) 16 *Criminal Reports* (4th) 125; Stone, *supra* note 36.

68. Conversation of the author with a former Alberta residential school student, October 1993, who planned to form a victim collective for male survivors of residential school discipline. He is searching for the nun, now in her 80s, who acted as discipline officer, in order to sue the Catholic Church for damages. Officials have confirmed that she is still alive, but will not say where she now lives.

69. The Committee Final Report, *No Quiet Place*. [Kimelman Report] Manitoba Community Services 1985 at 201.

70. Aboriginal Justice Inquiry, *supra* note 5 at 514–515. See Ing, *supra* note 55 for accounts by former pupils. But see Cariboo Tribal Council, *supra* note 55 at 180, suggesting that "The type of school attended by the respondents' mothers did not seem to affect family life, while respondents whose fathers had attended residential school had somewhat different experiences from those whose fathers had attended non-residential school." While perhaps the majority of Indian children did not attend residential school, studies and personal accounts suggest far-reaching effect on the quality of family life and community cohesion where even one family member, especially a father, did so. The picture is complex. Christian corporal punishment values even without the residential school experience have suggested to elders that the birch switch is somehow part of traditional Aboriginal values, while domestic violence and child sexual abuse in "closed" stressed communities can spread rapidly. "Culture" may deny as well as protect.

71. Miller 1989, *supra* note 33 at 199. Miller also cites state parsimony as a cause of the failure of the system.

■ ■ ■

Discussion and Writing Suggestions

1. McGillivray describes how and why the Canadian government employed two key institutions of society—the school system and organized religion—in its attempt to assimilate Aboriginal people into a British version of civilization. Under pressure of objections that presenting any one religious perspective is problematic in a culturally diverse society, the Church has generally been sidelined in the public school system. Is the school system now ideology-free? Or is it still used for purposes of social engineering?

2. Why would McGillivray see "the reserve, the residential school, the child protection system, young offender facilities and jail" as a "Foucauldian carceral archipelago"? (If you don't know these terms, start by investigating their meanings.)

3. McGillivray makes the claim that strong resistance by Aboriginal people caused the project of residential schooling to fail dismally. What are the implications of her claim for other instances of oppression and resistance in the school system?

Residential Schools Story More Complicated

RODNEY A. CLIFTON

As a professor of sociology of education at the University of Manitoba who has also worked at Memorial University in Newfoundland, the University of Stockholm in Sweden, and the Australian Council for Educational Research, Melbourne, Australia, Rodney Clifton has occupied influential positions. Further, he has been extensively published in various academic and policy journals, including Policy Options, *the* Canadian Journal of Education, Sociology of Education, *and the* International Encyclopaedia of Education. *In this article that appears on the website of the conservative Frontier Centre for Public Policy (www.fcpp.org/), Clifton argues that not all schools were abusive and that the church employees who worked in them were devoted to caring for the children in their charge.*

I spent the 1966–67 year as a supervisor in an Anglican residential school,   1
Stringer Hall, in Inuvik, N.W.T. Previously, I spent four months living at Old Sun School, an Anglican residential school, on the Siksika (Blackfoot) Reserve in southern Alberta. Much earlier, my wife (a Siksika) spent eight years at Old Sun, and even earlier, her parents attended the same school for eight years. All of us recognize many of the positive things that happened in residential schools. My wife, in fact, insists on calling Old Sun a "private Anglican school," my father-in-law was ordained as an Anglican priest, and my mother-in-law worked in the local church for more than 60 years. None of us heard a word—not even a murmur—about children being sexually abused.

It is now widely acknowledged that some people working in residential   2
schools abused the children under their care. But no one has acknowledged that
some children abused other children. Of course, people who abused others
should be charged, and if convicted, they should pay for their crimes. Moreover,
administrators from the churches and from Indian and Northern Affairs who
covered up these crimes should be charged, convicted, and punished.

But before joining the feeding frenzy of lawyers who want to extract bil-   3
lions of dollars from Canadian taxpayers, it may be worthwhile considering
some of the positive things that happened in residential schools. Surprisingly,
church leaders have rarely mentioned the benefits these schools provided for
their students:

- Most children who went to residential school learned how to read, write and
  calculate. Many also learned other skills necessary for living in a modern
  society. Aboriginal citizens, like other people, use these skills every day.
- Some children had serious illnesses—TB, chronic ear infections and rup-
  tured appendices, for example—which were diagnosed while they were in
  school. Doctors and dentists made regular visits to residential schools to
  treat sick children, something that may not have happened if they had been
  living in their home communities, for those in southern Canada, or if they
  had been out on the land hunting and fishing with their parents, for those
  in the North.
- Throughout the sad history of residential schools, there have been numerous situations—during epidemics and fires, for example—in which non-
  aboriginal and aboriginal people worked together to save "their children."
  Often, these people continued to work even when it was a danger to their
  own health and safety.
- Some school administrators and supervisors were aboriginals. At Stringer
  Hall, for example, two of the six residential supervisors were Inuit women.
  Did aboriginal supervisors abuse the children under their care? Do both the
  children and the supervisors deserve compensation?
- Some children in residential schools were not aboriginals. I myself attended
  a United Church residential school in the early 1960s, and when I was a supervisor at Stringer Hall, about 12 per cent of the 280 students were non-aboriginal.
  Children of school administrators, white trappers, missionaries and merchants
  attended these schools. If aboriginal people are going to receive compensation,
  do the non-aboriginal students also deserve compensation?

Shockingly, the churches have failed to honour the dedicated service of   4
most residential school employees, both aboriginal and non-aboriginal. They
have failed to defend their own integrity and they have failed to defend the
integrity of their innocent employees. They have done little to correct the
impression, in the minds of some Canadians, that many residential school
supervisors were child abusers and pedophiles.

Nevertheless, most people who worked in residential schools wanted to   5
help children receive the type of education necessary to survive in the modern
world. In the 1960s, when I lived and worked in residential schools, it was the
evangelistic calling for committed Christians similar to rebuilding houses
following disasters in South America. Most residential school employees

worked for very little pay, less recognition, and many sleepless nights. Most of them will never acknowledge that they worked in residential schools because they fear the denigration from other church members. Not surprisingly, many of them also fear the charges they may face from the wolf-pack of hungry lawyers hunting for compensation.

I do not fear the denigration, and I'm not afraid of the lawyers. But, I am afraid that this feeding frenzy will tear the churches apart while further alienating non-aboriginal Canadians from their aboriginal brethren. I fear the alienation of one side of my family, including our son, from the other. This will happen because people who were never responsible for any crimes, people who never covered up for any criminal activities, are being forced to pay substantial sums to people who were never abused. If the scales of justice are to be rebalanced, it is important that those who actually committed crimes against their charges pay for these crimes. It is important that Canadians, including church members and even lawyers, should honour the vast majority of people, both aboriginal and non-aboriginal, who selflessly dedicated their lives to helping aboriginal children. Moreover, citizens who did not know that abuse was taking place in residential schools should not be forced to pay for the crimes that other people committed.

■ ■ ■

Discussion and Writing Suggestions

1. What kinds of evidence does Rodney Clifton use in his defence of the employees of the Residential School System? Do an analysis of his use of *ethos*, *pathos*, and *logos*.
2. What do you think of his contention that some children were abused by other children in the school? How might we account for this as a further effect of abuse by the adults supervising them?
3. Grand Chief Phil Fontaine argues that the existence of the schools was a crime in itself, and that anyone who attended was therefore a victim of abuse and deserves compensation. Do you agree with Chief Fontaine's reasoning? Or do you find Dr. Clifton's argument more persuasive?

Schooling and Society: Perspectives on Knowledge, Culture, and Difference

RATNA GHOSH AND ALI A. ABDI

Dr. Ratna Ghosh is Professor of Education at McGill University in Montreal, Member of the Order of Canada, Officer of the Order of Quebec 2005, Fellow of the Royal Society of Canada, and Full Member of the European Academy of

Arts, Sciences and Humanities. Ghosh has received several awards from national and international organizations for her work. Among her many contributions to the cause of working across differences is the playing of an important leadership role in the development of the Shastri Indo-Canadian Institute and serving on the Board of Directors of the Canadian Human Rights Foundation.

Dr. Ali A. Abdi is Associate Professor of Education at the University of Alberta in Calgary where he teaches courses on international issues in education. His research interests include comparative and international education, citizenship and development education, cultural studies in education, African philosophies of education, and postcolonial studies in education and, like Ghosh, he has published widely in a variety of journals and books.

This article is drawn from their book, Education and the Politics of Difference: Canadian Perspectives. *Ghosh and Abdi review various progressive approaches to education to build their argument that it is not enough to teach students to be good "citizens," that a multicultural society in a globalized world needs teachers "to advance the welfare and interests of all who inhabit this earth."*

Education, if formulated and implemented with the practices of justice and equity, is the great engine of social development.

—Nelson Mandela

Inquiries in the social sciences have produced substantial research on the relationship between school and society, specifically between the knowledge transmitted by schools, and societal position and power. Some traditions of schooling and theories on the social construction of knowledge imply that constructions of reality, their selection, and their organization legitimize the knowledge and culture of the dominant group, with the resulting elevation and ensured continuity of this group's bodies of knowledge at the expense of others (Apple, 2000; Banks, 1993).   1

The process by which this happens through the agency of the public schools is a complex one. As societies have experienced social, economic, and political shifts as well as globalization-induced movements there has been a critical public debate over the role of educators and educational institutions. Schools have also been the domain of intense conflict in the controversy over whose knowledge and culture are to be communicated. In heterogeneous societies, education plays a significant role in the development of moral and political skills necessary to pursue a democratic vision of the common good. The issues are political because they involve power struggles among different groups, and conflict with democratic ideals of equal and just participation by all groups. In schools, as in society, power is exercised through the hierarchical classification of differences as binary opposites (i.e., man/woman; rich/poor; black/white) to which meaning is given through social construction. These meanings and stereotypes are rigid and hierarchical, but remain concealed in the ideology of the school and society.   2

The expansion of mass education, complemented by global migrations   3
and the mixing of people from previously detached geographies, has resulted
in heterogeneity of the student population. In North America, the dramatic
change in the elite and male nature of schools with universal education is
exacerbated because its history is closely linked to immigration. Difference is
not only based on the inclusion of female and working class students, but also
on racial, ethnic, and cultural diversity. At stake is the equality issue in
modern democracies—due to the inclusion of the other—and the school's role
as an equalizing force. An education founded on the democratic principles of
equality and social justice, however, involves an emancipatory vision of all
segments and members of the community (Giroux, 2002). This goes well
beyond pedagogical skills for economic and citizenship requirements, and
includes ethical and moral issues that will work towards human freedom. An
equitable and just community is not necessarily an ethical and caring community. Legislation and regulations do not guarantee the transformation of
the societal vision. The need is for change in the affective, ethical, and cognitive domains. As such, in an age of global interdependence, the concept of one
world economy, one earth, one environment, one humanity can be cultivated
through the ethical dimensions of caring and compassion, and not merely
because of pragmatic reasons (Nussbaum, 1998). To achieve this in tangible
measure, one must take into account the new expansive possibilities that
must be undertaken with a higher sense of sustainable economic development,
equitable distribution of resources, overall social justice, and attendant security guarantees for all segments of society. The point is to change the world
positively while still seeking new possibilities. Education must help us understand the world in order to change it. To achieve this, we must ask a number
of critical questions, including, for example, why are various others systematically marginalized? What changes would bring about a more just society in
which all humans would have the right to define the terms of their existence?
How can education advance the welfare and interests of all who inhabit this
earth?

The Role of Education

At least three groups of educational theorists have influenced the main forums   4
that analyzed the role as well as the objectives of education in society, before
the first initiatives to challenge the old order began in earnest. The first of
these were the consensus theorists, who viewed education's role as that of cultural transmission and human capital formation. These traditional theories
remained relatively unchanged in a number of educational settings until the
1960s. They emphasized consensus and viewed the school as providing equal
access. Several other researchers began to emphasize the legitimization of the
inequality function of the school system through supposedly objective testing,
which made unequal results of different groups appear justifiable. The transmission of culture model was seen by conflict theorists as depoliticizing differences as well as the function and process of schooling, because of the

connection between knowledge and power. The debate over inequality had shifted from the liberal to the socialist interpretation of equality.

The second group were the structuralist-functionalists (people like Talcott   5
Parsons and Robert Merton) who analyzed inequalities of educational opportunities in terms of assimilation in education and society, and human resource development as a means of gaining mobility by maintaining equilibrium in society. Differences were neither accepted nor considered important. They were deficiencies that could be overcome, and to which non-dominant individuals and groups could aspire if they were successfully shaped in the mold of the dominant group.

The third group of theorists were those who espoused liberal views and   6
who based their assumptions on an ideology of cultural pluralism. They saw adaptation by the dominant group as the means to enable disadvantaged groups to gain access to status as well as economic and political power. Cultural pluralists accepted the plurality of society in terms of fragmented groups—based on racial and ethnocultural characteristics—and recognized the correspondence between the groups, and socio-economic status and class. Here, the dominant group would make some overtures to help subordinate groups adjust. However, the ideal to be achieved was to attain the dominant group characteristics, by which others would be measured for entrance to dominant social institutions. As such, these educational theories were, unlike current multicultural education programs that welcome and accept differences, structurally oblivious to them and, by commission and omission, disguised the exclusion of the other.

To challenge the normalized but problematic corridors of writing and   7
provision, radical theorists, for example, explained the persistence of inequality by viewing the school's role essentially as reproducing the dominant ideology through maintenance of the hierarchical structures in society. Borrowing from the earlier theories of the German social theorists Karl Marx and Max Weber, these thinkers not only saw the problematic of the habitualized continuities of educational and related inequalities in society, but also realized the urgency with which new and inclusive discursive as well as practical platforms should be created if the dominant ideology was ever to be diluted. In addition, correspondence theorists such as Bowles and Gintis, in their well-known work *Schooling in Capitalist America* (1976), pointed out how the hierarchical structure of values is reflected in classroom interactions. There were also a number of independent researchers such as John Ogbu (1992), who made the distinction between class and minority group problems in education and society. Ogbu used the term *caste-like minorities* to describe the structural legacy of some minority groups, and distinguished their educational and economic problems from those of the working class.

With the introduction of issues other than social class-based economics   8
directly influencing education, perspectives on cultural reproduction and the important role of cultural capital as the ensemble of all linguistic and expressive skills children learn from their family and social environments gained

momentum primarily with the work of the prominent French sociologist Pierre Bourdieu (1973, with Passeron, 1990). These important works were complemented by Bernstein's (1971) work on language codes in education that had detrimental effects on the learning success of minority students, and by Willis' landmark book, *Learning to Labour*, which showed how conventional programs of learning were, in effect, making sure that the dominant order was maintained by preparing, for example, working class children to find working class jobs, thus discounting any possibilities for viable social mobility and concomitant social advancement. The sustainability of the theoretical threads created by these earlier works was strengthened through the 1970s and into the current debate on the problems of education as an agent of social development, by the related works of critical theorists (mainly from the Frankfurt School) such as Max Horkheimer (1972), Herbert Marcuse (1964) and Jürgen Habermas (1979).

Over the last decades, a number of studies have utilized critical theory [9] from the humanities and social sciences to focus on culture and cultural production through the daily experiences of teachers and students. Integrating neo-Marxist social theory with microcosmic descriptions of everyday life, they illustrate the dynamics of accommodation, conflict, and resistance that shape the often antagonistic daily experiences of students and teachers' lives (McRobbie, 1991). Cultural resistance involves opposition to dominant cultural codes, or withdrawal from one's assigned position in society. It poses a challenge to dominant patterns of gender, class, ethnicity, and forms of oppression; for example, white, middle class control or male domination. Resistance theories focus their attention on oppressed groups and emphasize human agency or action in the internal workings of the school (McLaren, 1994). One of the weaknesses in resistance theories has been the lack of historical analyses of the conditions that give rise to simultaneous modes of resistance and struggle. Again, challenging a developmentally restraining school environment with any attendant immediacy may be the best option, especially when conditions of life do not allow for the long-term study and analysis of why things are what they are. Here, the main point, *ipso facto*, becomes what one can do now to alleviate current regimes of deprivation that are directly affecting people's lives. The emergence of postmodern theories, primarily through the widely diffused writings of French thinkers such as Jacques Derrida (1976) and Jean-François Lyotard (1984) would also have a lasting impact on how education and knowledge are defined, even if they were not intended to do so in the first place. Postmodern theory, as anti-modernity (modernity as an enlightenment-driven project) usually accords legitimacy, at least theoretically, on all forms of knowledge and ways of knowing. In addition, the analytical as well as the temporal relationships between these and the previous theories, as well as philosophical and discursive attachments, all would have to do with the now *au courant* post-colonial studies area (e.g., Achebe, 2000; Said, 1993, 2000; Bhabha, 1994; Ashcroft et al., 1995). In the new cultural and educational formations that have emerged, not only from education but also from other social science disciplines (poststructuralism, postmodernism, postcolonialism, etc.), the most important pedagogical and knowledge/power deconstructions and reconstructions would involve (a) the delegitimization of meta-narratives or overarching philosophies that are meant to represent universal truths; (b) the emphasis on a cultural politics of difference; and (c) a new and apparently sustainable focus on identity, culture, and power.

Protesting the lack of vision and strategies, as well as gender bias in radical theories, critical radical educators have taken the opportunity provided by contemporary social theories to start to question the knowledge produced in schools and its impact on students of different backgrounds. These theories have enabled educators to rethink the purpose of schooling, and the means by which one can struggle for social justice. Over the past fifteen years, critical pedagogy and a critical feminist pedagogy have been emerging, based on a wide variety of writings. These are inspired by the analytical forces of the Frankfurt School as well as the work of the postmodern scholars and students, with the added but conjecturally primary support of educational philosophers and thinkers such as John Dewey (1952, 1929), Paulo Freire (1985, 1998, 2000), and Antonio Gramsci (1990). Dewey was indeed ahead of his time in advocating for a culturally inclusive education, albeit one with more Euro-American platforms, which was to allow the child to slowly integrate into the new school environment while still expecting to see something of his or her background in the different structures of schooling.

The works of these theorists were again complemented by the important and gender-sensitive books of a number of writers who first highlighted the world of women in educational settings (see, among others, Gilligan, 1982; Lorde, 1984; DeLauretis, 1987; Lewis, 1990; Luke and Gore, 1992; Hooks, 1984; Narayan and Harding, 2000) Here again, in the same way that liberal theories of education were challenged from the margins, liberal feminist perspectives that initially formed the vanguard of the movement met new schemes of resistance from, among others, coloured women, who correctly pointed out that analysis of difference solely on the basis of gender was not enough to deal with the multiple levels of marginalization that many women faced. In addition, the new crop of feminist scholars highlighted the fact that mainstream Western women cannot represent the voice of women from Third World countries or those who could be, for a variety of reasons, marginalized in industrialized Western democracies (Collins, 2000 [1990]; Mohanty, 1995). Critiquing the case from the assumed perspective of Third World women, Mohanty writes:

> [In the Western, liberal feminist discourse], a homogenous notion of the oppression of women as a group is assumed, which, in turn, produces the image of an 'average third world woman.' This average third world woman leads an essentially truncated life based on her feminine gender (read: sexually constrained), and being 'third world' (read: ignorant, poor, uneducated, tradition-bound, domestic, family-oriented, victimized, etc.).

This, I suggest, is in contrast to the (implicit) self-representation of Western women as educated, modern, as having control over their own bodies and sexualities, and the freedom to make their own decisions. . . . These distinctions are made on the basis of the privileging of a particular group as the norm or referent [with Western feminists constructing] themselves as the referent in such a binary analytic. (1995, p. 261)

With these clusters of empowering approaches to education for tradi- 12 tionally disadvantaged groups, the very identity of power brokers is at stake, thus implying a change in relations between the traditionally powerful and powerless. Critical pedagogy not only challenges racism, sexism, and classism, but changes the precepts of their foundation. It also implies an integrated society and classroom in which differences do not divide individuals or groups. Hence, the continuing focus on the development of critical citizenry as well as literacy programs that tangibly focus on the relationship between education, learning possibilities, and public enfranchisement (Giroux, 2001).

The now-established literature on critical pedagogy reveals a variety of 13 discourses. Two main strands can be identified. Both are associated with a socialist vision and based on a critique of dominant approaches to education (Gore, 1993). One stresses social vision and sees the role of the school as being a site for equality and social justice. Pointing out that a critique of schools is not enough, it stresses the need to speak the language of possibility and hope in order to change the system and debunk the myth of equality in the present system.

The second strand, represented by those who focus on pedagogy as class- 14 room practice, is consistent with the politics of liberation, and epitomized as a struggle against injustice and inequality. This is undoubtedly influenced by the writings of the late Brazilian philosopher, Paulo Freire (1985, 2000 [1970]). Although Freire's radical pedagogy has been criticized as having neglected gender issues (Weiler, 1991) his broad social vision, symbolized by Third World politics and identity, corresponds with the politics and social vision of critical as well as feminist pedagogy, and can be adapted, across many cultures, into pedagogical practices.

Theories of critical pedagogy are united in focusing on a program that 15 aims to empower those who have been and are being subjected to the equalities and inequities that, more often than not, permeate public spaces and programs of education (McLaren, 1994, 1997). While these theories reveal a diversity in emphasis, they are bound together by their common concern with race, class, and gender oppression. Multiculturalism thus becomes an integral part of the critical pedagogy program. It offers possibilities to educators for going beyond the apolitical and ahistorical conceptions of multicultural education, and instead enables them to focus on issues of power, subordination, and struggle within a progressive vision, which includes both theory and practice. In these critical theories of production, knowledge is considered to be a major productive force of schools. The legitimization, organization, and distribution of the functions of knowledge by schools results in a social hierarchy based on difference. This makes knowledge an object for investigation.

The Concept of Knowledge

Theories of Knowledge

Knowledge characterizes the way we look at the world. Where we are located   16
in society affects how we understand the world. In traditional educational theories, an assimilationist model of education, rooted in the positivist period, insisted on one truth because it was assumed that there was one way of knowing, and knowledge was thought to be value-free. The connection between knowledge and power was not made. In critical pedagogy, of which multiculturalism must be an integral component, knowledge and power are inherently connected. Truth is based on different ways of knowing, made more complex as a result of differences in human experience. The function of knowledge is to lead one towards freedom, and that can only happen when it increases awareness of the hidden aspects of power. That is, when it deliberately diffuses and accords emancipatory knowledge.

Philosophical and epistemological debates have raged through both the   17
social and natural sciences. While realists have argued for universal knowledge that is value-free and neutral, idealists argued that knowledge (in the physical as well as in the social sciences) is contextual, defined by socio-cultural and historical forces. Therefore, it is neither neutral nor value-free. For Freire, knowledge is praxis, primarily for use in action. Knowledge is to be used by marginalized people to change their situation of oppression by challenging the knowledge of the oppressor. This, indeed, is where Freire's well-known program of conscientization (see Freire, 2000 [1970]) comes along. Here, as people become conscious of the conditions as well as the nature of their oppression, they acquire the critical faculties to proactively respond to their relationship with their social and physical environments, becoming capable, in the process, of transforming their lives vis-à-vis their oppressors. In the newly forming, post-conscientization contexts, knowledge is interpreted by its purpose, and produced in a manner that is multi-perspectively relational. As Lusted (1986, p. 4) pointed out earlier, "Knowledge is not the matter that is offered so much as the matter that is understood."

In addition, feminist pedagogy is also largely a response to the traditional   18
theory of knowledge in which the white middle class male (classified as the norm) represents all human experience as universal (validating certain methodologies). Pointing out that what is claimed as universal is largely inapplicable to the historical experiences of women (and peoples of other races, ethnicities, and classes), feminist scholars raised questions about the kind of knowledge and the particular means available to men for obtaining universal knowledge. In an attempt to put women's experiences within a broad framework of human civilization, feminist scholarship points to the social, historical, and political aspects in the construction of knowledge.

Knowledge in Educational Theories

Critical pedagogy demands a reformulation of theories of knowledge that focus 19 on the relationship between knowledge and subjectivity, i.e., self-conscious awareness. A central assumption is that knowledge is not produced only by experts. The deconstruction of boundaries between traditional knowledge and power has raised new questions that suggest different ways of knowledge construction representing different worldviews. For example, student experiences and their historical, social, and cultural conditions must be viewed as primary sources of knowledge if they are to be subjects, and involved in the productive educational process. By rejecting metanarratives and universalistic theories—which are from the Eurocentric male, middle class perspective—and by asserting the contextual nature of knowledge and the plurality of meanings, they broaden the base to include marginalized groups and expand knowledge about themselves and their world. This challenges the validity of Eurocentric knowledge "as the exclusive referent for judging what constitutes historical, cultural, and political truth." It asserts that "there is no tradition or story that can speak with authority and certainty for all of humanity" (Giroux, 1991, p. 231).

Schools promote specific notions of knowledge and power by rewarding 20 specific forms of behaviour. School knowledge is influenced by structures of economic/social class power, notions, and assumptions about race, and differences on the basis of gender (Apple, 1999, 2000). When knowledge is politically based, historically embedded, and socially constructed, and therefore subjective (Banks, 1997), then questions that involve the validity of what constitutes acceptable knowledge arise. The social location of those who produce school knowledge and use it as a neutral object to be transmitted to subjects who have different social locations (Freire, 2000 [1970]), in combination with the politics of location (Rich, 1986), have brought into focus the relations of power resulting in injustice that underlie these politics. Moreover, the recognition that school knowledge is far from neutral provides a significant explanation as to how it serves students of different groups unequally. If knowledge and power are inextricably linked, then in order to empower students, attention must be paid to the ways in which students acquire knowledge and are given the opportunity to construct, analyze, and deconstruct knowledge to uncover the values and assumptions of curriculum canons or precepts.

The Politics of Difference

Audre Lorde's (1984) point that it is not the differences in themselves, but the 21 social construction and conceptualization of these differences that divide people has, even after so many years, a powerful theoretical and practical resonance. Power relations invariably denote oppressive consequences, whether conscious (and obvious) or not. Those who are different become the other, and their histories, cultures, and experiences are denigrated and/or eradicated. In the literature of postmodern thought, Jacques Derrida (1973) coined the neologism *différance* to imply the unheard and abstract element in conceptualizing difference, because the *a* in differance is only seen and not heard.

From a straightforward definitional perspective, the Oxford Dictionary 22 defines *difference* as "that which distinguishes one thing from another." Difference is a comparative term; it is relational and it is created. The creation of the other implies deviance from the norm—in standards of excellence, achievement, and evaluation. Giroux writes that "to take up the issue of difference is to recognize that it cannot be analyzed unproblematically" (1992, p. 171). The idea of difference as such hides its profoundly political aspect that results in prejudice (the attitude) and discrimination (the behaviour). For those who are different, their inability to challenge these interpretations (their silence and powerlessness) oppresses them. It violates their sense of worth, self-esteem, and overall individual and social identities. The fear of difference is perhaps the greatest impediment to understanding among different people because it creates barriers. Further, it puts the onus on those who are different to cross the distance between their realities and the dominant consciousness, while those who represent the norm avoid their responsibility.

These issues indicate that not only is there a diversity of meaning of the 23 concept of difference, but also that this meaning is not fixed in time and place. Here, difference is taken as a process of construction of meanings in the interplay of power and identity, which brings together groups on the basis of their subordination. It recognizes differences both within and between groups. Democracy implies that despite differences, human beings have equal dignity, and therefore equal rights. Although there is still controversy as to the extent of rights, especially in the economic sphere (due to the inability of many nations to provide those rights), there is a global consensus on basic rights for all (citizenship and voting rights). Education, for example, is considered a basic right, even when the majority of non-industrialized countries are unable to provide education for all.

The Politics of Recognition

The paradox is that democracy entails universal acceptance of equal dignity 24 on one level (notwithstanding differences), but recognition of individual identity on another (acknowledging differences). As such, democracy signifies recognition. In his seminal essay "The Politics of Recognition," Charles Taylor (1994) defines identity as a person's understanding of who she or he is, of her/his fundamental defining characteristics as a human being. And how one defines oneself is partly dependent on the recognition, misrecognition, or absence of recognition by others. As Taylor notes, non-recognition and/or misrecognition can inflict harm, and literally constitute a form of oppression that incarcerates people in a false, deformed, and existentially reduced mode of being.

Contemporary conceptions of identity are also influenced by postmod- 25 ernist/poststructuralist writers who seek to deconstruct what they call the logic of identity in Western philosophical and theoretical discourse. The logic of identity conceptualizes objects as measurable (unity and substance) rather than as process. Earlier discussions of identity were located in the area of personality. Social identity research challenged this individualistic frame and subjective definition of the notion of identity as a stabilized factor, an essential personality trait. Identity is no longer seen as a static, unitary trait; nor is it merely a result of socialization. People construct their identities within the social framework. Identity is now seen as being formed in social processes, and in terms of relations because human beings are always in the making. As such, identities are constantly shifting and renegotiable, and the search for new or modified identities, even in places historically largely Anglo-Saxon, such as North America, is continuous.

In terms of difference, then, questions arise. Different from what?   26
Different in what way? And, perhaps more importantly, different from whom? The operative concepts in theorizing difference are both power and identity. The answer to the first question—different from what—requires a definition of the norm, or dominant groups who enjoy dominance over others and are the repositories of power. Those who are not from the norm are different, and this in itself may be the underlying factor for discrimination. Likewise, those who are from the working class suffer from classism, and females are exposed to sexism. As Gilroy (1990) keenly pointed out, these categories stand for hierarchies, and not difference. The concept of power is implicit in the terms racism, classism, and sexism; a domination of white over black; middle class over working class; male over female. The relational equation, then, is that of power. The educational project must be to expose and uncover the patterns of power relations and inequalities.

The second question—different in what way—brings issues of identity of   27
the other into the portrayal of the category of otherness. Those who are different (they; the outsiders) are defined by the dominant group (we; the insiders). Both we and they are artificially constructed in unitary fashion, disregarding the differences within each construct. The physical and economic differences that are used to categorize groups and define people also reproduce inequalities through relations of domination and subordination. The pedagogical issue is the social and historical construction of identity, which is in flux. Essentially, racial, ethnic, gender, and class differences are as irrelevant to the educational process as are the size and shape of students.

Finally, different from whom? By remaining invisible—because whites do   28
not give themselves a racial identity—the dominant group remains outside the hierarchy of social relations, and in that way is not part of the politics of difference. Its supremacy in the ladder of power is ensured (Carby, 1992), while relegating a subaltern status to the other. Pedagogically, the issue is how the historical and social constructions of whiteness and difference are learned. More critically, what opportunities are given to students to deconstruct these conceptions as implying reality? In pedagogical terms, the object is to discern how students "learn to identify, challenge, and rewrite such representations" (Giroux, 1993, p. 21).

Difference, as a historical and social idea, has a long history in the West,   29
and can be traced back to the Enlightenment. From that perspective, human
differences are simplistically seen in binary oppositions: difference/sameness,
we/them; white/black, male/female, middle class/working class; good/bad,
superior/inferior, strong/weak. Binary oppositions were used by conservative
theorists to justify inequality and discrimination by associating difference
with deficiency and deviance. Liberals recognized difference but avoided the
issue, and were blind to the unequal power relations and institutional discrimination that accompanied the conceptions of difference. The other was
conceived as static and made peripheral by the domination of a unified norm.
Radical theorists focus on the changing social construction of difference and
identity and their multiplicity.

The concept of difference has also been the focus of feminist theories in   30
the West. Initially, this was in defence of their difference as women from men
in a patriarchal society. More recently, it has focused on the differences
among women, specifically between privileged white middle class women
and the disadvantaged working class and/or ethnic minority women. Minority
feminist scholars, as discussed above, have pointed out how the experiences
of minority women differ from those of white women: not only are they subjected to two forms of oppression (sexism and racism), but the combination
of the two makes it different, and not simply more acute. The multiple
instances and levels of oppression may induce what Carty (1991) and
Mohanty (1995) have called multi-layered platforms of marginalization in the
lives of non-European women. Not to recognize this difference in experiences is to deny the difference in the sexism that black and white women
experience, and the racism that men and women encounter.

These conceptualizations and their possible pragmatics create very real   31
discrepancies for those who are different in terms of race, sex and class. The
salient point is that the dominant group and minority groups (racial, ethnic,
class, or gender) have very different conceptions of how difference works.
Dominant group responses to differences may vary in several ways, including
silence, guilt, and fear. It is the refusal to recognize the effects of distorted connotations given to differences, therefore, that has to cease (see Hartman,
1997). As such, Stuart Hall would still be right:

> Identities are a matter of "becoming" as well as of "being" .... Far from
> being eternally fixed in some essentialised past, they are subject to the con-
> tinuous "play" of history, culture and power .... Identities are the names
> we give to the different ways we are positioned by, and position ourselves
> within, the narratives of the past (Hall, 1990, p. 225).

Identity is formed along multiple axes that include, among others, race,   32
gender, and social class. Identity surfaces at the individual level, but each
person has many social identities (such as ethnic, sexual, and class identities)
that develop meaning in people's lives both at the ideological/political and
social/cultural levels. People's multiple identities are not apparent in all

contexts, and represent different spheres of reality in everyday life. Different ones are important at different times. Generally, what people define as "real" are real in their consequences, and reality is defined socially by individuals and groups of individuals who serve as definers of reality.

At the individual level, those who identify with a group can redefine the meaning and norms of group identity. Individual and collective identities are constructed in three areas: the biological, the social and the cultural (Aronowitz, 1992). Our biological attributes—gender, race, and ethnicity— become meaningful and are defined in our interactions with people. While gender, race, and ethnic identities are ascribed and cannot usually be changed, class position, which is also assigned at birth, can be changed. The given characteristics do not have meaning in themselves, but become defining factors. Identity is, therefore, constructed relationally.   33

Cultural identities are a "conjuncture of our past with the social, cultural and economic relations we live within" (Rutherford, 1990, p. 19). Although we may be a précis of the past (Gramsci, 1988), our cultural identities are not fixed. Identity is a constructed sense of self that also incorporates views of self-help by others. Identity is influenced by one's location in relation to others and the way others identify and define us. It is influenced by the dilemma of differences (Minow, 1990) and by the notion of different degrees of othering (Mercer, 1992). In this construction, schools play a significant role in reproducing racial, gender, and class differences.   34

Culture

Culture refers to the way in which a group of people responds to the environment in terms of cognition, emotion and behaviour. In that sense, "culture is . . . excerpted by human thought from . . . world history, and invested with sense and meaning" (Hartman, 1997, p. 27). Culture, therefore, is a dynamic rather than a static phenomenon. Despite being bound up with the most fundamental epistemological questions, the issue of culture has been considered superfluous within the economic and political challenges of daily life. If culture is a way of seeing the world, and if seeing the world has any relevance to changing the world, then it would be necessary to understand effectively and respond pragmatically to issues that concern the way in which we see the world. The purpose of multicultural education is to create new possibilities in confronting the ways in which we see the world. Culture plays a significant role in production and reproduction in schools. Cultural struggle is essential to political and economic struggle. Multiculturalism represents that cultural struggle.   35

Moreover, formations of difference, whether in schools or in the generalized, societal interactions of people, are now influenced by rapidly emerging global constructions of culture. Here, as globalization affects all aspects of people's lives, the mediating of difference and related issues that are undertaken in schools will have to deal with the homogenizing forces of global media and information technology that are incessantly shaping the way learners, teachers, and others define, operationalize, and eventually manage or problematize dif-   36 ference. The irony in this is that while globalization is supposedly opening up the world's cultures and differences to one another, by default and primarily via the hegemonic cultural forces of its major sponsors, it is actually indirectly advancing the Westernization of the world. In this regard, the role of education and educators to welcome and sustain multi-centric notions of culture and difference cannot be overestimated.

The emergence of the discourses of the new politics of cultural difference   37
in the social sciences has important implications for redefining diverse conceptions of culture. Culture here signifies special ways in which particular classes and social groups live and make sense out of the world and their life situations. As such, the concept of culture is directly related to how people's relations are structured in terms of the differences discussed above, and selectively explains the discrepancies that arise in defining and using the practices of knowledge and experience.

In modernist discourse, culture is an organizing principle, which homog-   38
enizes and creates borders around ethnicity, class, and gender, despite its emphasis on democratic ideals. However, neither dominant nor minority cultures are homogenous. Individuals see the world from their own perspectives and have multiple consciousness. The politics of location, as Rich (1986) and Bhabha (1994) have discussed, explains how people are grounded and confined because they are located unequally in terms of race, ethnicity, class, and gender. Multicultural connotes numerous cultures. Cultural aspects based on biological differences of race and ethnicity are the ones most obviously perceived. However, gender differences are cultural too, and these are also constructed around biological differences.

The notion of multiculturalism is closely related to the concepts of race   39
and ethnicity. The question of hierarchy in categories of oppression leads to the view that issues are often different for different groups, and the impact is weakened when dealt with simultaneously. Yet everyone is a member of some racial or ethnic group, and of other groups simultaneously. Discrimination based on perception of difference is the problem. And multiculturalism speaks about and advances the right to difference (Ghosh, 1996). Here, the need is to question structures and patterns of relationships, not to prioritize groups. Instead of giving credibility to the current limited interpretation of multiculturalism, it is the commonality and intersection of experiences in terms of race and ethnicity, class and gender, which we need to understand.

Women, for example, may manifest differences in thought processes that   40
correspond to their difference in status and lack of power in society. It would be possible that all knowledge is gendered, classed, and culture-based. The concept of multiculturalism must contain within it all these cultures because the effects of their social definition and construction are similar. The end result is that the segregation of populations is eliminated. The root factors innate within the concept are political, thinly concealing the twin facets of dominance and exclusivity, and symbolizing some kind of primeval power struggle (Goldberg, 1992). Multiculturalism must challenge both marginalization and

incorporation by recognizing disadvantage as intersecting with class, colour, gender, and culture, and as being embedded in history.

The challenge to the dominant Eurocentric domination that "colonizes   41
definitions of the normal" (Giroux, 1991, p. 225) is central to multicultural philosophy. That challenge comes as much from racial and ethnic groups as from women and the working class. Each of these groups is identified by their particular culture, but they often converge to make individual and group experiences complex and multiple. Linking the experiences of minority groups, and making connections between different experiences enables recognition of similarities and variations.

Dominant Group

Multiculturalism is a controversial issue, and hotly debated at the educational   42
level. This implies that it is an arena of power struggles, where different constituencies are struggling with their different interests. One problem with the notion of existing concepts of multiculturalism has been its almost exclusive concern with the other. It has failed to question the norm of whiteness and the domination of white culture by being invisible. By remaining concealed, and removing the dominant group from race and/or ethnicity, the focus on difference is depoliticized. Thus, asymmetrical relations of power are maintained. Subordinate groups do not own the categories of race, gender, and class. Surely the dominant or majority groups belong to some race if Homo sapiens are to be categorized. They must also have gender and class affiliations. Race, gender, and class categories have been socially constructed by dominant discourse and practice to determine the social location of the other; multiculturalism, in its present form, does not challenge the dominant group's understanding of the world (Carty, 1991). Yet it is the very encounter with the dominant group that produces the subordinate groups; "the marginal [is] a consequence of the authority invested in the centre" (Julien and Mercer, 1988, p. 3). Multiculturalism must conceptualize issues of race and ethnicity, gender and class as part of a wider discourse on power and powerlessness, not only the latter. The dominant group must be a part of the multicultural ideology because it has to take part of the responsibility for the emerging sociocultural conditions, which threaten democracy and global stability. For the dominant group, multiculturalism must be "the desire to extend the reference of 'us' as far as we can" (Rorty, 1991, p. 23) if democracy is to have any meaning.

Fusion of Cultures

Our future survival as human beings in the face of global human and envi-   43
ronmental problems is contingent upon interdependence. We must develop the ability to relate within a framework of equality, which involves an ameliorated vision of our future. Multiculturalism must analyze the meaning of race and ethnicity, gender, and class as social and historical constructs that involve all citizens of a democracy, both dominant and subordinate. Difference is "a dynamic human force, one which is enriching rather than threatening to the

defined self, when there are shared goals" (Lorde, 1984, p. 45). Multiculturalism involves majority and minority groups alike, and must formulate new goals in a new paradigm where definitions of power enable relating across differences. In the new terrains of social comportment among previously disjointed groups, "commitments to cultural diversity [anticipate] . . . accommodation, integration and transformation" (Goldberg, 1994, p. 7). These should all enhance the global interdependence that is now becoming a universal fact of life.

Multiculturalism as such refers, therefore, to a community in the making   44 and not to a plurality of cultures. Its meaning encompasses the creation of spaces within which different communities (defined by race/ethnicity, gender, and/or class) feel encouraged and are able to grow. The creation of public spaces enables interaction. In this genre and possible action, the construction of a syncretic culture is characterized by consensus while maintaining separate identities. Postmodern thought resists the idea of culture as an organizing principle, which creates borders around ethnicity, class, and gender. Creating borders homogenizes cultures within a culture, although neither dominant nor minority cultures are homogeneous. Taylor (1994) points out that we cannot judge other cultures, for a culture that sufficiently diverges from the norm would speak about, and stand for, situations that constitute different historical and life possibilities for people in different locations, conditions, and relationships. So, what has to happen is a fusion of horizons (a term Taylor borrows from Gadamer), which involves a broader horizon in which we negotiate what Homi Bhabha calls the third space (Bhabha, 1994). This means developing new ideas and vocabularies, which will enable us to make the comparisons partly through transforming our own standards. To do that effectively, three points need to be made:

- The third space is not an extension of established values; it is rather a rene-   45 gotiation of cultural space. Interpreting one level of experience and transposing that to another is creating a multidimensional condition. The words *syncretic* and *hybridity* are useful to imply culture as process. Syncretic suggests the union of opposite principles and practices, while hybridity means to create and innovate by articulating a new way. The third space offers the opportunity to create conventions and practices within and between different modes of meaning. It is the harmonization of cultures, not their dissolution, disappearance, or disintegration.
- The fusion of cultures does not imply difference-blindness, which is neither   46 desirable nor possible. Human beings are different from each other in various ways, and this does not translate into deficiency or deviance when they differ from a traditional norm. It simply means that they are different, but also that they have the right to be different. Indeed, the validation of their cultural, social, and gender differences, and the development of their individual identities, should be a focus of multicultural education. The aim of multicultural education is thus to empower all students with an ethical and democratic vision of society within which they can make a variety of contributions appropriate to their talents, needs, and aspirations.

- Fusion does not mean homogenization; rather, it emphasizes identity   47
  because individuals see the world from their own perspectives and have
  multiple identities, some of which may be contradictory. This makes their
  experiences dialectical. An example is being bilingual or multilingual. We
  do not forget one language when we speak another; rather, we are enriched
  by the knowledge of the other. Diversity will diminish in importance not
  because we will be the same but because it is natural.

Implications for Education

Crisis in Epistemology

The questions arising from the evolution of the concept of knowledge and the   48
function of schooling are central to the teaching profession. What kinds of
knowledge will best ensure that students are critical and participating citizens?
Who produces school knowledge, and who speaks for society? How are the
various groups of students socially and culturally located in terms of the
socio-cultural point of view of school knowledge: the curriculum? Does the
curriculum serve students differently depending upon their gender, race,
ethnic, and class differences? Do teachers assume that their pedagogical practices are suitable for all students even though there are differences in ways of
knowing and learning?

These questions transform the process of teaching. They focus on the   49
relation between discursive practices and the practical subjectivity of those
who produce and/or consume them. They also change the student-teacher
equation where, as Freire (2000) pointed out, knowledge is not an object to
be transmitted from the teacher who has it to the students who do not.
Knowledge is seen increasingly as resulting from specific social and historical
relations, rather than as static entities that are context and value-free. As such,
students are active knowers at the centre of the learning process, knowing
subjects, rather than at the receiving end acquiring knowledge as objects.
The changes in curriculum content and process implied by the major shifts
challenge the knowledge taught by schools as the only legitimate form of
learning. The politics of location become central to the teaching and learning
act. Conventional teaching practices and knowledge are, therefore, at stake.

These challenges to traditional pedagogy confront all societies, but they   50
are particularly crucial in multicultural societies where the complex needs of
students with cultural differences are usually ignored. Critical pedagogy focuses
attention on culturally determined content and practices, and provides the
basic framework for multicultural pedagogy. In the multicultural arrangements of learning, therefore, "students must develop multicultural literacy and
cross-cultural competency if they are to become knowledgeable, reflective,
and caring citizens in the twenty-first century" (Banks, 1997, p. 13).

Multiculturalism as a philosophy must be translated into education. Lived   51
realities cannot be expressed without formal mediation. While realities are
always mediated, the need for radical transformation involves how people
view their specific situations and needs, i.e., from the assimilationist mode of

traditional education rooted in conservative theories (the monocultural), and the accommodation of pluralist theories, to the multicultural mode of critical pedagogy (the heterogeneous). This change must be transformative, not incremental. Transformative change is radical because it is a change in view, perspective, and methodology. It alters the relationship between teacher and student, and between student and the learning environment. It is characterized by a paradigm switch, and thus internally generated, not externally controlled.

Education and the Politics of Difference and Recognition

The cultural pluralist approach to multicultural education by those who consider themselves liberal is additive, and the focus is upon culture as exotic. Education that addresses the needs of a multicultural society deals with social inequalities and inequities, and links power and empowerment with race, gender, and class (among other social constructions) for social change. It attempts to close we/they dichotomies, which maintain inequality. It challenges the prevailing understanding of the process of knowledge generation of Eurocentric subjugated knowledges.   52

Knowledge is directly tied to people's differences, because it locates and situates them in relation to the dominant group in terms of race and ethnicity, gender, and class. The central issue is not merely acknowledging difference (Mohanty, 1990). Multicultural education should enable us to express our differences in other ways (Lewis, 1990), going beyond the equality concept that remains within the existing traditional structure, to a configuration that would encompass differences. Schools need to legitimize multiple traditions of knowledge. And to do that inclusively, multicultural education must address issues to the politics of difference, not just descriptively furnish the components of plurality that will only highlight difference per se.   53

A significant aspect of multicultural education is to teach dominant groups to challenge oppression, especially because their privileged position tends to make it difficult for them to see the world critically. Multicultural education is for *all* students and *all* teachers, not only for oppressed groups. However, equal treatment implies that because all students are not on a level playing field, schools need to give the marginalized students situation-specific treatment that is primarily designed to level the uneven historical and current appropriations in resources, skills, and achievements. As a philosophy, it needs to permeate the school culture, in order for all students to be empowered to cope with existing realities, and have a vision for the future. In the final analysis, it is what Freire (1985) has called education for critical consciousness that could deploy new programs of leaning that may furnish novel and hopefully effective strategies and practices for liberation. Again, the persistence of educational, and therefore socio-economic, inequities, especially in Western multicultural societies, is creating some doubt in the minds of critical pedagogy educators, who urgently call for the pragmatic operationalization and not just the academic discussion of the project to achieve the still-evasive forums of equity and development for all. In this regard, McLaren (1998, p. 452) writes: 54

The critical pedagogy to which I am referring needs to be made less in-formative and more per-formative, less a pedagogy directed toward the interrogation of written texts than a corporeal pedagogy grounded in the lived experiences of students. Critical pedagogy, as I am revisioning it from a Marxist perspective, is a pedagogy that brushes against the grain of textual foundationalism, ocular fetishism, and the monumentalist abstraction of theory that characterizes most critical practice within teacher education classrooms. I am calling for a pedagogy in which a revolutionary multicultural ethics is performed—is lived in the streets—rather than simply reduced to the practice of reading texts (although the reading of texts with other texts, against other texts, and upon other texts is decidedly an important exercise). Teachers need to build upon the textual politics that dominates most multicultural classrooms by engaging in a politics of bodily and affective investment, which means "walking the talk," and working in those very communities one purports to serve.

If and when we decide to achieve McLaren's recommendations, as well as   55
other suggestions that could be contextually effective, then the implications of power differentials must be comprehensively examined. Here, one can see that in order to aim for a practically functioning and situation-changing pedagogy, one must critically develop a relentless program of understanding the enduring but still malleable contours of the social and historical construction of difference that is, somehow, still succeeding in devaluing and excluding the knowledge, and as dangerously, the contemporary realities of the other. The question then should involve how schools organize differences in social and pedagogical interactions that influence the way in which teachers and students define themselves and each other. In Harstock's earlier but still relevant question, does the school "construct an understanding of the world that is sensitive to difference" (Harstock, 1987, p. 189)?

Schools, generally speaking, not only sustain asymmetrical social rela-   56
tions of power, but foster the binary oppositions in society by confirming that the primary term (the "white" in white/black; the "male" in male/female) is superior. Students are socialized to react to human differences in diverse ways: with dislike and fear (racism); with the option of disregarding differences (consensus theories), of accommodating them (liberal theories), or incorporating them (critical multiculturalism). Differences have been used to separate and create walls, rather than to be related across on an equal basis. Those who are different become the other, and their histories, cultures, and experiences are disparaged and/or obliterated and effaced (for example, Native populations in North America and colonized cultures around the world). Pedagogy must be developed around the politics of difference in order to cross borders, not construct barriers. This suggests transcending boundaries of language, culture, and perspectives. Welch (1991) recommended several ways to do this. First, the learning process must represent the construction of subjectivities and identities that link experiences of the other to school curriculum and practices. Race, ethnicity, gender, and class experiences combine to shape identity in complex and contradictory ways.

Secondly, the historical differences that manifest themselves as ideologies   57
such as racism, sexism, and classism need to be dealt with, in order to reveal
how asymmetrical power relations create different conditions for different
groups and individuals. Furthermore, the ways in which differences within
and between groups result in social hierarchy through school structures need
to be understood. The idea is to construct knowledge in which multiple voices
and worldviews are legitimized so that new patterns of relating are forged. It
is essential for both insider and outsider to understand the politics of difference. It is especially important for the different to be allowed to define themselves: "It is axiomatic," says Audre Lorde (1984), "that if we do not define
ourselves for ourselves, we will be defined by others—for their use and to our
detriment" (p. 45). Finally, the creative function of difference needs to be recognized so that it can become the strength necessary for interdependence:
"Difference is that raw and powerful connection from which our personal
power is forged" (Lorde, 1984, p. 112).

Children's experiences and identities are constructed in relation to their   58
gender, class, and race, as well as their ethnicity (which is mediated by culture)
and their location in history. For example, children of immigrant parents are not
what their parents are or were because of their positional identities in history and
culture. The question, then, is how educators can facilitate students' attempts at
making sense of the self and the other in the process of empowerment.

The differences in cultural content of children result in differences in   59
communication and interaction styles, as well as cognitive and learning styles.
This makes it necessary for the teacher, as mediator in the education process,
to develop a knowledge base on which to build understanding. Knowledge of
students is imperative if teachers are to guide their learning experiences, and
lead students to see the connections between what is learned in school and
their lived experiences. Education is not merely collecting disjointed knowledge; rather, it is acquiring conceptual schemes. Learning is to connect, to
make meaning, and must be built on students' experiences and what they
know. It behooves us as educators to understand student experiences, and
how identities are produced differently. Only then can teachers provide students with the analytical tools to deal with problems of unresolved identities
and challenge experiences of racism, sexism, and other inequities.

The effect of difference on identity is one's location in relation to others,   60
and more importantly, how that location produces a concept of self in relation
to the way others identify and define us. As Hall (1997, p. 174) notes, "[for
example] to be English is to know yourself in relation to the French, to the hot-
blooded Mediterraneans, and to the passionate, traumatized Russian soul.
You know that you are what everybody else on the globe is not." In these constructions of identity, schools play a significant role in perpetuating racial,
gender, and class differences. The dynamics of identity and identification in
modern society are complex. The daily experiences that shape the identities of
minority group students, the psychosocial impact of prejudice, and discrimination based on race and ethnicity, gender, and class, are of great significance,
especially with increasing ethnic and racial tensions in schools and society. Key

questions relate to the implications of identity for self-esteem and school achievement, and of ethnic identity for integration and relationship to the dominant culture. The development of oppositional identities is a rejection of the dominant culture, knowledge, and norms by some minority group students.

To incorporate the transformative change, we must redefine multicultural   61 education as radically different from an apolitical representation of education that views culture as artifact, which emphasizes difference but nonetheless attempts to provide strategies to accommodate these differences through equity policies within the dominant traditional structure. It does not change the situation of sexism, racism, and classism in society. It is this that prevents people with differences from maximizing their potential. It places them unfairly and invisibly in a supposedly democratic society. Multicultural education must recognize the politics of difference and culture, and capitalize on the potential offered by difference to develop it as a creative force rather than treat it as a deficiency.

Conclusion

How we come to know, and what we know, defines our position in the   62 world. In their present framework, multicultural educational programs generally emphasize pluralism and benign versions of culture as artifact. This has become part of the problem and discourages change. These programs do not address the real problematic of the politics of difference, power, and dominant hegemony. They remain ineffective because the focus is on addressing the other: those who do not belong to mainstream culture. When the salient issues are not addressed, the inequalities in society are perpetuated. The current levels of racism, sexism, and class discrimination stand witness to the failure of multicultural education to lead students to an understanding of the possibilities of an integrated, rather than a segregated, society.

It is obvious that an educational model of assimilation, which serves the   63 needs of a monocultural society, cannot provide equal opportunity to all groups. The change to a recast multicultural model implies a dramatic shift in worldview, a paradigm shift. However, because this has not been recognized as such, multicultural education has failed to achieve its true objectives due to a paradigm blindness. As Edelsky (1990) pointed out, paradigm blindness is not politically innocent.

"The contemporary search for educational choices is a reflection of the   64 tensions between a changing social reality and an inherited system held captive by its past" (Singh, 1992, p. 12). Traditional theorists have ignored the structural causes of inequality, negated the importance of identity (racial, ethnic, cultural, class, and gender) and blamed the victim for failure. Radical theorists have emphasized the political aspects of schooling because of its functions of reproduction and legitimization of the dominant culture. The theoretical advances made by radical theorists provide valuable insights in explaining the means by which inequality for difference is perpetuated through the content (explicit and implicit), process, and psychological dimensions of an unfair school system.

Critical pedagogy enables an analysis of the dialectics of consciousness 65
and cultural domination by race, class, and gender. Given the nature and magnitude of changes in society, a new kind of education to create a better future
is imperative. Students who are different must be seen in a new light in a
system that has hitherto excluded and marginalized them. A major problem
with the federal Multicultural Policy is that it cannot be effectively implemented in education because education is a provincial responsibility, and
neither legal nor political remedies are available in the absence of a substantive rights guarantee. The legal. provisions (or protections) to prevent discrimination on grounds of ethnicity or race in the Charter of Rights and
Freedoms have implications for education. It is significant, however, that the
Multiculturalism clause for education is vague. It is true that the Canadian
federal government assists multicultural programs and research in education
through a department (originally set up as a Multiculturalism Directorate in
1972 under the Secretary of State). But the lack of federal control over education, and provincial legislation in general, has limited federal ability to
influence education in this direction to any meaningful degree.

Across the country, multiculturalism has been variously interpreted in 66
education. Notwithstanding the fact that Canada is an immigrant country, the
provincial departments of education have historically maintained a policy of
assimilation. The education of various groups in Canada has been assimilationist towards an Anglo-dominated culture, although at least a quarter of the
population has been French and concentrated in Quebec. Furthermore, the
country was built by immigrants from Europe and the Third World.
Following consensus theories, education's role was seen as cultural transmission in the process of human capital formation, and therefore essential for
developing Canada. Within the vision of a monocultural society, it implied
non-recognition or non-acceptance of cultural differences (except for the
dominant English and the subordinate French) for ethnic group relations in all
of Canada, including Quebec. Racial and ethnic (as well as gender and class)
differences were negated in an attempt to devalue non-dominant group characteristics. The exclusion of the other was structural. To achieve more inclusive and effective notions and practices of multiculturalism, the role of
multicultural education becomes paramount. And this paramountcy is again
elevated by the reality of the globalization of difference (discussed in chapter
four) that should force us not only to share spaces of schooling, but also to
coexist, peacefully and productively, in multi-ethnic, multi-racial, and multilinguistic locations of work and residency.

References

Achebe, Chinua (2000). *Home and Exile*. Oxford, UK: Oxford University
Press.
Apple, Michael (1999). *Power, Meaning and Identity: Essays in Critical
Educational Studies*, New York, NY: Peter Lang.
Apple, Michael (2000). *Official Knowledge*, (2nd edn.). New York, NY:
Routledge.

Aronowitz, Stanley (1992). *The Politics of Identity: Class, Culture, Social Movements*. New York, NY: Routledge.

Ashcroft, Bill, Griffiths, Gareth, and Tiffin, Helen, eds. (1995). *The Post-Colonial Studies Reader*. New York, NY: Routledge.

Banks, James (1993). The Canon Debate, Knowledge Construction, and Multicultural Education. *Educational Researcher* (June–July), 4–14.

Banks, James (1997). *Educating Citizens in a Multicultural Society*. New York, NY: Teachers College Press.

Bernstein, Basil (1971). *Class, Codes and Control*. London, UK: Routledge.

Bhabha, Homi (1994). *The Location of Culture*. London, UK: Routledge.

Bourdieu, Pierre (1973). Cultural Reproduction and Social Reproduction. In Richard Brown (ed.), *Knowledge, Education and Cultural Change*. London, UK: Tavistock.

Bourdieu, Pierre and Passeron, Jean-Claude (1990). *Reproduction in Education, Society, and Culture*. London, UK: Sage.

Bowles, Samuel and Gintis, Herbert (1976). *Schooling in Capitalist America: Educational Reform and the Contradictions of Economic Life*. New York, NY: Basic Books.

Carby, Hazel (1992). The Multicultureal Wars. *Radical History Review* 54 (1992 Fall), 7–18.

Carty, Linda (1991). Women's Studies in Canada: A Discourse and Praxis of Exclusion. *Resources for Feminist Reseach* 20(3/4), 12–18.

Collins, Patricia (2000). *Black Feminist Thought: Knowledge, Consciousness and the Politics of Empowerment* (2nd revision, 10th Anniversary edn.) New York, NY: Routledge.

De Lauretis, Teresa (1987). *Technologies of Gender*. Bloomington, IN: Indiana University Press.

Derrida, Jacques (1976). *Of Grammatology* (G. Spivak, Trans.). Baltimore, MD: Johns Hopkins University Press.

Dewey, John (1929). *Democracy and Education: An Introduction to the Philosophy of Education*. New York, NY: Macmillan.

Dewey, John (1952). *Experience and Education*. New York, NY: Macmillan.

Edelsky, Carole (1990). Whose Agenda is this Anyway? A Response to McKenna, Robinson, and Miller, *Educational Researcher* 19(8), 7–11.

Freire, Paulo (2000). *Pedagogy of the Oppressed* (M. Bergman Ramos, Trans.) (30th Anniversary edn). New York, NY: Continuum.

Freire, Paulo (1985). *The Politics of Education: Culture, Power, and Liberation* (D. Macedo. Trans.). South Hadley, MA: Bergin and Garvey.

Freire, Paulo (1998). *Politics and Education* (P. Lindquist Wong, Trans.). Los Angeles, CA: UCLA Latin American Center Publications.

Ghosh, Ratna (1996). *Redefining Multicultural Education*. Toronto, ON: Harcourt Brace.

Gilligan, Carol (1982). *In a Different Voice*. Cambridge, MA: Harvard University Press.

Gilroy, Paul (1990). One Nation Under a Groove: The Cultural Politics of "Race" and Racism in Britain. In D. Goldberg (ed.), *Anatomy of Racism*. Minneapolis, MN: University of Minnesota Press.

Giroux, Henry (1991). Postmodernism As Border Pedagogy: Redefining the Boundaries of Race and Ethnicity. In Henry Giroux (ed.). *Postmodernism, Feminism and Cultural Politics: Redrawing Educational Boundaries.* Albany, NY: State Universtiy of New York Press.

Giroux, Henry (1992). *Border Crossings: Cultural Workers and the Politics of Education.* New York, NY: Routledge.

Giroux, Henry (1993). Living Dangerously: Identity Politics and the New Cultural Racism: Towards a Critical Pedagogy of Representation. *Cultural Studies* 7(1), 1–27.

Giroux, Henry (2001). *Public Spaces, Private Lives: Beyond the Culture of Cynicism.* Lanham, MD: Rowman and Littlefield.

Goldberg, David (1992). The Semantics of Race. *Ethnic and Racial Studies* 15(4), 543–569.

Goldberg, David (1994). Introduction: Multicultural Conditions. In David Goldberg (ed.), *Multiculturalism: A Critical Reader.* Cambridge, MA: Blackwell.

Gore, Jennifer (1993). *The Struggle for Pedagogies: Critical and Feminist Discourses As Regimes of Truth.* New York, NY: Routledge.

Gramsci, Antonio (1990). *Selections from the Prision Notebooks.* (Quintin Hoare and Geoffrey Smith, trans. and eds.). Minneapolis, MN: University of Minnesota Press.

Gramsci, Antonio (1988), *Gramsci's Prison Letters: A Selection* (H. Henderson, trans.). London, UK: Zwan in association with the *Edinburgh Review.*

Habermas, Jürgen (1979). *Communication and the Evolution of Society* (Thomas MsCarthy, trans.). Boston, MA: Beacon Press.

Hall, Stuart (1990). Cultural Identity and Diaspora. In J. Rutherford (ed.), *Identity: Community, Culture, Difference.* London, UK: Lawrence and Wishart.

Hall, Stuart (1997). The Local and the Global: Globalization and Ethnicity. In Anne McClintock, Amir Mufti, and Ella Shohat (eds.), *Dangerous Liaisons: Gender, Nation and Postcolonial Perspectives.* Minneapolis, MN: University of Minnesota Press.

Hartman, Geoffrey (1997). *The Fateful Question of Culture.* New York, NY: Columbia University Press.

Hartstock, Nancy (1987). Rethinking Modernism: Minority vs. Majority Theories. *Cultural Critique* 7, 187–206.

hooks, bell (1984). *Feminist Theory from Margin to Center.* Boston, MA: South End Press.

Horkheimer, Max (1972). *Critical Theory* (Matthew O'Connell, trans.). New York, NY: Herder and Herder.

Julien, Isaac and Mercer, Kobena (1988). De Margin and De Centre. *Screen* 29(4), 2–10.

Lewis, Magda (1990). Interrupting Patriarchy: Politics, Resistance, and Transformation in the Feminist Classroom. *Harvard Educational Review* 60(4), 467–88.

Lorde, Audre (1984). *Sister Outsider*. Trumansburg, NY: Crossing Press.

Luke, Carmen and Gore, Jennifer, eds. (1992). *Feminism and Critical Pedagogy*. New York, NY: Routledge.

Lusted, David (1986). Why Pedagogy? *Screen* 27(5), 2–14.

Lyotard, Jean-Francois (1984). *The Postmodern Condition: A Report on Knowledge* (G. Bennington and B. Massumi, trans.). Minneapolis, MN: University of Minnesota Press.

Marcuse, Herbert (1964). *One-Dimensional Man*. Boston, MA: Beacon Press.

McLaren, Peter (1994). *Critical Pedagogy and Predatory Culture: Oppositional Politics in a Postmodern Era*. New York, NY: Routledge.

McLaren, Peter (1997). *Revolutionary Multiculturalism: Pedagogies of Dissent for the New Millennium*. Boulder, CO: Westview Press.

McLaren, Peter (1998). Revolutionary Pedagogy in Post-Revolutionary Times: Rethinking the Political Economy of Critical Education. *Educational Theory* 48(4), 431–462.

McRobbie, Angela (1991). *Feminism and Youth Culture*. Houndmills, UK: Macmillan.

Mercer, Cecil (1992). *Students with Learning Disabilities*. New York, NY: Maxwell Macmillan Internationl.

Minow, Martha (1990). *Making all the Difference: Inclusion, Exclusion, and American Law*. Ithaca, NY: Cornell University Press.

Mohanty, Chandra (1990). On Race and Voice: Challenges for Liberal Education in the 1990s. *Cultural Critique* 14 (Winter 1989–90), 179–208.

Narayan, Uma and Harding, Sandra (2000). *Decentering the Center: Philosophy for a Multicultural, Postcolonial, and Feminist World*. Bloomington, IN: Indiana University Press.

Ogbu, Johh (1992). Understanding Cultural Diversity and Learning. *Educational Researcher* 21(8), 5–14.

Rich, Adrienne (1986). Notes Toward a Politics of Location. In Adrienne Rich (ed.), *Blood, Bread and Poetry: Selected Prose 1979–1985*. New York, NY: W.W. Norton and Co.

Rutherford, Jonathan (1990). *Identity: Community, Culture, Difference*. London, UK: Lawrence and Wishart.

Said, Edward (1993). *Culture and Imperialsim*. New York, NY: Knopf.

Said, Edward (2000). *Reflections on Exile and Other Essays*. Cambridge, MA: Harvard University Press.

Singh, Raja Roy (1992). Changing Education for a Changing World. *Prospects* 22(1), 7–18.

Taylor, Charles (1994). The Politics of Recognition. In D. Goldberg (ed.) *Multiculturalism: A Critical Reader*. Cambridge, MA: Blackwell.

Weiler, Kathleen (1991). Freire and a Feminist Pedagogy of Difference. *Harvard Educational Review* 61(4), 449–474.

Welch, Sharon (1991). An Ethic of Solidarity and Difference. In H.A. Giroux (ed.), *Postmodernism, Feminism, and Cultural Politics*. Albany, NY: State University of New York Press.

■　■　■

Discussion and Writing Suggestions

1. To what extent does your experience of the education system match the authors' perception that the typical school approach to multiculturalism is assimilationism? Do you have any experience of a more critical multiculturalism that works against anglo-centrism in Canada?

2. Do you agree with the authors that it is not enough to educate for citizenship—that we must educate "to advance the welfare and interests of all who inhabit this earth"?

3. Choose one of the educational theories introduced in this article and test its current status by searching for journal articles that apply the theory to issues of multiculturalism and human rights. Which theories seem to be most useful to the scholars writing in education journals?

Teaching Children Peacekeeping to Avoid Violence in the Schools and in the World

HETTY VAN GURP

Hetty van Gurp (formerly Hetty Adams) is a Nova Scotia educator who suffered the death of her son Ben in a bullying incident at school. Since then she has dedicated herself to promoting the need to teach peace in the schools. In 2001 van Gurp founded Peaceful Schools International (http://peacefulschoolsinternational.org/) in response to requests for support from schools throughout Canada and beyond.

*Van Gurp is a recipient of the Principal of Distinction Award, a Bahá'í commendation for "Promoting Racial Harmony," and the Queen's Golden Jubilee Medal for service to youth. She is the author of three books—*Peace in the Classroom: Practical Lessons in Living for Elementary Age Children; *The Peaceful School: Models that Work; *and *Peer Mediation: The Complete Guide to Resolving Conflict in Our Schools.

Van Gurp delivered the following speech to the Lester B. Pearson Canadian International Peacekeeping Training Centre in Nova Scotia five years after the death of her son.

We all share a common bond through the children in our lives. I am sure that all of us hope that they may live their lives to the absolute fullest in a world that is continually learning better ways to deal with the conflicts we face—whether they be local or global.

My own experience has been primarily with young people in the school system, although I am a member of the Federal Human Rights Tribunal, a panel created by the Government of Canada to conduct inquiries to determine whether the Canadian Human Rights Act has been contravened. The Tribunal has jurisdiction over matters that come within the legislative authority of the

Parliament of Canada. It has quasi-judicial powers and the legal authority to stop discriminatory practices. For enforcement purposes, a Tribunal order is made an order of the Federal Court of Canada.

Most of the panel members have a background in law, but there are also   3
a few ordinary people, such as me. My nomination came as a result of my work with mediation within our public school system and my strong personal commitment to peacemaking.

I consciously use the word commitment as opposed to involvement. To   4
understand the difference, I'd like you to think about a plate of bacon and eggs. It's easy to appreciate that in creating the bacon and eggs, the hen was simply involved while the pig was definitely committed. That's the level of my commitment.

My commitment has its roots in a personal tragedy. My 14-year-old son   5
died five years ago while in school as a result of an act of aggression by another student. In order to help myself cope with the loss, I decided to do whatever I could to teach other children alternatives to violence within my own world, which was a kindergarten classroom at the time.

My approach was to create a curriculum in peacemaking which I call   6
Lessons in Living. These are basically lessons to enlighten young people to believe in themselves—to believe that they can be a powerful influence for bringing about needed changes in our society and in the world at large. Lessons in Living includes teaching such skills as co-operation, effective communication, tolerance, empathy, and conflict resolution, including mediation. I truly believe that if the youth can be empowered by a combination of factual knowledge of the world situation while being convinced of their own ability to change that situation for the better, your jobs will be a lot easier.

I used to ask myself this question: If peace is what every government says   7
it seeks and it is the yearning of every heart, then why are we not teaching it and studying it in schools?

I believe that many educators have arrived at the conclusion that we   8
must now teach our children peacemaking skills. We recognized that we cannot change behaviour simply by creating behaviour codes, any more than a country can eliminate crime by creating more law. In both cases it would be much like hanging a poster of Einstein on your bedroom wall in the hope that this will make you brilliant.

The skills you have learned here over the past weeks should be a part of   9
our education. Why didn't we learn these skills in school?

Students in our schools today do not have to wait until they are adults to   10
realize that there are effective alternatives to violence. In my own school, every student receives Lessons in Living. We have students trained in mediation who handle most of the conflicts that occur between students. Our school is a safe and peaceful place, and as a result our students enjoy being there. As a principal, I feel that the first assurance I need to make to parents is that their children will feel safe in school, and then I know that learning will take place.

I am reading a book by Neil Postman about the current state of education   11
in America. He examines alternative strategies that we can use to instill our

children with a sense of global citizenship. I'd like to share with you a fable that appears in this book. (I have shortened it just a bit.)

A Classroom Fable

Once upon a time in the city of New York, civilized life very nearly came to an end. The air and rivers were polluted, and no one could cleanse them. The schools were rundown and no one believed in them. Each day brought new hardships. Crime and strife, intolerance and disorder were to be found everywhere. The young fought the old. The poor fought the rich. The politicians fought with everyone. 12

When things came to the most desperate moment, the mayor declared a state of emergency. Our city, he said, is under siege like the ancient cities of Troy and Jericho but our enemies are indifference, hatred and violence. 13

One of the mayor's aides, in order to prepare for his exodus from the city, began to read Henry David Thoreau's *Walden*, which he had been told was a useful handbook on how to survive in the country. While reading the book he came upon this passage: Students should not play at life or study it merely while the community supports them at this expensive game, but earnestly live from beginning to end. The aide explained to the mayor that the students in the public schools who had heretofore been part of the general problem, with some imagination and a change of perspective might easily become part of the general solution. 14

But how can we use them? asked the mayor. What would happen to their education if we did? 15

To this the aide replied, They will live their education in the process of trying to save our city. As for their lessons, we have ample evidence that the young do not exactly appreciate them and are now even turning against their teachers and schools. The aide pointed out that the city was spending $1 million a year merely replacing broken windows and nearly one-third of all students enrolled in the schools did not show up on any given day. 16

The Emergency Education Committee and the state at once made plans to remove 400 000 students from their dreary classrooms and their even drearier lessons so that their energy and talents might be used to repair their desecrated city. When these plans became known to the teachers, they complained that their contract made no provision for such unusual procedures. To this the aide replied, "It is not written in any holy book that an education must occur in a small room with chairs in it." And so, the curriculum of the public schools of New York became known as Operation Survival, and all the children became part of it. 17

Here are some of the things they were obliged to do: 18

First, the students cleaned up their neighbourhoods. They swept and painted, cleaned and tidied. They planted flowers and trees and even repaired rundown buildings, starting with their own rundown schools. Some students were given responsibility to assist in hospitals, some helped with the elderly. They published a newspaper to include good news. They helped in day care centres, in food banks, and in libraries. Students trained in mediation helped 19 ease the burden of the court system. They helped register voters, organized seminars and lectures. The city began to come alive.

Amazingly, the students soon learned that while they did not receive an   20
education, they were able to create one.

They lived their lessons in social studies, geography and communication   21
and many other things that decent and proper people know about. It even
came to pass that the older people, who had regarded the young as unruly and
parasitic, came to respect them. There followed a revival of courtesy and a
decrease in crime. Now it would be foolish to deny that there were not some
problems attending this adventure. For instance, thousands of children who
would otherwise have known the principal rivers of Uruguay had to live out
their lives in ignorance of these facts. Hundreds of teachers felt that their
training had been wasted because they could not educate children unless it
were done in a classroom.

But the mayor promised that as soon as the emergency was over, every-   22
thing would return to normal. Meanwhile, everyone lived happily ever after.

The moral of this fable might be that a sense of responsibility for the   23
planet is born out of a sense of responsibility for one's own neighbourhood.
It is also important that we look at the things we are teaching young people
and that we begin to reexamine our priorities. We cannot afford to waste the
energy and potential idealism of the young. We need to continually look for
ways to encourage youthful participation in social reconstruction.

Last week when I was working with a group of five-year-olds in my   24
school, I told them that I would be coming here and that I would have an
opportunity to meet some adult peacekeepers who might find themselves in
situations of conflict and danger. I asked if they had any advice for you.
Some of the advice reflects that even at the age of five, children can be very
wise. I call this Words of Wisdom for Peacekeepers.

WORDS OF WISDOM FOR PEACEKEEPERS
(from the Primary Students of William King Elementary School)

Make sure you don't make any deals so you won't join sides.
Be careful, because in a war, even the people on the good team could
get hurt.
Run away and when the coast is clear, come out and help. If you can't
run fast, use a Jeep.
Always bring a guard with you.
Talk it out. They might listen if you are peaceful.
When a gun shoots, duck.
Give the job to somebody else.
Hide behind a rock or a tree or a haystack.
Watch out for swinging swords.
Don't bring guns into countries.
Plant flowers.
Keep up the good work.

Alternatives to Violence

I have often been accused of being an optimist. Although I realize that violence, civil strife, and even war may never be totally eliminated, I do believe that we can make great strides towards that goal if we continue to teach both young people and adults in positions of authority and power that there are alternatives to violence. 25

To cynical people who say that we are wasting our time, I remind them that, in our society, there are many things that we have been able to make totally unacceptable. From drinking and driving to smoking in public places, from slavery to segregation, we have made great progress. Why, then, can't we make senseless acts of violence and ultimately war, universally shameful? 26

I realize that there are both opponents and proponents of the thesis that humankind is naturally aggressive. Certainly man has a potential for violence that cannot be denied—but human nature only makes war possible, it does not make war inevitable. 27

Over the course of the past 4000 years of experimentation and repetition, warmaking has become a habit. For our own survival, we now need to unlearn this habit which we have taught ourselves. 28

In my optimism, I see this as being a hopeful time in human history—a time of effective disarmament and a time of the adoption of humanitarianism as a principle in world affairs. The majority of people in all parts of the world spend their days in a spirit of fellowship and seek to avoid discord and to diffuse confrontation. 29

I feel a deep sense of pride that Canada has a strong commitment to peacekeeping and Canada's leadership in this role is incontestable. By its historic association with peacekeeping, Canada is universally recognized as a prime mover in putting United Nations peacekeeping capacities on a more solid footing. 30

The world community needs, more than ever before, skilled and disciplined peacekeepers—protectors of civilization. 31

When I think of peacekeepers, I think of men and women who dress like soldiers, organize like soldiers, live like soldiers, and are often equipped like soldiers, but in terms of traditional images, they behave in an unsoldierly way: they prefer compromise to conquest, and persuasion and prevention to punishment. 32

The example you set for our young people and the potential for creating partnerships between military peacekeepers and non-military peacekeepers, no matter how small or seemingly insignificant, is reason enough to be optimistic. 33

Recently, I was honoured to be chosen as this year's recipient of the YMCA Peace Medal. The YMCA Statement on Peace says: 34

Peace has many dimensions. It is not only a state of relationships among nations. We cannot expect to live in a world of peace if we are unable to live in peace with those close to us—even those who differ from us.

The responsibility for peace begins with each person, in relationships   35
with the family and friends, and extends to community life and national
activities. There are no simple recipes.

Because of my work in promoting the need for teaching our students   36
skills in peacemaking, I often get calls from parents and teachers who are
faced with a serious problem. Recently I got a call from a mother whose 13-
year-old son lay in a coma in the hospital after a senseless beating by some of
his peers. This boy was different from his classmates and for them this seemed
to be enough of a reason to beat him. This mother was looking for a quick fix
or a simple solution to the problems in her son's school. I had to tell her that
there is no easy answer. But there is a solution—one that takes time and commitment (there's that word again). That solution is for us to create a climate
in our schools where aggression of any kind is totally unacceptable.

Within my own school, and now on a broader scale, I work with stu-   37
dents, teachers, and parent groups to introduce them to the skills of peacemaking. As you know, some schools can be extremely intimidating with
gangs and bullies tyrannizing the playground.

In some ways, the world is like a big schoolyard where we often feel pow-   38
erless to stop fights or keep the bullies from hurting each other or innocent
victims. With bullies in school, and possibly with global bullies as well, we
need to look at the underlying causes of insecurity and aggression.

Children today are saturated with violence—from games to television and   39
movies, to schoolyards, the streets, and homes. The sad part is that often we
don't recognize it. Because of this, children become desensitized to violence.
The average young person in North America watches 22 hours of television
per week. By high school graduation, a young person will have witnessed over
18 000 murders on TV. In an effort to balance this, I feel, therefore, that it is
incumbent upon us to saturate these young people with more peaceful ways
of living together.

If young people have become more violent in recent years, then unfortu-   40
nately this is our legacy to them. Children are born into a world not of their
own making. We all recognize that children are not born with a compelling
urge to hurt others, whether verbally or physically. This is a behaviour they
learn.

But on the positive side, it is also possible to unlearn such behaviours, and   41
this is how I see my role as an educator.

In our mediation training, there is one activity that carries a strong mes-   42
sage in its predictable outcome. It's an activity where we break the students
into three groups and send each of the groups off with a task. The first group
is asked to make a list of the things children typically argue or fight about,
and how they handle these conflicts. The second group does the same, but
they look at the things adults argue or fight about. The third group deals with
world leaders. When they finish this task and return to the group, we examine the commonalties among the three groups. Are there things that all three
groups fight about? Are there ways in which all three groups handle their con-

flicts in the same manner? Inevitably, there are many commonalties. Sadly enough, when we ask the question, So, what have we learned about handling conflict from childhood, through adulthood and even to positions of world power? The answer is always a resounding, Nothing!

I think we would all agree that conflict is a normal, unavoidable part of 43 life. Human beings are continually involved in conflicts. However, our response to that conflict is what determines its outcome. We can either respond in a confrontational, adversarial way, or attempt to resolve conflict in a more positive, creative manner. The list from the third group of students often cites war as a common way that world leaders handle conflicts. Some of these leaders believe (and perhaps deserve credit for the intensity of their beliefs) that violence is the only way to stop violence.

Gwynne Dyer, author and narrator of the television series *War*, said: 44

Some generation of mankind was eventually bound to face the task of abolishing war, because civilization was bound to endow us, sooner or later, with the power to destroy ourselves. We happen to be that generation though we did not ask for the honour and we do not feel ready for it. There is nobody wiser who will take responsibility and handle this problem for us. We have to do it ourselves.

I am not suggesting that we can dismiss a country's legitimate security 45 needs, but plainly, a military response forms only a small part of that security. A deeper level of security is assured if a network of valued relationships can be formed. A peaceful, relationship-building international approach is as much a national defence strategy as war, weapons, or confrontation.

Ordinary people, solving problems effectively, build the conflict-resolving 46 community, and conflict-resolving communities are the building blocks of a peaceful world.

Peacekeepers, both at a school level as well as an international level, 47 need to reach beyond confrontation to remove the causes as well as the symptoms of violence and strife.

In teaching tolerance, anger management, and conflict resolution skills to 48 young people, we are equipping them with the tools to do that. We are providing them with the attitudes, knowledge, and skills to become responsible, fully-participating members of society. Tolerance, especially, is essential to the realization of human rights and the achievement of peace.

Our classrooms are microcosms of the cultural diversity of the global 49 economy. Cross-cultural understanding has become a primary requirement of a healthy learning climate, in schools and around the world.

We have a quote by Lester B. Pearson in our school: 50

We are now emerging into an age when different civilizations will have to learn to live side by side in peaceful interchange, learning from each other, studying each other's history, ideals, arts and culture; mutually enriching each other's lives.

My guess is that much of that has been happening here over the past few   51
weeks. I have written a book, *Peace in the Classroom,* in which I devote a
chapter to ideas for classroom activities to promote acceptance of differences. If we do not diligently address the problem of intolerance we are destined to live with stereotyping, prejudice, scapegoating, discrimination,
bullying, and segregation. We need to educate children and young people with
a sense of openness and comprehension toward other people, their diverse cultures and histories, and their fundamental, shared humanity.

I dream sometimes. I think it goes with the territory of being an optimist.   52
I dream that one day, each school across this nation, and maybe even the
world, will have earned the right to proudly fly a flag from its flagpole declaring itself to be a peaceful school. What if, one day, every nation on this
planet could fly such a flag? Part of my vision would require that all people
inheriting or elected to positions of political power would be required to
have some formal training in mediation and negotiation.

The young people learning mediation skills in our school system will be   53
entering society as adults well equipped with the tools needed to resolve conflict with a sense of fairness, patience, and compromise.

Earlier, I read to you some advice from five-year olds. Now I will read a   54
letter from one of my 11-year-old students who is also a mediator.

Dear Peacekeepers:

I am 11 years old and I am a mediator in my school.

Sometimes it is hard to be someone who helps out. People don't
always listen, but when they do and we get through to them it's a wonderful feeling to know you helped someone.

What you are doing in the world is brave and awesome. You are
doing a good job trying to stop people from making war. I wish there was
not a need for peacekeepers but we all know that there are many things
in the world that need to change first. Things like hunger and racism.

War seems so pointless. What does it prove? That one country is better
at fighting than the other? If only the whole world could learn mediation.

My advice to you is to keep your eye on the goal of world peace. Thanks   55
for trying to make the world a better place for us. I wish you all the best in the
future.

■ ■ ■

Discussion and Writing Suggestions

1. Visit the website of van Gurp's organization (http://peacefulschoolsinterna-
   tional.org/) and try to find other organizations and programs that promote
   an ethic of care in the school system such as The Roots of Empathy program. What similarities and differences do they have? Which seem the most
   radical in the sense of getting at the root causes of violence?

2. Like many other educators, van Gurp sees strong connections between bullying in the schoolyard and aggression in the larger world. Is there a causal connection between the two, or are they simply different levels of analysis of the same social problem?

■ WRITING AND RESEARCH ACTIVITIES

1. This chapter covers topics as far afield as poverty, racism, homophobia, teachers as participants in oppressive systems, and residential schools. Although the authors do not make the connections explicitly, all of these topics can be seen as related aspects of the abuse of power in the school system. Using some of these readings as source material, write an essay from the perspective that all of these are symptomatic of a more general problem in the way schools work in and for our society.

2. The readings in this chapter are one-sided in the sense that they include only one article (Clifton's) offering the perspectives of educators, students, or parents who believe that many schools fulfill their mandates very well indeed by offering students an education that prepares them for post-secondary education and the workplace. Write an essay in which you critique the liberationist outlooks of some of the readings in this chapter. Develop the position that schools should be in the business of preparing students to succeed in society as it is, not of disturbing the status quo.

3. Research the issue of residential schools in more depth, including legal documents, scholarly articles and books that present the testimonies of former students. Write a research essay in which you try to account for the cruelties, both official and unofficial, of the residential school system.

4. Aboriginal Canadians are not the only people to have been colonized under British rule. Find research sources on the topic of the education of indigenous peoples in another part (or parts) of the former British Empire: Africa, Asia, Australia, New Zealand, India, Hong Kong, the United States, or the Caribbean. Write an essay in which you compare and contrast the Canadian residential school system to the systems of education established elsewhere under British colonial rule.

5. Some people argue that the residential school system was a product of its time, a time when schooling was not only racist but harsh in its treatment of all students. Investigate the validity of this claim by finding sources about the treatment of students in the Canadian public school system in the first part of the twentieth century and comparing that system with the residential school system.

6. Many educators across the country are starting to integrate anti-homophobia education into the curriculum, some of them with the support of school authorities, and some without. Write a research essay investigating the state of anti-homophobia education in Canadian schools. After doing some preliminary research, narrow your focus to one

level of education (university, high school, junior high, or elementary) or one site (say, Vancouver, Winnipeg, Ottawa, or Toronto, to name the cities most prominent in the effort) or one issue. (What form should it take? Should any school be exempt from implementing it?)

The Brave New World of Biotechnology

What is biotechnology? Broadly speaking, biotechnology encompasses "all the studies and techniques that combine the ideas and needs of biology and medicine with engineering" (Grolier's *Academic American Encyclopedia*). In the public mind, however, biotechnology has mainly come to be associated with a range of controversial applications in the areas of genetic engineering, medicine, human genetics, crop and food production, and the forensic use of DNA. In this chapter, we will focus on some of these controversies—on the science behind them and on the ethical, social, political, and legal issues that make them important.

Genetics, the science of inherited characteristics, has figured in human history (in a rough and ready way) for thousands of years—in the breeding of domesticated plants and animals to obtain desired types. Formal scientific studies in genetics, however, date only from the experiments of the Austrian botanist Gregor Mendel (1822–1884). Mendel established some of the basic laws of inheritance by crossbreeding plants with certain characteristics and noting how those characteristics were distributed in subsequent generations. But the means for understanding the molecular basis of those laws was not developed until 1953, when James Watson, an American, and Francis Crick, a Briton, published a landmark article in the scientific journal *Nature* that first elucidated the molecular structure of DNA (deoxyribonucleic acid). It had been known for some time that DNA is the chemical compound forming the genetic material (chromosomes and genes) of all organisms, but understanding how DNA functions in the process of inheritance required knowledge of DNA's molecular structure. Watson and Crick showed that DNA has the structure of a double helix—that is, two interconnected helical strands (see illustration, p. 384).

Each of the two strands of the DNA molecule consists of a sugar-phosphate "backbone" and sequences of nucleotides, or bases, attached to the backbone. The bases pair up in specific ways to connect the two strands. In most organisms, DNA is present in all cells in the form of chromosomes gathered in a cell's nucleus. Genes are parts of chromosomes—that is, they are segments of DNA. Each gene is a sequence of bases that governs the production of a certain protein, so the sequence of bases that forms a gene can be viewed as a "code" for producing a protein; hence, the term *genetic code*. Acting separately and together, the proteins produced by the genes determine many of the organism's physical and behavioural characteristics, including the way in which the organism progresses through its life cycle. And because genes are passed along from one generation to the next, they are the basis for heredity.

Watson and Crick's discovery and the subsequent advances in genetics provided the foundation for genetic engineering, and the techniques developed for genetic engineering made possible the controversial applications in medicine and human genetics that are the focus of this chapter.

Genetic engineering (a branch of biotechnology) is "the application of the knowledge obtained from genetic investigations to the solution of such problems as infertility, diseases, food production, waste disposal, and improvement of a species" (Grolier's *Academic American Encyclopedia*). Genetic engineering is also known as "gene splicing" and as "recombinant DNA technology" because it involves combining the DNA (that is, splicing together the genes) of different organisms. For example, a gene with a certain desired function (e.g., that of generating a particular antibody) could be taken from the cells of one person and inserted into the cells of a person lacking that gene, thus enabling the second person to produce the desired antibody.

In another kind of application, genes that generate desired products can be inserted into the DNA of bacteria or other types of cells that replicate rapidly. When the "engineered" cells replicate, they copy the foreign genes along with their own and generate the products specified by those genes. Populations of such cells can function as "factories" to produce large quantities of useful products.

The following ad hasn't appeared anywhere yet; but many people are afraid that something like this could result if the revolution in biotechnology continues, unchecked by ethical considerations:

> Career competition in the twenty-first century will be tough. The prizes will go only to those with the right combination of high-level physical and mental attributes. Why take a chance? You can guarantee that your unborn child will have what it takes to succeed in this demanding environment. Our highly trained medical staff stands ready to assist you in designing and executing a genetic profile for your offspring. Call today for an appointment with one of our counsellors.
>
> —GenePerfect, Inc.

The moral dilemmas now enveloping biotechnology would not be so hotly debated if the technology itself were not so remarkable and effective. Thanks to its successes so far—in making possible, for instance, the cheap and plentiful production of such disease-fighting agents as insulin and interferon—numerous people have been able to live longer and healthier lives. Its promise in improved agricultural production is exciting. And even without considering the practical consequences, we have the prospect of a new world of knowledge about life itself and the essential components of our own humanity—our own individuality—as revealed in our distinctive genetic codes.

Gene splicing can be done by means of special enzymes ("restriction enzymes") that can split DNA from one organism into fragments that will combine with similarly formed fragments from another organism, thus forming a new DNA molecule. Copies of this new molecule can be obtained by inserting it into a host cell that replicates the molecule every time it divides, as in the examples just described. In 1985, however, a more efficient method of gene splicing was developed, called *polymerase chain reaction* (PCR), done in a test tube rather than with living cells. PCR allows the double helix of the new DNA molecule to be split into its two complementary strands. When mixed with DNA polymerase from certain bacteria, the two strands function as templates for the generation of two copies of the new molecule. Thus PCR allows a repeated, rapid doubling in the number of desired molecules.

Gene splicing experiments began in the early 1970s, at first involving DNA exchanges between unicellular organisms, such as viruses and bacteria. But recipients of "foreign" DNA soon included more complex organisms, such as fruit flies and frogs (although no humans, at this stage). During this early period of experimentation, some people began to worry about the possibility of a genetic disaster. What if some newly engineered microbes escaped from the lab and caused an epidemic of a new and unknown disease, for which there was no known cure? What if the delicate ecological balance of nature or the course of evolution were drastically affected? (Fears of DNA experimentation gone haywire were expertly—and thrillingly—exploited by Michael Crichton's novel [and Steven Spielberg's movie] *Jurassic Park*, in which a new race of rampaging dinosaurs is cloned from ancient DNA and spliced with frog DNA.) Some proposed an outright ban on genetic engineering experiments. At an international conference in Asilomar, California, in 1975, scientists agreed on a set of guidelines to govern future research.

In time, these early fears turned out to be groundless, and the restrictions were eased or lifted. Meanwhile, considerable strides were made in genetic engineering, with new applications discovered in agriculture, pollution control, and the fight against a host of diseases. Genetic engineering became big business, as many scientists abandoned the academy to found and work for firms with names such as Genentech and Genex.

But reservations persist. Some people are uncomfortable with the fact of genetic engineering itself, considering it an unwarranted intrusion by human beings into the fragile structure of Nature, with too little knowledge or care about the consequences. Others have no philosophical objections to genetic engineering but worry about its effects on the environment and on humans. Or they worry about the kind of ethical problems raised by the new field of *genetic therapy*—the kind of problems suggested by the imaginary ad in this chapter's introduction. Of course, this is an extreme example. Most people would have no problem with using genetic therapy to cure life-threatening diseases or conditions. For example, in a pioneering experiment in 1992, genes were injected into the blood cells of three infants lacking an enzyme whose

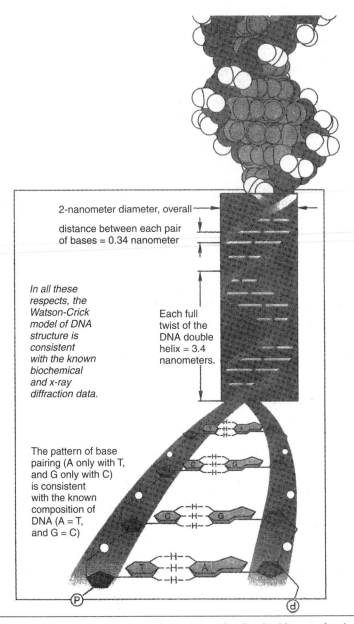

2-nanometer diameter, overall

distance between each pair
of bases = 0.34 nanometer

*In all these
respects, the
Watson-Crick
model of DNA
structure is
consistent
with the known
biochemical
and x-ray
diffraction data.*

Each full
twist of the
DNA double
helix = 3.4
nanometers.

The pattern of base
pairing (A only with T,
and G only with C)
is consistent
with the known
composition of
DNA (A = T,
and G = C)

The double helix structure of DNA (deoxyribonucleic acid). The "backbone" of each strand is composed of sugar-phosphate molecules. Nucleotide bases are attached to the back-bones, and the two strands are linked by pairs of these bases. There are four different bases in DNA—the nucleotides adenine (A), cytosine (C), guanine (G), and thymine (T)—and they pair up in a highly restricted way: A pairs only with T, and C pairs only with G. Each unit of three successive base pairs (i.e., a "triplet") governs the production of an amino acid. Proteins are composed of amino acids. Thus, a gene is a sequence of triplets governing the production of a protein that consists of the amino acids specified by those triplets.

Source: Cecie Starr and Ralph Taggart, *Biology: The Unity and Diversity of Life*

absence prevented their bodies from fighting off potentially deadly viral and bacterial infections. Three years later, the infants' cells appeared to be producing on their own the enzyme that is crucial to their survival.

There is little controversy over such forms of genetic therapy. But should genetic therapy be conducted to "correct" left-handedness? Nearsightedness? Baldness? Or even to *detect* such potential conditions? A recent survey for *Redbook* magazine revealed that while only 18 percent of respondents disapproved of *genetic testing* and manipulation to discover whether a child would have a disease or disability, an overwhelming 86 percent disapproved of using such a tool to select the sex of a child; 91 percent, to increase the child's IQ; and 94 percent, to improve the child's athletic ability. (Of course, such figures could change dramatically when the possibilities become real instead of abstract.)

There are other troubling aspects of biotechnology. Genetic testing may be used as a *screening* device by employers and insurance companies—in other words, it may be used as a means of genetic discrimination. Employers may be disinclined to hire prospective employees for whom genetic screening has revealed a present or potential health problem, such as heart disease. Since many genetic traits are linked to race or sex, genetic discrimination could be another form of racial or gender discrimination. Another area of concern is the Human Genome Project, a massive scientific undertaking begun in the late 1980s to determine the complete genetic makeup of human chromosomes. Armed with the knowledge of what each gene does and where it is located, scientists (it is feared) would be able to manipulate human cells to create individuals with qualities considered desirable, while eliminating qualities considered undesirable. For many, such possibilities bring to mind the notorious Nazi eugenics programs aimed at creating an Aryan "master" race and exterminating "inferior" races. And, as the O. J. Simpson trial has dramatically demonstrated, there is controversy over the *forensic* use of DNA—the use of DNA testing in legal proceedings to determine guilt. While many suspects, and some convicted persons, have been exonerated as a result of DNA testing, some defence attorneys have contested the validity and reliability of DNA evidence when it is used by the prosecution.

For most, then, the problem is not so much biotechnology itself as its possible abuses. This chapter explores the controversies surrounding the application of genetic engineering in the areas of human health and agriculture. In our first readings, related to genetics and human biology, we begin with the opening chapter of Aldous Huxley's dystopian novel *Brave New World*, which for more than 60 years has served as an unforgettable warning of the dark side of scientific progress. Here we see human ova fertilized outside the womb, the embryos and fetuses conditioned and then decanted (born) from bottles, prepared to do specific jobs and to be contented and productive citizens in a stable society. Later in the chapter, sobering views emerge again in Michael Valpy's piece, in which he consults an international panel of medical researchers who comment on the promise and the danger of biogenetics.

Huxley's dark vision is followed by Cecie Starr and Ralph Taggart's article (an excerpt from their science text), which explains the mechanics of genetic engineering as well as some of the ethical problems involved in its use. From here, we look at several largely supportive responses to genetic engineering. Canadian scientist Henry Friesen expounds the view that this work will improve health and the general quality of life in Canada and the developing countries. Next, journalist Virginia Postrel defends genetic therapies from the libertarian perspective that the rights of individuals should come first. She argues that professional ethicists and government should stay out of the business of mandating which genetic therapies are socially acceptable. The needs of patients and the services of physicians and surgeons—that is, the free market—should determine which services, including cloning, should become available. Peter Calamai and Rey Pagtakhan are also optimistic about the role of biogenetics in the context of Canadian society.

Brave New World

ALDOUS HUXLEY

The title of Aldous Huxley's novel Brave New World *(1932) derives from a line in Shakespeare's final comedy,* The Tempest. *In that play, Miranda is a young woman who has grown up on an enchanted island; her father is the only other human she has known. When she suddenly encounters people from the outside world (including a handsome young prince), she remarks, "O brave [wondrous] new world that has such people in it!" Shakespeare used the line ironically (the world of* The Tempest *is filled with knaves and fools); and almost three hundred years later, Huxley employed not only the language but also the irony in labelling his nightmare society of* A.F. *632 (After [Henry] Ford).*

In comparison with other dystopias, like George Orwell's 1984*, Huxley's brave new world of creature comforts seems, at first glance, a paradise. People are given whatever they need to keep happy: unlimited sex, tranquilizers, and soothing experiences. No one goes hungry; no one suffers either physical or spiritual pain. But the cost of such comfort is an almost total loss of individuality, creativity, and freedom. Uniformity and stability are exalted above all other virtues. The population is divided into castes, determined from before birth, with the more intelligent Alphas and Betas governing and managing the society, while the less intelligent Deltas, Gammas, and Epsilons work at the menial tasks. Epsilons are not unhappy with their lot in life because they have been conditioned to be content; in fact, they are incapable of conceiving anything better. Love, art, and science are suppressed for all castes because they lead to instability, and instability threatens happiness. Idle reflection is discouraged for the same reason; to avoid the effects of any intense emotions—positive or negative—the inhabitants of this brave new world are given regular doses of the powerful tranquilizer "soma."*

Huxley's brave new world, then, is a projection into the future of disturbing or dangerous tendencies he saw in his own world. In the context of our present chapter on biotechnology, we are most interested in Huxley's portrait of a "hatchery," where human ova are removed from the womb and fertilized, and where the embryos and fetuses grown in bottles are programmed before "birth" to produce an assortment of the kind of people who will be most desirable to society. In the following passage, the first chapter of Brave New World, *we are taken on a tour through the Central London Hatchery and Conditioning Centre, where we follow an egg from fertilization through conditioning. To many people today, Huxley's dramatic portrait of the manipulation of human germ cells is uncomfortably close to what modern genetic engineers are beginning, with ever greater facility, to make possible: the substitution of "more desirable" for "less desirable" genes in order to create "better" people.*

Born in Surrey, England, Aldous Huxley (1894–1963), grandson of naturalist T. H. Huxley, intended to pursue a medical career, but after being stricken with a corneal disease that left him almost blind, he turned to literature. Among his works are Crome Yellow *(1921),* Antic Hay *(1923),* Point Counter Point *(1928), and* Eyeless in Gaza *(1936). Huxley moved to the United States in 1936, settling in California. In the latter part of his life, he tended toward the mystical and experimented with naturally occurring hallucinogenic drugs—the subject of his* Doors of Perception *(1954).*

A squat grey building of only thirty-four stories. Over the main entrance the   1
words, Central London Hatchery and Conditioning Centre, and, in a shield, the World State's motto: Community, Identity, Stability.

The enormous room on the ground floor faced towards the north. Cold   2
for all the summer beyond the panes, for all the tropical heat of the room itself, a harsh thin light glared through the windows, hungrily seeking some draped lay figure, some pallid shape of academic gooseflesh, but finding only the glass and nickel and bleakly shining porcelain of a laboratory. Wintriness responded to wintriness. The overalls of the workers were white, their hands gloved with a pale corpse-coloured rubber. The light was frozen, dead, a ghost. Only from the yellow barrels of the microscopes did it borrow a certain rich and living substance, lying along the polished tubes like butter, streak after luscious streak in long recession down the work tables.

"And this," said the Director opening the door, "is the Fertilizing   3
Room."

Bent over their instruments, three hundred Fertilizers were plunged, as the   4
Director of Hatcheries and Conditioning entered the room, in the scarcely breathing silence, the absent-minded, soliloquizing hum or whistle, of absorbed concentration. A troop of newly arrived students, very young, pink and callow, followed nervously, rather abjectly, at the Director's heels. Each of them carried a notebook, in which, whenever the great man spoke, he desperately scribbled. Straight from the horse's mouth. It was a rare privilege. The D.H.C. for Central London always made a point of personally conducting his new students round the various departments.

"Just to give you a general idea," he would explain to them. For of course some sort of general idea they must have, if they were to do their work intelligently—though as little of one, if they were to be good and happy members of society, as possible. For particulars, as every one knows, make for virtue and happiness; generalities are intellectually necessary evils. Not philosophers but fret-sawyers and stamp collectors compose the backbone of society.

"To-morrow," he would add, smiling at them with a slightly menacing geniality, "you'll be settling down to serious work. You won't have time for generalities. Meanwhile ... "

Meanwhile, it was a privilege. Straight from the horse's mouth into the notebook. The boys scribbled like mad.

Tall and rather thin but upright, the Director advanced into the room. He had a long chin and big, rather prominent teeth, just covered, when he was not talking, by his full, floridly curved lips. Old, young? Thirty? Fifty? Fifty-five? It was hard to say. And anyhow the question didn't arise; in this year of stability, A.F. 632, it didn't occur to you to ask it.

"I shall begin at the beginning," said the D.H.C. and the more zealous students recorded his intention in their notebooks: *Begin at the beginning.* "These," he waved his hand, "are the incubators." And opening an insulated door he showed them racks upon racks of numbered test-tubes. "The week's supply of ova. Kept," he explained, "at blood heat; whereas the male gametes," and here he opened another door, "they have to be kept at thirty-five instead of thirty-seven. Full blood heat sterilizes." Rams wrapped in thermogene beget no lambs.

Still leaning against the incubators he gave them, while the pencils scurried illegibly across the pages, a brief description of the modern fertilizing process; spoke first, of course, of its surgical introduction—"the operation undergone voluntarily for the good of Society, not to mention the fact that it carries a bonus amounting to six months' salary"; continued with some account of the technique for preserving the excised ovary alive and actively developing; passed on to a consideration of optimum temperature, salinity, viscosity; referred to the liquor in which the detached and ripened eggs were kept; and, leading his charges to the work tables, actually showed them how this liquor was drawn off from the test-tubes; how it was let out drop by drop onto the specially warmed slides of the microscopes; the eggs which it contained were inspected for abnormalities, counted and transferred to a porous receptacle; how (and he now took them to watch the operation) this receptacle was immersed in a warm bouillon containing free-swimming spermatozoa—at a minimum concentration of one hundred thousand per cubic centimetre, he insisted; and how, after ten minutes, the container was lifted out of the liquor and its contents re-examined; how, if any of the eggs remained unfertilized, it was again immersed, and, if necessary, yet again; how the fertilized ova went back to the incubators; where the Alphas and Betas remained until definitely bottled; while the Gammas, Deltas and Epsilons were brought out again, after only thirty-six hours, to undergo Bokanovsky's Process.

"Bokanovsky's Process," repeated the Director, and the students under-   11
lined the words in their little notebooks.

One egg, one embryo, one adult—normality. But a bokanovskified egg   12
will bud, will proliferate, will divide. From eight to ninety-six buds, and
every bud will grow into a perfectly formed embryo, and every embryo into
a full-sized adult. Making ninety-six human beings grow where only one
grew before. Progress.

"Essentially," the D.H.C. concluded, "bokanovskification consists of a   13
series of arrests of development. We check the normal growth and, paradox-
ically enough, the egg responds by budding."

Responds by budding. The pencils were busy.   14

He pointed. On a very slowly moving band a rack-full of test-tubes was   15
entering a large metal box, another rack-full was emerging. Machinery faintly
purred. It took eight minutes for the tubes to go through, he told them. Eight
minutes of hard X-rays being about as much as an egg can stand. A few died;
of the rest, the least susceptible divided into two; most put out four buds;
some eight; all were returned to the incubators, where the buds began to
develop; then, after two days, were suddenly chilled, chilled and checked.
Two, four, eight, the buds in their turn budded; and having budded were
dosed almost to death with alcohol; consequently burgeoned again and
having budded—bud out of bud out of bud—were thereafter—further arrest
being generally fatal—left to develop in peace. By which time the original egg
was in a fair way to becoming anything from eight to ninety-six embryos—a
prodigious improvement, you will agree, on nature. Identical twins—but not
in piddling twos and threes as in the old viviparous days, when an egg would
sometimes accidentally divide; actually by dozens, by scores at a time.

"Scores," the Director repeated and flung out his arms, as though he were   16
distributing largesse. "Scores."

But one of the students was fool enough to ask where the advantage lay.   17

"My good boy!" The Director wheeled sharply round on him. "Can't   18
you see? Can't you see?" He raised a hand; his expression was solemn.
"Bokanovsky's Process is one of the major instruments of social stability!"

Major instruments of social stability.   19

Standard men and women; in uniform batches. The whole of a small fac-   20
tory staffed with the products of a single bokanovskified egg.

"Ninety-six identical twins working ninety-six identical machines!" The   21
voice was almost tremulous with enthusiasm. "You really know where you
are. For the first time in history." He quoted the planetary motto.
"Community, Identity, Stability." Grand words. "If we could bokanovskify
indefinitely the whole problem would be solved."

Solved by standard Gammas, unvarying Deltas, uniform Epsilons.   22
Millions of identical twins. The principle of mass production at last applied
to biology.

"But, alas," the Director shook his head, "we *can't* bokanovskify indef- 23
initely."

Ninety-six seemed to be the limit; seventy-two a good average. From the 24
same ovary and with gametes of the same male to manufacture as many
batches of identical twins as possible—that was the best (sadly a second best)
that they could do. And even that was difficult.

"For in nature it takes thirty years for two hundred eggs to reach matu- 25
rity. But our business is to stabilize the population at this moment, here and
now. Dribbling out twins over a quarter of a century—what would be the use
of that?"

Obviously, no use at all. But Podsnap's Technique had immensely accel- 26
erated the process of ripening. They could make sure of at least a hundred and
fifty mature eggs within two years. Fertilize and bokanovskify—in other
words, multiply by seventy-two—and you get an average of nearly eleven
thousand brothers and sisters in a hundred and fifty batches of identical
twins, all within two years of the same age.

"And in exceptional cases we can make one ovary yield us over fifteen 27
thousand adult individuals."

Beckoning to a fair-haired, ruddy young man who happened to be pass- 28
ing at the moment, "Mr. Foster," he called. The ruddy young man
approached. "Can you tell us the record for a single ovary, Mr. Foster?"

"Sixteen thousand and twelve in this Centre," Mr. Foster replied without 29
hesitation. He spoke very quickly, had a vivacious blue eye, and took an evident pleasure in quoting figures. "Sixteen thousand and twelve; in one hundred and eighty-nine batches of identicals. But of course they've done much
better," he rattled on, "in some of the tropical Centres. Singapore had often
produced over sixteen thousand five hundred; and Mombasa has actually
touched the seventeen thousand mark. But then they have unfair advantages.
You should see the way a negro ovary responds to pituitary! It's quite astonishing, when you're used to working with European material. Still," he added,
with a laugh (but the light of combat was in his eyes and the lift of his chin
was challenging), "still, we mean to beat them if we can. I'm working on a
wonderful Delta-Minus ovary at this moment. Only just eighteen months
old. Over twelve thousand seven hundred children already, either decanted or
in embryo. And still going strong. We'll beat them yet."

"That's the spirit I like!" cried the Director, and clapped Mr. Foster on 30
the shoulder. "Come along with us and give these boys the benefit of your
expert knowledge."

Mr. Foster smiled modestly. "With pleasure." They went. 31

In the Bottling Room all was harmonious bustle and ordered activity. 32
Flaps of fresh sow's peritoneum ready cut to the proper size came shooting up
in little lifts from the Organ Store in the sub-basement. Whizz and then,
click! the lift-hatches flew open; the bottle-liner had only to reach out a hand,
take the flap, insert, smooth-down, and before the lined bottle had had time
to travel out of reach along the endless band, whizz, click! another flap of

peritoneum had shot up from the depths, ready to be slipped into yet another bottle, the next of that slow interminable procession on the band.

Next to the Liners stood the Matriculators. The procession advanced; one by one the eggs were transferred from their test-tubes to the larger containers; deftly the peritoneal lining was slit, the morula dropped into place, the saline solution poured in ... and already the bottle had passed, and it was the turn of the labellers. Heredity, date of fertilization, membership of Bokanovsky Group—details were transferred from test-tube to bottle. No longer anonymous, but named, identified, the procession marched slowly on; on through an opening in the wall, slowly on into the Social Predestination Room. 33

"Eighty-eight cubic metres of card-index," said Mr. Foster with relish, as they entered. 34

"Containing *all* the relevant information," added the Director. 35

"Brought up to date every morning." 36

"And co-ordinated every afternoon." 37

"On the basis of which they make their calculations." 38

"So many individuals, of such and such quality," said Mr. Foster. 39

"Distributed in such and such quantities." 40

"The optimum Decanting Rate at any given moment." 41

"Unforeseen wastages promptly made good." 42

"Promptly," repeated Mr. Foster. "If you knew the amount of overtime I had to put in after the last Japanese earthquake!" He laughed good-humouredly and shook his head. 43

"The Predestinators send in their figures to the Fertilizers." 44

"Who give them the embryos they ask for." 45

"And the bottles come in here to be predestinated in detail." 46

"After which they are sent down to the Embryo Store." 47

"Where we now proceed ourselves." 48

And opening a door Mr. Foster led the way down a staircase into the basement. 49

The temperature was still tropical. They descended into a thickening twilight. Two doors and a passage with a double turn insured the cellar against any possible infiltration of the day. 50

"Embryos are like photograph film," said Mr. Foster waggishly, as he pushed open the second door. "They can only stand red light." 51

And in effect the sultry darkness into which the students now followed him was visible and crimson, like the darkness of closed eyes on a summer's afternoon. The bulging flanks of row on receding row and tier above tier of bottles glinted with innumerable rubies, and among the rubies moved the dim red spectres of men and women with purple eyes and all the symptoms of lupus. The hum and rattle of machinery faintly stirred the air. 52

"Give them a few figures, Mr. Foster," said the Director, who was tired of talking. 53

Mr. Foster was only too happy to give them a few figures. 54

Two hundred and twenty metres long, two hundred wide, ten high. He   55
pointed upwards. Like chickens drinking, the students lifted their eyes
towards the distant ceiling.

Three tiers of racks: ground floor level, first gallery, second gallery.   56

The spidery steel-work of gallery above gallery faded away in all direc-   57
tions into the dark. Near them three red ghosts were busily unloading demi-
johns from a moving staircase.

The escalator from the Social Predestination Room.   58

Each bottle could be placed on one of fifteen racks, each rack, though   59
you couldn't see it, was a conveyor travelling at the rate of thirty-three and a
third centimetres an hour. Two hundred and sixty-seven days at eight metres
a day. Two thousand one hundred and thirty-six metres in all. One circuit of
the cellar at ground level, one on the first gallery, half on the second, and on
the two hundred and sixty-seventh morning, daylight in the Decanting Room.
Independent existence—so called.

"But in the interval," Mr. Foster concluded, "we've managed to do a lot   60
to them. Oh, a very great deal." His laugh was knowing and triumphant.

"That's the spirit I like," said the Director once more. "Let's walk round.   61
You tell them everything, Mr. Foster."

Mr. Foster duly told them.   62

Told them of the growing embryo on its bed of peritoneum. Made them   63
taste the rich blood surrogate on which it fed. Explained why it had to be
stimulated with placentin and thyroxin. Told them of the *corpus luteum*
extract. Showed them the jets through which at every twelfth metre from zero
to 2040 it was automatically injected. Spoke of those gradually increasing
doses of pituitary administered during the final ninety-six metres of their
course. Described the artificial maternal circulation installed on every bottle
at Metre 112; showed them the reservoir of blood-surrogate, the centrifugal
pump that kept the liquid moving over the placenta and drove it through the
synthetic lung and waste-product filter. Referred to the embryo's troublesome
tendency to anaemia, to the massive doses of hog's stomach extract and fetal
foal's liver with which, in consequence, it had to be supplied.

Showed them the simple mechanism by means of which, during the last   64
two metres out of every eight, all the embryos were simultaneously shaken
into familiarity with movement. Hinted at the gravity of the so-called "trauma
of decanting," and enumerated the precautions taken to minimize, by a suitable training of the bottled embryo, that dangerous shock. Told them of the
tests for sex carried out in the neighbourhood of Metre 200. Explained the
system of labelling—a T for the males, a circle for the females and for those
who were destined to become freemartins a question mark, black on a white
ground.

"For of course," said Mr. Foster, "in the vast majority of cases, fertility   65
is merely a nuisance. One fertile ovary in twelve hundred—that would really
be quite sufficient for our purposes. But we want to have a good choice. And
of course one must always leave an enormous margin of safety. So we allow

as many as thirty per cent of the female embryos to develop normally. The others get a dose of male sex-hormone every twenty-four metres for the rest of the course. Result: they're decanted as freemartins—structurally quite normal ("except," he had to admit, "that they *do* have the slightest tendency to grow beards), but sterile. Guaranteed sterile. Which brings us at last," continued Mr. Foster, "out of the realm of mere slavish imitation of nature into the much more interesting world of human invention."

He rubbed his hands. For of course, they didn't content themselves with   66
merely hatching out embryos: any cow could do that.

"We also predestine and condition. We decant our babies as socialized   67
human beings, as Alphas or Epsilons, as future sewage workers or future
. . . " He was going to say "future World controllers," but correcting himself,
said "future Directors of Hatcheries," instead.

The D.H.C. acknowledged the compliment with a smile.   68

They were passing Metre 320 on Rack 11. A young Beta-Minus mechanic   69
was busy with screwdriver and spanner on the blood-surrogate pump of a
passing bottle. The hum of the electric motor deepened by fractions of a tone
as he turned the nuts. Down, down . . . A final twist, a glance at the revolution counter, and he was done. He moved two paces down the line and began
the same process on the next pump.

"Reducing the number of revolutions per minute," Mr. Foster explained.   70
"The surrogate goes round slower; therefore passes through the lung at longer
intervals; therefore gives the embryo less oxygen. Nothing like oxygen-
shortage for keeping an embryo below par." Again he rubbed his hands.

"But why do you want to keep the embryo below par?" asked an ingen-   71
uous student.

"Ass!" said the Director, breaking a long silence. "Hasn't it occurred to   72
you that an Epsilon embryo must have an Epsilon environment as well as an
Epsilon heredity?"

It evidently hadn't occurred to him. He was covered with confusion.   73

"The lower the caste," said Mr. Foster, "the shorter the oxygen." The   74
first organ affected was the brain. After that the skeleton. At seventy per cent
of normal oxygen you got dwarfs. At less than seventy eyeless monsters.

"Who are no use at all," concluded Mr. Foster.   75

Whereas (his voice became confidential and eager), if they could discover   76
a technique for shortening the period of maturation what a triumph, what a
benefaction to Society!

"Consider the horse."   77

They considered it.   78

Mature at six; the elephant at ten. While at thirteen a man is not yet sex-   79
ually mature; and is only full-grown at twenty. Hence, of course, that fruit of
delayed development, the human intelligence.

"But in Epsilons," said Mr. Foster very justly, "we don't need human   80
intelligence."

Didn't need and didn't get it. But though the Epsilon mind was mature at   81
ten, the Epsilon body was not fit to work till eighteen. Long years of superfluous and wasted immaturity. If the physical development could be speeded
up till it was as quick, say, as a cow's what an enormous saving to the
Community!

"Enormous!" murmured the students. Mr. Foster's enthusiasm was infec-   82
tious.

He became rather technical; spoke of the abnormal endocrine coordina-   83
tion which made men grow so slowly; postulated a germinal mutation to
account for it. Could the effects of this germinal mutation be undone? Could
the individual Epsilon embryo be made to revert, by a suitable technique, to
the normality of dogs and cows? That was the problem. And it was all but
solved.

Pilkington, at Mombasa, had produced individuals who were sexually   84
mature at four and full-grown at six and a half. A scientific triumph. But
socially useless. Six-year-old men and women were too stupid to do even
Epsilon work. And the process was an all-or-nothing one; either you failed to
modify at all, or else you modified the whole way. They were still trying to
find the ideal compromise between adults of twenty and adults of six. So far
without success. Mr. Foster sighed and shook his head.

Their wanderings though the crimson twilight had brought them to the   85
neighbourhood of Metre 170 on Rack 9. From this point onwards Rack 9
was enclosed and the bottles performed the remainder of their journey in a
kind of tunnel, interrupted here and there by openings two or three metres
wide.

"Heat conditioning," said Mr. Foster.   86

Hot tunnels alternated with cool tunnels. Coolness was wedded to dis-   87
comfort in the form of hard X-rays. By the time they were decanted the
embryos had a horror of cold. They were predestined to emigrate to the tropics, to be miners and acetate silk spinners and steel workers. Later on their
minds would be made to endorse the judgment of their bodies. "We condition
them to thrive on heat," concluded Mr. Foster. "Our colleagues upstairs will
teach them to love it."

"And that," put in the Director sententiously, "that is the secret of hap-   88
piness and virtue—liking what you've *got* to do. All conditioning aims at that:
making people like their unescapable social destiny."

In a gap between two tunnels, a nurse was delicately probing with a   89
long fine syringe into the gelatinous contents of a passing bottle. The students
and their guides stood watching her for a few moments in silence.

"Well, Lenina," said Mr. Foster, when at last she withdrew the syringe   90
and straightened herself up.

The girl turned with a start. One could see that, for all the lupus and the   91
purple eyes, she was uncommonly pretty.

"Henry!" Her smile flashed redly at him—a row of coral teeth.   92

"Charming, charming," murmured the Director and, giving her two or three little pats, received in exchange a rather deferential smile for himself. 93

"What are you giving them?" asked Mr. Foster, making his tone very professional. 94

"Oh, the usual typhoid and sleeping sickness." 95

"Tropical workers start being inoculated at Metre 150," Mr. Foster explained to the students. "The embryos still have gills. We immunize the fish against the future man's diseases." Then, turning back to Lenina, "Ten to five on the roof this afternoon," he said, "as usual." 96

"Charming," said the Director once more, and with a final pat, moved away after the others. 97

On Rack 10 rows of next generation's chemical workers were being trained in the toleration of lead, caustic soda, tar, chlorine. The first of a batch of two hundred and fifty embryonic rocket-plane engineers was just passing the eleven hundred metre mark on Rack 3. A special mechanism kept their containers in constant rotation. "To improve their sense of balance," Mr. Foster explained. "Doing repairs on the outside of a rocket in mid-air is a ticklish job. We slacken off the circulation when they're right way up, so that they're half starved, and double the flow of surrogate when they're upside down. They learn to associate topsyturvydom with well-being; in fact, they're only truly happy when they're standing on their heads. 98

"And now," Mr. Foster went on, "I'd like to show you some very interesting conditioning for Alpha Plus Intellectuals. We have a big batch of them on Rack 5. First Gallery level," he called to two boys who had started to go down to the ground floor. 99

"They're round about Metre 900," he explained. "You can't really do any useful intellectual conditioning till the fetuses have lost their tails. Follow me." 100

But the Director had looked at his watch. "Ten to three," he said. "No time for the intellectual embryos, I'm afraid. We must go up to the Nurseries before the children have finished their afternoon sleep." 101

Mr. Foster was disappointed. "At least one glance at the Decanting Room," he pleaded. 102

"Very well then." The Director smiled indulgently. "Just one glance." 103

■ ■ ■

Review Questions

1. What is the Bokanovsky Process? Why is it central to Huxley's "brave new world"?
2. How does Huxley comment sardonically on the racism of the Hatchery's personnel—and of Europeans in general?
3. What is the difference—and the social significance of the difference—among Alphas, Betas, Deltas, Gammas, and Epsilons?

4. What technological problems concerning the maturation process have the scientists of *Brave New World* still not solved?

Discussion and Writing Suggestions

1. How does the language of the first two paragraphs reveal Huxley's tone, that is, his attitude toward his subject? For example, what is the function of the word "only" in the opening sentence: "A squat grey building of only thirty-four stories"? Or the adjectives describing the building?

2. What does the narrator mean when he says (paragraph 5) that "particulars, as every one knows, make for virtue and happiness; generalities are intellectually necessary evils. Not philosophers but fret-sawyers [operators of fret-saws—long, narrow, fine-toothed hand saws used for ornamental detail work] and stamp collectors compose the backbone of society"? To what extent do you believe that such an ethic operates in our own society? Give examples of the relatively low value placed on "philosophers" and the relatively high value placed on "fret-sawyers."

3. Throughout this chapter, Huxley makes an implied contrast between the brisk, technological efficiency of the Hatchery and the ethical nature of what takes place within its walls. What aspects of our own civilization show similar contrasts? (Example: We are now able to build more technologically sophisticated weapons of destruction than ever before in history.) Explore this subject in an essay, devoting a paragraph or so to each aspect of our civilization that you consider.

4. In the Hatchery, bottled, fertilized eggs pass into the "Social Predestination Room." In that room, their future lives will be determined. Is there an equivalent of the Social Predestination Room in our own society? (In other words, are there times and places when and where our future lives are determined?) If so, describe its features, devoting a paragraph to each of these features.

5. Foster explains how the undecanted embryos are conditioned to adapt to certain environments—for instance, conditioned to like heat so that, years later, they will feel comfortable working in the tropics or working as miners; or they may be conditioned to improve their sense of balance, so that they will be able to repair rockets in midair. What evidence do you see in our own society that people are or will be subject to conditioning to "like their unescapable social destiny"? Consider, for example, the influence of the conditioning exerted by parents, siblings, teachers, friends, or various social institutions.

6. As we noted in the headnote, Huxley's *Brave New World* (like much science fiction) is a projection into the future of contemporary aspects of culture that the author finds disturbing or dangerous. Select some present aspect of our culture that *you* find disturbing or dangerous and—in the form of a short story, or chapter from a novel, or section from a screenplay—dramatize your vision of what *could* happen.

Recombinant DNA and Genetic Engineering

CECIE STARR AND RALPH TAGGART

Many of the public policy dilemmas of our modern world—the use of nuclear weapons, for example, or the debate about when to "pull the plug" on persons near death, or the debate about privacy from electronic snooping—have arisen as a direct result of scientific breakthroughs. Much of this chapter will deal with various aspects of the public policy debate surrounding biotechnology. But we thought it would be illuminating to precede these discussions with a scientific description of just what is entailed in a key aspect of the new field—genetic engineering.

In the following selection, reprinted from a textbook widely used in introductory university-level biology courses, the authors survey the field of genetic engineering, describe some recent developments in the field, and conclude by discussing some of the social, legal, ecological, and ethical questions regarding its benefits and risks.

Cecie Starr is a science writer who lives in Belmont, California. Ralph Taggart teaches biology at Michigan State University. This passage is from their textbook Biology: The Unity and Diversity of Life.

Mom, Dad, and Clogged Arteries

Butter! Bacon! Eggs! Ice cream! Cheesecake! Possibly you think of such foods as enticing, off-limits, or both. After all, who among us doesn't know about animal fats and the dreaded cholesterol? 1

Soon after you feast on such fatty foods, cholesterol enters the bloodstream. Cholesterol is important. It is a structural component of animal cell membranes, and without membranes, there would be no cells. Cells also remodel cholesterol into a variety of molecules, such as the vitamin D necessary for the development of good bones and teeth. Normally, however, the liver itself synthesizes enough cholesterol for your cells. 2

Some proteins circulating in blood combine with cholesterol and other substances to form lipoprotein particles. *High*-density lipoproteins, or *HDLs*, transport cholesterol to the liver, where it's metabolized. Usually, *low*-density lipoproteins, or *LDLs*, end up inside cells that store or use cholesterol. But sometimes too many LDLs form. The excess infiltrates the elastic walls of arteries and helps form atherosclerotic plaques (Figure 16.1 [not included]). These abnormal masses interfere with blood flow. If they clog one of the tiny coronary arteries that deliver blood to the heart, a heart attack may result. 3

How well you handle dietary cholesterol depends on which alleles you got from your parents. For example, one gene specifies a protein receptor for LDLs. If you inherited two "good" alleles and don't go overboard on the fatty foods, your blood level of cholesterol may stay low to moderate and your 4 arteries may never clog up. Inherit two copies of a certain mutated allele, and you will develop *familial hypercholesterolemia*, a rare genetic disorder. Cholesterol levels get so high, many of those affected die of heart attacks in childhood or their teens.

In 1992 a woman from Quebec, Canada, became a milestone in the history of genetics. She was thirty years old. Like two brothers felled in their early twenties by heart attacks, she had inherited the mutant allele for the LDL receptor. She survived a heart attack at sixteen. At twenty-six, she had coronary bypass surgery.

At the time, people were hotly debating the risks and the promises of **gene therapy**—the transfer of one or more normal or modified genes into an individual's body cells to correct a genetic defect or boost resistance to disease. The woman opted for an untried procedure to give her body working copies of the good gene.

Surgeons removed about 15 percent of her liver. Researchers put cells from it in a nutrient-rich medium to promote cell growth and division. *And they spliced the functional allele for the LDL receptor into the genetic material of a harmless virus.* The modified virus infected the cultured liver cells, thereby inserting copies of the good gene into them. When the liver cells went on to reproduce, they made copies of the good gene, also.

About a billion modified cells were infused into the woman's portal vein, a blood vessel that leads directly to the liver. Some cells took up residence in the liver and started to make the missing cholesterol receptor. Two years later, a fraction of the woman's liver cells were behaving normally and sponging up cholesterol from blood. Her LDL blood levels declined nearly 20 percent. There was no sign of the arterial clogging that nearly killed her. Her cholesterol levels were still higher than normal. Yet the intervention demonstrated the safety and feasibility of gene therapy for some patients.

As you might gather from this pioneering clinical work, recombinant DNA technology has huge potential for medicine, agriculture, and industry. Think of it! For thousands of years, we humans have been changing genetically based traits. By artificial selection practices, we produced new plants and new breeds of cattle, cats, dogs, and birds from wild ancestral stocks. We were selective agents for meatier turkeys, sweeter oranges, seedless watermelons, spectacular ornamental roses, and big juicy corn kernels (Figure 16.2 [not included]). We conjured up hybrids such as the mule (horse × donkey) and plants that bear tangelos (tangerine × grapefruit).

Of course, we have to remember we're newcomers on the evolutionary stage. During the 3.8 billion years before we even made our entrance, nature conducted uncountable numbers of genetic experiments. Nature's tools have included mutation, crossing over, and other events that introduce changes in genetic messages. The countless changes gave rise to life's rich diversity.

But the striking thing about human-directed change is that the pace has picked up. Researchers analyze genes with **recombinant DNA technology**. They cut and recombine DNA from different species and insert it into bacterial, yeast, or mammalian cells. The cells replicate their DNA and divide rapidly. They copy the foreign DNA as if it were their own and churn out useful quantities of recombinant DNA molecules. The technology also is the basis of **genetic engineering**. By this process, genes are isolated, modified, and inserted into the same organism or into a different one. Protein products of the modified genes may cover the function of their missing or malfunctioning counterparts.

A Toolkit for Making Recombinant DNA

Restriction Enzymes

In the 1950s, the scientific community was agog over the discovery of DNA's   12
structure. The excitement gave way to frustration. No one could figure out the sequence of nucleotides, the order of genes and gene regions along a chromosome. Robert Holley and his colleagues did sequence a small tRNA. They used digestive enzymes that broke the molecule into fragments small enough to be chemically characterized. But DNA molecules? These are far longer than RNAs. No one knew how to cut one into fragments long enough to have unique, and thus analyzable, sequences. Digestive enzymes can cut DNA, but not in any particular order. There was no telling how the fragments had been arranged in the molecule.

Then, by accident, Hamilton Smith discovered that *Haemophilus influen-*   13
zae chops up foreign DNA inserted into it by a bacteriophage. Extracts from *H. influenzae* cells included an enzyme that restricts itself to a specific kind of site in DNA. It was named a **restriction enzyme**.

In time, several hundred strains of bacteria offered up a toolkit of restric-   14
tion enzymes that recognize and cut specific sequences of four to eight bases in DNA. They are among many that make *staggered* cuts, which leave single-stranded "tails" on the end of a DNA fragment. Tails made by *Taq*I are two bases long (CG). *Eco*RI makes tails four bases long (AATT).

How many cuts do restriction enzymes make? That depends in part on   15
the molecule. *Not*I only recognizes a rare eight-base sequence in the DNA of mammals, so when it makes its cuts, most of the fragments are tens of thousands of base pairs long. That is long enough for studying the **genome**—all of the DNA in a haploid number of chromosomes for a species. For the human species, the genome is about 3.2 billion base pairs long.

Modification Enzymes

DNA fragments with staggered cuts have sticky ends. "Sticky" means a   16
restriction fragment's single-stranded tail can base-pair with a complementary tail of any other DNA fragment or molecule cut by the same restriction enzyme. *Mix DNA fragments cut by the same restriction enzyme, and the sticky ends of any two fragments having complementary base sequences will base-pair and form a recombinant DNA molecule:*

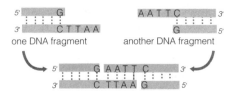

one DNA fragment   another DNA fragment

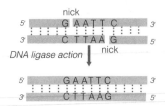

Notice the nicks where such fragments base-pair. **DNA ligase**, a modification enzyme, can seal these nicks:

Cloning Vectors for Amplifying DNA

Restriction and modification enzymes make it possible to insert foreign DNA   17
into bacterial cells. As you know, each bacterial cell has only one chromosome, a circular DNA molecule. Many also inherit plasmids. A plasmid is a very small circle of extra DNA that has just a few genes and that gets replicated along with the bacterial chromosome (Figure 16.3 [not included]). Bacteria usually can survive without plasmids, but some of the genes offer benefits, as when they confer resistance to antibiotics.

Under favorable conditions, bacteria divide rapidly and often—every   18
thirty minutes, for some species—so that huge populations of genetically identical cells form. Before cell division, replication enzymes duplicate the bacterial chromosome. They also replicate the plasmid, sometimes repeatedly, so a cell can hold many identical copies of foreign DNA. In research laboratories, foreign DNA typically is inserted into a plasmid for replication. The outcome is called a **DNA clone**, because bacterial cells have made many identical, "cloned" copies of it.

A modified plasmid that accepts foreign DNA is a **cloning vector**. It can   19
insert foreign DNA into a host bacterium, yeast, or some other cell that can be the start of a "cloning factory." It may give rise to a population of rapidly dividing descendant cells, all with identical copies of the foreign DNA (Figure 16.4).

How Is DNA Sequenced?

In 1995, researchers accomplished what was little more than a dream a few   20
decades ago. They determined the full DNA sequence for a species: *Haemophilus influenzae*, a bacterium that causes human respiratory infections. Since then, the genomes of other species have been fully sequenced. A draft sequence of the human genome has now been completed.

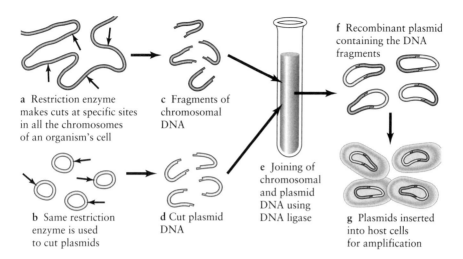

a Restriction enzyme makes cuts at specific sites in all the chromosomes of an organism's cell

c Fragments of chromosomal DNA

f Recombinant plasmid containing the DNA fragments

b Same restriction enzyme is used to cut plasmids

d Cut plasmid DNA

e Joining of chromosomal and plasmid DNA using DNA ligase

g Plasmids inserted into host cells for amplification

FIGURE 16.4 (A—F)   Formation of recombinant DNA—in this case, a collection of either chromosomal DNA fragments or cDNA sealed into bacterial plasmids. (g) Recombinant plasmids are inserted into host cells that can rapidly amplify the foreign DNA of interest.

The molecular sleuths are using **automated DNA sequencing**. This laboratory method gives the sequence of cloned DNA or PCR-amplified DNA in a few hours.   21

Researchers use the four standard nucleotides (T, C, A, and G) for automated DNA sequencing. They also use four modified versions, which we can represent as T*, C*, A*, and G*. Each modified version is labeled with a molecule that fluoresces a certain color when it passes through a laser beam. Every time one of these modified nucleotides gets incorporated into a growing DNA strand, it arrests DNA synthesis.   22

Before the reactions, researchers mix the eight kinds of nucleotides together. They add millions of copies of the DNA to be sequenced along with a type of primer and molecules of DNA polymerase. Then they separate the DNA into single strands, and the reactions begin.   23

The primer binds with its complementary sequence on one of the strands. DNA polymerase synthesizes a new DNA strand starting at one end of the primer. One by one, it adds nucleotides in the order dictated by the exposed sequence in the template strand. Each time, one of the standard nucleotides *or* one of the modified versions may be attached.   24

Suppose that DNA polymerase encounters a T in a DNA template strand. It will catalyze the base-pairing of either A or A* to it. If A is added to the new strand, replication will continue. But if A* is added, replication will stop; the modified nucleotide will block addition of any more nucleotides to that strand. The same thing happens at each nucleotide in a template strand.   25

When a standard nucleotide is attached, replication proceeds; when a modified version is attached, replication stops.

Remember, the starting mixture contained millions of identical copies of   26
the DNA sequence. Because either a standard or a modified nucleotide could be added at every exposed base, the new strands end at different locations in the sequence. The mixture now contains millions of copies of tagged fragments having different lengths. These can now be separated by length into sets of fragments. And each set corresponds to only one of the nucleotides in the entire base sequence.

The automated DNA sequencer is a machine that separates the sets of   27
fragments by gel electrophoresis. The set having the shortest fragments migrates fastest through the gel and reaches the end of it first. The last set to reach the end has the longest fragments. Because the fragments have a modified nucleotide at the 3′ end, each set fluoresces a certain color as it passes through a laser beam (Figure 16.8*a*). The automated sequencer detects the color and indicates which nucleotide is on the end of the fragments in each set. It assembles the information from all nucleotides in the sample, and in this way it reveals the entire DNA sequence.

Figure 16.8*b* is a printout from an automated DNA sequencer. Each   28
peak along that tracing represents the detection of a particular color as the sets of fragments reached the end of the gel.

From Haystacks to Needles—Isolating Genes of Interest

Any genome consists of thousands of genes. *E. coli* has 4,279, for instance,   29
and humans apparently have about 30,000. What if you wanted to learn about or modify the structure of any one of those genes? First, you'd have to isolate that gene from all others in the genome.

There are several ways to do this. If part of the gene sequence is already   30
known, you can design primers to amplify the entire gene or part of it by PCR. Often, though, researchers must isolate and clone a gene. First they make a gene library. This is a mixed collection of bacteria that contain different cloned DNA fragments. One is the gene of interest. A *genomic* library contains cloned DNA fragments from an entire genome. A *cDNA* library contains DNA derived from mRNA. Often it is the most useful because it is free of introns. But the gene is still hidden like a needle in a haystack. How can you isolate it? One way is to use a nucleic acid probe.

What Are Probes?

A **probe** is a very short stretch of DNA labeled with a radioisotope so that it   31
can be distinguished from other DNA molecules in a given sample. Part of the probe must be able to base-pair with some portion of the gene of interest. Any base-pairing that takes place between sequences of DNA (or RNA) from different sources is called **nucleic acid hybridization**.

How do you acquire a suitable probe? Sometimes part of the gene or a   32
closely related gene has already been cloned, in which case it can be used as

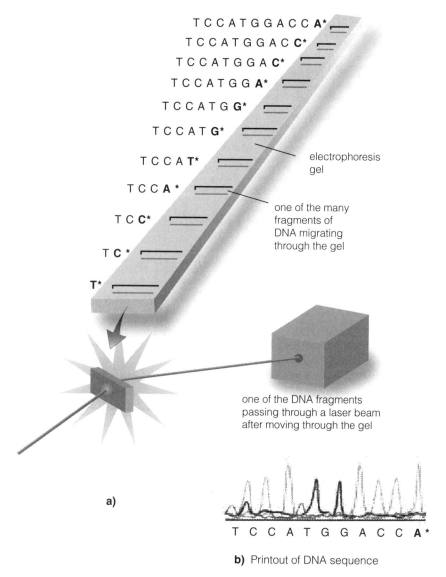

a)

b) Printout of DNA sequence

FIGURE 16.8   Automated DNA sequencing. (a) DNA fragments from an organism's genome become labeled at their end with a modified nucleotide that fluoresces a certain color. (b) Printout of the DNA sequence used in this example. Each peak indicates absorbance by a particular labeled nucleotide.

the probe. If the gene's structure is a mystery, you still may be able to work backward from the amino acid sequence of its protein product, assuming that protein is already available. By using the genetic code as a guide . . . , you could build a DNA probe that is more or less similar to the gene of interest.

Screening for Genes

Once you have a gene library and a suitable probe, you are ready to hunt   33
down the gene . . . . The first step is to take bacterial cells of the library and
spread them apart on the surface of a gelled growth medium in a petri plate.
When spread out sufficiently, individual cells undergo division. Each cell
starts a colony of genetically identical cells. The bacterial colonies appear as
hundreds of tiny white spots on the surface of a culture medium.

After colonies appear, you lay a nylon filter on top of the colonies. Some   34
cells stick to the filter at locations that mirror the locations of the original
colonies. You use solutions to rupture the cells, and the DNA so released
sticks to the filter. You denature the DNA to single strands and then add the
probes. The probes hybridize only with DNA from the colony that took up
the gene of interest. If you expose the probe-hybridized DNA to x-ray film,
the pattern formed by the radioactivity will identify that colony. With this
information you can now culture cells from that colony alone, knowing that
it will be the only one that can replicate the cloned gene.

Using the Genetic Scripts

As researchers decoded the genetic scripts of species, they opened the door to   35
astonishing possibilities. For example, genetically engineered bacteria now
produce medically valued proteins. Huge bacterial populations produce useful
quantities of the desired gene products in stainless steel vats. Diabetics who
must receive insulin injections every day are among the beneficiaries. At one
time, medical supplies of this pancreatic hormone were extracted only from
pigs and cattle. Later on, synthetic genes for human insulin were transferred
into *E. coli* cells. The cells were the start of populations that became the first
large-scale, cost-effective bacterial factory for proteins. Besides insulin, human
somatotropin, blood-clotting factors, hemoglobin, interferon, and a variety of
drugs and vaccines are also manufactured with the help of genetically engineered bacteria.

Other kinds of modified bacteria hold potential for industry and for   36
cleaning up environmental messes. For instance, as you know, many microor-
ganisms can break down organic wastes and help cycle nutrients through
ecosystems. Certain modified bacteria can break down crude oil into less
harmful compounds. When sprayed onto oil spills, as from a shipwrecked
supertanker, they might help avert an environmental disaster. Others are
genetically engineered to sponge up excess phosphates or heavy metals from
the environment.

In addition, bacterial species that contain plasmids offer benefits for   37
basic research, agriculture, and gene therapy. For instance, deciphering the
messages encoded in bacterial genes helps us reconstruct the evolutionary history of life . . . .

What about the "bad" bunch—the pathogenic fungi, bacteria, and viruses? 38
Natural selection favors mutated genes that improve a pathogen's chances of
evading a host organism's natural defenses. Mutation is frequent among
pathogens that reproduce rapidly. So designing new antibiotics and other
defenses against new gene products is a constant challenge. But if we learn
about the genes, we may have advance warning of the "plan of attack." The
story of HIV, a rapidly mutating virus that causes AIDS, gives insight into the
magnitude of the problem . . . .

Gene Transfers in Animals

Supermice and Biotech Barnyards

The first mammals enlisted for experiments in genetic engineering were lab- 39
oratory mice. Consider an example of this work. R. Hammer, R. Palmiter,
and R. Brinsfer corrected a hormone deficiency that leads to dwarfism in
mice. Insufficient levels of somatotropin (or growth hormone) cause the
abnormality. The researchers used a microneedle to inject the gene for rat
somatotropin into fertilized mouse eggs, which they implanted in an adult
female. The gene was successfully integrated into mouse DNA, and the eggs
developed into mice. Young mice in which that foreign gene was expressed
grew 1-1/2 times larger than their dwarf littermates. In other experiments,
researchers transferred the gene for human somatotropin into a mouse
embryo. The gene became integrated into mouse DNA, and the modified
embryo grew up to be a "supermouse" (Figure 16.14 [not included]).

Today, human gene transfers are being attempted in research into the 40
molecular basis of genetic disorders. "Biotech barnyards" have animals that
compete with bacterial factories as genetically engineered sources of proteins. Goats produce CFTR protein (to treat cystic fibrosis) and TPA (to
counter effects of a heart attack). Cattle may soon be producing human col-
lagen, which can help repair cartilage, bone, and skin.

Remember the first case of cloning a mammal from an adult cell? 41
A nucleus extracted from a mammary gland cell of a ewe was inserted into an
enucleated egg. Signals from the egg cytoplasm sparked development of
an embryo, which was implanted into a surrogate mother. This resulted in
Dolly . . . .

For years, researchers had been cloning animals from embryonic tissue, 42
but not adults that already displayed some sought-after trait. Now, however,
if they could just refine the steps of their cloning processes, they might be able
to maintain some genotype indefinitely.

Not long after Dolly's debut, genetically engineered clones of mice, cattle, 43
and other animals were produced. Example: Steve Stice and his colleagues
produced designer cattle. They started with a culture of cells from cattle.
They induced the development of six genetically identical calves. They also
engineered targeted changes in the cloning cell lineage.

Stice would like to genetically engineer cattle resistant to bovine spongi- 44
form encephalopathy (mad cow disease . . .). His method also has been used

to put the human serum albumin gene into the chromosomes of dairy cows. Albumin can be used to control blood pressure. At present, this protein must be separated from large quantities of donated human blood. It would be easier to get quantities of the protein from bountiful supplies of milk.

Given how rapidly the technologies are developing, is the genetic engi-   45
neering and cloning of humans not far behind?

Mapping and Using the Human Genome
In the late 1980s, biologists were in an uproar over a costly proposal before   46
the National Institutes of Health (NIH) to map the entire human genome. Many argued that benefits for medicine and pure research would be incalculable. Others said the mapping couldn't be done and would divert funding from "worthy" endeavors. But then the molecular biologist Leroy Hood invented automated DNA sequencing, and the race was on.

By 1990, the Human Genome Initiative was under way. The interna-   47
tional effort came with a projected price tag of 3 billion dollars—about 92 cents for each base pair in the heritable script for human life. By 1991, not even 2,000 genes had been sequenced. The pace picked up after Craig Venter realized even a bit of cDNA could be used as a molecular hook to drag the whole sequence of its parent gene out of a cDNA library. He named the hooks ESTs (for *Expressed Sequence Tags*).

Later, Venter and Hamilton Smith used a software program, the TIGR   48
Assembler, to decipher the first full genome of an organism—the bacterium *H. influenzae*. In 2000, researchers of the Human Genome Initiative along with Venter's team jointly announced that they had completed a rough draft of the human genome. Its extensive noncoding portions are now being analyzed.

Today, studies of the genome of humans and other organisms are now   49
grouped together as a new research field: **genomics**. The branch called *structural* genomics is concerned with actual mapping and sequencing of genomes of individuals. The branch called *comparative* genomics is more concerned with possible evolutionary relationships of groups of organisms. The similarities and differences being discovered among the different genomes are analyzed.

Comparative genomics has practical applications as well as potential for   50
research. The starting premise is that the genomes of all existing organisms are derived from common ancestral ones. For example, pathogens share some conserved genes with their human hosts, although their ancestors diverged long ago from the lineage that led to humans. By comparing the shared gene sequences, how those sequences are organized, and where they have come to differ, it may be possible to advance understanding of where immune defenses against pathogens are strongest and where they are the most vulnerable. In such ways, it is helpful to think of genomes as the keys to ancient molecular locks that became more and more complicated over time.

Genomics obviously has potential for human gene therapy. However,   51
now that the human genome is fully sequenced, it still is not easy to manipu-

late it. Genetic researchers have to insert a modified gene into a host cell of a particular tissue. They have to be sure the gene gets inserted at a suitable site in a given chromosome. They must also make sure that the targeted type of cell will synthesize the specified protein at suitable times, in suitable amounts.

Today, most experimenters employ stripped-down viruses as vectors that put genes into cultured human cells. They know cells are able to incorporate foreign genes into their DNA. But viral genetic material can undergo rearrangements, deletions, and other changes that can shut down or disrupt gene expression. What about developing synthetic, streamlined versions of human chromosomes? Maybe the machinery for DNA replication and protein synthesis will work on them. 52

Some gene therapies simply put modified cells into a tissue. This may help, even if the cells only make 10 to 15 percent of a required protein. But no one can yet predict where the genes will end up. The danger is that the insertion will disrupt the function of other genes, including those controlling cell growth and division. One-for-one gene swaps by homologous recombination are possible. Oliver Smithies, one of the best at using this process, can put genes right where they should go, but only once every 100,000 or so tries. 53

Safety Issues

Many years have passed since foreign DNA was first transferred into a plasmid. That gene transfer ignited a debate that will continue well into the next century. The issue is this: *Do potential benefits of gene modifications and gene transfers outweigh potential dangers?* 54

Genetically engineered bacteria are "designed" so they cannot survive except in the laboratory. As added precautions, "fail-safe" genes are built into the foreign DNA in case they escape. These genes are silent unless the captives are exposed to environmental conditions—whereupon the genes get activated, with lethal results for their owner. Say the package includes a *hok* gene next to a promoter of the lactose operon . . . . Sugars are plentiful in the environment. If they were to activate the *hok* gene, the protein product of that gene would destroy membrane function and the wayward cell. 55

What about a worst-case scenario? Remember how retroviruses are used to insert genes into cultured cells? If they escape from laboratory isolation, what might be the consequences? 56

And what about genetically engineered plants and animals released into the environment? For example, Steven Lindlow thought about how frost destroys many crops. Knowing that a surface protein of a bacterium promotes formation of ice crystals, he excised the "ice-forming" gene from bacterial cells. As he hypothesized, spraying "ice-minus bacteria" on strawberry plants in an isolated field prior to a frost would help plants resist freezing. He actually had deleted a *harmful* gene from a species, yet a bitter legal battle ensued. The courts ruled in his favor. His coworkers sprayed a strawberry patch; nothing had happened. 57

Then there was one potato plant designed to kill the insects that attack it. It also was too toxic for people to eat. Or think of how crop plants compete 58 poorly with weeds for nutrients. Many have been designed to resist weed-killers so farmers can spray for weeds and not worry about killing their crops. Some of the herbicides do have toxic effects on more than their targets. If crop plants offer herbicide resistance, will farmers be less or more apt to spread them about?

And what if engineered plants or animals transfer modified genes to 59
organisms in the wild? Think of how the advantage in acquiring resources would tilt toward vigorous weeds blessed with herbicide-resistant genes. Such possibilities are why standards for rigorous and extended safety tests are in place *before* the modified organisms enter the environment.

Biotechnology in a Brave New World

Before you leave this unit of the book, reflect on what you have learned so far. 60
You started out by examining cell division mechanisms, the means by which parents pass on their DNA to each new generation. You then moved on to the chromosomal and molecular basis of inheritance. You continued with a glimpse into the gene controls that guide the continuation of life from one generation to the next. The sequence you followed parallels the history of genetics research.

And now, with this chapter, you have arrived at a point in time when 61
molecular geneticists hold keys to the kingdom of inheritance. They are now unlocking and changing genomes at a stunning pace. They are making **DNA microarrays**, or gene chips, each with thousands of DNA sequences from a genome stamped onto a glass plate the size of a business card. Within days instead of years, researchers can now find out which genes are silent and which are being expressed in a tissue, pinpoint mutations, track host–microbe interactions, diagnose genetic diseases, and see how drugs or therapies influence gene expression.

Each gene chip is bathed in a solution containing labeled probes. These 62
probes are RNA transcripts that were extracted from the cells being studied—say, cancer cells from a patient. The probes bind only to complementary base sequences on the gene chip and make them glow in fluorescent light. Analysis of the glowing spots on the chip can reveal which of the thousands of genes in the cells are inactive and which are switched on. This kind of molecular knowledge is about to revolutionize how we diagnose, treat, and prevent the many diverse forms of cancer.

And we as a society are working our way through bioethical aspects of 63
such astonishing research even as it is swirling past us.

Who Gets Well?

Think about the potential of gene therapy. The historic case mentioned at the 64
start of this chapter was the first proof that medical applications of genetic engineering might alleviate suffering and save lives. More proof comes from two male infants with a severe combined immune deficiency called *SCID-X1*. With this genetic disorder, having two copies of a certain mutant allele dis-

ables the immune system. The infants were living as "bubble boys," in germ-free isolation tents, because they could not fight infections. Then geneticists used a viral vector to insert copies of the nonmutated gene stem cells from the boys' bone marrow. They infused the genetically modified cells into the marrow. Months later, both boys left their isolation tents. For the past year, at least, their immune system is working as it should. The boys are healthy and living at home.

We already have identified more than 15,500 genetic disorders. Should   65
we dismiss them simply because they are rare in the population at large? Whose lives will they touch? In any given year, genetic disorders affect 3 to 5 percent of all newborns and underlie 20 to 30 percent of all infant deaths. They account for 50 percent of all people who are mentally impaired and close to 25 percent of all hospital admissions. And what of the age-related disorders that await all of us? Critics who would like to put a lid on genetic research would do well to put a face on those among us who are badly and painfully bent or broken.

Who Gets Enhanced?

To many of us, human gene therapy to correct genetic disorders seems like a   66
socially acceptable goal. Now take this idea one step further. Is it socially desirable or even acceptable to change some genes of a normal human (or sperm or egg) to alter or enhance traits?

The idea of being able to select desirable human traits is called *eugenic*   67
engineering. Yet who decides which forms of a trait are most "desirable"? Would it be desirable to engineer taller or blue-eyed or fair-skinned boys and girls? Would it be okay to engineer "superhumans" with amazing strength or intelligence?

For a survey conducted not long ago, more than 40 percent of the   68
Americans interviewed said that it would be okay to use gene therapy to make smarter or better looking babies. One poll of British parents found 18 percent willing to use genetic enhancement to prevent children from being aggressive and 10 percent willing to keep them from growing up to be homosexual.

Through gene transfers, J. Z. Tsien and others have produced mice with   69
enhanced memory and learning abilities. Maybe their work heralds help for those who have Alzheimer's disease or dementia, perhaps even for those who just want to have more brain power.

Geneticist Dean Hamer even predicts we will soon be tinkering with   70
genes in order to change forms of behavior held to be socially undesirable. Violent forms of aggression and drug addictions come to mind.

Send in the Clones? Don't Bother, They're Here

Each year, about 75,000 people are on waiting lists for an organ transplant   71
from a human donor, but donors are in short supply. There is talk of harvesting organs from pigs, which function very much like organs from humans do. Transferring an organ from one species to another is called **xenotrans-plantation**.

But the human immune system battles anything that it recognizes as   72
"nonself," and it would reject an unmodified pig organ at once. At the free
surface of cells of a pig organ's blood vessels is a certain sugar component of
a glycoprotein. Antibodies circulating in human blood would bind at once to
the sugar. Binding would doom the transplant. It would trigger a cascade of
reactions that would, within hours, cause massive coagulation inside the vessels . . . . Potent drugs can suppress the immune response, but they make the
organ recipient vulnerable to infections.

Pig DNA contains two copies of *Ggta1*, the gene for alpha-1,3-galacto-   73
syltransferase. This enzyme catalyzes a key step in the biosynthesis of the
sugar that human antibodies latch on to. Knowing this, biotechnologists
worked to knock the two copies of the gene out of pig DNA. Recently, they
did succeed in excising one of the copies. They went on to transfer "knockout
cells" (those with the excised gene) into enucleated pig eggs . . . .

Some eggs developed into embryos, which were implanted in a host sow.   74
The embryos developed into a clone of piglets, each without one copy of the
Ggta1 gene. Two piglets died shortly afterward; another died a few weeks
later. The survivors appear to be healthy even though one piglet has a defec-
tive eye and small ear flaps. Biotechnologists plan to breed the cloned pigs by
conventional methods to produce offspring in which both copies of the *Ggta1*
gene are knocked out. (Remember your Mendelian genetics? If both parents
lack one copy of the *Ggta1* gene, there is one chance in four that one of their
offspring will have no copies.)

A potential problem for xenotransplantation is that pigs carry a virus   75
similar to the one that causes AIDS in humans. For the experiments just
described, the researchers used miniature pigs, which apparently cannot trans-
mit the virus to human cells.

Pigs are mammals. So are humans. Is human cloning next? Are there   76
people willing to fund research that might yield a clone of a child, either "as
is" or with genetically engineered "enhancements"? Will a human female be
able to reproduce copies of herself without involving men? Will men be able
to pay to have their DNA inserted into a cell stripped of its nucleus, have the
cell implanted in a surrogate mother, and make a little repeat of themselves?

Lee Silver, a biologist at Princeton University, has suggested that anyone   77
who thinks human cloning will move slowly is naive. One couple has already
pledged up to 500 million dollars to a controversial company to clone their
dead infant. The company says it has lots of potential customers and surrogate mothers lined up.

At this writing, several countries have now banned human cloning, but   78
the bans leave room for cloning technology with uses in basic research.
Nonscientists and scientists alike are actively debating whether any form of
human cloning should be allowed.

Weighing the Benefits and Risks

Some say that the DNA of any organism must never be altered. Put aside the   79
fact that nature itself has been altering DNA ever since the origin of life. The

concern is that we as a species simply do not have the wisdom to bring about beneficial changes without causing irreparable harm to ourselves or to the environment.

To be sure, when it comes to altering human genes, one is reminded of our very human tendency to leap before we look. And yet, when it comes to restricting genetic modifications of any sort, one also is reminded of another old saying: "If God had wanted us to fly, he would have given us wings." Something about the human experience did give us a capacity to imagine wings of our own making—and that capacity carried us to the frontiers of space.   80

Where are we going from here? To gain perspective on our future, spend some time reading about our past. Ours is a history of survival in the face of challenges, threats, bumblings, and sometimes disasters on a grand scale. It is also a story of our connectedness with the environment and with one another.   81

The basic questions now confronting you are these: Should we be more cautious, believing the risk takers may go too far? And what do we as a species stand to lose if risks are not taken? There are no simple answers.   82

Discussion and Writing Suggestions

1. What do researchers do with recombinant DNA technology?
2. What is the basic procedure, and the basic goal, of genetic engineering? Provide one example of genetic engineering.
3. Write a one-page summary of this selection.
4. This selection originally appeared in an introductory university biology text. To what extent did you find it difficult to comprehend? Locate those passages that gave you particular trouble. Does the problem lie in the terminology Starr and Taggart use? The scientific concepts under discussion? The organization or writing style? See if your instructor or other, more scientifically inclined, students can throw light on these troublesome sections.
5. Describe (in scientific report format, if possible) an experiment that you conducted in high school, or that you are conducting now in chemistry, physics, or biology. Write in language that your non-scientific readers will be able to follow.

Canada and the Genomic Revolution

HENRY FRIESEN

After acquiring post-graduate medical training as an endocrinologist in Boston, Dr. Friesen entered the Department of Medicine at McGill University, where he carried out research on human growth hormone (HGH) that enabled successful replacement therapy in hormone-deficient children. Further endocrine research led to the isolation and purification of the hormone prolactin; and, in collaboration with researchers in the pharmaceutical industry, Dr. Friesen developed the drug Bromocriptine, which proved to be effective in the treatment of infertility in women.

As an administrator, Dr. Friesen served on the Medical Research Council of Canada for 20 years, and was its President from 1991 to 2000. He was appointed an Officer of the Order of Canada in 1992.

What follows is the transcript of a speech delivered by Dr. Friesen to the Canadian Club in Toronto. The event was co-sponsored by the Club and the Gairdner Foundation, an organization that funds medical research.

Two thousand years ago, the great Chinese philosopher, Lao Tzu, observed   1
that "each leaf is a tree." Since then, modern science has confirmed the truth of this ancient wisdom, not only as allegory, but as fact. We know that in the cells of each leaf there is, indeed, the genetic pattern for an entire forest.

Now, with the mapping of the human genome, we have been given,   2
quite literally, the language of life itself—the pattern not simply for a forest, but for every living thing on earth.

For the first time, we are on the verge of understanding the biological   3
basis of our shared humanity—of understanding the tiny genetic differences that contribute to the colour of our eyes, the shape of our mouths or our susceptibility to certain diseases.

Today, I would like to talk very briefly about what genomics can mean   4
to our society—about the potential it offers and the challenges it presents. And I want to tell you why I believe it is so important that Canada become a leader in genomic research.

But first, some definitions. I suppose it's inevitable that new areas of sci-   5
entific research bring with them their own specialized vocabulary, designed to confound the public and professionals alike.

So I thought it might be useful to provide you with some of the key   6
buzzwords that you will be hearing more and more in the days ahead.

First, "genome." Genome is not the mapping, or sequencing that was   7
announced a few months ago. That was the Human Genome Project. "Genome" is simply all of the genetic information stored within our cells.

I say "simply," but in fact it is a tremendous amount of information. If   8
the genome was a book, it would be the equivalent of 800 Bibles. And if I were to start reading it to you at the rate of one "word" per second, for eight hours a day, we would all still be sitting here 100 years from now!

The truly amazing thing is that all of this information is held inside the   9
microscopic nucleus of a cell so tiny that it could easily fit on the head of a pin.

And this is information that our bodies are constantly producing, divid-   10
ing and replicating. In the next 60 seconds, as you sit here, your body will produce enough new DNA that if it was linked together, would stretch 100 000 kilometres. One hundred thousand kilometres in 60 seconds!

And every bit of information—every instruction that keeps us growing,   11
thinking and breathing—must be reproduced precisely. That is the miracle of
DNA.

Perhaps equally remarkable is the similarity of our individual genomes.   12
Humans have about 80 000 genes and 99.9 per cent of them are identical.
That means that only one chemical letter in a thousand is different in the
genome of, say Tie Domi and Albert Einstein. Makes you want to treat Tie
with a little more respect, doesn't it?

We're also discovering that our genes are remarkably similar to those of   13
other life forms. For example, about 40 per cent of the genes found in worms
are also found in humans. The genetic overlap between mice and humans is
almost 75 per cent. And chimps share more than 98 per cent of our DNA.

That's important because finding similar genes in simpler organisms can   14
save scientists thousands of hours of rummaging through our own—much
larger—genome.

So that's the "genome"—an amazing concentration of genetic informa-   15
tion printed on the DNA inside the nucleus of every cell in our body.

As you know, our DNA is made up of four molecules, identified as A, T,   16
C and G. Just four letters, over and over, in random order. More than three
billion of them.

It was the researchers' job to put them in the right order. That's akin to   17
being handed a dictionary and told to reproduce the works of Shakespeare.
But they did it.

Now we have an idea of the sequence, but there's still much more to   18
learn.

It's like knowing the street address and telephone number of every person   19
in Canada. That's important information, but it doesn't tell us what those
people do or how their society is structured.

Similarly, having the human genome mapped out doesn't tell us how   20
genes function or interact, only their location along our DNA.

Moreover, genes themselves are not the big players in molecular processes.   21
They're more like a text book, providing information that the cell refers to.

The real work horses are proteins. Which leads me to the next word-of-   22
the-day: proteomics.

"Proteomics" is part of genomics and is just a fancy way of saying "cat-   23
aloguing proteins and studying what they do in the body."

Why is this so important? Well, as I've said, proteins are the key players,   24
responsible for every chemical reaction essential to life.

They are the hormones that course through our veins, the guided missiles   25
that target infections; they're the enzymes that build up and break down our
energy reserves and the circuits that power movement and thought.

Little wonder, then, that proteomics is often referred to as "the next big   26
thing" in biotechnology.

What they do depends on their shape and their shapes are complex; their   27
surface covered with bumps and grooves sort of like popcorn.

The interesting thing is that these bumps and grooves are perfectly   28
formed to receive molecules, just as a lock receives a key.

By knowing the exact shape and form of each protein, we should be able   29
to develop drugs that will fit into their grooves and either activate them or
prevent them from being activated. And by doing this, we will really be able
to control disease and a host of other chemical functions inside our bodies.

Well, enough definitions. Let me give you a sense of what genomics   30
might mean to you and me in our daily lives.

But before I do, one caveat: predictions can be perilous—especially when   31
trying to extrapolate current trends into future events. Just consider that in
1972, there were 457 Elvis impersonators in the United States. By 1993, that
number had grown to 2700. If this trend continues, it will mean that by
2005, one out of every four Americans will be an Elvis impersonator!

So we have to be careful when we look ahead and make predictions   32
about what genomics can do. That said, the potential really is remarkable.

Indeed, we are already starting to reap the benefits.   33

We've made enormous progress, for example, in the area of single-gene   34
diseases. Here in Toronto, Dr. Lap-Chee Tsui discovered the gene responsible
for cystic fibrosis and Dr. Ron Worton identified the gene tied to muscular
dystrophy.

While we haven't been able to translate these discoveries into cures, at   35
least now we know the target we're aiming at—an enormous step forward.

In addition, the hepatitis B vaccine, the growth hormone for children,   36
new treatments for breast cancer and MS patients are all products of biotechnology that are in our clinics now and helping Canadians today.

One of the areas where genomics has tremendous potential is drug ther-   37
apy. This is because the drugs we consume today are based on average
responses. Clinical trials measure how well a drug works on a group of
people in general, not on how it will work on you, in particular.

Take hypertension. This is one of the most common health problems of   38
modern life and, as a result, anti-hypertensive drugs are the single most prescribed medication group—over $1 billion worth in Canada alone.

These drugs are very effective at preventing heart attacks, but some   39
research shows that as many as 40 per cent of those receiving conventional
therapy either don't respond or suffer side-effects leading to hospitalization or
even death. In fact, severe side-effects from these drugs are the fifth largest
cause of mortality in the United States. The problem is we don't know which
people will respond positively, or worse, negatively.

Genomic researchers are working hard to find the genetic markers that   40
will tell us if you're in that 40 per cent group. Think of the benefits to the individual of avoiding months of treatment that may be doing more harm than
good. And think of the savings to the health system by avoiding hospitalization of these patients.

A few years ago, a major international team which included Dr. Johanna   41
Rommens here in Toronto and Dr. Jacques Simard at Laval discovered BRCA

I and BRCA 2—two gene mutations that greatly increase the likelihood of breast cancer, particularly in younger women.

By identifying the women with BRCA 1 or 2, we can monitor them more   42
closely, detect the cancer sooner and begin treatment earlier—all key elements to improving their care and enhancing their lives.

More generally, it is estimated that 10 to 40 per cent of people taking   43
medication—any medication—respond less than perfectly to it. As a result, two million Americans are hospitalized for adverse reactions every year and 100 000 die.

Genome research will also revolutionize the way medicine is practised. It   44
will tell us which genes turn on when a wound heals, when a baby cries, when a head becomes bald or a brow wrinkled, when a song is learned or a memory recalled, when hormones surge or stress overwhelms—and they will learn how to manipulate these genes.

Think of the typical check-up at your doctor's. Today, it's like going to   45
a mechanic who diagnoses your car by listening to the engine. If the engine sounds good, the mechanic says the car is fine. But internally, the car could be on the verge of a major collapse. As you drive away, your brakes could fail, or your steering wheel could come off.

Similarly, a physical exam consists of tests such as taking a blood sample   46
or determining your blood pressure. What's actually happening in your body, at the genetic and molecular level, is completely unknown. Even after having an electrocardiogram, you could still have a fatal heart attack as you leave the doctor's office.

But imagine going into your doctor's office and handing her a CD-ROM   47
with your complete DNA sequence. She could then determine if you have any of the roughly 5000 known genetic diseases or are likely to get them.

Based on this information, she could recommend preventive measures,   48
years before any symptoms appear. Think of that—*before any symptoms appear!* This is early detection with a difference!

This would also allow your doctor to determine, for example, whether or   49
not you are likely to contract a particular disease that has run through your family for generations—and if so, what to do now to prevent it or at least minimize its effects.

And it could also mean avoiding preventative measures—such as a mas-   50
tectomy—where your genes say you're unlikely to contract a particular disease.

Quite simply, your personalized DNA sequence will be the foundation for   51
the treatment you receive.

This will revolutionize how doctors practise medicine because diagnoses   52
will become biology-based, not symptom-based, ushering in a whole new era of individualized medicine.

In other words, we are moving from reactive to proactive medicine, from   53
intervention based on what your doctor sees to intervention based on what your DNA says.

Well, the possibilities of genomics on health and health care are mind-   54
boggling, and I could talk about them for hours, but let me just touch on one
other area where genomics could have a dramatic effect on our lives and our
society and that's agriculture.

Through genomics, we will be able to dramatically increase the volume of   55
food and fibre grown. Working in laboratories, in tissue cultures in giant bacteria baths, we will be able to produce more food, at a fraction of the cost,
than growing staples on land.

This will have enormous consequences for poorer nations, allowing them   56
to advance from mere subsistence to true development.

And by developing disease resistant crops, farmers in all parts of the   57
world will benefit. Hunger may indeed go the way of polio or smallpox.

So there is little doubt that genomics holds the power to transform our   58
lives, from the drugs we receive to the food we eat.

It is also a vital component of the new, "knowledge" economy.   59

Genomics is a classic example of the new economy. It puts a premium on   60
invention and imagination. It requires special skills and higher education.

And it is extremely knowledge-intensive. Indeed, the tidal wave of data   61
which genomics is producing is giving rise to a whole new discipline—bioinformatics, which applies the power of information technologies to classifying, analyzing and organizing the more than three billion bits of information
in the genome.

Discussion and Writing Suggestions

1. Friesen is a scientist who is enthusiastic about the promises of genetic
   research. Can you think of ways to counter some of his claims about the
   advantages of genetic research?
2. Friesen is optimistic about the outcome of genetic research. Are there points
   where he engages the opposition and responds to the serious concerns many
   have raised about the problems associated with genetic research? Friesen is
   giving a speech to businessmen, some of whom may contribute to funding
   his research project. In this situation, would he sound defensive or unsure
   of himself if he were to devote a lot of attention to addressing concerns and
   complaints about his work?

Fatalist Attraction: The Dubious Case against Fooling Mother Nature

VIRGINIA POSTREL

*Some challenge the wisdom of "defying" Nature by tinkering with the genetic
blueprints of life. But as Virginia Postrel points out, Nature in its unmodified state
can be a brutal breeding ground of illness, suffering, and disease. What genetic*

researchers are doing now is not so very different (at least in intent) from what medical researchers have done for centuries: that is, sought ways to block the development of disease and to offer patients long and healthy lives. If patients are willing to create "demand" for new medical techniques (even human cloning) and researchers are willing to deliver them, then what role—if any—should medical ethicists and government administrators play in deciding whether these techniques should go to market?

Virginia I. Postrel is editor of Reason *magazine, in which this selection appeared in July 1997. Reason presents a libertarian perspective that advocates against government interference in personal affairs. (The magazine's signature phrase is "Free Minds and Free Markets.") Postrel also writes commentaries for other national publications and appears regularly as a commentator on national television.*

Twenty years ago, the bookstore in which I was working closed for a few   1
hours while we all went to the funeral of one of our colleagues. Herbie was a delightful guy, well liked by everyone. He died in his 20s—a ripe old age back then for someone with cystic fibrosis. In keeping with the family's wishes, we all contributed money in his memory to support research on the disease. In those days, the best hope was that scientists would develop a prenatal test that would identify fetuses likely to have C.F., allowing them to be aborted. The thought made us uncomfortable. "Would you really want Herbie never to be?" said my boss.

But science has a way of surprising us. Two decades later, abortion is no   2
longer the answer proposed for cystic fibrosis. Gene therapy—the kind of audacious high-tech tool that generates countless references to *Brave New World* and *Frankenstein*—promises not to stamp out future Herbies but to cure them.

This spring I thought of Herbie for the first time in years. It was amid the   3
brouhaha over cloning, as bioethicists galore were popping up on TV to demand that scientists justify their unnatural activities and Pat Buchanan was declaring that "mankind's got to control science, not the other way around."

It wasn't the technophobic fulminations of the anti-cloning pundits that   4
brought back Herbie's memory, however. It was a letter from my husband's college roommate and his wife. Their 16-month-old son had been diagnosed with cystic fibrosis. He was doing fine now, they wrote, and they were optimistic about the progress of research on the disease.

There are no Herbies on *Crossfire*, and no babies with deadly diseases.   5
There are only nature and technology, science and society, "ethics" and ambition. Our public debate about biotechnology is loud and impassioned but, most of all, abstract. Cowed by an intellectual culture that treats progress as a myth, widespread choice as an indulgence, and science as the source of atom bombs, even biotech's defenders rarely state their case in stark, personal terms. Its opponents, meanwhile, act as though medical advances are an evil, thrust upon us by scheming scientists. Hence Buchanan talks of "science" as

distinct from "mankind" and ubiquitous Boston University bioethicist George Annas declares, "I want to put the burden of proof on scientists to show us why society needs this before society permits them to go ahead and [do] it."

That isn't, however, how medical science works. True, there are research   6
biologists studying life for its own sake. But the advances that get bioethicists exercised spring not from pure science but from consumer demand: "Society" may not ask for them, but individual people do.

Living in a center of medical research, I am always struck by the people   7
who appear on the local news, having just undergone this or that unprecedented medical procedure. They are all so ordinary, so down-to-earth. They are almost always middle-class, traditional families, people with big medical problems that require unusual solutions. They are not the Faustian, hedonistic yuppies you'd imagine from the way the pundits talk.

And it is the ambitions of such ordinary people, with yearnings as old as   8
humanity—for children, for health, for a long and healthy life for their loved ones—of which the experts so profoundly disapprove. As we race toward what Greg Benford aptly calls "the biological century," we will hear plenty of warnings that we should not play God or fool Mother Nature. We will hear the natural equated with the good, and fatalism lauded as maturity. That is a sentiment about which both green romantics and pious conservatives agree. And it deserves far more scrutiny than it usually gets.

Nobody wants to stand around and point a finger at this woman [who   9
had a baby at 63] and say, "You're immoral." But generalize the practice and ask yourself, "What does it really mean that we won't accept the life cycle or life course?" Leon Kass, the neocons' favorite bioethicist, told *The New York Times,* "That's one of the big problems of the contemporary scene. You've got all kinds of people who make a living and support themselves but who psychologically are not grown up. We have a culture of functional immaturity."

It sounds so profound, so wise, to denounce "functional immaturity" and   10
set oneself up as a grown-up in a society of brats. But what exactly does it mean in this context? Kass can't possibly think that 63-year-olds will start flocking to fertility clinics—that was the quirky action of one determined woman. He is worried about something far more fundamental: our unwillingness to put up with whatever nature hands out, to accept our fates, to act our ages. "The good news," says Annas of human cloning, "is I think *finally we have a technology that we can all agree shouldn't be used.*" (Emphasis added.) Lots of biotech is bad, he implies, but it's so damned hard to get people to admit it.

When confronted with such sentiments, we should remember just what   11
Mother Nature looks like unmodified. Few biotechnophobes are as honest as British philosopher John Gray, who in a 1993 appeal for greens and conservatives to unite, wrote of "macabre high-tech medicine involving organ transplantation" and urged that we treat death as "a friend to be welcomed." Suffering is the human condition, he suggested: We should just lie back and accept it. "For millennia," he said, "people have been born, have suffered pain

and illness, and have died, without those occurrences being understood as treatable diseases."

• • •

Gray's historical perspective is quite correct. In the good old days, rich   12
men did not need divorce to dump their first wives for trophies. Childbirth and disease did the trick. In traditional societies, divorce, abandonment, annulment, concubinage, and polygamy—not high-tech medicine—were the cures for infertility. Until the 20th century, C.F. didn't need a separate diagnosis, since it was just one cause of infant mortality among many. Insulin treatment for diabetes (highly unnatural) didn't exist until the 1920s. My own grandmother saw her father, brother, and youngest sister die before she was in middle age. In 1964 a rubella epidemic left a cohort of American newborns deaf.

These days, we in rich countries have the wonderful luxury of rejecting   13
even relatively minor ailments, from menstrual cramps to migraines, as unnecessary and treatable. "People had always suffered from allergies. . . . But compared to the other health problems people faced before the middle of the twentieth century, the sneezing, itching, and skin eruptions had for the most part been looked at as a nuisance," writes biologist Edward Golub. "In the modern world, however, they became serious impediments to living a full life, and the discovery that a whole class of compounds called antihistamines could control the symptoms of allergy meant that allergic individuals could lead close to normal lives. The same story can be told for high blood pressure, depression, and a large number of chronic conditions."

Treating chronic conditions is, if anything, more nature-defiant than   14
attacking infectious diseases. A woman doesn't have to have a baby when she's 63 to refuse to "accept the life cycle or life course." She can just take estrogen. And, sure enough, there is a steady drumbeat of criticism against such unnatural measures, as there is against such psychologically active drugs as Prozac. We should, say the critics, just take what nature gives us.

In large part, this attitude stems from a naive notion of health as the nat-   15
ural state of the body. In fact, disease and death are natural; the cures are artificial. And as we rocket toward the biological century, we will increasingly realize that a bodily state may not be a "disease," but just something we wish to change. Arceli Keh was not sick because her ovaries no longer generated eggs; she was simply past menopause. To say she should be able to defy her natural clock (while admitting that mid-60s parenthood may not be the world's greatest idea) doesn't mean declaring menopause a disease. Nor does taking estrogen, any more than taking birth control pills means fertility is a sickness.

"The cloned human would be an attack on the dignity and integrity of   16
every single person on this earth," says German Research Minister Juergen Ruettgers, demanding a worldwide ban, lest such subhumans pollute the planet. (The Germans want to outlaw even the cloning of human cells for

medical research.) Human cloning is an issue, but it is not *the* issue in these debates. They are really about whether centralized powers will wrest hold of scientists' freedom of inquiry and patients' freedom to choose—whether one set of experts will decide what is natural and proper for all of us—and whether, in fact, nature should be our standard of value.

Ruettgers is wildly overreacting and, in the process, attacking the human- 17 ity of people yet unborn. As Ron Bailey has noted . . . human cloning is not that scary, unless you're afraid of identical twins, nor does it pose unprecedented ethical problems. No one has come up with a terribly plausible scenario of when human cloning might occur. Yet judging from the history of other medical technologies, the chances are good that if such a clone were created, the parents involved would be ordinary human beings with reasons both quite rare and extremely sympathetic. We should not let the arrogant likes of Ruettgers block their future hopes.

Review Questions

1. According to Postrel, who should control decisions regarding which technologies medical researchers (and patients) should pursue?
2. What distinction does Postrel make between "natural" and "unnatural" interventions in human health?
3. Postrel claims that professional ethicists and politicians tend to make their objections to high-tech medicine in abstract, not personal, terms. Postrel sees this as a problem. Why?

Discussion and Writing Suggestions

1. To what extent do you see human cloning as a difference in degree or in kind from the medical research that has been done in the past? Researchers have developed elaborate techniques, for instance, to help infertile couples conceive and give birth. In what ways is cloning a radical departure from this kind of science?
2. How comfortable are you in allowing someone—or some government entity—to decide which medical investigations and technologies ought to be permitted? To take a particular case, should it be the government's decision to restrict or ban research on human cloning? Explain your answer.
3. Explain the significance of Postrel's title for this selection. What is a "fatalist" attraction? What is the case against Mother Nature? Why is this a "dubious" case?
4. What, in your view, is the distinction between healing a diseased person naturally versus unnaturally? What would be an example of each type of treatment? Explain the distinctions between the natural and the unnatural treatments.
5. "For millennia," writes Postrel, quoting the British philosopher John Gray, "people have been born, have suffered pain and illness, and have died, without those occurrences being understood as treatable diseases." In

Gray's view of the life cycle, what is the function of medicine and what is the role of medical research?

6. If the decision to make genetic interventions (whether in one's own body or, perhaps, in that of a child or embryo) were left to individuals, as Postrel advocates, some observers predict that two classes, if not species, of humans would inevitably arise—one that insisted on being "natural" and the other that freely made genetic "enhancements." To what extent does this prediction argue for decisions about genetic intervention being made *not* by individuals but by broader cultural authorities—governments, say, or international bodies of scientists?

Human Genome Projection

G. CLEMENT

Source: G. Clement/*National Post*. Reprinted with permission.

Perfection, but at What Price?

MICHAEL VALPY

Michael Valpy began his journalism career at The Vancouver Sun *in 1961 and went on to serve as national affairs columnist. For* The Globe and Mail, *he has been a member of the editorial board, Ottawa national affairs columnist, Africa correspondent and deputy managing editor.*

He has produced numerous public affairs documentaries for CBC Radio, received community awards for his writings from organizations such as Daily Bread Food Bank, the Ontario Psychological Foundation, and the Canadian Nurses Association, and won three National Newspaper Awards. In 1997, Trent University awarded him an honorary doctorate of letters for his work.

He is co-author of two books on the constitution, The National Deal *(1982) and* To Match a Dream *(1998), and a co-author with Judith Maxwell and others of* Family Security in Insecure Times *(1994).*

In the following article, "Perfection, but at What Price?" Valpy consults an international panel of medical researchers to canvass their opinions on various issues of biogenetics.

The Panel

Dr. Alan Bernstein has been a molecular and medical genetics professor at the   1
University of Toronto since 1984. He has made key contributions to the study of embryonic development, hematopoiesis, cancer, the cardiovascular system, gene therapy, and mammalian development. He is the president of the Canadian Institute for Health Research.

Dr. Peter Doherty, who originally studied veterinary medicine in   2
Australia, is now chairman of the department of immunology at St. Jude Children's Research Hospital in Memphis and a pathology professor at the University of Tennessee, Memphis. He won a Gairdner Award in 1986 and the Nobel Prize for physiology in 1996.

Dr. Judah Folkman developed the first implantable pacemaker and dis-   3
covered anti-angiogenesis, the eradication of tumours by cutting off their blood supply. Before devoting himself to research, the Cleveland native became a professor of surgery at Harvard Medical School in 1967 and served as surgeon-in-chief at Children's Hospital Medical Center in Boston for 14 years. He received the Gairdner in 1991.

Dr. Judith Hall is a clinical geneticist and the head of the pediatrics   4
departments at the University of British Columbia and B.C.'s Children's Hospital. Born in Boston, her main areas of research are human congenital anomalies, including the genetics of short stature and monozygotic (identical) twins. She is an officer of the Order of Canada.

Dr. Joseph Martin, born in Bassano, Alta., is the dean of Harvard　5
Medical School. His specialties include the molecular genetics of neuro-
degenerative disease. His early work led to the discovery of the genetic marker
for Huntington's disease. He won the Abraham Flexner Award for distinguished service to medical education in 1999.

Sir Keith Peters is the Regius Professor of Physic (medicine) at the　6
University of Cambridge. His research interests include diseases of the kidneys
and blood vessels and immunological mechanisms in disease. He is a fellow of
Christ's College, Cambridge, and served on the Advisory Council on Science
and Technology from 1987 to 1990.

The Gairdner Foundation

Dr. John Dirks is president of the Toronto-based Gairdner Foundation, which　7
presents an annual international award for excellence in medical science. A
native of Winnipeg, he became the dean of medicine at U of T in 1987 and is
currently a professor emeritus of medicine there. His work is concentrated in
renal pathophysiology. He has served on the Medical Research Council of
Canada and received the medical award of the Kidney Foundation of Canada
in 1985.

• • •

Scientists in Britain received parliamentary approval this week to create　8
human embryos for research into treating disease. In two words, therapeutic
cloning.

It is the first legal green light given to the Western world's biomedical　9
community to actually create human life. The terms are stringent: The
embryos must be destroyed after 14 days; they must never be allowed to
grow into human beings; a select parliamentary committee is to come up with
detailed regulatory controls before the first research licences are granted.

Now, from the moral principles of Westminster's lawmakers, let's travel　10
to this month's issue of *Wired* magazine, the widely read periodical of the
North American software industry, a sort of *New England Journal of
Medicine* for computer nerds. The cover story is about the Creator and the
Client. It is not fiction.

The Creator is described by writer Brian Alexander as "an intense dark-　11
haired man in his thirties [who] looks a little like Peter Lorre in *The Beast
With Five Fingers.*"

He has a PhD in molecular biology, a list of peer-reviewed publications,　12
a research job at a major U.S. university, an entrepreneurial spirit and a
shortage of ethical scruples. He has "just enough skill to make human cloning
work," Mr. Alexander writes.

And he has attracted a customer—the Client—a businessman living in　13
Western Europe whose son died from disease a year ago. The Client found
him by cruising the underworld of the Internet.

The Client wants the Creator to clone his dead son. He has consulted   14
experts and keeps tissue samples from the body stored in liquid nitrogen and
paraffin blocks. The Creator has found an in vitro fertilization laboratory that
can do the work, with a compliant director skilled in the handling of human
eggs and the IVF embryo manipulations that closely resemble the techniques
used in cloning.

At last report, Mr. Alexander writes, the Creator and the Client had   15
fallen to bickering over whether the Creator could guarantee success.

Then there is the story of the Quebec-based New Age cult, the UFO   16
worshipping Raelians, and their project, Clonaid. They announced last year,
through much salacious press coverage around the world, that they had found
a U.S. couple ready to pay $500 000 to have their dead baby cloned from
saved tissue.

The cult said it has the medical know-how to do the job. It, too, may   17
have found the Creator and his lab.

"The Creator's spirit," Mr. Alexander writes, "has been awakened by the   18
historical moment we're in right now, a convergence of under-the-radar pro-
cloning agitation, falling taboos, and the inexorable march of science."

Or, as Dr. Joseph Martin, the Alberta-born dean of Harvard University's   19
school of medicine, explains: "The technology isn't that difficult and it will
happen probably before we'd like it to.

"Cloning of the monkey has already been done. So the possibility of   20
reproducing ourselves, humankind, within the next few years is really not a
question of whether or if you can, but a question of 'who does it.'"

• • •

And so here we have the chills travelling up the world's spine.   21

Hidden from view in corporate-financed research laboratories, human-   22
cloning experiments already may be well under way, Dr. Martin told a recent
breakfast gathering attended by some of the world's outstanding clinical and
basic-science researchers in genetics, immunology and molecular biology.

The Globe and Mail had invited the scientists to talk about the morals   23
and ethics required to frame the relentless advance of biomedical research.

Britain has now taken the step to the leading edge. The U.S. National   24
Institutes of Health has just begun to finance research using surplus human
embryos from in vitro fertilization clinics (manufacturing embryos remains
prohibited), which the new Bush administration is being strongly lobbied to
halt.

The Canadian government, wishy-washy to a fault, twice has backed   25
away from regulatory legislation of any kind, relying on a voluntary morato-
rium by the biomedical community that may well have served to drive
research underground. In any event Canadian scientists have described human
embryo-cell research in the country as having gone nowhere.

The publicly funded Canadian Institutes of Health Research (the rein-   26
carnated Medical Research Council) has a committee working on research

guidelines. A Health Canada discussion paper given media attention this week says the government may permit therapeutic cloning similar to the British model when it finally gets around to making laws to govern human reproductive technology.

Religious groups, with the Roman Catholic Church in the forefront, immediately announced their opposition.   27

A brief look at the science before we get to *The Globe*'s breakfast: 28

Dolly the sheep was cloned in Scotland four years ago. This month, scientists announced the cloning of ANDi the rhesus monkey (named for "inserted DNA") in Oregon. Mice and other forms of life have been cloned in university and private labs around the world.   29

This is how it works: The nucleus is removed from a fertilized egg to be replaced by a new cell nucleus from the tissue of the "parent" animal (or "brother" or "sister"—the language hasn't yet found the right comfortable word) in a process called somatic cell nuclear transfer. The new cloned egg is then grown into an embryo.   30

Within the embryo are stem cells, the body's master cells that go on to diversify into organs, bones, nerves, muscles, skin and blood. Researchers want to understand, using the knowledge of genetic codes, how stem cells can be grown into new organs and body parts that can replace those that are diseased or genetically disordered.   31

In Britain, before the House of Lords passed amendments this week to the Human Fertilisation and Embryology Act, scientists were restricted to research on fertilization, contraception and congenital disorders using existing, surplus embryos.   32

British researchers are still expected to rely on surplus embryos rather than to create new ones. But the legal authority now exists, and the limits on research have been lifted.   33

Against this backdrop is an engulfing debate over both the ethical issues of creating life as "disposable organic material"—as one British church leader has termed it—and the scientific issues of whether devoting so many resources to genetic research is going down the wrong path and raising invalid public expectations.   34

And, of course, there is the worry about the Creator and for-profit corporate interest in what can be done with our bodies.   35

To date, private companies, universities and charitable organizations working to eradicate various diseases and disorders have filed patents on 127 000 genetic bits of the human body—the gene sequences and chemical codes that are the software of life. The race to buy life, it has been called.   36

• • •

The scientists who met *Globe* journalists for breakfast were in Toronto to serve as jurors for medical science's prestigious Gairdner Award, known as the Baby 'Bel because many winners subsequently receive the Nobel Prize.   37

The group included Harvard medical dean Joseph Martin; Australian   38
immunologist Peter Doherty; Sir Keith Peters, regius professor of physic (medicine) at Cambridge University; Harvard surgeon Judah Folkman; Judith
Hall, clinical geneticist at the University of British Columbia; and Alan
Bernstein, president of the Canadian Institutes for Health Research, the pre-
eminent agency for funding medical research in Canada.

John Dirks, president of the Gairdner Foundation and former dean of   39
medicine at University of Toronto, was also at the breakfast.

The job of the Gairdner Award jurors, Dr. Dirks said, "will be to decide   40
what ideas are important and what will last." It will be interesting to speculate on what values are embodied in the selection of this year's winner, whose
name will be announced this spring.

What they had to say, in sum, was this: 41

- The biggest obstacle to growing cloned embryos into human beings is   42
  that there is not a mass market for it. Yet. Which is not the same as
  saying there isn't a market.
- It is not the role of scientists to determine the ethical limits to research   43
  or the application of genetic knowledge to the delivery of public health.
  That is the role of legislatures and the public. The job of scientists, Dr.
  Bernstein said, is to be canaries in the coal mine, saying: "Hey, there's
  an issue coming up here, and we should have a full discussion."
- The public and the news media generally have an inaccurate and exag-   44
  gerated—the best word might be naïve—idea of where genetics
  research is leading and what can be accomplished in treating and erad-
  icating disease and other human imperfections.
- The debate over stem-cell research will probably end, or at least   45
  become more muted, once researchers learn how to work usefully with
  adult stem cells and no longer need embryos.
- The primary ethical issue for medical scientists is not about genetics and   46
  cloning but the rapidly widening gulf between the developed and developing worlds in the availability of medical knowledge and treatment.

The market for genetics research will be created by the demand for genet-   47
ically engineered human tissue (preferably a person's own) or genetic pharmacology to replace or compensate for diseased and disordered parts of the
body. To that end, private corporations have invested billions of dollars in
biotechnology and applied for tens of thousands of patents (one French company alone holds more than 38 000).

But the reality, Sir Keith Peters said, is that the market for cloning   48
embryos for human life is not absent.

"In most Western societies, there's a tremendous amount of hand-waving   49
about how human cloning is not going to happen, it's absolutely unacceptable, the society will reject it.

"And then I ask the question of my friends: 'Okay, your only child, age   50
21, is killed in a motor accident and you had a chance to take a little tissue

from him or her and you're beyond reproductive age yourself almost certainly—
would you like to have another child, [because we] have this technology?' And
I've yet to come across an answer no.

"I think there are all kinds of reasons why we should not do that. But   51
when people are faced with it as a real possibility, the answer is yes."

Why should science not do that? Because genetic determinism, however   52
much it comes eventually to be understood, will never replicate a human
being.

The parents who want their dead 21-year-old cloned will get a 21-year-   53
old, Sir Keith said. But they won't get back the 21-year-old child who died.

Patricia Baird, the University of British Columbia geneticist whose report   54
from the 1993 Royal Commission on New Reproductive Technologies has
been left by Ottawa to gather dust, pointed out in a public Vancouver lecture
this month that genetic constitutions—even if they could be exactly replicated—
can never overcome human nurture, human experience and the million and
one other environmental factors that from conception give shape to a human
being.

$$\bullet \ \bullet \ \bullet$$

What of genetic manipulation, or the application of transgenic technol-   55
ogy? What do scientists say about therapies to deal with, for example, the
genetic mutation for cystic fibrosis identified in a human embryo?

The CF gene has been known for 11 years, since it was discovered by   56
University of Toronto geneticist Lap-Chee Tsui.

To date, there is no proven gene-based therapy to correct it, to replace the   57
mutated gene with one that is not.

Dr. Bernstein asked whether a couple wanting a child free of the muta-   58
tions would be willing to undergo all the required genetic manipulations,
most of which would fail. Maybe one in 50 would succeed. Dr. Doherty
said. It took 300 tries to get Dolly.

Dr. Bernstein posed further questions. Should genetic screening for the   59
mutation become required? Do we move to some sort of social consensus that
all fetuses identified with the mutation should be routinely aborted?

And what would that say to people living with cystic fibrosis—the people   60
with a mutation that wasn't identified?

To date, 950 mutations of the cystic-fibrosis gene have been identified,   61
only 30 of which are routinely screened for in laboratories. In 1 to 15 per cent
of affected patients, the mutation is not identified either during a natural pregnancy or before an in vitro embryo is implanted.

Dr. Bernstein said: "It's not up to the research community to decide   62
whether fetuses with the cystic fibrosis gene should be aborted. It's for the
public through their lawmakers to either regulate or legislate."

"Those questions," Dr. Doherty said, "rest with the community values   63
and ethical considerations in a particular society."

The scientists at the *Globe* breakfast spoke enthusiastically about revo-   64
lutionary advances in genetics-based medical knowledge. They talked about
developments in genetic pharmacology leading to drugs that will compensate
for genetic disorders.

They predicted major therapeutic advances in the next few years for   65
cancer, diabetes, muscular dystrophy, coronary diseases and neurological disorders such as Alzheimer's.

They also repeatedly tempered their enthusiasm with warnings against   66
unreal public expectations.

"One of the things we've learned from the genetic revolution . . . is the   67
uniqueness of every individual and how much environment plays a role," Dr.
Hall said. "So although we can talk broadly about Alzheimer's, there are
major environmental factors and there will be individual susceptibilities
because of the interaction of various biochemicals."

Dr. Baird, in her public lecture, put the issue succinctly with two exam-   68
ples: There are 256 different identified risk factors for heart disease, and a
B.C. study of one million individuals followed from birth to age 25 found that
single-gene disorders occur in only 3.6 per 1000 live births.

"The vast majority of illnesses in humans are the result of complex inter-   69
actions, over time, between their genetic constitutions and [their environ-
ment]," she said. "The evidence is overwhelming that the determinants of the
common chronic diseases of modern life are complex, interrelated, act over
time and are embedded in a social context."

Which suggests that the breakthroughs in the treatment of humanity's   70
horrible disorders are not going to come from genetic discoveries alone but
from a partnership of medical scientists doing both basic and clinical research.

Harvard's Judah Folkman said: "I continue to be fascinated by the   71
absolute, unexpected and surprising discoveries that come when clinicians
work with basic scientists which would not come at all if their work was separate."

He cited as an example the isolation by basic researchers of an enzyme in   72
hemangiomas—benign facial tumours that appear at birth and usually disappear by age 7 or 8. Clinical researchers then discovered that these tumours
destroyed thyroid hormones and are a leading factor in causing mental retar-
dation in children.

Then Dr. Folkman spoke of the moral issue that is most in his mind: "All   73
our arguments about cloning and ethics will pale before the fact that we will
be judged by not worrying about places . . . that can't afford the treatments
we discover."

He recalled one of his medical residents who returned from working in a   74
children's hospital in New Delhi. The resident described how every morning
there were 20 children on the hospital's doorstep who had died overnight
from simple diarrhea.

"They don't do the fancy surgery we do," Dr. Folkman said. The assaults   75
on the frontiers of medical science have not been matched by assaults on
miserly foreign aid.

Sir Keith said the endemic presence of diseases such as AIDS in Africa— 76 where, in countries, 40 per cent of women arriving in clinics and hospitals for childbirth are HIV-positive—puts all other medical ethical issues on the back burner.

(In an article in *The Globe and Mail* yesterday, Stephen Lewis, former 77 Canadian ambassador to the United Nations, called AIDS in southern Africa one of the greatest human tragedies of our age on which the West is willfully turning its back.)

Dr. Doherty spoke of recently visiting the University of California's vet- 78 erinary school and seeing dogs on dialysis at a cost of $7000 a year. "Think about it. It's these people's money. They could just as well spend the money on a new Cadillac every year, but they choose to spend it on their dog.

"Ethically, it's appalling. Look at AIDS. In this country and in Australia 79 and in the U.S., everyone gets triple drug therapy. In Africa, . . . they can't afford these drugs."

At a guess, there will be more public fuss in the West about the Creator. 80

Discussion and Writing Suggestions

1. Of the panelists, who seems the most supportive of biotechnology? Who seems most critical? Who do you think makes the best case? What is the strongest argument?
2. Define the word "ethics" using a dictionary. Then look at the way medical researchers define ethical issues. Does the term shift as it is applied by individuals?
3. Valpy consults a panel of experts, in the sense that they are medical researchers. What do you think would occur if Postrel were added to a panel like this? Would Postrel be "out of her league," on the basis of her article that indicated that she was working with, at best, a generalist knowledge-base of biotechnological issues?

Ethics under the Microscope

PETER CALAMAI

In this article which appeared in The Toronto Star *in 2002, Peter Calamai describes the struggles and limited successes of a panel of medical experts convened to develop regulations to govern stem-cell research practices in Canada. As he points out, even if this body had been able to hammer out a roster of guidelines, their rules would have applied only to public sector research, and not to "the Wild West of private sector." In the process of explaining what needs to be done, Calamai's article also indicates why guidelines are urgently needed.*

Peter Calamai is currently the national science reporter with The Toronto Star *based in Ottawa. He is a founder of the Canadian Science Writers Association.*

Six men and four women gathered in the windowless boardroom of a down-   1
town office building here on Nov. 22, 2000, to be handed a whole sack of hot
potatoes: writing Canada's rules for stem-cell research.

For most people whose biology lessons stopped with high school, stem   2
cells are the stuff of headlines about growing new organs for transplants, stopping cancer in its tracks or reversing the ravages of Parkinson's and
Alzheimer's.

But for the 10 experts in that boardroom, stems cells also represented an   3
ethical minefield, a cauldron of bubbling scientific controversies and a major
test of whether Canadians will control the biotechnology revolution or be
controlled by it.

As well, those medical researchers, lawyers and ethics specialists faced   4
worries of what might happen if they got the rules wrong—a Wild West
research free-for-all that could spur attempts at human cloning or the spectre
of labs creating creatures that are part-man/part-animal, such as mice with
human brain cells.

"With the great potential of stem cells to treat disease, we needed a   5
framework of rules that Canadians would be comfortable with but that
would also allow the scientific work to go forward," says Alan Bernstein.

A former researcher at the Samuel Lunenfeld Research Institute in   6
Toronto, Bernstein is president of the Canadian Institutes of Health Research
(CIHR), the federal agency that funds the studies of most medical scientists at
universities and hospitals across the country.

It was the CIHR that selected the 10 experts and handed them that sack   7
of hot potatoes. But the agency also gave them an advance okay to sidestep
what most Canadians consider the hottest issue of them all—where stem
cells come from.

Right now, stem-cell research includes what some consider a Faustian   8
bargain, a pact to eventually deliver our souls to the Devil. That's because the
most medically promising stem cells are found, so far, mainly in human
embryos and fetuses.

These particular stem cells seem to be immortal. They keep reproducing   9
indefinitely in a laboratory dish, unlike ordinary human tissue cells that
quickly die off.

And with the right prodding, these stem cells also appear capable of   10
transforming into any of the body's 260 varieties of specialized cells, such as
brain, liver, bone and blood. This changeling ability raises the prospect of
growing new tissues and organs to replace any damaged by disease or injury.

Yet extracting these "mother" cells destroys the embryo. To some people,   11
this is as morally unacceptable as abortion, since they consider an embryo to
be a person. To others, causing the destruction of an embryo isn't the same as
killing a person and is justified by the immense potential to relieve human suffering.

When the working group gathered for its first and only face-to-face meet- 12
ing on that November morning, federal research rules in place since 1987 said
scientists could experiment with embryos that were "surplus" at fertility clinics or with aborted fetuses.

With the approval of the CIHR, the experts decided they wouldn't recon- 13
sider the moral status of the human embryo. That core issue in Canada's
research approach remained unchanged, despite the accusations of radical liberalization protested by special interest groups since the new rules were made
public Monday.

"There is no change at all. We simply didn't address that issue," says 14
Bernstein.

But the experts did tackle other hot potatoes in the stem-cell sack, result- 15
ing in greater restrictions on what experiments Canadian medical researchers
will be allowed to perform.

University of Alberta law professor Tim Caulfield says the working group 16
members devoted nights and weekends without complaint to reading complex
documents and going through draft rules line by line.

"Everyone was tremendously committed to hammering this report out. 17
We all knew it was going to have an impact."

Because the CIHR began applying the new rules this week, Canada likely 18
now has some of the most ethically consistent and scientifically sound guidelines for stem-cell research in the world. And these rules will undoubtedly
strongly shape a new human reproduction law now before Parliament.

Major advances were made in four contentious areas: 19

- Rigorous rules for ensuring that people give informed consent to any 20
  stem-cell research use of embryos and fetuses in which they have a stake.
- The first-ever national body to approve the ethics of each proposed 21
  stem-cell research project, a task previously left to the very institutions
  that benefited from the federal research dollars.
- A mandatory national data bank where researchers must register the 22
  stem-cell lines they grow from embryos, agreeing to provide them at
  cost to other Canadian researchers.
- Sweeping prohibition of stem-cell research where genetic material from 23
  different humans, or from humans and other animals, is melded to
  create uniquely new creatures—called chimera after a fire-breathing
  female monster in Greek mythology that combined a lion's head, goat's
  body and serpent's tail.

The working group last year circulated a draft recommendation that 24
would have allowed some restricted research in this field, such as grafting
human stem cells into a mouse embryo but then killing the mother mouse
before it gave birth.

But that proposal faltered because of what one member called the "yuck" 25
response. Instead, the final report urges further study by a new panel with
deeper expertise.

The 10 working group members had better success reaching agreement 26
on other heated issues. Some of the group's practising researchers, although

initially opposed, were gradually won around to the need for yet another layer of bureaucratic approval for stem-cell projects, a national ethics screening panel.

The group also urged Health Canada to add similar, additional national 27 ethics screening for other "novel and contentious" areas of research. The message is unmistakable—the existing system of local ethics review doesn't provide enough openness and independence for public confidence.

In addition, the members devoted a lot of e-mailing and teleconferencing 28 time to word-by-word crafting of the airtight rules for how researchers must get informed consent from all parties to use their surplus embryos and then get consent a second time.

'We've definitely made everything more restrictive than the current 29 atmosphere," says Barbara Beckett, a senior officer with the Stem Cell Network who served as co-ordinator for the working group.

Unfortunately, these carefully crafted rules apply only to stem-cell 30 research funded by the CIHR's $560 million annual budget.

Stem-cell researchers in industry or with private funding through a foun- 31 dation or a medical charity don't have to comply, although some charities have pledged to enforce the CIHR rules voluntarily.

As a result of this week's guidelines, the contrast is stark between tight 32 controls on stem research in the public sector and the prospect of a Wild West private sector. Many experts predict Parliament won't be able to keep stalling on a law governing human reproductive technology, more than a decade after a royal commission urged such legislation.

Adding to such political pressure may well be one reason why the CIHR 33 pushed ahead with its stem-cell guidelines even after the working group's preliminary recommendations a year ago were incorporated almost completely in the government's draft legislation.

For the record, the CIHR's Bernstein says it would have been irresponsi- 34 ble not to provide an ethical and scientific framework for Canadian researchers as soon as possible.

Unlike their counterparts in other parts of the world, Canadian scientists 35 have voluntarily refrained from carrying out research with human embryonic stem cells since November, 1988, when three separate, privately funded scientific experiments first signalled their immense potential.

Using surplus embryos or fetuses to gather human stem cells was per- 36 missible back then under the long-existing rules, as well as under the newest national guidelines, announced in August, 1998, by the CIHR's predecessor, the Medical Research Council of Canada, and the two other federal granting councils that provide funds to university researchers in the physical and social sciences.

Yet Canadian medical scientists held back because these Tri-Council 37 guidelines had been written before the potential of human embryonic stem cells became well-known. They worried aloud about the risk of a public backlash for appearing rash or opportunistic.

But the researchers were also obviously anxious to get going. Canadians 38
have been leaders in using embryonic stem cells in other animals, especially
mice, to develop new techniques to investigate the genetic aspects of disease
and test potential therapies.

Janet Rossart, for example, a Lunenfeld Institute geneticist who headed 39
the CIHR group, is ranked second in the world for most-influential scientific
papers about mouse embryonic stem cells, published between 1991 and 2001.

Rossart's colleague on the working group and a specialist in bone 40
marrow research, Dr. Keith Humphries of the B.C. Cancer Research Centre,
sums up the feelings of researchers:

"If we didn't get guidelines in place, Canada was going to be left in the 41
dust," he says.

Falling behind in the global knowledge stakes was far from the only 42
reason that the CIHR working group felt Canada needed quick action on scientifically sound and ethically rigorous stem-cell guidelines.

A little-realized fact is that Canada has very few spare embryos—too few 43
to waste even one on anything but the most medically compelling research,
argues Françoise Baylis, a member of the working group and, since January,
also a member of the CIHR governing council.

Writing in her capacity as a bioethicist at Dalhousie University, Baylis 44
lays out the mathematics:

Canada's fertility clinics are probably storing somewhere around 500 45
embryos in cryogenic deep freeze. Some belong to couples still trying to have
children and some are needed for training and testing. Perhaps 250 "surplus"
embryos would be available for stem-cell research.

Based on experience, roughly half would survive being thawed. Of these 46
125 surviving embryos, no more than nine could be expected to progress all
the way to generating some sort of stem-cell line. Fewer still would meet the
exacting scientific criteria to qualify for human embryonic stem-cell research.

Fertility clinics are already creating the maximum number of embryos
required for reproductive success. So any increases would expose women to 47
unethical extra risk from the high-drug doses and amount to creating extra
human embryos specifically for research purposes, which is expressly banned
in Canada under both the old Tri-Council and new CIHR guidelines.

Instead, Baylis predicts that the number of "surplus" embryos available 48
for stem-cell research in Canada is likely to fall in coming years because
improved techniques will allow frozen preservation of women's eggs, just as
sperm is now. As well, some fertility clinics are likely to close once stricter
operating standards are enforced nationally under new federal human reproduction legislation.

No one knows how many different stem-cell lines are necessary to make 49
the move from laboratory potential to therapeutic reality. But the best estimates are that scores, and quite possibly more than a hundred, will be needed
to provide the required genetic diversity.

Some people who oppose the use of embryos and fetuses on ethical   50
grounds are touting heavily another approach—finding stem cells in adult tissues that have the same changeling ability as the embryonic stem cells.

Isolated scientists support such claims, but the leading researchers in the   51
field mostly agree that the few experiments reported so far with these adult
cells, including work at McGill University, fall far short of making the case.

And while much is contentious in the area of stem-cell-research, law   52
professor Caulfield expresses a view that seems to be universally agreed.

"This issue is never going to end," he says. "We are always going to have   53
continuing talk, continuing schemes. This is the dawn of the biotech century."

Discussion and Writing Suggestions

1. What is the link between the prominence of our Canadian researchers and
   the respect our researchers are willing to show for ethical procedures?
2. How is this article, examining the issue of ethics and biotechnology, different in tone and purpose from Postrel's article on a similar topic?

Biosciences Will Help Shape Our Future

REY PAGTAKHAN

*Writing for government publication in 2003, in his role as our National Minister
of Veterans Affairs and Secretary of State (Science, Research and Development),
Dr. Pagtakhan views the promises of bioscience with optimism, with particular
emphasis on its potential for overcoming viral mutations. He explains the presence
and significance of research undertakings in our country.*

*Born in the Philippines, Rey Pagtakhan was trained as a doctor and became
a professor of pediatric and child health. He served as MP for Winnipeg North
from 1988 to 2004, and was a cabinet minister in both the Chrétien and Martin
governments.*

The United Nations is projecting that the global population will reach 8.9 bil-   1
lion by 2050, up from 6.3 billion today. When we consider the societal challenges we face now, the global demographic pressures, and, more recently, the
threat of bioterrorism, there is cause for concern. How will our world feed so
many people, care for them, maintain our security and do all of these things
without degrading our natural environment?

Such challenges may seem daunting, even insurmountable. In fact, thanks   2
to the rapidly-growing sector known as the "biosciences," our world can look
forward to a very bright future. Take the example of biotechnology.
Biotechnology is a transformative technology that will revolutionize many traditional businesses, and other aspects of our society. It also brings together

many other research fields, including information technology, bioinformatics, nanotechnology and biophotonics. Indeed, biotechnology is driving the use of individualized medicine and offering new treatments and potential cures for many currently intractable conditions. The economic benefits for Canada within the health sector are now beginning to flow from high value-added research and development activities and from focused manufacturing opportunities in such areas as nutriceuticals, or foodstuffs with enhanced characteristics.

There are many sectors other than health services where bio-based products and processes will be applied, and I am pleased to underline the fact that several of these can be developed and commercialized in Canada. For example, the resource industries, like mining and forest products, can benefit from bio applications that result in cleaner, lower-cost processes. The chemical and energy industries can also benefit from biotech derived products. And after the health sector, agriculture and agrifood is a leader in biotechnology research and applications. 3

Our country is in an excellent position to benefit from the coming biotech revolution. Currently, Canada has the world's third largest biotechnology industry, in terms of revenue. We have the second largest, in terms of number of companies. And we are the first in terms of producing R&D workers, and first in terms of the tax treatment of R&D investments. 4

Furthermore, Canada's biotechnology sector is growing at a phenomenal rate. Annual revenues reported by the publicly-traded biotech companies now exceed $3.5-billion, more than 300 per cent higher than in 1997. 5

How has this happened? Well, the Government of Canada has made research and innovation one of its top priorities and has made direct investments in the biosciences sector. 6

The federal government has invested in a number of internationally respected organizations that are breaking new ground in this exciting new field of research. One of them is Genome Canada, an organization that is dedicated to making Canada a world leader in selected areas of genomics research. Already, it has contributed $291-million to 54 large-scale projects. These funds have been matched by other partners. 7

Another scientific body is the Canadian Institutes of Health Research, with an annual budget of $176-million for biotech-related projects. The Canada Foundation for Innovation, established to modernize the infrastructure of our universities and hospitals, has already awarded research grants to more than 2,400 projects, many of which are in biotechnology. 8

Canada's National Research Council is a leader in biotechnology research. In addition to its Biotechnology Research Institute in Montreal, which has attracted a number of large foreign research-based firms, the NRC has several institutes specializing in different aspects of biotechnology, including plant biotech in Saskatoon, marine biosciences in Halifax, and biodiagnostics in Winnipeg. 9

As well, the federal government has established 2,000 Canada Research Chairs, which assist our universities in attracting and retaining the best faculty 10 in the world. Already, $214.5-million has been invested to create 93 research chairs focussed on biotechnology. And finally, I want to mention our Networks of Centres of Excellence, which bring together the highest quality of research in government, academia and the private sector. Several of these centres are involved in biotech-related work.

Also, the government has a number of grant and investment programs   11
administered through the Industrial Research Assistance Program, the Business Development Bank of Canada and Technology Partnerships Canada, that support development and pre-commercialization activities of companies. These programs include over $80-million annually for biotech firms. This is above and beyond the indirect support provided through the Scientific Research & Experimental Development Tax Credit.

With the commitments made in its most recent budget, the Government   12
of Canada will have invested a cumulative total of over $11-billion in research and innovation between 1998–1999 and 2004–2005.

As the regional minister for Manitoba, I am pleased that our govern-   13
ment's investment in this crucial sector has been distributed throughout the country. The biotechnology and health research sector in Manitoba employs some 3,500 people in the biomedical and agricultural fields, with an emerging environmental field. This high-skills, high-wage sector exported a total of $125-million in 2002.

Now these investment numbers are all very encouraging, but what do   14
they mean in concrete terms? How is Canada benefiting from our government's commitment to the biosciences?

Well, take the example of the $95-million Structural Genomics   15
Consortium launched last April in Toronto, led by a young Canadian scientist, Dr. Aled Edwards of the University of Toronto. As a physician, I am proud of the fact that this is the largest medical research project ever funded in Canada.

The Structural Genomics Consortium will be focussing on proteins. You   16
see, while scientists have mapped out what genes look like, the proteins that carry their messages remain a mystery. Once we know what the proteins look like we will be able to make drugs that either boost the work of good proteins or block the work of "bad" proteins, for instance, those that make a cancer cell multiply and spread.

It is the first time that Canada will lead an international genomics project   17
of this magnitude, and it is also the first time that the Wellcome Trust, Britain's private sector medical research body, is investing outside of the U.K.

This ground-breaking project, which will certainly have all kinds of ben-   18
efits for Canadians, was made possible because the Government of Canada came forward with other partners to invest the money needed. Together, Genome Canada and CIHR invested $21-million, while the Ontario government, the Wellcome Trust and GlaxoSmithKline provided the balance. As a result, instead of a "brain drain," our government is now fostering a "brain gain," holding onto Canada's top scientists, and attracting their colleagues from other countries.

Another recent Canadian success story is the sequencing of human chro-　19
mosome 7. Last spring it was announced that scientists at The Hospital for
Sick Children in Toronto had compiled the complete DNA sequence of
human chromosome 7. The research involved an international collaboration
of 90 scientists from 10 countries, and the information generated by the
chromosome 7 project has been put in a publicly accessible database that can
be used to facilitate disease gene research. It's a public good.

In an era of new diseases like SARS and West Nile Virus, this kind of　20
research is more important than ever. And while on the subject of SARS, I am
proud to note that it was the Michael Smith Genome Sciences Centre, in
British Columbia, that completed the first publicly available draft sequence of
this new virus. Clearly, biotechnology is a crucial tool in our ongoing campaign to overcome mutations in viruses, so that we can respond to today's
health threats, and the unknown ones that will emerge in the years ahead.

Thanks to the policies adopted by our government and the significant　21
investments made, Canada is well-positioned to play a leadership role in the
biosciences sector in the years ahead. By doing so we will foster prosperity
here at home, but we will also be developing the technologies and the products that will help build a cleaner, healthier, safer world, for us and for our
neighbours around the globe. Here I am reminded of a wonderful initiative of
the University of Toronto Joint Centre for Bioethics called, "Top 10
Biotechnologies for Improving Health in Developing Countries." It provides
us with an inspiring vision of the future. We Canadians have the biotechnology tools and the know-how to make it a reality.

Discussion and Writing Suggestions

1. Why would Pagtakhan write this piece? For what audience and purpose?
2. There is no reference to outside sources in order to validate the facts and
   claims the author makes here. On what basis does the reader accept
   Pagtakhan as an expert in this field?

■ WRITING ACTIVITIES

1. Suppose you are writing a survey article on biotechnology for a general
   audience magazine, such as *Time* or *Maclean's*. You want to introduce
   your readers to the subject, tell them what it is and what it may become,
   and you want to focus, in particular, on the advantages and disadvantages
   of biotechnology. Drawing on the sources you have read in this chapter,
   write such an article (i.e., an explanatory research essay). For background
   information on the subject, you can draw on sources such as Starr and
   Taggart and the introduction to this chapter. Other sources, such as
   Postrel, use examples to illustrate advantages and disadvantages. And, of
   course, Huxley warns against the kinds of thing that *could* happen if
   biotechnology were to be used for unethical purposes.

2. Write an editorial (i.e., an argument essay) arguing that additional regulations need to be placed on biotechnology. Specify the chief problem areas, as you see them, and indicate the regulations needed to deal with these problems.

    You may want to begin with a survey of biotechnology (in which you acknowledge its advantages) but then narrow your focus to the problem areas you choose to emphasize. Categorize the problem areas (e.g., problems for prospective parents, for the workplace, for the courtroom, for the commercial applications of biotechnology). The suggested regulations—and explanations of why they are necessary—might be discussed throughout the editorial or saved for the end.

    In developing your editorial, devote one paragraph to Virginia Postrel's position (that the free market, not government regulations, should determine which genetic technologies get used). Devote another paragraph to rebutting her position.

3. *Brave New World* represents one artist's view of how scientific knowledge might be abused to ensure social stability and conformity. Huxley focused on the possibility of dividing fertilized human ova into identical parts and then conditioning the ova before "birth." Write a short story (or a play or screenplay) that represents your own nightmare vision. You may want to focus on other aspects of genetic engineering: the problem of forced genetic testing, of eugenics (creating "perfect" people or eliminating "imperfect" ones), of fostering uniformity among the population, of some fantastic commercial application of bioengineering, or even of some aspect of cloning (among the films dealing with cloning are Woody Allen's *Sleeper*, Steven Spielberg's *Jurassic Park* and, more recently, *The Island*).

    Decide whether the story is to be essentially serious or comic (satirical)—or something in between. Create characters (try to avoid caricatures) who will enact the various aspects of the problem, as you see it. And create a social and physical setting appropriate to the story you want to tell.

4. Write an article for a magazine such as *Maclean's* or *Time* on the current status of biotechnology—as of August 2050. Try to make the article generally upbeat (unlike the nightmare vision called for in the previous question), but be frank also about the problems that have been encountered, as well as the problems that remain. Refer, at some point in your article, to views of biotechnology from the late 1980s and the early 1990s to establish some basis for comparison between what they thought "then" and what they think "now."

5. Genome research is made possible by the investments of pharmaceutical companies, which bet that research will reveal the genetic foundations of certain diseases that can then be corrected with specially designed drugs. Certainly, without private investment, human genome research would proceed far more slowly than it is proceeding at present. How comfortable are you with the commercial direction that human genome research

has taken? Is the DNA map that researchers seek "larger" than the interests of particular pharmaceutical companies? What kinds of profits (if any) should companies be making in this field? Write an essay in which you take a position on this topic, drawing on relevant selections.

■ RESEARCH ACTIVITIES

1. The main focal points of the debate over genetic engineering and testing have been (1) whether the new biotechnologies are safe and ethical; (2) whether they will benefit agriculture and food processing; (3) whether they require stricter regulation (and if so, what kind); (4) whether genetic testing (or the use of genetic testing) by employers and insurance companies is ethical; (5) whether genetic testing of fetuses is ethical; (6) whether work should proceed on the Human Genome Project and/or the Human Genome Diversity Project; (7) whether geneticists should work on biological weapons. Select *one* of these areas and research the current status of the debate.

   In addition to relevant articles, see Jeremy Rifkin, *Declaration of a Heretic* (1985); Joseph Fletcher, *Ethics of Genetic Control* (1988); David Suzuki and Peter Knudtson, *Genetics* (1989); Andrew Linzey, *Slavery: Human and Animal* (1988); Daniel J. Kevles and Leroy Hood, *The Code of Codes: Scientific and Social Issues in the Human Genome Project* (1992); and Ingeborg Boyens, *Unnatural Harvest* (1999).

2. In August 1992, researchers announced that they had managed through genetic engineering to produce mice that developed cystic fibrosis. Scientists believed that by studying the course of this disease in mice, they would be able to devise new therapies for the treatment of this usually fatal disease in humans. Follow up on either this development or some other development involving the genetic engineering of laboratory animals to further medical research. Describe what is involved in the procedure, how it was developed, the results to date, and the ethical debate that may have ensued about its practice.

3. Research and discuss some aspect of the early history of genetic engineering as it developed in the 1970s. Begin with a survey of Watson and Crick's work with DNA in the early 1950s, describe some of the early experiments in this area, discuss some of the concerns expressed both by scientists and laypersons.

4. Research some of the most significant recent advances in biotechnology, categorize them, and report on your finding. You may wish to narrow your topic by dealing with biotechnology in relation to human health, agriculture, or the law. Focus on what is currently being done, on who is doing it, on the obstacles yet to overcome, and on the anticipated benefits of the research and development.

5. In 1989 James D. Watson was appointed to head the National Institutes of Health (NIH) Human Genome Project. Watson's appointment and his subsequent work as director of the project generated some controversy. Research Watson's professional activities since his discovery with Francis Crick of the structure of DNA, focusing on his more recent activities. See especially, the article on Watson, "The Double Helix," which appeared in *The New Republic*, July 9 and 16, 1990. How do Watson's professional colleagues—and others—assess his more recent work?

6. Research the current status of either the Human Genome Project or the Human Genome Diversity Project. To what extent has the project you selected made progress in achieving its goals?

7. Recently, our Parliament has debated regulating biogenetic research with particular interest in curtailing stem-cell research on human embryos that may lead to curing some serious illnesses but that sets off ethical alarm bells. Research and report on some of the most significant regulations imposed on the biotechnology industry, consider the views of critics and of scientists themselves, and indicate your own position (and possibly some of your own proposals) on existing and additional regulations.

8. If your college or university has scientists on its faculty who are working on DNA research, interview them to find out what they are doing. Ask them how they feel about some of the ethical issues covered in this chapter. Ask them to recommend references in the professional literature that will enable you to understand more fully the aims of their research; then consult some of these references and use them to provide context for your discussion of this research.

9. Conduct a survey on student attitudes about some facet of biotechnology and write a summary report based on this survey. Devise questions that focus on the main areas of controversy (see Research Activity 1). Phrase your questions in a way that allows a range of responses (perhaps on a scale of 1 to 5, or using modifiers such as "strongly agree," "agree somewhat," "disagree somewhat," "strongly disagree"); don't ask for responses that require a yes/no or approve/disapprove response. Attempt to correlate the responses to such variables as academic major, student status (lower division, upper division, graduate), gender, ethnic background, geographical area of origin (urban, suburban, rural). Determine whether respondents personally know someone with a disease for which a genetic cure is either possible or under consideration. Determine also how much prior knowledge of biotechnology your respondents have.

Canadian Identities

The topic of Canadian identity is always undergoing redefinition. It's a cliché that while Americans and Britons can be easily described, Canadians can't, which makes us think that we must be a bland lot, lacking in distinctive qualities. The definition is indeed elusive, perhaps because it is plural and dynamic. The articles in this chapter explore various aspects of Canadian identity—or identities—and the reasons why we are so difficult to pin down. In John Ralston Saul's words, we are a people who, unlike our American and British cousins, have not imposed "a monolithic mythology" on ourselves (pp. 446–451). In our selection from his book, *Reflections of a Siamese Twin*, Saul argues that our failure to enforce a unified public mythology reflects our genuine complexity.

To look at Canadian identity through the lens of cultural studies means to examine the complex processes of "representation" by which people's world view is formed: how they see themselves and each other, how they see other people, how they define their values. We can think of these processes of representation as the stories we tell about ourselves. These stories get told in the form of history books, newspapers, songs, plays, and novels. An article in our collection that refers to some of the popular images and themes that represent Canada is Anna Hudson's "The Art of Inventing Canada"; for many of us, as she points out, what comes to mind when we think about being Canadian is taking a road trip down the Trans-Canada Highway, singing campfire songs— "Land of the Silver Birch" among them—or viewing a painting by one of our Group of Seven.

Maybe the overriding myth or story we tell ourselves is that we are not like Americans. In the excerpt from *The Border*, James Laxer attempts to establish two contrasting histories. Douglas Coupland argues that Canada is distinct as a nation and that we need to resist the political and economic pull exerted by the U.S. in order to maintain our way of life. Lloyd Axworthy examines the question of our relation to our powerful neighbour, recommending that we resist the pressure they bring to bear in such a way as to foster a sense of community between us rather than hostility.

Another story we tell about ourselves is that Canadians are concerned for each other's welfare. In a recent poll on CBC, the founder of Medicare, Tommy Douglas, was voted the most important Canadian. Many refer to the safety net that supposedly guarantees all Canadians equal access to needed medical care. This is a powerful representation, but during the present "Crisis in Health Care," a competing vision of Canada is emerging, with many people arguing for the privatization of health care. Although it is hard to see anything but the self-interest of the wealthy as a motive for allowing fee-for-service health care, its advocates claim that they are not disturbing the medicare system that is a cherished part of Canadian identity, but in fact improving it for the general good of all.

Another dominant, even defining, story we tell ourselves is that we are a tolerant country more committed to human rights than is the U.S. We point to our less racist past and, some would say, present. The Liberal government under Paul Martin referred constantly to the importance of full commitment to the Charter of Rights in the months leading up to the enactment of same-sex marriage legislation in 2005—repeating that we cannot "cherry-pick" the Charter, extending rights to some Canadians and withholding rights from others. Yet this story, too, is challenged by other Canadians who see the Charter of Rights as interfering with Canadian tradition, where marriage "has always been between a man and a woman." To understand this conflict from the viewpoint of cultural studies, those in favour of same-sex marriage privilege allegiance to the Charter as essential to Canadian identity, and those opposed privilege allegiance to social tradition.

The stories we tell tend to represent the way things have been as the way things should be. Sometimes the message is explicit, as in the same-sex marriage debate, and sometimes it is a little more subtle. For example, if we look at Canadian history books used in the schools, Aboriginal history is generally represented only until about the time of the Riel rebellions in 1871. Even when the representations are not explicitly racist, First Nations, Inuit, and Métis people all but disappear from the history books once Canada is formally established, giving students the message that European settlement is the important story and that Aboriginal people don't matter to modern Canada. Daniel Francis examines how twentieth-century Canadian school books supported the interests of dominant culture by representing the "Indian" as culturally inferior and needing to be assimilated. Even powerful myths are fictions—and no matter how widely accepted as reflecting reality, they will be opposed by people whose interests are damaged when the story being told is accepted as reality.

These stories and representations aren't inconsequential—they aren't just innocent stories we amuse ourselves with. They're the terms through which people's lives are lived—not only our sense of self but our social and political life. For example, while "race" is widely recognized as a fiction that was constructed to justify the oppressive practices of imperialist nations, the story of Canada is nevertheless a highly racialized story where white-skinned people end up being represented as real Canadians and everyone else as "other." In cultural studies, scholars pay particular attention to the way that ethnicity, language, gender, class, and sexuality get represented in the interests of the status quo. The stories told in dominant culture tend to represent the way things *have* been as the way they *should* be, thus benefiting the *status quo* and opposing the aspirations of members of more marginalized groups. Peter Li addresses the persistence with which non-white-skinned people are cast as "other" in our culture in his article "Social Inclusion of Visible Minorities and Newcomers," and Susan Judith Ship writes of the seeming impossibility of attaining "Canadian" status as a Jew.

The Art of Inventing Canada

ANNA HUDSON

Anna Hudson is an assistant professor of Canadian art history and curatorial studies in the Department of Visual Arts at York University, Toronto. Hudson has also served as Associate Curator of Canadian Art at the Art Gallery of Ontario in Toronto. Her interests range from the connection between art and social progress to First Nations visual culture. She curated an exhibition of historical and contemporary Canadian art titled "Inventing Canada."

Do you remember writing about your summer vacation in grade school? I was mystified why my summer spent cramped in the back seat of a Pontiac travelling across endless stretches of highway mattered. I remember the Trans-Canada highway signs, especially the one that said it was a thousand miles to our next destination. How many pine trees, pit stops, and mosquito bites could it possibly take to make a country? So many families seemed to be on the same national circuit. I got to know a lot of campsite kids and brazen chipmunks. By the end of our trip, I had redefined Canada in terms of scale: i.e., extra large. 1

The daily drive through the vast landscape was relieved each night when campers drew closely around Parks Canada campfires. Where are you from? Where are you going? The campfire inspired us to trade stories about being Canadian. In the blazing and crackling light of the fire, we forged a sense of our collective selves. It was an exercise in understanding the reality of our country's multiple personalities. We could have called this campfire storytelling *Inventing Canada*. 2

> Boom de de boom boom
> Boom de de boom boom
> Boom de de boom boom
> Bo-o-o-m

Land of the Silver Birch remains a popular if amusing campfire song: "Land of the silver birch, home of the beaver, where still the mighty moose wanders at will. . . . My heart cries out for thee, hills of the north. . . . high on a rocky ledge I'll build my wigwam." But no allusion to "Indian-ness," no large amphibious broad-tailed rodent of the genus *castor* (even if the beaver appears on Roots™ bags), no moose nor caribou, no mounted policeman, no hockey player, no maple leaf, and not even the Queen of England (even if she 3 appears on most of our currency), can replace our campfire tales for sheer binding power. The simple lyrics of *Land of the Silver Birch* and the familiar icons only remind us of our complex present, and our vulnerability as a country to fracture along many sociopolitical and cultural fault lines. Moreover, by virtue of our size, we are a country with permeable borders. Fortunately we have a head start on cultural diversity. We pride ourselves on a flexible or expandable concept of union. Canada, after all, was born as a pair of Siamese twins—one French, one English—compellingly described by the Canadian essayist and political philosopher John Ralston Saul. *Inventing Canada* (or what I did on my summer vacation) is, at its core, a national tradition.

If Canadians have always known that Canada is a country conceived   4
from cooperative relationships (however much in need of constant maintenance), why do such symbols of national identity as the moose and the beaver and the mounted policeman still clutter our visual culture?

National crises sometimes fuel simplification of Canada's multiple per-   5
sonalities and narrow our view of Canadian art. In World War II, Tom Thomson's 1917 painting *The West Wind* became a symbol of national tenacity and resilience. He and the Group of Seven, still Canada's most recognized artists, were canonized, culturally speaking, during the war at the height of an unprecedented explosion of political propaganda. Perhaps we should reimagine Tom for contemporary Canada as a camper who spun visual yarns and who continues to spark our collective imagination with his stories of camping in Algonquin Park. No wonder artist Joyce Wieland idolized him so.

Canada's centennial celebration further imposed simplification. In an   6
effort to distance the country from both its old colonial master (Britain) and from its powerful neighbour (the United States), Expo '67 promoted a narrow notion of Canada suggested by the title of the world fair—Man and His World—a place where white, Western, and well-heeled values were paramount. But Expo was a last gasp for a Canadian identity that marginalized the voices of women, Quebecois, aboriginal peoples, and new Canadians, even while it celebrated world culture. Multiculturalism was in the air, and with it came a new concept of Canadian identity, the root of our contemporary ideals of plurality. Multiple interpretations of nation surged alongside static symbols of citizenship.

In 1970–71, Joyce Wieland took one of those static symbols, the Canadian   7
flag, and in *Flag Arrangement* reinterpreted it from a woman's point of view, hiring Nova Scotia knitter Valerie McMillan to knit four Canadian flags in cream and glowing red wool. The colours are classic Wieland—distinctly feminine and sensual—and the knitting beautifully demonstrates three basic stitches—stocking, ribbed, and box. Wieland's variation on a theme is a provocative invitation to revise our understanding of Canada in accordance with the knitter's hand, the weight of the wool, the variation in texture, and our inevitable association of wool to warmth, protection, and intimacy—and our favourite sweater or cardigan. Arguably as iconic as *The West Wind*, *Flag Arrangement* clearly addresses an anxious ideal of Canadian national identity welded along fault lines of race, gender, and class.

A generation after Wieland's visual metaphor of a nation carefully knit-   8
ted together, we continue to drop the aboriginal stitch. In other words, the
storytelling we embrace around a campfire remains separate from the First
Nations council fire. Jeff Thomas, an Iroquois/Onondaga photographer and
curator, feels the constant need to remind nonaboriginal Canadians that a
"vanishing race" of First Nations, popularized during the nineteenth century,
didn't vanish. Thomas points out, "Aboriginal people are still here today."

In *Indians on Tour: Place d'Armes, Montreal*, one of an ongoing series of   9
chromogenic prints he has been producing since 2001, Thomas sets plastic
representations of "Indianness"—figures from our childhood (or colonial
past)—against the backdrop of our contemporary present. By placing such figures in Place D'Armes, which marks the spot where European settlers, as the
monument inscription reads, "defeated Iroquois warriors in bloody hand-to-
hand fighting," Thomas reminds us of our responsibility to listen to the
voices of the oppressed. The story of Canada grows increasingly complex
according to the inflection of the speaker's voice. The campfire around which
we speak can only burn in the oxygen-rich air of an open gathering.

Inventing Canada suggests an alternative to any generalized account or   10
superficial representation of Canadianness. "Canada is a land of multiple bor-
derlines," wrote Marshall McLuhan, "psychic, social, and geographic." The
sentiment is echoed in *Green Grass, Running Water*, Thomas King's 1993
novel. In it, King criticizes Northrop Frye and his singular vision of the country, whose voice is heard through the character Dr. Joe Hovaugh (Jehova).
Nevertheless, Frye believed culture is communication, a view with which
King's narrator concurs: "There are no truths . . . only stories."

Discussion and Writing Suggestions

1. In this chapter you will encounter various efforts to examine the simple,
   unchanging myths many Canadians have come to associate with Canada,
   and the oftentimes much more complex realities of Canadian society. Why
   would a nation invent simple stories of itself, and who would be most likely
   to want to hold onto those simple stories?
2. Hudson refers to various artists who have undertaken to represent Canada:
   Tom Thomson, Joyce Wieland, and Jeff Thomas. Do some web or library
   research to find the works referred to here. Do you see what Hudson sees in
   their work?

Reflections of a Siamese Twin: Canada at the End of the Twentieth Century

JOHN RALSTON SAUL

John Ralston Saul is best known for his philosophical essays, which began with a philosophical trilogy: "Voltaire's Bastards: The Dictatorship of Reason in the West"; the polemic philosophical dictionary "The Doubter's Companion"; and "The Unconscious Civilization." The following reading is drawn from a more recent book, Reflections of a Siamese Twin, *where he argues that Canada is a "soft" country in terms of having a flexible and complex identity, in contrast to a static, monolithic one. Because he is married to Adrienne Clarkson, who was Canada's Governor-General at the time of the publication of the book, the book was met with controversy over its critical stance toward some aspects of American nationalism.*

Victims of Mythology

Canada, like other Nation-States, suffers from a contradiction between its   1
public mythologies and its reality. Perhaps we suffer more than most. Perhaps
the explanation is that, while all countries are complex, the central characteristic of the Canadian state is its complexity.

Mythology often turns into a denial of complexity that can become its   2
purpose.

On a good day it can provide relief from the endlessly contradictory   3
burdens of reality. Mythology thus helps citizens to summon up enough
energy to consider the public good—the good of the whole. And that simple
act of consideration—of doubting—is an affirmation of their self-confidence
as citizens. That self-confidence allows us to question how the public good
might be served. In place of fear, and the certitude fear demands, we are able
to question and to think.

On a bad day, mythology encourages the denial of reality. As if in a bank   4
of fog we stumble into illusion, which in turn produces an impression of
relief or rather a state of delusion. In that atmosphere a rising undercurrent of
fear creates that self-demeaning need for certitude. Absolute answers and
ideologies prosper. These are asserted to be natural and inevitable. In this way
mythology becomes not so much false as mystification.

And so it suddenly is rumoured or promised that prosperity is around the   5
corner, the quarrelling will end, la fin des chicanes, inflation will be strangled
along with unemployment, debts will be outlawed, duplication and overlap
evaporate, efficiency reign, outsiders disappear. In such an atmosphere of cer-
titudes the citizen feels defenceless against the forces of superstition and the
manipulation of false prophets.

Whatever their region or language or background, Canadians have no   6
particular desire for mythologies gone wrong. Anglophones, francophones,

Natives, Westerners, Maritimers, Northerners, new immigrants, whatever—none of us are more susceptible than the others to delusionary mythologies. And yet, our increasing inability to deal with our own reality suggests that we have somehow become the victims of mythology.

Mythologies gone wrong tend to turn on heroics and victimization.   7
Sometimes the Hero is also a victim. A martyr on behalf of a group. Sometimes this status of the Heroic victim is assumed by the whole collective. Suddenly we are dealing with or acting as if we are an Heroic, victimized people or region. All of this we have seen in the West, in Quebec, in Ontario.

The very act of brandishing slogans and flags, when done in the name of   8
heroics or victimization, necessitates the identification of villains. Usually, in this careful society, those who require a villain also deny their need. And yet the concept is there, often in a code—a word or a phrase which believers understand to identify the enemy, unnameable because they are a race or a language group or believers in another religion.

This victim psychology has melted its way ever further into Canadian   9
society. Scarcely a discussion goes on, between linguistic groups or regions or even within cities and towns, which is not a struggle between competing myths of victimization.

There is one other facet of public mythology. It involves specific qualities   10
which are asserted or assumed. Often these are just good fun—harmless clichés. One group claims that it produces the best lovers, another appropriates the qualities of niceness or warmth or looks or food or courage or common sense or honesty. One claims the talent for making money. Another cares about others.

Why not? If it makes an individual or a group feel better about them-   11
selves and also fills the trough of social banter and self-congratulation, which we all seem to need, why not? There is nothing wrong with a bit of innocent comic relief. We know that, as the mythology of these specific qualities is approached, so it mysteriously recedes without damaging our convictions. However, if these appropriations of qualities are taken seriously, they quickly slip into assumptions about race or about loyalty versus betrayal or indeed salvation versus damnation. The asserted qualities of one become the unacceptable flaws of the other.

Like other western nations, we went down that road in the latter part of   12
the last century and we have spent much of the twentieth century trying to rid ourselves of the resulting tics.

> With hearts as brave as theirs,
> With hopes as strong and high,
> We'll ne'er disgrace
> The honoured race
> Whose deeds can never die.

This nineteenth-century "Song for Canada"[1]—an apparently Anglo-Saxon Canada—isn't very different from the historian François-Xavier Garneau's "that which characterizes the French race above all others is this hidden force of cohesion and resistance, which guarantees national unity."[2]

Far worse was said on all sides and by well-known, well-educated people   13
who should have known better. Pages can be and have been filled with these nineteenth-century mythological delusions. The word 'race' was then bandied about with the greatest of ease. It was shorthand for nationalism and national interests. The catastrophes that these assumptions would lead to in the twentieth century were still unknown.

That many of our intellectual and political leaders, from one end of the   14
country to the other, went on talking that way beyond the middle of the twentieth century is quite another matter. Sensible, responsible people in the nineteenth and early-twentieth centuries knew that this sort of mystification of mythologies was dangerous, but didn't yet know how catastrophic it could be. Once that became clear, between the 1930s and the end of the Second World War, no room was left for naïveté on the subject of race. Those who continue to use the nineteenth-century formulae, or modern versions of them, do not deserve the respect which an attempt to understand their specific case would imply.

• • •

Whatever the situation, none of us believes that we live by myth alone.   15
It's just that, during brief moments of excitement—when raging emotion is set loose, and often manipulated—we convince ourselves of what we don't really believe. Even these can be moments of healthy or harmless celebration or of necessary mourning.

But they can also turn into explosions of anger or despair, as if only   16
unleashed mythology can permit their expression. And so the complexities of reality are tunnelled and filtered down to the dangerous false clarity of mythological truth.

Clearly we cannot live without myth. Nor should we, any more than we   17
can or should live without the various expressions of myth. We need a reasonable level of identity, nationalism, self-respect, pride and, for that matter, fantasy. But taken beyond the reasonable, these identification marks become the tools of deformed mythology and victimization. This is the territory not so much of mythology or even of false mythology, if such a concept can exist, but of mystification. Perhaps, to use an old term, this is fouled mythology. Suddenly the believers believe themselves to be alone in their sufferings and therefore in their rights. The *other*—the neighbour in another region, in the city, up north, speaking another language, of another colour—recedes ever further into the abstract meaningless typology of just that—the *other*. Too bad for him. Too bad for her. Too bad for them. They are merely the *other*.

Our difficulty is how to avoid myth being deformed into a negative force   18
which breeds—among other things—a victim psychosis. If we fail, these shadowy simplifications will restrict and deform how we see ourselves and others. With that, we lose a great force—the ability to imagine what we might do if we embraced the complexity of our reality.

Not that reality is easy to seize. Myth, after all, is a marriage of the past 19
and the present. And that past is itself wrapped up in myriad myths. "The
memory that we question," Saint-Denys Garneau wrote, "has heavily cur-
tained windows." He was echoed a half-century later by bp Nichol:

the lack of substantial fact
makes history the memory of
an amnesiac
makes anything his
who works it with his hands
& such lies as we make myths
accepted
as planned.[3]

We cannot live without myth. But even a cursory glimpse through history 20
suggests that more have died by that than have blossomed, once they become
its servant.

• • •

Since the arrival of the nation-state only a few hundred years ago, most 21
countries have tried to manage their real complexity by creating a manageable
appearance of simplicity—a single language, a single culture, a single or dominant race. All of this has been dressed up in a centralized mythology. But
these myths invariably required the real and prolonged use of state force. This
violence has included repeated wars against minorities, the forbidding of
minority languages, the centralization of government and, of great importance, the writing of a centralized justificatory history.

The centralization of government has often been close to total—as in 22
Britain and France—or clearly dominant, as in the United States. The force
required to accomplish this state of being has created mythologies which
could be described as enforced realities. With time, these become expressions
of acquiescence by the various groups of citizens, who agree to forget what
they once were. They don't necessarily forget everything, but usually enough
to permit the enforced realities to function as if they were real.

Canada is no innocent in these matters. We have engaged in state violence 23
against various minorities, particularly the Métis. We have attempted to
forbid various languages in particular circumstances.

But most of this—by the standards of our friends and neighbours, the 24
other nation-states—adds up to small potatoes. That hardly justifies what has
been done. But none of it has come close to enforcing a reality which could
produce a centralized mythology. In truth, none of those efforts have even
been seriously aimed at producing the standard monolithic mythology of the
other nation-states.

This is described by most federalists and anti-federalists alike as the fail- 25
ure of Canada. The failure to become like the others. To regularize a monolithic mythology. Some weep before the ever-retreating mirage of the

unhyphenated Canadian. Others say its continued existence proves that the country is not real and cannot exist. For me, this failure to conform is in fact our greatest success. A proof of originality which we refuse to grasp as a positive.

In *Les Aurores montréales*, Monique Proulx's wonderful portrait of   26
Montreal in the nineties, she talks of Canada as "*un grand pays mou*—a big soft country."[4] Soft because the classic nation-state is hard—hard in the force of its creation and its maintenance. Hard in the clarity of its enforced mythology. In the simple, monolithic model, the very concept of non-conformity is a simile for weakness. In general it is recuperated and reduced to a self-indulgent description of occasional, non-threatening non-conformity by individuals. Non-conformity becomes nothing more than personal particularities.

In the standard nation-state mythology of enforced reality, soft is unnat-   27
ural and therefore not real. Big, soft and weak. But is this a fair definition of 'soft'? Perhaps the opposite is true.

Surely it is fear and a sense of inferiority which make a people require the   28
defence of a monolithic, simplistic model. Was the violence required to enforce their mythology a sign of toughness, or the bravado of the insecure bully? Or did it simply reflect the determination of one group to dominate the others? And is softness not another word for self-confidence? Self-confident enough to live with complexity. Tough enough to assume complexity.

The essential characteristic of the Canadian public mythology is its com-   29
plexity. To the extent that it denies the illusion of simplicity, it is a reasonable facsimile of reality. That makes it a revolutionary reversal of the standard nation-state myth. To accept our reality—the myth of complexity—is to live out of step with most other nations. It is an act of non-conformity.

My own sense is that the citizenry accept their non-conformity with   30
some ease. They live it and so it makes sense. The élites, on the other hand, fret at being out of sync with élites in other countries, particularly those in the business and academic communities. But politicians also seem increasingly affected by a need to conform on some level perceived to be higher. It is an emotional or psychological problem. They don't want to feel out of step.

• • •

So long as Canada was a small, marginal place, more or less invisible on   31
the world scene, the best of our élites embraced the originality of the project. And by élites I mean those who occupy any of the positions of responsibility in government or business or academia or public service. The growth of Canada and the growth of visible global models has triggered their inferiority complex. What we now call globalization, like it or not, is a great force for conformity. In this context the élites don't like not fitting in. They long to conform, each in their own way, to the old monolithic national models and the new monolithic international economic models.

"We have quietly accepted the disappearance of the past," writes the   32
Swedish poet and novelist Kjell Espmark.[5] How can those who hold the var-

ious reins of power throughout society play their role if they are cut off from the reality of the society's past? I am not suggesting that they turn towards the past or act as its prisoners. But that reality and its mythology are always the key to the future.

Change may come at supersonic speeds and give the impression of anar- 33 chy all around us. But no matter how radical the forces of change, societies do not fly about in the air and transform themselves as if this were a matter of changing clothes. Those who successfully embrace change do so from the solid basis of what they are. Reality and a healthy mythology are the key to change.

Our élites have largely lost contact with our reality. They are so caught 34 up in a need to conform that they have forgotten—perhaps wilfully forgotten—that the very originality of the Canadian experiment has always been to stay out of step with the norm. That's what makes it interesting. Not cliché patriotism, flag waving and simplistic emotional evocations.

What might be called Canada's moments of failure can usually be traced 35 to those periods when we feel ourselves—or rather the élites feel themselves and so try to convince the population of the same—too insecure, too weak, too tired to carry the burden of an essentially complex nature. Then anglophones begin preaching unhyphenated Canadianism and francophones claim singularity as the key to survival. The models they reach for are imported, and are not intended to complement the local reality or improve it or strengthen it, but to replace or rather deny it.

This is the provincial, colonial mind at its most insecure. Social, cultural, 36 educational and economic models from the Rome of the day are dragged back home as proof of sophistication. Local circumstances become embarrassing reminders to this élite that it is not really Roman. And so, in place of the classical weapons of enforced realities, the élites use their positions to engage in a modern form of violence. Their desire is to turn these models into mythologies divorced from reality.

How is this done? Practical memory is eliminated. The modern tools of 37 communication become the tools of propaganda. And fear of the consequences of non-conformity is propagated.

Notes

[1]Charles Sangster, "Song for Canada," *Canadian Songs and Poems* (London: Walter Scott, 1892), 25.

[2]Francois-Xavier Garneau, Histoire du Canada (Quebec: 1845–1848), 1:24.

[3]Hector de Saint-Denys Garneau, "Monde irrémédiable désert," *Regards et Jeux dans l'espace* (Bibliotheque quebecoise, 1993), 144. Originally published 1949. bp Nichol, "Familiar," *An H in the Heart: A Reader* (Toronto: McClelland & Stewart, 1994), 10.

[4]Monique Proulx, *Les Aurores montréales* (Montreal: Boreal, 1996), 109.

[5]Kjell Espmark, *L'Oubli* (Paris: Gallimard, 1987), 58.

Discussion and Writing Suggestions

1. Saul claims that "most countries have tried to manage their real complexity by creating a manageable appearance of simplicity." Does Canada seem any different from the U.S. in this regard? How?
2. Is America the "hard" nation that Saul has in mind in this reading? Does his description of the qualities of a hard nation fit the U.S.? Do you agree with Saul that Canada is a soft nation, and that the qualities he calls soft are desirable in a nation? Why or why not?
3. In recent years, Canada has begun to come to terms with its history of state violence in the forms of internment of various ethnic minorities and the treatment of Aboriginal people generally. Why would Saul see the Métis as particularly aggrieved?

How to Make Love to a Porcupine

LLOYD AXWORTHY

Lloyd Axworthy's political career involved 6 years in the Manitoba legislature and 21 in the Canadian parliament, where he held several cabinet positions, but he is best known as Canada's Minister of Foreign Affairs in the Chrétien government. Dr. Axworthy is internationally known for his advancement of the human security concept. In particular, he was nominated for the Nobel Peace Prize for his instrumental role in achieving the Ottawa Treaty—a landmark global treaty banning anti-personnel landmines.

He is the recipient of many honours from organizations as diverse as the Vietnam Veterans of America Foundation (for his leadership in the international effort to outlaw landmines, to end the use of child soldiers, and to bring war criminals to justice), Princeton University (for his record of outstanding public service) and CARE (from which he received their International Humanitarian Award). He was elected Honorary Fellow of the American Academy of Arts and Sciences. He has been named to the Order of Manitoba and to the Order of Canada. He became President of the University of Winnipeg in 2004.

In this chapter from his book Navigating a New World: Canada's Global Future, *Axworthy takes up the thorny issue of Canada–U.S. relations, arguing that Canadians must take pains not to "surrender our freedom of action" under pressure from American demands that would undermine key Canadian values such as community, openness to immigration, and even the Charter of Rights.*

Sitting across the table from me in a huge, ornate hall in Kiev in the fall of   1
1996 was the newly elected president of Ukraine, Leonid Kuchma. When I asked him how best Canada could aid Ukraine's efforts at building an independent state out of the wreckage of the Soviet Union, the president answered without hesitation, "Can you send someone who will tell us how to live next door to a very large, powerful neighbour?"

Who better to ask than a Canadian? But whom to send, considering 2
how divided opinions were on the subject among the various factions and
forces in DFAIT, to say nothing of the government as a whole or Canadians
in general? What passed through my mind was the answer to the classic
Canadian question of how to make love to a porcupine—"carefully." I
refrained from offering that particular piece of advice.

I wasn't quite so cautious a few years later during an exchange at a uni- 3
versity in Taiwan. In my new role as a lecturer, unbound from the restraint of
departmental briefing notes, I responded to a question about what advice I
might have for the Taiwanese in dealing with China, based on my experience
with the U.S. I offered my advice on connubial relations with a porcupine.
The next day, as I attended a breakfast meeting with Taiwanese business-
people, I noticed some reservation among the group. When I asked my host
if I had committed a protocol error, he replied that it might have something
to do with the account of my speech in that morning's newspaper. It reported
that when asked what I would advise as an action in dealing with a powerful
neighbour, I had said, "It should be like making love to a concubine." Take
it as a variation on the debated use of hard vs. soft power.

Back to the question posed by President Kuchma, which, for as long as I 4
can remember, has been at the heart of Canadian public debate and decision.
Much of my own political history has been wound around this central issue.
I recall lining up at the microphone with my brother Tom at a Liberal Party
policy convention in 1966 to support Walter Gordon, then minister of
finance, in his motion to limit foreign ownership in Canada. Those were the
days when the party actually had such debates even while in government.
Some saw the takeover of Canadian industry as a threat to our independence
in decision making; others, as a source of investment and economic growth.
This is the same fundamental debate that played itself out before the 1988
federal election over free trade with the U.S.—economic advantage versus
control of choices on how we define ourselves.

The free trade debate caused great soul-searching in Liberal ranks, as tra- 5
ditionally we were the party of free trade. We had been strong advocates of
multilateral trade liberalization under the General Agreement on Tariffs and
Trade, whose broad-based rules applied to everyone. And there was no denying the attraction of a continental policy that could only facilitate what had
already become a close and active Canada–U.S. market.

What was of major concern to us was the kind of pact being negotiated 6
by the Mulroney government. There was not any effective dispute-resolving
mechanism to protect Canadian industry from the marauding tactics of U.S.
businesses using their political clout in Washington. In 2003 we continue to
see how this major omission results in big problems for key sectors of the
economy, most notably in the softwood lumber dispute. There was also a fear
that under the agreement we would lose control of institutions essential to
Canada, such as health care, culture and, on the resource side, the sale of fresh
water.

We were at pains to point out that Liberals weren't against the concept   7
of free trade. Our problem was with this particular treaty. We argued instead
for an updated multilateral round of negotiations where Canada would not be
so vulnerable to the weight of U.S. power, and where the dispute-resolution
system wasn't grounded in national trade law. Yet this wasn't a debate about
specific trade options; it was about closer ties with the commercial business
system of the U.S., even though the message of the advocates of the deal was
all about job creation and improved standards of living.

It was a fierce battle, and we lost. We were up against a very powerful   8
business lobby led by the Business Council on National Issues (now the
Canadian Council of Chief Executives), who mounted a highly successful
public relations campaign to discredit the Liberal position. I well recall a
meeting I had with John Turner shortly after he had taken a skiing holiday in
Collingwood, a favourite spot for many of the Bay Street businessmen he
knew well from his law-practice days. He was clearly shaken by the experience, saying to me, "These guys don't believe in Canada any more." . . .

September 11 and Canadian Choices

Nothing dramatized more for me the crucial responsibility that elected rep-   9
resentatives have in defending Canadian values, institutions and programs
than the experience over free trade. Along with others, I was vilified in the big
business community for my opposing position. Later, when I considered running for the Liberal leadership, it was obvious from the start that I was being
black-balled in my fundraising efforts because of my opposition to the
Mulroney Free Trade Agreement. Ever since, I've been labelled anti-American,
a charge I reject. It is not anti-American to be pro-Canadian on issues on
which our national interests diverge. Nor is it anti-American to take a pro-
Canadian stand when many of the ideas, values and institutions we have
stood for and fostered as liberal-minded Canadians are under attack by a
right-wing administration in the U.S.

However, attacks on the legitimacy of the Canadian nationalist stance   10
involve powerful forces not only in business but in the media and the academic world. Too many in our elite structures define the Canadian interest primarily as following the American lead without question. The stronger the pull
towards North American integration, the more insistent they are that we
simply bow to the inevitable, ignoring the oft-stated preference by most
Canadians for keeping our own identity. Our political system is crucial in
counteracting this blind attachment. The onus is on our public representatives
to maintain our capacity to act in the best Canadian interest and preserve our
autonomy. This will be put to the test as the leadership changes in the Liberal
Party at the November convention. Jean Chrétien came into office vowing to
keep a respectful distance. He is leaving office having kept Canada out of the
Iraq war, but then feeling compelled to seek a peace offering to the Bush
administration on missile defence. It is an example of how our elected leaders
are in a constant tug of war in trying to steer a balanced course for Canada
between the U.S. push and the internationalist pull.

In the meantime, various academics, think-tank gurus, business leaders, and senior Liberals are calling for even greater continental integration, including a common currency. Wendy Dobson of the C. D. Howe Institute, a pro-business think-tank, recommends that we concede to all demands for "interoperability of defence forces" in the name of keeping the trucks rolling across the border.[2] The CanWest publication empire ran front-page editorials in all its newspapers castigating anyone who has the temerity to question U.S. policy on Iraq and most other matters, arguing that it is un-Canadian to criticize the wisdom and the ways of the Bush administration. The Canadian Council of Chief Executives has established a high-powered action group to push the linkage between economic security and an integration of defence operations.

In light of these constant efforts to acquiesce to perceived American demands, one can't help wondering if we are about to pass the point of no return in surrendering our freedom of action. Borders shape the character of our country, especially in determining who is invited to come and join the distinctive cultural mix of Canada. I agree with Ron Atkey, the former Conservative employment and immigration minister, who once told me that the minister responsible for immigration has a sacred trust to keep Canada's doors open against all pressure to restrict entry. In general, successive governments have striven to attain that ideal, even though many immigration officials are congenitally opposed to open immigration. But under relentless pounding from the right-wing press, and the Alliance Party, especially since September 11, we are now witnessing a change. Refugees have become suspect. Immigrants coming for family reasons will be increasingly scarce. This in a country desperately in need of people to populate our vast land and provide a renewed workforce and which, since the Second World War, has provided leadership internationally on the right of sanctuary for the dispossessed.

Given that so much of our economy is dependent on trade and investment with Americans, it's no surprise that the threat of retaliation in the form of restrictive border measures raises the blood pressure in both federal and provincial cabinet rooms and corporate boardrooms. Shortly after September 11, a respected businessman in Vancouver told me with great conviction that if the Americans wanted perimeter defence then we should give it to them just to keep the border free from hassle. A few days later, in Ottawa, a DFAIT official said to me that there was only one foreign policy that Canada had to follow and that was to keep the Americans happy and show that we were loyal.

Such a stance implies that in addition to giving military support to actions in Afghanistan, muting criticism of the U.S.-led attack on Iraq, abandoning basic positions on arms control, tightening border controls and harmonizing other related policies, we should not take issue with the U.S. government on any of their actions. So if they abandon the Anti-Ballistic Missile (ABM) treaty, set up military tribunals rather than rely on international law, or advance any other form of unilateralism or exceptionalism, nary a cross word should be spoken? In that case, the war on terrorism not only changes the ground rules for Canada–U.S. relations but also impinges on our ability or interest in advancing a distinctive global agenda.

In a speech he gave in 2002 at Cornell University, former defence minis-   15
ter Art Eggleton spoke of his increasing discomfort with U.S. unilateralism and recounted a meeting in which U.S. Secretary of Defense Donald Rumsfeld told him that "the mission defines the coalition" and not the other way around. In other words, terms are to be dictated, not mutually agreed. This approach is repeated in many spheres of our relations with the U.S. and has created a Pavlovian response in many Canadian decision makers, who believe there is no choice but to go along, The fierce response and second-guessing that took place after the prime minister decided not to join in the Iraq adventure shows how prevalent such attitudes are, even amongst Liberals.

This could be tactical and short term, taking into account the public   16
mood of sympathy for the American tragedy of September 11. But it may also reflect a serious calculation that the risk presented by global terrorism over-rides other concerns, although, as this book aims to show, it is not the only human security risk. Nor is the predominantly military approach necessarily the best way to respond. There is a delicate and difficult balance to be struck in our relations with the U.S. Tactical and temporary concessions may tip the balance in such a way that we permanently lose precious elements of our independence.

The war on terrorism could clearly be a turning point for the broader   17
international community as well. What we do in carving out a separate, if connected, trajectory from our powerful neighbour has meaning for many others in the world. As President Kuchma's request for a Canadian sage clearly demonstrates, the Canada–U.S. sharing of a continent through an elaborate system of treaties, more than two hundred in number, and an extensive range of contacts and relationships has been seen by many as a model for how to manage border affairs in a peaceful way, and on how to respect differences even when there is a disparity in power. Many other medium-power states feel we have maintained the right balance between our relations with the U.S. and our wider international relations. If, however, the undefended frontier is now to be subsumed into a North American security fortress dominated by the imperatives of homeland defence, then a very different model appears, with sobering lessons for all those countries who are struggling to construct political space for themselves in proximity to bigger, stronger nations—which, in the global system of interdependence, basically means most other countries. Canada is better equipped than most to ride the waves of globalization without going under. If we can't keep our identity, who can?

The key choices we make in answering the Kuchma question are not for   18
the future but are with us now. Will buying into the anti-missile strategy of the Bush administration mean abandoning our long and constructive role in promoting multilateral arms agreements? How will we maintain an immigration policy that remains reasonably open and in fact is one of the few left

that recognizes the legitimacy of refugee determination? Is the rush to amend the Criminal Code to give police more power to apprehend terrorists going to affect the protection of Charter rights? What will be the consequence of continued big-business pressure to push us into closer economic dependence? How do we work out an acceptable agreement with our North American cohabitants on vital issues of energy, climate change and water resources? Does being compliant with American international policies mean abandoning a human security agenda?

There have been occasions when we have stood up to the U.S. on matters   19 of principle—when we resisted American efforts to scuttle the International Criminal Court, when we signed the Kyoto Accord or when Prime Minister Chrétien and Bill Graham were strong advocates of having the Iraq issue dealt with by the UN. On the other hand, the decision to proceed on missile defence negotiations and to become part of a joint planning unit on continental defence against terrorism is just a disguised way of setting the stage for a full integration of our land and sea forces, carrying with it major consequences for our own territorial integrity.

Muddling through these issues won't get us very far. And responding in   20 haste to self-interested domestic pressures or American demands real or perceived is a mistake. No, we need a game plan based on public discussion and consensus. The time has come for a clear blueprint for managing our U.S. relations in the context of evolving North American interdependence. Can we build this based on the principles of a community where we share responsibility for decisions on common problems, or do we simply leave it to the market or Uncle Sam to decide? . . .

Security vs Rights in North America

Security is a particularly crucial issue now. The September 11 attacks affected   21 the American psyche in very profound ways. Protection of the "heartland" has become a driving force in U.S. politics. The pressure is on Canada to join in a North American perimeter defence strategy against terrorism. The Pentagon has announced a Northern Command overseeing U.S. forces from Mexico to Canada, and there is strong pressure to have our own forces come under its jurisdiction. A continental anti-missile defence system will further involve Canadians in what military jargon calls interoperability, which is another way of saying "takeover." Duke University Professor Mike Byers spelled out the implications of this increasing military integration: we would lose our capacity to make independent choices on deployment of troops and their uses and find ourselves having to backtrack or renege on various policies and treaty agreements.[4]

A redefining of North American security is necessary. There are different   22 threats, new-style weapons, invasion of our common space by traffickers and terrorists. Unfortunately we have accepted analysis and prescriptions supplied by the U.S. administration instead of engaging in our own assessment of what the serious risks are from our perspective and sharing this Canadian "risk assessment" with our neighbour. Instead of working up a lather about NORAD being threatened if we don't join a missile defence program (a patent exercise in fear mongering), we should be working on recommendations for amending the role of NORAD to give it an updated mission for cooperative continental security in the new century. The most serious problem in meeting post-September 11 security issues is not peremptory American demands but our own lack of creative policy-making and a lame willingness to simply follow their direction without injecting our definition of what would be a good security regime.

The same fault lies in the treatment of civilian border management. The   23
mammoth new Department of Homeland Security, amalgamating many U.S. governmental agencies and organizations that deal with border issues and focused almost single-mindedly on anti-terrorist activities, will increase the demand for closer harmonization of cross-border matters as defined by the terrorist mission. The Canadian government has already signed a comprehensive border agreement that incorporates a thirty-point action plan covering everything from immigration to infrastructure, customs control and schemes for detecting suspicious persons seeking refugee asylum. There is no doubt that some of these measures are necessary. They lead inexorably, however, to a greater harmonization of key policies. And it is fair to say that most Canadians have little knowledge of the nature of the agreements or their implications. Of greatest concern are those dealing with immigration and the joint exercise of police powers. The agreement signed with some fanfare dealing with the return of refugees who claim asylum in Canada to American authorities for processing is a capitulation from our commitments to a liberal refugee policy. As we saw during the eighties, we had very different views from the U.S. on what constituted a refugee from Central America. We were able to give sanctuary to many from that wartorn area who came to Canada through the U.S. Now they would be sent back.

The opaque nature of the cooperation is a worry. Take, for example, the   24
extensive surveillance system authorized under the Homeland Security Act. This is a plan to establish a data pool on a broad sweep of individuals by mining various sources such as credit-card accounts, bank accounts and other confidential files—a version of Orwellian spying that is about to come true. How Canadians who travel to the U.S. will be affected is not yet determined, but already significant registration and information requirements are being imposed. Our new border arrangements could very well incorporate cooperation with the Homeland Security Big Brother. The minister of immigration has already called for the introduction of an identity card for Canadians, a drastic step in limiting rights of privacy. It is important that the government be far more transparent on the cross-border cooperative arrangements and spell out directly what is entailed.

The call of continental security also has troublesome implications for vital   25
areas of Canadian domestic policy. If we too readily accept American notions of who is a security threat, we could risk undermining distinctive elements of

our multicultural society. I say this based on my experience during very tough negotiations with the Americans between 1998 and 2000 over amendments to the International Traffic in Arms Regulations. Since the Second World War, Canada and the U.S. had agreements that allowed for the free exchange of defence-related goods and information. In July 1998, in the wake of a U.S. technology-secrets scandal, with minimal notice and no consultation the State Department advised us that they were changing these regulations and imposing an export licence requirement on Canada. Such sweeping changes coming in such an arbitrary fashion would have put Canadian-based defence industries (a $10-billion annual enterprise) at a severe disadvantage in competing for procurement contracts against their American counterparts.

Shortly after learning of this peremptory move I asked Madeleine   26
Albright for a delay until we could discuss these amendments. There ensued a protracted negotiation. We began by acknowledging that if there was a security risk in transfers of technology information to Canadian industry, then we would fix it, in accordance with our own rules. The American negotiators began with the assertion that they would lift the proposed amendments only if we complied with their conditions, a key one being that any Canadian company receiving classified technology could employ only Canadian citizens. They were totally unmoved when told that this contravened our Charter of Rights that grants equal rights to landed immigrants as to citizens. To State Department officials our Charter of Rights was irrelevant to their security concerns. Irrelevant, too, was the fact that many of our high-tech industries recruit skilled workers from other countries, based on Canadian rules that encourage economic immigration (at least until the latest round of changes that make economic immigration highly selective). Eventually I was able to work out with Madeleine Albright a compromise that would replace the citizenship test with a security-screening system for each company, one designed and implemented by Canadian officials. Even then her officials dragged the details on for several months until agreement was secured.

Politicians and bureaucrats in Washington, as this case demonstrates,   27
have little regard for what we consider our fundamental values, especially when security is at stake. In the absence of clear rules, muscle prevails, and serious damage can be done to our interests. We need to define our own strategy for managing those interests and not just be in a reactive mode. The place to start is by defining the border security issue in the mode of a community, not a fortress.

[2]Wendy Dobson, "Shaping the Future of the North American Economic Space," *C.D. Howe Institute Commentary* 162 (April 2002).

[4]Michael Byers, "Canadian Armed Forces Under U.S. Command." Report of the Simons Centre for Peace and Disarmament Studies, Liu Institute for Global Issues, University of British Columbia, May 2002.

Discussion and Writing Suggestions

1. Axworthy begins on a relatively light, personal note. How does this stance affect the reader's response to his argument about international relations? How does it affect the reader's sense of the writer's authority?
2. In a similar vein, comment on the title of the selection. Is it appropriate? How does it shape the reader's response to the writer's more serious thesis about the need for mutually co-operative cross-border relations?
3. Can you summarize Axworthy's view of positive U.S.–Canadian relations?

The Meaning of the Border

JAMES LAXER

James Laxer is a professor of political science at York University in Toronto. Prominent among his fields of specialization are global and Canadian political economy, American and European politics, the Canadian Left, and issues of social class. He is the author of eight books, including False God: How the Globalization Myth Has Impoverished Canada; In Search of a New Left: Canadian Politics after the Neo-Conservative Assault; The Undeclared War: Class Conflict in the Age of Cyber Capitalism; *and* Stalking the Elephant: My Discovery of America. *The following is an excerpt from the first chapter of his book,* The Border: Canada, the U.S. and Dispatches from the 49th Parallel.

A great debate has raged over many decades about Canada's border with the   1
United States, between those who think it an artificial boundary and those who want to keep it securely in place as marking off a society worth preserving next door to what is now the world's only superpower. Historians and economists, as well as politicians and poets, have shaped our conception of the border.

In the late nineteenth century, Canadian historians typically belonged to   2
what can be called the "blood is thicker than water" school of Canadian history. To these thinkers, steeped in the worthiness of the British connection, Canada was a country that had emerged in defiance of geography. When they looked at maps of North America, they saw the continent cordoned off into regions that marched along north-south lines. There was the West Coast, flanked by the Rocky Mountains, which in turn butted up against the Great Plains. East of the Great Plains were the Appalachian Mountains and beyond them the Eastern Seaboard. From this point of view it seemed that North America had been designed along north-south lines. For patriotic historians, the moral of the story was that Canada had been forged by those loyal to the crown despite the counter-pull of geography. The great event in Canadian history, then, had been the northern migration of the United Empire Loyalists at

the end of the American Revolution. These worthy believers in the British cause had left their comfortable homes in the south to make new ones in the northern wilderness.

Thinkers with a very different outlook used the same view of North   3
American geography to reach a contrary conclusion. According to late-nineteenth-century writers like the English-born Canadian historian Goldwin Smith, who favoured the union of Canada with the United States, Canada was nothing more than a series of northern extensions of continental regions loosely tethered together through Confederation. And these Canadian regions, Smith believed, had more in common with neighbouring U.S. regions than they did with each other. The idea of Canada as a freak in defiance of the natural lines of the continent has survived to the present day, particularly among economists who fervently espouse economic union between Canada and the United States. Especially for economists who believe in the perfection or near perfection of the market system, Canada's historic reliance on government intervention to sustain an east-west economy has been seen as a denial of sacred principles.

The view of Canada as a country composed of regions whose logic ran   4
north-south was reinforced by an influential interpretation of U.S. history that first appeared in the 1890s. The American historian Frederick Jackson Turner developed the thesis that what differentiated America from Europe was the continual presence of the frontier from the early seventeenth century to the last decade of the nineteenth century. It was not accidental that he came up with his seminal idea when he did. It was in the 1890s that the U.S. Department of the Interior announced that there was no longer an open frontier in the continental United States. At the moment of the passing of the frontier, Turner seized on it as having been the central influence in American life. His argument will be easily recognized since what came to be called "the frontier thesis" has had such a huge impact on American culture. Turner contended that the frontier, that zone on the edge where Americans could migrate to leave behind settled ways and hierarchies, constantly re-created a society populated by free people who had not yet made a compact to form a government. To Turner, the experience of individuals in a virtual state of nature on the frontier was an intensely democratizing force in American life. He contended that the experience on the frontier, where it mattered what you did, not who you were, had a determining impact on the rest of America. From the frontier, individualism and a penchant for democracy helped break down hierarchies and established ways in the East, in the long-settled regions of the country. The frontier thesis is the paradigm that underlies that staple of Hollywood films, the western. The cowboy, the hardy worker-frontiersman, became the quintessential character in the America of the margin.

Boiled down to its essence, Turner's thesis held that the open frontier had   5
allowed Americans who were tired of settled social norms to take off on their own to start life over. Not surprisingly, some historians in Canada were influenced by the thesis and used it as a tool for analyzing the development of

early Upper Canada and other regions of the country in the nineteenth century. When Canadian historians picked up the frontier thesis, their work suggested that Canadian development involved variations on the same themes that were evident south of the border. By its very logic, the frontier thesis emphasized those things common to the American and Canadian experience. Canada, seen this way, was a northern extension of the United States.

Beginning in the 1920s, the Canadian political economist Harold Innis   6
developed a sharply different outlook on Canada, its geography and its history. Innis and the historian Donald Creighton became the foremost exponents of the view that far from being a creation in defiance of geography, Canada was shaped by its natural setting and the commercial-communications systems that grew out of it. Innis and Creighton were not impressed by the theory that the regions of North America ran along north-south axes. What they looked at as the key to development were the continent's waterways. Understood this way, the logic of a Canada that was separate from the United States jumped out at them. For Innis and Creighton, the first fact of Canadian existence was the Great Lakes–St. Lawrence waterway, which thrust right into the heart of the continent. It was a natural route for the extraction of the treasures of North America by Europeans.

Harold Innis observed that west of the Great Lakes, the Great Plains were   7
divided at close to the forty-ninth parallel—the boundary between Canada and the United States—between north-flowing and south-flowing rivers. North of the forty-ninth parallel, the major rivers flow north into Hudson Bay and the Arctic Ocean. South of the parallel, most of the major rivers flow south into the Missouri and Mississippi rivers and their tributaries. Innis made the point that in the era when the United States and the British North American provinces that later formed Canada were developing, major waterways were the lifelines of commerce and communications. North of the forty-ninth parallel, these waterways pulled commerce along the east-west lines that had grown up with the fur trade, whose ultimate market lay in Europe. Innis and Creighton concluded that Canada emerged from its natural setting, and that its waterways and the resources of the Canadian Shield gave it the potential for an existence distinct from that of the United States.

In their approach to the political economy of North America, Innis and   8
Creighton turned the assumptions of Frederick Jackson Turner upside down. Turner had stressed how the frontier transformed American society. Innis and Creighton, however, insisted that metropolitan centres shaped the life and values of satellite settlements and of the hinterland. In their interpretation, it was the centre that shaped the margin, not vice versa. This understanding of Canadian history placed Montreal, with its English-speaking commercial capitalists, at the focus of nineteenth-century Canadian life. From there, along the pathways of commerce and communications, influence was directed outward to satellite centres and from there to the resource-producing hinterland. By the end of the nineteenth century, with the Canadian Pacific Railway completed, Montreal's main satellite in the West was Winnipeg. Winnipeg

remained the largest city in western Canada until the completion of the Panama Canal, on the eve of World War I, promoted the takeoff of Vancouver. With the opening of the canal, shipments from the port of Vancouver gained access to markets in eastern North America at competitive shipping rates.

For Innis and Creighton, the American cowboy myth was not convincing.   9
It was the powerful in London, New York, Montreal and Winnipeg who called the tune in the hinterland, not the other way around. In any case, the very geography of Canada conspired against the development of a cowboy myth on the northern side of the border. In the United States, it was possible for those seeking new land and a new life in the West to set out on their own or with a few others to head for the new territory. We can all recall those movies with wagon trains taking settlers west. But the Canadian Shield, the barrier between Central Canada and the Prairies, meant there could be no wagon trains to the Canadian West. Large-scale migrations from Central Canada to the West had to wait for the completion of the CPR. When settlers migrated to the Prairies, they did not arrive in a covered wagon in a lawless territory. They took the CPR, detraining in a region where the North West Mounted Police were on duty; and where the eastern banks had set up shop. Government, railway and banks were already on the scene. There was no return to a "state of nature" on the Canadian side of the line.

The American experience and, even more, the relating of that experience   10
promoted the notion of a stark conflict between the individual and society. In *High Noon*, Gary Cooper, deserted by the townspeople, walks down the main street to face the four desperadoes. When he has dispatched them, he throws down his sheriff's badge in disgust and leaves town with his bride. Escaping from society and its norms and avoiding the grasp of government remain powerful, almost instinctual, responses in American culture. The American theory of society and government as a coming together of individuals in a state of nature to form a limited compact has its roots in the writings of John Locke and is enshrined in the Declaration of Independence and the U.S. Constitution. Frederick Jackson Turner's insistence on the frontier as the feature that most distinguished America from Europe reshaped the legacy of Locke and the founding documents. The emphasis on the frontier elevated the role of a very particular kind of common man in American myth and culture. It was not the labourer, the factory worker or even the farmer who was the exemplar of this culture. Rather it was the free spirit, the cowboy, the rancher, the troubadour, the outlaw, the solitary avenger. The anti-societal loner became the hero.

In contrast, the Canadian experience promoted important variations   11
within a common North American culture. Developing a country with a colder climate and a more forbidding terrain pressured British North Americans and then Canadians to temper individualism and to promote a strong belief in the utility of social cohesion. Consider the settlement of the Canadian West from this perspective. The point has already been made that

for large numbers of settlers to move from Central Canada to the Canadian West, the railway had to be in place. And the building of the CPR required not only a change of government policies in Canada but the reconstruction of the Canadian state itself.

In the 1860s, the Canadian state was completely overhauled. The 12 Confederation of 1867 was undertaken to cope with a number of threats to the viability of the British North American provinces. Those threats included the undoing of the balance of power on the continent as a consequence of the American Civil War. Early in the Civil War, the British government was sufficiently sympathetic to the Southern cause that it sold two warships to the Confederacy, an act that enflamed the relationship between Britain and the United States. A consequence of Anglo-American tension was the abrogation of the reciprocity trade deal with British North America by the U.S. government. By the end of the Civil War, not only had the federalists regained control over the South, but the Union army had become the supreme military force in North America. The British government had to recognize that its forces in British North America could not conceivably hold out against an invasion by the United States. Under the circumstances, the British inclination was to support the drive for union among the British North American provinces and to give up its military bases on British North American soil, apart from its naval base in Halifax.

British North Americans were impelled to union for other reasons too, 13 which do not concern us in detail. Among them was the need to overcome the deadlock between English and French in the post–1841 Province of Canada through a move to federalism and the division of Quebec and Ontario into two separate provinces. And by the time of Confederation, there was a shortage of arable land in the Province of Canada. That fact, along with the loss of reciprocity with the U.S., increased the desire of British North Americans to expand westward into the lands held in the Prairies by the Hudson's Bay Company. It would surely be a race against time. If the newly formed Dominion of Canada was unable to extend its sway to British territory in the West, it would not be long before the United States would do so. And for Canada to move west, there would have to be a transcontinental railway.

Confederation gave the federal government the political and financial 14 clout to oversee the construction of the Pacific railway. But political scandal and disagreement about how to get the job done delayed the completion of the railway until the 1880s. Returned to power in 1878, Sir John A. Macdonald's Conservatives came up with a set of national development policies that finally led to the completion of the CPR in 1885. To build the railway, the government had to make extraordinary deals with the CPR. The railway was granted a twenty-year monopoly of the traffic of the West. In addition, the federal government granted the CPR $20 million and twenty million acres (eight million hectares) of land. The land was some of the most valuable in the Prairies, since it was taken along the rail line right-of-way. Especially valuable were the portions that ended up in the hearts of the cities that rose along with the line, such as Regina and Calgary. Just to make the pie especially delectable for the CPR, the government declared those lands exempt from property tax.

The second prong of Macdonald's east-west nation-building effort was   15
the introduction of a protectionist tariff policy. In 1879, John A. Macdonald did what he had promised during his successful election campaign the preceding year. He unveiled a revision of the tariff schedule whose purpose was to promote manufacturing in Canada. The average tariff on manufactured goods was nearly doubled, to over 30 percent. The manufacturing tariff was to have a long and controversial history. Its first consequence was to encourage Canadians and foreigners to set up manufacturing establishments in Canada, a fact of particular importance for Ontario and Quebec. A further consequence, and one that fostered long-term resentment, was that westerners were pressured to purchase their finished products from Central Canada. For prairie farmers, who had to sell their grain in world markets, it seemed immensely unfair that they were impelled to purchase their farm machinery and other manufactured goods from protected central Canadian manufacturers rather than from the U.S. A longer-term consequence was the branchplant economy in Canada, which emerged when U.S. firms jumped over the tariff and set up subsidiaries in Canada.

The Canadian experience, in which government policies were absolutely   16
crucial to the development of a transcontinental economy, embedded Canadians in a web of corporate and state relationships. They could not look back in fond remembrance to a golden age when rugged individuals did their thing unencumbered by large institutions. For Canadians, there never was a Garden of Eden, real or imagined. Prairie farmers, wage earners, eastern railway owners and manufacturers were all driven by their circumstances to pressure the state to act on their behalf, and just as often against the interests of others. As they did so, there was much less inclination than in the United States to raise the cry that the state should get off their backs and leave them alone.

No region of Canada has ever surpassed Saskatchewan for the level of cit-   17
izen involvement in community or provincial affairs, farm politics or formal politics. In 1944, when the social democratic Co-operative Commonwealth Federation (CCF) won office in Saskatchewan, the party had thirty thousand members. Out of a population of one million, that represented about 7 percent of the active adult population, an extraordinarily high level of participation compared with other parties in other regions or countries. It was no exaggeration to say that the CCF could achieve office if party members won over their relatives and close friends. By the time the CCF came to power, the people of Saskatchewan had had a long experience of wide popular involvement in public and farm community affairs. The Saskatchewan Wheat Pool, established by farmers to market grain collectively, had been a quasi-public institution in which thousands of farmers gained experience in how to engage in politics. Co-operation, not rugged individualism, was the ethic that took hold in Saskatchewan.

In the Saskatchewan case, the effects of terrain and climate were rein- 18
forced by a national culture that contained elements distinct from that of the
United States to produce and sustain a political movement that would not
have fitted anywhere south of the border. Crucial to that political culture was
the Canadian tie to Britain that continued as a vital force for more than 150
years after the American Revolution.

The Canada–U.S. border is intimately connected to the great struggle that 19
tore the English-speaking world apart in the late eighteenth century, when the
Thirteen Colonies fought for their independence from Britain. The revolution
that led to the founding of the United States played a critical role in reinforcing a very particular set of values among Americans. To this day, Americans
are profoundly influenced by the social ideas embodied in the Declaration of
Independence and the Constitution of 1787. In the United States, these founding documents are the living texts in an American civic religion. The notions
of the market economy and of individuals coming together to form a limited
government—a compact between the governors and the governed—are the
very essence of Americanism. The newly created United States locked itself
into its very particular version of a bourgeois revolution at about the moment
when the Industrial Revolution was beginning to transform Britain.

To the north, where British rule remained intact, a different experiment 20
was getting under way in the aftermath of the American Revolution. If the
United States was born of revolution, Canada was the product of counter-
revolution, and that includes both French Canada and English Canada,
although in different ways. France ceded New France to Britain in 1763, following the Conquest of 1759. When the French Revolution erupted in 1789,
French Canada remained subject to British rule, and as a consequence the
society of the St. Lawrence missed out on the political and social effects of the
great upheaval. While the revolution vastly lessened the role of the Church in
French society, the Church, if anything, grew even more important in French
Canada. When the Conquest devastated New France, the only important
indigenous institution to remain intact was the Church. It became the intellectual and even political centre of French-Canadian society. It is not surprising that Church leaders in French Canada came to see the fact that their
society was spared the apostasy of the French Revolution as a kind of salvation. For them, perverse as this may seem, the British Conquest came to be
understood as God's way of sparing them what befell their brethren in France.
During the nineteenth century and well into the twentieth, French-Canadian
thinkers exhibited an ambivalent attitude toward their old mother country.
On the one hand, they saw it as an essential source of cultural nourishment
for their small society, which was surrounded by the preponderance of
English-speaking North America. On the other hand, they feared the potential infection of their Catholic society with republican, liberal, socialist and
anti-clerical nostrums. It was only with the Quiet Revolution of the 1960s
that Quebec shed its old Catholic outlook and adopted a much more
favourable attitude to France.

In English Canada, the counter-revolution was directly linked to the 21 American Revolution. The patriots fought and defeated the British and the Tories. Some of the Tories came north to British North America as Loyalists. The first English-speaking settlers in what was to become Canada had settled in Nova Scotia decades before the American Revolution, and there were some English settlers in Quebec by the time of the revolution. But substantial settlement in Upper Canada and New Brunswick began with the United Empire Loyalists. It certainly overstates it to picture the Loyalists as a band of migrants who had a well thought out vision of society and of the British connection that marked them off from the supporters of the revolution. That said, it is clear that the Loyalists brought an outlook to English Canada that differed from the American outlook in important ways. As American historian Louis Hartz once remarked in a felicitous phrase, English Canada has a "Tory touch." The Loyalists, while sharing many of the social attitudes of their fellow colonists, were most distinguished from them on one single point: their attitude to the British connection. The patriots in the Thirteen Colonies had fought a lengthy war for their independence. The Loyalists gave up their homes, often forced to do so by the victors, because they had supported the losing British side. When they crossed the newly established frontier into British North America, the Loyalists were embittered refugees who were sure about one thing—their detestation of the new regime south of the border.

Three decades after the Loyalists made their trek north, they and their 22 descendants were given a new reason to detest the United States when American armies invaded their territory. Particularly in Ontario, where American troops burned down farmhouses and villages, seized food and livestock, and paid farmers with worthless paper money, the legacy of the War of 1812 was long and bitter. A century after the war, tens of thousands of Ontario schoolchildren were taken to Queenston Heights, near Niagara Falls, to celebrate Sir Isaac Brock's victory over the American invaders.

In 1883, there was a huge centenary celebration of the coming of the 23 Loyalists to Canada. A distinct Tory Anglo-Canadian sensibility had grown up by this time, and it formed a clear contrast to the outlook on the other side of the border. It has often been observed that the conscious rejection of the United States is and has been stronger in English Canada than in French Canada. Quebec nationalists have often attributed this to the fact that English Canadians, who speak the same language as Americans, are therefore much more vulnerable to American domination than are francophones. While this explanation is not entirely without merit, what it misses is the cogent fact that English Canada and the United States were created out of the two sides in a very bitter civil war. Civil wars leave behind them people with long memories, particularly among those on the losing side. Witness the enduring identity of the U.S. South, nearly a century and a half after the defeat of the "lost cause." English Canada, of course, was more successful than the South. It succeeded in making itself the majority component of a large country that managed to stay clear of the American republic, in a formal sense at least.

Just what was the difference in outlook that was being nurtured in   24
English Canada? The first difference was a tendency to reject the American
political model in favour of the English. In the nineteenth century, indeed
during the first half of the twentieth century, the American political system
was eyed with deep suspicion in English Canada. I can remember, as a child
attending a public school in Toronto in 1950, being taught by my teacher the
conventional Canadian wisdom about politics; in my eyes the teacher was
ancient; I figured she had probably known Queen Victoria personally. She
taught our class that we were privileged to live in the greatest empire in the
history of the world, by which she meant, of course, the British Empire. In
Kiplingesque language, she informed us that the British had shouldered the
heavy burden of civilizing a very large part of the world. As Canada grew in
population and importance, we could expect to take up a larger part of the
burden of sustaining the empire. Our teacher had a much less positive view of
the United States, which she insisted on calling "the Thirteen Colonies," in a
derisive tone. The problem with the neighbour to the south, she told us, was
that a republic was more or less fated to become a tyranny, as had happened
to Rome. Canadians, on the other hand, lived in a constitutional monarchy,
by far the best guarantee of our liberty, because of the separation between the
monarch, the head of state, and the prime minister, the head of government.
In the U.S., the president is the head of state, the head of government and the
commander-in-chief of the armed forces—a very dangerous cocktail.

The folk wisdom I was receiving from my teacher was the Canadian   25
image of the United States that was the Canadian Tory outlook. This outlook
was in part a legacy of the historic relationship with the United States, dating
back to the American Revolution, and in part the product of Canada's continuing connection with Britain. On display in this perspective is what we can
call "colonial nationalism." The colonial nationalism of English Canada was
cultural as well as political. The heirs to the Loyalist tradition saw the United
States as a violent, corrupt country, where aggressive business practices were
the norm. It was a place where innocents had to be constantly on their guard.
In the minds of northerners, the violence of the United States was reflected
both in individual behaviour and in great historical events.

In the minds of Canadians, there was a definite link between the revolu-   26
tionary origins of the United States, the terrible Civil War of the mid-
nineteenth century and the lawlessness of the American frontier. The
Canadian Methodist Magazine in 1880, in a self-congratulatory tone, wrote:
"We are free from many of the social cancers which are empoisoning the
national life of our neighbours. We have no polygamous Mormondom; no
Ku-Klux terrorism; no Oneida communism; no Illinois divorce system; no
cruel Indian massacres."

There was an ingrained conviction in the conservative Canadian con-   27
sciousness that the United States was an inherently unstable society, that its
experiment in excessive democracy was fraught with peril. In the 1880s,
when Loyalist sentiment was at a peak in Canada, it was not difficult for

Canadians to perceive the United States as deeply flawed. The Civil War, with its terrible casualties—there were as many Unionist and Confederate deaths at Gettysburg in a three-day battle in 1863 as there were Canadians killed in World War II—was fresh in the minds of Canadians. And the Civil War was followed in the 1870s and 1880s by an epoch in American politics that was chiefly noteworthy for its venality.

Discussion and Writing Suggestions

1. What are some of the reasons that Canadians do not embrace the myth of the cowboy hero and the lure of frontier?
2. Are Harold Innis and Donald Creighton still referred to (in Canadian history books and classes and in media discussions of our past) as influential Canadian historians?
3. Laxer ends his discussion of the different forces at work in Canadian and American history with the "Canadian Tory" vision of Canadian superiority based on our Britishness. Can traces of this pride in Canada's British heritage still be found in our school system?

Social Inclusion of Visible Minorities and Newcomers: The Articulation of "Race" and "Racial" Difference in Canadian Society

PETER S. LI

Peter Li, a professor of sociology at the University of Saskatchewan, has written many articles on ethnic relations in Canada and, in particular, on the impact of racism on the experience of people who immigrate to Canada. In the following extracts from a paper prepared for the Conference on Social Inclusion which was held March 2003 in Ottawa, Li discusses how the concept of "race" works to keep outsiders to the dominant White Anglo culture in a subordinate position.

Normative Value of "Race"

Historically, Canada has institutionalized policies and practices aimed at lim-   1
iting the rights and livelihood of people deemed to belong to undesirable "races". Over time, the oppressed conditions and marginal status of racialized minorities became part of their defining features. Thus, the colonial history of the Aboriginal peoples and their present-day dependence on the state (see for example, Frideres and Gadacz, 2001; Patterson, 1972; Ponting, 1986; Satzewich and Wotherspoon, 2000) contribute to the social meaning of the term *Indians* to refer not only to a "racial" group of a remote past, but also

a contemporary people that is economically burdensome, socially marginal and political militant. In the same way, the history of Chinese in Canada illustrates how the state resorted to using the notion of a foreign "race" to manage and control a segment of the workforce deemed undesirable but useful to capitalist expansions (Li, 1998a). Over time, their marginal social and economic position and their "foreign" cultural background became defining features of Chinese. Throughout the late 19th and early 20th century, Asians in Canada were considered belonging to an inferior "race", with loathsome values, foreign customs and questionable behavioural standards that would corrupt the morality and culture of Europeans (Anderson, 1991; Li, 1998a; Roy, 1989; Satzewich, 1989; Ward, 1978). The notion of Asians in general, and Chinese in particular, as "racially" distinct and culturally inferior was well articulated in the ideology and practice of Canada; as well, a normative order that upheld the desirability of European culture and "race" was well entrenched in Canadian society (Anderson, 1991; Berger, 1981; Li, 1998a). Canada's historical treatment of "racial" minorities provided concrete substance to the concept of "race". In turn, "race" has come to symbolize essential differences of people articulated in the normative order as well as social and economic relations.

The entrenchment of the Canadian Charter, the official multiculturalism policy and employment equity policy throughout the 1980s has contributed to *de jure* racial equality. However, "race" remains a value-laden notion that is articulated meaningfully in norms and social behaviours, in apparent contradiction to the principles of a democratic society (Henry et al., 2000; Li, 1995; Zong, 1994). As Henry, et al. (2000) point out, racism can be articulated in a democratic society in "racial" myths and stereotypes without requiring its followers to denounce the democratic principles. Li (1994, 2001a) also argues that "race" and "racial" differences can be articulated forcefully by adopting a discourse that makes use of codified concepts and syntax to sanctify "racial" messages and make them appear not in contradiction to the principles of equality and non-discrimination.

Researchers and pollsters have consistently reported that in surveys and public polls, Canadians have attributed unequal social value to people based solely on the "racial" origin of the people they are asked to rate (Driedger and Peters, 1977; Filson, 1983; Pineo, 1977; Richmond, 1974). In other words, respondents appear to have accepted the legitimacy of rank ordering the social desirability of people based on "race", and have done so regularly in public polls.

For example, Pineo (1977) found in a national study that English Canadians regarded "Negroes", "Coloured", and "Japanese" to have the lowest social standing, while French Canadians considered "Chinese", "Negroes", "Coloured", and "Japanese" the lowest social ranks. Filson (1983) indicated that Canadian respondents in a 1977 national survey were most hostile towards immigrants from India and Pakistan, followed by those from West Indies; in contrast, British and American immigrants received the least hostility. In a 1991 national survey conducted by Angus Reid Group on behalf of Multiculturalism and Citizenship Canada, respondents gave strong support to various elements of the multiculturalism policy, but at the same time, displayed varying degrees of "comfort" towards individuals of different origins (Angus Reid Group, 1991). Respondents were given a list of ethnocultural groups and asked to indicate how comfortable they were with members from each group, ranging from "not at all comfortable" to "very comfortable". Those of European origins received higher comfort ratings from respondents than those from non-white origins, mostly Asians and blacks. Those of non-white origins, irrespective of whether they were immigrants or native-born, were seen as being less likely to provide high comfort level to respondents (Li, 1998b). As well, in a 2000 national survey commissioned by Citizenship and Immigration Canada and conducted by Ekos Research Associates, respondents were asked to indicate how they felt about someone from a given country moving into their neighbourhood. The results, similar to those found in a 1992 survey, show that respondents were more positive towards those from the UK and France than those from China, Jamaica, or Somalia (Ekos Research Associates, 2000). Asking respondents to indicate how much they accept members of a different "race" has long been adopted in social science as an acceptable way to measure the "social distance" between the dominant group and minority groups (see Berry and Kalin, 1995; Berry, Kalin and Taylor, 1977; Kalin and Berry, 1996).

Canadian respondents are also routinely being asked to indicate whether they think that there are too many, too few or just the right amount of visible minorities coming to Canada as immigrants. In other words, respondents are asked to place a value on immigrants based solely on their "racial" origin (Li, 2001a). Results of these surveys are used typically to gauge Canadians' level of tolerance or acceptance of immigrants of visible minority origin (see Palmer, 1997).

These studies indicate that while Canadians endorse many elements of the multiculturalism policy, they also have no difficulty attributing unequal social value and desirability to people based on "race" and "origin". The findings also confirm that in surveys conducted over a period of over 20 years, Canadians consistently rate Europeans more favourably than those of non-white origin. If such ratings were based on subjective criteria in addition to superficial information of "race" and "origin", then such subjectivity can only be said to have been internalized as social norms which provide the consistency and meaning to the notion of "race". The very fact that both pollsters and respondents have accepted the legitimacy of ranking people based on "race" or "origin" and have asked and answered such questions routinely further suggests that the concept of "race" is socially entrenched in the normative order of Canada. . . .

Life Chances of Racialized Groups

Substantial evidence is also available to suggest that racialized minorities' life [7] chances have been adversely affected because of their "racial" origin (see Abella, 1984; Li, 1988; Reitz and Breton, 1994). Despite disagreements over John Porter's vertical mosaic thesis (Porter, 1965) about the precise influence of ethnic origin on socio-economic performance (see Brym with Fox, 1989; Darroch, 1979), findings are consistent regarding the disadvantage of non-whites in occupational status and earnings (Lautard and Loree, 1984; Lautard and Guppy, 1999; Li, 1988; Geschwender, 1994). Analyses based on Canadian censuses and survey data clearly indicate that Canadians of European origins had an income advantage over visible minorities, and a substantial earnings disparity remains after controlling for variations in human capital, demographic features and other job related factors (Beach and Worswick, 1993; Boyd, 1984, 1992; Li, 1992, 2000; Pendakur and Pendakur, 1998). Using the 1991 census data to reassess the vertical mosaic thesis, Lian and Matthews (1998: 475–6) concluded that "similar educational qualifications carried different economic values in the Canadian labour market for individuals of different 'racial' origins" and that a "coloured mosaic" now exists, in which "educational achievement at any level fails to protect persons of visible minority background from being disadvantaged in terms of income they receive".

Other research has also shown that non-white immigrants tend to be par- [8] ticularly disadvantaged because their foreign credentials are devaluated in conjunction with their "racial" features, immigrant status and linguistic characteristics (Basavarajappa and Verma, 1985; Li, 2001b; Rajagopal, 1990; Reitz, 2001; Trovato and Grindstaff, 1986). In other words, non-white immigrants' "racial", linguistic and gender features become social markers that are evaluated or devaluated along with their educational credentials (Li, 2001b).

The disadvantage of visible minorities affects not only the foreign born, [9] but also those born in Canada. A systematic analysis of earnings gaps between native-born visible minorities and white workers using data from multiple censuses indicates that there was a mild improvement in relative earnings of visible minorities between 1971 and 1981, but their relative earnings, for both visible minority men and women, fell further below that of male and female white workers between 1991 and 1996 (Pendakur and Pendakur, 2002). However, the authors cautioned that the broad category of "visible minorities" aggregated specific groups that differed in terms of the degree to which they were disadvantaged. Pendakur and Pendakur (2002: 510) concluded that despite measures of employment equity adopted over a decade ago, "racial" inequity has been on the rise, and that the labour market cannot be said to be "colour blind" nor "moving towards employment equity".

Conclusion

Social inclusion of visible minorities and new immigrants of "non-white" [10] origin necessitates rejecting using "race" and "racial" features to signify the value of people and to reward or penalize people accordingly. Social signification based on "race" facilitates social exclusion and hinders social inclusion. This paper argues that despite Canada's constitutional and legislative commitment to the principles of equality and non-discrimination, "race" and "racial differences" are meaningfully articulated in the normative order, public discourse and economic relations.

The literature indicates that Canadians have consistently attached unequal social value to people of different "racial" origin, and have accepted the legitimacy of doing so in opinion polls. Over twenty years of research on the topic suggests that Canadians have attributed a higher value, in terms of social comfort level and social desirability, to people of European origin than those of visible minority origin. The very fact that the findings are consistent and that both pollsters and respondents have accepted the legitimacy of rating people by "race" indicates that "race" and "racial" differences continue to be powerful normative constructs in Canadian society.   11

In public discourse of immigration, it is also apparent that "racial" issues have been articulated liberally using a codified language that clearly conveys "racial" subtexts, without resorting to blatant "racial" references. Thus, value-laden terms such as "diversity" and "problems of diversity" become codified concepts used to articulate the concerns and reservations over "non-white" immigrants and over the social problems which such immigrants have supposedly brought to Canada. In short, "racial" discourse reifies the significance of "race" in its subtle vocabulary, implied logic and careful syntax, and legitimizes "racial" significance by transforming blatant "racial" references to reasonable citizens' concerns.   12

Studies of inequality in labour market outcomes also consistently indicate that Canadians of visible minority origin do not enjoy the same life chances as others. Many studies have confirmed that visible minorities are penalized in the labour market in earnings and occupation status, and that such penalty tends to persist after variations in human capital and other factors have been taken into account. In particular, the life chances of "non-white" immigrants tend to be particularly disadvantaged because of their "race", and also because of problems of credential devaluation and market discrimination of "racial" markers as reflected in origin, birthplace, and linguistic characteristics. Recent research indicates that "race" also adversely affects the life chances of visible minorities born in Canada, and that the income gap of visible minorities, relative to white workers, in fact widens at a time when measures of employment equity have been in place.   13

It has long been recognized that there is no scientific basis in using skin colour and other phenotypic features to racialize people, and that the social significance of "race" can only be socially constructed (see Li, 1999; Satzewich, 1998). It appears that the social significance of "race" and "racial" differences has been continuously reified in Canadian society. The paper shows how the articulation of "race" is well entrenched and accepted in Canada's normative order, public discourse and economic relations. These are by no means the only domains in which the articulation of "race" is evident;   14 other research has shown that the discourse of "race" is pervasive and robust in the arts as well as in the media (Henry and Tator, 2002; Tator, Henry, and Mattis, 1998). The complexity and subtlety in which "race" is articulated in Canadian society suggest that convention approaches to studying blatant "racial" discrimination are inadequate, and that confronting the problem of "racial" signification remains a daunting challenge in the social inclusion of visible minorities and racialized immigrants.

References

Abella, Rosalie S.
  1984 *Report of the Royal Commission on Equality in Employment*. Ottawa: Minister of Supply and Services.

Angus Reid Group
  1991 *Multiculturalism and Canadians: Attitude Study, 1991 National Survey Report*. Submitted to Multiculturalism and Citizenship Canada.

Anderson, Kay J.
  1991 *Vancouver's Chinatown: Racial Discourse in Canada, 1875–1980*. Montreal and Kingston: McGill-Queen's University Press.

Basavarajappa, K.G., and R.B.P. Verma
  1985 'Asian immigrants in Canada: Some findings from 1981 Census', *International Migration* 23(1): 97–121.

Beach, Charles M., and Christopher Worswick
  1993 'Is There a Double-Negative Effect on the Earnings of Immigrant Women?' *Canadian Public Policy* 19(1): 36–53.

Berger, Thomas R.
  1981 *Fragile Freedoms: Human Rights and Dissent in Canada*. Toronto and Vancouver: Clarke, Irwin and Company Limited.

Berry, John W., Rudolf Kalin, and Donald Taylor
  1977 *Multiculturalism and Ethnic Attitudes in Canada*. Ottawa: Minister of Supply and Services Canada.

Berry, J.W., and Rudolf Kalin
  1995 'Multicultural and Ethnic Attitudes in Canada: An Overview of the 1991 National Survey', *Canadian Journal of Behavioural Science*, 27(3), 301–320.

Boyd, Monica
  1992 'Gender, Visible Minority and Immigrant Earnings Inequality: Reassessing Employment Equity Premise', in Vic Satzewch, ed., *Deconstructing a Nation: Immigration, Multiculturalism & Racism in '90s Canada*. Halifax: Fernwood Publishing, pp. 279–321.

  1984 'At a Disadvantage: The Occupational Attainments of Foreign Born Women in Canada', *International Migration Review* 18(4): 1091–1119.

Brym, Robert J. with Bonnie J. Fox
  1989 *From Culture to Power: The Sociology of English Canada*. Toronto: Oxford University Press.

Darroch, Gordon, A.
  1979 'Another Look at Ethnicity, Stratification and Social Mobility in Canada', *Canadian Journal of Sociology* 4: 1–25.
Driedger, Leo, and Jacob Peters
  1977 'Identity and Social Distance', *Canadian Review of Sociology and Anthropology* 14(2): 158–173.
Ekos Research Associates
  2000 *National Immigration Survey.* Presentation to the Hon. Elinor Caplan, P.C. M.P., Minister of Citizenship and Immigration.
Employment and Immigration Canada
  1989 *Immigration to Canada: Issues for Discussion.* IM 061/11/89.
Filson, Glen
  1983 'Class and Ethnic Differences in Canadian's Attitudes to Native People's Rights and Immigrants', *Canadian Review of Sociology and Anthropology* 20(4): 454–482.
Frideres, James S., and René R. Gadacz
  2001 *Aboriginal Peoples in Canada: Contemporary Conflicts.* Toronto: Prentice Hall.
Geschwender, James A.
  1994 'Married women's waged labor and racial/ethnic stratification in Canada', *Canadian Ethnic Studies* 26 (3): 53–73.
Henry, Francis, and Carol Tator
  2002 *Discourses of Domination: Racial Bias in the Canadian English-Language Press.* Toronto: University of Toronto Press.
Henry, Francis, Carol Tator, Winston Mattis and Tim Rees
  2000 *The Colour of Democracy: Racism in Canadian Society*, 2nd edition. Toronto: Harcourt Brace & Company, Canada.
Kalin, Rudolf, & Berry, J.W.
  1996 'Interethnic Attitudes in Canada: Ethnocentrism, Consensual Hierarchy and Reciprocity', *Canadian Journal of Behavioural Science,* 28(4): 253–261.
Lautard, Hugh E., and Donald J. Loree
  1984 'Ethnic stratification in Canada, 1931–1971', *Canadian Journal of Sociology* 9: 333–343.
Lautard, Hugh, and Neil Guppy
  1999 'Revisiting the Vertical Mosaic: Occupational Stratification Among Canadian Ethnic Groups', in Peter S. Li, ed., *Race and Ethnic Relations in Canada*, 2nd edition, Toronto: Oxford University Press, pp. 219–52.
Li, Peter S.
  2001a 'The Racial Subtext in Canada's Immigration Discourse', *Journal of International Migration and Integration* 2(1): 77–97.
  2001b "The Market Worth of Immigrants' Educational Credentials', *Canadian Public Policy* 27(1): 1–16.
  2000 'Earning Disparities between Immigrants and Native-Born Canadians', *Canadian Review of Sociology and Anthropology* 37(3): 289–311.
  1998a *Chinese in Canada*, 2nd edition. Toronto: Oxford University Press.

1998b 'The Market Value and Social Value of Race', in Vic Satzewich, ed., *Racism & Social Inequality in Canada*. Toronto: Thompson Educational Publishing, pp. 115–130.

1995 'Racial Supremacism Under Social Democracy', *Canadian Ethnic Studies* 27(1): 1–17.

1994 'Unneighbourly Houses or Unwelcome Chinese: The Social Construction of Race in the Battle Over "Monster Homes" in Vancouver, Canada', *International Journal of Comparative Race and Ethnic Studies* 1(1): 47–66.

1992 'Race and Gender as Bases of Class Fractions and Their Effects on Earnings', *Canadian Review of Sociology and Anthropology* 29(4): 488–510.

1988 *Ethnic Inequality in a Class Society*. Toronto: Wall and Thompson.

Li, Peter S., ed.
1999 *Race and Ethnic Relations in Canada*, 2nd edition. Toronto: Oxford University Press.

Lian, Jason Z., and David Ralph Matthews
1998 'Does the Vertical Mosaic Still Exist? Ethnicity and Income in Canada, 1991', *Canadian Review of Sociology and Anthropology* 35(4): 461–81.

Palmer, Howard
1997 *Canadians' Attitudes Towards Immigration: November and December 1996, and February 1997 Surveys*. Report prepared for Program Support, Strategic Policy, Planning and Research Branch, Citizenship and Immigration Canada.

Patterson II, E. Palmer,
1972 *The Canadian Indian: A History Since 1500*. Don Mills, Ontario: Collier Macmillan Canada.

Pendakur, Krishna, and Ravi Pendakur
2002 'Colour My World: Have Earnings Gaps for Canadian-born Ethnic Minorities Changed over Time?' *Canadian Public Policy* 28(4): 489–512.

1998 'The Colour of Money: Earnings Differentials among Ethnic Groups in Canada', *Canadian Journal of Economics* 31(3): 518–48.

Pineo, Peter
1977 'The Social Standings of Racial and Ethnic Groupings', *Canadian Review of Sociology and Anthropology* 14(2): 147–157.

Ponting, J. Rick, ed.
1986 *Arduous Journey: Canadian Indians and Decolonization*. Toronto: McClelland and Stewart.

Porter, John
1965 *The Vertical Mosaic: An Analysis of Social Class and Power in Canada*. Toronto: University of Toronto Press.

Rajagopal, Indhu
1990 'The Glass Ceiling in the Vertical Mosaic: Indian Immigrants to Canada', *Canadian Ethnic Studies* 22(1):96–105.

Reitz, Jeffery G.
  2001   'Immigrant Skill Utilization in the Canadian Labour Market:
         Implications of Human Capital Research', *Journal of International
         Migration and Integration* 2(3): 347–78.
Reitz, Jeffery G., and Raymond Breton
  1994   *The Illusion of Difference: Realities of Ethnicity in Canada and the
         United States.* Toronto: C.D. Howe Institute.
Richmond, Anthony
  1974   *Aspects of Absorption and Adaptation of Immigrants.* Ottawa:
         Minister of Supply and Services of Canada.
Roy, Patricia E.
  1989   *A White Man's Province: British Columbia Politicians and Chinese and
         Japanese Immigrants, 1958–1914.* Vancouver: University of British
         Columbia Press.
Satzewich, Vic
  1989   'Racisms: The Reactions to Chinese Migrants in Canada at the Turn of
         the Century', *International Sociology* 4: 311–37.
Satzewich, Vic, ed.
  1998   *Racism & Social Inequality in Canada.* Toronto: Thompson
         Educational Publishing.
Satzewich, Vic, and Terry Wotherspoon
  2000   *First Nations: Race, Class and Gender Relations.* Regina: Canadian
         Plains Research Centre.
Tator, Carol, Frances Henry, and Winston Mattis
  1998   *Challenging Racism in the Arts: Case Studies of Controversy and
         Conflict.* Toronto: University of Toronto Press.
Trovato, Frank, and Carl F. Grindstaff
  1986   'Economic Status: A Census Analysis of Immigrant Women at Age
         Thirty in Canada', *Canadian Review of Sociology and Anthropology*
         23(4): 569–87.
Ward, W. Peter
  1978   *White Canada Forever: Popular Attitudes and Public Policy Toward
         Orientals in British Columbia.* Montreal: McGill-Queen's University
         Press.
Zong, Li
  1994   'Structural and Psychological Dimensions of Racism: Towards an
         Alternative Perspective', *Canadian Ethnic Studies* 26 (3): 122–134.
  1997   'New Racism, Cultural Diversity and the Search for a National
         Identity', in Andrew Cardoza and Louis Musto, eds., *The Battle Over
         Multiculturalism: Does it Help or Hinder Canadian Unity?* Ottawa:
         Pearson-Shoyama Institute, pp. 115–126.

Discussion and Writing Suggestions

1. There is an extensive list of references attached to this article. What does this tell the reader about Li's treatment of his topic, and what purpose does a research-based approach serve?
2. Does Li conform to APA conventions when he cites sources for his quotations and paraphrases?
3. This piece was published after the publication of his edited book on a similar topic. If your library houses the book, take a look at Li's article in it to see the extent to which he has shifted ground.

Jewish, Canadian, or Québécois? Notes on a Diasporic Identity

SUSAN JUDITH SHIP

Susan Judith Ship is an independent consultant and policy analyst with extensive experience in the design and implementation of First Nations and Inuit community health initiatives and intercultural/anti-racist education programs for children. She has also taught at the University of Ottawa. In the following excerpts from this self-reflective piece, she writes about the elusiveness of full Canadian or Québécois status for Jewish people in this country.

I must confess that when I was first invited to write about Jewish   1
identity and experience in Canada and more specifically in Quebec, I only
reluctantly agreed. My immediate reaction was one of profound discomfort.
Perhaps more curious is why I felt so ill at ease. After all, it should be relatively easy for a Jewish woman to write about Jewish identity and experience
in the country where she was born. My starting point, then, became the need
to interrogate more closely the sources of my discomfort in writing about
these issues.

Part of the difficulty in defining my own sense of Jewish identity and Jews   2
is that as a social collectivity with a unique history, we defy the neat categories
of sociological and political analysis. Do Jews constitute a people, a nation, a
religious group, an ethnic group, or a cultural group? Is Jewish identity a religious, cultural, ethnic, or political identity, or simply a matter of ancestry? In
the end it proved much easier to speak about the identity of Jews as "outsiders" in Quebec and in the rest of Canada than about my own sense of
Jewish identity. The complexities of identity at the individual level of consciousness and lived experience stand in stark contrast to the social construction of Jews as a simple category of "otherness."

Despite the historically changing definitions of Jews, as a "race," as a   3
people, as a nation, and as an ethnic minority, cultural minority, and/or reli-

gious minority, what has remained constant in our diasporic experience and identity in Quebec and Canada, as in Europe or elsewhere, is the construction of Jews as a social category of "otherness" on the basis of religion, culture, and/or physical appearance and the persistence of anti-Semitism in its various, changing forms and faces. This pervasive tendency to view identity—ethnic, "racial," religious, class, or gender, for that matter—in singular, homogenizing, static, and totalizing terms is, in part, the legacy of outmoded categories and ways of classifying peoples that inhere from a historically specific Eurocentric perspective and experience whereby a single social signifier becomes the indelible mark of "otherness," of difference if not inferiority.

   . . . The relative homogeneity and dominance of Anglo/French culture in most of Canada and Quebec still make me ill at ease even though I was born here. Too many people, particularly in Quebec, still ask me where I was born, what my nationality is (I thought I was Canadian), where my parents were born, and what languages I speak. Although some people, perhaps most, are genuinely curious, I am, however, reminded of my status as "other" and somehow obviously "different." But then I understand. I speak French with a funny accent. I don't have blond hair or blue eyes. I don't look Nordic or Norman. I don't belong to either of the "two founding nations." Therefore I must be in that "other" category—the eternal immigrant.   4

   The reaffirmation of "otherness" is also conveyed in everyday experience and in the language of exclusion embodied in the collective representation of "us" and "them" that underpin the politics of national identity in Quebec. I was enrolled as a student in the political science department at the Université du Québec à Montréal in the early 1980s, and I can recall a heated discussion on the topic of immigrants and French-language usage in one of my classes. The professor, a sympathetic and open person, did her best to explain the complexities and difficulties of integration faced by newcomers to Quebec. I cannot fault her. However, in typically Québécois fashion, the terms "us" and "them"—"*nous et les autres*"—were bandied about. I suddenly wondered, as an anglophone Jew born in Quebec: where am I in all of this?   5

   That question was soon to be answered for me. When I was taking a course on Quebec-Canada relations, Louise Harel, the Parti Québécois MNA and long-time ardent *indépendantiste,* came to our class to speak about the strategy of creating a federal wing of the Parti Québécois. While listening to her speak, I began to notice that she was directing most of her comments to the right side of the lecture hall and rarely to the side where I was sitting. I wondered why she was ignoring our section of the room. When I looked around, I saw that all the students of African, Haitian, and North African origins were sitting together—with me—to her left. The message from her nonverbal behaviour and body language reinforced the growing discomfort I already felt. I understood. We were not "Québécois" but "*les autres*"—*les Noirs, les Arabes, les Juifs, et les Anglais*—and we weren't really a part of their political project anyway, as Jacques Parizeau was to remind us years later on the night of the Quebec referendum on sovereignty in October 1995,   6 when he said that the defeat of the independence option was the result of "money and the ethnic vote."

The reaffirmation of "otherness" and "difference" was no less evident in the 1996 Canadian census. I found the census form profoundly disturbing. On a rational level I understand the desire to collect data on the religious, ethnic, and "racial" backgrounds of Canadians for purposes of improving employment equity and specialized services to specific minority communities. Nevertheless, on a deeper level I was reluctant to officially identify myself as Jewish. I felt uneasy about "Jewish" being the most salient aspect of my identity. I understand my hesitancy. It harks back to an older and darker period of Canadian history when only Jews and Blacks were identified as distinct categories of "otherness" in government documents (see the Canadian immigration statistics prior to 1967; these two distinct categories reappeared in the 1996 census). While the context in Canada is now different, more so for the Jewish community than for people of African descent, both social collectivities remain identified as the two primary and distinct categories of "otherness"—the former by religion and culture and the latter by reference to skin colour or "race." Old ways of thinking and seeing die hard. Despite the profoundly multicultural, multireligious, multi-"racial," and multilinguistic character of Canada, the dominant collective representation remains that of a country that is white and Christian, of predominantly British Isles or French ancestry.

Recently *La Presse* ran a series of articles on the evolution of the Jewish community in Quebec. The articles were informative, well-documented, and positive in perspective. They bore none of the traces of the anti-Semitism of Lionel Groulx's Quebec, but rather revealed the significant changes that have taken place in the status of the Jewish community and its relations with the larger francophone society. Yet I still found myself disturbed by these articles. The Jewish presence in Quebec dates back to 1738, and the oldest synagogue in North America is in Montreal, yet they still speak of *"les Québécois et les Juifs."* At what point do we cease to be outsiders in the country where we were born or choose to live?

Everyday terms to distinguish Quebeckers, such as *"Québécois pure laine"* or *"Québécois de vieille souche"* on the one hand and *"Québécois de nouvelle souche," "Néo-Québécois,"* Jews, or Blacks on the other hand, serve as continual reminders to those of us who are not of French or British Isles origins of our status as "outsiders." The language of exclusion and inclusion is deeply embedded not only in everyday speech and popular culture but also in the formal, legal-political discourse.

Identifying social collectivities in the Canadian context in terms of "nations" and "ethnic minorities or "cultural communities," as we are called in Quebec (or visible minorities, for that matter), is not simply about preserving cultural heritages, the affirmation of the right to be different, or the demarcation of socio-cultural boundaries between social groups. It is also a means of structuring and legitimating unequal power relations between social collectivities, of creating and maintaining an operative ethnic and "racial" hierarchy. Formal political labels, developed by academics and government bureaucrats and enshrined in policy, and which distinguish social categories of citizens, carry with them attendant rights and privileges. They establish a hierarchy of belonging.

I was born here and I do have roots here. I am tired of being referred to   11
as an ethnic minority. I am tired of being referred to as a cultural community. I do not want to be integrated as a member of a minority whose rights need to be protected. When do I cease to be a member of an ethnic minority in Canada or a cultural minority in Quebec? When do I cease to be a Jew and become Québécoise? When do I cease to be a Jew and become Canadian?

Discussion and Writing Suggestions

1. What does Ship suggest is unique about Jewish identity?
2. What bothers Ship about the cultural positioning of Jewish and other minority groups in Quebec, a province whose population is particularly sensitive to linguistic and ethnic differences?
3. Does this article run the risk of offending some Québécois activists? Is Ship's use of personal voice a way of shouldering responsibility for sometimes controversial or contentious views?

Your Majesty's Realm: The Myth of the Master Race

DANIEL FRANCIS

Daniel Francis is a Vancouver-based historian and the author and editor of more than 15 books including The Imaginary Indian: The Image of the Indian in Canadian Culture; Imagining Ourselves: Classics of Canadian Non-Fiction; Copying People: Photographing British Columbia First Nations; A History of World Whaling; Discovery of the North; *and* Partners in Furs, *as well as several textbooks published by Oxford University Press. An excerpt from a chapter in his book* National Dreams: Myth, Memory, and Canadian History *traces the systematic construction of a myth of British superiority to all other cultures, in part through the equally systematic representation in school textbooks of Aboriginal culture as inferior.*

One fine morning in turn-of-the-century Alberta, a young newcomer from   1
England, Abee Carter Goodloe, went out to sample some local culture at Fort Macleod, only to find herself overwhelmed by the sense that she was back in the Old Country. "In the morning there is polo," she wrote, "and one sees

young English fellows in patent-leather boots and baggy khaki riding trousers, for which they have sent all the way to England, dashing up and down and 'running the whole show.' The Indians standing around look like aliens, like visiting strangers. The Englishman doesn't insult or bully the Indian. He simply ignores him, and by pursuing a life as nearly as possible like the one he would lead in England, and by appropriating whatever suits his interest or fancy, he makes the Indian understand that it is his country."[36]

Goodloe captures the arrogance of a colonial elite at its leisure, what Sid   2
Marty calls the "Raj on the Range."[37] This vision of cowboys in polo helmets was replicated everywhere across the country, with regional variations, whether it was the tea-sipping, croquet-playing gentlefolk on Vancouver Island, or the colony of remittance men at Saskatchewan's Cannington Manor, or the ersatz Ontario gentry familiar from the best-selling Jalna novels of Mazo de la Roche. These were the self-confident purveyors of the British ideal who anticipated molding the new dominion of Canada in the image of the Mother Country. Blacks, Jews, Asians of any type, Slavs, need not apply for membership in this elite. In the words of Professor W.G. Smith, an "expert" on immigration, "British-born Canadians" were "the elect of the earth."[38] This was the dark side of Canada's British inheritance, a virulent sense of racial superiority which placed beyond the pale anyone who was not English speaking, fair skinned, and devoutly Christian.

As Goodloe's description makes clear, one group which in particular   3
suffered the fallout from this ethnocentric view of the country was the Aboriginal people, whom the newcomers pushed aside as if they hardly existed. The past three decades have seen an explosive growth in interest in the history and traditional culture of Canada's Native population. Treaty rights and land claims have shot to the top of the public agenda, and the century-long policy of assimilation has been discarded in favour of a formal commitment to some form of Native self-government. There has been nothing short of a revolution in the thinking of non-Native Canadians about the Aboriginal "question." Given such a changed climate of opinion, it is easy to forget how different the mainstream Euro-Canadian view was just a generation ago when Aboriginals, if they were considered at all, were dismissed as backward savages. No matter how familiar one is with the sad history of Aboriginal–white relations in Canada, one is not prepared for the sorry stew of smug, racist propaganda which, until quite recently, passed for informed opinion about Indians.   4

Just as school textbooks are an excellent place to examine the ideology of imperialism, they are also an excellent source for the kinds of stereotypes non-Native Canadians used when they thought about Aboriginal people. What emerges from the pages of these books is a cluster of images which might collectively be labelled the Textbook Indian. The Textbook Indian was the Indian in whom Abee Goodloe's polo-playing cowboys believed, the Indian which the anglocentric view of Canada invented in order to justify its own hegemony.

The earliest schoolbooks virtually ignored the Indian. A few pages at best, a few lines at worst, this was about all the attention Aboriginal societies received. W.H.P. Clement, for example, in his award-winning 1898 text, took eleven sentences to sum up the "character and habits" of the Indian. Another book concluded a brief discussion of the subject by dismissing its importance: "Much more might be said, but it would be tedious to do so in this place."[39] John George Hodgins's text, *A History of Canada*, in wide use in Ontario at the time of Confederation, included a nine-page chapter on "The Principal Indian Tribes," but prefaced it with the following note "The Teacher can omit this chapter at his discretion."[40] Perhaps it was just as well that many teachers did, for the chapter is an appalling collection of stereo-types and misinformation. By the 1920s, the status of the Textbook Indian had improved to the point that most books presented at least some sort of an overview of Native societies. Still, as late as mid-century, the Canadian and Newfoundland Education Association, the national organization of educators, proposed a standardized outline of Canadian history that did not even include Native people as a topic worth studying.

Textbooks which did mention Native people adopted a fairly standard approach, beginning with a brief overview of the Indian Tribes, then moving on to more important matters. Students could not help but notice that French and English colonists received far more attention than the indigenous people. At the same time as Clement devoted eleven sentences to the Indians, for instance, he took eight and a half pages to describe the career of Samuel de Champlain.

The material which was devoted to Aboriginal cultures focussed almost entirely on what they lacked. Texts made much of the fact that Indians did not have a written language and therefore had no books, no laws, no schools; that they did not have sophisticated technology; that they did not live in houses; that they had no discernible religions ("As they were heathens, of course, they knew not the true God of the Christians."[41]). Native people were portrayed as overawed by the superiority of European technical achieve-ments. Here is George Wrong, head of the history department at the University of Toronto, describing the meeting between Jacques Cartier and a party of Micmac: " . . . he scattered among them glass beads, combs and other trinkets for which they scrambled like eager children. They were a wretched company, and Cartier thought they must be the poorest people in all the world!"[42] Cartier may well have thought so, but the textbooks did noth-ing to suggest their readers might think otherwise. A relentless ethno-centrism pervaded all descriptions of the Textbook Indian.

The dominant theme of all these books was the expansion of European civilization in America. Given that way of framing the story, there was no real place for Native people, except insofar as they obstructed this process. History was something that happened to white people. "They had no history or writ-ten language," John Calkin assured his young reader.[43] Once the Iroquois wars end, the Indians go missing from the textbooks, reappearing briefly during the War of 1812 and again during the disturbances in western Canada in 1869 and 1885. Otherwise they have no role to play. By their very nature they were inimical to the main story line.

Until the 1960s, Textbook Indians were sinister, vicious figures, without   9 history or culture. They inhabited the New World as wild animals inhabited the forest. They were introduced to young readers not as another civilization with which Europeans came into contact, but as part of the landscape, which had to be explored and subdued. Contact, a term familiar to modern readers, implies that two civilizations meet and interact. This was not the way young-sters thirty years ago, myself included, were taught to understand what took place. We were taught that the Indians were savages; that is, beings without civilization—and that the arrival of Europeans in America was a process of discovery and conquest, not contact.

Early texts portrayed Indians as bright-eyed animals peering out from   10 their hiding places in the dark woods; "wolf-eyed, wolf-sinewed, stiller than the trees," as the poet Marjorie Pickthall put it. Descriptions focussed on their physical characteristics. The Indians were "a strange race," wrote Duncan McArthur. "They belonged to the country almost as the trees or the wild roaming animals."[44] They were "human wolves," wrote W.L. Grant.[45] Like animals, their senses were particularly keen. "They had bright; black eyes that could see ever so far, and ears that could hear clearly sounds that you would never notice."[46] And their strength was notable. "The Indians . . . were tall athletic people with sinewy forms . . . . They were capable of much endurance of cold, hunger and fatigue; were haughty and taciturn in their manners; active, cunning, and stealthy in the chase and in war."[47] Their lodges were crowded and filthy like animal dens, and their ferocity was like the wild beasts tearing at the heart of the European settlements.

War was the favourite, almost the exclusive, pastime of Textbook   11 Indians. "But to go to war was the most important part of an Indian's life," wrote J.N. McIlwraith in *The Children's Study of Canada*; "he cared for nothing else."[48] "The customs and character of the American aborigine turned, mainly, upon war," declared Castell Hopkins.[49] Before the arrival of whites, Textbook Indian life was taken up by fighting amongst themselves; afterwards they made a sport of preying on the colonists. And sport it seemed to be, since the textbooks never seriously paid attention to any rational motives Native people might have had for their behaviour. Colonists had political and economic objectives; Textbook Indians ("these forest tigers, these insatiable scalp-hunters"[50]) had only appetites and superstitions. Like beasts, they seemed to lack the ability to reason out their own best interests.

The double standard employed by Charles G.D. Roberts was typical.   12 After condemning Iroquois bloodthirstiness for a hundred pages, he turns to a description of the expulsion of the Acadians from Nova Scotia by the British in 1755. Not surprisingly, Roberts finds reason to forgive this admittedly ruthless act. There was a war going on, he explains, and bad things happen in wartime. "If the step now decided upon seems to us a cruel one, we must

remember to judge it by the standards of that day rather than this."⁵¹ An
excellent piece of advice but one which Roberts had not thought to give
when he was portraying the Indians as "painted butchers," "shrewd red
schemers." It was simply not admitted that Native people had a point of view
worth trying to understand.

Textbook authors did admire certain martial qualities attributed to   13
Textbook Indians, who were held to be fiercely brave in combat and, when
captured, "gloried in showing that they could not be made to heed pain."⁵² As
far as the texts were concerned, however, these qualities were corrupted by
the Natives' whole approach to warfare: whereas Europeans fought hon-
ourably, out on the open battlefield, Textbook warriors skulked through the
forest and attacked from ambush. They did not abide by the code of the gentleman; the textbooks use words like *ruthless, cunning, cruel, sinister, fero-
cious*, and *bloodthirsty* to describe their behaviour. Indians were not soldiers,
they were predators. "War is not a pretty thing at any time," wrote Agnes
Laut, a popular writer for children, "but war that lets loose the bloodhounds
of Indian ferocity leaves the blackest scar of all."⁵³ Textbooks liked to linger
over the hideous tortures inflicted on the colonists, entertaining their readers
with the smell of burning flesh and the sound of tearing limbs.

The entire approach to the early history of Canada in these textbooks,   14
both French and English, serves to demonize the Indians. The history of New
France is depicted as the struggle of a small band of brave colonists to gain a
toehold in the St. Lawrence Valley while fighting off first the Indians, then the
English. The bold *habitant* farmers with a plow in one hand, a gun in the
other. The founding colonists endure unspeakable suffering; Indians are the
implacable foe which give meaning to this suffering. Every text highlights the
same familiar series of events as they review the history of New France for
their readers. First, Adam Dollard des Ormeaux singlehandedly holds off an
Iroquois war party at the Long Sault. This was "Canada's Thermopylae,"
declare the textbooks. Then Madeleine de Verchères, the teenaged farm girl,
defends the family fort against marauding Iroquois; and the Iroquois attack
on Lachine in 1689 is always presented as the worst instance of Indian
depravity. It hardly matters that modern historians have shown that many of
these events did not happen the way the textbooks say they happened. These
stories long ago transcended mere fact to become the myths which explain the
origins and survival of the country. Together they established what has been
called our "trial-by-fire tradition," a tradition of suffering and sacrifice which
animated, and to a great extent still animates, the textbook version of the earlier history of Canada.⁵⁴

An important premise of the trial-by-fire tradition is that colonists were   15
the innocent victims of Indian aggression. This premise is usually taken for
granted. When made explicit, however, it shows how even the most glaring
contradictions appear to make sense in the absence of an alternative point of
view. In his *History of Canada*, J. George Hodgins spends about a hundred
pages on the wars between the French colonists and the Iroquois, including

the several attacks by French soldiers on Iroquois villages, after which he concludes, rather astonishingly, "that Canada was one of the few countries which
was not originally settled by (or for purposes of) conquest. The pursuits of her
inhabitants were always peaceful, not warlike. She has always acted on the
defensive, and never as the aggressor."[55] Hodgins never offers his readers the
opposite point of view, that Native people were fighting to protect their
homelands against what amounted to an armed invasion by European soldiers
and settlers. Instead, students were encouraged to believe that no colonist ever
killed an Indian who wasn't asking for it.

At the centre of the trial-by-fire tradition is the figure of the Jesuit mis-   16
sionary. Textbooks pull out all the stops when they come to describe the
efforts of these itinerant priests to convert the Native people not just to
Christianity, but to civilization itself. "Their record among the savages is one
of imperishable glory," wrote Charles Roberts, whose praise of the missionaries is bathed in eroticism. "Their faith was a white and living flame, that
purged out all thought of self. Alone, fearless, not to be turned aside, they
pierced to the inmost recesses of the wilderness."[56] The Jesuits were "pioneers
of civilization," "a glorious army" sent to subdue the savage heart of
America. The Indian represented the untamed, uncivilized essence of the New
World. The Jesuits were special heroes because they went up against that
essence armed only with a bible and a cross. Their suffering gave the colonial
enterprise a moral purpose. And so it was described in gory detail, often
purely imaginary: the necklace of red-hot hatchets, the dripping heart torn
from the chest and devoured, the severed tongues and roasting flesh, the
screams of agony. "The boys and girls who read these pages will never be
called upon to witness such scenes in our country again" writes G.U. Hay in
his *Public School History of Canada*; "but it is well that they should know of
the toil, suffering and hardship of its founders, and be themselves willing to
undergo, in a less degree, trials that may come to them. This is the duty of the
patriot."[37]

The deification of the Jesuits meant the demonization of the Indians: 17
Native people were the villains of New France. As one historian has written,
"martyrs must have murderers."[58] That was the role assigned to the Textbook
Indians: they stood in the way of civilization; it was natural that they should
be brushed aside. Textbooks constructed the story of New France in such a
way as to justify policies of forced assimilation which the government had
been practicing in Canada since Confederation. The derogatory image of the
Textbook Indian was not created in a vacuum. It reflected the inferior status
of Native people in Canadian society and Canadian historiography. In
Quebec, prior to the Quiet Revolution of the 1960s, the Catholic Church
exercised pervasive power and influence. The Church operated the school
system and priests wrote the textbooks. Not surprisingly, the Catholic version
of Canadian history disparaged Native people as superstitious savages and
praised French colonists and missionaries for planting the One True Faith in
the New World. To Catholics, which meant to the majority of Quebeckers,

New France represented the triumph of Christianity over the dark forces of paganism. This was the meaning of Quebec's early history.

Until only recently, Native people everywhere in Canada were considered second-class citizens, and the declared aim of government policy was their assimilation. Most Canadians firmly believed that Indians had no future as Indians, that their culture was unsuited to modern, industrial civilization, that their only hope for survival was to join mainstream, white society. Natives were segregated socially, silenced politically, and marginalized economically. No wonder, then, that textbooks read back into history the inferior status of the Native which was everywhere evident in contemporary Canada.

18

When early textbooks turned their attention to the Métis of western Canada, it was usually with the same superficiality that characterized their treatment of the First Nations of New France. The Métis only appear in early textbooks when they clash with European settler society, so readers meet them for the first time at Seven Oaks on the Red River in 1816 when a party of Métis led by Cuthbert Grant skirmished with a party of Lord Selkirk's settlers. Responsibility for this event, which resulted in the deaths of twenty-two people, has been argued by historians ever since, but the textbooks show no hesitation in handing out blame. Seven Oaks was a "crime," declared A.L. Burt, committed by "half-civilized Métis" under the thumb of unscrupulous fur traders.[59] Chester Martin agreed that the Métis had no will of their own, that their "Indian blood" was "aroused to frenzy," that the "hideous massacre" was all their fault. It was "the worst orgy of bloodshed among men of British race that ever stained the western prairie," he told his readers.[60] The Selkirk settlement on the Red River represented an extension of European civilization into the wilderness; by opposing it, the Métis were seen to have put themselves beyond the pale. None of the textbooks admit that the Métis possessed a unique culture or played a pivotal role in the economy of the West. Charles G.D. Roberts was typical when he contemptuously dismissed their claim to be a "New Nation" as simply "vainglorious."[61]

19

The next textbook appearance of the Métis is the Red River insurrection of 1869–70. Most authors admit that the federal government was to blame for not dealing sooner with the legitimate fears of the Métis for the security of their land tenure. But this did not mean that they condoned armed rebellion. To the contrary, they invariably portray the Métis and their leader, Louis Riel, as impatient, excitable, and unstable. Whatever cause the Métis may have had to complain about their treatment at the hands of an indifferent federal government, they are said to have had no cause to take the law into their own hands. What especially outraged the textbook authors, as it did most English-speaking Canadians at the time, was the death of Thomas Scott at the hands of a Métis firing squad. The execution was "cold-blooded murder"; Scott was shot "like a dog." "It was not an execution," wrote Charles Roberts, "it was a murder, and a peculiarly brutal one."[62]

20

The North-West Rebellion in 1885 was similarly treated as an act of lunacy. While again admitting that the Métis may have had legitimate

21

grievances, most authors concentrated on Louis Riel and the question of his stability. He was mad, they wrote, a wild fanatic. Chester Martin thought Riel was insane and raises the spectre of an Indian bloodbath. "None but a madman could think of bringing the savage Indians from their reserves on such a mission against settlers with their innocent women and children."[63] Others portray Riel as clever but "unstable" and "deluded." Once again the distinctive culture of the Métis is ignored, as are their claims to being a "new nation." In the early textbooks, the rebellion is important chiefly for the strain it placed on French–English relations; its implications for the West are largely ignored.

By the 1930s and 1940s the textbook view of the western rebellions was becoming a bit less black and white. The language used to describe the events was less hyperbolic, and more credence was given to the Métis point of view. Some books—not all, but some—began to lay a heavier weight of blame on the government of John A. Macdonald for not responding sooner to Métis grievances. Riel still emerges from the books as a highly erratic character, but his cause is considered just. "'With all his faults,'" admits Arthur Dorland somewhat reluctantly in 1949, "Riel's aims in standing up for the rights of the Métis and Indians were not entirely unworthy."[64] Evident in these books are the first glimmerings of the transformation of Riel into the folk hero he would become to later generations.   22

With the execution of Riel, Native people virtually disappear from the early textbooks, having served their purpose of providing a standard against which the superiority of Euro-Canadian civilization was measured. They had given Canadian youngsters like myself a reason to consider our country superior to the United States. And they had provided a rationale for the policy of forced assimilation which the government of our parents was implementing against Native people. No one cared that Textbook Indians were never really taken seriously as distinct cultures. Their contributions to Canadian history are not mentioned in the books. Issues which affect them are not discussed. There are almost no references to the contemporary land question, to the treaties, to life on the reserves. It is quite probable that as a student in high school during the 1960s I would not even have known that reserves existed. As in contemporary Canada, so in the textbooks, Indians are marginalized and silenced. Their spirituality is dismissed as nothing more than superstition. Their claims to their traditional territories are never even discussed.   23

Imagine for a moment the impact these ideas would have had on Native students when they encountered them in the residential schools which were established to accomplish their acculturation. Richard Nerysoo, a northern Native man, told Justice Thomas Berger at the hearings of the Mackenzie Valley Pipeline Inquiry in the mid-1970s: "When I went to school in Fort McPherson I can remember being taught that the Indians were savages. We were violent, cruel and uncivilized. I remember reading history books that glorified the white man who slaughtered whole nations of Indian people. No one called the white man savages, they were heroes who explored new horizons or   24 conquered new frontiers . . . ."[65] An analysis of social studies texts in use in Ontario schools during the 1960s concludes: "It is bad enough that any group should be subjected to prejudicial treatment, but the fact that Indians are the native people of this country and that their children are required to read these texts compounds the immorality of such treatment."[66]

Of course, the curriculum was not devised for Native students like   25 Richard Nerysoo. Their discomfort, their shame, was incidental. The curriculum was devised for white youngsters like myself. It was supposed to teach us a view of history which rationalized the assimilationist policies being carried out by our government. In effect, we were being educated for racism. Textbook Indians were vicious children who did not have the good sense to recognize the superiority of the British heritage which could have been their rightful inheritance as citizens of Canada. Assimilation was presented as the only alternative to their extinction. We were taught that we were doing them a favour.

Notes

[36]From Abee Carter Goodloe, "At the Foot of the Rockies," *Alberta History*, vol. 34, no. 2 (1986); cited in Sid Marty, *Learning on the Wind* (Toronto: Harper-Collins, 1995), p. 78.

[37]Marty, p. 78.

[38]W.G. Smith, *A Study in Canadian Immigration* (Toronto: The Ryerson Press, 1920), p. 349.

[39]Henry H. Miles, *The Child's History of Canada* (Montreal: William Dawson, 1910), p. 22.

[40]J. George Hodgins, *A History of Canada and of the Other British Provinces in North America* (Montreal: John Lovell, 1857), p. 123.

[41]Miles, p. 22.

[42]George Wrong, et al., *The Story of Canada* (Toronto: The Ryerson Press, 1929), p. 14.

[43]John Calkin, *A History of the Dominion of Canada* (Halifax: A & W MacKinlay, 1898), p. 3.

[44]Duncan McArthur, *History of Canada for High Schools* (Toronto: The Educational Book Co., 1927), p. 2.

[45]W.L. Grant, *History of Canada* (Toronto: T. Eaton Co., 1914), p. 51.

[46]E.L. Marsh, *Where the Buffalo Roamed* (Toronto: Macmillan, 1923), p. 2.

[47]William Withrow, *A History of Canada for the Use of Schools and General Readers* (Toronto: Copp, Clark & Co., 1876), p. 19.

[48]J.N. McIlwraith, The Children's Study of Canada (London: Fisher Unwin, 1899), p. 52.

[49]J. Castell Hopkins, *The Story of Our Country* (Toronto: John C. Winston, 1912), p. 52.

[50]W.L. Grant, p. 48.

[51]Charles G.D. Roberts, *A History of Canada for High Schools and Academies* (Toronto: Morang Educational Co., 1897), p. 129.

[52]Miles, p. 20.

[53]Agnes Laut, *Canada: The Empire of the North* (Toronto: William Briggs, 1904), p. 171.

[54]James W. St.G. Walker, "The Indian in Canadian Historical Writing," *Canadian Historical Assoc. Historical Papers* 1971, p. 37.

[55]Hodgins, p. 144.

[56]Roberts, p. 28.

[57]G.U. Hay, *Public School History of Canada* (Toronto: Copp, Clark Co., 1902), p. 218.

[58]Walker, p. 36.

[59]Burt, p. 200.

[60]Wrong, et al., p. 263.

[61]Roberts, p. 256.

[62]Ibid., p. 364.

[63]Wrong, et al., p. 293.

[64]Dorland, *Our Canada*, p. 256.

[65]Thomas Berger, *The Report of the Mackenzie Valley Pipeline Inquiry, vol. 1* (Ottawa: Supply and Services Canada, 1977), p. 91.

[66]Garnet McDiarmid and David Pratt, *Teaching Prejudice* (Toronto: Ontario Institute for Studies in Education, Curriculum Series 12, 1971), p. 88.

■ ■ ■

Discussion and Writing Suggestions

1. Consider some of the ways in which the image of early British settlers as "cowboys in polo hats" aptly captures the misplaced confidence of colonialists. To add another level to your thinking, look back to what Laxer said about our collective rejection of the American myth of the cowboy hero.

2. Imagine, as Francis suggests, being an Aboriginal student receiving instruction from "social studies" texts depicting natives and Métis as enemies and intruders. How is this sort of cultural story similar to the one Li says is told to/about non-white immigrants?

3. Can you draw some connections between this reading and some of the articles discussing residential schools and native education in the chapter about power and privilege in education?

End: Zed

DOUGLAS COUPLAND

In this vignette which ends Souvenir of Canada *(Volume 1), Coupland reflects on why he opposes any move toward opening the border between Canada and our U.S. neighbour. He suggests that Canada is more than a business venture, and needs to preserve its character, history and geography.*

Douglas Coupland is a Canadian author and cultural commentator born in Vancouver in 1961. His breakthrough novel Generation X: Tales for an Accelerated Culture *(1991) was praised for capturing the Zeitgeist of his peer group—those born before 1970. The term "Generation X" in the title provided a convenient label for this group, and the novel awaits movie production. Coupland has since written several popular novels, and produced two volumes of* Souvenir of Canada, *studies of our country that combine visual images with Coupland's written commentary.*

A few days ago, two national newspapers ran simultaneous front-page articles touting the elimination of border crossings between Canada and the United States. They offered photos of long line-ups of cars: *Just think, no more messy and boring waiting in line if we eliminate the border!* They spoke with some politicians: *Some of the politicians we spoke with think it might be a good idea to open the border!* These articles discussed how an open border might be good for business: *More money!* Yet nowhere in these articles did they speak with the average citizen, most likely because the average citizen would puke on the spot if they heard the border was being eliminated.   1

In the next few days, I polled everybody I came in contact with, and rarely have I found an issue that everybody was so passionately *against*. It really made me wonder if someone (who knows who) phoned up the papers and forcefully suggested that they run some articles on the topic of border removal and see if the skids could be greased for some impending legislation about which the Canadian public will have no say. The same sort of thing has also been happening with mysterious clusters of articles touting the elimination of the Canadian dollar.   2

Yes, the elimination of the border *à la Europe* might well be a bit better for business (and most likely U.S. business, not Canada's) and ditto for scrapping the Canadian dollar. Is that all we are then, as a country? A *business*? Of course not. But it makes me angry when a solely mercantile vision of Canada is put forth. In a hundred years we'll all be dead, like it or not. Yes, I fear death, and I also fear for the death of Canada. Not in a big noisy way, but in a first-get-rid-of-the-dollar-and-then-get-rid-of-the-border way. What if we become a vast crack-ridden, highway-strangled, ecologically sterilized hunk of nothingness glued onto the United States? That would be death, even though the maps might still technically say Canada.   3

At the moment I'm in a 767 en route from Vancouver to Toronto, a flight   4
I call "The Elevator" because it's essentially three hours and fifty-eight minutes inside a comfortable box that has chicken, salmon or lasagna entrées, and
bilingual audio programming. I'm in an "A" seat, looking north up the
prairies and over, what I'm guesstimating, is southern Saskatchewan. The
fields are like 1970s mural art—rectangles and circles in browns and ochres.
Amid the grid are splotches—it's hard to tell whether I'm seeing a lake or the
shadow of a cloud—and there are ten thousand popcorn clouds, and maybe
as many farmers waking up and looking to the sky and singing, "Oh What a
Beautiful Morning!" I briefly develop superpowers and can see radio waves
covering the sky like lace: the songs of other eras—the latest dance craze—a
documentary about Inuit carvings.

If I were an astronaut looking down, details would vanish, but a larger   5
picture would emerge, a swath of land cloaked in snow and wheat and clean
water and pine trees and glaciers which, for much of the world, remains a
vision of freedom and of heaven, and rightly so. And from space it would be
impossible to miss how northerly a country Canada is, and I could only begin
to imagine the lives of the pioneers for whom survival was a far bigger issue
than matters of politics or nationhood. Survival has always dominated
Canada's history, from the time of the last ice age up until the day you read
these words. And it will continue to do so, but survival no longer means
portaging through unmapped birch forests that stretch past the horizon, or
wintering inside a hut while the wind blows at minus 60°Celsius (–75°F)
outside. Survival now means not being absorbed into something else and not
being seduced by visions of short-term financial gain.

Canada is not a country that is out to grab more land. People around the   6
world like Canada and Canadians because they know we're not out to colonize them or take their land away from them. Because Canada is not acquis-
itive this way, the other implication is that Canada is never going to be larger
than it already is. Never. So without permanent alertness, Canada can only
ever shrink.

An hour later, outside the plane's window, I see Lake Superior. Some   7
clouds are bumping into each other, and it looks like there's going to be
rain. This is August, so most of the mosquitoes are gone, the blackflies, too—
a lovely time of year to be outside. It's so easy to conjure up images of peace
and calm—of summer nights with the neighbourhood kids out on the road
playing kick the can or road hockey, hoping not to be called in because
everything is just so *perfect*. It's easy to imagine pictures of home and the
smell of dinner cooking. It's easy to imagine sitting on deck chairs, sifting
through old snapshots: the dog you once had who may well have been your
best friend—the seedling outside the bedroom window that grew into the tall
strong maple.

But Canada as a country has other images, too—images vanishing with   8
time, but so haunting and potent that to know them is to never forget them—
the American ship *Caroline*, set on fire by Canadians in the rebellions of

1837 as it was moored in the Niagara River and sent blazing over the misty edges of Niagara Falls. From the 1700s we have images of bodies of the plague dead weighted with stones and dropped into fissures in the grey-blue ice of the St. Lawrence River. We have images of dusty Depression-era prairies, of clotheslines hung with laundry eaten by locusts, of mountainsides collapsing and swallowing villages.

There is also an image of my father, a finer man it is hard to imagine, in   9
his mid-twenties, flying bush planes in the unmapped wilds of Labrador, camped out at the end of an inlet, seeing a water spout ripping down the fjord, directly at him, a tall twisted tube of white water operating with the force of an atomic bomb. I see my father head from the beach into the nearby forest, grabbing onto the roots and trunk of a pine tree, expecting at any moment to be wrenched away from the earth and be delivered up into the sky, as Canadian a death as can be imagined. Then the waterspout comes suddenly to an end. Peace descends once more onto the water and the land. But for one brief moment there, the sky and earth and water together conspired to deliver the message to my father—and to us all—that we are the land, and the land is us—we are inseparable—that the land makes us who we are, and continues to do so—and that this knowledge binds us together in a covenant that is as sacred and precious as any written under the eyes of God or otherwise, since the creation of the world.

O Canada.   10

■ ■ ■

Discussion and Writing Suggestions

1. Coupland is a renowned Canadian writer. Can you find examples of an ease of style that is reflective of the work of a successful professional writer?

2. Coupland suggests that geography is important to our sense of ourselves as Canadians. Can you connect this to Hudson? To Laxer? How do each of these authors make a slightly different point about our sense of identity and the landscape?

■ RESEARCH AND WRITING ACTIVITIES

1. Look for definitions or written discussions of each of these terms: cultural identity, Canadian identity, cultural studies. Write an essay arguing why it is useful to consider Canadian identity from a cultural studies perspective.

2. Earlier in the book (in Chapter 2) are excerpts from Northrop Frye and Gordon Laird, each providing insight into the author's view of what it means to be Canadian. Do one of the following: (1) review some of Frye's work on Canadian literature and identity, considering whether his

ideas continue to make sense some 25 years later; or (2) read and review Laird's book (*Slumming It at the Rodeo*), considering whether his thesis from the '90s about the harm done by our cost-cutting conservatives remains current and convincing. If you are ambitious, you might look at both, to consider whether commentary about art has a longer "shelf life" than does social/political commentary. Is Frye, as humanist literary critic, able to unearth some truths that hold up over time?

3. Many of the writers link our identity to the character of our relationship with the United States. In relation to recent events (such as the War in Iraq, the devastation of New Orleans, the ongoing softwood lumber dispute, or the banning [followed by the lifting of the ban] of Canadian livestock) assess the status of our neighbourly relations. Have we responded with dignity, civility, thoughtfulness and resourcefulness, as Axworthy counsels? Have we been active or inactive, and has there been something distinctly Canadian in our stance of doing?

4. Li, Francis, and Ship point out that exclusion is an unspoken practice in our culture, so that too little or harmful consideration is given to Aboriginals, people of colour, immigrants, and, really, any Canadians whose lives fall outside the mainstream population groups. Does this continue to be true? Are people "othered" on matters beyond race and ethnicity? How do we make more room for the stories and lives of people who are outside the mainstream on matters of sex and gender, or class, or religion, so that we are culturally more responsive to the stories of gays, women, the poor and homeless, and those of non-Christian (or, perhaps, of non-Christian/Jewish) faiths.

Literary Credits

"For the Infertile, a High-Tech Treadmill," by Sheryl Gay Stolberg, from *The New York Times*, December 14, 1997, p. 1, 36.

"The Nature and Meaning of Data," by Bryan Glastonbury and W. Lamendola from *The Integrity of Intelligence: A Bill of Rights for the Information Age*. Palgrave Publishers, September 1992. Reprinted with permission of Macmillian Ltd.

"Roll Back the Red Carpet for the Boys," by Donna Laframboise. Reprinted with permission of the author.

"Our Daughters, Ourselves," by Stevie Cameron. From *The Act of Writing: Canadian Essays for Composition*, Fifth Edition, by Ronald Conrad. Reprinted with permission of the author.

"Ban the Bargains," by Bob Ortega as appeared in *The Wall Street Journal*, October 11, 1994. Copyright © 1994. Permission conveyed through the Copyright Clearance Center, Inc.

"Eight Ways to Stop the Store," by Al Norman, reprinted by permission from the March 28, 1994 issue of *The Nation*.

Sarah Anderson, "Wal-Mart's War on Main Street." *The Progressive*, Nov. 1994: 19–21. Reprinted by permission from *The Progressive*, 409 E. Main Street, Madison, WI 53703.

"Who's Really the Villain?" by Jo-Ann Johnson, *Business Ethics*, May–June 1995. Reprinted with permission from *Business Ethics*, P.O. Box 8439, Minneapolis, MN 55408.

James F. Moore. Chart: "Wal-Mart Takes Off" in "Predators and Prey," *Harvard Business Review*, May–June 1993, p. 82.

"Mall Owners Vent Anger at Wal-Mart," by David O'Brien, copyright *Winnipeg Free Press*, January 12, 2000. Reprinted with permission.

"Wal-Mart's Cheer: My Short Life as an Associate," by Mary McAlister, *Catholic New Times*, February 11, 2001. *Catholic New Times*, Vol. 25, issue 3, p. 6.

Excerpt from "The Last Retailer in Canada?" by Kevin Libin. *Canadian Business*, Toronto, March 18, 2002. CB Media Ltd., Vol. 75, issue 5, p. 30.

The Canadian Charter of Rights. Copyright her Majesty the Queen in the Rights of Canada.

"I'm Tired of Being a Slave to the Church Floor," by Jack Stackhouse, from *The Globe and Mail*, December 22, 1999. Reprinted with permission from *The Globe and Mail*.

"The Homeless: Are We Part of the Problem?" by Jack Layton, from *The Globe and Mail*, Dec. 22, 1999. Reprinted with permission of Jack Layton.

"Life on the Streets," by Thomas O' Reilly Fleming, from *Down and Out in Canada: Homeless Canadians*, copyright © 1993, Thomas O'Reilly Fleming. Reprinted by permission of Canadian Scholars' Press.

From *Someone To Talk To: Care and Control of the Homeless*, by Tom C. Allen. Printed with permission of Fernwood Publishing Co. Ltd.

From *The War at Home: An Intimate Portrait of Canada's Poor*, by Pat Capponi. Copyright © Pat Capponi, 1999. Reprinted by permission of Penguin Group (Canada), a Division of Pearson Penguin Canada Inc.

"Notes on Prejudice," by Isaiah Berlin. Reproduced with the permission of Curtis Brown Group Ltd., London, on behalf of The Isaiah Berlin Literary Trust. Copyright © Isaiah Berlin Literary Trust, 2001.

"Group Minds," by Doris Lessing, from *Prisons We Choose to Live Inside*. Copyright © 1988 by Doris Lessing. Reprinted by permission of HarperCollins Publishers, Inc.

"Opinions and Social Pressure," by Solomon E. Asch, *Scientific American*, November 1995. Copyright © 1995 by Scientific American, Inc. All rights reserved.

"The Perils of Obedience," by Stanley Milgram, abridged and adapted from *Obedience to Authority*. Published in